GW00322640

The Sunday Telegraph
GOOD WINE GUIDE

1 9 9 4

𝔗𝔥𝔢 𝔖𝔲𝔫𝔡𝔞𝔶 𝔗𝔢𝔩𝔢𝔤𝔯𝔞𝔭𝔥

in association with

WINE
MAGAZINE

GOOD WINE *Guide*

1994

ROBERT JOSEPH

PAN BOOKS
London, Sydney and Auckland

Editor: Robert Joseph
Deputy Editor: Simon Woods
Editorial Assistants: Laura Pragnell, Colin Gent, Harry Dickinson, Elena Urrutia
Editorial Production/Coordination: Sheila Keating
Author photograph: Christopher Hawkins

Published in Great Britain 1993
by the Sunday Telegraph
1 Canada Square, Canary Wharf
London E14 5DT
in association with Pan Books

First edition published 1983
Copyright © Robert Joseph and
The Sunday Telegraph 1993

ISBN 0 330 33182 5

Designed by Peter Ward
Typeset by R J Publishing Services
Printed and bound in Great Britain by
BPCC Hazell Books Ltd
Member of BPCC Ltd

CONTENTS

INTRODUCTION

Buying a bottle of wine used to be wonderfully easy. Without descending to the level of the tabloid editor-turned-broadcaster who once proudly declared, 'I only know about three types of wine: red, white and Beaujolais', it used to be that the only names anyone needed to remember were those of a few tried-and-trusted regions of France, Italy, Germany and Spain.

Today, even the least ambitious supermarkets are filling their shelves with wines made in Australia by Frenchmen, in Portugal by Australians and just about everywhere else by an Englishman called Hugh Ryman.

Just as we've finally come to grips with grapes such as Chardonnay, Cabernet and Sauvignon Blanc, suddenly we're faced with the Irsay Oliver from Slovakia, the Bacchus in England and the Malbec in Argentina.

Then there's the question of where to buy your wine. When the first edition of the *Guide* appeared 12 years ago, supermarkets had only just begun to take wine seriously. Sainsbury and Waitrose offered good ranges but the Tesco and Safeway selections were a hit and miss affair. Today, both these chains have world-class wine departments and even former wine wildernesses such as Spar, the Co-op and Kwik Save now stock stuff which even the sniffiest wine snobs would be unable to turn their noses up at.

The big chains haven't had it all their own way, however. Throughout the country, independent merchants have struggled to find good-quality individual wines, and to offer the kind of service with which no large company could ever hope to compete. But small isn't always beautiful, and how is anyone to know which merchants are reputable and which are not?

Since its first edition, *The Sunday Telegraph Good Wine Guide* has cleared a path through this minefield, offering clear advice on what to buy, where to find it and how much it ought to cost.

The *Guide* includes the names of 250 commendable merchants throughout the British Isles, from pioneering one-man (or woman) bands to City specialists and the biggest supermarket and high-street chains.

As in previous editions, the 500 wines recommended in this year's *Guide* have been chosen from the winners at the *1993 International Wine Challenge*. Organised annually by *WINE Magazine*, this event has become the world's biggest, toughest and most respected comparative tasting, and an award won at the *Challenge* is the one most coveted by winemakers from Cahors to California.

More than 6,300 wines of every nationality, style and price were judged in the 1993 *Challenge*. Of these, 3,000 received no award and only 2,000 won medals. It was almost exclusively from this last group that we have picked the 500 wines featured in this edition of the *Guide*.

Also in the *Guide*, you will find a unique 1,000-entry A-Z glossary offering definitions of common and uncommon wine terms and recommending specific examples.

Plus there's some advice on wine investment, details of the ultimate corkscrews and glasses, the best specialist merchants, the finest wine courses, and the pros and cons of importing wine directly from France.

In short, if you enjoy wine, you will find the *Guide* an invaluable and a money-saving companion – and the only wine book you will need in 1994.

ACKNOWLEDGEMENTS

To ensure that its contents are as fresh and relevant as possible, each edition of the *Guide* is entirely revised every year (unlike some annual publications) and produced to deadlines as tight as the ones used for weekly magazines and daily newspapers.

The clock starts ticking in early May with the *WINE* Magazine International Wine Challenge, the world's biggest wine competition which this year involved the pulling of some 10,000 corks. Next comes the collation of literally thousands of wine names, descriptions and wine merchant addresses, a process requiring a highly sophisticated computer system and the day-and-night toil of a number of knowledgeable, dedicated and extraordinary hard-working people.

Led by Simon Woods, Deputy Editor of the *Guide* and coordinator of the 1993 International Wine Challenge, the team that made it possible to produce the book in the available time consisted of Harry Dickinson, Elena Urrutia, Matthew Rochfort, together with Colin Gent and Laura Pragnell, both of whose contribution to the *Stockists* section were crucial to the book. Sheila Keating had the awful task of pulling all of the strands of the *Guide* together and shoe-horning it all into its compact format with the help of Di Spencer. I am also indebted for their forebearance and support to Angela and Peter Muir, Jill Woods and Tim and Liam White.

Equally essential in a different way were the members of the British and international wine trade listed below who spent a week in Harbour Yard, Chelsea Harbour, tasting their way through over 6,300 wines (and half of these twice) to select 3,500 award winners.

To ensure that the right bottles of wine were placed in front of the right tasters at the right time, Charles Metcalfe, associate editor of *WINE* Magazine led a team of wine enthusiasts consisting of the above-listed staff. But for these people, for Eric Verdon Roe and Damian Riley-Smith, publishers of *WINE* Magazine, Ruth Arnold, its editor, and her staff, the desktop publishing wizardry of Francis Jago of Fingal in Fulham, for Piers Russell-Cobb, Jas Singh, Catherine Hurley and Ingrid Connell at Pan and Marilyn Warnick at Telegraph Books, this *Guide* would never exist.

THE TASTERS

Edward Adams MW, Nick Adams, Jim Ainsworth, Liz Aked, Colin Akers, Richard Allisette, Keith Anderson, Susan Anderson, Ruth Arnold, Tim Atkin, Susy Atkins, Rob Atthill, John Avery MW, John Axon MW, Lucy Bailey, Richard Bailey, Chris Baker, Julian Baker, Sally Baker, Richard Balls, Richard Bampfield MW, Abigail Barlow, Anne Barlow, Ken Barlow, Anthony Barne, Philip Barnett, Terry Barr, Stephen Barrett, Andrew Barros, Gerard Basset, Joaquin Bauza, David Baverstock, Nicolas Belfrage MW, Elizabeth Belok, Stephen Bennett, Richard Berrington, Liz Berry MW, Vicky Bishop, Julia Black, Charles Blagden, Hew Blair, Bill Blatch, Neville Blech, Hugh Boileau, Jeremy Bolam, David Boobbyer, Nick Borst-Smith, Philippe Boucheron, Paul Boutinot, P.F Bowen, Caspar Bowes, Paul Bowness, John Boys MW, Mark Brandon, Brandt, Joanna Brear, Jayne Bridges, Julia Bridgwater, Peter Bright, Julian Brind MW, Peter Broadbent, Nick Brookes, Richard Brooks, Paul Brown, Ross Brown, Tony Brown MW, Jim Budd, Brian Burch, Richard Burgess, Debra Buzan, Brian Cable, Hugo Campbell, Judith Candy, Philippa Carr MW, J Chamberlen, Penny Champion, Henry Chebanne, Guy Chisenhale-Marsh, Stanley Cholaj, Nick Clarke, Oz Clarke, Paul Cleeton, Philip Clive, Gordon Coates, Hugh Cochrane MW, Deborah Collinson, Michael Collyer, John Comyn, R.M. Conn, Chris Connolly, Mike Conolly, B. O. Cowan, Michael Cox, Robin Crameri MW, Charles Crawfurd MW, Jan Critchley-Salmonson MW, Tim Cross, Peter S. Crosse, John Cruse, David Cudd, Robert Dale, Steve Daniel, Christophe Daviau, Robin Davis, Paul Day, Louisa De Faye Perkins, Sergio de Luca, Jenny De Montfort, Mark de Vere, Carlos De Witt, Simon Deakin, Michael

Dean, Annabel Dearlove, Joanna Delaforce, Sally Denbigh, Mark Denison, Robert Di Massimo, David Dickinson, Harry Dickinson, Alison Dillon, Chris Dolby, Claudia Dowell, Jim Dowling, Annette Duce, Gerald Duff, Helena Duff, Adrian Eastaugh, Alison Easton, Maria Edney, Julian Eggar, Nick Elliott, Martin Everett MW, Liz Eyre, Nick Faith, Simon Farr, Nicola Fearnhead, Sinead Ferramosca, Alfie Fiandaca, Alex Findlater, Jon Firmin, James Fleetwood, Charlotte Fleming, David Forbes, G. Fortune, Chris Foss, Anthony Foster MW, Martin Fowke, Emma Fox, Lance Foyster MW, Margaret J Francis, Elizabeth Gabay, Graham Gardner, Tim Garland, Michael Garner, Colin Gent, Alastair Gibson, Dr Caroline Gilby MW, David Gleave MW, Claire Gordon-Brown, Vince Gower, Maxwell Graham-Wood, Nigel Gray, Lara Grayburn, Peter Greet, Jeff Grier, Rhett Griffiths, Patrick Grubb MW, Julie Gubbins, Richard Guest, David Gummer, Bill Gunn MW, Peter Hallgarten, James Handford, Caroline Hansberry, Roger Harris, Stephen Harrison, Mark Harrison, John Hart, John Harvey MW, Margaret Harvey MW, Helena Harwood, Peter Hastings, John Hawes, Lucy Hawes, Charles Hawkins, Harold Heckle, Piarina Hennessey, Piers Hillier, Rodney Hogg, Ian Hollick, J.T. Holmes, David Holt, Pamela Holt, Christian Honorez, Andrew Hooper, Simon Hore, Terry Horton, Justin Howard-Sneyd, Anne Howarth, Caroline Howells, Oliver Howells, Ben Howkins, Jane Hughes, Mark Hughes, Mike Hunt, Jane Hunt MW, David W Hunter, Lena Inger, Nicholas Ingham, Keith Isaac MW, Julie Jackson, Tim Jackson, Nikki Jacoby, Daniel Jago, Geraldine Jago, Phil James, Hugh Janus, Mark Jarman, Bobby Jeaux, Andrew Jefford, Cherry Jenkins, Phillip John, Eluned Jones, Martyn Jones, Quentin Jones, Robin Jones, Stephen Jones, Robert Joseph, Matthew Jukes, Jacqueline Kay, Richard Kayne, Richard Kelley, John Kemp, Tony Keys, Stephen Kyjak-Lane, Henrietta Laitt, Adrian Lake, Robin Lane, Catriona Lapsley, Michael Larn, Gareth Lawrence, Antony Le Ray-Cook, Willy Lebus, Peter Ledgerwood, Janet Lee, Geoff Leigh, Angela Leighton, Jon Leighton, A Leisk, Paul Levy, Alastair Llewellyn-Smith, Michael Lo, Jerry Lockspeiser, William Long, Lorna Loose, Wink Lorch, Peter Lowe, Debbie Lush, Kevin Lyle, Luciana Lynch, Giles MacDonogh, Caroline Mack, Bruce MacKenzie, Judy Manwell, Simon March, Sally Marriage, S Marsay, Douglas Marshall, Donald Mason, Nick Mason, Tony Mason, Anne Matthews, David Matthews, Judy Maxwell, Richard Mayson, David McDonnell, Patrick McGrath, Chris McIndoe, Clive McLaughlin, Maggie McNie MW, Ken Meek, Charlie Melton, Olivier Merotto, Paul Merritt, Charles Metcalfe, Piers Methuen, David Mikitka, Anne Monnot, Andrew Montague, Evan Moore, Maurice Moore, Liz Morcom MW, David Morgan, Jasper Morris MW, Lewis Morton, Clifford Mould, Angela Mount, Angela Muir MW, Chris Murphy, Monica Murphy, Simon Nash, Rosemary Neal, Zue Newton, Geoff Nicholls, Hugh Nicholson-Lailey, Richard Nurick, Keith Olds, Steve Olley, Robert Osborne, Tudor Owen, Sue O'Connell, Bernard O'Kane, Mark O'Neill, Grant Page, Michael Palij, Jeremy Palmer, Neil Palmer, David Park, Steve Parsons, Richard Pass, Diana Patterson Fox, Luis Pato, Sebastian Payne MW, Michael Peace MW, David Peppercorn MW, David Perry, Jordanis Petridis, Patrick Porritt, Lynn Power, Laura Pragnell, Eloise Price, Keith Price, John Pride, Jethro Probes, Chris Pughe-Morgan, Mira Puskasora, Ali Quinnell, John G Radford, Lewis Ragbourn, Barry Ralph, Margaret Rand, Jeremy Randall, Carlos Read, Monique Reedman, Philip Reedman, Raymond Reynolds, Howard Ripley, Jeremy Roberts, N.K Robinson, Matthew Rochfort, Bill Rolfe, Anthony Rose, Hugo Rose, David Round, Richard Royds, Tony Russell, Finola Ryan, Corinne Samson, David Sandys-Renton, Michael Saunders, Hector Scicluna, Marcus Scriven, Ted Searle, Philip Shaw, Gabrielle Shaw, Richard Sheedy, Michael Sheeres, Geoff Sheppard, Paul Shinnie, Pat Simon MW, James Simpson MW, Jane Skilton, Chris Smales, Derek Smedley MW, Barney Smith, Caroline Smith, Neil Sommerfelt MW, Mark Soudah, Richard Speirs, Steven Spurrier, Joanna Standen, Tim Stanley-Clarke, D Stanton, Simon Staples, Kit Stevens MW, Tom Stevenson, John Stott, Helen Sugarman, Peter Symington, Hendryk Szterbin, Nick Tarayan, Christopher Tatham MW, Nick Tatham MW, Charles Taylor MW, James Taylor, Simon Taylor, Katherine Terry, Nicky Thompson, Edward Thornton, John Thorogood, Christine Thorpe, Simon Thorpe, Marcus Titley, Kym Tolley, Eve Tomkins, Debbi Tomkinson, Giles Townsend, Julia Trustram-Eve, Rachel Tully, Nick Underwood, Tim Underwood, Jean Denis Vacheron, Rene Vannetelle, Gerard Varennes, Helen Verdcourt, Roger Voss, Tim Wacker, Monty Waldin, Robert Walker, Simon Walker, Tim Walker, Peter Wallis, Stuart Walton, Justin Waples, Penny Ward, Andrea Warren, Marcia Waters MW, Ashley Webb, Chris Wells, Lilyane Weston, Robert Wheatcroft, Anthony Whitaker, Paul J White, Phil Wiehe, Guy Wilkes, Andrew Williams, D R Williams MW, Deborah Williams, Laurence Williams, Andrew Willy, Andrew Wilson, Charles M Wilson, Liz Wilson, Geraldine Wood, Arabella Woodrow MW, Richard Woodrow, Pippa Woods, Simon Woods, Anthony Woollams, Thomas Woolrych, John Worontschak, Debbie Worton, David Wright, Sarah Wykes, B. Yardley, Guy Young, Nick Zalinski

THE SUNDAY TELEGRAPH GOOD WINE GUIDE & *WINE* MAGAZINE WINES AND MERCHANTS OF THE YEAR

The recommendations that form the main body of the *Guide* are taken from *WINE* Magazine's annual *International Wine Challenge*. Since its launch in 1985, this event has become the biggest international competition of its kind.

The wines are entered – and judged – by representatives of every part of the UK wine trade, from the smallest English vineyard and one-man-band importer, to the most venerable of City merchants and the biggest High Street chains and supermarkets, plus an increasing number of overseas winemakers.

A full list of the award-winning wines is sent to 1,000 retailers (whether or not they competed), enabling them to indicate those that they stock. Where companies have submitted wines, we first compare the number of successful wines with the number entered into the Challenge – so the success rate of a merchant with 15 recommendations out of 25 entries is recognised as being greater than that of a firm that submitted 100, of which 30 won awards. Then we compare the total number of award-winning wines from each company with their full wine lists to see whether the recommended wines are representative of their range as a whole.

Finally, we select the merchants that will feature in the *Guide*. Where companies declare that they have sufficient stocks to expect to be able to supply them in the early part of 1994, the wines in question are listed.

More difficult is the task of selecting the best from Britain's wealth of independent merchants. Paramount in our considerations are the breadth of choice and the range of services offered to customers. While our regional awards reflect the national scope of the *Guide*, our category winners, for different styles of businesses, take account of the diversity of ways in which British wine drinkers may choose to shop for their wine.

To avoid companies from winning the same award thrice running, last year, we instituted a 'no-hat-trick' rule. This affected Adnams (twice Wine Merchant of the Year), Winecellars (twice Italian Specialists of the Year); Wine Rack (twice winner of High Street Chain Award), the Wine Society (twice By-the-Case Merchant of the Year) and James Nicholson (twice Northern Ireland Wine Merchant of the Year).

This year, in recognition of the often daunting hurdles confronting Britain's smaller merchants, we have introduced a new award for any merchant with less than four full-time employees: Small Independent Merchant of the Year.

THE JUDGES

These sought-after awards were judged this year by an expert panel consisting of: **Tim Atkin**, wine writer for *The Guardian*; **Oz Clarke** of BBC2's *Food & Drink Programme* and *The Daily Telegraph*; **Ruth Arnold**, editor of *WINE*; **Jill Goolden**, also of *Food & Drink*; **Eluned Jones**, editor of *Wine & Spirit International*; **Kathryn McWhirter**, wine writer of the *Sunday Independent*, and former editor of both the *Which? Wine Guide* and *Wine & Spirit* Magazine; **Charles Metcalfe** of *WINE*, *Homes & Gardens* and Granada Television's *This Morning*; **Jancis Robinson MW** of *The Financial Times* and *The Wine Spectator*; **Anthony Rose**, wine correspondent of *The Independent*; **Joanna Simon**, former editor of *WINE* and wine correspondent of *The Sunday Times*; and **Simon Woods,** coordinator of the *International Wine Challenge*. Robert Joseph, the *Guide* editor, excluded himself from the judging.

THE MERCHANTS

East of England – Winner: Adnams

The toughest part of the country for our judges, this is the award for which Adnams, Thos Peatling, T&W and Lay & Wheeler had to fight, each winning votes for one or other aspect of their service. In the end, though, it was a previous winner, Adnams, which took the prize, for the 'extraordinary quality and variety of its wines'.

Scotland – Winner: Raeburn

Scottish wine drinkers are extraordinarily well served, with a choice between Peter Green, Bute Wines, Gelston Castle, Raeburn Fine Wines and Valvona & Crolla. Bute Wines put up a good fight to win this prize, but, ultimately, it was another former winner, Raeburn Fine Wines, who took the award.

Wales – Winner: Celtic Vintner

David Baker, CPA's and Tanners were all in the running for this prize, but none of them could keep it from The Celtic Vintner, whose list of Challenge winners and the support of loyal customers gave it just the edge it needed.

North of England – Winner: EH Booth

Another region with a fast-improving set of wine merchants. The contest here was between BH Wines, D. Byrne, Great Northern Wine Co, Portland Wine Co and our winners, the highly impressive EH Booth.

Central England – Winner: Windrush

Anthony Byrne, last year's winner, fought hard to take the award again, against strong competition from Bennets of Chipping Campden, Croque-en-Bouche, Connollys, Gauntleys of Nottingham and Tanners. He was, however, just pipped at the post by New and Old World specialist, Windrush.

West of England – Winner: Nobody Inn

Reid Wines, Averys, Richard Harvey, Christopher Piper... this quartet of first class merchants were all beaten to the finish by Nick Borst-Smith and his encyclopaedic range of wines at the Nobody Inn.

London/South East – Winner: Winecellars

The region, unsurprisingly, with the greatest number of worthy contenders, ranging from shops like The Hermitage, Lea & Sandeman, La Vigneronne and Roberson to traditional merchants like Corney & Barrow and Justerini & Brooks. Then there are the chains like Davisons and Fullers and warehouses such as Bibendum (last year's winner) and Winecellars. Ultimately, it was Winecellars who won the prize, thanks in part to this company's ability to conquer wine regions and countries beyond their specialist country, Italy.

Northern Ireland – Winner: Direct Wine Shipments

James Nicholson having been excluded (because of our 'no-hat-trick' rule), the choice in Ulster was between Direct Wine Shipments, Winemark and Stewarts Wine Barrel. In the event, the Award went to Direct Wine Shipments.

CATEGORY AWARDS

Wine List –Winner: John Armit

Despite the recession, wine merchants' lists get better every year. Would this year's winner be John Armit, Bottoms Up, Thos Peatling or Lay & Wheeler? In a photo-finish between Adnams, Bottoms Up and John Armit, ultimately it was the stylish John Armit catalogue which won the prize.

Regional Chain – Winner: Davisons

This South-east chain regularly surprises wine buffs with its combination of mature Bordeaux, Burgundy and port – and well chosen daily drinking. It faced tough competition from Thos Peatling, EH Booth and Fullers.

National Chain – Winner: Oddbins

Victoria Wine, Thresher, Majestic and Oddbins contested this (Wine Rack having won for the last two years). The winner was a familiar contender: Oddbins: 'still a really exciting place to buy wine'.

By-the-Case / By Mail – Winner: Adnams

The Wine Society being ineligible, the fight here was between Lay & Wheeler ('laudably efficient'), Majestic ('back on form') and the winner ('brilliantly enticing special case offers') Adnams.

'Going Places' – Winner: Asda

Kwiksave's sudden emergence as a supplier of drinkable, good value wine won it a place on the short-list, alongside the Co-op and Spar. The chain the judges felt to have developed most over the last 12 months, however, was Asda, which has become a source of a remarkable range of well-chosen wine.

Supermarket – Winner: Waitrose

Sainsbury's ('greatly improved') Tesco and Safeway ('innovative') were beaten by more than a head by Waitrose, whose 'already excellent range seemed to take a further leap ahead this year'.

Small Independent – Joint Winners: The Hermitage and Helen Verdcourt

Gill Reynolds and Helen Verdcourt exemplify precisely what we intended when creating this award: two fiercely independent merchants who work extraordinarily hard to choose, talk about and sell (at fair prices) ranges of first class wine. Also worthily shortlisted were the Australian Wine Centre, Derek Smedley, Nadder Wine Co, Summerlee, Roger Harris and BH Wines.

SPECIALIST MERCHANTS

'Fine & Rare' – Winner: T&W

The expression 'Fine and Rare' is especially appropriate for this East Anglian merchant which offers its customers a choice between the rarest classics of the Old World, and the finest of the New World. The other contenders were Reid Wines, Farr Vintners and Turville Valley.

Burgundy – Winner: Howard Ripley

Good Burgundy is becoming easier to buy – from merchants like Anthony Byrne, Berkmann/Le Nez Rouge, Bibendum, Gelston Castle, Justerini & Brooks, Domaine Direct, Haynes Hanson & Clarke and Morris & Verdin. However, no one is more exclusively obsessive about getting Burgundy right than Howard Ripley.

Bordeaux – Winner: Thos Peatling

Short listed for two other awards, Thos Peatling wrested this prize from the jaws of Averys, Davisons and the Wine Society. The judges were especially impressed by the range of vintages offered and the fairness of the prices.

Rhône – Winner: Justerini & Brooks

Adam Bancroft, Gauntleys of Nottingham and – a *very* close second – Yapp Bros were all chasing Justerini here, but none of them quite made it. This is a really impressive list of producers and wines.

German – Winner: Berry Bros & Rudd

An embattled group of merchants still try to specialise in German wines, despite the apathy of their customers. Our shortlist included Summerlee, Gelston Castle and the Wine Schoppen, but it was Berry Bros & Rudd which most impressed the judges with the depth and breadth of its range.

Italian – Winner: Valvona and Crolla

Winecellars, Valvona's deadly rival for this award, were not eligible, but the Scottish specialist still had to compete with the ranges offered by Lea & Sandeman and Adnams.

Spanish – Winner: Oddbins

Moreno and Laymont & Shaw both fight the good fight for Spain and Thresher has certainly tried to broaden its range. Even so, Oddbins won this award for doing the difficult thing of going out to find interesting *new* wines in a country where few such beasts exist.

New World – Winner: Wine Rack

If the flavour of New Zealand wines has become familiar to tens and probably hundreds of thousands of Britons, much of the credit must go to Kim Tidy and his team of buyers at Wine Rack. Adnams, Lay & Wheeler, Oddbins and the Australian Wine Centre were all worthily shortlisted.

WINE MERCHANT OF THE YEAR
Joint Winners: Winecellars and Wine Rack

If choosing winners for each of the categories was tough, selecting an overall winner gave our judges a greater headache. There were too many impressive contenders. Ultimately, as in the last two years, they felt forced to give the award to a pair of equally deserving companies: Winecellars and Wine Rack.

Winecellars is an extraordinary phenomenon: a first class merchant which has actually got even better. Over the last year, an already dazzling Italian selection has been increasingly complemented by brilliantly chosen wines from just about everywhere else. The service in the shop and by telephone is as efficient as it is friendly. In short, this is a great wine merchant.

The fight between Wine Rack and Oddbins was the toughest of all. Ultimately, the judges turned to the results of the International Wine Challenge. Oddbins did not directly enter the competition this year. Wine Rack submitted a large number of wines and won a large number of medals and commendations. But, as we say, companies are not exclusively judged on the number of awards achieved but on the *proportion* of successful entries. Wine Rack's entry, despite its size, was proportionally the most successful of any chain. It was this success, coupled with its efforts to train its staff, and to introduce customers to an ever-growing range of exciting wines, which won Wine Rack this award.

WINES OF THE YEAR

Over the past decade, the *Guide* has proved remarkably prescient in spotting (and helping to nurture) new trends. It was the *Guide*, for example, that first drew public attention to such now-familiar wines as New Zealand's Montana Sauvignon Blanc, Grassa's Vin de Pays des Côtes de Gascogne and Penfolds Bin 28 Shiraz. The 1992 *Guide*'s three Sparkling Wines of the Year – the Mumm Cuvée Napa Rosé, Lindauer and Salinger – were the focus of heated debate on Champagne, while the success of last year's tremendous Stratford Zinfandel enabled Britain's professional wine buyers to stand their ground when arguing with the Californians who claimed it was impossible for them to produce a high-quality wine to sell in the UK for less than £5.

Any wine which wins this award has a lot to live up to.

Joint Red Wines of the Year: Albor Rioja Tinto 1991; Michel Lynch Bordeaux Rouge 1989; Mas de Figaro, Vin de Pays de l'Hérault 1992

Three very different wines, each of which reveals a fresh approach. Most wine drinkers think they know how Rioja and Bordeaux taste but the Albor and Michel Lynch both demonstrate the exciting direction in which modern winemaking is heading. Traditionally, Bordeaux drinkers who didn't wish to splash out on a Cru Classé or Cru Bourgeois had the choice between taking pot luck with a *Petit Chateau* or accepting the mediocrity of a branded or own-label Bordeaux Rouge, Medoc or St Emillion.

Joint White Wines of the Year: Hardy's Moondah Brook Estate Chenin Blanc 1992; Chardonnay Gyongyos 1992

Last year the Hardy Wine Company made the Gewürztraminer-Riesling; this year they've hit the target again with an oaked Chenin Blanc, one of the few affordable whites to win a Gold Medal in the Challenge. The Gyongos reveals both the progress made in white winemaking in Eastern Europe over the past couple of years and the key role played by Hugh Ryman (maker of this and two previous wines of the year) in that process.

Sparkling Wines of the Year: Le Grand Pavillon de Boschendal Cuvée Brut Blanc de Blancs; Victoria Wine Vintage Champagne 1986

After all the brouhaha surrounding Grande Marque Champagnes over the past couple of years, and the stunning success of fizz from Australia, New Zealand and California, we were delighted to choose two Sparkling Wines of the Year which broaden the debate still further. The Le Grand Pavilion de Boschendal is a lovely rich South African fizz made by the Champagne method from a blend of three types of white grape: the Chardonnay, Semillon and Riesling. (Who says Pinot and Chardonnay are the *only* varieties to use?)

The Victoria Wine Vintage Champagne comes from Marne et Champagne, one of the biggest producers in the region, but one that somehow rarely gets mentioned by writers extolling the virtues of the big names who offer the hospitality and pay for all the advertising. In three Wine Challenges, this wine – and the previous vintage – has proved to be more consistently good than any big-name fizz.

AVAILABILITY

Among the gratifyingly large number of letters we receive from our readers there is the occasional complaint that one or other of the merchants named has run out of a particular recommended wine. We would love to be able to guarantee availability. Indeed, we specifically ask retailers to confirm that they have sufficient stock to ensure availability through the spring. They should also be selling at prices quoted in the *Guide* – though obviously merchants may be affected by changes in currency and duty rates.

Last year, almost 50,000 people bought copies of the *Guide*. If only half that number purchased a single bottle of one of our recommended wines, merchant's cellars would be emptied. Were we to restrict our recommendations to wines made in huge quantities, this would be a very dull book.

HOW TO USE THE GUIDE

The *Guide* is split into three main sections. First, on p.33, is the **A-Z** glossary which includes definitions of 1,000 wine-related terms, recommended vintages, approximate prices, producers and stockists. Where a wine features elsewhere in the *Guide*, its code number will appear; otherwise a typical example and a stockist is given.

Secondly, on p.69, there is the the list of 500 recommended wines (**The Wines**), listed by style in order of price. Every wine in this section has a code number which features elsewhere in the *Guide*, plus one or more stockist's codes, indicating where the wine may be bought. And we list coded food sugestions, explained in the **Wine With Food** chapter (p.16).

Finally, the **Stockists** section (p.115) lists and describes 250 wine merchants alphabetically, along with the recommended wines they sell.

HOW TO READ THE ENTRIES

The Wines Listing

304[1]   **ROSSO SECONDO**[2] VINATTIERI[3] 1985[4] TUSCANY[5] (IT)[6]
£9.65 [7]   ☛BI [8]   ↻ j, k, m [9]

From a partnership of three of Italy's best wine experts, this is a deep purple, blackcurranty wine with dusky tannin and rich tarry fruit right to the finish – very New World style.[10]

1   The code number that refers to this wine
2   The wine name
3   The producer, though with New World wines in particular, this may already feature in the wine name – for example:
     MONTANA[3] **SAUVIGNON BLANC**[2] 1989[4] Marlborough[5] (NZ)[6]
4   The vintage
5   The region in which the wine was made
6   The country in which the wine was made
7   The price we would expect you to pay, not an average price
8   The stockists – for codes, see p.16
9   Foods that might go well with this wine – for codes, see p.66
10 Tasting notes

Wine names printed in red indicate particularly good quality and value.

The Stockists' Listing

Recommended wines are listed beneath each merchant thus:

354 [1] **£10.75** [2] **CORNAS** [3], **Guy de Barjac** [4], **Rhône (F)** [5] **1986** [6]

1. The code number – refer to **The Wines** for tasting notes
2. The price which the stockist charges for the wine
3. The wine name
4. The producer
5. The region/country
6. The vintage

Wine names printed in red indicate particularly good quality and value.

The Stockists' Codes

A	Asda Stores Ltd	**CWI**	A Case of Wine
AB	Augustus Barnett Ltd	**CWM**	Cornwall Wine Merchants Ltd
ABA	Adam Bancroft Assocs	**CWS**	Co-operative Wholesale Society
ABB	Abbey Cellars	**CWW**	Classic Wine Warehouses Ltd
ABY	Anthony Byrne Fine Wines Ltd	**C&A**	Chennell & Armstrong Ltd
ADN	Adnams Wine Merchants	**C&B**	Corney & Barrow Ltd
AF	Alexr Findlater & Co	**D**	Davisons Wine Merchants
AK	Arriba Kettle & Co	**DAL**	David Alexander
AMA	Amathus	**DBW**	David Baker Wines
AMW	Amey's Wines	**DBY**	D Byrne & Co
AUC	Australian Wine Centre	**DD**	Domaine Direct
AV	Averys of Bristol	**DHM**	Douglas Henn-Macrae
BAL	Ballantynes of Cowbridge	**DIR**	Direct Wine Shipments
BAR	Barwell & Jones	**DWL**	The Sunday Times Wine Club
BBR	Berry Bros & Rudd Ltd	**DX**	Mayfair Cellars
BD	Bordeaux Direct	**EBA**	Ben Ellis & Associates Ltd
BE	Bin Ends (London)	**ECK**	Eckington Wines
BEN	Bennetts	**EE**	Eaton Elliot Wine Merchant
BFI	Bedford Fine Wines Ltd	**EP**	Eldridge Pope & Co plc
BGC	Borg Castel	**ES**	Edward Sheldon
BH	B H Wines	**EVI**	Evingtons Wine Merchants
BI	Bibendum Wine Ltd	**FAR**	Farr Vintners Ltd
BLS	Balls Brothers Ltd	**FDL**	Findlater Mackie Todd
BN	Bin Ends (Rotherham)	**FNZ**	Fine Wines of New Zealand Ltd
BNK	The Bottleneck	**FSW**	Frank E Stainton
BOO	Booths of Stockport	**FUL**	Fuller Smith & Turner plc
BRO	Broad Street Wine Co	**FV**	Fernlea Vintners
BTH	E H Booth & Co	**FWC**	The Fulham Road Wine Centre
BU	Bottoms Up	**F&M**	Fortnum & Mason
BUT	The Butlers Wine Cellar	**G**	Gateway Foodmarkets Ltd
BWC	Berkmann Wine Cellars/Le Nez Rouge	**GBY**	Elizabeth Gabay and Partners
BWI	Bute Wines	**GDS**	Garrards
BWS	The Barnes Wine Shop	**GEL**	Gelston Castle Fine Wines
CAC	Cachet Wines	**GEW**	Great English Wines
CAP	Cape Province Wines	**GH**	Goedhuis & Co Ltd
CC	Chiswick Cellar	**GHS**	Gerard Harris Fine Wines
CEB	Croque en Bouche	**GI**	Grape Ideas
CFT	Clifton Cellars	**GLY**	Gallery Wines
CHF	Chippendale Fine Wines	**GNW**	The Great Northern Wine Co
CIW	City Wines Ltd	**GON**	Gauntleys of Nottingham
CNL	Connolly's	**GRO**	Grog Blossom
COK	Corkscrew Wines	**GRT**	Great Western Wine Company
COR	Corn Road Vintners	**G&M**	Gordon & Macphail
CPS	CPA's Wine Ltd	**HAM**	Hampden Wine Co
CPW	Christopher Piper Wines Ltd	**HEM**	The Hermitage
CRC	The Claret Club	**HFV**	Harcourt Fine Wine
CRL	The Wine Centre/ Charles Steevenson Wines	**HHC**	Haynes, Hanson & Clarke
CT	Charles Taylor Wines Ltd	**HLV**	Halves Ltd
CUM	The Cumbrian Cellar	**HOL**	Holland Park Wine Co
CVR	The Celtic Vintner Ltd	**HOT**	House of Townend

HOU	Hoult's Wine Merchants
HPD	Harpenden Wines
HR	Howard Ripley
HUD	Hudsons Fine Wines
HUN	Hungerford Wine Co
HV	John Harvey & Sons
HVW	Helen Verdcourt
HW	Hedley Wright & Co Ltd
H&D	Hicks & Don
H&H	Hector & Honorez Wines Ltd
JAG	J A Glass
JAR	John Armit Wines
JAV	John Arkell Vintners
JCK	J C Karn
JEH	J E Hogg
JFD	John Ford Wines
JFR	John Frazier Ltd
JN	James Nicholson
JOB	Jeroboams
JS	J Sainsbury Plc
J&B	Justerini & Brooks Ltd
KS	Kwiksave
K&B	King & Barnes Ltd
LAV	Les Amis du Vin
LAY	Laytons Wine Merchants Ltd
LEA	Lea & Sandeman Co Ltd
LEF	Le Fleming Wines
LES	C R S Ltd - Leos
LV	La Vigneronne
LWE	London Wine Emporium Ltd
LWL	London Wine Ltd
L&S	Laymont & Shaw Ltd
L&W	Lay & Wheeler Ltd
MAD	Madeleine Trehearne Partners
MAR	Marco's Wines
MAW	M & A Winter
MC	Master Cellar
MCL	McLeod's
MFW	Marcus Fyfe Wines
MG	Matthew Gloag & Son Ltd
MM	Michael Menzel Wines
MOR	Moreno Wine Importers
MRN	Wm Morrison Supermarkets
MTL	Mitchells Wine Merchants Ltd
MWW	Majestic Wine Warehouses
MYS	Mayor Sworder & Co Ltd
M&S	Marks & Spencer plc
M&V	Morris & Verdin Ltd
NAD	The Nadder Wine Co. Ltd
NI	Nobody Inn
NIC	Nicolas UK Ltd
NRW	Noble Rot Wine Warehouse Ltd
NY	Noel Young Wines
N&P	Nickolls & Perks Ltd
OD	Oddbins Ltd
ORG	The Organic Wine Co Ltd
OWL	O.W. Loeb & Co Ltd
P	Parfrements
PEY	Philip Eyres Wine Merchant
PGR	Patrick Grubb Selections
PHI	Philglas & Swiggot
PLA	Playford Ros Ltd
PMR	Premier Wine Warehouse
PON	Le Pont de la Tour
POR	The Portland Wine Co
PRW	Protea Wines
PTR	Peter Green & Co
PUG	Pugsons of Buxton
PWY	Peter Wylie Fine Wines
R	R S Wines
RAE	Raeburn Fine Wines
RAM	The Ramsbottom Victuallers
RAV	Ravensbourne Wine
RBS	Roberson Wine Merchant
RD	Reid Wines (1992) Ltd
RES	La Reserve
RHV	Richard Harvey Wines
RIB	Ribble Vintners Ltd
RN	Rex Norris Wine Merchants
ROD	Rodney Densem Wines
ROG	Roger Harris Wines
RTW	The Rose Tree Wine Co
RWC	Rioja Wine Co Ltd
RWW	Richmond Wine Warehouse
R&I	Russell & McIver Ltd
SAC	Le Sac a Vin
SAF	Safeway Stores plc
SAN	Sandiway Wine Co
SAS	Sherston Wine Co
SEB	Sebastopol Wines
SEL	Selfridges
SHG	Wine Shop on the Green
SHJ	S. H. Jones & Co Ltd
SHV	Sherborne Vintners
SK	Seckford Wines
SOM	Sommelier Wine Co Ltd
SPG	Springfield Wines
SPR	Spar UK Ltd
STW	Stewarts Wine Barrels
SUM	Summerlee Wines Ltd
SUP	Supergrape Ltd
SV	Smedley Vintners
SWB	Satchells of Burnham Market
TAN	Tanners Wines Ltd
TH	Thresher Wine Shops
THP	Thos Peatling
TO	Tesco Stores plc
TOJ	Tony Jeffries Wines
TP	Terry Platt Wine Merchant
TRE	Tremaynes
TRW	Trinity Wine
TVW	Turville Valley Wines
T&W	T & W Wines
U	Unwins Wine Merchants
UBC	Ubiquitous Chip
VDV	Vin du Van
VER	Vinceremos Wines & Spirits Ltd
VIL	Village Wines
VLW	Villeneuve Wines Ltd
VR	Vintage Roots
VT	The Vine Trail
VW	Victoria Wine
V&C	Valvona & Crolla Ltd
W	Waitrose Ltd
WAC	Waters of Coventry Ltd
WAW	Waterloo Wine Co Ltd
WBM	Wine Byre Merchants
WCE	Winecellars
WDW	Windrush Wines Ltd
WE	The Wine Emporium/ Cockburn's of Leith Ltd
WEP	The Welshpool Wine Company
WES	Wessex Wines
WGW	Woodgate Wines
WHC	Whiclar & Gordon Wines Ltd
WIN	The Winery
WL	William Low & Company plc
WMK	Winemark Wine Merchant
WNS	Winos Wine Shop
WOC	Whitesides of Clitheroe Ltd
WOI	Wines of Interest
WR	Wine Rack
WRB	Robbs of Hexham
WRW	The Wright Wine Co
WSC	The Wine Schoppen Ltd
WSO	The Wine Society
WTL	Whittalls Wines
WTR	The Wine Treasury Ltd
WWT	Whitebridge Wines
YAP	Yapp Brothers

MERCHANTS BY REGION

The following pages will help you to find the nearest wine merchant in any part of the country. Companies marked in red are regional chains, and the the area they cover is indicated in brackets after the company name.

LONDON
E2
Balls Brothers Ltd
EC1
Corney & Barrow Ltd
EC3
Russell & McIver Ltd

N2
Grog Blossom
N7
Berkmanns Wine Cellars/Le Nez Rouge
N10
The Hermitage
N13
Amathus
N21
Howard Ripley

NW1
Bibendum
Laytons Wine Merchants Ltd
NW3
Madeleine Trehearne
NW5
Fine Wines of New Zealand
NW6
Grog Blossom
NW10
Les Amis du Vin

SE1
O W Loeb
Mayfair Cellars
Le Pont de la Tour
Waterloo Wine Co
SE10
Ravensbourne Wine Co
SE11
London Wine Emporium Ltd
Mayor Sworder

SW1
Berry Brothers & Rudd
Farr Vintners
Jeroboams
Justerini & Brooks
Laytons
Morris & Verdin
The Wine Treasury Ltd

SW2
Trinity Wine
SW3
La Réserve
SW6
Fulham Rd Wine Centre
Haynes Hanson & Clark
Premier Wine Warehouse
Le Sac a Vin
SW7
La Vigneronne
SW8
Goedhuis
SW10
London Wine Co
Lea & Sandeman
SW11
Philglas & Swiggot
SW12
Fernlea Vintners
SW13
The Barnes Wine Shop
SW15
Hudsons
SW18
Marco's
Supergrape
Winecellars
SW19
Findlater Mackie Todd
SW20
Elizabeth Gabay

W1
Adam Bancroft
Fortnum & Mason
Harcourt Fine Wine
Selfridges
W2
Moreno Wine Importers
W4
Chiswick Cellars
Fuller Smith & Turner plc (South East)
W8
Bute Wines
Haynes Hanson & Clark
Nicolas
W9
Moreno Wine Importers
The Winery
W11

John Armit Wines
Grog Blossom
Holland Park Wine Co
W14
Protea

WC1
Bin Ends
Domaine Direct
WC2
Australian Wine Centre

AVON
Bath
Great Western Wine
Bristol
Averys of Bristol
Clifton Cellars
John Harvey & Sons
R S Wines
Reid Wines (1992) Ltd
Vine Trail

BEDFORDSHIRE
Bedford
Bedford Fine Wines Ltd
Luton
Smedley Vintners

BERKSHIRE
Bracknell
Waitrose (South, East Anglia and Midlands)
Hungerford
The Claret Club
The Hungerford Wine Co
Maidenhead
David Alexander
Helen Verdcourt Wines
Reading
Bordeaux Direct
Great English Wines
The Sunday Times Wine Club
Wargrave
Vintage Roots

BUCKINGHAMSHIRE
Amersham
Philip Eyres
Aston Clinton

Gerard Harris
Fine Wines
Great Missenden
Turville Valley Wines
High Wycombe
The Organic Wine Co

CAMBRIDGESHIRE
Cambridge
Noel Young
Kimbolton
Hector & Honorez Wines Ltd
Ramsay
Anthony Byrne

CHESHIRE
Alderley Edge
Eaton Elliot
Buxton
Pugsons of Buxton
Chester
Classic Wine Warehouses
Nantwich
Rodney Densem Wines
Sale
Portland Wine Co
Sandiway
Sandiway Wine Co
Stockport
Booths of Stockport

CORNWALL
Cambourne
Cornwall Wine Merchants
Truro
Laymont & Shaw

CUMBRIA
Carlisle
Corkscrew
B H Wines
Cockermouth
Garrards
Kendall
Frank E Stainton
Lowick
Woodgate Wines
Penrith
The Cumbrian Cellar

DEVON
Doddiscombsleigh
The Nobody Inn
Ottery St Mary
Christopher Piper Wines
Plymtree
Peter Wylie Fine Wines
Tavistock
The Wine Centre/Charles
Steevenson Wines

DORSET
Blandford St Mary
Hicks & Don

Bridport
Wessex Wines
Dorchester
Eldridge Pope (South)
Sherborne
Sherborne Vintners
Wareham
Richard Harvey Wines

ESSEX
Chigwell
M&A Winter
Colchester
Lay & Wheeler

GLOUCESTERSHIRE
Cheltenham
J C Karn & Son
The Rose Tree Wine
Windrush Wines Ltd
Chipping Campden
Bennetts Wine & Spirit

**HEREFORD &
WORCESTERSHIRE**
Bromsgrove
Noble Rot Wine W'house
Evesham
Arriba Kettle
Malvern Wells
Croque en Bouche

HERTFORDSHIRE
Bishops Stortford
Hedley Wright & Co
Harpenden
Harpenden Wine
Le Fleming Wines
St Albans
Sherston Wine Co
Stevenage
The Wine Society

HUMBERSIDE
Hull
House of Townend
(Humberside)

KENT
Appledore
Vin du Van
Aylesford
Douglas Henn-Macrae
Bexley
Village Wines
Broadstairs
The Bottleneck
Dartford
Unwins (South East)
Wittersham
La Solitude

LANCASHIRE
Bury

The Ramsbottom Victuallers
Co Ltd
Clitheroe
D Byrne & Co
Whitesides of Clitheroe
Oldham
Winos Wine Shop
Preston
Borg Castel
E H Booth (North West)
Ribble Vintners

LEICESTERSHIRE
Leicester
Evingtons

LINCOLNSHIRE
Louth
McLeods

MIDDLESEX
Staines
Cape Province Wines

NORFOLK
Burnham Market
Satchells
Norwich
Adnams
City Wines
Thetford
T&W Wines
Weston Longville
Roger Harris Wines

NORTHAMPTONSHIRE
Northampton
Tony Jeffries Wines
Summerlee
Wines Ltd

NORTHUMBERLAND
Hexham
Robbs of Hexham
Morpeth
Corn Road Vintners

NOTTINGHAMSHIRE
Nottingham
Gauntley's of Nottingham

OXFORDSHIRE
Bicester
Patrick Grubb
Selections
S H Jones & Co Ltd
Blewbury
Sebastopol Wines
Henley-on-Thames
Tremaynes
Oxford
Grape Ideas
Thame
The Hampden Wine Co

SHROPSHIRE
Ludlow
Halves
Shrewsbury
Tanners (Central England
and Wales)

SOMERSET
Yeovil
Abbey Cellars

STAFFORDSHIRE
Stone
Whitebridge Wines

SUFFOLK
Bury St Edmunds
Thos Peatling (E. Anglia)
Halesworth
Alexr Findlater
Ipswich
Barwell & Jones (East
Anglia)
Seckford Wines
Wines of Interest
Newmarket
Corney & Barrow
Southwold
Adnams
Sudbury
Amey's Wines

SURREY
Brockham
Ben Ellis & Associates
Croydon
Davisons (South East)
The Master Cellar
Dorking
Whiclar & Gordon
Wines Ltd
Epsom
Charles Taylor Wines
Richmond
Richmond Wine
Warehouse

SUSSEX (East)
Haywards Heath
Rex Norris
Brighton
The Butlers Wine
Cellar
Hove
John Ford Wines

SUSSEX (West)
Horsham
King & Barnes

WARWICKSHIRE
Coventry
Parfrements
Shipston on Stour

Edward Sheldon
Warwick
The Broad St Wine Co
Waters of Coventry Ltd

WEST MIDLANDS
Birmingham
Connolly's
Solihull
John Frazier
Stourbridge
Nickolls & Perks Ltd
Wallsall
Whittalls Wines

WILTSHIRE
Mere
Yapp Brothers
Salisbury
Hicks & Don
Nadder Wine Co
Swindon
John Arkell Vintners

YORKSHIRE (North)
Skipton
The Wright Wine Co
Thirsk
Playford Ros Ltd
York
Cachet Wines
Chennell & Armstrong

YORKSHIRE (South)
Rotherham
Bin Ends
Sheffield
Eckington Wines
Michael Menzel
Mitchells Wine
Merchants Ltd
The Wine Schoppen Ltd

YORKSHIRE (West)
Huddersfield
Hoults Wine Merchants
Springfield Wines
Otley
Chippendale
Springfield
Leeds
The Great Northern
Wine Co
Ossett
Vinceremos Wines
& Spirits
Wakefield
Wm Morrison
Supermarkets (North)

N IRELAND
Co Down
James Nicholson
Belfast

Direct Wine Shipments
Stewarts Wine Barrels
(N. Ireland)
Winemark Winemerchant
(N. Ireland)
Londonderry
Gallery Wines

SCOTLAND
Argyll
Marcus Fyfe
Castle Douglas
Gelston Castle
Fine Wines
Dundee
William Low & Co plc
(Scotland)
Edinburgh
Peter Green
J E Hogg
Justerini & Brooks
Raeburn Fine Wines
Valvona & Crolla
The Wine Emporium/
Cockburns of Leith Ltd
Fife
J A Glass
Wine Byre
Glasgow
The Ubiquitous Chip
Isle of Bute
Bute Wines
Moray
Gordon & McPhail
Peebles
Villeneuve Wines Ltd
Perth
Matthew Gloag
& Son

WALES
Clwyd
Rioja Wine
Company
Dyfed
A Case Of Wine
Wine Shop on
the Green
Llandudno Junction
Terry Platt
Mid Glamorgan
David Baker
Powys
The Welshpool Wine Co
South Glamorgan
Ballantynes of
Cowbridge
Swansea
The Celtic Vintner
CPAs Wine

CHANNEL ISLANDS
Guernsey
Sommelier Wine Co

THIS YEAR

Adventurous wine lovers in the Pas de Calais owe rather a lot to the not entirely lamented Norman Lamont. Until the former Chancellor allowed his compatriots to fill their car boots with duty-free wine in France, the range on offer in Calais and Boulogne was less than exciting. Now, scarcely a week goes by without the opening of yet another British-owned 'Cash et Carry', packed to the gills with Australian, Californian and Chilean wines previously unheard of in France. Not to mention regional French wines which had escaped the notice of Gallic supermarket buyers obsessed with finding the cheapest Muscadet on the market, no matter how nasty its flavour.

Unfortunately for British merchants, Mr Lamont's largesse and his subsequent raising of the duty on wine (in direct contravention of our undertaking to harmonise rates with our European neighbours) compounded the effects of a devalued pound and swingeing business rates to make life just a little closer to impossible.

And, what's bad for those merchants is bad for those of us who buy our wine in Clapham or Carlisle rather than Calais or Cherbourg. This year's *Guide* is partly dedicated to the hard-working wine merchants whose businesses either had to be sold or closed completely. Firms like Italian specialists Millevini, who shut their doors, and Haughton Fine Wines who – rather more happily – became part of Adnams.

As one of the survivors, Patrick Toone put it, 'I very much fear that the independent personal wine merchant, like the individual fishmonger and butcher, will soon become a rarity.' Is this really what any of us wants?

By the time you read this, Britain's high streets will most probably have seen yet another takeover – by Victoria Wine of Augustus Barnett– which will leave the nation's drinking in the hands of Whitbread (Thresher, Wine Rack, Bottoms Up, Drink Stores), Seagram (Oddbins), Allied-Lyons (Victoria Wine, Augustus Barnett, Haddows) and a handful of big supermarkets.

Just as WH Smith and John Menzies now more or less control book and magazine distribution and Boots and Superdrug dictate the way we clean our homes and skin, wine producers wanting to sell their produce in Britain have only around a dozen telephone numbers to call.

This does nothing to encourage diversity. British wine drinkers are fortunate that the buyers of Britain's biggest chains are a more quality-conscious bunch than their counterparts on the other side of the Channel, where price and appellation are paramount. Even so, there are worrying trends here, too.

When Wine & Spirit International held a round table discussion in April, the buyers from Marks & Spencer and Sainsbury questioned why they should want to encourage their customers to buy wine at over £3 or £4 a bottle. And over the past few years, as cheap wine has been better made, far too many of us have fallen into the trap of saying: 'If the Bulgarian Cabernet tastes okay for £3, why lash out a fiver – let alone a tenner – on a bottle of Bordeaux?'

But there's another side to that coin: quality. Sometimes, even when you can't really afford it , it's worth paying a a little more for things that give you pleasure. Silk and cashmere are more sensual than man-made fibres; extra virgin olive oil tastes better than soya; Ferraris are more exciting to drive than Ford Escorts. And, yes, a £7 bottle of Australian fizz can wipe the floor with all sorts of £14 Champagne but not *good* £14 Champagne. And *that* is what this *Guide* is all about.

1993 was, in more ways than one, the year of Eastern Europe, with rampant privatisation leading to a plethora of new wine sources. Unfortunately, escape from state control does not automatically bring the ability to produce the style and quality of wine demanded by foreign buyers, which is where the 'flying winemakers' come in.

In 1992 and 1993, Australian-trained winemakers like Hugh Ryman, Nick Butler and Kym Milne and their teams rushed from winery to winery throughout the old Eastern bloc, overseeing the production of vats of Chardonnay, Cabernet, Sauvignon and Rkatsateli, ensuring that the grapes were crushed cleanly, fermented at the right temperature and the wine bottled in a hall from which birds (frequent visitors to one 'traditional' winery bottling line in Slovakia) have been excluded. This year, the *Guide* recognises this marriage of Eastern European potential and Antipodean expertise by making Hugh Ryman's Hungarian Gyongos Chardonnay one of our White Wines of the Year.

The flying winemakers have been just as busy in other parts of the world. Spain has seen the arrival of Jacques Lurton, whose Rueda Sauvignon shows just how easy it would be for the Spaniards to join the international market in fresh, characterful white wine. Things *are* changing in Iberia, as the buyers of Oddbins and Victoria Wine have proven with impressive new additions to their lists, but these are revolutionary exceptions to a conservative rule.

The Spaniards will have to watch out, though, if they are not to be overtaken by their neighbours to the west. Last year's Red Winemaker of the Year, Peter Bright, now has competition in Portugal from fellow Australian Peter Baverstock, who's helping to show what this country's indigenous grapes can do.

Italy, like Spain, a beneficiary of a devalued currency, is offering more interesting and increasingly affordable wines than ever. The bargains come from the south, Sicily and Sardinia, but the exciting flavours are to be found in Piedmont, where a young band of winemakers is proving that the tough, tannic reds with which their region is associated could soon be a thing of the past.

Germany is increasingly paying for its past mistakes. Just as some of the best German wines in years are hitting the German market, British merchants are giving up the struggle to sell anything more ambitious than an own-label hock. Oddbins deserves credit for plugging on with its excellent range but, revealingly, it's a two-producer show.

France, after the spectacular series of vintages in the 1980s, began the 1990s less happily. After frost cut the crop in half in 1991, rain diluted it almost everywhere in 1992. France's wine makers are also belatedly coming to terms with the fact that once-faithful foreign customers are regularly being seduced by wines produced in the New World.

Almost all the classic areas are feeling financially dejected. By far the worst effects have been felt in Champagne, where redundancies have led to public protests in the once-calm towns of Reims and Epernay and prices have returned to earth. Champagne of questionable quality was on sale in French supermarkets last year for 40 francs a bottle – less than the cost of the grapes from which it was made – and although big-name brands were officially holding out for big-name prices, most were doing deals galore.

Matters were calmer in Burgundy, though smaller merchants were alarmed at the speed by which one firm, Boisset, was swallowing up their neighbours and competitors. In Bordeaux, the merchants appeared to be slightly healthier financially than they had been in 1992, after successfully emptying their cellars of unimproving stocks of 1984 and 1987 reds. Now they have to find buyers for all those 1985s, 1986s 1988s and 1990s. And until they do, they're in neither the position nor the mood to buy very much new wine from the chateaux, even if it is sublime. In other words, the *en primeur* business is effectively dead and shows little likelihood of being revived.

Ironically, some of the strongest competition for regions like the Loire, Bordeaux and Burgundy, comes from close to home, with wines like Mas de Figaro, our joint Red Wine of the Year. The 1990s will be a boom time for the producers of Languedoc Roussillon, who have cast off their image of rustic red winemakers and taken on the mantle of high-tech Euro-Californians.

However, the French authorities believe that the greatest threat to their traditional regions lies in 'varietal' wines from other countries. Accordingly, they have banned the use of 'Chardonnay' from white Burgundy labels, outlawed 'Sauvignon Blanc' from Bordeaux, and so on. In effect, they are changing the lock on a door which is hanging on very fragile hinges.

What they *should* do is take a good look at the quality of the stuff *in* the bottles. As we go to press, the French are launching an expensive advertising campaign to persuade us all to look out for wines with the words 'Appellation Contrôlée' on their labels, because they are supposed to indicate reliable quality. But, as Dave West of the East Enders wine warehouse in Calais, famous for its Vino Collapso, cheerily says, 'We stock an awful Muscadet. We tell people not to buy it.' So much for appellation reliability.

In the New World, Australia continues to carve itself a reputation for value for money across the board. And in case people are tiring of big ripe wines, the Aussies are wheeling out subtler fare at just as attractive prices.

New Zealand has built a similarly enviable image among even less adventurous wine buyers, and Kiwi Sauvignon is now one of the wines most readily recognised when it is served 'blind'. Unfortunately, a pair of tricky and short harvests and the phylloxera louse, which is beginning to lay waste to New Zealand's best vineyards, may make wines like these less available and affordable. Enjoy them while you can.

South Africa's wines are beginning to live up to the promise prematurely hailed a couple of years ago, but they are handicapped by years of isolation and a UK wine trade which has been too ready to welcome *anything* from the Cape. But watch this space. 1994 could bring some far more exciting, good value wines.

In South America, Chile is the victim of its successful economy: a strengthening currency against the dollar has made exports less attractive. There are some highly commercial wines, but too few stars. Investment and expertise are flooding in, with Bordeaux names ranging from Eric de Rothschild of Château Lafite to Bruno Prats of Cos d'Estournel, but so far there has been little to show beyond basic good value wine. Given the success of wines from competitors in Argentina and Mexico in this year's International Wine Challenge, that's not good enough.

California, by contrast, produces loads of brilliant wines – though affordable, daily drinking is a concept with which California's producers have yet to come to grips, with the exception of the commendable wines of Stratford, Fetzer and Glen Ellen, and the forgettable ones of E&J Gallo and Sebastiani.

Closer to home, if there is one thing English winegrowers do not like, it is being informed periodically that they have 'come of age'. It must be as tedious as it is for a child to hear: 'My, how he has grown'. 1993 did, however, mark a turning point. First there was the belated announcement (long called for by the *Guide*) that the reconstituted, fermented Cyprus grape jelly which currently calls itself 'British' wine will no longer be able to do so. Secondly there was the opening of Denbies, the £5m, 100-acre winery-cum-vinous-theme-park near Dorking. Next there was the creation of the Harvest Group of vineyards under the leadership of superstar Australian winemaker John Worontschak.

For the first time, too, a group of English wine producers joined forces to promote themselves in Britain and overseas. I should like to thank the Government for following the lead of other countries in helping to support this export drive. But I can't. Because it didn't.

WINE AND HEALTH

Over the past year, the Wine-Is-Healthy bandwagon has gathered speed. It has a lot of ground to make up before it can draw level with All-Alcohol-Is-A-Dangerous-Drug which seems to have become a slogan in the US, but it is now increasingly acknowledged that moderate consumption of red wine in particular reduces the risk of heart disease by as much as 40%. Surveys are being conducted around the world, but the focus of attention is currently on Toulouse, where the so-called 'French Paradox' is most apparent. The rest of their diet ought to condemn the Toulousians to an early grave, but their wine intake is thought to play a major part in breaking down cholestrol.

Mind you, according to another report published by the Common Cold Research Unit in 1993, moderate wine drinkers also suffer less from colds than their teetotal neighbours. All of which puts a fresh twist on the tradition of clinking glasses and saying 'your health...'

ORGANIC WINES

As Britain's wine drinkers have sought out ever-cheaper bottles, higher priced organic wines have inevitably suffered. The good news for would-be green wine fans, though, is that, with every harvest, the number of organic wine producers grows, the quality of their products improves and, thanks to the EC, their organic status is more easily established. Encouragingly, too, organic wines are becoming more affordable. Adam Wynn has led the way in the New World but, by the time the 1995 *Guide* hits the streets, we expect a range of affordable organic wines to have arrived from Fetzer in California. In the meantime, organic wine fans should seek out the following recommended 'green' wines in the *Guide*, consult our specialist chart on p.254, or contact Cornucopia Health Foods (081-579 9431).

86   The Millton Vineyard Chardonnay, 1992
166 Terres Blanches Blanc, Aix en Provence les Baux 1992
221 Terres Blanches Vin Rosé, Aix en Provence, 1992
247 Domaine Anthea Merlot, 1992
289 Domaine Richeaume Cabernet Sauvignon, AOC Côtes de Provence, 1991
339 Botobolar Vineyard Shiraz, 1990
340 Côtes du Rhône, Domaine St. Apollinaire, Cuvée Cepage Syrah, 1990
354 Châteauneuf du Pape, Pierre Andre, 1990
364 Châteauneuf du Pape, Chateau de Beaucastel, 1988

LEARNING ABOUT WINE

Local authority-run classes are widely available but in London the best courses are run by Michael Schuster, Leith's School of Food and Wine and the Fulham Road Wine Centre, where you may end up tasting with the editor of the *Guide* (well, nothing's perfect). The premise behind these classes is that wine should be unpretentious, unprejudiced and, above all, fun.

For those who want more classical training, Christie's and Sotheby's run tastings often hosted by the winemakers themselves. Anyone wanting to join the wine trade, however, should make for the Wine & Spirit Education Trust, where you can take the basic (*very* basic) 'Certificate', the useful 'Higher Certificate' and the testing 'Diploma'. Only after you have cleared all three hurdles may you try the real high jump, the Master of Wine written and tasting exams. But be warned: it's now a two-year course, and fewer than 200 people have earned this qualification in three decades. Incidentally, if you know of good local authority courses and lecturers, please let us know.

Recommended wine courses: Michael Schuster (071-254 9734); Fulham Road Wine Centre (071-736 7009; fax 071-736 6648); Christie's Wine Course (071- 839 9060; fax 071-839 1611); Sotheby's (071-924 3287; fax 071-493 8080); Wine & Spirit Education Trust (071-236 3551; fax 071-329 0298); Leith's School of Food and Wine (071-229 0177 fax 071-937 5257) Grant's of St James (0483 506691); German Wine Academy (010 39 61 31 28 29 50); Lay & Wheeler (0206 764446; fax 0206 564488). Ecole de Vin, Chateau Loudenne (010 33 56 09 05 03; fax 010 33 56 09 02 87).

Tastings

For many people, a course is quite unnecessary; much can be learned by attending tutored tastings given by wine merchants – see chart beginning on p.244. Whether you attend a structured class or simply a tutored tasting, what you get out of it will depend largely on your teacher. The following people are especially worth travelling to hear: David Molyneux-Berry MW, Liz Berry MW, Jane Hunt MW, Charles Metcalfe, Michael Schuster, John Vaughan Hughes MW, Maggie McNie MW, Angela Muir MW, Richard Harvey MW, Oz Clarke, Michael Broadbent MW, David Gleave MW, Steven Spurrier, Pamela Vandyke Price, Serena Sutcliffe MW, Richard Hobson MW and Richard Mayson.

THE CASE FOR JOINING A WINE CLUB

As Waitrose, Sainsbury and Marks & Spencer join the wine-by-mail band-wagon, the *raison-d'etre* of wine clubs becomes increasingly questionable. The *Sunday Times* Wine Club still offers an enjoyable annual tasting in London and good wine tours, but very few vinous bargains for those whose only contact with the club is by mail. The Wine Society, which genuinely belongs to its members, *is* worth joining, if only to benefit from its depot in northern France. If, however, you want a club whose existence is not geared towards purchasing, there are all sorts of local wine appreciation societies that organise tastings presented by merchants and producers, plus theme dinners. In addition to those listed below, clubs with vacancies for new members are listed in the diary pages of both *WINE Magazine* and *Decanter*.

Wine merchant clubs

The Vintner (0923 51585; fax 0923 251585); Vin de Garde / Vintage Expectations (0372 463251); Châteaux Wines (0454 613959). For more see chart on p.244

Non-merchant wine clubs

Cofradia Riojana/Gallo Nero Wine Club (081-863 2135; fax 081-427 9944); The International Food and Wine Society (071-370 0909; fax 071-495 4191); Wine & Gastronomic Societies (081-427 9944); North East Wine Tasting Society (091-438 4107); Northern Wine Appreciation Group (0484 531228); The Wine and Dine Society (071-274 9484); The Winetasters (081-997 1252); For local wine groups see *WINE Magazine* or *Decanter* .

BUYING AT AUCTION

As Lloyds 'names' have to sell their cellars to pay their debts and restaurants and merchants call in the receivers, auction houses can prove a better than ever source of all sorts of wine. But don't get carried away. It's still worth keeping a check on what you end up paying per bottle. Auctions are not inevitably cheaper than wine merchants.

For details of the 'right' prices for top-flight wines, check *WINE Magazine*'s Fine Wine section, which gives examples of merchants' and auction prices. Remember, too, that a 'bargain' £50 case of Chablis can be a little less of a snip by the time you have added on the 10% buyer's premium, a pound or so a bottle duty and 17.5% VAT, and driven to Edinburgh to pick it up.

Among fine wines today, the 1978 and 1979 clarets are still underpriced and, when compared with the prices of the 1988s, 1989s and 1990s *en primeur*, the 1986s and 1985s look positively cheap. The 1983s and lesser 1982s are already looking surprisingly mature, but the best of the latter vintage are holding up wonderfully and deserve to be left alone for a long while yet. 1985s are generally delicious and should last, too, though 1986 (possibly an auction bargain) is going through a tough phase. The 1975s are finally 'coming round', but most 1970s show little sign of ever wanting to do so.

Auction Houses

Christie's Auction House (Wine Department 071-839 9060; fax 071-839 1611); Sotheby's (071-924 3287; fax 071-924 3287); Bigwood Auctioneers (0789 269 415; fax 0789 294168); Lacy Scott (0284 763531; fax 0284 704713); Lithgow Sons and Partners (0642 710158; fax 0642 712641); Phillips (0865 723524; fax 0865 791064); Jean Pierre et Fils (0273 308 422).

BUYING *EN PRIMEUR*/ INVESTING IN WINE

If you're thinking of buying wine as a 'future', we have one word of advice: don't. If you absolutely *must* put your money into wine, we'd recommend sticking to 'blue chip' first growths, but, in this post-Lloyds world, you'll still have to tread carefully. As we go to print, an auction which will include a single vendor's 100 cases of Château Mouton Rothschild 1982 has just been announced. Batches like this of what ought to be a rare wine are hardly likely to help a market that has already lost a lot of momentum following the surfeit of good vintages in the 1980s and their dearth since then. Sensible buyers have learned to wait until at least a year after the wine is initially offered – by which time it is often on offer for rather less at Oddbins.

The following companies should all offer good advice on wine investment: The Claret Club; Justerini & Brooks, who put together 'portfolios'; The Wine Society; Lay & Wheeler; Thos Peatling; and Berry Bros & Rudd (see *The Stockists* p.115 for addresses) and Pat Simon (081-455 8255; fax 081-458 6825)

Specialists in fine, rare and old wines

For ready-matured wine, contact the merchants listed in the chart starting p.254, or Wine on the Green (071-794 1143); Domaine Direct (071-837 1142; fax 071-837 8605).

WINE TOURS and WINE WEEKENDS

1993 was as tough a year for wine tour organisers as it was for the rest of the travel industry. Before making your booking – through a wine merchant or directly through a tour operator – be sure to check that you are protected through some kind of bond.

Wine tours and weekends are rather like any other holiday organised for a group of like-minded people. They can be enormously successful – or extraordinarily tedious. In our experience, enjoyment depends only partly on one's fellow travellers; how well the trip has been organised has a much greater bearing. Make sure you know the name of the 'expert' leading the trip and, in the case of tours, the producers to be visited. A quality-conscious tour operator will take the trouble to choose high-quality winemakers; travel agents who are playing at wine tours will often opt for 'big names' irrespective of their worth.

From personal experience, we recommend World Wine Tours (0865 310344; fax 0865 310299); Arblaster & Clarke (0730 66883; fax 0730 68620) and The *Sunday Times* Wine Club (see *The Stockists*). Other companies include Blackheath Wine Trails (081-463 0012); Classic Wine Tours (0626 334233/010 33 53 58 81 48); Ian Dickson Travel (031-556 6777); Facet Travel (0825 732266; fax 0825 733330); Francophiles (0272 621975); Gourmet Espionnage (0379 71234); Grants of St James's (0483 64861); Knights of Languedoc (071-704 0589); Moswin Tours Ltd (0533 714982; fax 0533 716016); Tanglewood Wine Tours (09323 48720; fax 0533 716016); Walking with Wines (0432 840649); Network Wine, South Africa, (0509 891159; fax 0533 302701); Vacances Cuisine (010 33 94 04 49 77); Vinescapes (0903 744279); Vintage Wine Tours (0225 315834; fax 0225 446093); Wine Trails (081-463 0012; fax 081-463 0011) .

Hotels running wine weekends include Gleneagles (with Jancis Robinson, 0764 62231; fax 0764 62134); Imperial Hotel (0493 851113); Millers House Hotel (0969 22630); Mynd House Hotel (0694 722212); Norton House Hotel (031-333 1275; fax 031-333 5305); Studley Priory Hotel (0865 351203; fax 0865 351613).

STARTING A CELLAR

A few simple rules: avoid areas in which the temperature varies – constant warmth is better than the variations in, say, a kitchen. Avoid areas that are too dry; well-insulated cupboards and attics can make ideal cellars, but be sure to keep the humidity up with a sponge left in a bowl of water. Try to find a space where there is at least some air movement; cut air holes in cupboards if necessary. If the area you have chosen is damp, remember not to store wine in cardboard boxes. It sounds obvious, but even experienced wine buffs have lost wine by letting it fall from soggy boxes.

Spiral Cellars Ltd (0372 842692; fax 0372 360142) sell (and install, if you like) a purpose-built kit that can be sunk into the floor of your kitchen, garage or garden. Wine racks custom-built to fit awkward areas are available from Majestic Wine Warehouses and most other helpful wine merchants. To buy direct, contact: RTA Wine Racks (0328 78666; fax 0328 78667); A & W Moore (0602 607012; fax 0602 491308).

A cellar book provides an invaluable means of keeping track of your wines, and elegant ones have been produced by Hugh Johnson (published by Mitchell Beazley) and by Grants of St James's. These make fine Christmas or birthday presents but a simple exercise book will work just as well. Simply rule it up to allow space for you to indicate where and when you bought each wine; the price you paid; its position in your racks; when you open each bottle; tasting notes; and the guests to whom you served it. Most home computers will enable you to log the same information electronically.

If you would prefer not to store your wine at home, there is always the option of cellaring it with the merchants from whom you bought it (see our Merchants' services chart, p.244), provided you ensure your stock is clearly marked. Or you can rent space at Prime Wine Cellars (071-613 0763; fax 071-613 0765); Smith & Taylor (071-627 5070; fax 071-622 8235); Abacus (081-991 9717; fax 081-991 9611); or Octavian (081-853 5551; fax 081-858 4402).

GLASSES AND VINOUS GIFTS

There is so much nonsense talked about the 'right' glasses for the 'right' wine that I am tempted to not discuss the subject at all. My advice is to use any kind of clear glass whose rim has a smaller circumference than its bowl, and which is large enough to hold more than a few mouthfuls.

For real luxury, however, there are no better glasses than those produced by Riedel. They're available from the Conran Shop (071-589 7401) or Bibendum (see *The Stockists*) but unfortunately cost an arm and a leg. More affordable are Cristal d'Arques' wine taster-designed glasses (from Roberson, see *The Stockists*). As an inveterate glass-breaker, though, I buy Royal Leerdam's bargain Bouquet range. Very happily used by tasters at the 1993 *WINE International Wine Challenge*, they can be bought from The Wine Glass Company (0234 721300; fax 0234 720759). Other good glass stockists include Richard Kihl (071-586 3838) and The Barnes Wine Shop (see *The Stockists*)

Although the Philips Electric Corkscrew seems thankfully to have disappeared, there is an increasing number of very silly vinous gifts around. For sensible items, try Harrods or The Fulham Road Wine Centre, which also offers a range of antiquarian wine books. Richard Stanford (071-836 1321) also stocks old wine books, while Richard Kihl (071-586 3838) is a good source of vinous antiques and curiosities; Birchgrove Accessories (048328 5369; fax 048328 5360) has modern items, as does Hugh Johnson's ultra-smart shop opposite Berry Bros & Rudd (071-491 4912; fax 071-493 0602)

CORKSCREWS

Despite earnest attempts by competitors, the best corkscrew is still made by Screwpull (0264 358036; fax 0264 356777) in a variety of styles from the simple 'Spin-handle' (our favourite) to the ultra-sophisticated (and ultra-pricy) lever model. Available from good wine shops and department stores.

WINE PRESERVATION DEVICES

After years of experimentation, I would temper my enthusiasm for the Vacuvin vacuum pump (0264 332821; fax 0264 358036) which seems to suck fruit out of some wines, and recommend the 'Winesaver' from Drylaw House (031-558 3666), which keeps wine fresh in the same way as most modern wineries, by creating a layer of harmless, heavier-than-air inert gas which sits on the wine surface and prevents oxidation. It was used to great effect in the 1993 *International Wine Challenge*. The Wine-keeper from Anthony Byrne Fine Wines (see *The Stockists*) works on the same principle but is rather pricier.

CHILL OUT

The 'Chilla' looks like an old-style gas cooker with four wells (instead of gas rings) filled with freezing brine. Pop in the bottle(s) and 90 seconds later, (a little longer for Champagne) the wine is cold. Half- bottles can get lost down the holes but don't put your hand in to fish them out unless you want severe frostbite (Chilla 0850 264582) . At £700, the Chilla is probably a little pricey for the home. Slightly more affordable at £6.99 is 'Rapid Ice' a foil jacket you keep in the freezer and which will cool bottles in six minutes and keep them that way for up to three hours (Rapid Ice 0264 332821; fax 0264 356777).

BRING YOUR OWN

Eating out in Australia can be far more fun than it is in Britain - simply because some of the best restaurants in Sydney, Melbourne and Adelaide welcome customers who arrive bearing their own bottles. In this country, BYOs are as rare as hen's teeth; of the ones that do exist, even fewer serve food most of us would want to eat with a decent glass of wine. We'd recommend the short list below, but would love to hear of other establishments of interest to Australian-minded wine lovers.

Olivers Cafe, 10 Russell Gdns, London W14 (071-603 7645); Museum Street Cafe, 47 Museum St, London WC1 (071-405 3211); Melbournes, 74 Park St, Bristol (0272 22 6996).

WINE IN PUBS

I've always admired people with the courage or foolhardiness to order a glass of wine in a pub. The risks are too great of being given a deep golden 'Blancs de Blancs' only distinguishable from sherry by the size of the measure or a Liebfraumilch too poor to be given shed-room by Britain's least choosy supermarkets. But pubs don't *have* to serve bad wine; after all, they have come round to offering real beer, a choice of malt whiskies and even, in some cases, edible food, which is why, with this edition, we are launching a search for Britain's best wine pubs. The list below includes the cream of the crop so far, but we'd be grateful to hear from readers and publicans about pubs we should include in the 1995 *Guide*.

Beetle & Wedge, Moulsford, Oxfordshire; The Cornish Arms, Pendoggett, Cornwall; The Crown, Southwold, Suffolk; La Galoche, Tunbridge Wells, Dorset; The Green Man, Toot Hill, Essex; The New Inn, Cerne Abbas, Dorset; The Nobody Inn, Doddiscombsleigh, Devon; The Plough, Blackbrook, Surrey; The Red Lion, Steeple Aston, Oxfordshire; The Royal Oak, Yattendon, Cornwall; The Wykeham Arms, Winchester, Hampshire.

BUYING ABROAD

One of Britain's best independent merchants ruefully complained as we were going to press that 'Even my own brother-in-law bought the wine for his daughter's wedding in France – and then had the gall to ask me if I'd lend him the glasses from which to drink it.'

There is no doubt that importing your own wine is worthwhile – a 9F Minervois could cost you twice as much in Britain, and you could even save on a bottle of Aussie fizz – but there are a few rules to follow: look for wines you already know (easiest when dealing with a French offshoot of a UK merchant, like the Wine Society, Marco's, Richard Harvey or Windrush, or when going directly to the producer), or try a bottle before buying a case.

In French supermarkets especially, watch out for 'almost' wines: those made by a producer with a name similar to the one you actually want – V (for Victor) Leflaive, say, rather than V (for the more famous Vincent) – or wines made in less inspiring years than the better vintages. Champagne can be a real trap, even for the experienced: we sampled three bottles of identically labelled 39F fizz from Carrefour and they ranged from good, through adequate to ghastly.

Be careful, too, when shopping for 'big name' appellations such as Muscadet, Côtes du Rhône and Burgundy – Sainsbury's buyers choose these more carefully than their Gallic counterparts. And tread warily when confronted by 'bargain' big-name Bordeaux. As long as the pound is worth less than 8F, these wines are often far cheaper in the UK (*WINE Magazine*'s Fine Wine section gives a useful guide to what you ought to be paying).

PARTY PLANNING – 50 WINES FOR LESS THAN £3.50

For descriptions of these wines and details of stockists, please refer to
them by number in *THE WINES* section of the *Guide*.

191	£2.39	Gateway Hock, Rudolf Müller
199	£2.39	Tesco Hock, Deutsches Weintor
433	£2.59	Leziria Vinho Tinto, Vega Co-operative Almeirim 1992
463	£2.59	Sainsbury's Auslese Bereich Mittelhaardt, QmP, Sichel 1990
223	£2.65	Hungarian Country Wine Kekfrankos/Zweigelt, Villany, Zoltan Bella 1992
35	£2.67	Pelican Bay Semillon
36	£2.75	Sainsbury's Romanian Sylvaner, Jidvei
192	£2.79	Tesco Dry Hock, Tafelwein, Zimmerman Graff
● 241	£2.85	Young Vatted Merlot, Russe Winery 1992
242	£2.85	Tesco Bulgarian Cabernet Sauvignon, Lovico
66	£2.89	Safeway La Mancha, Rodriquez & Berger 1992
243	£2.89	Asda Merlot, Vin de Pays d'Oc, Skalli
244	£2.89	Russe Cabernet Cinsault
37	£2.95	Sainsbury's Do Campo Branco Terras do Sado, J.P. Vinhos
125	£2.95	Blaye Blanc, Ginestet 1992
324	£2.95	Tesco Côtes du Rhône, Michel Bernard
410	£2.95	Cortenova Merlot, Pasqua 1991
434	£2.95	Sainsbury's Do Campo Tinto, JP Vinhos
435	£2.95	Sainsbury's Arruda
67	£2.99	Safeway Californian White, Heublein 1992
● 187	£2.99	Morio Muskat, St Ursula 1992
193	£2.99	Rhine Riesling Great Plain, Mor Winery 1992
224	£2.99	Domaine Sapt Inour, Sincomar Parlier & Fermaud
225	£2.99	Victoria Wine French Full Red, Skalli
226	£2.99	Tesco Australian Red, Penfolds
411	£2.99	Tesco International Winemaker Basilicata Rosso, Jacques Lurton 1992
456	£2.99	Sainsbury's Muscat de St Jean de Minervois, Val d'Orbieu
38	£3.09	Vin de Pays de L'Hérault Blanc, Skalli 1992
227	£3.09	Spar Coteaux du Languedoc
457	£3.09	Safeway Moscatel de Valencia, Gandia
68	£3.19	Somerfield Australian Dry White
212	£3.19	Clairet de Gaston, Bordeaux, Peter A. Sichel
325	£3.19	Casa del Campo Syrah, Bodegas Santa Ana 1992
126	£3.25	Vin de Pays d'Oc, Sur Lie, J & F Lurton 1992
245	£3.25	Coop California Ruby Cabernet, P. Flemming France
246	£3.25	Dunavar Connosseur Collection Merlot, Danubiana Bonyhad 1990
228	£3.29	Frankovka, Vino Nitra 1991
412	£3.29	Tesco Monica di Sardegna, Dolianova
● 39	£3.35	Chardonnay Gyongyos, Hugh Ryman 1992
40	£3.35	Safeway Chardonnay del Triveneto, G.I.V. 1992
127	£3.35	La Coume de Peyre, Vin de Pays des Cotes de Gascogne, Plaimont 1992
436	£3.35	Safeway Cariñena, Bodegas Coop San Valero 1988
128	£3.39	Tesco Sauvignon Blanc, Univitis
● 229	£3.39	Val Du Torgan, Les Producteurs du Mont Tauch
230	£3.39	Somerfield Californian Dry Red
69	£3.49	Tolleys Pedare Chenin Colombard 1990
129	£3.49	Tesco Nuragus, Dolianova
194	£3.49	Tollana Dry White 1992
247	£3.49	Domaine Anthea Merlot, Serge Ziggiotti 1992
464	£3.49	Monbazillac Domaine du Haut Rauly, Alard 1990

THE COUNTRIES

Australia

The Antipodean revolution goes on. Sales have gone up by another 100% and, most hearteningly, Jacob's Creek overtook E&J Gallo, despite the Californians' multi-million-dollar advertising campaign, proving that British wine drinkers prefer value for money to marketing muscle.

When we came to analyse the results of the International Wine Challenge, the findings confirmed what we have all suspected: Australia is the world's most reliable source of decent, drinkable wines at every price level. In the process of examining the wine lists of some 350 or so merchants to select the 250 that we have finally chosen to appear in the *Guide*, it also became clear that Aussie wines are no fashion item; they're here to stay.

More interesting, however, is the new trend towards lighter, and subtler styles, alternatives to the oaky blockbusters with which regions like the Hunter Valley first seduced us.

For specialist stockists, see the chart beginning on p.254, plus: The Wine Spot (061-748 2568); Bow Wine Vaults (071-248 1121; fax 071-248 8673); Peter Watts Wines (0376 561130; fax 0376 562925)

Austria

As Bordeaux discovered in the early 1970s, scandals can do a wine region a lot of good. A decade after Austria's winemakers hit the headlines for all the wrong reasons, they are back winning medals and praise for brilliantly made, ripely dry and spicily sweet wines. So far they are still rarities in Britain, though T&W Wines (see *The Stockists*) offer the extraordinary Willi Opitz wines that should give you an idea of what Austria can do.

For specialist stockists, see the chart beginning on p.254, plus: Caxton Tower (081-758 4500; fax 081-568 9149).

Eastern Europe

Watching the wine industry of Eastern Europe is rather like examining a colony of exceptionally hard-working ants. Everybody is heading in every which way. Countries are splitting apart (last year's Czechoslovakian wines are this year's Czech and Slovakian wines); privatisation is in full swing (the Bulgarian Vintners monopoly has been challenged by three competitors in Britain); and foreign investors and buyers are flooding in, bearing dollars and bringing equipment and expertise.

This year's joint White Wine of the Year, the 1992 Gyongos Hungarian Chardonnay from Hugh Ryman, is the best widely available example of the new wave and a role model for white wine producers aiming to update such dull-as-ditchwater wines as the Khan Khrum range. But fellow flying winemakers are at work throughout the region and new wines are arriving in the shops almost every week.

The result is a deliciously confusing array of new styles, from Ryman's Moldovan Rkatsateli to Safeways' brilliant Young Vatted Merlot, a fresh young wine that should serve as an excellent role model for all those tired, stewy, Eastern European reds.

For specialist stockists, see the chart beginning on p.254, plus: Bulgaria: Wines of Westhorpe (0283 820285; fax 0283 820631); Slovakia: Heart of Europe Wine Co (071 384 2588; fax 071 736 6648); Slovenia: Teltscher Brothers (071-987 5020; fax 071- 515 3957); Vitkovitch Bros (071-261 1770; fax 071-633 9123).

Eastern Mediterranean

Greece

'We keep trying to find and sell good Greek wines, but neither activity's easy.' This comment, from one of Britain's biggest wine buyers, says it all. Things *are* changing, but on the shelves of British wine merchants, decent Greek wine is still the exception rather than the rule.

The exasperated buyer quoted above was murmuring about the possibility of sending in a flying winemaker to see what could be done with Greece's native grapes. I hope one lands there soon. In the meantime, try the Gentile wines from Bibendum (see *The Stockists*).

For specialist stockists, see the chart beginning on p.254, plus: The Greek Wine Centre (0743 364636; fax 0743 367960); Chris Milia (071-485 5032; fax 071-482 4557).

Israel

Little news to report since the last *Guide*. The Golan Heights winery's Muscat and Cabernet Sauvignon are still worth looking out for.

Specialist stockists: Selfridges; Tesco (see *The Stockists*); Peter Hallgarten (071-722 1077).

England

Besides the fact that they were working in one of the few European countries to produce attractive wines in 1992, English winemakers have other reasons to celebrate. For the first time, a couple of their wines have beaten more established competitors to win Gold medals in the *WINE Magazine* International Wine Challenge; the Denbies Winery opened to the public, offering visitors the chance to enjoy a vinous theme park to match any in the New or Old World; and English winemakers finally began working together to promote their wines.

And their efforts seem to be getting results, with English labels finding their way on to the shelves of almost every supermarket in the country.

For specialist stockists, see the chart beginning on p.254, plus: The English Wine Centre (0323 870532; fax 0323 870005).

France

Alsace

Thrust into the spotlight by Thresher, whose Alsace Club was launched in May, this region is continuing to win new friends. But the Alsatians will have to beware. There are some very disappointing wines from 1990, 1991 and 1992 that display a tendency to squeeze too much juice out of every acre. Great winemakers like Olivier Zind Humbrecht still show what can be done, but it remains a region in which buyers would do well to tread warily.

For specialist stockists, see the chart beginning on p.254, plus: Farthinghoe (0295 710018; fax 0295 711495); Curzon Wine Co (071-499 3327).

Bordeaux

After the frost-hit vintage of 1991, the Bordelais ought to have been happy with a large crop in 1992. Unfortunately, the deluge of wine owed much of its bulk to the rain that punctuated the harvest. Skilled wine-making enabled the more quality-conscious properties to produce far better wine than they might have a few years ago under similar conditions, but, overall, these two years saw few wines of real class. Top chateaux wines and ambitious Bourgeois may be worth buying, but petits chateaux should be treated with circumspection.

As an alternative, seek out the delicious 1989s, including Michel Lynch our Joint Red Wine of the Year! The rather tough 1988s are still developing and should be left to themselves for a while yet. Much the same could be said for the 1986s, but the 1985s are growing lovelier by the day. As for 1983 and 1982, the younger of the two is ageing quite gracelessly. Buy carefully.

For specialist stockists, see the chart beginning on p.254, plus: Curzon Wine Co (071-499 3327); Robert Rolls & Co (071-248 8382; fax 071-236 1891); Pavilion Wine Co (071-628 8224; fax 071- 628 6205); Classic Wines (081-500 7614); Fine Vintage Wines (0865 72486; fax 0865 79159); Andrew Mead Wines (05476 268); Buckingham Vintners (0753 21336); Wine on the Green (071-794 1143).

Burgundy

As white Burgundy prices have dropped there have been all sorts of un-familiar Mâcons and Bourgogne Blancs on offer. Few are good and most compare unfavourably with Chardonnays from non-Appellation regions further south. Go a little upmarket and seek out the Côte d'Or 1989 whites, which can be wonderfully well-balanced wines.

Red Burgundy is less of a bargain but a better buy than it has been for years following a succession of good vintages (including the 1992 that was so poor elsewhere). The vintage to keep is still 1988, but 1989, 1990 and 1992 are all to be taken seriously.

For specialist stockists, see the chart beginning on p.254, plus: Curzon Wine Co (071- 499 3327); Robert Rolls & Co Ltd (071-248 8382; fax 071-236 1891); Ferrers le Mesurier (0832 732660); Andrew Mead Wines (05476 268); Evertons of Ombersley (0905 620282; fax 0905 794660).

Champagne

Still a minefield in which spending large amounts of money guarantees you nothing special. Cheap fizz looks as though it's here to stay now that the Champagne houses can fix their own price for grapes, so there'll be no shortage of real Champagne for Bucks Fizz. Sadly, that's all most £7.50 Champagne is good for. Among the big names, variability in the quality and style of non-vintage wines is such a problem that one (very) big chain has resorted to tasting every batch against control samples.

For specialist stockists, see the chart beginning on p.254, plus: Curzon Wine Co (071-499 3327); The Champagne House (071-221 5538).

The Loire

A varied vintage; some reds were as juicily good as the 1990s, others were picked too early and tasted green and acidic. There were some good Sancerres and a few delicious late-harvest Chenins. Wine making is still a problem, though. Overdosing sweet whites with sulphur dioxide was unacceptable even when they were left a decade or so before opening. Today, it is too evident too early. Heavy-handed users should learn from New World producers that clean wineries need far less protection from sulphur.

For specialist stockists, see the chart beginning on p.254, plus: Ian Howe (0636 704366; fax 0636 610502); Christopher Milner Wines (071-266 2245; fax 071-286 7631); F&E May (071-405 6249; fax 071-404 4472); Ferrers le Mesurier (0832 732660); La Cave de Bacchus (0903 892933; fax 0903 892422); Bromley-Stephens (0533 768471; fax 0533 460459).

The Rhône

The Rhône fared no better in 1992 than elsewhere in France, but there are some lovely 1991s around, especially from the northern Rhône, where winemaking is improving with every vintage. The wave of Rhônophilia predicted in the *Guide* a few years ago is already apparent, especially in the US, and I'm not expecting boredom to set in for quite a while yet.

For specialist stockists, see the chart beginning on p.254, plus: Ian Howe (0636 704366; fax 0636 605 248); Robert Rolls (071-248 8382; fax 071-236 1891); Wine on the Green (071-794 1143).

Germany

Sainsbury's and Victoria Wine both held media tastings as we were preparing the *Guide*. How many German wines did they show? As many as they did from Zimbabwe, Albania and Iceland. It is a sad irony that just as Germany is making some of its best wines in years, British wine merchants seem to have given up selling anything other than very basic fare. However, decent Kabinett is being served as an aperitif at smart London dinners, so perhaps there is hope. Personally, I'm far from certain.

For specialist stockists, see the chart beginning on p.254, plus: Robert Mendelssohn

(081-455 9895; fax 081-455 4533); Bromley-Stephens (0533 768471; fax 0533 460459); Dennhöfer Wines (091-232 7342; fax 091-261 0926).

Italy

After the extravagant 1980s, when fashion victims were as ready to pay through the nose for Italian designer wines as they were for Armani jeans, commonsense is back in vogue. Good value wines are more widely available than they have been for years, and regions like Basilicata, Sicily and Sardinia are thrusting their way to the fore. Despite all the hype over Tuscany, the most exciting area remains Piedmont, where a new wave of winemakers led by Elio Altare and a few of the more established wineries, such as Mascarello, are revealing flavours in the Nebbiolo and Barbera grapes that few people ever suspected.

For specialist stockists, see the chart beginning on p.254, plus: Cantino Augusto (071-242 3246; fax 071-831 3962); Geoffrey Roberts Agencies; Continental Wine House (071-262 2126); Caledonian Wines (0228 43172); Gardavini (081-549 2779); Wineforce (071-586 5618); Organics (071-381 9924); Alfie Fiandaca (081-952 8446; fax 081-951 0694).

New Zealand

With every passing year, the Kiwis prove increasingly successful at offering a fresher, tangier alternative to Australian wine. Good winemaking has overcome the problems of two less-than-wonderful vintages, but the 1992 and 1993 crops were very short and, with the Phylloxera louse at work in the vineyards, there are doubts about the Kiwis' ability to meet the demand they have so successfully created.

For specialist stockists, see the chart beginning on p.254, plus: Kiwi Fruits (071-240 1423; fax 071-930 4587); Fine Wines of New Zealand (071-482 0093).

Portugal

Following the success of last year's Red Winemaker of the Year, Peter Bright, and Tinto da Anfora, his Red Wine of the Year, Portugal has found itself another star Australian in David Baverstock, formerly of Dows port. Both men are leading the way in making flavoursome red wines using local grapes while, embarrassingly, apart from the ubiquitous Leziria, a brilliant-value red from an ultra-modern cooperative, there are, as yet, no modern world-beaters being made by the country's own winemakers.

For specialist stockists, see the chart beginning on p.254, plus: AOL Grilli (0580 891472); Fine Vintage Wines (0865 724866); Wineforce (071-586 5618); RS Pass Wines (0843 584161; fax 0843 584161).

Spain

Britain's wine merchants have become used to not being able to find exciting new Spanish wines, or even sufficient reliable traditional ones. But, as Victoria Wine and Oddbins have proved, there are some good unfamiliar labels to be found, and new classics such as Remelluri are getting better with every vintage. Perversely, Spain's handicap remains the readiness of British wine drinkers to accept some very dull stuff.

For specialist stockists, see the chart beginning on p.254, plus: Paul Sanderson (031-312 6190); Wine on the Green (071-794 1143); Bodegas Direct (0243 773474 ; fax 0243 530034).

South Africa

As predicted, the South African invasion was received less enthusiastically over here than wine makers in the Cape must have hoped. Britain doesn't need overpriced, dilute Chenin Blanc or old-fashioned stewy reds and the message is obviously getting through to the producers, with many of the wines on offer today being far better value than their counterparts of a year ago. Quality is still variable, however, as the Cape's poor medal tally proved. While waiting for Antipodean-style consistency, I'd recommend heading straight for the wonderful Boschendal Grand Pavilion, our joint Sparkling Wine of the Year.

For specialist stockists, see the chart beginning on p.254, plus: Quellyn Roberts (0244 310455; fax 0244 346704); Edward Cavendish & Sons (0794 516102; fax 0704 512213); Southern Hemisphere Wines Ltd (071-731 4661; fax 071-736 5061).

South and Central America

A few years ago in the *Guide*, I predicted that Argentina would soon rival Chile in its wine sales to Britain. It hasn't happened yet, but both Argentinian and Mexican wines have leaped on to the shelves. In the meantime, embattled Chilean winemakers have suffered from a rare frost-bitten vintage in 1992, a strengthening of the nation's currency that has made its exports less competitive, and the eagerness of US wineries to treat them as a source of very basic fare. Despite big investment by even bigger names, Chile has yet to produce a truly dazzling wine.

For specialist stockists, see the chart beginning on p.254, plus: AL Vose (05395 33328).

USA

Californian winemakers scored exceptionally highly in the Challenge, winning an impressive proportion of medals and commendations. Where they fell down was on the matter of price. There were very few entries under £7, and even fewer worth drinking. I love some of those higher-priced wines but, sadly, they find few buyers in Britain, where a £5 bottle is still rather a luxury. It's a pity that so many people have been persuaded by advertising to buy such dull examples as the E&J Gallo Chardonnay.

Hopefully, other wineries will follow the lead of Tony Cartledge, maker of the Stratford Zinfandel, last year's brilliant, affordable Red Wine of the Year. It cannot please California and Napa-obsessed marketeers in San Francisco to see their small corner of the Bottoms Up list headed simply 'North American wines'.

For specialist stockists, see the chart beginning on p.254.

A-Z

HOW TO READ THE ENTRIES

Hermitage (Rhône) Top-class northern RHONE[1] long-lived wines; superb,
  complex, long-lived reds and sumptuous, nutty whites. Also
  Australian name for the SYRAH grape. 76 78 79 82 83 85[2] *££££-£££££*[3]
  Chave 179[4] (OD YAP ADN)[5]

1 Words that appear in SMALL CAPITALS have their own entry elsewhere
  in the *A-Z*.
2 Only those vintages that are good have been listed. The years that
  appear in bold are ready to drink.
3 Price guide: £ = under £3.50 ££ = £3.50-5.50 £££ = £5.50-9 ££££ = £9-15
  £££££ = £15 and over
4 This is a recommended example of the wine. Where possible we
  recommend one of the *Guide*'s 500 wines, in which case it will appear
  as a number, in this example 179
5 Stockists, see page 16 for an explanation of merchants' codes. If the
  merchant is not featured in the *Guide*, its phone number will appear.

Abbocato (Italy) Semi-dry
Abfüller/Abfüllung (Germany) Bottler/bottled by
Abocado (Spain) Semi-dry
Abruzzi (Italy) Region on the east coast. Often dull TREBBIANO whites. Finer
  MONTEPULCIANO reds 82 83 85 86 87 88 90 91 *£-££* 413
AC (France) See APPELLATION CONTROLEE
Acetic acid This volatile acid (CH_3COOH) features in tiny proportions in all wines.
  In excess (as a result of careless winemaking) it can turn wine to vinegar.
Acidity Essential natural balancing component (usually TARTARIC) that gives
  freshness. In hotter countries (and sometimes in cooler ones) it may be added.
Aconcagua Valley (CHILE) Central valley region noted for its CABERNET SAUVIGNON
Adega (Portugal) Winery – equivalent to Spanish BODEGA
Adelaide Hills (Australia) Cool, high-altitude vineyard region, producing top-
  class RIESLING, but now also growing more fashionable varieties such as
  Sauvignon Blanc, Chardonnay and Pinot Noir 82 88 90 91 *£££-£££££* 25 93 305
Aglianico del Vulture (BASILICATA) Full-bodied, best-known and best DOC red from
  this region, made from a grape used by the ancient Greeks 85 86 87 88 90
  £££
Agricola vitivinicola (Italy) Wine estate
Aguja (LEON) So-called 'needle' wines which owe their slight SPRITZ to the addition
  of ripe grapes to the fermented wine
Ahr (Germany) Northernmost ANBAUGEBIET, producing light red wines little seen in
  the UK. Walporzheimer Klosterberg 1988 (WSC)
Aix-en-Provence (Coteaux d') (S France) Pleasant floral whites, up-and-coming
  reds and dry rosés using BORDEAUX and RHONE varieties. A recent AC 85 88 89
  90 91 *££-£££* 166
Albana di Romagna (Italy) Improving but traditionally dull white wine which, for
  political reasons, was made Italy's first white DOCG, thus making a mockery
  of the whole Italian system of denominations
Albariño (Spain) The Spain's name for the Portuguese ALVARINHO. Can produce
  spicily attractive wine in GALICIA *£££* Galician Albarino, Laricja Alta 1992 (TO)
Aleatico (S Italy) Red grape producing sweet, Muscat-style, often fortified wines. Gives
  name to DOCs A. di PUGLIA and A. di Gradoli Aleatico di Sovana Avignones (V&C)

Alella (Spain) DO district of CATALONIA, producing better whites than reds 86 87 89 90 91 92 ££ 153

Alentejo (Portugal) Up-and-coming province north of the Algarve 446, 449

Algeria Hearty, old-fashioned mostly red wines produced by state-run cooperatives

Aligoté (BURGUNDY) The region's lesser white grape, making dry, sometimes sharp white wine that is traditionally mixed with cassis to make KIR. Also grown in Eastern Europe where they think a lot of it 89 90 91 92 ££-£££ 163

Almacenista (JEREZ) Fine, old, unblended sherry from a single SOLERA – the sherry equivalent of a single malt whisky. Lustau are specialists ££-£££££ Almacenista Manzanilla, Emilia Lustau (H Sichel & Sons 071-930 9292))

Aloxe-Corton (BURGUNDY) COTE DE BEAUNE commune producing slow-maturing reds (including the GRAND CRU Corton) and whites (including Corton Charlemagne). Invariably pricey; variably great 78 83 85 87 88 89 90 92 £££££ Tollot-Beaut 88 (ADN)

Alsace (NE France) Dry (and occasionally sweeter) whites and pale reds pitched in style between France and Germany and named after grape varieties 83 85 86 88 89 90 91 £-£££££ 22 181-186 211

Alto-Adige (NE Italy) Aka ITALIAN TYROL and SUDTIROL. DOC for a range of exciting, mainly white, wines, often from Germanic grape varieties. Also light and fruity reds made from the LAGREIN and VERNATSCH. 85 88 89 90 91 £-£££ Sainsbury's Chardonnay Alto-Adige Tiefen Brunner (JS)

Alvarinho (Portugal) White grape at its best in VINHO VERDE blends and in the DO Alvarinho de Monção

Amabile (Italy) Semi-sweet

Amador County (California) Region noted for quality ZINFANDEL

Amaro (Italy) Bitter

Amarone (VENETO) Also 'bitter', used particularly to describe RECIOTOS Amarone Recioto della Classico 1986, Zenato (TH)

Amontillado (JEREZ) Literally 'like MONTILLA'. In Britain, medium-sweet sherry; in Spain, dry, nutty wine ££-£££££ 481

Amoroso (JEREZ) Sweet sherry style devised for the British ££-££££

Amtliche Prüfüngsnummer (Germany) Official identification number relating to quality. Appears on all QBA/QMP wines

Anbaugebiet (Germany) Term for 11 large wine regions (eg RHEINGAU). QBA and QMP wines must name their ANBAUGEBIET

Ancenis (Coteaux d') (LOIRE) Light reds and deep pinks from the CABERNET FRANC and GAMAY, and MUSCADET-style whites 89 90 92 ££

Anjou (LOIRE) Many dry and DEMI-SEC whites, mostly from the CHENIN BLANC. Usually awful rosé but good, light, claretty, CABERNET reds 85 86 90 92 £-££££ Anjou Rosé 1992, Caves De La Loire (AB)

Annata (Italy) Vintage

Año (Spain) Year: preceded by a figure – eg 5 – indicates the wine's age at the time of bottling. Banned by the EC since 1986

AOC (France) See APPELLATION CONTROLEE

AP (Germany) Abbreviation for AMTLICHE PRUFUNGSNUMMER

Appellation Contrôlée (AC/AOC) (France) Designation for 'top quality' wine: guarantees origin, grape varieties and method of production – but not quality.

Apremont (E France) Floral, slightly PETILLANT white from skiing country 88 89 90 92 ££ St Andre des Marches P Boniface 90 (EE)

Apulia (Italy) See PUGLIA

Arbois (E France) Light reds from Trousseau and PINOT NOIR , dry whites from the JURA, most notably VIN JAUNE and fizz £££-£££££ 10

Ardèche (Coteaux de l') (RHONE) Light country reds, made mainly from the SYRAH and CHARDONNAY grapes by certain Burgundians 88 89 90 91 92 £-££ Grand Ardèche 1990, Vin de Pays de L'Ardèche

Argentina The great white (and red) hope of the 1990s? 84 85 86 88 90 91 288 325

Asciutto (Italy) Dry

Asenovgrad (BULGARIA) Demarcated northern wine region. Reds from CABERNET SAUVIGNON, MERLOT and MAVRUD 85 87 88 89 90 91 ££ Asenovgrad Mavrud 85 (MWW)

Assemblage (France) The art of blending wine from different grape varieties in a CUVEE. Associated with BORDEAUX and CHAMPAGNE

Asti (PIEDMONT) Town famous for sparkling SPUMANTE, lighter MOSCATO D'ASTI and red BARBERA D'ASTI 2 414 424

Astringent Mouth-puckering. Mostly associated with young red wine. See TANNIN

Asz (HUNGARY) The sweet 'syrup' made from 'nobly rotten' grapes (see BOTRYTIS) used to sweeten TOKAY

Aubance (Coteaux de l') (LOIRE) Light wines (often semi-sweet) grown on the banks of a Loire tributary 83 85 88 89 90 92 ££

Aude (Vin de Pays de l') (SW France) Prolific *département* producing much ordinary red, white and rosés 83 85 86 88 89 90 91 92 £ Campagnard Vin de Pays de L'Aude, Les Vignerons (TH)

Ausbruch (AUSTRIA) Term for wines sweeter than German BEERENAUSLESEN but less sweet than TROCKENBEERENAUSLESEN

Auslese (Germany) Sweet wine from selected ripe grapes usually affected by BOTRYTIS. Third rung on the QmP ladder 207-209 463

Austria Home of tangy, dry, white GRUNER VELTLINER, usually drunk within a year of the harvest, plus light fresh PINOT NOIRs and sweet Germanic-style whites, including good-value dessert styles 81 83 85 87 88 89 90 91 ££-£££££ 461

Auxerrois (LUXEMBOURG) Locals' name for the PINOT GRIS – and their fresh, clean wine. In Alsace, a separate but often indistinguishable grape variety ££ 184

Auxey-Duresses (BURGUNDY) Best known for buttery rich whites but produces greater quantities of raspberryish reds. A slow developer 83 85 87 88 89 90 92 £££-££££ Auxey-Duresses Jaffeun (RIB)

Avelsbach (MOSEL-SAAR-RUWER) RUWER village producing delicate light-bodied wines 83 85 86 87 88 89 90 £££

Avize (CHAMPAGNE) Fine white grape village

Ay (CHAMPAGNE) Ancient regional capital growing mainly black grapes 79 82 83 85 88 89 ££££-£££££

Ayl (MOSEL-SAAR-RUWER) Distinguished SAAR village producing steely wines 85 86 87 88 89 90 ££-£££ Ayler Kupp Riesling Spätlese 1990 Bischöfliches Konvikt (ADN)

Azienda (Italy) Estate

Bacchus White grape, a MULLER-THURGAU -RIESLING cross, making light, flowery wine. Grown in Germany and also England 82

Bad Durkheim (RHEINPFALZ) Chief Rheinpfalz town and source of some of the region's finest whites. Small production of reds 83 85 88 89 90 91 92 ££-£££££ Durkheimer Schenkenbohl Huxelrebe Beerenauslese 90 Kloster Limbourg (OD)

Bad Kreuznach (NAHE) Chief and finest wine town of the region, giving its name to the entire lower Nahe 83 85 88 89 90 91 92 ££-£££££ 207

Badacsony (HUNGARY) Wine region particularly renowned for full-flavoured whites

Baden (Germany) Southernmost ANBAUGEBIET, largely represented by the huge ZBW cooperative. Among the ripest, fullest, driest wines in Germany. Rarely classy, but can stand up well to food 83 85 86 88 89 90 91 92 ££-£££££ 197

Baga (Portugal) High-quality, spicily fruity red grape varieties – used in BAIRRADA

Bairrada (Portugal) DO wine region south of Oporto, producing dull whites and good value reds, often from the BAGA 83 85 88 90 92 £-£££ 453

Balance Harmony of fruitiness, ACIDITY, alcohol and TANNIN. Balance can develop with age but should also be evident in youth

Balaton (HUNGARY) Wine region producing fair-quality reds and whites

Ban de vendange (France) Officially sanctioned harvest date

Bandol (PROVENCE) AOC red and rosé. MOURVEDRE reds are particularly good and spicy. Worth keeping 79 83 85 86 89 90 91 £££ Chateau de la Rouvière 90 (YAP)

Banyuls (PROVENCE) France's answer to port. Fortified, GRENACHE-based VIN DOUX NATUREL 82 85 86 88 89 90 91 92 ££-£££ Château de Jau Banyuls, Robert Doutres1989 (Val D'Orbieu Wines 071-736 3350)

Barbaresco (PIEDMONT) DOCG red from the NEBBIOLO grape, with spicy fruit plus depth and complexity. Approachable earlier (three to five years) than neighbouring BAROLO 82 83 84 85 86 87 88 89 90 92 ££-£££££ Barbaresco Rabaja 1985, Giuseppe Cortese (LAV)

Barbera (PIEDMONT) Grape making fruity, spicy wine (eg B. d'Alba and B. d'Asti) with robust ACIDITY. Now grown in California 86 87 88 89 90 92 ££-££££ 419

Bardolino (VENETO) Light and unusually approachable for a traditional DOC Italian red. Refreshing with a hint of bitter cherries. Best drunk young 88 89 90 91 92 £-£££ Tesco Bardolino

Barolo (PIEDMONT) Noblest of DOCG reds, made from NEBBIOLO. Old-fashioned versions are undrinkably dry and tannic when young but, from a good producer and year, can last and develop extraordinary complexity. Modern versions are ready earlier, but still last. 83 84 85 86 87 88 89 90 92 ££-££££ 429

Barossa Valley (Australia) Established region north-east of Adelaide, famous for traditional SHIRAZ, 'ports' and RIESLINGS which age to oily richness. CHARDONNAY and CABERNET are now taking over **80 84 86 87** 90 91 ££-££££ 98-99 337 495

Barrique French barrel, particularly in BORDEAUX, holding 225 litres. Term used in Italy to denote barrel ageing

Barsac (BORDEAUX) AC neighbour of SAUTERNES, with similar, though not quite so rich, SAUVIGNON/SEMILLON dessert wines **75 76 83 86 88** 89 90 91 £££-£££££ 473

Basilicata (Italy) Southern wine region chiefly known for AGLIANICO DEL VULTURE and some improving VINI DA TAVOLA **85 86 87 88 90** 91 92 £-£££ 411

Bastardo Red grape used widely in port and previously in MADEIRA where there are a few wonderful bottles left. Shakespeare refers to a wine called 'Brown Bastard'

Bâtard-Montrachet (BURGUNDY) Biscuity-rich white GRAND CRU of CHASSAGNE and PULIGNY MONTRACHET. Very fine, very expensive. **78 79 81 82 83 85 86 87** 88 89 90 92 £££££ Bienvenues Bâtard-Montrachet 1991, Henri Clerc (ABY)

Baux-en-Provence (Coteaux des) (S France) Inexpensive fruity reds, whites and rosés of improving quality **85 86 88 89 90** 91 92 £-££££ Domaine de Trévallon

Beaujolais (BURGUNDY) Light, fruity red from the GAMAY, good chilled and for early drinking; B.-Villages is better, and one of the 10 CRUS better still, as they take on pronounced Burgundian characteristics with age. See B.-VILLAGES, MORGON, CHENAS, BROUILLY, COTE DE BROUILLY, JULIENAS, MOULIN A VENT, FLEURIE, REGNIE, ST AMOUR, CHIROUBLES **88 89 91** ££-££££ 374 376-381

Beaujolais Blanc (BURGUNDY) From the CHARDONNAY, rarely seen under this name. Commonly sold as ST VERAN **87 88 90 91** 92 ££-£££ Somerfield Beaujolais Blanc 1990 (G)

Beaujolais-Villages (BURGUNDY) From the north of the region, fuller flavoured and more alcoholic than plain BEAUJOLAIS, though not necessarily from one of the named 'CRU' villages **85 88 89** 91 ££-££££ 374

Beaumes de Venise (RHONE) Sweet, grapey, fortified VIN DOUX NATUREL from the MUSCAT and spicy reds which are just beginning to make their appearance in the UK (White) **88 89 90** 91 Muscat de Beaumes de Venise, Domaine de Coyeux (OD) (Red) **86 88 89 90 91**

Beaune (BURGUNDY) Reliable commune for soft, raspberry-and-rose-petal PINOT NOIR. The walled city is the site of the famous HOSPICES charity auction. Also (very rare) whites **78 80 82 83 85 87** 88 89 90 92 £££-££££ 402 405

Beerenauslese (Australia, AUSTRIA, Germany) Luscious sweet wines from selected ripe grapes (*beeren*), hopefully affected by BOTRYTIS ££££-£££££ 475-476

Bellet (PROVENCE) Tiny AC behind Nice which produces good red, white and rosé from local grapes including the ROLLE, the Braquet and the Folle Noir. (Excessively) pricey and rarely seen in the UK **83 85 87 88 89 90 91** 92 £££-££££ Bellet 1990, Charles Bagnis (YAP)

Bentonite Type of clay used as a clarifying agent to attract and absorb impurities. Popular as a non animal-derived FINING material

Bereich (Germany) Vineyard area, subdivision of an ANBAUGEBIET. On its own indicates simple QBA wine, eg NIERSTEINER. Finer wines are followed by the name of a GROSSLAGE subsection; even better ones by the names of individual vineyards

Bergerac (BORDEAUX/SW) Lighter, often good-value alternative to everyday claret or dry white BORDEAUX. Fine sweet MONBAZILLAC is produced here, too **85 86 88 89** 90 £-£££ 148 276

Bernkastel (MOSEL-SAAR-RUWER) Town and vineyard area on the MITTELMOSEL making some of the finest RIESLING (including the famous Bernkasteler Doktor) and, sadly, a lake of poor-quality cheap wine **83 85 86 88 89 90 91** 92 ££-£££££ Bernkastler Lay Riesling 1989, Prum (D)

Bianco di Custoza (VENETO) Widely exported DOC, a reliable, crisp, light white from a blend of grapes. A better alternative to most basic SOAVE **88 89 90 91** 92 £-££ Bianco di Custoza, Pasqua 1992 (AB)

Bingen Village giving its name to a RHEINHESSEN BEREICH that includes a number of well-known GROSSLAGEN **76 83 85 88** 89 90 91 92 £-£££ 475

Biscuity Flavour of biscuits (eg Digestive or Rich Tea) often associated with the CHARDONNAY grape, particularly in CHAMPAGNE and top-class mature BURGUNDY, or with the yeast that fermented the wine

Black Muscat Grown chiefly as a table grape, also produces very mediocre wine – except that made at the Quady winery in California Quady Elysium 89 (DAL)

Blanc de Noirs White (or pink) wine made from black grapes

Blanc de Blancs White wine, usually sparkling, made solely from white grapes. In CHAMPAGNE, denotes 100% CHARDONNAY 8 26 28 30

Blanquette de Limoux (MIDI) METHODE CHAMPENOISE sparkler, at its best appley and clean.
Takes on a yeasty, earthy flavour with age ££-£££ Blanquette de Limoux 1991, Vurgres (U)

Blauburgunder (AUSTRIA) The PINOT NOIR, making light, sharp reds

Blauer Portugieser Red grape used in Germany and Austria for light, pale wine

Blaye (Côtes de/Premières Côtes de) (BORDEAUX) Reasonable Blayais whites and
sturdy AC reds. Premières Côtes are better 82 83 85 86 88 89 90 £-£££ 125

Bodega (Spain) Winery or wine cellar; producer

Body Usually used as 'full-bodied', meaning a wine with mouth-filling flavours
and probably a fairly high alcohol content

Bommes (BORDEAUX) SAUTERNES COMMUNE and village containing several PREMIERS
CRUS 75 76 79 80 81 83 86 88 89 90 ££££-£££££

Bonnezeaux (LOIRE) Delicious sweet whites produced from the CHENIN BLANC. They
last for ever 71 76 83 85 88 89 90 92 ££-£££££ Domaine des Gagneries 90 (LV)

Bordeaux (France) Largest quality wine region in France, producing reds from
CABERNET SAUVIGNON, CABERNET FRANC, PETIT VERDOT, and MERLOT, and dry and
sweet whites from (principally) blends of SEMILLON and SAUVIGNON. See *THE
WINES* section for numerous examples

Botrytis *Botrytis cinerea*, a fungal infection that attacks and shrivels grapes,
evaporating their water and concentrating their sweetness. Vital to SAUTERNES
and the finer German and Austrian sweet wines

Bottle-fermented Commonly found on the labels of US sparkling wines to indicate
the METHODE CHAMPENOISE, gaining wider currency. Beware, though – it can
indicate inferior 'transfer method' wines

Bouquet Overall smell, often made up of several separate aromas

Bourg (Côtes de) (BORDEAUX) Inexpensive, fast-maturing, everyday AC reds with
solid fruit; lesser whites 85 86 88 89 90 92 £-£££ Château Puy Barbe 1989 (G)
Orlandi (SAF)

Bourgueil (LOIRE) Red AC in the TOURAINE area, producing crisp, grassy 100 per cent
CABERNET FRANC wines 83 85 86 88 89 90 92 ££-£££ Bourgueil 1990, Domaine du Petit (FUL)

Bouzeron (BURGUNDY) Village in the COTE CHALONNAISE, principally known for
ALIGOTE 88 89 90 92 ££-£££ Bourgogne Aligote Bouzeron 1992, Chanzy Freres (ABY)

Bouzy Rouge (CHAMPAGNE) Sideline of a black grape village: an often thin-bodied,
rare and overpriced red wine 88 89 90 92 ££££-£££££

Braquet (MIDI) Grape variety used in BELLET

Brauneberg (MOSEL-SAAR-RUWER) Village best known in UK for the Juffer vineyard
Brauneberger Juffer Sonnenuhr Riesling Spätlese 89, Haag (LV)

Bricco Manzoni (PIEDMONT) Non-DOC red blend of NEBBIOLO and BARBERA grapes,
round and fruity. Drinkable young 83 85 86 87 88 89 90 92 £££-£££££ Bricco
Roche dei Manzoni 86 (V&C)

British Wine 'Made' wine from diluted grape concentrate bought in from a
number of countries. Avoid it. ENGLISH wine is the real stuff, produced from
grapes grown in England

Brouilly (BURGUNDY) Largest of the BEAUJOLAIS CRUS producing pure, fruity GAMAY
85 88 89 91 ££-£££ 376 379

Brunello di Montalcino Prestigious DOCG red from a SANGIOVESE clone. Needs at
least five years to develop complex and intense fruit and flavour 83 85 87 88 89
90 91 £££-£££££ Brunello Di Montalcino Riserva 1986, Val di Suga (DIR)

Brut Dry, particularly of CHAMPAGNE and sparkling wines. *Brut nature/sauvage/zéro*
are even drier

Bual MADEIRA grape producing a soft, nutty wine that is good with cheese 490

Bucelas (Portugal) DO area near Lisbon, best known for intensely coloured yet
delicate and aromatic white wines. Rare in Britain

Bugey (E France) SAVOIE district producing a variety of wines, including white
ROUSSETTE DE BUGEY from the grape of that name

Bulgaria Losing its way after apparently conquering the 'noble' grapes with the
help of massive state-aided technology and advice from California. Source of
decreasingly good value CABERNET SAUVIGNON and MERLOT, making (slow)
progress with SAUVIGNON and CHARDONNAY. MAVRUD is the traditional red variety
81 83 84 85 86 87 £-££ 241-242 244 250

Burgenland (AUSTRIA) Wine region bordering HUNGARY, climatically ideal for fine, sweet
AUSLESEN and BEERENAUSLESEN ££-£££ Bouvier Trockenbeerenauslese 89 Apetlan (ADN)

Burgundy (FRANCE) Home to PINOT NOIR and CHARDONNAY; wines ranging from
banal to sublime, but never cheap £££-£££££. See *THE WINES* section for
numerous examples

Buttery The rich fat smell often found in good CHARDONNAY. Sometimes found in wine which has been left on its LEES

Buzbag (TURKEY) Rich, dry red wine. Sadly, it is rarely well made and often oxidised (SEL)

Buzet (Côtes de) (BORDEAUX) AC region adjoining BORDEAUX, producing light claretty reds, and whites from SAUVIGNON **88 89 90 92** £-££ 264

Cabernet d'Anjou/de Saumur (LOIRE) Light, fresh, grassy, blackcurranty rosés, typical of their grape, the CABERNET FRANC **85 86 87 88 89 90** 92 £-£££££ Cabernet D'Anjou Perray Jouannet 90 (YAP)

Cabernet Franc Red grape, the CABERNET SAUVIGNON's younger brother. Produces simpler, blackcurranty wines, particularly in the LOIRE and Italy, but plays a more sophisticated role in BORDEAUX, especially in ST EMILION

Cabernet Sauvignon The great red grape of BORDEAUX, where it is blended with MERLOT and other varieties. The most successful red VARIETAL, grown in every reasonably warm winemaking country. See *THE WINES* section for numerous examples.

Cadillac (BORDEAUX) Known for sweet whites (not quite as sweet or fine as SAUTERNES) for drinking young and well chilled £-£££

Cahors (SW France) 'Rustic' BORDEAUX-like reds produced mainly from the local TANNAT and the Cot (MALBEC), full-flavoured and still quite full-bodied, though have lightened recently **83 85 88 89 90 91** £-£££ 239

Cairanne Named COTES DU RHONE village for powerful reds **82 83 85 88 89 90 91** £££

Calabria (Italy) The 'toe' of the boot, making little-seen Gaglioppo reds and Greco whites ££ Ciro Rosso Classico Librandi 89

Campania (Italy) Region surrounding Naples, best known for TAURASI, LACRYMA CHRISTI and GRECO DI TUFO **85 86 87 88 90** 91 92

Canada Surprising friends and foes alike, the winemakers of British Columbia and, more specifically, Ontario are producing very good CHARDONNAY and RIESLING

Cannonau Heady, robust DOC red from SARDINIA **82 83 84 85 86 88 89 90** 91 92 £-££ Cannonau di Alghero, Sella & Mosca 88 (Alivini 081-880 2525)

Canon Fronsac Small AC bordering on POMEROL for sound attractive reds from some good-value PETIT CHATEAUX **78 79 81 82 83** 85 86 88 89 90 ££-£££££ Château Moulin Pev Labrie 1989 (C&B)

Cantenac (BORDEAUX) Haut Médoc Commune with several top CHATEAUX including Palmer 78 79 81 **82 83** 85 86 88 89 90 ££-£££££ Reserve du General 1989 (MWW)

Cantina (Sociale) (Italy) Winery cooperative

Capsule The lead or plastic sheath covering the cork on a wine bottle

Carbonic Maceration See MACERATION CARBONIQUE

Carcavelos (Portugal) Sweet, usually disappointing fortified wines from a region close to Lisbon. Rare in Britain

Carignan Prolific red grape making usually dull, coarse wine for blending, but classier fare in CORBIERES and FITOU £-££

Cariñena (Spain) Important DO of Aragon for rustic reds, high in alcohol. Also some whites **88 89 90 91 92** £-££ 436

Carmignano (TUSCANY) Exciting alternative to CHIANTI, in the same style but with the addition of CABERNET grapes **82 83 85 86 87 88 89 90 91** £££-££££ 423

Carneros (California) Small, cool, high-quality region shared between the NAPA and SONOMA VALLEYS, and producing top-class CHARDONNAY and PINOT NOIR **85 86 87 88 89 90** 91 £££-££££ 107 396

Casa vinicola (Italy) Firm buying and vinifying grapes

Casa (Italy, Spain, Portugal) Firm (company)

Cassis (PROVENCE) Rare, spicy white made from UGNI BLANC, CLAIRETTE and MARSANNE Clos Ste Magdeleine 91 (YAP)

Cat's pee Describes the tangy smell often found in typical – and frequently delicious – MULLER-THURGAU and SAUVIGNON

Cava (Spain) Sparkling wine produced by the METHODE CHAMPENOIS. Traditionally 'earthy' but now much improved ££-£££ 3

Cave (France) Cellar

Cave Cooperative (France) Cooperative winery

Cépage (France) Grape variety

Cerasuolo (ABRUZZI) A pink wine from the grape, greatly benefiting from newer, cool fermentation techniques £££

Cérons (BORDEAUX) Bordering on SAUTERNES with similar, less fine, but cheaper wines ££

Chablis (BURGUNDY) Often overpriced and overrated white, but a fine example still has that steely European finesse that New World CHARDONNAYS have trouble capturing 78 79 81 85 86 87 88 89 90 ££-£££££ 55 57-60

Chai (France) Cellar/winery

Chalonnais/Côte Chalonnaise (BURGUNDY) Increasingly sought-after source of lesser-known, less complex BURGUNDIES – GIVRY, MONTAGNY, RULLY and MERCUREY. Potentially (rather than actually) good-value 85 86 87 88 89 90 92 £-££££ 103 397

Chambolle-Musigny (BURGUNDY) One of the finest red wine communes, producing rich, fragrant, deeply flavoured wines. Le Musigny is the GRAND CRU 78 83 84 85 88 89 90 92 £££-£££££ Roumier 89 (FUL)

Champagne (France) In the north-east of France, source of the finest and greatest (and most jealously guarded) sparkling wines, from the PINOT NOIR, PINOT MEUNIER and CHARDONNAY grapes ££££-£££££ 26-28 30-34

Chaptalisation The legal (in some regions) addition of sugar during fermentation to boost a wine's alcohol content

Charbono Obscure grape variety grown in California but thought to come from Italy. Makes interesting full-bodied reds

Chardonnay The great white grape of BURGUNDY, CHAMPAGNE and now the New World. As capable of fresh simple charm in BULGARIA as of buttery, hazelnutty, richness in MEURSAULT. See *THE WINES* section for numerous examples

Charmat The inventor of the CUVE CLOSE method of producing cheap sparkling wines

Charta (Germany) Syndicate of RHEINGAU producers using an arch as a symbol to indicate their new dry (TROCKEN) styles

Chassagne-Montrachet (BURGUNDY) COTE DE BEAUNE COMMUNE making grassy, biscuity, fresh yet rich whites and mid-weight, wild fruit reds. Pricey but recommended 85 86 88 89 90 92 ££££-£££££ 118

Chasselas Widely grown, prolific white grape making light, often dull fruity wine principally in Switzerland, eastern France and Germany

Château (usually BORDEAUX) Literally 'castle'; practically, vineyard or wine estate

Châteauneuf-du-Pape (RHONE) Traditionally the best reds (rich and spicy) and whites (rich and floral) from the southern Rhône valley 78 79 80 81 83 85 86 88 89 90 91 £££-£££££ 354 356 364

Château-Chalon (E France) Speciality JURA AC for a VIN JAUNE of good keeping quality

Château-Grillet (RHONE) Tiny, pricey property region and APPELLATION producing (once) great VIOGNIER white 88 89 90 91 92 £££££ Château-Grillet 1990 (YAP)

Chef de culture (France) Vineyard manager

Chénas (BURGUNDY) One of the 10 BEAUJOLAIS CRUS, the least well-known but well worth seeking out 88 89 90 91 £££ 381

Chêne (France) Oak, as in FUTS DE CHENE (oak barrels)

Chenin Blanc The white grape of the LOIRE, neutral and with high acidity; can produce anything from bone-dry to very sweet, long-lived wines with a characteristic honeyed taste. Also grown with success in South Africa, the US and Australia. See VOUVRAY, QUARTS DE CHAUMES, BONNEZEAUX, SAUMUR 146, 177, 478-479

Cheverny (LOIRE) Light, floral VDQS whites from the SAUVIGNON and CHENIN BLANC 76 83 85 86 88 89 £-££

Chianti (CLASSICO, PUTTO) (TUSCANY) Famous red DOCG, round and extrovert but of variable quality. The cockerel or cherub insignia of the Classico or Putto growers should indicate a finer wine 82 83 85 86 87 88 89 90 91 ££-££££ 417 422

Chiaretto (LOMBARDY) Commendable light reds and rosés from around Lake Garda Chiartetto Classico Bardolino, Rizardi 92 (BAR)

Chile Rising (if rather old-fashioned) source of CABERNET SAUVIGNON, SAUVIGNON/ SEMILLON whites and some experimental CHARDONNAY 81 82 83 84 85 86 88 89 90 91 £-££££ 54 143 175 265

Chinon (LOIRE) CABERNET FRANC-based reds, rosés and whites that are light and grassy when young. Reds from a hot summer can age for up to 10 years 83 85 86 88 89 90 ££-£££ 222 285

Chiroubles (BURGUNDY) One of the 10 BEAUJOLAIS CRUS, drinks best when young and full of almost *nouveau*-style fruit. 88 89 90 91 £££ La Seigneronce Gobet (EYP)

Chorey-les-Beaune (BURGUNDY) Modest warm reds once sold as COTE DE BEAUNE VILLAGES, now beginning to be appreciated 78 80 83 85 86 88 89 90 92 £££

Chusclan (RHONE) Named village of COTES DU RHONE with perhaps the best rosé of the area ££ La Barque Vieille Cotes du Rhone 91 (BD)

Cinsaut/Cinsault Prolific, hot climate, fruity, red grape with high acidity, often blended with GRENACHE. One of the 13 permitted varieties of CHATEAUNEUF-DU-PAPE, and also in the blend of Château Musr in the Lebanon

Cissac (BORDEAUX) HAUT-MEDOC village close to ST ESTEPHE, producing similar though less fine wines 78 79 81 82 83 85 86 88 89 90 £££-££££ Chateau Cissac 1982 (CWS)

Clairette de Die (RHONE) Pleasant, if rather dull, sparkling wine. The Cuvée Tradition made with MUSCAT is far better; grapey and fresh – like a top-class French ASTI SPUMANTE £££ Clairette de Die Tradition J Pachard (U)

Clairette Dull, white, workhorse grape of southern France

Clare Valley (Australia) Well-established region producing high-quality Rieslings which age well. (Look for Tim Knappstein, Pikes, Lindemans Watervale) 80 84 86 88 89 90 91 Shiraz Tim Adams 90 (A&N)

Clarete (Spain) Term for light red wine frowned on by the EC

Classico (Italy) May only be used on a central, historic area of a DOC, eg CHIANTI CLASSICO, VALPOLICELLA CLASSICO

Climat (BURGUNDY) An individual vineyard

Clos (France) Literally, a walled vineyard – and often a finer wine

Colares (Portugal) DO region near Lisbon for heavy, tannic red wines. The vines are grown in deep sand. Surprisingly hard to find in the UK ££-£££

Colheita (Portugal) Harvest or vintage

Colle/colli (Italy) Hill/hills

Colli Berici (VENETO) DOC for red and white – promising CABERNETS

Colle Orientali del Friuli (Friuli-Venezia Giulia) Excellent, fresh, lively whites from near the Yugoslav border 85 88 89 90 91 92 £££ Tocai Friuliano Collio, Scellopetto 90 (PON)

Colombard White grape grown in SW France principally for distillation into Armagnac, but sometimes blended with UGNI BLANC to make a crisp dry wine. Also planted in Australia and the US, where it is known as French Colombard £ Best's Victoria Colombard 92 (C&A)

Commandaria (Cyprus) Traditional dessert wine with rich raisiny fruit £-££

Commune (France) Small demarcated plot of land named after its principal town or village. Equivalent to an English parish

Condrieu (RHONE) Fabulous pricey white from the VIOGNIER grape – old-fashioned, rich, aromatic wine 86 87 88 89 90 91 92 £££££ Château du Rozay 91 (YAP)

Consejo Regulador (Spain) Spain's administrative body for the enforcement of the DO laws

Consorzio (Italy) Syndicate of producers, often using their own seal of quality

Coonawarra (Australia) Important, southerly, cool climate area of South Australia, famed for excellent RIESLING, minty CABERNET SAUVIGNON and, more recently, CHARDONNAY (Red) 82 84 85 86 87 88 90 91 92 (White) 86 87 88 90 91 92 ££-£££££ 272 298 352

Corbières Highly successful everyday red of variable quality. At its best a full, fruity, country wine 85 86 88 89 90 91 £-££ 217 238

Corked Unpleasant, musty smell, caused by fungus attacking cork

Cornas (RHONE) Dark red from the SYRAH grape, hugely tannic when young but worth tucking away 76 78 79 82 83 85 88 89 90 91 ££££ 362 367

Corsica (France) Mediterranean island making robust reds, whites and rosés, often high in alcohol

Cortese (Italy) Grape used in Piemonte and to make Gavi.

Cosecha (Spain) Harvest or vintage

Costières du Gard (SW France) Good fruity reds, lesser-seen whites and rosés

Cot The red grape of CAHORS and the LOIRE, also the MALBEC of BORDEAUX £-££ 239

Côte de Beaune (Villages) A geographical distinction; with Villages on a label, indicates red wines from one or more of the villages in the Côte de Beaune. Confusingly, wine labelled simply 'Côte de Beaune' comes from a small area around Beaune itself. These wines (red and white) are very rare 78 79 80 82 83 85 87 88 89 90 92 £££-££££ 85

Côte de Brouilly (BURGUNDY) One of the 10 BEAUJOLAIS CRUS; distinct from BROUILLY and often finer. Floral and ripely fruity; will keep for a year or two 88 89 90 91 £££ 380

Côte de Nuits (BURGUNDY) Northern, and principally 'red' end of the COTE D'OR 78 80 82 83 84 85 86 87 88 89 90 92

Côte des Blancs (CHAMPAGNE) Principal CHARDONNAY-growing area 78 83 85 86 88 90 Gimonnet 1 er Cru Blanc de Blancs (CD)

Côte d'Or (BURGUNDY) Geographical designation for the central, finest slopes running down the region, encompassing the COTE DE NUITS and COTE DE BEAUNE

Côte Rôtie (RHONE) Powerful yet refined SYRAH reds from the northern Rhône, need at least six (better 10) years 76 78 79 82 83 85 88 89 90 91 ££££-£££££ 366 368 371

Coteaux Champenois (CHAMPAGNE) APPELLATION for the still wine of the area, thin and light 88 89 90 92 £££££ Veronique-Sylvie, Georges Vesselle (JOB)

Côtes de Provence Improving, good value fruity rosés and whites, and ripe spicy reds 85 86 87 88 89 90 91 £-£££ Domaine du Jas d'Esclans 89 (LAV)

Côtes du Rhône (Villages) Large APPELLATION for warm, fruity, spicy reds both medium and full-bodied, and full spicy reds. Villages, particularly if named, are finer and very good value 83 85 86 87 88 89 90 91 £-£££ 331 335 340

Cotesti (ROMANIA) Easterly vineyards growing some French varieties

Côte(s), Coteaux (France) Hillsides – prefixed to, eg Beaune, indicates finer wine

Cotnari (ROMANIA) Traditional white dessert wine of good repute

Coulure Vine disorder caused by adverse climatic conditions, causing grapes to shrivel and fall

Cream sherry Popular style produced by sweetening an OLOROSO ££-£££

Crémant (France) In CHAMPAGNE, lightly sparkling. Elsewhere, eg Crémant de Bourgogne, de Loire and d'Alsace, MÉTHODE CHAMPENOISE fizz 7 18 22

Criado y Embotellado (por) (Spain) Grown and bottled (by)

Crianza (Spain) Literally 'keeping' – 'con crianza' means aged in wood

Crisp Fresh, with good acidity

Crouchen (France) Obscure grape variety capable of producing agreeable whites. Previously known as Clare Reisling in Australia and Paarl in South Africa

Crozes-Hermitage (RHONE) A few nutty white wines – better known for pleasing, light, SYRAH reds which drink young but will keep. Hermitage's kid brother 78 79 82 83 85 88 89 90 91 ££-££££ 333 338 344

Cru artisan Antiquated classification for sub-CRU BOURGEOIS wines

Cru bourgeois (BORDEAUX) Wines beneath the CRUS CLASSES, satisfying certain requirements, which can be good value for money and, in certain cases, better than supposedly classier classed growths

Cru classé (BORDEAUX) The best wines of the MEDOC are *crus classés*, divided into five categories from first (top) to fifth growth (or *cru*) in 1855. The GRAVES, ST EMILION and SAUTERNES have their own classifications

Cru grand bourgeois (exceptionnel) An estate-bottled HAUT-MEDOC cru bourgeois, which is aged in oak barrels. *Exceptionnel* wines must come from the area encompassing the *crus classés*. Future vintages will not bear this designation, as it has fallen foul of the EC

Crusted (port) Affordable alternative to vintage port, a blend of different years bottled young and allowed to throw a deposit 491

Curico (CHILE) Up-and-coming wine region 54 133

Cuve close The third-best way of making sparkling wine, where the wine undergoes secondary fermentation in a tank and is then bottled. Also called the CHARMAT or TANK method

Cuvée Most frequently a blend, put together in a process called ASSEMBLAGE

Cuvée de Prestige What the producer considers a finer blend, or cuvée

Dão (Portugal) DO reds and whites, fairly full. 88 89 90 92 £-££ Catedral Dão, Capiver (STW)

Dealul Mare (Romania) Carpathian region once known for whites, now producing reds from 'noble' varieties

Dégorgée (dégorgement) The removal of the deposit of inert yeasts from CHAMPAGNE after maturation. See **RD**

Deidesheim (Rheinpfalz) Distinguished wine town producing quality, flavoursome RIESLINGS. Deidesheimer Bacchus, Vollmer (AB)

Demi-sec (France) Medium-dry

Deutscher Tafelwein (Germany) Table wine, guaranteed German as opposed to Germanic-style EC TAFELWEIN

Deutches Weinsiegel (Germany) Seals of various colours awarded for merit to German wines, usually present as neck labels

Diabetiker Wein (Germany) Indicates a very dry wine with most of the sugar fermented out (as in a Diät lager), thus suitable for diabetics

DLG (Deutsche Landwirtschaft Gesellschaft) Body awarding medals for excellence to German wines

DO Denominaci/on/ão d'Origen (Spain, Portugal) Demarcated quality area, guaranteeing origin, grape varieties and production standards

DOC(G) Denominazione di Origine Controllata (é Garantita) (Italy) Quality control designation based on grape variety and/or origin. 'Garantita' is supposed to imply a higher quality level but it is not a reliable guide.

Dolcetto (d'Alba, di Ovada) (PIEDMONT) Red grape making anything from soft, everyday wine to more robust, long-lasting DOCs 83 85 86 88 89 90 92 £££ 414 424

Dôle (SWITZERLAND) Light reds from the PINOT NOIR and/or GAMAY

Domaine (France) Wine estate, can encompass a number of vineyards

Dosage The addition of sweetening syrup to CHAMPAGNE, that is naturally dry

Douro (Portugal) The great port region and river, producing much demarcated and occasionally good table wines 79 80 82 83 85 88 89 ££ 437 439 443

Doux (France) Sweet

Dumb As in dumb nose, meaning without smell

Duras (Côtes de) (BORDEAUX) Inexpensive whites from the SAUVIGNON, often better value than basic Bordeaux Blanc 88 89 90 92 £-££ Domaine Petitot 92, Hugh Ryman (MWW)

Durbach (BADEN) Top vineyard area of this ANBAUGEBIET

Edelfäule (Germany) BOTRYTIS CINEREA, or 'noble rot'

Edelzwicker (ALSACE) Generic name for white wine from a blend of grape varieties. Increasingly rare

Eger (HUNGARY) Official wine district best known for 'Bulls' Blood'

Einzellage (Germany) Single vineyard; most precise and often the last part of a wine name, finer by definition than a GROSSLAGE

Eiswein (Germany) The finest QmP wine, made from BOTRYTIS-affected grapes naturally frozen on the vine. Concentrated, delicious, rare but often underpriced. Can now be made only from grapes of BEERENAUSLESE or TROCKENBEERENAUSLESE quality

Eitelsbach (MOSEL-SAAR-RUWER) One of the top two Ruwer wine towns, site of the famed Karthäuserhofberg vineyard

Elaborado y Anejado Por (Spain) 'Made and aged for'

Elba (Italy) Island off the Tuscan coast making full dry reds and whites

Elbling Inferior Germanic white grape

Elever/éleveur To mature or 'nurture' wine, especially in the cellars of the BURGUNDY NEGOCIANTS, who act as *éleveurs*

Eltville (RHEINGAU) Town housing the Rheingau state cellars and the German Wine Academy, producing good RIESLING with backbone 83 85 88 89 90 91 92 ££-££££

Emerald Riesling (California) Bottom of the range white hybrid grape, at best fresh, fruity but undistinguished

Emilia-Romagna (Italy) Region surrounding Bologna best known for LAMBRUSCO

En primeur New wine, usually BORDEAUX – specialist merchants buy and offer wine 'en primeur' before it has been released; customers rely on their merchant's judgement to make a good buy

English wine Produced from grapes grown in England (or Wales), as opposed to BRITISH WINE, which is made from imported concentrate 88 89 90 91 ££-££££ 82 96 176 196

Enoteca (Italy) Literally, wine library or, nowadays, wine shop

Entre-Deux-Mers (BORDEAUX) Up-and-coming source of basic Bordeaux Blanc, principally dry SAUVIGNON 88 89 90 92 £-££ Somerfield Entre-deux-mers, Y Mau (G)

Epernay (CHAMPAGNE) Centre of Champagne production, where famous houses such as Mercier, Moët & Chandon, Perrier Jouët and Pol Roger are based.

Erbach (RHEINGAU) Town noted for fine, full RIESLING, notably from the Marcobrunn vineyard 85 86 88 89 90 91 92 ££-£££££

Erden (MOSEL-SAAR-RUWER) Northerly village producing full, crisp, dry RIESLING. In the Bernkastel BEREICH, includes the famous Treppchen vineyard 83 85 86 88 89 90 91 92 £££-£££££ 204

Erzeugerabfüllung (Germany) Bottled by the grower/estate

Espum/oso/ante (Spain/Portugal) Sparkling

Esters Chemical components in wine responsible for a variety of odours, mainly fruity

Estufa The vats in which MADEIRA is heated, speeding maturity and imparting its familiar 'cooked' flavour

Eszencia (HUNGARY) Essence of TOKAY, once prized for its supposedly miraculous properties. Now virtually unobtainable, though supplies may improve as Hungary's winemakers benefit from privatisation and foreign investment £££££

Etna (Italy) From the Sicilian volcanic slopes, hot-climate, soft, fruity DOC reds, whites and rosés. Can be flabby

Fattoria (Italy) Estate, particularly in Tuscany

Fat Has a silky texture which fills the mouth. More fleshy than meaty

Faugères (MIDI) Good, full-bodied AC reds, some whites and rosés, a cut above the surrounding COTEAUX DU LANGUEDOC **88 89 90 91** £-££ Château La Liquieres 91 (TH, WR)

Fendant (SWITZERLAND) The CHASSELAS grape and its white wines, so called in the VALAIS area

Fermentazione naturale (Italy) 'Naturally sparkling' but, in fact, indicates the CUVE CLOSE method

Fining The clarifying of young wine before bottling to remove impurities, using a number of agents including ISINGLASS and BENTONITE

Finish What you can still taste after swallowing

Fino (Spain) Dry, delicate sherry, the finest to aficionados. Drink chilled and drink up once opened ££-££££ Safeway Fino, Garcia de Leaniz (SAF)

Fitou (MIDI) Reliable southern AC, making reds from the CARIGNAN grape. Formerly dark and stubborn, the wines have become more refined, with a woody warmth **88 89 90** 91 £-££ Terroir de Tuchan Fitou 91 (TH)

Fixin (BURGUNDY) Northerly village of the COTE DE NUITS, producing lean, tough, uncommercial reds which can mature splendidly **85 87** 88 89 90 92 £££-££££ 401

Flabby Lacking balancing acidity

Flagey-Echezeaux (BURGUNDY) Prestigious red COTE DE NUITS COMMUNE. Echezeaux and Grands Echezeaux are the two best GRANDS CRUS **78 80 82 83** 85 88 89 90 92 £££££ Echezeaux Vallet Freres 89 (Paul Boutinot Wines 061-477 1171)

Fleurie (BURGUNDY) One of the 10 BEAUJOLAIS CRUS, fresh and fragrant as its name suggests. Much admired but most expensive Cru **85 87 88 89 90 91** £££ 379

Flor Yeast which grows naturally on the surface of some maturing sherries, making them potential FINOS

Flora Grape, a cross between SEMILLON and GEWURZTRAMINER best known in Brown Brothers Orange Muscat and Flora

Folle Blanche Widely planted workhorse white grape, high in acidity. Known as the GROS PLANT in MUSCADET. Some success in California

Folle Noir (MIDI) Grape used to make BELLET

Forst (RHEINPFALZ) Wine town producing great, concentrated RIESLING. Famous for the Jesuitengarten vineyard **75 76 79 83 85 86** 88 89 90 91 92 ££-£££££ Forster St Ursula Collection 90 (OD)

Franciacorta (LOMBARDY) DOC for good, light, French-influenced reds and a noted sparkler, Franciacorta Pinot **85 86 88 89 90** 92 £-£££ Franciacorta Rosso Bellavista (Alivini 081 880 2525)

Franken (Germany) ANBAUGEBIET making charracterful, sometimes earthy, dry whites, traditionally presented in the squat, flagon-shaped 'bocksbeutel' on which the Mateus bottle was modelled **83 85 86 87 88 89 90** 91 92 ££-££££

Frascati (Italy) Clichéd dry or semi-dry white from LATIUM, at best soft and clean, more usually dull. Drink within 12 months of vintage £-££££ Frascati Superiore Selezione, San Marco 92 (U)

Friuli-Venezia Giulia (Italy) Northerly region containing a number of DOCs, successful with MERLOT, PINOT BIANCO and GRIGIO **85 88 89 90** 91 92 ££-££££ 65 170 410

Frizzante (Italy) Semi-sparkling

Fronsac/Canon Fronsac (BORDEAUX) Below ST EMILION, producing comparable but tougher, often robust reds. Canon Fronsac is better and often good value **81 82 83 85 86 88** 89 90 £££-££££ Château La Vieille Cure 89 (JS)

Frontignan (Muscat de) (PROVENCE) Rich, sweet, grapey fortified wine from the Bandol area in Provence. More forceful (and cheaper) than BEAUMES DE VENISE. Also a synonym for Muscat à Petits Grains ££-£££ Château de la Peyrade (ADN)

Frontonnais (Côtes du) (SW France) Up-and-coming inexpensive red (and some rosé), full and fruitily characterful **85 86 88** 89 90 ££

Fruska Gora (YUGOSLAVIA) Hilly wine region best known for white wines. Improving success with French grape varieties

Fumé Blanc Name invented by Robert Mondavi for the SAUVIGNON grape, derived from POUILLY BLANC FUME

Fürmint Eastern European white grape, used for TOKAY in HUNGARY

Fûts de Chêne (France) Oak barrels, as in *é leve en* (matured in)

Gaillac (SW France) Light, fresh, good-value reds and whites, the result of an invasion of the GAMAY and SAUVIGNON grapes. PERLE is lightly sparkling **88 89 90 91** ££ Gaillac Cave de la Bastide 92 (VW)

Galestro (TUSCANY) A light, grapey white ££ Galestro Antinori 1990 (V&C)

Gamay The BEAUJOLAIS grape, making wine with youthful, fresh, cherry/plummy fruit. Also successful in the LOIRE and GAILLAC

Gamay Beaujolais A misnamed variety of PINOT NOIR grown in California

Gamey Smell or taste reminiscent of hung game

Gard (Vin de pays du) (MIDI) Huge VIN DE TABLE producing area with one fair VDQS, COSTIERES DU GARD **89 90 91 92**

Garganega (Italy) Uninspiring white grape used chiefly for SOAVE

Garrafeira (Portugal) Indicates a producer's 'reserve' wine, selected and given extra ageing **78 80 82 83 85 86** 88 90 ££ Garrafeira D Fuas 83 (STW)

Gascogne (Côtes de) (SW France) Source of Armagnac, good-value, fresh, floral whites and increasingly good light reds. Source of our White Wine of the Year in 1989, made by Grassa **90 91 92** £ 127 131 134

Gattinara (PIEDMONT) Red DOC from the NEBBIOLO, varying in quality but at least full-flavoured and dry **82 85 88 89 90** 92 ££-££££

Gavi (TUSCANY) Full, dry white from the CORTESE grape. Compared to white BURGUNDY (often for no good reason). Gavi and Gavi di Gavi tend to be creamily pleasant and overpriced **88 90 91 92** ££-££££ Gavi Tenute Neirano 92 (GRD, U)

Geelong (Australia) Vine growing area of VICTORIA, cool and well suited to CHARDONNAY and PINOT NOIR. Look for Bannockburn, Idyll and Hickinbotham **85 86 88 89 90** 91 92

Geisenheim (RHEINGAU) Town and the home of the German Wine Institute, the most famous wine school in the world **83 85** 88 89 90 91 92 ££-£££££

Generoso (Spain) Fortified or dessert wine

Gevrey Chambertin (BURGUNDY) Best-known red CÔTE DE NUITS COMMUNE, much exploited but still capable of superb, plummy rich wine from the best vineyards. The GRAND CRU is Le Chambertin **78 80 82 83 85** 88 89 90 92 ££££-£££££ 407

Gewürztraminer White grape making dry, full, fleshy, spicy wine, best in ALSACE but also grown in Australasia, Italy, the US and E Europe 179-180 182-183

Gigondas (RHONE) Côtes du Rhône COMMUNE producing good value, reliable, full-bodied, spicy/peppery, blackcurranty reds, best with food **79 82 83 85 86 88** 89 90 91 ££-£££ Gigondas Tour de Queyron 90 (JS)

Giropalette Machines which, in MÉTHODE CHAMPENOISE, automatically perform the task of REMUAGE

Gisborne (New Zealand) North Island vine growing area since 1920s. Cool, wettish climate, mainly used for (good) Chardonnay **89 90 91** ££-££££ 86 121 252

Givry (BURGUNDY) CÔTE CHALONNAISE commune, making typical and affordable, if sometimes unexciting, PINOT NOIRS and creamy whites **83 85 87 88 89** 90 92 £££ Givry M Derain 89 (SMJ)

Graach (MOSEL-SAAR-RUWER) MITTELMOSEL village producing fine wines. Best known for Himmelreich vineyard **83 85 86 88** 89 90 91 92 ££-££££ Graacher Himmelreich Auslese 1988 Gymnasium (TO WOC)

Gran reserva (Spain) A quality wine aged for a designated number of years in wood and, in theory, only produced in the best vintages

Grand cru (France) The finest vineyards. Official designation in BORDEAUX, BURGUNDY and ALSACE. Vague in Bordeaux and Alsace, but in Burgundy denotes a single vineyard with its own AC, eg Montrachet

Grandes marque Syndicate of the major CHAMPAGNE houses

Grave del Friuli (Friuli-Venezia Giulia) DOC for young-drinking reds and whites. CABERNET and MERLOT increasingly successful **85 86 87 88 90** 91 92 ££ 410

Graves (BORDEAUX) Large, southern region producing vast quantities of white, from good to indifferent. Reds have a better reputation for quality. See also PESSAC LEOGNAN (Red) **78 79 81 82 83 85 86 88** 89 90 (White)**78 79 81 82 83 85** 86 88 89 90 ££-£££££ 101 300

Greco di Tufo (Italy) From Campania, best-known white from the ancient GRECO grape; dry, characterful southern wine Greco di Tufo

Grenache Red grape of the RHONE (the GARNACHA in Spain) making spicy, peppery, full-bodied wine. Also increasingly used to make fruity rosés across Southern France and California 218

Grignolino (PIEDMONT) Red grape and its modest, but refreshing, wine, eg the DOC Grignolino d'Asti **85 86 87 88** 90 91 ££-£££

Gros Plant (du Pays Nantais) (LOIRE) Light, sharp white VDQS wine from the same region as MUSCADET, named after the grape elsewhere known as the FOLLE BLANCHE **89 90 92** £-££

Groslot/Grolleau Workhorse grape of the Loire, particularly ANJOU, used for white, rosé and base wines for sparkling SAUMUR

Grosslage (Germany) Wine district, the third subdivision after ANBAUGEBIET (eg RHEINGAU) and BEREICH (eg NIERSTEIN). For example, Michelsberg is a GROSSLAGE of the Bereich PIESPORT

Grüner Veltliner White grape of AUSTRIA and Eastern Europe, producing light, fresh, aromatic wine **87 88** 89 90 ££-£££ Grüner Veltliner Winzerhaus 91 (TO)

Gumpoldskirchen (AUSTRIA) Town near Vienna famous for full, rather heady characterful wines **87 88 89 90 91 92** ££

Gutedel German name for the CHASSELAS grape

Halbtrocken (Germany) Off-dry. Rising style intended to accompany food. Halbtrocken Riesling Kabinett 92 Rudolf Ermann (VR)

Hallgarten (RHEINGAU) Important town near Hattenheim producing robust wines

Haro (Spain) Town at the heart of the RIOJA region, home of many BODEGAS, eg CVNE, La Rioja Alta

Hattenheim (RHEINGAU) One of the greatest Johannisberg villages, producing some of the best German RIESLINGS **76 79 83** 85 88 89 ££-££££ Hattenheim Nussbrunner riesling Auslese Von Simmern 1990 (ADN)

Haut-Médoc (BORDEAUX) Large APPELLATION which includes nearly all of the well-known CRUS CLASSES. Basic Haut-Médoc should be better than plain MÉDOC **78 81 82 83** 85 86 88 89 90 91 ££-£££££ 296 302 308

Haut Poitou (LOIRE) Often boring VDQS red but reliable, good value SAUVIGNON and CHARDONNAY whites **89 90 92** ££ La Cave Du Haut Poitou Sauvignon 92 (LWL)

Hautes Côtes de Beaune (BURGUNDY) Sound, soft, strawberry PINOT NOIR from a group of villages **85 86 87 88 89** 90 92 ££-£££££ 385

Hautes Côtes de Nuits (BURGUNDY) Slightly tougher than HAUTES COTES DE BEAUNE, particularly when young **85 86 87** 88 89 90 92 ££-££££ Thorin 1990 (ER)

Hawkes Bay (New Zealand) Major North Island vineyard area **87 89 90 91** ££-££££ 112 136 220

Hérault (Vin de pays de l') (France) Largest vine growing *département*, producing some 20 per cent of France's wine, nearly all VIN DE PAYS or VDQS, of which COTEAUX DU LANGUEDOC is best known. Also home of the extraordinary Mas de Daumas Gassac, where no expense is spared to produce easily the best of France's 'country wines' **82 83** 85 86 88 89 90 91 £-££££ 38 233

Hermitage (RHONE) Top-class, long-lived northern Rhône wines; superb, complex reds and sumptuous, nutty whites. Also Australian name for the SYRAH grape and, confusingly, the South African term for CINSAULT **76 78 79 82 83** 85 88 89 90 91 ££££-£££££ Hermitage Cave de Tain 89 (PBW)

Hessische Bergstrasse (Germany) Smallest ANBAUGEBIET, rarely seen in the UK

Hochfeinste (Germany) 'Very finest'

Hochgewächs QbA Recent official designation for RIESLINGS which are as ripe as a QmP but can still only call themselves QbA. This from a nation dedicated to simplifying what are acknowledged to be the most complicated labels in the world

Hochheim (RHEINGAU) Village whose fine RIESLINGS gave the English the word 'Hock'. HochheimerKonigen Victoria Deinhard 89 (Deinhard 071-261 1111)

Hock English name for Rhine wines, derived from HOCHHEIM in the RHEINGAU 191-192 195 199

Hospices de Beaune (BURGUNDY) Charity hospital, wines from whose vineyards are sold at an annual charity auction on the third Sunday in November, the prices setting the tone for the COTE D'OR year. Beware that although price lists often merely indicate 'Hospices de Beaune' as a producer, all of the wines bought at the auction are matured and bottled by local merchants, some of whom are more scrupulous than others

Huelva (Spain) DO of the Estremadura region, producing rather heavy whites and fortified wines

Hungary Country previously known for its famous TOKAY, infamous Bull's Blood, and OLASZ RIZLING. Now a popular destination for flying winemakers – a country to watch 39 193 223 246 487

Hunter Valley (Australia) Famous region of New South Wales, producing many reds (often from SHIRAZ) and full, fleshy whites from SEMILLON and CHARDONNAY (Red) **83 86 87 88 90** 91 92 (White) **83 86 87 88 90** 91 92 ££-£££££ 79 87

Huxelrebe Minor white grape, often grown in England 201

Hybrid Cross-bred grape, usually *Vitis vinifera* (European) x *Vitis labrusca* (N American)

Hydrogen sulphide Naturally occurring gas given off by especially young red wine, resulting in smell of rotten eggs. Often caused by insufficient racking

Imbottigliato nel'origine (Italy) Estate bottled

Imperiale Large bottle containing six litres of wine

Inferno (Italy) LOMBARDY DOC, chiefly red from NEBBIOLO, which needs to be aged for at least five years.

Institut National des Appellations d'Origine (INAO) French administrative body which designates and polices quality areas

Irancy (BURGUNDY) Light reds and rosés made near CHABLIS from a blend of grapes. Little known 88 89 90 92 £££ Andre Sorin (ABY)

Irouléguy (SW France) Earthy, spicy reds and rosés, duller whites 219

Irsay Oliver (Slovakia) Native white varietal giving aromatic, spicy but dry wines. Excellent value for money. Slovakian Irsay Oliver, Vino Nitra (VW)

Isinglass FINING agent derived from the sturgeon fish

Israel Once the source of appalling stuff, but the new-style VARIETAL wines are improving

Italian Riesling Not the great RHINE RIESLING, but a lesser version, going under many names, and widely grown in Northern and Eastern Europe

Jardin de la France (Vin de Pays du) Marketing device to describe VINS DE PAYS from the LOIRE £ Sainsbury's VdP du Jardin de la France (JS)

Jasnières (LOIRE) Rare, sweet CHENIN BLANC wines from TOURAINE 88 89 90 92

Jeunes Vignes Term occasionally seen in BURGUNDY, denotes wine from vines too young for their classified destiny, eg CHABLIS

Jerez (de la Frontera) (Spain) Centre of the SHERRY trade, gives its name to entire DO sherry-producing area 480-485

Jeroboam Large bottle containing three litres, usually of CHAMPAGNE

Jesuitengarten (RHEINGAU) One of Germany's top vineyards. Forster Jesuitgarten Riesling Spätlese 88, Bassermann Jordan (VW)

Johannisberg (RHEINGAU) Village making superb RIESLING, which has lent its name to a BEREICH covering all the Rheingau 75 76 79 83 85 88 89 90 91 92 £-£££££ 210

Johannisberg Riesling Californian name for RHINE RIESLING

Jug wine American term for quaffable VIN ORDINAIRE

Juliénas (BURGUNDY) One of the 10 BEAUJOLAIS CRUS producing classic, vigorous wine which often benefits from a few years in bottle 88 89 90 91 ££-£££ 378

Jumilla (Spain) Improving DO region, traditionally known for heavy, high-alcohol wines but increasingly making lighter ones 82 83 84 85 86 87 88 £-££ Taja 88 (RWC BOO)

Jura (E France) Region containing ARBOIS and SAVOIE, home of the SAVAGNIN grape and best known for specialities such as VIN GRIS, VIN JAUNE and VIN DE PAILLE 10

Jurançon (SW France) Rich, dry apricotty white and excellent long-living sweet wines 86 87 88 89 90 91 ££-££££ 477

Kabinett First step in German quality ladder, for wines which fulfil a certain natural sweetness rating. Semi-dry wines 200 205-206 210

Kaiserstuhl (BADEN) Finest BADEN BEREICH with top villages producing rich, spicy RIESLING from volcanic slopes. Kaiserstuhl Winkleberg Gewurztraminer Spatlese 89 Ihringer(SAF)

Kallstadt (RHEINPFALZ) Village containing the best known and finest vineyard of Annaberg, making luscious, full RIESLING. Kallstadter Kobnert Riesling Kabinett 90 Muller Ruprecht (TRW)

Kalterersee (Italy) Germanic name for the LAGO DI CALDARO in the SUDTIROL/ALTO ADIGE

Keller/kellerei/kellerabfüllung (German) Cellar/producer/estate-bottled

Keppoch/Padthaway (Australia) Vineyard area north of COONAWARRA 84 85 86 87 88 90 91 92 ££-£££££ Penfolds Padthaway Chardonnay 92 (PEF, OD)

Kerner White grape, a RIESLING cross, grown in Germany and now England. Barkham Manor Kerner 90 (BAK)

Kiedrich (RHEINGAU) Top village high in the hills with some renowned vineyards 75 76 79 83 85 88 89 90 91 92 £-£££££

Kir White wine with a dash of cassis syrup, good for disguising a disappointing buy. With sparkling wine (properly CHAMPAGNE), a Kir Royale

Klusserath (MOSEL-SAAR-RUWER) Small village best known in UK for Sonnenuhr and Konigsberg vineyards 76 79 83 85 88 89 90 91 92 £-£££££ (WSC) Klusserather Bruderschaft, Moselland 88 (MWW)

Krems (AUSTRIA) Town and WACHAU vineyard area producing Austria's most stylish Rieslings from terraced vineyards

Kreuznach (NAHE) Northern BEREICH, with fine vineyards around the town of Bad Kreuznach 207

La Mancha (Spain) Over a million acres of vineyard on the central plain. Mostly VIN ORDINAIRE, but with some startling exceptions, for example, Castillo de Alhambra, the *Guide*'s Wine of the Year in 1989 **88 89 90 91 92** £ 66

Labrusca *Vitis labrusca*, the North American species of vine, making wine which is often referred to as 'foxy'. All VINIFERA vine stocks are grafted on to PHYLLOXERA-resistant Labrusca roots, though the vine itself is banned in Europe

Lacryma Christi (Campania) Literally, 'tears of Christ'; melancholy name for some amiable, light, rather rustic reds and whites. Those from Vesuvio are DOC **86 87 88 89 90 92** ££ LAC CHR 87 Mastro Berdardino (LV)

Lago di Caldaro (TRENTINO-ALTO ADIGE) Also known as the KALTERERSEE, making cool, light reds with slightly unripe, though pleasant fruit **88 89 90 91** £-££

Lagrein Red grape grown in the TRENTINO-ALTO ADIGE region making dry, light, fruity DOC reds and rosés

Lake County (California) Vineyard district salvaged by improved irrigation techniques and now capable of some fine wines **86 87 88 89 90 92** ££-£££ Konocti Merlot 90 (BI)

Lalande de Pomerol (BORDEAUX) Bordering on POMEROL with similar, but less fine wines. Some good value PETITS-CHATEAUX **81 83 85 86 88 89 90** ££-££££ 294

Lambrusco (EMILIA-ROMAGNA) Famous, rather sweet, red fizzy wine, and now some white versions produced for the Anglo-Saxon palate. Variable quality but the best are the dry, Italian-style versions, ideal for picnics **90 91 92** £-££ Tesco Lambrusco Rosso Cantine Del Duca (TO)

Landwein (Germany) A relatively recent quality designation – the equivalent of a French VIN DE PAYS from one of 11 named regions (ANBAUGEBIET). Often dry

Langhe (PIEDMONT) A range of hills

Languedoc (Coteaux du) (MIDI) Big VDQS, a popular source of everyday reds from RHONE and southern grapes **85 86 88 89 90 91** £-£££££ 144 227 329

Laski Riesling/Rizling YUGOSLAV name for poor quality white grape, unrelated to the RHINE RIESLING. Aka WELSCH, OLASZ and Italico

Late-bottled vintage (port) (LBV) Bottled either four or six years after a specific vintage; the time in wood softens them up so they're ready to drink younger 494

Late Harvest Made from grapes which are picked after the main vintage, giving a higher sugar level ££-£££££ 471-472

Latium/Lazio (Italy) The vineyard area surrounding Rome. Avoid most of its Frascati, although there are some exciting Bordeaux-style reds **88 89 90 92** £-££ Villa Fontana, Fontana Candida (MWW)

Laudun (RHONE) Named village of COTES DU RHONE, with some atypical fresh, light wines and attractive rosés

Layon, Coteaux du (LOIRE) Whites from the CHENIN BLANC grape, slow to develop and long lived. Lots of lean dry wine but the sweet BONNEZEAUX and QUARTS DE CHAUME are superior **71 76 83 85** 89 90 92 ££-£££££ 478

Lazio SEE LATIUM

Lean Lacking body

Lebanon Chiefly represented in the UK by the remarkable Château MUSr, made in BORDEAUX style but from CABERNET SAUVIGNON, CINSAULT and SYRAH **78 79 80 81 82 86 87 89 90** ££-£££££ 346

Lees Or *lies*, the sediment of dead yeasts let fall as a white wine develops. See SUR LIE

Length How long the taste lingers in the mouth

Léognan (BORDEAUX) GRAVES COMMUNE containing many of the finest white CHATEAUX **82 83 85 86 88 89 90** ££-£££££ Château Brown (AB)

Leon (Spain) North-western region producing acceptable dry, fruity reds and whites ££ Palacio de Leon 86 (VW)

Liebfraumilch (Germany) The most seditious exploitation of the German QbA system – a good example is perfectly pleasant but the vast majority, though cheap, are money down the drain. Responsible for the ruination of the German wine market in the UK **90 91 92** £-££ Carl Reh 92 (AB)

Lie(s) See LEES/SUR LIE

Liqueur de Tirage (CHAMPAGNE) The yeast and sugar added to base wine to induce secondary fermentation (bubbles) in bottle

Liqueur d'Expédition (CHAMPAGNE) The sweetening syrup used for DOSAGE

Liquoreux (France) Rich and sweet

Liquoroso (Italy) Rich and sweet

Lirac (RHONE) Peppery, TAVEL-like rosés, and – increasingly impressive – deep, berry-fruit reds **80 81 85** 89 90 91 ££-£££ Château d'Aqueria Rouge 90 (LAV)

Listrac (BORDEAUX) Look out for Châteaux Clarke, Fourcas-Hosten & Fourcas-Dupré **82 83 85 86** 88 89 90 ££-££££

Livermore (Valley) (California) A warm climate vineyard area with fertile soil producing full, rounded whites, including increasingly fine CHARDONNAY

Loir (Coteaux du) Clean vigorous whites from a LOIRE tributary; JASNIERES is little seen but worth looking out for **85 89 90** 92 £££ Jasnières Les Tuffières 85 (YAP)

Loire (France) An extraordinary variety of wines come from this area – dry whites such as MUSCADET and the classier SAVENNIERES, SANCERRE and POUILLY FUME; grassy, summery reds; buckets of rosé – some good, most dreadful; glorious sweet whites and very acceptable sparkling wines. Refer to sub-categories for recommended wines

Lombardy (Italy) The region (and vineyards) around Milan, known mostly for sparkling wine but also for some increasingly interesting reds, and the whites of Lugana 13 61 71 157

Loupiac (BORDEAUX) Bordering on SAUTERNES, with similar, but less fine wines **83 85 86 87** 88 89 90 ££-£££ Château de Ricaud 88 (LAV)

Luberon (Côtes du) (RHONE) Reds, like light COTES DU RHONE, pink and sparkling wines; the whites CHARDONNAY-influenced. A new APPELLATION and still good value **88 89 90** 91 92 £-£££ 234

Ludon (BORDEAUX) HAUT-MEDOC VILLAGE and COMMUNE **81 83 85 86** 88 89 90 £££-£££££ Château Ludon Pomies Agassac 88 (SAF)

Lugana (LOMBARDY) grown on the shores of Lake Garda, smooth, pungent white wine, a match for food. Lombardy's best wine **90 91 92** ££ 61 71 157

Lugny (BURGUNDY) See MACON

Lussac-St-Emilion A satellite of ST EMILION **78 79 81 82 83 85** 86 88 89 90 £££ Château Lyonnat 88 (ABY)

Lutomer (Slovenia) Wine producing area still known mostly for its (very basic) LUTOMER RIESLING, but now doing better things with CHARDONNAY £ Chardonnay 91, Slovenijavino (TEL)

Luxembourg Source of pleasant, fresh, white wines from ALSACE-like grape varieties ££-£££ (EP)

Lyonnais (Coteaux du) (RHONE) Just to the south of BEAUJOLAIS, making some very acceptable good value wines from the same grapes **89 90 91** £-££

Macau HAUT-MEDOC COMMUNE possessing some useful CRUS BOURGEOIS **79 81 82 83 85 86** 88 89 90 £££-££££ Baron Villeneuve de Cantemerle 88 (TH)

Macération carbonique Technique in which uncrushed grapes burst and ferment under pressure of a blanket of carbon dioxide gas to produce fresh, fruity wine. Used in BEAUJOLAIS, South of France and becoming increasingly popular in the New World

Mâcon/Mâconnais (BURGUNDY) Avoid unidentified 'rouge' or 'blanc' on restaurant wine lists. Mâcons with the suffix VILLAGES, SUPERIEUR or PRISSE, VIRE, LUGNY or CLASSE are better and can afford some pleasant, good value CHARDONNAY **89 90 91 92** ££-££££ 50 62 109 382-383

Madeira Atlantic island producing famed fortified wines, usually identified by style: BUAL, SERCIAL, VERDELHO or MALMSEY £££-££££ 491 493 499

Maderisation Deliberate procedure in MADEIRA, produced by the warming of wine in ESTUFAS. Otherwise undesired effect, commonly produced by high temperatures during storage, resulting in a dull, flat flavour tinged with a sherry taste and colour

Madiran (SW France) Heavy, robust country reds, tannic when young but which age extremely well **82 85 86 88** 89 90 ££ 240

Maître de chai (France) Cellar master

Malaga (Spain) Andalusian DO producing dessert wines in varying degrees of sweetness, immensely popular in the 19th century £££ 460

Malbec Red grape, now rare in BORDEAUX but widespread in Argentina and CAHORS, where it is known as the COT or AUXERROIS

Malmsey Traditional, rich MADEIRA – the sweetest style, but with a dry finish £££-££££ Cossart Gordon 15 year old (ADN)

Malolactic fermentation Secondary effect of fermentation in which 'hard' malic acid is converted into the softer lactic acid

Malvasia MUSCATTY white grape vinified dry in Italy, but far more successfully as good, sweet traditional MADEIRA 499

Malvoisie (LOIRE) Local name for the PINOT GRIS 89 90 92 ££ J-P Guindon 90 (YAP)

Manseng, Gros & Petit (Jurançon) Gros = dry whites; Petit = sweet vendange tardives 477

Manzanilla Dry, tangy SHERRY – a FINO-style wine widely (though possibly mistakenly) thought to take a salty tang from the coastal BODEGAS of SANLUCAR DE BARRAMEDA ££-£££ 480

Maranges (Burgundy) Brand-new hillside appellation promising potentially affordable Côte d'Or wines

Marc Residue of pips, stalks and skins after grapes are pressed – often distilled into a woody unsubtle brandy of the same name, eg Marc de Bourgogne

Marches (Italy) Central region on the Adriatic coast best known for ROSSO CONERO and good, dry, fruity VERDICCHIO whites (Red) 85 86 87 88 89 90 92 (White) 89 90 91 92 ££-££££ 53 145 427

Marcillac (SW France) Full-flavoured country reds principally from the Fer grape – may also contain CABERNET and GAMAY. Le sang du pays Dom du Cros 1988 (LV)

Margaret River (Australia) Cool(ish) vineyard area on Western Australia coast, gaining notice for CABERNET SAUVIGNON and CHARDONNAY. Also Australia's only ZINFANDEL from Cape Mentelle (best known wineries are Moss Wood, Cape Mentelle, Leeuwin, Cullens Vasse Felix and Chateau Xanadu) 86 87 89 90 93 £££-££££ 105 307

Margaux (BORDEAUX) Large, variable-quality COMMUNE that boasts a concentration of CRUS CLASSES, the most famous being the first growth Château Margaux 78 79 81 82 83 85 86 88 89 91 ££-£££££ 297 319

Marlborough (New Zealand) Increasingly important wine area with cool climate in the South Island making excellent Sauvignon 90 91 92 93 ££-££££ 104 155 161-162 169 178 269

Marmandais (Côtes du) (SW France) Uses the BORDEAUX grapes plus GAMAY, SYRAH and others to make pleasant, inexpensive wines. Domaine de Beaulieu 91 (TO)

Marsala Dark, rich, fortified wine from SICILY essential in a number of recipes, such as zabaglione ££-£££££

Marsannay (BURGUNDY) Pale red and rosé from the PINOT NOIR 85 87 88 89 90 92 £££-££££ 386

Marsanne With Roussanne, grape responsible for most northern RHONE whites. Also successful in the Goulburn Valley in VICTORIA for Chateau Tahbilk and Mitchelton and in California for Bonny Doone 85 86 88 89 90 91 92 ££-£££ 150

Martinborough (New Zealand) Up-and-coming region for PINOT NOIR and CHARDONNAY. Martinborough Pinot Noir 91 (L&W)

Master of Wine (MW) One of a small number (less than 200) who have passed a gruelling set of trade exams

Mavrodaphne Greek red grape and its wine. Dark and strong; needs ageing ££ Tsantali 91 (GWC)

Mavrud (BULGARIA) Traditional red grape and characterful wine

Médoc (BORDEAUX) As a generic term, implies sound, everyday claret to be drunk young. As an area, that region of Bordeaux south of the Gironde and north of the town of Bordeaux 78 79 82 83 85 86 88 89 90 £-££ 291

Melon de Bourgogne White grape producing a dry, not very exciting wine that can nevertheless be good in Muscadet 139 151 156 158

Mendocino (California) Northern, coastal wine county successfully exploiting cool microclimates to make 'European-style' wines 83 84 85 86 87 88 90 91 92 ££-££££ 23 95 268 282 295 306 336

Ménétou-Salon (LOIRE) Bordering on SANCERRE making similar, less pricey Sauvignon and some PINOT NOIR red 87 88 89 90 92 ££-£££ 164

Mercaptans See HYDROGEN SULPHIDE

Mercurey (BURGUNDY) Good value wine from the Côte CHALONNAISE – tough, full reds worth waiting for, and nutty buttery whites 85 87 88 89 90 92 £££ 397

Merlot Red grape making soft, honeyed, even toffeed wine with plummy fruit. Used to balance the TANNIC CABERNET SAUVIGNON throughout the MEDOC but the main grape of POMEROL and ST EMILION. Also increasingly successful in Washington State, VENETO, HUNGARY and Australia 247 250 268 275 292 309

Merlot di Pramaggiore (VENETO) Plummy red wine from the BORDEAUX grape

Méthode Champenoise As a term, now restricted by law to wines from CHAMPAGNE but in effect used by all quality sparkling wines; labour-intensive method where bubbles are produced by secondary fermentation in bottle

Methuselah Same as an IMPERIALE, usually applied to CHAMPAGNE

Meursault (BURGUNDY) Superb white Burgundy; the CHARDONNAY showing off its nutty, buttery richness in mellow, full-bodied dry wine 81 82 85 **86 88** 89 90 92 £££-£££££ Meursault Les Genevrières 89, Ropiteau (JS)

Midi (France) Vast and vastly improved region of southern France, including CORBIERES, ROUSSILLON, LANGUEDOC, MINERVOIS and the VIN DE PAYS departments of GARD, AUDE and HERAULT. See *THE WINES* section for several examples.

Millesime (France) Year or vintage

Minervois (SW France) Firm and fruity suppertime reds 88 89 90 91 £-££ Caves Pouzol 89 (TH, WR)

Mis en Bouteille au Château/Domaine (France) Bottled at the estate

Mittelhaardt (RHEINPFALZ) Central and best BEREICH **86 87 88** 89 90 91 92 ££ 463

Mittelmosel (MOSEL-SAAR-RUWER) Middle and best section of the Mosel, including the BERNKASTEL BEREICH **85 86** 87 **88** 89 90 91 92 £-£££

Mittelrhein (Germany) Small, northern section of the RHINE. Good RIESLINGS little seen in the UK 83 **85 86 88** 89 90 91 92 ££-£££

Moelleux (France) Sweet 479

Moldova Newly created republic next to Rumania, with exciting vinous potential

Monbazillac (SW France) BERGERAC AOC, using the grapes of sweet BORDEAUX to make improving inexpensive alternatives to SAUTERNES 76 83 85 86 88 89 90 ££-£££ 464 470

Monica (di Cagliari/Sardegna) (Italy) Red grape and wine of SARDINIA producing dry and fortified spicy wine £-££ Tesco Monica di Sardegna, Dolianova (TO)

Monopole (France) Literally, exclusive – in BURGUNDY denotes single ownership of an entire vineyard

Montagne St Emilion (BORDEAUX) A 'satellite' of ST EMILION. Often good-value reds 82 83 85 **86 88** 89 90 92 ££-£££ 283

Montagny (BURGUNDY) Tiny Côte CHALONNAISE commune producing good, lean CHARDONNAY, a match for many POUILLY FUISSÉS **83 85** 87 88 89 90 92 £££ Montagny 1er Cru 91, Domaine Bernard (CT)

Montalcino (TUSCANY) Village near Sienna known for BRUNELLO DI MONTALCINO

Montepulciano (Italy) Red grape making red wines in central Italy; also see VINO NOBILE DI MONTEPULCIANO and ABRUZZI

Monterey (California) Underrated region south of San Francisco, producing slightly tangier, 'grassier' wines. Monterey Vineyard Chardonnay 90 (OD)

Monthélie (Burgundy) Often overlooked COTE DE BEAUNE village producing potentially stylish reds and whites **83 85 87** 88 89 90 ££-££££ 398

Montilla (-Moriles) (Spain) DO region producing SHERRY-type wines in SOLERA systems, often so high in alcohol that fortification is unnecessary £-££ Tesco Montilla, Vinicola del Sud (TO)

Montlouis (LOIRE) Neighbour of VOUVRAY making similar, lighter-bodied, wines 85 88 89 90 ££-££££ Domaine des Liards Demi-Sec Vieilles Vignes, Berger Frères 89 (ADN)

Montravel (Cotes de) (SW France) Dry and sweet whites from, and comparable to, BERGERAC ££-£££ Lou Cache 90 (BD)

Mor (HUNGARY) Hungarian town making clean, aromatic white wine – Mori Ejerzo 193

Morey St Denis (BURGUNDY) COTES DE NUIT village which produces deeply fruity, richly smooth reds, especially the GRAND CRU Clos de la Roche 78 **82 83 85 86** 88 89 90 92 £££-£££££ Rue de Vergy 89, Rossignol-Trapet (ABY)

Morgon (BURGUNDY) One of the ten BEAUJOLAIS CRUS, worth maturing, when it can take on a delightful chocolate/cherry character **88 89 90 91** ££-£££ Marcel Jonchet 91 (WMK)

Morio Muskat White grape grown in Germany making full, fragrant wine £-££ 187

Mornington Peninsula (VICTORIA) Some of Australia's newest and most southerly vineyards which are producing minty CABERNET, tasty PINOT and fruity CHARDONNAY **84 85 86** 87 **88** 89 90 91 £££ 286 395

Moscatel de Valencia (Spain) Delicious, honeyed, fortified dessert wine. Spanish examples are deliciously grapey, Portuguese ones are richer and age indefinitely ££-£££££ 457

Moscato The MUSCAT grape in Italy, at its best in fruity, low-strength Spumante wines (eg Moscato d'Asti) or in sumptuous dessert wines ££-££££ 2

Moselblumchen MOSEL-SAAR-RUWER, equivalent to the Rhine's LIEBFRAUMILCH

Mosel/Moselle River and loose term for MOSEL-SAAR-RUWER wines, equivalent to the 'HOCK' of the Rhine 85 **86 87** 88 89 90 91 92 £-£££££ 204-205 208

Mosel-Saar-Ruwer (MSR) (Germany) Major ANBAUGEBIET capable of superb RIESLINGS, differing noticeably in each of the three regions **76 78** 82 83 85 88 89 90 91 92

Moulin-à-Vent (BURGUNDY) One of the 10 BEAUJOLAIS CRUS, big and rich at its best and, like MORGON, benefits from ageing a few years 88 89 90 ££-£££ E Loron 91 (U)

Moulis (BORDEAUX) Red wine village of the HAUT-MEDOC; like LISTRAC, some good-value lesser growths 81 82 83 85 86 88 89 90 ££-££££ 290

Mount Barker (W Australia) Cooler climate, great Riesling and Verdelho

Mourvèdre RHONE grape usually found in blends. Increasingly popular in France and California 326

Mousseux (France) Sparkling. *Vin mousseux* tends to be cheap and unremarkable

Mousse The bubbles in CHAMPAGNE and sparkling wines

Mudgee (Australia) High-altitude, isolated region undergoing a revival; previously known for robust, often clumsy wines. (Botobolar and Montrose are probably the best known producers) 82 84 88 89 90 91 92 ££-£££

Müller-Thurgau Workhorse white grape, a RIESLING-SYLVANER cross, making much unremarkable wine in Germany. Very successful in England

Murfatlar (ROMANIA) Major vineyard and research area having increasing success with the CHARDONNAY

Murray River Valley (Australia) Vineyard area between VICTORIA and NEW SOUTH WALES producing much of the Antipodes' cheapest wine.

Murrumbidgee (Australia) Area formerly known for bulk dessert wines, now improving irrigation and vinification techniques to make good table wines and some stunning BOTRYTIS-affected sweet wines (look out for de Bortoli)

Muscadet (LOIRE) Area at the mouth of the Loire making dry, appley white from the Melon de Bourgogne. Clean and refreshing when good; sadly this is rare. SUR LIE is best. May be barrel-fermented 92 £-££££ 139 151 156 158

Muscat à Petits Grains Aka FRONTIGNAN, the grape responsible for MUSCAT DE BEAUMES DE VENISE, ASTI SPUMANTE, Muscat of Samos, Rutherglen Muscats and Alsace Muscats 2. Also see *THE WINES*

Muscat of Alexandria Grape responsible for MOSCATEL DE SETUBAL, Moscatel de Valencia and some sweet South Australian offerings. Also known as Lexia and not of as high quality as MUSCAT À PETITS GRAINS 457

Muscat Ottonel Muscat variety grown in Middle and Eastern Europe

Must Unfermented grape juice

MW See MASTER OF WINE

Nackenheim (RHEINHESSEN) Village in the NIERSTEIN BEREICH, producing good wines but better known for its debased GROSSLAGE, Gutes Domtal

Nahe (Germany) ANBAUGEBIET producing increasingly popular wines which combine a delicacy of flavour with full body 87 88 89 90 91 92 £-£££ 207 209

Naoussa (Greece) Dry red wines from the Xynomavro grape ££-£££ Boutari Xinomavro Naoussis 91 (SAF)

Napa Valley (California) Established, top-quality vineyard area. 'Napa' is the American-Indian word for 'plenty' (Red) 85 86 87 88 90 91 92 (White) 85 86 87 88 90 91 92 ££-££££. See *THE WINES* for plenty of examples

Navarra (Spain) Northern DO, traditionally for rosés and heavy reds but now producing some good-value, exciting wines, easily rivalling those from neighbouring RIOJA 85 86 87 88 89 90 91 £-£££ 454

Nebbiolo Great red grape of Italy, producing wines which are slow to mature, then richly complex and fruity, epitomised by BAROLO 429

Négociant (-Eléveur) A BURGUNDY merchant who buys, matures and bottles wine

Négociant-manipulant (NM) Buyer and blender of wines for CHAMPAGNE, identifiable by NM number mandatory on label

Neusiedlersee (AUSTRIA) Burgenland region on the Hungarian border, best known for its fine, sweet, BOTRYTISED wines 173

New South Wales (Australia) Major wine-producing state including the HUNTER VALLEY, MUDGEE and MURRUMBIDGEE regions

New Zealand New, superstar nation, increasingly successful with Sauvignon Blanc and Chardonnay

Nierstein (RHEINHESSEN) Village and, with PIESPORT, BEREICH best known in the UK. Some very fine wines, obscured by the notoriety of Gütes Domtal 83 85 88 89 90 91 92 £-£££ Niersteiner Rehbach Riesling Kabinett 88, Balbach (VW)

Noble rot Popular term for BOTRYTIS CINEREA

Nose Smell

Nouveau New wine, most popularly used of BEAUJOLAIS

Nuits St Georges (BURGUNDY) COMMUNE producing the most claret-like of red Burgundies, properly tough and lean when young but glorious in age **82 83 85 88 89 90** £££-£££££ 124 403 406 408

NV Non-vintage, meaning a blend of wines from different years

Oaky Flavour imparted by oak casks. 'Woody' is usually less complimentary

Ockfen (MOSEL-SAAR-RUWER) Village producing the best wines of the Saar-Ruwer BEREICH, especially from the Bockstein vineyard ££-£££££ Ockfener Scharzberg Riesling 90, Rheinart Erben (RTW)

Oechsle (Germany) Sweetness scale used to indicate the sugar levels in grapes or wine

Oenology The study of the science of wine

Oidium Insidious fungal infection of grapes, causing them to turn grey and shrivel

Olasz Rizling (HUNGARY) Term for the inferior WELSCHRIESLING

Oloroso (JEREZ) Style of full-bodied SHERRY, dry or semi-sweet ££-£££ 483

Oltrepó Pavese (Italy) Red and white LOMBARDY DOC for a range of wines from varying grape varieties ££

Opol (YUGOSLAVIA) Source of dry, light, slightly spicy rosé

Oppenheim (RHEINHESSEN) Village in NIERSTEIN BEREICH best known, though often unfairly, for Krottenbrunnen vineyard. Elsewhere produces soft wines with concentrated flavour **76 83 85 86** 88 **89 90 91 92** ££-£££££ Oppenheimer Sacktraegar 90, Kuehling-Gillot (WSC)

Orange Muscat Yet another member of the MUSCAT family, best known for dessert wines in California and VICTORIA Brown Brothers Late Harvest Orange Flora Muscat 92 (TH)

Oregon (US) Fashionable wine-producing state best known in the UK for its skill with the PINOT NOIR **83 85 86 87 88** 90 91 92 ££-£££££ 387

Oriahovitza (BULGARIA) Major source of reliable CABERNET SAUVIGNON and MERLOT **87 88 89 90** 91 £-££

Orvieto (Italy) White Umbrian DOC responsible for a quantity of dull wine. Orvieto CLASSICO is better **89 90 91 92** ££-£££££ Vigneto Torricella 91, Bigi (F&M)

Oxidation The effect (usually detrimental) of oxygen on wine

Pacherenc-du-Vic-Bilh (SW France) Dry or fairly sweet white wine, a speciality of MADIRAN growers. Very rarely seen, worth trying ££-£££ St Albert 88 Plaimont (WR)

Padthaway See KEPPOCH/PADTHAWAY

Pais CHILEAN red grape and its wine

Palate The taste of a wine

Palatinate (Germany) Region (ANBAUGEBIET) now known as the RHEINPFALZ

Pale Cream (Spain) A heavily sweetened FINO sherry ££ Sainsbury's Pale Cream, Duff Gordon (JS)

Palette (PROVENCE) AC rosé, a cut above the average. Also some fresh white 86 88 89 90 91 ££-£££££ Ch Simone 88 (YAP)

Palo Cortado (SHERRY) A rare SHERRY-style wine pitched between an AMONTILLADO and an OLOROSO ££-£££ Osborne y Cia Palo Cortado (BAR)

Palomino White grape responsible for virtually all fine SHERRIES

Pasado/Pasada (Spain) Term applied to old or fine FINO and AMONTILLADO sherries £££-£££££

Passe-Tout-Grains (BURGUNDY) Wine made of two-thirds GAMAY, one-third PINOT NOIR **86 87 88 90** 92 ££-£££££ D Lafouge 91 (ABY)

Passito (Italy) Sweet raisiny wine, usually made from sun-dried grapes ££££-£££££ Bukkuram Moscato Passito di Pantelleria (V&C)

Pauillac (BORDEAUX) The home of Châteaux Lafite, Latour and Mouton – the epitome of full-flavoured, blackcurranty Bordeaux, very classy (and expensive) wine **78 79 81 82 83 85 86** 88 **89 90** £££-£££££ 312 317 320 322

Pécharmant (SW France) In the BERGERAC area, producing light, Bordeaux-like reds. Worth trying **85 86 88 89 90** 91 Ch Tiregand 90 (JS)

Pedro Ximenez (PX) White grape dried in the sun for sweet, curranty wine, added to produce the mellower SHERRY styles. Also produces one very unusual wine at de Bortoli's in Australia £££-£££££ 485

Pelure d'Oignon 'Onion skin'; distinctive orangey tint of some rosé

Peñafiel (Portugal) District producing some good VINHO VERDE **90 91 92**

Penedés Largest DOC of Catalonia, with improving table wines following the example of the Torres BODEGA. More importantly, the centre of the CAVA industry **86 87 88 89 90 91** ££-£££££ 3 123

Perlé/Perlant (France) Lightly sparkling

Perlwein (Germany) Sparkling wine

Pernand-Vergelesses (BURGUNDY) COMMUNE producing rather clumsy, jammy reds but fine whites, some of the best buys on the COTE D'OR **82 83 85** 88 89 90 92 £££-££££ Olivier Leflaive 90 (ADN)

Pessac-Léognan (BORDEAUX) GRAVES COMMUNE recently given its own APPELLATION and containing all the better Graves CHATEAUX **85 86 88** 89 90 £££-£££££ 300

Pétillant (FRANCE) Lightly sparkling

Petit Chablis (BURGUNDY) Less fine than plain CHABLIS **85 86 87 88 89 90** 91 ££-£££ 59

Petit château (BORDEAUX) Minor property, beneath CRU BOURGEOIS

Petit Verdot (France) Spicy, tannic, hard-to-ripen variety used in tiny proportions in red Bordeaux and (rarely) California

Petite Sirah Red grape, aka Durif in the MIDI and grown in California. Has nothing to do with the SYRAH but can produce very good, spicy red. L A Cetto 88 (BTH)

Petrolly A not unpleasant overtone often found in mature RIESLING

Pfalz (Germany) See RHEINPFALZ

Phylloxera Dastardly louse that wiped out Europe's vines in the 19th century. Foiled by the practice of grafting VINIFERA vines on to resistant American rootstock. Isolated pockets of pre-PHYLLOXERA vines still exist in Australia, Chile and Portugal, but a new breed of the louse is so devastating areas of California that Napa Valley growers who (mostly) planted on insufficiently resistent rootstock may have to replant 90% of their vines.

Piave (VENETO) Area covering a number of DOCs, including reds made from a Bordeaux-like mix of grapes **86 87 88 89 90** 91 92

Piedmont/Piemonte (Italy) Increasingly ancient-and-modern north-western region producing old-fashioned, tough, tannic BAROLO and BARBARESCO and increasing amounts of brilliant new-style, fruit-packed wines. Also the source of OLTREPO PAVESE, ASTI SPUMANTE and DOLCETTO D'ALBA 1-2, 41, 46, 414, 424, 426, 428-429

Piesport (MOSEL-SAAR-RUWER) With its GROSSLAGE Michelsberg, infamous for dull wine. Try one of its single vineyards – Guntersley or Goldtroppchen – for something more drinkable **85 86** 87 88 89 90 91 92 £-£££ Piesporter Goldtroppchen 90, von Kesselstaat (MWW)

Pineau d'Aunis Red grape grown in the LOIRE valley for red and rosé

Pineau de la Loire The CHENIN BLANC grape

Pineau des Charentes (SW France) White grape juice fortified with cognac – best chilled as an aperitif or with cheese ££-£££ J Brard (ORG)

Pinot Blanc Not as classy or complex as its PINOT NOIR or CHARDONNAY relations, but fresh and adaptable. Widely grown, at its best in ALSACE (Pinot d'Alsace) and the ALTO ADIGE in Italy (as Pinot Bianco). In California, a synonym for MELON DE BOURGOGNE 65 173 181

Pinot Chardonnay Misleading name for the PINOT BLANC

Pinot Gris White grape of uncertain origins, making full, rather heady, spicy wine. Best in ALSACE (also known as TOKAY D'ALSACE) and Italy (as Pinot Grigio).

Pinot Meunier Dark pink-skinned grape that plays an unsung but major role in CHAMPAGNE, where it is the most widely planted variety. In England, it is grown as the Wrotham Pinot or Dusty Miller; Bests in VICTORIA produce a VARIETAL wine from it

Pinot Noir Noble red grape with the unique distinction of being responsible for some of the world's greatest red (BURGUNDY) and sparkling white (CHAMPAGNE) wine. Also grown, with varying degrees of success, in the New World 384-409

Pinotage Red grape, a PINOT NOIR-CINSAULT cross used in South Africa and (decreasingly in) New Zealand. Kanonkop 90 (SAF)

Pomerol (BORDEAUX) With ST EMILION, the Bordeaux for lovers of the MERLOT grape, which predominates in its rich, soft, plummy wines. Château Pétrus is the big name **78 81 82 83 85** 86 88 89 90 £££-£££££ 313-314

Pommard (BURGUNDY) Variable quality commune, theoretically blessed with a higher proportion of old vines, making slow-to-mature, then solid and complex reds **83 85** 88 89 90 92 £££-£££££ Pommard Les Epenots 86, Parent (CAC)

Port (Portugal) Fortified, usually red wine made in the upper Douro valley. Comes in several styles; see TAWNY, RUBY, LBV, VINTAGE, CRUSTED and WHITE 489 491-492 494 496-498

Pouilly Fuissé (BURGUNDY) White beloved by the Americans, and consequently sold at vastly inflated prices. Other Mâconnais wines are affordable and often its equal, unless your purse can stretch to the very finest examples **85 86 87 88 89** 90 92 ££-£££££ Clos Reissier 91, Georges Duboeuf (BWC)

Pouilly Fumé (LOIRE) Distinguished, elegant SAUVIGNON BLANC with classic gooseberry fruit and 'flinty' overtones 86 87 88 89 90 92 ££-£££££ 167 174

Pourriture noble (France) BOTRYTIS CINEREA or NOBLE ROT

Prädikat (Germany) Short for QUALITÄTSWEIN MIT PRADIKAT (QMP), the higher quality level for German wines

Precipitation The creation of a harmless deposit, usually of tartrate crystals, in white wine

Premier Cru Principally a BURGUNDY ranking, indicates wines second only to a GRAND CRU

Primeur (France) New wine, eg BEAUJOLAIS Primeur

Propriétaire (-Récoltant) (France) Vineyard owner-manager

Prosecco (VENETO) Dry and sweet sparkling wines, less boisterous than ASTI SPUMANTE and often less fizzy £-£££ 1

Provence (France) Southern region producing a quantity of honest, country wine with a number of minor ACs. Rosé de Provence should be dry and fruity with a hint of peppery spice 166 221 289

Puisseguin St Emilion (BORDEAUX) Satellite of ST EMILION 82 83 85 86 88 89 90 ££-££££ Ch Durand Laplagne 88 (ADN)

Puligny-Montrachet Aristocratic white COTE D'OR COMMUNE that shares the Montrachet vineyard with CHASSAGNE 78 79 81 83 85 86 88 89 90 92 ££££-£££££ 113 122

Putto (Italy) As in CHIANTI PUTTO, wine from a consortium of growers who use the cherub (*putto*) as their symbol

Puttonyos (HUNGARY) The measure of sweetness (from 1 to 6) of TOKAY 487

PX See PEDRO XIMENEZ

QbA (Germany) *Qualitätswein bestimmter Anbaugebiet*: basic quality German wine meeting certain standards from one of the 11 ANBAUGEBIET, eg RHEINHESSEN

QmP (Germany) *Qualitätswein mit Prädikat*: QBA wine with 'special qualities' subject to rigorous testing. The QMP blanket designation is broken into five sweetness rungs, from KABINETT to TROCKENBEERENAUSLESEN plus EISWEIN

Qualitätswein (Germany) Loose 'quality' definition to cover QBA and QMP wines, whose labels will carry more informative identification of their exact status

Quarts de Chaume (LOIRE) Luscious but light sweet wines, uncloying, ageing beautifully, from the COTEAUX DU LAYON 76 83 85 88 89 90 92 £££-£££££ Domaine des Beaumard 90 (SAC)

Quincy (LOIRE) Dry SAUVIGNON, lesser-known and often good value alternative to SANCERRE or POUILLY FUME 89 90 92 ££-£££ Denis Jaumier 92 (YAP)

Quinta (Portugal) Vineyard or estate, particularly in port where 'single quinta' wines are much prized 498

Racking The drawing off of wine from its LEES into a clean cask or vat

Rainwater (MADEIRA) Light, dry style of Madeira popular in the US

Rancio Term for the peculiar yet prized oxidised flavour of certain fortified wines, particularly in France and Spain

Rasteau (RHONE) Southern village producing sound, spicy reds with rich berry fruit, and some dessert wine 86 88 89 90 91 ££-£££ 335

RD (CHAMPAGNE) Récemment DEGORGEE — a term invented by Bollinger to describe their delicious vintage Champagne, which has been allowed a longer than usual period on its LEES. Other producers make their own versions but may not call them 'RD' ££££ Bollinger 82 (WR)

Recioto (Italy) Sweet or dry alcoholic wine made from semi-dried, ripe grapes 432

Récoltant-manipulant (RM) (CHAMPAGNE) Individual winegrower and blender, identified by mandatory RM number on label

Récolte (France) Vintage, literally 'harvest'

Refosco (FRIULI-VENEZIA GIULIA) Red grape and its DOC wine, dry and full-bodied, benefits from ageing Refosco Giovanni 91 Collavini (LAV)

Régisseur In BORDEAUX, the manager of a CHATEAU and its wine production

Régnié (BURGUNDY) Recently created the tenth BEAUJOLAIS CRU 88 89 91 ££-£££ Regnie Domaine des Buyats, Marc Dudet (C&B)

Reichensteiner Hybrid white grape popular in England (and Wales) 82

Reims (CHAMPAGNE) Capital town of the area, base of many GRANDES MARQUES, eg Krug, Roederer

Remuage (CHAMPAGNE) Part of the METHODE CHAMPENOISE, the gradual turning and tilting of bottles so that the yeast deposit collects in the neck ready for DEGORGEMENT

Reserva (Spain) Indicates the wine has been aged for a number of years specific to the DO

Réserve (France) Legally meaningless, as in 'Réserve Personelle', but implying a wine selected and given more age

Residual sugar Tasting term for wines which have retained sugar not converted to alcohol by yeasts during fermentation

Retsina (Greece) Distinctive dry white wine with a piney, resinated flavour

Reuilly (LOIRE) White AC for dry SAUVIGNONS, good value alternatives to Sancerre. Some spicy PINOT rosé **89 90 91** 92 ££-£££ Reuilly 91, G Cordier (YAP)

Rheingau (Germany) Produces the finest German RIESLINGS of the eleven ANBAUGEBIETE, some extremely expensive **83 85 88** 89 90 91 92 £-£££££ 206 210

Rheinhessen (Germany) Largest of the eleven ANBAUGEBIET, producing fine wines but better known for LIEBFRAUMILCH and NIERSTEINER **83 85 88** 89 90 91 92 £-£££££ 195 200 475

Rheinpfalz (Gemany) Formerly known as the Palatinate, southerly ANBAUGEBIET noted for riper, spicier RIESLING **83 85 88** 89 90 91 92 £-£££££ 203

Rhine Riesling/Rheinriesling Widely used name for the noble RIESLING grape

Rhône (France) Rich, round, warm, spicy reds from the GRENACHE and SYRAH; increasingly fashionable, and thus pricey. Some highly prized (and rightly so) rich, peachy, nutty wines **83 85 86 88** 89 90 91 £-£££££ see *THE WINES* for numerous examples

Ribatejo (Portugal) DO area north of Lisbon making much white wine and good, full-bodied reds, especially GARRAFEIRAS **85 86 87 88** 89 90 £-£££ Safeway Ribatejo 88, Borbosa (SAF)

Ribera del Duero (Spain) Northern DO region bordering Portugal, source of VINHO VERDE-type whites and newer stylish reds **82 83 85 86** 89 90 ££-£££££ 450

Riesling The noble grape producing Germany's finest offerings, ranging from light, floral everyday wines to the delights of the BOTRYTIS-affected sweet wines, which still retain their freshness after several years. Also performs well in ALSACE, California and the BAROSSA/EDEN VALLEY (Australia) See *THE WINES* section for numerous examples

Riesling Italico See ITALIAN RIESLING

Rioja Alavesa (Spain) Minor subregion of the RIOJA area, with some fine reds **81 82 85 86 87 88** 89 ££-£££££

Rioja Alta (Spain) The best subregion of the RIOJA area **81 82 84 85 86** 87 88 89 ££-£££££

Rioja Baja (Spain) Largest subregion of the RIOJA area, producing less fine wines, most of which are blended with wine from the Alta and Alavesa regions **81 82 85 86 87** 89

Ripasso (Italy) VALPOLICELLA which, having finished its fermentation, is pumped into fermenting vessels recently vacated by RECIOTO and AMARONE, causing a slight fermentation. This increases the alcohol and body of the wine

Riquewihr (ALSACE) Town and COMMUNE noted for RIESLING. Riesling d'Alsace, Marcel Deiss (WC BD L&S)

Riserva (Italy) DOC wines aged for a specified number of years

Rivaner The MULLER-THURGAU grape with reference to its RIESLING/SYLVANER parents

Rivesaltes (MIDI) Fortified dessert wine of both colours, the white made from Muscat is lighter and more lemony than that of BEAUMES DE VENISE, the red made from GRENACHE is almost like liquid Christmas pudding ££-£££ 486

Rolle (MIDI) Variety used to make BELLET

Romania Traditionally making sweet reds and whites, but trying to develop drier styles from classic European varieties £-£££ 36

Rosato (Italy) Rosé

Rosé d'Anjou (LOIRE) Widely exported, usually dull pink from the CABERNET FRANC. Semi-sweet but getting drier

Rosé des Riceys (CHAMPAGNE) Rare and delicious AC still rosé from the PINOT NOIR

Rosso Conero (Italy) Big DOC red from the MARCHES, from the MONTEPULCIANO and SANGIOVESE grapes with a hint of bitter, herby flavour. Needs five years 427

Roussillon (Côtes du) (MIDI) Up and coming for red, white and rosé, though not always worthy of its AC. Côtes du Roussillon Villages is better **85 86 88** 89 90 91 £££ Côtes du Roussillon Villages 91, Caves Co-op (D, MC)

Rubesco di Torgiano (UMBRIA) Popular red DOC **82 83 85 86 87 88** 89 90 **91** ££-£££££ Torgiano Riserva Monticchio 80 Lungarotti (ADN, WSO)

Ruby Cabernet (California) A cross between CABERNET SAUVIGNON and CARIGNAN producing big, fruity wines which tend to lack subtlety

Ruby (port) Cheapest, basic port; young, blended, sweetly fruity wine

Rudesheim (RHEINGAU) Tourist town producing, at their best, rich and powerful RIESLINGS

Rueda (Spain) DO for clean dry whites and a traditional, FLOR growing sherry-type wine **82 84 85 86** £-£££ Hermanos Lurton Bianco (TH, WR)

Rufina (TUSCANY) Subregion of the CHIANTI DOC **81 83 85** 86 88 ££-£££££ 431

Ruländer German name for the PINOT GRIS grape

Rully (BURGUNDY) COTE CHALONNAISE COMMUNE, the 'poor man's Volnay'. Much white is destined for Crémant de Bourgogne £££-£££££ 103

Ruppertsberg (RHEINPFALZ) Top-ranking village with a number of excellent vineyards making vigorous, fruity RIESLING 83 85 88 89 **90 91 92**

Russian River Valley (California) Cool vineyard area north of SONOMA and west of NAPA. Ideal for good fizz, as is proven by Iron Horse.

Rust (AUSTRIA) Wine centre of BURGENLAND, famous for Ruster AUSBRUCH, sweet white wine. Ruster Beerenauslese 81, Weinkellerei Burgenland (U)

Rutherglen (Australia) VICTORIA wine area on the MURRAY RIVER noted for rich, MUSCATTY dessert and port-style wines, and incredibly tough reds £££-£££££ 461-462

Saar (Germany) Tributary of the MOSEL river **83 85 88 89** 90 91 92 ££-££££

Sablet (RHONE) A named COTES DU RHONE village

Sacramento Valley (California) Another name for the CARNEROS region

St Amour (BURGUNDY) One of the ten BEAUJOLAIS CRUS, tends to be light and delicately fruity **83 85 86 87 88 89** 90 91 ££-£££ St Amour Loron 89 (AV)

St Aubin (BURGUNDY) Underrated COTE D'OR VILLAGE for reds and rich, flinty, nutty white affordable alternatives to MEURSAULT **85 86 88 89** 90 92 £££ Jean Germain 91 (D, MC)

St Bris (Sauvignon de) (BURGUNDY) Burgundy's only VDQS, an affordable alternative to SANCERRE from the CHABLIS region **89 90 91 92** ££ Sauvignon De St Bris 90, Bersan (OD)

St Chinian (SW France) AC in the COTEAUX DU LANGUEDOC producing mid-weight, good-value wines **88 89 90 91** ££ Château de Salvanhiac 92 (JS)

St Emilion (BORDEAUX) COMMUNE for soft, MERLOT-dominated claret. Its lesser satellite neighbours — LUSSAC, PUISSEGUIN, etc — often prefix the name with theirs **81 82 83 85 86** 88 89 90 ££-£££££ 310

St Estèphe (BORDEAUX) Northern MEDOC COMMUNE, often a shade more rustic than its neighbours, tough when young but very long-lived **81 82 83 85** 86 88 89 90 ££-£££££ 301 323

St Georges St Emilion (BORDEAUX) Satellite of ST EMILION **82 83 85 86 88** 89 90 ££-£££ Ch Macquin-St-George (ADN)

St Joseph (RHONE) Vigorous, fruity reds from the northern Rhône, with the spice of the SYRAH. Good value **85 86 88 89 90** 91 £££-£££££ 345 347 355 360

St Julien (BORDEAUX) Aristocratic MEDOC COMMUNE producing classic rich wines, full of cedar and deep, ripe fruit **82 83 85 86** 88 89 90 £££-£££££ 304

St Nicolas de Bourgueil (LOIRE) Lightly fruity CABERNET FRANC, needs a warm year to ripen its raspberry fruit **85 86 87 88 89** 90 92 (CT)

St Péray (RHONE) AC for full-bodied, still white and METHODE CHAMPENOISE sparkling wine **88 89** 90 91 £££ St Péray Nature (YAP)

St Pourçain (Central France) The local wine of Vichy, AC for red, white and rose. Saint Pourcain sur Sioule 89 (YAP)

St Romain (BURGUNDY) High in the hills of the HAUTES COTES DE BEAUNE, a village producing undervalued fine whites and rustic reds **83 85 87** 88 89 90 92 £££ St Romain Blanc 91, Barolet (TO)

St-Véran (BURGUNDY) Affordable alternative to POUILLY FUISSE, delicious young. Head and shoulders above its MACONNAIS neighbours **88 89 90 91** £££-££££ St Véran Les Pierres 90, Cave de Prissé (CT)

Sainte Croix-du-Mont (BORDEAUX) Neighbour of SAUTERNES, with comparable though less fine wines **83 85 86 87 88** 89 90 ££-£££ 465

Sakar (Mountain) (BULGARIA) Source of much of the best CABERNET SAUVIGNON **86 88 89** 90 ££ Sakar Mountain Cabernet 86 (TO)

Samos (Greece) Aegean island producing sweet, fragrant, golden MUSCAT once called 'the wine of the Gods' ££-£££ 459

San Luis Obispo Californian region gaining a reputation for Chardonnay and Pinot Noir. Wild Horse (OD)

Sancerre (LOIRE) Much exploited AC, but at its best the epitome of elegant, steely dry SAUVIGNON. Quaffable pale reds and rosés from the PINOT NOIR **89 90 91 92** ££-£££££ 168 172 393

Sangiovese The red grape of CHIANTI, used elsewhere but not to such great effect

Sanlúcar de Barrameda (Spain) Town neighbouring JEREZ, centre of production for MANZANILLA sherry

Santa Barbara Increasingly succesful southern-Californian cool-climate region for Pinot Noir and Chardonnay

Santenay (BURGUNDY) Pretty white CHARDONNAYS and good, though occasionally rather clumsy, reds from the southern tip of the CÔTE D'OR **83 85 87 88 89 90 92** £££-£££££ Santenay Foulot 89, Château Perruchot (A)

Sardinia (Italy) Good, hearty, powerful reds, robust whites and a number of interesting DOC fortified wines 129, 412

Saumur (LOIRE) White and rosé MÉTHODE CHAMPENOISE sparklers which are reliably clean and appley, fresh fruity whites plus reds and pinks made from CABERNET FRANC ££-£££££ 17 277

Saumur Champigny (LOIRE) Crisp, refreshing CABERNET FRANC red; like BEAUJOLAIS, serve slightly chilled **85 86 88 89 90 92** ££-£££ La Grande Vignolle 90, Filliatreau (YAP)

Sauternes (BORDEAUX) Nobly rich, honeyed dessert wines, SAUVIGNON and SEMILLON blends, properly BOTRYTIS-affected. Worth splashing out on **80 83 85 86 88 89 90** £££-£££££

Sauvignon (Sauvignon Blanc) White grape making gooseberry-fruity wine with a steely backbone, classically elegant in fine LOIRE but equally successful in the New World, particularly New Zealand ££-£££££. See *THE WINES* section for numerous examples

Savagnin Jura variety used for VIN JAUNE and blended with CHARDONNAY for ARBOIS. Also, confusingly, the Swiss name for the GEWURZTRAMINER

Savennières (LOIRE) Fine, rarely seen, vigorous and characterful whites, very long-lived. Coulée de Serrant and La Roche aux Moines are the top names **82 83 84 85 86 88 89 90 92** £££-££££ 177

Savigny-lès-Beaune (BURGUNDY) Rarely seen whites and delicious plummy/raspberry reds, at their best can compare with neighbouring BEAUNE **83 85 87 88 89 90 92** £££-£££££ 399

Savoie (E France) Mountainous region best known for crisp, floral whites such as APREMONT, Seyssel and Crépy

Scharzhofberg (MOSEL-SAAR-RUWER) Top-class Saar vineyard, producing quintessential RIESLING £££-£££££ Scharzhofberger Riesling 89, von Hovel (TH, WR)

Schaumwein (Germany) Low-priced sparkling wine

Scheurebe White grape, RIESLING/SYLVANER cross, grown in Germany and in England, where it imparts a grapefruity tang

Schilfwein (Austria) Luscious 'reed wine' - Austrian VIN DE PAILLE pioneered by Willi Opitz (T&W)

Schloss (Germany) Literally 'castle', often (as in CHATEAU) designating a vineyard or estate

Schlossbockelheim (NAHE) Village giving its name to a large Nahe BEREICH, producing elegant, balanced Riesling. Best vineyard: Kupfergrube ££-£££ Schlossbockelheimer Konigfels Riesling Spätlese 71 (LV)

Schluck (AUSTRIA) Generic term for a light, blended white wine from the WACHAU

Sciacarella (CORSICA) Corsican red grape variety, making smooth, aromatic, RHONE-style wine **88 89 90 91**

Second label (BORDEAUX) Wines produced principally by Bordeaux CHATEAUX which, because of the youth of the vines or a lessening of quality in a particular year, are sold under a 'second' name 297, 304, 310, 312

Sec/secco/seco (France/Italy/Spain) Dry

Sekt (Germany) Not dry, but sparkling wine. Only the prefix 'DEUTSCHER' guarantees German origin 15

Sélection de Grains Nobles (ALSACE) Equivalent to German BEERENAUSLESEN: rich, sweet BOTRYTISED wine from selected grapes £££££ Tokay Sélection des Grains Nobles 91, Zind Humbrecht (ABY)

Sémillon Grape blended with SAUVIGNON in BORDEAUX to give fullness in both dry and sweet wines, notably SAUTERNES and, vinified separately, in Australia 93, 98, 101, 102, 116, 188

Sercial Grape used for MADEIRA, making the driest and some say the finest wines Henriques & Henriques 10 year old Sercial (JS)

Servir frais (France) Serve chilled

Setúbal ([Portugal) See MOSCATEL DE SETUBAL

Sèvre-et-Maine (Muscadet de) (LOIRE) Demarcated area producing a cut above plain Muscadet. (Actually, it is worth noting that this 'higher quality' region produces the vast majority of each Muscadet harvest) ££ 151

Seyval blanc Hybrid grape, a cross between French and US vines. Unpopular with EC authorities but successful in eastern US and England

Sherry (Spain) The fortified wine made around Jerez. Similar--style wines made elsewhere should not use this name 480-485

Shiraz The SYRAH grape in Australia

Sicily (Italy) Best known for MARSALA, but produces a variety of unusual fortified wines, also much sturdy 'southern' table wine. Terre di Ginestra 92 (TO)

Sin crianza (Spain) Not aged in wood

Skin contact The longer the skins are left in with the juice after the grapes have been crushed, the greater the TANNINS and the deeper the colour

Slovakia Very up-and-coming country, especially for whites made from grapes little seen elsewhere 228, 242

Soave (VENETO) Irredeemably dull white wine; the best one can hope for is that it is fresh and clean. Soave CLASSICO is better, single vineyard versions are best. Sweet RECIOTO di Soave is delicious 86 87 88 89 90 91 £-£££££ Pasqua 92 (VW)

Solera SHERRY-ageing system, a series of butts containing wine of ascending age, the older wine being continually 'refreshed' by the younger

Somlo (HUNGARY) Ancient wine district, now source of top-class whites. See FURMINT

Sonoma Valley (California) Region containing some of the state's top wineries, subdivided into the Sonoma, Alexander and RUSSIAN RIVER Valleys and Dry Creek 29, 111, 316, 349, 369

South Africa Oldest winemaking country in the New World (300 years), and increasingly the focus of interest today. First class Chenins, surprisingly good Pinotages; otherwise very patchy in quality 4, 6, 81, 89, 149, 159, 179, 267, 299, 341, 471-472

Spanna (Italy) In PIEDMONT, the NEBBIOLO grape, main ingredient of BAROLO. Spanna del Piemonte 89, Agostino Brugo (OD)

Spätburgunder The PINOT NOIR in Germany. Spätburgunder Trocken, Lingenfelder (ADN)

Spätlese (Germany) Second step in the QMP scale, late-harvested grapes making wine a notch drier than AUSLESE 201, 203

Spritz Slight sparkle or fizz. Also PETILLANCE

Spritzig (Germany) Lightly sparkling

Spumante (Italy) Sparkling

Stalky or stemmy Flavour of the stem rather than of the juice

Steely Refers to young wine with evident acidity. A compliment when paid to CHABLIS and dry SAUVIGNONS

Steen Grape grown widely in South Africa, thought to be the CHENIN BLANC of the LOIRE. Swartland Steen 92 (SAF)

Structure All the component flavours fit well together. A young wine with structure should age well

Suhindol (BULGARIA) Source of good reds, particularly CABERNET SAUVIGNON 85 87 88 89 90 91 £-££ 242

Sulfites (America) American term now featuring as a labelling requirement alerting those suffering from an (extremely rare) allergy to the presence of sulphur compounds

Supérieur (BORDEAUX) Technically meaningless in terms of discernible quality, but denotes wine with 1-2 per cent more alcohol

Superiore (Italy) As in France, indicates a degree or two more alcohol but not necessarily finer wine

Sur lie 'On its LEES', most commonly seen of MUSCADET, one of the few wines that benefits from ageing with its own dead YEASTS

Süssreserve (Germany) Unfermented grape juice used to bolster sweetness and fruitiness in German and ENGLISH wines, in a process known as back-blending

Swan River (W Australia) Well-established, hot and generally unexciting vineyard area. 85 86 89 90 92 93 Evans & Tate Shiraz 1987 (AF)

Switzerland Produces, in general, enjoyable but expensive light, floral wines for early drinking.

Sylvaner/Silvaner White grape, originally from Austria but adopted by other European areas, particularly ALSACE, as a prolific yielder of young, crisp, quaffable wine 36

Syrah The red RHONE grape, an exotic mix of ripe fruit and spicy, smokey, gamey, leathery flavours. Skilfully adopted by Australia where it is called SHIRAZ or HERMITAGE. See *THE WINES* section for numerous examples

Tafelwein (Germany) Table wine. Only prefix 'DEUTSCHER' guarantees German origin

Tannat Rustic French grape variety used in CAHORS and Uruguay

Tannin Astringent component of red wine which comes from the skins, pips and stalks and helps the wine to age

Tarry Red wines from hot countries often have an aroma and flavour reminiscent of tar. The SYRAH grape in particular exhibits this characteristic

Tartrates Harmless white crystals often deposited by white wines in the bottle

Tasmania (Australia) Up-and-coming area with great potential which is producing more than adequate CHARDONNAY, PINOT NOIR and CABERNET SAUVIGNON. (Look out for Heemskerk, Moorilla, Piper's Brook) 64

Tastevin The silver BURGUNDY tasting cup. Much adopted as an insignia by vinous brotherhoods *(confréries)* and much used as ashtrays by wine buffs. The Chevaliers de Tastevin organise an annual tasting of Burgundies; successful wines may bear an ugly *Tastevinage* label

Taurasi (CAMPANIA) Big red from the AGLIANICO grape, needs years to soften. Develops a characteristic cherryish taste 83 85 88 89 90 91 ££-£££ Antonio Masteroberadino 85 (V&C)

Tavel (RHONE) Spicy, peppery, characterful dry rosé, usually (wrongly) said to age well 88 89 90 91 ££ Château d'Aqueria Rosé 92 (LAV)

Tawny (port) Either ruby port that has been barrel-matured to mellow and fade or a cheap blend of RUBY and WHITE PORT. Examples with an indication of their age (eg 10-year-old) are the real thing 496

Tempranillo (Spain) The red grape of RIOJA, whose sturdy fruit is a match for the vanilla/oak flavours of barrel-ageing

Tenuta (Italy) Estate or vineyard

Terlano/Terlaner (TRENTINO-ALTO-ADIGE) Northern Italian village/its wines, usually fresh, crisp and carrying the name of the grape 87 88 89 90 91 £-££££

Teroldego (TRENTINO-ALTO-ADIGE) Dry reds, quite full-bodied with lean, slightly bitter berry flavours 85 86 87 88 89 90 91 £-££ Teroldego Rotaliano 90, Gaierhof (SAF)

Tête de Cuvée (France) A producer's finest wine, or the one he is proudest of

Thouarsais (Vin de) (LOIRE) VDQS for a soft, light red from the CABERNET FRANC and whites from the CHENIN BLANC ££ Vin de Thouarsais Rouge 1990 M Gigon (YAP)

Tinta Negra Mole Versatile and widely used MADEIRA grape, said to be a distant cousin of the PINOT NOIR

Tocai White grape and its wines of northern Italy, of Venetian origin 89 90 91 £-££££ Tocai Friulano 91, Eno Friulia (WCE)

Tokay (HUNGARY) Legendary dessert wine made only from NOBLE ROT-affected grapes 76 79 81 £££-£££££ 487

Tokay d'Alsace See PINOT GRIS 177

Toro (Spain) Region on the Portuguese border lying on the DOURO producing up-and-coming wines £-££ Tesco Toro 90, Bodegas Farina (TO)

Toscana See TUSCANY

Touraine (LOIRE) Area encompassing the ACs CHINON, VOUVRAY and BOURGUEIL, also an increasing source of quaffable VARIETAL wines — SAUVIGNON, GAMAY DE TOURAINE etc 12

Touriga (Nacional) Red port grape, also seen in the New World

Traminer Alternative name for the GEWURZTRAMINER grape, particularly in Italy and Australia

Trebbiano Much appreciated and widely planted white grape in Italy, though less vaunted in France where it is called the UGNI BLANC. Cortenova Trebbiano del Emilia 91, Pasqua (MWW)

Trentino-Alto Adige (Italy) Northern wine region variously known as the Italian Tyrol or Süd Tirol. Cool, fresh VARIETAL wines, non-Italian in style and often with Germanic labels 88 89 90 91 £-££££

Tricastin (Coteaux du) (RHONE) Southern Rhône APPELLATION, emerging as a source of good value, soft, peppery/blackcurranty reds. Domaine de Montine 91 (TH)

Trittenheim (MOSEL-SAAR-RUWER) Village whose vineyards are said to have been the first in Germany planted with RIESLING, making soft, honeyed wine 76 79 83 85 86 88 89 90 91 92 ££-££££ 208

Trocken (Germany) Dry . Often aggressively so. Avoid Trocken Kabinett from the Mosel, Rheingau and Rheinhessen. QbA and Spatlese Trocken wines are better

Trockenbeerenauslese (Germany) Fifth rung of the QmP ladder, wine from selected dried grapes, with concentrated sugar and usually BOTRYTIS-affected. Only made in the best years, rare and expensive

Trollinger The German name for the Black Hamburg grape, used in Wurttemburg to make light red wines

Tunisia Best known for dessert MUSCAT wines

Turkey Producer of big, red, often oxidised table wine, rarely seen in the UK

Tursan (Vin de) (SW France) MADIRAN VDQS whose big, country reds are most likely to be seen in the UK. Château de Bachen 90 (C&B)

Tuscany (Italy) Major wine region, the famous home of CHIANTI and some of the more intractable reds, BRUNELLO DI MONTALCINO and VINO NOBILE DI MONTEPULCIANO 110, 160, 171, 421-423, 431 .

Ugni Blanc Undistinguished white grape of southern France — comes into its own as the TREBBIANO in Italy, particularly in TUSCANY

Ull de Llebre (Spain) Literally 'hare's eye' – a pink wine from the TEMPRANILLO in Catalonia

Ullage Space between surface of wine and top of cask or, in bottle, cork. The wider the gap, the greater the danger of OXIDATION

Umbria (Italy) Central wine region, best known for white ORVIETO 86 87 88 89 90 91 ££-££££ 418 430

Utiel-Requeña (Spain) DO of VALENCIA, producing heavy reds widely used for blending and some of Spain's best rosé. Viña Carmina 92 (GI)

Vacanzay (LOIRE) Near CHEVERNY, making comparable whites, light, clean and rather sharp

Vacqueyras (RHONE) COTES DU RHONE VILLAGE and COMMUNE producing fine, full-bodied, peppery reds 85 86 87 88 89 90 91 ££-£££ Cuvée les Templiers 90 (ADN)

Valais (SWITZERLAND) Vineyard area on the upper RHONE, making good FENDANT (CHASSELAS) and some reds

Valdepeñas (Spain) LA MANCHA DO striving to refine its rather hefty, alcoholic reds and whites 86 87 88 89 90 91 £-££ Los Llanos Reserva 88 (TO)

Valencia (Spain) Produces quite alcoholic red wines and also deliciously sweet, grapey MOSCATEL DE VALENCIA

Val d'Aosta (Italy) Small winemaking area between PIEDMONT and the French/Swiss border

Valpolicella (VENETO) Light red very similar in composition to BARDOLINO; should be nuttily pleasant but more often, in UK, is rather dull. It really is worth paying more for a bottle of AMARONE or RECIOTO 78 79 81 83 85 86 88 89 90 £-££££ 415 432

Valréas (RHONE) Peppery and inexpensive red AOC 85 86 88 89 90 91 ££

Valtellina (LOMBARDY) Red DOC from the NEBBIOLO grape, of variable quality but improves with age Inferno Valtellina Nino Negro 85 (V&C)

Varietal A wine made from and named after a single grape variety, eg California CHARDONNAY, GAMAY DE TOURAINE

Vaucluse (RHONE) COTES DU RHONE region producing much rosé and good reds from certain villages, eg VACQUEYRAS

VDQS (France) *Vin Délimité de Qualité Supérieur*; official designation for wines better than VIN DE PAYS but not fine enough for an AC. Source of much good value everyday drinking

Vecchio (Italy) Old

Vegetal Often used of SAUVIGNON BLANC and CABERNET FRANC, like 'grassy'. Frequently complimentary - though rarely in California or Australia.

Velho/velhas (Portugal) Old, as of red wine

Veltliner See GRÜNER VELTLINER

Vendange (France) Harvest or vintage

Vendange Tardive (France) Particularly in ALSACE, wine from late harvested grapes, usually lusciously sweet 211

Vendemmia (Italy)/**Vendimia** (Spain) Harvest or vintage

Venegazzú (VENETO) Remarkably good VINO DA TAVOLA from the CABERNET SAUVIGNON, almost claret-like. Needs five years Venegazzú Loredan Gasparini 86 (V&C)

Veneto (Italy) North-eastern wine region, the home of SOAVE, VALPOLICELLA and BARDOLINO 425, 432, 474

Ventoux (Côtes du) (RHONE) Improving source of everyday, country reds 88 89 90 91 £-££ Domaine des Anges Clos de la Tour 90 (BWI)

Verdelho White grape used for MADEIRA and WHITE PORT AND FOR TASTILY LIMEY TABLE WINE IN AUSTRALIA 154, 493

Verdicchio (Italy) White grape seen as a number of DOCs in its own right; in UMBRIA, a major component of ORVIETO 88 89 90 91 £-££ 53 145

Verduzzo (FRIULI-VENEZIA GIULIA) White grape making a dry and a fine AMABILE style wine in the COLLI ORIENTALI

Vermentino (LIGURIA) The dry white wine of the Adriatic. Best drunk *in situ* with seafood

Vernaccia White grape making the Tuscan DOC Vernaccia di San Gimignano and Sardinian Vernaccia di Oristano, at best with a distinctive, characterful flavour 88 89 90 91 ££-££££ 160

Victoria (Australia) Huge variety of wines from the liqueur MUSCATS of RUTHERGLEN to the peppery SHIRAZES of Bendigo and the elegant CHARDONNAYS AND PINOT NOIRS of the YARRA VALLEY. See these, plus MURRAY RIVER, MORNINGTON PENINSULA, GOULBURN VALLEY, GEELONG and PYRENEES

VIDE (Italy) A marketing syndicate supposedly denoting finer estate wines

Vieilles Vignes (France) Wine from a producer's oldest, best vines

Vigneto (Italy) Vineyard

Vignoble (France) Vineyard; vineyard area

Villages (France) The suffix *'villages'* after e.g. Côtes du Rhône or Mâcon generally indicates a slightly superior wine (in the way that Classico does in Italy)

Vin de Corse Corsican wine

Vin de garde (France) Wine to keep

Vin de paille (Jura) Speciality of the region; rich and sweet golden wine from grapes laid out and dried on straw mats

Vin de pays (France) Lowest/broadest geographical designation, simple country wines with certain regional characteristics. Especially successful as whites in Vin de Pays des Côtes de Gascogne and in various styles in Vin de Pays d'Oc

Vin de table (France) Table wine from no particular area

Vin doux naturel (France) Fortified dessert wines, best known as the sweet, liquorous MUSCATS of the south, eg BEAUMES DE VENISE

Vin gris (France) Chiefly from ALSACE and the JURA, pale rosé from red grapes pressed before, not after, fermentation

Vin jaune (JURA) A speciality of ARBOIS, golden yellow, slightly oxidised wine, like a dry SHERRY. Château d'Arlay (LV)

Vin santo (Italy) Powerful Italian white dessert wine made from grapes dried on the vine and after picking, especially in TUSCANY. Traditionally used for dunking nut biscuits 82 84 85 87 88 89 90 91 £££££ 467

Vinho Verde (Portugal) Young, literally 'green' wine, confusingly, red or pale white often tinged with green. At best delicious, refreshing, slightly fizzy 92 £-££ Asda Vinho Verde, Aveleda (A)

Vinifera Properly *Vitis vinifera*, the species name for all European vines

Vino de pasto (Italy) Table wine

Vino da tavola (Italy) Table wine, but the DOC quality designation net is so riddled with holes that producers of many superb - and pricey - wines content themselves with this 'modest' APPELLATION

Vino Nobile di Montepulciano (TUSCANY) CHIANTI in long trousers; truly noble, made from the same grapes, ages superbly to produce a traditional full red 83 85 86 88 89 90 91 £££-££££ Le Casalte 89 (TH, WR)

Vino novello (Italy) New wine from this year's harvest, equivalent to French NOUVEAU

Vintage (port) Only produced in 'declared' years, aged in wood then in bottle for many years. In 'off' years, port houses release wines from their top estates as single QUINTA ports. Must be decanted. 70 75 77 80 83 85 £££££ 498

Vintage Champagne A wine from a single, good 'declared' year 27, 31, 33-34

Vintage character (port) Supposedly inexpensive alternative to vintage, but really an up-market Ruby made by blending various years' wines. £££-££££ 489

Viognier The white grape of the finest RHONE wines (eg Condrieu) making richly nutty, peaches-and-cream wine. Chateau du Trignon Viognier 92 (TP)

Viticulteur (-Propriétaire) (France) Vine grower/vineyard owner

Viura (Spain) White grape of the RIOJA region

Vivarais (Côtes du) (PROVENCE) Light southern Rhône-like reds, a great deal of fruity rosé and occasional fragrant, light whites

Volnay (BURGUNDY) Village producing reds of such delicacy and complexity that tasters wax lyrical 78 79 82 83 85 86 87 88 89 90 ££££-£££££ Robert Ampeau 85 (L&W)

Vosne Romanée (BURGUNDY) The red wine village which numbers Romanée-Conti among its many grand names 78 80 82 83 85 86 87 88 89 90 ££££ Domaine Grivot 88 (D, MC)

Vougeot (BURGUNDY) COTE DE NUITS COMMUNE comprising the famous GRAND CRU Clos de Vougeot and a great number of growers of varying skill 78 80 82 83 85 87 88 89 90 92 ££££-£££££ Clos Vougeot 'Musigni' 86, Gros Frères (J&B)

Vouvray (LOIRE) White wines from the CHENIN BLANC, from clean, dry whites and refreshing sparklers to astonishingly long-lived, sweet wines with massive acidity 69 71 75 76 83 85 88 89 90 92 ££-£££££ 21 479

Wachau (AUSTRIA) Major wine region, producing some superlative RIESLING from steep, terraced vineyards

Wachenheim (RHEINPFALZ) Full, rich, unctuous RIESLING in all but the best years from this superior MITTELHAARDT village 75 76 79 83 85 86 88 89 90 91 92 ££-£££££

Walschriesling/Welschriesling The LASKI, ITALIAN RIESLING or OLASZ RIZLING, unrelated to RHINE RIESLING, but widely cultivated in Central Europe

Washington State US region to watch for its RIESLING and MERLOT 292

Wehlen (MOSEL-SAAR-RUWER) MITTELMOSEL village making fresh, sweet, honeyed wines; look for the Sonnenuhr vineyard 75 76 79 83 85 86 88 89 90 91 92 ££-£££££

Weingut (Germany) Wine estate

Weinkellerei (Germany) Cellar or winery

Weissburgunder The PINOT BLANC in Germany and Austria

White port (Portugal) Made from white grapes, an increasingly popular dry or semi-dry aperitif , though it's hard to say why. Tesco White Port (TO)

Wiltingen (MOSEL-SAAR-RUWER) Distinguished Saar village, making elegant, slaty wines. Well-known for the Scharzhofberg vineyard 76 79 83 85 86 88 89 90 91 92 ££-£££

Winkel (RHEINGAU) Village with an established reputation for complex, delicious wine, housing the famous Schloss Volrads estate 75 76 79 83 85 86 88 89 90 91 92 ££-£££££ 206

Winzerverein/Winzergenossenschaft (Germany) Cooperative

Wurttemburg (Germany) ANBAUGEBIET surrounding the Neckar region, producing more red than any other. Little seen in the UK

Yarra Valley (Australia) Revived historic wine district of VICTORIA, re-populated by small, adventurous, 'boutique' wineries using grapes such as Pinot Noir 82 84 86 88 90 91 92 ££££-£££££ 24 370 394

Yeasts Naturally present in the 'bloom' on grapes, they convert sugar to alcohol, or, in sparkling wines, create carbon dioxide. Some wines, eg CHAMPAGNE and MUSCADET — benefit from ageing in contact with their yeasts — or 'SUR LIE'

Yonne (BURGUNDY) Wine department, home of CHABLIS

Zell (MOSEL-SAAR-RUWER) BEREICH of lower Mosel and village, making pleasant, flowery RIESLING. Famous for the Schwarze Katz (black cat) GROSSLAGE 76 79 83 85 86 88 89 90 91 92 ££-£££

Zentralkellerei (Germany) Massive, central cellars for groups of cooperatives in six of the ANBAUGEBIET – the MOSEL-SAAR-RUWER is Europe's largest

Zinfandel (California) Versatile red grape producing everything from dark, jammy, leathery reds to pale pink, spicy 'blush' wines. Also grown by Cape Mentelle in MARGARET RIVER, Australia ££-£££££ 334 336 349 351 358 363

WINE WITH FOOD

Experimenting with the kaleidoscope of wine and food flavours can be a great adventure – so who needs rules? The fact is, there *are* a few wines and foods which fight the moment they are put together – just as there are some marriages made in heaven. Here are a few tips and suggestions gleaned from the monthly food-and-wine tastings in *WINE Magazine*. The letters which denote each style of food appear alongside the wine descriptions on the following pages. The rest is up to you…

a	Smoked fish

b	Smoked meat

The distinctive tastes and often oily textures of smoked fish and meat cry out for something robust. Avoid light, lemony wines and opt instead for fat oaky Chardonnays or good fino sherries. Smoked meats are also well matched with light fruity reds or warm spicy rosés – and though pairing smoked salmon with Champagne is now something of a cliché, it's with very good reason – it works.

c	Light starters

Salads tossed in vinaigrette, Californian concoctions of citrus fruits and leaves – in fact any palate-cleansing starter – are difficult to pair with wine. Those with good acidity such as the lighter style of Chardonnay or Muscadet are good bets. Delicately flavoured dishes such as vegetable terrines need the gentle touch of a soft white, such as a St Veran, while patés are well suited to fruity reds. You could, of course, play safe and top up those glasses of pre-prandial fizz or sherry.

d	Egg Dishes

Eggs served neat benefit from the clean crispness of a Sauvignon, Muscadet, a good English wine, or even a light north Italian red. However, if the dish contains an assertive ingredient such as strong cheese, try something a little more robust.

e	White meat without sauce

Grilled or roasted chicken, pork or veal will happily partner a range of wines from White Burgundy to Cabernet Sauvignon, but to do justice to the rich flavours of plainly cooked duck or goose, choose the fattest, ripest, fruitiest wine you can find.

f	Fish without sauce

Though there's nothing to stop you serving a light red with fish, delicate flavours are happiest with a light Chardonnay or a Soave with gentle acidity. Oily fish, such as sardines, need the refreshing bite of a good Muscadet or Vinho Verde.

g	White meat or fish in a creamy sauce

Complement the delicate flavours of dishes such as salmon in a cream sauce with a fairly soft wine such as an unoaked Chardonnay. Chicken can take something with firmer acidity, a fresh gooseberryish Sauvignon, perhaps, or a dry Vouvray.

h	Shellfish

In the time-honoured tradition, serve a steely Sancerre or Chablis with oysters. Richer shellfish can take something a little fruitier. Garlic butter or aioli will clash violently with most wines, but a fino sherry or retsina will stand its ground.

i	White meat or fish in a Provençale-type sauce

New World Chardonnays with strong acidity and freshness are the natural partners for forceful, tangy sauces – or choose a red with strong fruit and some tannin.

j	Red meat

Fine light clarets complement the flavour of plain roast lamb or beef, but richly sauced dishes require something more powerful. Hearty regional European casseroles made with cheaper cuts of meat are happiest served with their local rustic reds.

k	Game

The strong tastes of hung game and venison need the gutsiness of big Italian and Portuguese reds, Rhônes, Zinfandels or Shirazes; lighter game is better with a fruity red without too much wood: a cru Beaujolais or Merlot-based Bordeaux perhaps?

l	Spicy food

The lychees and spice of a great Gewürztraminer go perfectly with Chinese food– or try a demi-sec Loire-style white. Champagne can work with Indian food but, if you really want to play safe, go for something completely different – ice-cold lager!

m	Cheese

Since the world of cheese is as diverse and exciting as the wine world, the fun is in experimenting. Forget the old notion that only red wine should be drunk with cheese; in tastings we've found that white wine is often more adaptable, especially with high-fat and creamy cheeses. And for sheer indulgence, do try a honeyed, late-harvest dessert wine with blue cheese!

n	Pudding

Good old-fashioned stodgy puddings are delicious with Sauternes or the stickier German wines – and positively sinful with Madeira or Rutherglen Muscat. Creamy desserts are trickier to partner. Try a sweet wine made from the Chenin Blanc or Sémillon grape, or go for a good-quality sparkling wine or Champagne.

o	Fresh fruit and fruit puddings

The delicious juicy sweetness of fresh fruit deserves its equivalent in a bottle of Muscat (not Australian fortified) or a German Riesling of Spätlese quality. Fruit tarts and puddings can handle slightly sweeter German or New World Rieslings.

p	Chocolate

Surely a hedonist's dream: chocolate *and* wine. Well, the only way to make it work is to go right over the top. Forget soft, subtly flavoured wines, and revel in the strong complementary flavours of Brown Brothers Orange Muscat or Flora, or a Christmas pudding-style fortified Muscat from Australia, Portugal, Spain or France.

q	Non-food wines

Some wines seem to have been made with food in mind. Others say simply: 'It's a balmy summer evening, the scent of jasmine is in the air…Drink me!' Or: 'It's snowing, put another log on the fire, an old film in the video, and I'll give you a warm glow!' There are also traditional non-food wines such as the semi-sweet Germans, and fizz – sure to lift your spirits without the help of so much as a peanut.

r	Party wines

Since there are as many ways of holding a party as there are wines to choose from, the easiest way to recognise a wine that gets itself invited to all the best bashes is: it's fun, doesn't take itself too seriously, keeps the conversation flowing, won't be left standing alone in the kitchen and is generally terrific value. For some name dropping see page 30.

s	Special occasions

It doesn't have to be expensive, but it usually has bubbles and there's something about it that is synonymous with celebration. All you need is the excuse. How about cracking open a bottle if there's a 'y' in the day and at least four weeks in the month?

THE WINES

Sparkling wine

Two cheers for cheaper Champagne. The only problem is that the stuff on offer at £7.50 rarely tastes very good– which is why we're recommending delicious inexpensive fizzes from other regions which will leave you with enough money to pay the price for a bottle or two of the real thing.

1 TESCO PROSECCO SPUMANTE, ZONIN Piedmont (It)

£4.69	☛ TO	↻ o,q,r

Ripe, with peaches and apples, a lively sparkle and a fine mousse. Fresh and well balanced.

2 TESCO MARTINI ASTI SPUMANTE, CASTELVERO Piedmont (It)

£5.89	☛ TO	↻ o,q,r

Brilliant Asti. A cocktail of freshly squeezed grape juice, smoke, sweet spice and lime. Perfect with fruit or as a thirst-quencher on a warm day.

3 SEGURA VIUDAS CAVA BRUT RESERVA Cava (Sp)

£5.99	☛ ABB AMA BTH BU DIR JEH MM NY OD TH WBM WR WRW
	↻ c,r

Unusually fresh modern Cava: subtly fizzy, full and rounded.

4 NEDERBURG 1ER CUVEE BRUT Paarl (SA)

£5.99	☛ AF CAP JCK JEH LWE POR	↻ c,n,q

Subtle, apple soft flavours and yeast building up to a clean finish.

5 GRAND DUCHESS RUSSIAN SPARKLING WINE (Ukr)

£6.29	☛ AF AMA BOO LWE TO WSC	↻ c, n,o,q

Once known as Champagnski. Creamy, biscuity strawberryish and rather interesting. *NO REAL APPEAL FOR ME.*

6 LE GRAND PAVILLON DE BOSCHENDAL, CUVEE BRUT BLANC DE BLANCS Paarl (SA)

£6.59	☛ LWE SAF	↻ a,n,q,r

Sparkling Wine of the Year

A great combination of ripe, New World fruit and yeasty Champagne style. Watch out Champagne! Watch out Australia!

7 CREMANT DE BOURGOGNE, LES CAVES DE VIRE 1989 Burgundy (F)

£6.89	☛ CVR JS TO	↻ c,o,q,r

Crisp, clean fizz, with solid fruit flavour. Ideal for a party.

8 DOMINIQUE CHARNAY BLANC DE BLANCS 1989 Burgundy (F)

£6.95	☛ BI	↻ c,n,q

Clean, concentrated, single-domaine fizz, with a yeasty, biscuity flavour.

9 EDMOND MAZURE VINTAGE BRUT, SEAVIEW 1990 South East Australia (Aus)

£6.99	☛ A AUC OD	↻ c,n,q

More delicate in style than most of the Australian fizzes on the market, and more complex. Fresh, ripe and yeasty. Classy.

10 ARBOIS-PUPILLIN, PAPILLETTE BLANC BRUT, FRUITIERE VINICOLE DE PUPILLIN Jura (F)

£6.99	☛ SPG	↻ a,c,n,

A lovely mouthful from the North-east of France with a rich, mature nose and palate full of toasty, creamy flavours of honey, biscuits and oranges.

11 MONTANA LINDAUER BRUT (NZ)

£7.49	☛ WIDELY AVAILABLE	◡ n,o,r

Instantly seductive, fruity fizz with no pretentions to be Champagne.

12 TOURAINE ROSE BRUT, CAVES DES VITICULTEURS DE VOUVRAY Loire (F)

£7.50	☛ ABY G	◡ o,q,r

The Loire at its rare best. Creamy, fruity, yeasty and full of character.

13 BERLUCCHI BIANCO IMPERIALE, VINO DA TAVOLA, GUIDO BERLUCCHI Lombardy (It)

£7.69	☛ V&C	◡ n,o,q,r

Stylish, rich, full-bodied, peachy wine.

14 ANGAS BRUT CLASSIC, YALUMBA WINERY South East Australia (Aus)

£7.79	☛ AB AMA BH HPD JN JS OD SOM SWB WBM WIN	
		◡ a,n,q

Powerful wine with lots of ultra-rich flavour.

15 DEINHARD LILA RIESLING BRUT, SEKT Mittelrhein (G)

£7.80	☛ ECK EVI JEH	◡ c,o,q

A rare good deed in the naughty world of German fizz. Appley and dry.

16 YALUMBA SPARKLING CABERNET CUVEE PRESTIGE South East Australia (Aus)

£7.95	☛ ADN LAV NY OD SOM WIN	◡ o,p,q,s

Ripe, yet dry, with spice, raspberry and blackcurrant flavours. A weirdly wonderful Aussie curiosity.

17 BOUVET LADUBAY SAUMUR BRUT Loire (F)

£7.99	☛ DBY ES GHS HUN J&B JAV JN MM NIC RBS	◡ c,n,o,q

Soft, fruity, full-flavoured, creamily attractive wine.

18 CREMANT DE LOIRE ROSE, CAVE DES VIGNERONS DE SAUMUR Loire (F)

£7.99	☛ NIC SOM TO YAP	◡ n,o,r

Perfect, clean, fresh bouquet; delicate nose with a hint of oranges. Dry, smooth and creamy with a good mousse.

19 CHAPIN ROSE, SAUMUR, CHAPIN & LANDAIS Loire (F)

£8.19	☛ CHF CWW RBS WNS	◡ n,o,q

Delightful salmon pink. Pronounced raspberries and strawberries; full, rich and creamy – a great quaffer.

20 OMAR KHAYYAM, CHAMPAGNE INDIA 1987 Maharashtra (Ind)

£8.49	☛ ADN AMA BH BOO CEB CHE CWS DBY DIR ECK HEM HOL	
	HOU HPD JFD LWE MM MRN MTL NRW POR TAN VER WBM WNS WRK	
		◡ l,n,q

Seriously! Good fizz from India. Maturing, appley, full and creamy.

21 SPARKLING VOUVRAY, CHEVALIER DE MONCONTOUR Loire (F)

£8.95	☛ BH TO	◡ a,n,o

Rich, biscuity, appley Chenin Blanc. Perfect with fruit.

22 MAYERLING CREMANT D'ALSACE, CAVE VINICOLE DE TURCKHEIM Alsace (F)

£8.99	☛ AMW BU DBY ECK HEM NIC NRW POR TDS TH U WGW WNS	
WR WRK		◡ c,o,q

Light, refreshing lemony fizz full of attractive fruit salad flavours.

(Arg) = Argentina; (Au) = Austria; (Aus) = Australia; (Bul) = Bulgaria; (Cal) = California; (Ch) = Chile; (F) = France; (G) = Germany; (Gr) = Greece; (Hun) = Hungary; (Is) = Israel; (It) = Italy; (Mad) = Madeira; (Mex) = Mexico; (NZ) = New Zealand; (P) = Portugal; (SA) = South Africa; (Slo) = Slovakia; (Sp) = Spain; (UK) = United Kingdom; (US) = USA, excluding California

23 SCHARFFENBERGER BRUT Mendocino County (Cal)

£9.99	🖝 A FWC	🍷 c,n,r

Crisp, refreshing and cleanly made up-front fizz to shame many a Champagne. We love the label too.

24 GREEN POINT, DOMAINE CHANDON 1990 Yarra Valley (Aus)

£9.99	🖝 AB ADN AF AUC CWS DBY FUL G G HHC JEH JS L&W LEF LV LWE MWW NIC OD PHI RAE RBS ROD SHJ THP TO TP VW W WCE WL WOC	
		🍷 c,n,q

Zesty and clean with good Chardonnay and Pinot character. Soft fruit with a touch of nuttiness. Will improve.

25 CROSER METHODE TRADITIONNELLE, PETALUMA WINERY 1990 Adelaide Hills (Aus)

£12.50	🖝 ABY AUC BEN BH FV HEM JN LAV OD RBS SOM WIN	
		🍷 c,n,q

Light, crisp and creamy with a delicate, yeasty nose and good mousse.

26 LE MESNIL BLANC DE BLANCS Champagne (F)

£14.95	🖝 ADN BU J&B RHV SHJ SOM TH WOI WR	🍷 a,n,q

Big and powerful with long, buttery, toasty Chardonnay flavours. Better than most pricier, big-name Champagnes.

27 SAFEWAY CHAMPAGNE ALBERT ETIENNE VINTAGE, MASSE 1988 Champagne (F)

£14.99	🖝 SAF	🍷 c,n,q

Classic, buttery, yeasty Champagne. Great value.

28 DRAPPIER BLANC DE BLANCS CHAMPAGNE Champagne (F)

£16.99	🖝 ABY BU ECK NI SPG TH WR	🍷 a,n,q,s

Toasty, buttery, creamy, slightly honeyed Champagne from an up-and-coming producer.

29 'J' JORDAN 1987 Sonoma (Cal)

£17.55	🖝 L&W	🍷 a,n,q,s

Toasty and complex with masses of seductive sweet flavour. Clean fresh and long. The bottle looks pretty special too.

30 CHAMPAGNE JACQUESSON BLANC DE BLANCS Champagne (F)

£18.25	🖝 CEB DX LWE YAP	🍷 c,n,q,s

Beautifully full and mature, with a bready nose and complex, full bodied Chardonnay character.

31 VICTORIA WINE VINTAGE CHAMPAGNE 1986 Champagne (F)

£18.59	🖝 VW	🍷 a,n,q,s

Sparkling Wine of the Year

This has everything. Mature and bready, with wonderful, long hazelnutty flavours. Very, very classy. QUITE GOOD, BUT OVERRATED IN MY OPINION

32 CHAMPAGNE HENRI BILLIOT Champagne (F)

£18.90	🖝 ADN BI SHJ UBC	🍷 a,n,o,s

Brilliant, strawberryish, toasty, aniseedy and liquoricey wine.

33 BOLLINGER GRANDE ANNEE 1985 Champagne (F)

£29.50	🖝 WIDELY AVAILABLE	🍷 c,n,q,s

Classic, full-bodied vintage Champagne typical of the Bollinger style at its best. Rich, nutty and toasty, with plenty of fruit and a lovely lingering finish.

34 CHAMPAGNE LOUISE POMMERY VINTAGE ROSE 1988 Champagne (F)

£45.00	🖝 ABY BI POR RBS ROD	🍷 d,e,n,o,s

Traditional rosé fizz with bags of fruit. Drink it with a meal as an alternative to Burgundy.

Richer dry whites

Oaky wines can be delicious but one can have too much of a good thing –
which is why we've put together this range of wholly recommendable
unoaked and lightly oaked examples.

35   PELICAN BAY SEMILLON (Aus)

£2.67	☛ KS	♡ e, g, q

Very attractive gentle wine; at once dry and honeyed. Great value.

36   SAINSBURYS ROMANIAN SYLVANER, JIDVEI (Rom)

£2.75	☛ JS	♡ e, g

An unusually aromatic example of what can be a dull grape. Rich,
floral and apricotty, yet clean and refreshing too.

37   SAINSBURYS DO CAMPO BRANCO TERRAS DO SADO, J.P. VINHOS(P)

£2.95	☛ JS	♡ e, g, q

From Peter Bright, last year's Red Wine Maker of the Year, this is softly
ripe, fruity stuff. The future face of Portuguese white wine?

38   VIN DE PAYS DE L'HERAULT BLANC, SKALLI 1992 Midi (F)

£3.09	☛ CPW NI VW	♡ c,f,q,r

From a reliable New World-style producer, a fresh appley party wine.

39   CHARDONNAY GYONGYOS, HUGH RYMAN 1992 (Hun)

£3.35	☛ BU CWS FUL JS MWW SAF TDS TH WR	♡ e, g, q

Joint White Wine of the Year

Chardonnay doesn't have to be oaky to taste good – nor does it have to
come from France or the New World. This is rich and buttery with subtle
peachy, currranty flavours and a dry, melony finish. Great winemaking
by British-born, French-bred, Australian-trained Hugh Ryman.

40   SAFEWAY CHARDONNAY DEL TRIVENETO, G.I.V. 1992 (IT)

£3.49	☛ SAF	♡ e, g, q

Sweetly ripe wine, with crisp acidity and a dry melony finish.

41   'LE MONFERRINE' CHARDONNAY DEL PIEMONTE, A.V.P. 1992 Piedmont (It)

£3.75	☛ SAF	♡ e, i

An intense wine from Barolo and Asti country. Well-balanced, with
good fruit and acidity and typical Chardonnay character.

42   ASDA CHARDONNAY, VIN DE PAYS D'OC, SKALLI Midi (F)

£3.75	☛ A	♡ c, g, q

Another Skalli winner. Easy-drinking, with a rich, clean, fruity style.

43   COTES DE ST MONT WHITE, PLAIMONT 1991 South West (F)

£3.99	☛ AB ABY ADN CFT FUL GH GI HHC L&W NIC SAC SHJ SV SWB	
TAN		♡ e,f,i

Modern wine from one of France's most reliable cooperatives. Rich
and fat with a touch of lime on the finish.

44   CHARDONNAY, VINO DA TAVOLA, CA DONINI 1992 Triveneto (It)

£3.99	☛ AB BTH CWS ES JAG JAV UBC V&C VLW WL WOC	
		♡ c, e, f, i

For people who hate big Aussie-oaky Chardonnays, this is at once
fruity and buttery, with a dry, flinty finish.

☛	For an explanation of the stockist abbreviations, see page 16
♡	For an explanation of food style codes, see page 67

45 NOBILO WHITE CLOUD 1992 (NZ)

£4.25	AV C&A CEB CWM CWS D DAL DBY ES GHS JAG JFD JS MM RIB	
	RTW TAN THP VLW VW WBM WNS WOC	♫ c, e, f

A very aromatic, peachy-floral wine with a good, long finish. New Zealand's most reliable white blend.

46 CHARDONNAY DEL PIEMONTE, ARALDICA 1992 Piedmont (It)

£4.29	ABY BEN BOO COK CWI DAL DBW DBY EE EVI G NRW NY PHI	
	POR SAF SAN SOM V&C VLW VW WCE WGW	♫ c, e, i

Clean, young wine with a really characterful fruity-spicy flavour. Will develop further.

47 WHITE BURGUNDY, LABOURE-ROI 1991 Burgundy (F)

£4.69	STW	♫ c, e, h

Stylish, creamy Chablis-like wine full of soft fruit and balancing acidity.

48 CHAIS BAUMIERE, CHARDONNAY VIN DE PAYS D'OC 1990 Midi (F)

£4.75	CVR G SHG VLW W WOC	♫ c, e, g

Made by an offshoot of Australian winery, Hardy's. Classy, medium-bodied, and toasty with just the right balance of butter and ripe fruit.

49 ORLEANAIS, COVIFRUIT 1992 Loire (F)

£4.95	YAP	♫ c, e, i

An appellation which is rarely seen. Judging by this example, that's a great pity. Full-bodied wine with lots of intense, peachy-appley fruit and a hint of peardrops. Will continue to improve.

50 TESCO MACON BLANC VILLAGES, LES CAVES DE VIRE 1992 Burgundy (F)

£4.99	TO	♫ c, e, i

A Mâcon which stands up to the challenge from further south. Fresh and fruity with lively acidity and a mouthfilling, long finish.

51 CHARDONNAY 'VIRGINIE', VIN DE PAYS D'OC, SARL DOMAINE VIRGINIE LIEURAN 1992 Midi (F)

£4.99	ADN DAL ECK J&B L&W M&V PON RD SHJ SOM TAN	
		♫ c, e, i, m

A name to watch in southern France. A beautifully balanced wine, with bags of fruit backed up with good citrussy acidity. Good enough to shame producers of Mâcon and Bourgogne Blanc.

52 DOMAINE DES DEUX RUISSEAUX CHARDONNAY, SKALLI 1991 Midi (F)

£4.99	BU TH WR	♫ c, e, i

A single-domaine wine from Skalli. Medium-bodied, nutty and buttery, with subtle ripe fruit. A cross between Burgundy and the New World.

53 'CASAL DI SERRA' VERDICCHIO CLASSICO, DOC, UMANI RONCHI 1991 Marches (It)

£5.45	AMA BH BTH BWS C&A C&B CWW DBY ES FUL FWC GHS GNW	
	HEM HVW JAG JN JS LV MM PHI PON RD V&C VW WOI	
		♫ c, e, g

A perfect Italian alternative to Chardonnay. Spicy, smoothly dry and light years away from all those dull Verdicchios in their 'Lollobrigida' bottles.

54 MONTES UNOAKED CHARDONNAY, DISCOVER WINES LTDA 1993 Curico (Ch)

£5.49	D DBY HW NY P SV SV VIL	♫ e,f,g

From one of Chile's top wineries, and made with a little help from Hugh Ryman. Rich, herbaceous and long.

55 TESCO CHABLIS, LA CHABLISIENNE 1992 Burgundy (F)

£5.49	TO	♫ f,h,i

Clean, crisp, typical Chablis combining ripe peach, spice and citrus fruit flavours. *Gently oaked. Quite good.*

56 SUNNYCLIFF CHARDONNAY 1992 Victoria (Aus)

| £5.49 | ☞ ADN G&M HHC L&W SHJ TAN WOM | ◎ e, g, i |

Rich, tropical flavours galore with crisp, appley acidity. A new wave Australian with intense fruit but none of the oak.

57 CHABLIS, LOUIS ALEXANDRE 1992 Burgundy (F)

| £5.99 | ☞ AMW BNK BOO BU BUT CAC CDE COK CVR DAL DBY ECK HOU NRW P PHI POR RN TDS TH TOJ WCE WES WGW WR | ◎ e,fg,h |

Well made young Chablis, combining juicy fruit with toasty, fat, buttery and slightly toffeed flavours.

58 ASDA CHABLIS, G. MOTHE 1991 Burgundy (F)

| £6.69 | ☞ A | ◎ e,f,h,i |

Powerful, classy, textured wine with ripe fruit, a rich, honeyed nose.

59 PETIT CHABLIS, GOULLEY 1991 Burgundy (F)

| £6.75 | ☞ BU G HEM TH WGW WR | ◎ f,h,i |

Far from 'petit' in style. Exotic and lemony with hints of cinnamon.

60 SOMERFIELD CHABLIS, LA CHABLISIENNE 1990 Burgundy (F)

| £6.95 | ☞ G | ◎ f,g,h |

An intense wine, with masses of lovely, peachy, buttery flavour.

61 LUGANA CA'DEI FRATI 1992 Brescia (It)

| £6.99 | ☞ ABY AMW BOO CAC CNL CWI DBY GRT HEM HOU LEF NRW NY POR SAN SOM SWB TAN V&C VLW WCE WGW | ◎ e, f, i |

Forget Soave; try this distinctive, floral Italian blend of peary fruit and spice.

62 MACON VIRE L'ARRIVE VIEILLES VIGNES, CAVES COOPERATIVE A. SARJEANT 1988 Burgundy (F)

| £7.25 | ☞ THP | ◎ e, g, m |

Dry, maturing, southern Burgundy with a mixture of rich, ripe pineappley fruit, vanilla, apple and lemon and an attractively dry finish.

63 LA MONT-NORMOND, DOMAINE DE L'ANCIENNE FORCE MAJEURE 1992

| £7.99 | ☞ SAC KED COS WLD NOT RES IGN | ◎ e, x, e, r, m |

A wine with lashings of whipped cream flavour but a distinctly bitter finish. Not for drinking in the short term but rates interest.

64 TASMANIAN WINE COMPANY CHARDONNAY, PIPER'S BROOK 1991 Tasmania (Aus)

| £8.50 | ☞ ABY AUC BH BNK BOO COK DBY FUL FWC HEM HVW POR RIB ROD WRW | ◎ c, e, g |

An unoaked but opulently seductive wine from the great Pipers Brook winery. Rich and reminiscent of honeysuckle, with delicious tropical fruit.

65 JERMANN PINOT BIANCO 1991 Friuli Venezia Giulia (It)

| £11.75 | ☞ ADN MM PON V&C VIL VLW | ◎ c, e, f, g, s |

One of the world's masters of this variety, Jermann makes wines with astonishing depth of fruit and richness. Lovely, classy, peary flavour.

Oaked whites

Until a few years ago, apart from a few 'big name' Graves, almost the only overtly oaked white wines around were old-fashioned Riojas, Burgundies and Chardonnays from the New World. Today, new barrels are being used almost everywhere – with a bewildering array of grape varieties.

(Arg) = Argentina; (Au) = Austria; (Aus) = Australia; (Bul) = Bulgaria; (Cal) = California; (Ch) = Chile; (F) = France; (G) = Germany; (Gr) = Greece; (Hun) = Hungary; (Is) = Israel; (It) = Italy; (Mad) = Madeira; (Mex) = Mexico; (NZ) = New Zealand; (P) = Portugal; (SA) = South Africa; (Slo) = Slovakia; (Sp) = Spain; (UK) = United Kingdom; (US) = USA, excluding California

PETULAMA CHARDONNAY £9.99   THRESHERS
Superb wine, oaked but not intensely.

66	SAFEWAY LA MANCHA, RODRIQUEZ & BERGER 1992 Central (Sp)	
£2.89	☛ SAF	⦿ c, e, r

Fresh and full of personality, with a gentle, soft, peachy nose and a tangy note of acidity.

67	SAFEWAY CALIFORNIAN WHITE, HEUBLEIN 1992 (Cal)	
£2.99	☛ SAF	⦿ c, e, f

Light, dry, subtly oaked wine with gentle, melony fruit.

68	SOMERFIELD AUSTRALIAN DRY WHITE (Aus)	
£3.19	☛ G	⦿ e, g, r

Lively flavours, warm fruit and hints of almond and angelica. Great value.

69	TOLLEYS PEDARE CHENIN COLOMBARD 1990 South Australia (Aus)	
£3.49	☛ OD	⦿ c, e, q

An Aussie blend of Loire and South-West French grapes, with rich vanilla and nicely balanced ripe fruit. Crisp, lingering and bright.

70	TIMARA WHITE, MONTANA 1991 (NZ)	
£3.99	☛ AB ADN AMA BNK BU DBY CWS HVW JCK MRN MTL OD PLA	
	RAV TDS TH TO WL WOC WR ⁄	⦿ e, i, q

From New Zealand's biggest winery, this is brilliant stuff, with just the right balance of oak and strawberries-and-cream.

71	LUGANA, SANTI 1991 North (It)	
£4.25	☛ AMA SAF	⦿ c, e, i

Great value from Italy: full-flavoured and ripely fruity, with crisp acidity.

72	CHASAN, DOMAINE SABLEYROLLE, VIN DE PAYS D'OC 1992 Midi (F)	
£4.30	☛ ADN CHF	⦿ a, e

A delicious rich wine; full-bodied, buttery and subtly characterful.

73	COTES DE SAINT MONT CUVEE PRESTIGE BLANC, ANDRE DAGUIN 1991 South West (F)	
£4.50	☛ ABY SWB	⦿ a, e, q

A maturing, richly fruity wine with lots of fruity-nutty flavour.

74	PENFOLDS KOONUNGA HILL CHARDONNAY 1992 South East Australia (Aus)	
£4.99	☛ WIDELY AVAILABLE	⦿ a, b, i

One of the best bargains around; a big, fat wine, with delicious, peachy-pineappley fruit.

75	BOURGOGNE CHARDONNAY, BOISSET 1992 Burgundy (F)	
£4.99	☛ VW	⦿ e, q, r

Gently oaked, easy-drinking Burgundy from the company which is quietly swallowing up an astonishing array of its rivals.

76	CHARDONNAY VIN DE PAYS D'OC, H RYMAN 1992 Midi (F)	
£4.99	☛ CVR FUL JS MWW NI OD STW	⦿ e, f, q

Brilliantly made, exotic, fruit salady wine from Hugh Ryman, with sweet vanilla oak. Refreshing and mouth-filling.

77	SALISBURY ESTATE CHARDONNAY 1992 South East Australia (Aus)	
£4.99	☛ AMW AUC BEN BOO C&B DAL EBA HAM HOU NRW NY OD PHI	
	PLA RAM SAN WCE WGW	⦿ a, b, i

Classy, buttery and smoky, with typical, ripe Aussie style.

78	CHARDONNAY BARREL FERMENTED, VINAS DEL VERO, COVISA 1991 Somontano (Sp)	
£5.50	☛ MOR PMR RBS SAC TP	⦿ a, b, i

Spain has been slow to join the Chardonnay bandwagon, but this blend of spicy-fruity flavours and (very) toasty oak shows how well they could do it.

79 ROSEMOUNT CHARDONNAY 1992 Hunter Valley (Aus)

| £5.99 | ☛ WIDELY AVAILABLE | ↺ a, b, e, i |

The wine most people associate with Hunter Valley Chardonnay and still reliable. Clean and ripe with lots of depth and just the right balance of oak and lemony acidity.

80 CHATEAU REYNELLA STONY HILL CHARDONNAY 1990 South Australia (Aus)

| £6.25 | ☛ ABY AMA AMW AUC BOO CVR DBY ECK HOU NRW OD POR | |
| | R SHG TOJ | ↺ a, b, e, i |

Another winner from Hardy's, with a green-gold colour, a full, oaky nose and flavours of lemon and pineapple.

81 CATHEDRAL CELLARS CHARDONNAY, KWV 1991 Coastal Region (SA)

| £6.75 | ☛ ABY AMA CAP CWS DBY ECK G&M MRN | ↺ a, e, i |

A very well made wine from the biggest winery in South Africa. Vanilla-oaky, with mouth-watering, fresh citrus fruit.

82 CARIAD GWIN DA O GYMRU BACCHUS/REICHSTEINER, LLANERCH VINEYARD 1990 Glamorgan (UK)

| £6.75 | ☛ CPS DBW SAF SHG | ↺ a, e, g |

Don't call this British (that's nasty reconstituted Cyprus grape jelly) or English. It's 100% Welsh, medium-dry, leafy, honeyed and slightly orangey.

83 VERNACCIA DI SAN GIMIGNANO, PODERI MONTENIDOLI 1991 Tuscany (It)

| £6.95 | ☛ ADN BI WSC | ↺ c, e, f |

Delicate, fresh and floral with zingy, appley fruit and a lovely long finish.

84 COVA DA URSA CHARDONNAY 1991 Terras do Sado (P)

| £6.99 | ☛ BU OD TO WR | ↺ a, e, i |

Portuguese Chardonnay is as rare as Burgundian port, but Peter Bright is leading the way with this example of New-World-Meets-Old lemony spice and oak.

85 COTES DE BEAUNE, LABOURE-ROI 1991 Burgundy (F)

| £6.99 | ☛ CPW MWW NAD SAF STW SWB | ↺ e, i |

Labouré Roi is one of the most reliable names in Burgundy. Good, sweetly oaky wine with a typically subtle Burgundian style.

86 THE MILLTON VINEYARD CHARDONNAY 1992 Gisborne (NZ)

| £6.99 | ☛ SAF VER | ↺ a, e, i |

From one of the world's best organic producers, this is broad-flavoured, ripe and oaky, with loads of tangy pineappley tropical fruit

87 BARREL FERMENTED CHARDONNAY, ROTHBURY ESTATE 1992 Hunter Valley (Aus)

| £7.25 | ☛ BEN DBY LAV NIC SAC WIN | ↺ a, b, e, i |

From Len Evans, the Welshman-turned-Australian who's been Godfather to the new wave of Aussie winemaking: a really intense, buttery wine with loads of spicy oak. The Hunter Valley at its best.

88 BOURGOGNE BLANC, HENRI CLERC 1991 Burgundy (F)

| £7.50 | ☛ ABY WOI | ↺ e, f, q |

Better than many Burgundies with village and premier cru names on their labels, this single estate wine marries apple, pear, hazelnuts and oak.

☛ For an explanation of the stockist abbreviations, see page 16
↺ For an explanation of the food style codes, see page 67

89 CHARDONNAY BATELEUR, DANIE DE WET 1991 Robertson (SA)

| £7.50 | ☞ CAP CWS HW WEP STW | ℧ a, b, i |

Danie de Wet is rapidly gaining a reputation as the best across-the-board Chardonnay maker in South Africa. This is like an oaky Burgundy from a very ripe year: creamy, full-bodied and deliciously smoky.

90 YARDEN CHARDONNAY, GOLAN HEIGHTS WINERY 1991 Golan Heights (Is)

| £7.75 | ☞ CFT ECK SAF WRW | ℧ a, b, e, i |

Full-bodied, buttery, pineappley-limey wine from vineyards overlooked by snow-capped mountains and burned out military hardware.

91 MARQUES DE MURRIETA RIOJA RESERVA BLANCO 1987 Rioja (Sp)

£7.99	☞ ADN AMA AMW BEN BH BI BOO BU D DBY ECK EE ES EVI FWC	
	GNW HEM HVW J&B JEH JN L&S LAV MM MOR MRN NY POR R RAM RBS	
	RIB TAN TH TP VLW VW WCE WIN WOC WOM WR WRK WRW	
		℧ b, e, i

Lovely, rich, toasty-nutty-oaky, old fashioned Spanish wine. Still the best example of this endangered species.

92 MONTANA CHURCH ROAD CHARDONNAY 1991 (NZ)

| £7.99 | ☞ AF BU JS LWE OD WR | ℧ a, e, i |

Yet more proof of New Zealand Chardonnay skills. Stupendous, stylish wine with a complex combination of peach and oak flavours.

93 SEMILLON, STEPHEN HENSCHKE 1991 Adelaide Hills (Aus)

| £7.99 | ☞ AUC L&W RIB | ℧ a, e |

The Bordeaux grape in top form down under. Bone dry, yet peachily rich.

94 VINAVIUS CHARDONNAY, DOMAINE DES COUSSERGUES, VIN DE PAYS D'OC 1991 Midi (F)

| £8.29 | ☞ BD WC | ℧ a, e, i |

Made by The *Sunday Times* Wine Club's Aussie 'Flying Winemakers', this is rich, spicy, powerful, lemony wine with lots of spicy oak.

95 BARREL SELECT CHARDONNAY, FETZER VINEYARDS 1991 Mendocino County (Cal)

| £8.50 | ☞ ABY AF BH DIR JN LAV SOM WIN | ℧ a, b, e, i |

In Britain at least, Fetzer are justifying our prediction that they would overtake Mondavi, by selling twice as much wine. Hardly surprising when you taste this classy, apricotty, creamy, subtly oaky example.

96 VALLEY VINEYARDS FUME BLANC 1991 Berkshire (UK)

| £8.50 | ☞ BI BU GI HWM NI WIN WR | ℧ c, e, f |

First class Australian winemaking in England from John Worontschak. Distinctive, rich, long, fruity flavours of lemon and green apples. This one really stands out from the crowd.

97 WAIPARA SPRINGS CHARDONNAY 1991 Canterbury (NZ)

| £8.75 | ☞ AF BU FV HEM LWE TH WAW WR | ℧ a, e, i |

Wonderful, rich, luscious limey, oaky wine from the south of the South Island. Really complex, with a flavour that goes on and on.

98 LOCAL GROWERS SEMILLON, ROCKFORD 1989 Barossa Valley (Aus)

| £8.75 | ☞ ADN AUC BTH DBY HOL NY OD RAM SAN WCE | |
| | | ℧ a, b, e, i |

Deep gold with a lovely rich nose; flavours of fruit and creamy, vanilla oak.

99 KRONDORF SHOW RESERVE CHARDONNAY 1991 Barossa Valley (Aus)

| £8.99 | ☞ AUC BH COR CWS D DBY HOU JS OD PHI ROD THP WNS | |
| | | ℧ a, b, e, i |

Full-bodied, traditional Aussie Chardonnay with plenty of toasty oak.

100	**FIRESTONE CHARDONNAY 1990 (Cal)**		
	£8.99	☛ AF BH C&A JEH JS LAV TRE VLW WIN	↻ a, e, i

Rich and full-bodied with lovely fruit, from a member of the family who brought you the tyres. Yes, 1990 was a Good Year.

101	**VIEUX CHATEAU GAUBERT, GRAVES 1991 Bordeaux (F)**		
	£8.99	☛ CT DBY GNW GRT RTW VIL	↻ a, e, i

New wave, rich, dry white Bordeaux with concentrated flavours of lychee, mango, pineapple and vanilla oak. Lovely, complex stuff.

102	**CHATEAU DOISY-DAENE SEC, BORDEAUX, P. DUBOURDIEU 1990**		
	Bordeaux (F)		
	£8.99	☛ OD	↻ e, f, i

Dry wine from a Sauternes chateau. Rich, long and fragrant with concentrated, aromatic fruit flavours and a really crisp finish.

103	**RULLY 1ER CRU, RABOURCE, OLIVIER LEFLAIVE 1991 Burgundy (F)**		
	£9.22	☛ C&B	↻ e, i, m

Rully is a Southern Burgundy village worth remembering – as is the merchant Olivier Leflaive. Gently ripe and classy with lovely length.

104	**CHARDONNAY, JANE HUNTER'S WINES 1991 Marlborough (NZ)**		
	£9.75	☛ AF BEN BU DBY HOL HVW LWE NAD NY POR TH VLW WR	
			↻ e, i, m

It really does smell of violets– with delicate passion fruit and oak flavours.

105	**CULLENS SAUVIGNON BLANC 1991 Margaret River (Aus)**		
	£9.99	☛ ADN CHF FV	↻ a, e, i

Made by Di and Vanya Cullen, increasingly famous mother-and-daughter winemakers. Classy wine with plenty of sweet new oak, concentrated ripe fruit and a zingy finish.

106	**EDNA VALLEY CHARDONNAY 1990 Edna Valley (Cal)**		
	£9.99	☛ BEN BH BU CPW CVR HLV JEH LAV LEA RBS SAC SAN TH	
	WCE WIN WR		↻ a, e, i

Under the same ownership as Acacia, but from further south and riper and more buttery in style, with lovely, lemony freshness and toasty oak.

107	**ACACIA CHARDONNAY, THE CHALONE GROUP 1989 Carneros (Cal)**		
	£10.50	☛ BH BU LAV TH WIN WR	↻ e, i

Larry Brooks of Acacia is one of the best respected winemakers in California and, thanks to first class Carneros grapes, makes one of its most stylish Chardonnays. Lemony and oaky, with a touch of mocha.

108	**SWANSON CHARDONNAY, NAPA VALLEY 1990 Napa Valley (Cal)**		
	£10.50	☛ AV DBY LEA WSC	↻ e, i, q

A very easy-going wine, with lovely ripe fruit flavour.

109	**MACON CLESSE, DOMAINE DE LA BONGRAN, J. THEVENET 1990**		
	Burgundy (F)		
	£11.20	☛ ADN J&B	↻ e, i, q

Jean Thevenet is that rare animal: a winemaker whose wines justify the existence of the Mâconnais appellation. This is honeyed and weighty with flavours of raspberries and lychees.

110	**POMINO IL BENEFIZIO, MARCHESI DE FRESCOBALDI 1990 Tuscany (It)**		
	£11.45	☛ ADN BH CPW GHS HLV LAV MM V&C WIN	↻ c, e

Tasty, toasty, lightweight wine from Tuscany for an aperitif or with food.

(Arg) = Argentina; (Au) = Austria; (Aus) = Australia; (Bul) = Bulgaria; (Cal) = California; (Ch) = Chile; (F) = France; (G) = Germany; (Gr) = Greece; (Hun) = Hungary; (Is) = Israel; (It) = Italy; (Mad) = Madeira; (Mex) = Mexico; (NZ) = New Zealand; (P) = Portugal; (SA) = South Africa; (Slo) = Slovakia; (Sp) = Spain; (UK) = United Kingdom; (US) = USA, excluding California

111	CHALK HILL CHARDONNAY 1991 Sonoma (Cal)		
£11.95	☛ BI BU TH TO WR		℧ c, e, f

California at its best. Subtle, attractive, long-lasting wine with a big, ripe nose and quite evident oak.

112	ELSTON CHARDONNAY, TE MATA ESTATE 1991 Hawkes Bay (NZ)	
£11.99	☛ ABY ADN AF AMA AMW BH BU DBY ES GHS GNW HPD L&W LWE NY PON ROD RTW SWB TOJ WIN WR	℧ a, e, i

John Buck is New Zealand's longest established top class winemaker. His Chardonnay is a complex wine, with an earthy nose, creamy and elegant fruit and light but delicious oak on the finish.

113	PULIGNY MONTRACHET, DOMAINE LOUIS CARILLON ET FILS 1991 Burgundy (F)	
£13.99	☛ A CT GI H&H RWC WCE	℧ c, e, m

Lightly wooded, with an equally light, flowery nose. Full-bodied, complex and packed with all sorts of fruit.

114	HOWELL MOUNTAIN CHARDONNAY, PETER MICHAEL 1990 Napa Valley (Cal)	
£14.65	☛ L&W	℧ c, e, i

Look out for regions like Howell Mountain; they often indicate far better wine than the 'Napa Valley' of which they are part. Made by an Englishman, this is at once light and spicy, fruity and toffeeish.

115	NEWTON UNFILTERED CHARDONNAY 1990 Napa Valley (Cal)	
£14.75	☛ ADN BH BU CHF ECK RAM RIB SOM WR	℧ b, e, i

A Californian wine made in the same way as the best traditional white Burgundy. Beautifully ripe, with rich fruit – peaches and pineapple – toasty, vanilla oak and a really creamy texture.

116	CHATEAU DE SENEJAC WHITE BORDEAUX 1989 Bordeaux (F)	
£14.75	☛ AF ECK LWE M&V	℧ a, e, i

Jenny Dobson is the only Kiwi-born, female winemaker in the Médoc and one of the very few people making white wine there. Complex stuff, with peaches, blackcurrants, tropical fruit and rich oak.

117	RIDGE CHARDONNAY 1990 St Cruz (Cal)	
£15.25	☛ BEN BH HVW LAV NI OD SOM WIN	℧ e, i, m

From the mountain-top winery best-known for its reds: a showstopper, with powerful-yet-restrained fruit and oak. Decidedly classy.

118	CHASSAGNE-MONTRACHET 1ER CRU, 'LES CHAMPS GAIN', DOMAINE JEAN PILLOT ET FILS 1991 Burgundy (F)	
£15.60	☛ CT	℧ a, b, e, i

Voluptuous, nutty, silky; lovely balance of oak and fruit. Leave a few years.

119	ROBERT MONDAVI RESERVE CHARDONNAY 1988 Napa Valley (Cal)	
£16.99	☛ ADN BEN CEB CVR DBY ES FV MM RIB WOC	
		℧ a, b, e, i

Back on form after a series of disappointing vintages, this is gorgeous, buttery and toasty Burgundian style, with a lovely roast coffee character.

120	CRICHTON HALL CHARDONNAY 1991 Napa Valley (Cal)	
£17.35	☛ MM	℧ a, e, i

Made by an English couple in California, this is creamily peachy wine with lovely vanilla oak.

121	ARARIMU CHARDONNAY, MATUA VALLEY 1991 Gisborne (NZ)	
£17.99	☛ AB	℧ a, e, i

A stunning full-bodied wine, with ripe and toasty vanilla oak and creamy, rich but discreet tropical fruit.

122 PULIGNY MONTRACHET 1ER CRU LES FOLATIERES, HENRI CLERC 1991 Burgundy (F)

£18.75	☛ ABY	♡ a, e, i, m

Classic Burgundy at its best. Complex lingering stuff with rich pineapple, oak, cloves, toffee and tangerines. Worth keeping.

123 TORRES MILMANDA CHARDONNAY 1991 Penedes (Sp)

£20.99	☛ CVR CWS DBY DIR MM NI PON POR RD RIB SWB WBM WOC	
		♡ a, b, e, i

Miguel Torres's most exciting white. Creamy and mouth-filling, with delicate, honeyed oak, weighty fruit, and a Burgundy-like, nutty finish.

124 NUITS ST GEORGES CLOS DE L'ARLOT BLANC, DOMAINE DE L'ARLOT 1990 Burgundy (F)

£28.50	☛ ABY BWI HR	♡ a, b, c, e

A true rarity; lovely, classy, velvety, peachy wine.

Dry Loire-style and country whites

A collection from the Loire itself, other regions of France and such varied countries as Spain and South Africa, and dry-but-fruity 'country' wines.

125 BLAYE BLANC, GINESTET 1992 Bordeaux (F)

£2.95	☛ SAF W	♡ c, d, e

A little known Bordeaux appellation, and a very stylish wine; drily fruity – apples and berries – with plenty of weight. Lingers well too.

126 VIN DE PAYS D'OC, SUR LIE, J & F LURTON 1992 Midi (F)

£3.25	☛ OD SAF TO VW	♡ c, d, e, f

An alternative to Muscadet. Slightly off-dry wine with a ripe, tropical flavour, good acidity and the yeasty-tangy "lift" which comes from prolonged time on the lees.

127 LA COUME DE PEYRE, VIN DE PAYS DES COTES DE GASCOGNE, PLAIMONT 1992 South West (F)

£3.35	☛ SAF	♡ c, e, f, g

A tangy wine, almost bone dry, with a perfumed nose, clean, fruity and herbaceous flavours and a good long finish.

128 TESCO SAUVIGNON BLANC, UNIVITIS Bordeaux (F)

£3.39	☛ TO	♡ c, e, g

Delicious wine with a fresh nose, excellent grassy flavours, lemon acidity and a lovely finish. Great value.

129 TESCO NURAGUS, DOLIANOVA Sardinia (It)

£3.49	☛ TO	♡ c, e, g

Clean and violet-scented with appley fruit and a good zip of acidity. An example of the great value wines this island can produce.

130 GAILLAC CAVE DE LABASTIDE DE LEVIS 1992 South West (F)

£3.59	☛ VW	♡ c, e, g, h

A wine to be drunk in jeans? Dry but creamy stuff from the South-west, with lots of ripe fruit and crisp acidity.

☛	For an explanation of the stockist abbreviations, see page 16
♡	For an explanation of food style codes, see page 67

131 DOMAINE DE ROBINSON VIN DE PAYS DES COTES DE GASCOGNE 1992 South West (F)

£3.79	☛ MWW	♉ c, e, l

Fresh and floral wine with flavours of lychees and lemon. A Premier Cru-soe, presumably.

132 SAUVIGNON BLANC, VREDENDAL COOP 1991 (SA)

£3.99	☛ WEP STW	♉ c, e, g

Clean, pale wine with a grassy nose and a full, but still surprisingly young-tasting blackcurrant leaf flavour.

133 NOGALES SAUVIGNON BLANC, DISCOVER WINES LTDA 1993 Curicó (Ch)

£3.99	☛ GLY OD P WL	♉ c, e, g

Fresh, well-made wine from Chile; fragrant, crisp and long. Great value.

134 DOMAINE DE MAUBET VIN DE PAYS DES COTES DE GASCOGNE, FONTAN 1992 South West (F)

£3.99	☛ AMW BEN COK CVR DBY GRT HOU HPD WGW	♉ c, e, i

From an individual domaine, this is a stunning example of Vin de Pays. Rich, zingy and gorgeously full of fruit.

135 SAUVIGNON BLANC RUEDA, HERMANOS LURTON 1992 Rueda (Sp)

£3.99	☛ JS OD	♉ c, e, g, m

More rounded. Made by Jacques Lurton of Châteaux Bonnet and La Louvière. Pale, with a surprising green gooseberry aroma and fresh, tangy acidity.

136 SAINSBURYS NEW ZEALAND SAUVIGNON BLANC FERNHILLS, DELEGATS 1992 Hawkes Bay (NZ)

£3.99	☛ JS	♉ c, d, g

Terrific value, typically ripe New Zealand Sauvignon. Crisp, grassy-gooseberry flavours, with a touch of spritz.

137 BORDEAUX BLANC, RAOUL JOHNSTON 1992 Bordeaux (F)

£3.99	☛ MWW	♉ c, d, g

Well-balanced modern wine with a fresh, slightly grassy aroma and tangy fruit.

138 RESPLANDY SAUVIGNON BLANC, VIN DE PAYS D'OC, VALD'ORBIEU 1992 Midi (F)

£4.45	☛ WTR	♉ c, d, g, q

A slightly off-dry wine with a refreshing, ripe strawberry flavour.

139 MUSCADET DOMAINE DES DEUX RIVES, D. HARDY & C. LUNEAU 1990 Loire (F)

£4.65	☛ CT	♉ c, g, q

Rich and smooth, with unusual flowery character and appley fruit.

140 CHATEAU LA BERTRANDE, AC BORDEAUX 1992 Bordeaux (F)

£4.65	☛ ABB VIL WTR	♉ c, d, i

Nicely balanced, full-bodied wine with a grassy nose and plenty of green, herbaceous fruit.

141 CUVEE DE CEPAGE SAUVIGNON, DOMAINE DU BREUIL 1992 Loire (F)

£4.75	☛ CPW CVR EBA WOI	♉ d, e, g

Full-bodied, tangy Sauvignon with a good, strong, long finish.

142 OZIDOC SAUVIGNON, VIN DE PAYS D'OC, J & F LURTON 1992 Midi (F)

£4.75	☛ ADN CHF	♉ c, d, e, g

A fresh, grapey, gooseberryish Loire-style wine made by the peripatetic Jacques Lurton.

143 SANTA RITA RESERVA SAUVIGNON 1993 Maule (Ch)

£4.75	☞ ABY BI CWW ECK	❍ a, d, e, g

Classy Sauvignon with a complex, smoky nose and a rich, almost over-the-top flavour.

144 COTEAUX DE LANGUEDOC PICPOUL DE PINET, DUC DE MORNY 1991 Midi (F)

£4.75	☞ DAL DBY DIR NRW PHI WCE WGW	❍ c, e, g

Made from one of France's most traditional, yet little-known grapes. Creamy, well-balanced and dry.

145 VERDICCHIO DEI CASTELLI DI JESI, BRUNORI 1991 (It)

£4.98	☞ BI	❍ c, e, i

Broad, full-flavoured, aromatic wine with tangy fruit. Well balanced, with an excellent long and rich finish.

146 HARDY'S MOONDAH BROOK ESTATE CHENIN BLANC 1992 Gingin, Western Australia (Aus)

£4.99	☞ ABY AMW BOO CVR CWS DBY ECK G GI HOU JS MTC NI POR R TO TOJ WL	❍ a, e, i, m

Joint White Wine of the Year

A brilliant alternative to Chardonnay, with ripe, appley fruit and rich, sweet oak. Fresh, mouthfilling and immediately seductive.

147 CASABLANCA WHITE LABEL SAUVIGNON BLANC 1992 (Ch)

£4.99	☞ MOR NY RWC	❍ c, e, i

One of the most exciting new wines to come out of Chile. Lovely, fresh and zingy with pungent greengage flavours.

148 BERGERAC, LA COMBE DE GRINOU 1992 South West (F)

£5.29	☞ C&B	❍ c, d, e

Fresh, floral wine with greengage and grass, and concentrated fruity flavours. Good length, too.

149 ZONNEBLOEM BLANC DE BLANC, STELLENBOSCH FARMERS WINERY 1991 Coastal Region (SA)

£5.45	☞ CAP DBY GI PGR PLA SAC WSC	❍ c, d, g

Clean, crisp, grassy-yet-buttery flavours. Stylish, mouth-filling and spicy.

150 KONOCTI SAUVIGNON BLANC 1991 Lake County (Cal)

£5.49	☞ BBR BI BU BWS TH WR	❍ d, e, g

Clear, light style of California Sauvignon. Fresh, crisp, well balanced and eminently drinkable.

151 MUSCADET DE SEVRE ET MAINE, GUY BOSSARD 1992 LOIRE (F)

£5.75	☞ A CUM ORG RAV RBS SAF VER VR	❍ d, e, f

Clean, crisp and dry wine with a slight sparkle (proof that, unlike some, it really has been bottled 'sur lie'). A very modern, well-balanced style.

152 DOMAINE DE GRANDCHAMP BERGERAC SAUVIGNON BLANC 1992 South West (F)

£5.95	☞ JS	❍ a, e, h

From Nick (Hugh's father) Ryman's Château la Jaubertie, this is more than a match for most Sancerre and Pouilly Fumé. Delicious, ripe, fat, gooseberry flavours. Outstanding value.

(Arg) = Argentina; (Au) = Austria; (Aus) = Australia; (Bul) = Bulgaria; (Cal) = California; (Ch) = Chile; (F) = France; (G) = Germany; (Gr) = Greece; (Hun) = Hungary; (Is) = Israel; (It) = Italy; (Mad) = Madeira; (Mex) = Mexico; (NZ) = New Zealand; (P) = Portugal; (SA) = South Africa; (Slo) = Slovakia; (Sp) = Spain; (UK) = United Kingdom; (US) = USA, excluding California

153 MARQUES DE ALELLA CLASSICO 1992 Alella (Sp)

£5.99	☛ MOR NY RWC TAN	🍽 c, e, q

A great Spanish summer wine; bright, fresh and full-bodied with delicate fruit flavours and just a little spritz.

154 VERDELHO, WYNDHAM ESTATE 1991 South East Australia (Aus)

£5.99	☛ ABB CVR D ECK FWC GI WOC WRB WSC	🍽 c, e, g

Made from a grape better known for Madeira, this is flowery, broad, smoky wine, with a ripe, limey flavour and a very long finish.

155 ROTHBURY SAUVIGNON BLANC 1992 Marlborough (NZ)

£6.19	☛ BH CPS CVR HVW PHI SAC SOM VDV WBM WCE WIN WOC	
		🍽 c, e, g, q

A New Zealand wine from a well-known Australian Hunter Valley winery. Typical Sauvignon, clearly defined, and packed with gooseberry flavours, building up to a rich creamy finish.

156 MUSCADET CHATEAU DU CLERAY, SAUVION ET FILS 1992 Loire (F)

£6.25	☛ BWC CPW DBY NI	🍽 c, e, f, m

Nutty, grassy traditional Muscadet with good, rich fruit.

157 LUGANA SANTA CRISTINA, VIGNETO MASSONI 1991 Lombardy (It)

£6.49	☛ A GNW RD V&C	🍽 c, e, f

An appley wine with a touch of ripely creamy sweetness.

158 MUSCADET CLOS DE LA SABLETTE, MARCEL MARTIN 1990 Loire (F)

£6.50	☛ RIB STW	🍽 c, e, f

Fruity Muscadet. Some (welcome) mistake surely! Lemony, appley wine with good, peppery acidity.

159 SAUVIGNON BLANC, VILLIERA 1992 Paarl (SA)

£6.75	☛ AF LWE RD	🍽 c, d, e, g

A lovely, earthy Loire-like wine; herbaceous, gooseberryish and slightly woody.

160 GROVE MILL SAUVIGNON 1992 Blenheim (NZ)

£6.75	☛ AF AMW BI BOO BTH BWI CNL CPW DAL DX EVI FNZ FUL FV	
	HHC LWE NY PHI RAV SAC VIL	🍽 c, e, g

Soft, rich gooseberry fool in a glass. Tremendous, intense, ripe-yet-dry.

161 JACKSON ESTATE SAUVIGNON BLANC 1992 Marlborough (NZ)

£6.99	☛ ADN BOO BTH BU CVR D HOU HPD HW J&B L&W NI NY P POR	
	PUG RAM SV SV TAN TH TO TP W WAC WOC WR WTL	
		🍽 c, d, e, g, i

From vines neighbouring Cloudy Bay. Aromatic, with a distinctive, tropical nose and mouthfilling, peachy flavour. A superstar in the making.

162 SELAKS MARLBOROUGH SAUVIGNON BLANC 1991 Marlborough (NZ)

£6.99	☛ ADN AMW BEN BU DBY CVR FV HVW RIB SAC SOM TH WOI	
WR WSO		🍽 c, d, e

A lightly floral, herbaceous Sauvignon, with soft, fruity flavours.

163 BOURGOGNE ALIGOTE, VALLET FRERES 1990 Burgundy (F)

£7.50	☛ BUT DBY ECK TOJ WGW	🍽 c, e, m

An unusual, ripe example of a normally acidic grape. Well-balanced, with fresh peach, lemon and apricot flavours.

164 MENETOU SALON LES MOROGUES HENRI PELLE 1992 Loire (F)

£7.55	☛ BOO BU DBY CVR ECK GH GNW H&H HHC HVW M&V NRW	
NY TH WGW WR WRK WSO		🍽 d, e, h

A full-bodied wine with a crisp, zesty, gooseberry nose, balanced fruity flavours and a clean finish. Far better value than most Sancerre.

165 KATNOOK ESTATE SAUVIGNON BLANC 1992 Coonawarra (Aus)

| £7.99 | ☛ BU TH WR | ¶OI d, e, g |

An excellent example - fresh, light and clean, with a pungent gooseberry nose, broad flavours and a zippy, almost peppery, finish.

166 TERRES BLANCHES BLANC, AIX EN PROVENCE LES BAUX, NOEL MICHELIN 1992 Midi (F)

| £8.30 | ☛ ABY NY ORG VR WAC | ¶OI b, e, g |

Top class organic winemaking. Creamy, round, ripe and welcoming.

167 POUILLY FUME, DOMAINE COULBOIS, PATRICK COULBOIS 1991 Loire (F)

| £8.75 | ☛ A TRE | ¶OI a, e, h, m |

Complex and aromatic with lots of fresh, lively flavours and a hint of gooseberries. Soft and subtle.

168 SANCERRE LES ROCHES, DOMAINE VACHERON 1992 Loire (F)

| £8.95 | ☛ ADN BEN BH CHF EE GI GNW JAV MWW RD U | |
| | | ¶OI a, e, h |

From one of the most reliable Sancerre estates: a well-balanced wine with nettly green nose and complex herbaceous and fruity flavours.

169 HUNTERS MARLBOROUGH SAUVIGNON BLANC 1992 Marlborough (NZ)

| £8.99 | ☛ AF AMA BBR BEN BU CFT CPW DBY DIR HOL HVW JCK LWE | |
| NAD NI NY PHI POR PTP TH UBC VLW WR | | ¶OI c, g, e |

Beautiful, typical, tropical New Zealand-style Sauvignon. Ripe, full-bodied, soft and beautifully balanced.

170 SAUVIGNON BLANC, KENWOOD 1991 Sonoma (Cal)

| £9.23 | ☛ H&D | ¶OI c, e |

An attractive, soft, wine with a pungent, slightly woody, gooseberry nose, soft sweet fruit and well-balanced acidity.

171 POGGIO ALLE GAZZE, TENUTA DELL'ORNELLAIA 1991 Tuscany (It)

| £9.50 | ☛ ABY CWI DBY HOU LEA PON POR RD SOM V&C WCE WGW | |
| | | ¶OI c, e, f |

From the superstar Ornellaia winery, this is beautifully balanced wine with all sorts of delicate, spicy flavours.

172 SANCERRE MD, H. BOURGEOIS 1991 Loire (F)

| £9.99 | ☛ FV JAV RIB SOM | ¶OI a, e, h |

A stylish and delicate wine with floral, fat, spicy fruit and a dry, soft finish. Beautifully balanced too. Everything a good Sancerre ought to be.

173 POUILLY FUME, TRADITION CULLU, MASSON-BLONDELET 1990 Loire (F)

| £10.55 | ☛ CPW SOM | ¶OI c, e, h, m |

Cheerful fruity wine with plenty of body, hints of lemony spiciness and a long, dry finish.

174 POUILLY FUME, DE LADOUCETTE 1990 Loire (F)

| £12.50 | ☛ BBR DBY EE FV HHC HOL HUN JEH MM PON RBS RIB SAC VLW | |
| WOC WOM WSO | | ¶OI a, e, h |

A justly famous Loire classic: crisp, dry, spicy and smoky with complex, ripe fruit flavours.

| ☛ | For an explanation of the stockist abbreviations, see page 16 |
| ¶OI | For an explanation of food style codes, see page 67 |

Medium-dry whites

The most debased category in the *Guide* – and in the wine world as a whole, now that the idea of semi-sweet wines has become so firmly associated with all that is unsophisticated. But who wants wines which only conform to a narrow definition of what is and isn't drily fashionable? This selection shows how deliciously hedonistic a touch of sweetness can be.

175	SAUVIGNON SEMILLON, MONDRAGON 1991 Santiago (Ch)	
	£3.59 ☞STW	ΙΟΙ a, e, l, m

A ripe, concentrated Bordeaux blend to teach the French a thing or two.

176	THAMES VALLEY VINEYARDS SWEET LEA 1990 Berkshire (UK)	
	£5.25 ☞HWM RAM	ΙΟΙ a, b, e

Fresh, elderflowery and raisiny, with a smooth, creamy, lemony finish.

177	SAVENNIERES, CHATEAU D'EPIRE, LUC BIZARD 1990 Loire (F)	
	£8.99 ☞NIC YAP	ΙΟΙ a, e, l

Complex, grapefruity-appley wine, with lovely, refreshing acidity.

Aromatic whites

Call them 'aromatic', call them 'spicy', these are the wines whose smells and flavours go beyond the fruit bowl and hedgerow to take in an extraordinary array of perfumes and spices. If blandness is what you're looking for in a wine, seek elsewhere.

178	CORBANS DRY WHITE RIESLING 1991 Marlborough (NZ)	
	£4.19 ☞AB JCK WES	ΙΟΙ a, e, l

Stylish, intensely perfumed and full of ripe, grapey fruit. Great value.

179	NEETHLINGSHOF GEWURZTRAMINER 1991 Stellenbosch (SA)	
	£4.29 ☞AB CAP LWE WL	ΙΟΙ a, e, l, m

An impeccably made, late harvest wine with a floral, honeyed nose, plenty of fruit and a satisfyingly long finish.

180	NEIL ELLIS INGLEWOOD GEWURZTRAMINER 1992 (SA)	
	£5.25 ☞AF ECK LEA LWE MTL	ΙΟΙ a, e

Very fragrant wine, with herbaceous, appley, yet spicy rich fruit.

181	ALSACE PINOT BLANC, DOMAINE JEAN-LUC MADER 1990 Alsace (F)	
	£5.30 ☞CT	ΙΟΙ c, e

Crisp and full-bodied with a distinctive, slightly coconutty aftertaste.

182	GEWURZTRAMINER D'ALSACE, CAVE VINICOLE DE TURCKHEIM 1992 Alsace (F)	
	£5.99 ☞AMW BTH BU CWM DBY ECK FUL G GRT HOL HVW NRW PHI POR RN RTW SAF TDS TH U WCE WES WGW WNS WR WRK	
		ΙΟΙ a, e, l, m

Typical, perfumed Gewürztraminer. Creamy, with a hint of nuts, yet crisp and refreshing with a tangy finish.

183	ARNEIS ROERO, MALVIRA 1992 PIEDMONT (IT)	
	£8.30 ☞ADN BI	ΙΟΙ a, e, l

One of the best-kept secrets of Piedmont, the Arneis makes wonderfully soft, spicy, melony wine. Like this.

184	PINOT GRIGIO, LA VIARTE 1991 Friuli Venezia Giulia (It)	
	£9.30 ☞BI	ΙΟΙ a, l, m

Intensely spicy, almost gingery wine, with perfectly balanced fruit and acidity. Deliciously long.

185 PINOT BLANC LATE HARVEST SPATLESE DRY, THE OPITZ WINERY 1990 (Au)

£10.28	☛T&W	🍴 c, e, m

From the extraordinary Willi Opitz: an extraordinary, ripe, spicy wine with plenty of soft mature fruit, good acidity and a very long finish.

186 TOKAY PINOT GRIS VIELLES VIGNES, DOMAINE ZIND HUMBRECHT 1990 Alsace (F)

£16.50	☛ABY RAM WR	🍴 a, c, e

Slightly spritzy, with a soft, limey nose, warm peachy flavours and a hint of pepper.

Grapey whites

A quartet of very different wines, made from different varieties in different countries. Their common quality is an intensely fruity style, which combines grapes with all sorts of ripe tropical flavours. Fun wine to enjoy well chilled.

187 MORIO MUSKAT, ST URSULA 1992 Rheinpfalz (G)

£2.99	☛SAFW	🍴 o, q, r

A wine made for fun, with all sorts of lychee, lavender and grapey flavours.

188 PETER LEHMANN SEMILLON 1992 Barossa Valley (Aus)

£5.99	☛ADN BOO CHF DBY ECK JS LEF VDV	🍴 o, q

Oaky and sherbetty with grapey, tropical fruit and a touch of coconut.

189 LAGAR DE CERVERA, RIAS BAIXAS, LAGAR DE FORNELOSSA 1992 Galicia (Sp)

£7.99	☛BOO BU EBA HEM L&S MOR NY PMR RIB RWC TH WR WTR	
		🍴 o, q

Fascinating modern Spanish wine, with flavours of tinned pears, lemon sherbet and peaches.

190 MUSCAT, DOMAINE ZIND HUMBRECHT 1991 Alsace (F)

£9.49	☛ABY WR	🍴 e, o, q

An extraordinary, complex mixture of nettles and freshly mown grass mingled with gooseberries and raspberries and spice. If you don't believe me, try it for yourself!

Drier Germanic whites

If you listen to the Germans, this is the style the world ought to be drinking. Well, perhaps, but we had to search hard to find this set of recommendations, some of which were made rather closer to home than the vineyards of the Rhine or Mosel.

191 GATEWAY HOCK, RUDOLF MULLER Rhein (G)

£2.39	☛G	🍴 c, e, i

Wonderfully zingy; a great mouthful of fruit.

192 TESCO DRY HOCK, TAFELWEIN, ZIMMERMAN GRAFF Rhein (G)

£2.79	☛TO	🍴 c, d, e

Honey and crunchy green apples with more than a hint of spice.

(Arg) = Argentina; (Au) = Austria; (Aus) = Australia; (Bul) = Bulgaria; (Cal) = California; (Ch) = Chile; (F) = France; (G) = Germany; (Gr) = Greece; (Hun) = Hungary; (Is) = Israel; (It) = Italy; (Mad) = Madeira; (Mex) = Mexico; (NZ) = New Zealand; (P) = Portugal; (SA) = South Africa; (Slo) = Slovakia; (Sp) = Spain; (UK) = United Kingdom; (US) = USA, excluding California

193	RHINE RIESLING GREAT PLAIN, MOR WINERY 1992 Mor (Hun)	
£2.99	☛ OD	⎮◯⎮ c, d, e

A real mouth-filler with loads of fresh, clean lemon fruit, crisp acidity and a hint of old wood.

194	TOLLANA DRY WHITE 1992 South East Australia (Aus)	
£3.49	☛ ABY BU ECK ECK GNW HOU POR SHJ SOM TDS TH VLW WAW	
	WOC WR WRB	⎮◯⎮ c, e, r

Crisp, spicy party wine with bags of fruit salad flavour. Chill well.

195	HOCK TAFELWEIN, RUDOLF MULLER Rheinhessen (G)	
£3.50	☛ BWI STW TAN	⎮◯⎮ c, e, q

Soft, clean and well-made with attractive, appley fruit.

196	DENBIES ENGLISH WINE 1991 Surrey (UK)	
£3.99	☛ A BTH CWS CWW JS TO	⎮◯⎮ c, d, e, q

From England's newest, biggest winery: soft, appley and gently spicy.

197	BADEN DRY, BADISCHER WINZERKELLER Baden (G)	
£3.99	☛ BTH BWS CPW CUM CWS G JEH MM NRW RAV RTW TRE VIL W	
	WCE	⎮◯⎮ c, e, q

Refreshing, ripe, dry Southern German wine with appley, peary fruit.

198	SAFEWAY'S STANLAKE, THAMES VALLEY VINEYARDS 1992 (UK)	
£3.99	☛ HWM SAF	⎮◯⎮ c, d, q

Great value, zingy, grapefruit-flavoured English wine. Why buy an import?

Medium Germanic whites

Forget sugar-water Liebfraumilch and the even worse Laski Rizling; these are wonderful examples of refreshing, well-balanced wines which display the unique appeal of the Riesling and the growing range of Germanic grapes.

199	TESCO HOCK, DEUTSCHES WEINTOR (G)	
£2.39	☛ TO	⎮◯⎮ c, e, q

A wine with a real taste of the grape – and appley, too. Great value and far classier than its name and label might lead you to suppose.

200	COOP KABINETT, QMP RHEINHESSEN, ST URSULA 1989 Rheinhessen (G)	
£3.75	☛ CWS	⎮◯⎮ c, d, e, q

Steely, characterful, ripe and surprisingly stylish, with a touch of spritz.

201	SAFEWAY SPATLESE, RHEINHESSEN, FRANZ REH 1990 Rhine (G)	
£3.99	☛ SAF	⎮◯⎮ c, e, q

Light floral bouquet, with lots of ripe fruit and good balancing acidity.

202	DANIE DE WET SINGLE ESTATE RHINE RIESLING RESERVE 1991 Robertson (SA)	
£4.25	☛ STW	⎮◯⎮ e, i, q

Another classic from Danie de Wet, with a lovely green-gold colour and intense, ripe, grapey fruit flavours.

203	TESCO KLOSTER STEINWEILER SPATLESE, QMP, DEUTSCHES WEINTOR Rheinpfalz (G)	
£4.49	☛ TO	⎮◯⎮ c, o, q

Traditional, rich, raisiny wine with good, mouthfilling intensity.

204	ERDENER TREPPCHEN RIESLING KABINETT, MONCHHOF 1989 Mosel Saar Ruwer (G)	
£6.91	☛ J&B	⎮◯⎮ e, q

Crisp, classy, honeyed; with the Mosel hallmark of fresh, spring flowers.

205 SAARSTEINER RIESLING KABINETT, SCHLOSS SAARSTEIN 1990
Mosel Saar Ruwer (G)

£7.24	☛ SUM	↻ c, d, e

Stylish wine with a rich, rounded, ripe-fruit flavour, but with more than a hint of steel. Typical Mosel Kabinett at its best.

206 WINKELER HASENSPRUNG RIESLING KABINETT, BARON VON BRENTANO 1990 Rheingau (G)

£7.29	☛ BU TH WR	↻ c, e, l

Seductive perfume; ripe and richly flavoured with a spicy, tangy finish.

207 KREUZNACHER BRUCKES RIESLING AUSLESE, SCHLOSS VON PLETTENBERG 1989 Nahe (G)

£8.99	☛ BU TH WR	↻ e, o, q

Crunchy green apples and acacia honey: everything good late harvest German wine ought to be.

208 TRITTENHEIMER APOTHEKE RIESLING AUSLESE, GRANS FASSIAN 1989 Mosel Saar Ruwer (G)

£9.99	☛ BU TH WR	↻ e, i, q

Pungent herby and stylish, with concentrated tangy fruit and rich length.

209 NEIDERHAUSER FELSEN REISLING AUSLESE, PAUL ANHEUSER 1989 Nahe (G)

£12.11	☛ SUM	↻ c, d, q

Delicate but mouthfilling , with lovely ripe, appley, Riesling flavour.

210 JOHANNISBERGER ERNTEBRINGER RIESLING KABINETT, BALTHASAR RESS 1990 Rheingau (G)

£12.36	☛ SUM	↻ e, i

Fruity, aromatic and intense wine, with a clean, sweet character.

211 RIESLING HERRENWEG VENDANGE TARDIVE, DOMAINE ZIND HUMBRECHT 1990 Alsace (F)

£17.75	☛ ABY	↻ o, q

Lovely, intense, lingering flavours of over-ripe grapes and sweet spice.

Rosés

A longer than usual list here - simply because they are all so good! Isn't it interesting, though, how few of these wines come from the regions traditionally associated with pink wines?

212 CLAIRET DE GASTON, BORDEAUX, PETER A. SICHEL Bordeaux (F)

£3.19	☛ JS WL	↻ b, c, e

Pear drops and black cherries with a really ripe, raspberry character. Well-made and quite intense with a long, crisp finish.

213 SYRAH ROSE, 'GASTRONOMIE', VIN DE PAYS D'OC, FORTANT DE FRANCE 1992 Midi (F)

£3.69	☛ SAF VW	↻ b, c, e

Full of spice, cherry, strawberry and bubblegum flavours. Drink with food.

214 DOMAINE DE LA TUILERIE MERLOT ROSE 1992 Midi (F)

£3.99	☛ JS	↻ b, c, e, i

Rich, weighty, blackcurranty wine with as much flavour as some so-called 'red' 1992 clarets.

☛   For an explanation of the stockist abbreviations, see page 16
↻   For an explanation of food style codes, see page 67

215	VALDEMAR ROSADA, MARTINEZ BUJANDA 1992 Rioja (Sp)	
£4.19	☞ BU JN TH WR	🝔 b, c, e, i

Ripe, berryish, full-bodied, slightly off-dry; from a top Rioja producer.

216	CHATEAU TOUR DES GENDRES BERGERAC ROSE 1992 South West (F)	
£4.64	☞ GNW GRT LEA	🝔 c, e,

Fresh, zingy wine with lovely, plummy-blackcurranty fruit.

217	CORBIERES, CHATEAU DE CARAGUILHES, LION FAIVRE 1991 Midi (F)	
£4.89	☞ ORG VER VR	🝔 b, e, q

Good, spicy, ripe, organic rosé from a region better known for its reds.

218	MOUNT HURTLE GRENACHE ROSE, GEOFF MERRILL 1992 McLaren Vale (Aus)	
£5.75	☞ AB AUC BH BOO BWS DBY ECK GNW L&W POR WRW	
		🝔 c, e, i, q

Very modern wine from the astonishingly moustachio'd Geoff Merrill, and every bit as voluble with loads of cherry fruit, pepper, and a lovely, long finish.

219	ROSE ARGI D'ANSA, LES MAITRES VIGNERONS D'IROULEGUY 1992 South West (F)	
£5.92	☞ ABY	🝔 b, c, e, q

From a little-known region. Unusual, almondy, spicy and intense.

220	VIDAL MERLOT ROSE 1992 Hawkes Bay (NZ)	
£6.95	☞ FNZ	🝔 c, e, i

Lovely plum and cherry packed rosé from a reliable Kiwi winery.

221	TERRES BLANCHES VIN ROSE 1992 Midi (F)	
£7.35	☞ ABY VR WAC	🝔 e, i, q

Organic, intensely fruity wine with a hint of spice.

222	CHATEAU DE LA GRILLE, CHINON ROSE, A GOSSET 1992 Loire (F)	
£9.95	☞ CFT HW LAV SAC SOM WIN	🝔 c, e

Chinon pink and white are unusual; this one is blackcurrant-leafy and more-ish.

Country reds

The French ought to be kicking themselves. It was they, after all, who introduced the world to the idea of 'vins de pays' and regional wines which displayed characteristics not found in wines from the big-name regions. Today, as the Cabernet Sauvignon and Merlot become increasingly ubiquitous, 'country wines' are beginning to appear from all sorts of places, offering a wide range of alternative flavours.

223	HUNGARIAN COUNTRY WINE KEKFRANKOS/ZWEIGELT, VILLANY, ZOLTAN BELLA 1992 (Hun)	
£2.65	☞ SAF	🝔 b, e, j

Fruit galore, with bubblegum, strawberries and cherries.

224	DOMAINE SAPT INOUR, SINCOMAR PARLIER & FERMAUD (Mor)	
£2.99	☞ SAF	🝔 e, i, j

Also known as 'Rabbi Jacob', this extraordinary wine tastes like lamb with mint sauce, with a dash of marzipan and a clean, fresh raspberry aftertaste.

225	VICTORIA WINE FRENCH FULL RED, SKALLI Midi (F)	
£2.99	☞ VW	🝔 b, e, j, r

Nice, clean and well made, with peppercorn tones. Great for parties.

226 TESCO AUSTRALIAN RED, PENFOLDS South Australia (Aus)

£2.99	☞ TO	ℸ⃝ b, c, e, i, j

Packed with lovely sweet fruit. Undemanding and very quaffable.

227 SPAR COTEAUX DU LANGUEDOC Midi (F)

£3.09	☞ SPR	ℸ⃝ e, i, j

Flavoursome, ripe, chewy and spicy with a hint of Angostura Bitters.

228 FRANKOVKA, VINO NITRA 1991 Pezinok (Slo)

£3.29	☞ FWC SPR VW	ℸ⃝ b, e, j

Soft, perfumed, blackcurranty wine made from a native Eastern European grape.

229 VAL DU TORGAN, LES PRODUCTEURS DU MONT TAUCH Midi (F)

£3.39	☞ AF BU EE JEH LAV LWE NIC STW TDS TH VLW WR	
		ℸ⃝ e, i, j

Berry flavours and freshly ground pepper. Very distinctive; very tasty.

230 SOMERFIELD CALIFORNIAN DRY RED (Cal)

£3.39	☞ G	ℸ⃝ e, i, j

Good hearty, deeply flavoured, plummy wine. A big mouthful.

231 MISTY MOORING RED, ANGOVES (Aus)

£3.59	☞ HOL MWW NAD ROD	ℸ⃝ b, c, e, j

Light, ripe, aromatic and fruity with creamy, redcurrant flavours.

232 DOMAINE DE ST LAURENT, VIN DE PAYS DES COTEAUX DU LIBRON 1991 Midi (F)

£3.65	☞ GI H&H JN TAN	ℸ⃝ b, e, j

Perfectly balanced, fruity-peppery wine from the warm south.

233 MAS DE FIGARO VIN DE PAYS DE L'HERAULT, AIME GUIBERT 1992 Midi (F)

£3.79	☞ ADN CHF JAR NY WL	ℸ⃝ b, e, i, j

Joint Red Wine of the Year

The antidote to all those oaky Cabernets. Great, unashamedly regional wine with all sorts of berry fruits. Shows all the class you'd expect from Aimé Guibert of the great Mas de Daumas Gassac.

234 DOMAINE DES BAUMELLES ROUGE, COTES DE LUBERON, VAL JOANIS 1991 Rhone (F)

£4.65	☞ TO	ℸ⃝ e, i, j

Elegant, meaty wine, full of the flavours of cherries and strawberries.

235 DAVID WYNN DRY RED 1992 Eden Valley (Aus)

£4.75	☞ ADN CHF NRW NY SOM VDV WL	ℸ⃝ e, i, j

First class, intense, cherry flavoured wine from Adam Wynn of Mountadam.

236 COTEAUX DU LANGUEDOC, DOMAINE DE L'HORTUS, JEAN ORLIAC 1991 South West (F)

£5.49	☞ BU RAE RAE RAM TH WR	ℸ⃝ b, e, j

Wonderfully rich, warm and spicy; full of chocolatey flavours.

237 CUVEE MYTHIQUE, VIN DE PAYS D'OC, VAL D'ORBIEU 1990 Midi (F)

£5.55	☞ AB BOO JN POR	ℸ⃝ e, i, j

A big powerhouse of a wine, packed with rich fruit cake flavours, blackberries, peppermint and cinnamon. More hit than myth.

(Arg) = Argentina; (Au) = Austria; (Aus) = Australia; (Bul) = Bulgaria; (Cal) = California; (Ch) = Chile; (F) = France; (G) = Germany; (Gr) = Greece; (Hun) = Hungary; (Is) = Israel; (It) = Italy; (Mad) = Madeira; (Mex) = Mexico; (NZ) = New Zealand; (P) = Portugal; (SA) = South Africa; (Slo) = Slovakia; (Sp) = Spain; (UK) = United Kingdom; (US) = USA, excluding California

£4.99. TESCO CHINON (Cabernet franc grape)
Oh, quite jammy, stewed fruit

238 CHATEAU DE LASTOURS CORBIERES, FUT DE CHENE 1989 Midi (F)

£6.29	☞ AMW BOO BU DBY CVR ECK GNW HOU PHI POR RBS RN TH	
	WGW WR WRK	❍ e, i, j, m

From a home for the mentally handicapped– and largely made by the residents. Rich, powerful, full bodied and generously fruity wine, with complex, cedary flavours.

239 CAHORS, PRINCE PROBUS, J. L. BALDES 1988 South West (F)

£9.25	☞ CWS H&H	❍ e, i, j

Full-bodied Cahors; meaty and full of hedgerow flavours. Still young-tasting, rich and big.

240 MADIRAN, MONTUS, ALAIN BRUMONT 1990 South West (F)

£9.99	☞ ADN BU H&H NY RD WR	❍ e, i, j

Soft, yet substantial wine from the leader of the modern band of Madiran producers. Plenty of character, with ripe, soft tannins.

Cabernet and claret-style wines

Inevitably the biggest red wine section in the *Guide* because these are the grapes winemakers throughout the world are most keen to master. But don't fall into the trap of imagining that these all taste similar. The range of flavours begins with the pure fruit flavours to be discovered in wines like Bulgaria's fresh-from-the-egg Merlot, to the complexity of classic claret.

241 YOUNG VATTED MERLOT, RUSSE WINERY 1992 (Bul)

£2.85	☞ SAF	❍ e, i, j, m

The shape of future reds from Eastern Europe: lively, young, light, fruitily dry and delicious.

242 TESCO BULGARIAN CABERNET SAUVIGNON, LOVICO Suhindol (Bul)

£2.85	☞ TO	❍ b, c, e, j

Still reliable: soft, ripe and mature-tasting with a flavour which lasts.

243 ASDA MERLOT, VIN DE PAYS D'OC, SKALLI Midi (F)

£2.89	☞ A	❍ b, c, e, j

A light, dry blackcurranty-plummy southern red. Very quaffable.

244 RUSSE CABERNET CINSAULT (Bul)

£2.89	☞ ABB AMA BU CHF CVR DBY ECK GLY SV TDS TH THP UBC	
	WES WR	❍ b, e, j

A blend of Bordeaux and obscure Rhône grape. Clean, fresh and spicy.

245 COOP CALIFORNIA RUBY CABERNET, P. FLEMMING FRANCE (Cal)

£3.25	☞ CWS	❍ e, i, j

A fruity cousin of the Cabernet Sauvignon. Deep red, dry and chunky, with a tangy blackcurrant flavour, good concentration and length.

246 DUNAVAR CONNOSSEUR COLLECTION MERLOT, DANUBIANA BONYHAD 1990 Szekszard (Hun)

£3.25	☞ COK VW	❍ e, i, j, m

Deep crimson, with delicious, ripe cherry jam flavour and a hint of pepper.

247 DOMAINE ANTHEA MERLOT, SERGE ZIGGIOTTI 1992 Midi (F)

£3.49	☞ SAF	❍ e, i, j, m

First class organic wine, with lots of curranty fruit and evident tannin.

248 SLOVAKIAN CABERNET SAUVIGNON, VINA NITRA 1992 (Slo)

£3.50	☞ FWC VW	❍ b, c, e, j

A light, soft, well balanced wine to appeal to people who don't like full-flavoured, oaky or tannic reds.

249 AUSTRALIAN CABERNET SAUVIGNON, RIVERINA WINES 1992 Riverina (Aus)

| £3.55 | ☛ SAF | 🍶 j, m, q |

A powerful mouthful of plummy fruit with cedar and tobacco.

250 STAMBOLOVO RESERVE MERLOT 1987 (Bul)

| £3.89 | ☛ AB AMA BU CVR DBY ECK G JFD MRN P SAF SWB TAN TDS TH | |
| | THP TOJ VLW WOI WR | 🍶 e, j, m |

Full-bodied, mature-tasting, with flavours of spicy fruit and bitter almonds.

251 LA SERRE CABERNET SAUVIGNON, VIN DE PAYS D'OC 1991 Midi (F)

| £3.98 | ☛ BI | 🍶 e, i, j |

Classy and straightforwardly attractive, with good, aromatic fruit.

252 TESCO NEW ZEALAND CABERNET MERLOT, COOKS NEWZEALAND WINE CO 1990 Gisborne (NZ)

| £3.99 | ☛ TO | 🍶 b, e, j |

A softly rich, blackcurrant wine with the leafy-herbaceous freshness typical of New Zealand.

253 TESCO AUSTRALIAN CABERNET SAUVIGNON, MILDARA Mildura (Aus)

| £3.99 | ☛ TO | 🍶 e, j, k |

Rich, ruby Aussie red with loads of ripe flavour, oak and spice.

254 CHATEAU CASTERA, BORDEAUX 1991 Bordeaux (F)

| £3.99 | ☛ SAF | 🍶 b, e, j |

Young and easy-going with light, soft flavours and loads of damson.

255 TESCO MEXICAN CABERNET SAUVIGNON, L A CETTO 1988 (Mex)

| £3.99 | ☛ TO | 🍶 e, j |

An exotic wine to confound your wine buff friends. Ripe but dry, with good fruit and soft oak. A model for Spain and Chile.

256 HARDYS NOTTAGE HILL CABERNET SAUVIGNON, BRL HARDY WINE CO 1991 South Australia (Aus)

| £4.19 | ☛ A AB ABB AMA AMW CVR CWS D DBY ECK FUL HOL HOU JAG | |
| | R SAF TOJ WBM WL | 🍶 e, j |

Very typical smooth, fruity, green peppery Cabernet.

257 SEAVIEW CABERNET SAUVIGNON/SHIRAZ 1990 South East Australia (Aus)

| £4.19 | ☛ AF ECK G HOU HVW OD TOJ VDV | 🍶 j, q |

A rich, mouthfilling wine with intense, fresh, blackcurranty-spicy flavours. Drink now or leave for a year or so.

258 DOMAINE DE RIVOYRE CABERNET SAUVIGNON, H RYMAN 1990 Midi (F)

| £4.29 | ☛ BU STW TH VW WR | 🍶 j, e, q |

Another Hugh Ryman success, with soft blackcurrants and a touch of oak.

259 GLEN ELLEN CABERNET SAUVIGNON 1989 (Cal)

| £4.49 | ☛ AMA G GLY JAG JEH LWE STW VLW WTL | |
| | | 🍶 e, j, q, r |

Silky-smooth, easy drinking wine, packed with ripe fruit. Precisely the kind of Californian wine E &J Gallo ought to be making.

| ☛ | For an explanation of the stockist abbreviations, see page 16 |
| 🍶 | For an explanation of food style codes, see page 67 |

**260 OLD TRIANGLE CABERNET SAUVIGNON, S SMITH & SONS 1991
Barossa Valley (AUS)**

| £4.65 | ☞ CNL COPK M&V SPG VDV | ♌ e, j, q |

Light and juicy with sweet, gentle, plummy flavours and a hint of oak.

261 CLARET, RAOUL JOHNSTON Bordeaux (F)

| £4.69 | ☞ MWW | ♌ b, j, q |

Soft, delicate wine with a light, minty nose and easy, oaky fruit flavours. Light but attractive.

**262 COOP AUSTRALIAN CABERNET SAUVIGNON, BERRI ESTATES
1989 South Australia (Aus)**

| £4.75 | ☞ CWS | ♌ e, i, j |

Rich, with lots of lovely, full fruit and a very satisfying, oaky finish.

263 MERCHANT VINTNERS CLARET, PETER A SICHEL Bordeaux (F)

| £4.75 | ☞ ADN G&M HHC L&W SHJ SPG WBM WOM | ♌ e, j, m |

Serious, traditional claret from Peter Sichel of Châteaux Palmer and Angludet. Quite tannic; could be worth leaving to soften.

264 BUZET TRADITION, LES VIGNERONS DE BUZET 1988 South West (F)

| £4.75 | ☞ BTH G SEB THP | ♌ e, j, m |

A middleweight claret-lookalike with attractive blackcurrant fruit.

265 ERRAZURIZ CABERNET SAUVIGNON, MAULE 1991 Maule (Ch)

| £4.89 | ☞ CEL HEM VDV VW | ♌ e, j, q |

Chewy, New World-style wine with plenty of intense, oaky, minty fruit. Nicely made, with a good long finish.

**266 SALISBURY ESTATE CABERNET SAUVIGNON 1991 South East
Australia (Aus)**

| £4.99 | ☞ AMW AUC BEN BOO COR DAL FWC HAM HOU NRW NY PLA POR RAM SAN WCE WGW WNS WOI | ♌ e, m, j, q |

Silky, ripe, fleshy stuff, with flavours of currants and sweet vanilla.

267 KANONKOP KADETTE, STELLENBOSCH 1991 Stellenbosch (SA)

| £5.19 | ☞ AF WEP SAF STW | ♌ b, e, j, q |

A young, quite light-bodied, berryish blend. Drinkable now but will improve. (Is Kadette Afrikaans for 'son-of-a gun'?)

**268 BEL ARBORS MERLOT, FETZER VINEYARDS 1991 Mendocino
County (Cal)**

| £5.25 | ☞ AB ABY BH LAV WES WIN WSC | ♌ b, e, j |

Almondy, redcurranty wine with refreshing, slightly grassy flavours. Worth chilling.

269 MONTANA CABERNET SAUVIGNON 1991 Marlborough (NZ)

| £5.29 | ☞ WIDELY AVAILABLE | ♌ j, m |

Spicy, with rich, crunchy, blackcurrant, cherry and green pepper flavours.

**270 HARDY'S MOONDAH BROOK ESTATE CABERNET SAUVIGNON 1989
Gingin, Western Australia (Aus)**

| £5.35 | ☞ ABY AMW BOO CVR ECK GI HOU POR R TOJ | ♌ e, i, j, m |

Ripe, fruity wine with big, mature flavours capable of taking on the tastiest dish.

271 CHATEAU TIMBERLAY, R. GIRAUD 1990 Bordeaux (F)

| £5.35 | ☞ AB D HHC | ♌ e, i, m |

Mature, fruity red with plenty of oak. Will come together very well over the next two or three years.

272 ROUGE HOMME CABERNET/SHIRAZ, COONAWARRA 1988
Coonawarra (Aus)

£5.45	☛ ABB AMW AV BH CEB COK DAL DBY EBA ECK FUL GNW GON	
	GON HAM JAG LEA PON PHI RAV RBS RHV RIB SAN WAW WNS WOC	
WRW WWT		🔾 e, i, j

One of Australia's top regions shows its best form in this rich, raisiny wine with eucalyptus and mint.

273 TALTARNI FIDDLEBACK TERRACE 1990 Pyrenees (Aus)

£5.75	☛ AMW BEN BH BOO CAC ECK HLV HOL HW JEH LEA NY POR	
RD ROD SOM SV SV WAC WOC		🔾 b, e, i, j

Made by a Frenchman whose father was winemaker at Château Lafite, this is ripe and very easy-going.

274 CHATEAU THIEULEY AC BORDEAUX ROUGE 1989 Bordeaux (F)

£5.75	☛ CPS CT GRT OD RTW SOM	🔾 e, j

Firm, ripe, minty-curranty Merlot. Very typical of modern Bordeaux.

275 RUSTENBERG MERLOT, STELLENBOSCH 1991 Stellenbosch (SA)

£5.75	☛ AV BH COR DBY LWE	

Modern South African winemaking, with none of the earthy flavours so often found in the past. Clean, mouthfillingly plummy, but slightly more tannic and less rich than most Australians.

276 CHATEAU DE LA JAUBERTIE BERGERAC ROUGE, HENRY RYMAN 1990
South West (F)

£5.99	☛ CWW JN L&W	🔾 e, i, j, m

Proof that Nick Ryman's winemaker doesn't keep stationary. Spicy wine with powerful cherry flavours and enough tannin to make it worth keeping. Classier than many a claret.

277 SAUMUR, CHATEAU FOUQUET, PAUL FILLIATREAU 1990 Loire (F)

£5.99	☛ SOM YAP	🔾 b, e, j, q

Stylish and deliciously more-ish. Floral, yet full of chunky, ripe fruit.

278 GOUNDREY LANGTON CABERNET/MERLOT 1991 Mount Barker (Aus)

£6.25	☛ FV GRT RAV RHV WRW	🔾 e, i, j

Soft and ripely sweet, spicy wine with lots of plummy-oaky flavour.

279 MICHEL LYNCH BORDEAUX ROUGE, COMPAGNIE MEDOCAINE 1989
Bordeaux (F)

£6.25	☛ ABY DBY FWC	🔾 e, j, m

Joint Red Wine of the Year

The wine Bordeaux drinkers have been waiting for. Beautifully made classic claret style from the makers of Château Lynch Bages, with 1989 ripeness but sufficient tannin to make it worth keeping. Precisely what Mouton Cadet ought to have been.

280 J WILE & SON CABERNET SAUVIGNON 1987 Napa Valley (Aus)

£6.25	☛ HW TP	🔾 e, i, j

Wonderful, seductive, beautifully balanced wine with plenty of lovely fruit and sweet tannins on the finish to give it longevity.

281 CHATEAU BONNET OAK AGED, A LURTON 1990 Bordeaux (F)

£6.29	☛ AMA BU CAC DBY HVW JN R TH WR	🔾 e, i, j, m

Classy Bordeaux made by Jacques Lurton in a region better known for Entre-Deux-Mers whites. Concentrated fruit with dusty tannin.

(Arg) = Argentina; (Au) = Austria; (Aus) = Australia; (Bul) = Bulgaria; (Cal) = California; (Ch) = Chile;; (F) = France; (G) = Germany; (Gr) = Greece; (Hun) = Hungary; (Is) = Israel; (It) = Italy; (Mad) = Madeira; (Mex) = Mexico; (NZ) = New Zealand; (P) = Portugal; (SA) = South Africa; (Slo) = Slovakia; (Sp) = Spain; (UK) = United Kingdom; (US) = USA, excluding California

282 VALLEY OAKS CABERNET SAUVIGNON, FETZER VINEYARDS 1990 Mendocino County (Cal)

£6.50	☞ AB ABY BEN BH CPS CVR GLY GNW HVW LAV OD RBS RIB
VLW W WIN WL	♡ e, i, j, m

Full-bodied, rich, blackcurrant wine with sweet oak and plenty of tannin.

283 MONTAGNE ST EMILION, CHATEAU BERTIN 1989 Bordeaux (F)

£6.64	☞ C&B	♡ e, j

St Emilion is often full of disappointments('satellite' communes like Montagne St Emilion can be a better bet), but this is attractive with lots of crunchy berry flavour.

284 CHATEAU CARIGNAN, PREMIERES COTES DE BORDEAUX 1990 Bordeaux (F)

£6.79	☞ VW	♡ e, i, j

Sharing its name with a grape used in Fitou and Corbières but banned from Bordeaux. Traditional claret with intense blackcurrant fruit.

285 CHINON, COULY-DUTHEIL 1990 Loire (F)

£6.99	☞ CPS GNW HLV H&H RTW WAC WAW WTL	♡ e, i, j, m

Classic Loire from a top-class producer, full of cherries and blackcurrants.

286 STONIER'S WINERY SELECTION CABERNETS 1991 Mornington Peninsula (Aus)

£7.49	☞ HOL LWE WAW	♡ e, i, j, m

From a new region close to Melbourne. Delicious, young wine with blackcurrant and redcurrant flavours. Very stylish.

287 KENDALL-JACKSON CABERNET SAUVIGNON 1989 (Cal)

£7.85	☞ GRT MWW	♡ b, e, j

Easy-drinking, eucalyptusy wine with lots of lovely, concentrated berry fruit.

288 CABERNET SAUVIGNON, BODEGA Y CAVAS DE WEINERT 1985 Mendoza (Arg)

£7.99	☞ ABB C&A CNL CVR DBW ES GHS GI HOL JAR NI PLA R RBS RD
RHV SHJ SV SV THP	♡ e, i, j

A lovely mature wine, holding up better than some Riojas of the same age. Rich, plummy and satisfying. Drink now.

289 DOMAINE RICHEAUME CABERNET SAUVIGNON, COTES DE PROVENCE 1991 Midi (F)

£7.99	☞ SAF VER	♡ e, i, j

Deep, young, purple, organic wine with a fabulous blackcurranty-woody flavour.

290 CHATEAU BISTON BRILLETTE, CRU BOURGEOIS MOULIS 1989 Bordeaux (F)

£8.75	☞ JFD SAF	♡ e, i, j, q

Vibrant blackcurrant and damson flavours overlaid with oak. Ready to drink, despite its youthfulness.

291 CHATEAU LA TOUR HAUT-CAUSSAN, MEDOC 1989 Bordeaux (F)

£8.95	☞ ADN DBY M&V SAN THP	♡ e, i, j

A Cru Bourgeois superstar in the making. Very classy stuff, with spicy, jammy fruit, subtle oak and loads of soft tannin.

292 COLUMBIA CREST MERLOT, STIMSON LANE 1989 Washington State (US)

£8.99	☞ C&B CEB ECK JFD NY RTW VIL WBM	♡ e, i, j

Washington State is getting a well-earned reputation for its Merlot. Full-bodied, plummy and oaky.

293 THE ANGELUS CABERNET SAUVIGNON, WIRRA WIRRA 1991 South Australia (Aus)

£8.99	☛ AMW AUC BBR OD RIB WOI WSO	♡ e, i, j, m

Beautifully made, with intense blackcurrant fruit and sweet new oak.

294 CHATEAU DE ANNEREAUX, LALANDE DE POMEROL 1989 Bordeaux (F)

£9.49	☛ ABY AMW BEN CVR DBY GI JCK ROD	♡ e, i, j, m

From a region close to Pomerol, this is good, earthy, plummy wine with more than a hint of oak and spice. Ripe, but not quite ready.

295 FETZER BARREL SELECT CABERNET SAUVIGNON 1989 Mendocino County (Cal)

£9.49	☛ ABY BH DIR FV JN LAV LEA OD SOM UBC WIN WSC	
		♡ e, i, j, q

Typical Californian Cabernet at its best: soft fruit with a hint of mint and vanilla oak.

296 CHATEAU TOUR DU HAUT MOULIN, HAUT MEDOC 1985 Bordeaux (F)

£9.75	☛ BWI CPS CT ECK GH RTW WRB	♡ e, i, j, m

From a good, ripe vintage, this is a ready-to-drink, beautifully-made wine with curranty-cedary flavours and soft, easy tannin.

297 CHATEAU NOTTON, MARGAUX 1988 Bordeaux (F)

£9.75	☛ JEH M&S VIL WIN	♡ e, j, m

The second label of Château Brane-Cantenac. Good, ripe, blackcurrant fruit with subtle spice. A tasty mouthful worth waiting for.

298 LINDEMANS ST GEORGE CABERNET SAUVIGNON 1989 Coonawarra (Aus)

£9.89	☛ ABY AMA AUC BOO BU ECK HOU HVW JAG OD POR SOM TH	
WL WR		♡ e, i, j

Classy, perfumed Aussie with delicious, intense, sweet, blackcurrant fruit.

299 MEERLUST MERLOT, STELLENBOSCH 1986 Stellenbosch (SA)

£9.99	☛ AF BAR BOO CAP DBY ECK JN LWE NAD PON TAN WGW	
		♡ e, i, j, m

A claret-like wine with sweet, ripe fruit and evident tannin.

300 L'ABEILLE DE FIEUZAL, PESSAC LEOGNAN 1990 Bordeaux (F)

£9.99	☛ BU WR	♡ e, i, j, k

The second wine of the great Château Fieuzal; upfront, spicy and juicily blackcurranty, but with lots of class. Leave for four or five years.

301 CHATEAU LA TOUR DE PEZ, ST ESTEPHE 1990 Bordeaux (F)

£10.25	☛ DBY WGW	♡ e, i, j

Classic, deep crimson wine with blackcurrants and vanilla oak. To keep.

302 CHATEAU DE LAMARQUE, HAUT MEDOC 1990 Bordeaux (F)

£10.40	☛ C&B	♡ e, i, j

Another one to keep; full of spicy new-oak, concentrated, rich, blackcurrant-and-plum fruit and evident tannin.

303 PETALUMA COONAWARRA RED 1988 Coonawarra (Aus)

£10.49	☛ ABY AF AUC BEN BH BU CEB DBY JN LAV OD PHI RBS SAC SAN	
SOM TH WIN WR		

From a patch of extraordinary red soil, and made by Brian Croser, Australia's top winemaker, this is a rich, concentrated wine with blackcurrant, plum and mint. Made to last.

☛ For an explanation of the stockist abbreviations, see page 16
♡ For an explanation of food style codes, see page 67

304 LES FIEFS DE LAGRANGE, ST JULIEN 1989 Bordeaux (F)

£10.99	☛ NIC RIB STW	♉ e, i, j

The second label from a Japanese-owned Château, this is a full, deep, eucalyptusy-spicy, blackcurrant-jammy wine. It just needs a little more time.

305 CYRIL HENSCHKE CABERNET SAUVIGNON, STEPHEN HENSCHKE 1988 Adelaide Hills (Aus)

£11.50	☛ AUC DBY L&W NI PHI RIB SEB WCE	♉ e, i, j, m

An Australian classic. Oaky and silky, with tons of intense, supple, lingering berry fruit flavours.

306 HUSCH CABERNET SAUVIGNON NORTHFIELD SELECTION 1988 Mendocino County (Cal)

£11.95	☛ J&B	♉ b, e, j, m

Californian class, with soft cassis, subtle oak and good touch of tannin.

307 LEEUWIN ESTATE CABERNET SAUVIGNON 1986 Margaret River (Aus)

£11.99	☛ DD GEL PLA	♉ e, j, m

A truly stylish, complex wine with flavours of cinammon, coffee, and mint. Tasting delicious at seven years old, but will last.

308 CHATEAU CANTERMERLE, HAUT MEDOC 1987 Bordeaux (F)

£12.50	☛ ECK JS THP TO	♉ e, i, j

A well made wine from a rainy vintage. Classy, tasty flavours of cedar and blackcurrant. Drinkable now, but will last another year or so.

309 NEWTON MERLOT 1990 Napa Valley (Cal)

£12.50	☛ ADN BH CHF ECK HVW LEF RIB SOM	♉ e, i, j, k

California's top Merlot? Certainly more interesting than most examples, thanks to hilltop vineyards and a blend which includes Cabernet Franc and Petit Verdot. Satisfying, sweetly ripe and tobaccoey.

310 LE CARILLON DE L'ANGELUS, ST EMILION 1990 Bordeaux (F)

£12.99	☛ BU WR	♉ e, i, j

The second wine from the greatly improved Château l'Angelus. Gorgeous, generous, cedar-woody, fruity and minty. Needs five years.

311 CHATEAU CISSAC, HAUT-MEDOC 1982 Bordeaux (F)

£13.99	☛ BWI CWS EVI FAR G&M HPD MM RBS VLW WRW	
		♉ e, i, j, m

A really typical, old-fashioned claret from a great vintage. Subtly spicy, but with a full, ripe, fruity flavour. Ready to drink.

312 RESERVE DE LA COMTESSE, PAUILLAC 1987 Bordeaux (F)

£14.50	☛ ABY BU GH J&B TAN WR	♉ e, i, j, m

A relatively affordable chance to taste Pichon Lalande winemaking. Deep, blackcurranty and cedary. A mouthful of class.

313 CLOS DU CLOCHER, POMEROL, BOUROTTE 1989 Bordeaux (F)

£15.80	☛ GRT J&B	♉ e, i, j, m

Impeccable Pomerol, with lots of complex berry fruit and a touch of oak. Give it at least three years.

314 DOMAINE DE L'EGLISE, POMEROL 1985 Bordeaux (F)

£15.95	☛ D	♉ e, i, j, m

Superb, plummy, chocolatey, licoricey; first class Pomerol.

315 MORMORETO CABERNET SAUVIGNON PREDICATO DI BITURICA, VINO DA TAVOLA, MARCHESI DE FRESCOBALDI 1988 Tuscany (It)

£15.95	☛ LAV V&C WIN	♉ e, i, j, k

Well-made, intense, herby-fruity young red from a top Tuscany producer.

316 LAUREL GLEN CABERNET SAUVIGNON 1987 Sonoma (Cal)

£15.95	☛ FWC	☋ e, i, j, k

Californian claret, with rich, warm flavours of juicy fruit and chocolate, coffee and oak. World class stuff.

317 CHATEAU HAUT BAGES AVEROUS, PAUILLAC 1988 Bordeaux (F)

£15.99	☛ ABY BU SAF TH WR	☋ e, i, j, m

From Château Lynch Bages, a deep, plummy, ripely fat wine.

318 ARARIMU CABERNET SAUVIGNON, MATUA VALLEY 1991 (NZ)

£16.99	☛ AB GRT	☋ e, i, j, m

Superb flavours ranging from rose water and cassis to roasted coffee.

319 CHATEAU LASCOMBES, MARGAUX 1988 Bordeaux (F)

£17.99	☛ AB MTL THP	☋ e, i, j, s

Classic Margaux; lovely, silky and youthful. Pungent and juicily blackcurranty. Needs time.

320 CHATEAU PICHON LONGUEVILLE BARON, PAUILLAC 1990 Bordeaux (F)

£21.99	☛ BWI CT EBA JAV OD SEB THP WTR	☋ e, i, j, s

Fast taking over the prestige of its neighbour and rival, Pichon Longueville Comtesse: concentrated, with complex fruit flavour and well-judged oak. Will be delicious early next century.

321 ORNELLAIA 1990 Tuscany (It)

£23.99	☛ ABY BEN BOO C&B CPW CWI DBW HOU L&W LEA NY PON	
	POR RD SEB SOM V&C VLW WCE WGW	☋ e, i, j, k

The newest Tuscan high-flying alternative to Bordeaux. Rich, powerful wine with blackcurrant, cherries and plums, vanilla, nutmeg and oak.

322 CHATEAU LYNCH-BAGES, PAUILLAC 1989 Bordeaux (F)

£27.50	☛ AV BWI CT FWC GH HUN J&B JAV L&W SEB THP	
		☋ e, i, j, m

A young, balanced wine with great colour and bags of tannin. Lovely, spicy blackcurrant fruit and excellent depth. Give it time.

323 CHATEAU COS D'ESTOURNEL, ST ESTEPHE 1982 Bordeaux (F)

£39.50	☛ BI BWI CT D FAR FV FWC NI RAM SWB WRK WRK	
		☋ e, i, j

Classic, mature and powerful, with flavours of ripe, plummy fruit.

Rhônes and spicy reds

With every *Guide*, we are delighted to record a greater number of really top class spicy red wines, both from the Rhône itself, from Rhône varieties grown elsewhere (including, this year, such unexpected places as Mexico) and from the Zinfandel which is at last getting the recognition it deserves.

324 TESCO COTES DU RHONE, MICHEL BERNARD Rhône (F)

£2.95	☛ TO	☋ b, j, k

Pungent and juicy with a gentle, redcurrant flavour. Great value.

325 CASA DEL CAMPO SYRAH, BODEGAS SANTA ANA 1992 Mendoza (Arg)

£3.19	☛ BTH SAF	☋ b, j, k

Youngish, yet dark in colour, with a perfumed nose and a soft, spicy flavour. Spanish-style winemaking meets Rhône-style grapes.

(Arg) = Argentina; (Au) = Austria; (Aus) = Australia; (Bul) = Bulgaria; (Cal) = California; (Ch) = Chile;; (F) = France; (G) = Germany; (Gr) = Greece; (Hun) = Hungary; (Is) = Israel; (It) = Italy; (Mad) = Madeira; (Mex) = Mexico; (NZ) = New Zealand; (P) = Portugal; (SA) = South Africa; (Slo) = Slovakia; (Sp) = Spain; (UK) = United Kingdom; (US) = USA, excluding California

326 RESPLANDY MOURVEDRE, VIN DE PAYS D'OC, VAL D'ORBIEU 1990 Midi (F)

| £3.75 | ☞ BOO GEL POR RWC WTR | 🌡 e, j, k, m |

Old-style wine with good gutsy flavour and wine gum fruit, aromas of barbecued meat and a touch of tobacco.

327 DOMAINE DE L'AMEILLAUD, VIN DE PAYS, N. THOMPSON 1992 Midi (F)

| £3.77 | ☞ AB WSO | 🌡 e, i, m |

Made by British-born Nick Thompson. Sweetly perfumed with parma violets and tasting of ripe, dark berries.

328 CEPAGE SYRAH, DOMAINE LA CONDAMINE L'EVEQUE 1991 Midi (F)

| £3.95 | ☞ TAN WSO | 🌡 e, i, j, k |

A full-bodied and mellow wine with spicy, mulberry fruit flavours.

329 MONASTERE DE TRIGNAN COTEAUX DU LANGUEDOC 1991 Midi (F)

| £3.99 | ☞ MWW | 🌡 b, e, j, k |

Outstanding, characterful wine, with soft, attractive fruit and peppery, spicy Syrah flavours.

330 VIN DE PAYS DES COLLINES RHODANIENNES CEPAGE SYRAH, CAVE DE TAIN L'HERMITAGE Rhône (F)

| £3.99 | ☞ AMW CAC COK CWM DBY EBA HVW NIC NRW OD RN TOJ VLW WCE WES WGW | 🌡 b, e, j, k |

Youngish, with an earthy, vegetal nose and soft, ripe peppery fruit. A good, light, well-balanced style for easy drinking.

331 CHATEAU DE MALIJAY, COTES DU RHONE, DOMAINE VITICOLES LISTEL C.S.M. 1990 Rhône (F)

| £3.99 | ☞ WMK | 🌡 e, j, k |

Flavours of smoke, treacle and just a touch of green pepper.

332 VIN DE PAY DES COLLINES RHODANIENNES SYRAH, VERRIER 1990 Rhône (F)

| £4.05 | ☞ EVI | 🌡 e, j, k, m |

Robust, with a savoury, smoky nose and rich, long-lasting, cherry flavour.

333 SAINSBURY'S CROZES HERMITAGE Rhône (F)

| £4.55 | ☞ JS | 🌡 e, j, k, m |

Lovely, peppery Syrah on the nose and palate. Full, fruity and far classier than you might expect at this price.

334 STRATFORD ZINFANDEL (Cal)

| £4.65 | ☞ MWW TO VW | 🌡 e, i, j, k |

Last year's Wine of the Year, now in a non-vintage blend. More proof that Englishman Tony Cartlidge can produce a bargain red packed with flavours of raspberries, plums and fresh, green pepper.

335 COTES DU RHONE DOMAINE DE TERRE BRULEE, CAVE DE VIGNERONS DE RASTEAU 1990 Rhône (F)

| £4.89 | ☞ AMW COK CVR D BY ECK P TOJ WGW | 🌡 e, i, j, k |

A lightly smoky wine with lots of intense, curranty fruit.

336 ZINFANDEL, FETZER VINEYARDS 1990 Mendocino County (Cal)

| £5.29 | ☞ ABY ABY BBR CAC CPS CPW CVR DBY GI HVW J&B JFD LAV OD RIB SAC SAF SOM TOJ VLW WIN WOC | 🌡 e, j, k |

A spicy, berryish and delicious example of California's 'own' grape.

337 GALWAY SHIRAZ, YALUMBA WINERY 1991 Barossa Valley (Aus)

| £5.75 | ☞ HPD LAV VDV WIN | 🌡 e, j, k, q |

An immediately approachable wine, with bags of raspberry fruit.

338 CROZES HERMITAGE ROUGE, JEAN-MARIE BORJA 1990 Rhône (F)

| £5.85 | ☞ CT YAP | 🌡 e, j, k |

Lovely wine with a smoky nose and crunchy youthful fruit.

339 BOTOBOLAR VINEYARD SHIRAZ, GIL WAHLQUIST 1990 Mudgee (Aus)

£5.99	☛ NY VDV VR	♡ e, i, j, k

Big, mature, meaty and smoky organic wine from an up-and-coming region.

340 COTES DU RHONE, DOMAINE ST. APOLLINAIRE, CUVEE CEPAGE SYRAH, FREDERIC DAUMAS 1990 Rhone (F)

£5.99	☛ ORG VR	♡ e, i, j, k

Fragrant, powerful, classy organic Syrah, with tar and violets galore.

341 KANONKOP PINOTAGE, VAN LOVEREN 1989 Stellenbosch (SA)

£6.75	☛ CAP COR COR WEP STW	♡ b, c, e, j

A great example of a grape variety that's almost unique to South Africa. Soft, ripe and lingering.

342 PETER LEHMANN 'CLANCY'S RED' 1990 Barossa Valley (Aus)

£6.99	☛ BBR BOO COK DBY ECK HOU JEH JS OD POR ROD VDV	
		♡ e, i, j, k

From the 'King of the Barossa', this is a big, gutsy wine, with an interestingly savoury, oaky character.

343 CUVEE DE L'ECU, CHATEAU DU GRAND MOULAS 1992 Rhône (F)

£7.29	☛ ADN TAN	♡ e, i, j

Young and intense, with damsons, spicy plums and sweetly satisfying length.

344 CROZES HERMITAGE LA PETITE RUCHE, CHAPOUTIER 1991 Rhône (F)

£7.49	☛ DIR MWW OD RIB TAN VLW	♡ e, i, j, k

Chapoutier used to have an unearned reputation for good winemaking; today it is deserved. This is classic, earthy, smoky, berryish Syrah.

345 ST JOSEPH, CAVES DE SAINT DESIRAT 1989 Rhône (F)

£7.85	☛ CVR W	♡ e, i, j, k

A strong, spicy wine with, full, rich, juicy fruit and soft, ripe tannins.

346 CHATEAU MUSAR, BEKAA VALLEY 1986 Bekaa Valley (Leb)

£8.25	☛ WIDELY AVAILABLE	♡ e, j, k

Still a classic, with mature, earthy, plummy richness. Perfect for lovers of old fashioned Rhônes.

347 ST. JOSEPH, COTE DIANE, CAVE CO-OPERATIVE DE ST. DESIRAT 1989 Rhône (F)

£8.25	☛ BU TH WR YAP	♡ e, j, m

Lovely oaky, cherryish Syrah. A great wine that will keep.

348 ROSEMOUNT SHOW RESERVE SYRAH 1990 McLaren Vale (Aus)

£8.25	☛ AF AMW BH BOO BU CEB DBW DBY GRT HOU HVW HW JN LWE NAD POR R SAN TH TOJ WNS WR	
		♡ e, i, j, k

Deliciously rich, modern wine; inky purple, with a pure spice nose, soft, ripe, plummy fruit and tannin and a very peppery finish.

349 ZINFANDEL, DRY CREEK VINEYARDS 1990 Sonoma (Cal)

£8.25	☛ BH DIR FV LAV WIN	♡ e, i, j, k

Richly full of brambly fruit and spice with some eucalyptus.

350 BROKENWOOD SHIRAZ 1991 South East Australia (Aus)

£8.49	☛ AUC BOO H&H LV LWE NY	♡ e, i, j, k

Hunter Valley Shiraz at its best: fruity, smoky and leathery (or 'sweaty saddley' if you prefer).

£7.49   ST HALLETT'S   SHIRAZ.   THRESHERS ✓

☛	For an explanation of the stockist abbreviations, see page 16
♡	For an explanation of the food style codes, see page 67

Excellent wine, strong fruit flavours, some pepper.

351 QUIVIRA ZINFANDEL 1989 Sonoma (Cal)

£8.75	☞ ABB ADN	↻ b, e, i, j

Creamy, youthful, deliciously fruity Zinfandel with sweet spice and a touch of green pepper.

352 PENLEY ESTATE SHIRAZ/CABERNET SAUVIGNON, COONAWARRA 1990 Coonawarra (Aus)

£8.99	☞ AUC BWS L&W NY PON POR WTR	↻ e, i, j

Beautifully balanced wine with lovely minty aromas and plenty of upfront, juicy, fruit and coffee flavours.

353 DAVID WYNN PATRIARCH SHIRAZ 1991 Eden Valley (Aus)

£9.49	☞ ADN BH BOO BU CHF FV HEM HVW NY PLA POR RIB SOM TH	
TOJ WR		↻ b, e, i, j, m

Lovely, rich mouthful, with a delicate, cherry nose, masses of sweet, mulberry fruit and an excellent finish. Silky and very attractive.

354 CHATEAUNEUF DU PAPE, PIERRE ANDRE 1990 Rhône (F)

£9.50	☞ OD VER VR	↻ e, i, j, m

Rich, velvety, organic wine, with mulberries and smoky bacon, plenty of ripe, mellow fruit and firm, peppery tannins.

355 ST JOSEPH GRISIERES, A PERRET 1990 Rhône (F)

£9.80	☞ J&B	↻ e, i, j, m

Lovely, spicy, eucalyptus nose, with rich cinnamon and blackcurrants.

356 CHATEAUNEUF DU PAPE, DOMAINE ANDRE BRUNEL 1989 Rhône (F)

£9.99	☞ DBY GON JS	↻ b, e, j

Traditional Châteauneuf with full, soft, sweet fruit and a peppery finish.

357 QUPE SYRAH, BOB LINDQUIST 1991 Central Coast (Cal)

£9.99	☞ M&V NY OD RD SOM	↻ e, i, j

Fresh and exciting, with powerful, youthful spice and berry flavours.

358 FROG'S LEAP ZINFANDEL 1990 Napa Valley (Cal)

£10.50	☞ CEB L&W M&V RIB SOM	↻ e, i, j, k

Gutsy, refreshing and satisfying, with an earthy, aromatic nose, and soft, creamy summer pudding fruit - with a hint of bell peppers.

359 LAWSON'S SHIRAZ, ORLANDO WINES PTY LTD 1987 South Australia (Aus)

£10.50	☞ AUC JCK	↻ e, i, j, k

Highly concentrated, spicy wine with deliciously smooth peppery fruit and new oak. Creamy, mellow and very elegant; built for a long life.

360 ST JOSEPH L'OLIVAIE, P COURSODON 1991 Rhône (F)

£10.99	☞ BU	↻ e, i, j, m

Classy, smoky, with meaty aromas, lovely fresh fruit and oak. To keep.

361 GEORGIA'S PADDOCK, JASPER HILL SHIRAZ 1990 Victoria (Aus)

£11.70	☞ ADN	↻ b, c, j

Subtle wine with a delicately oaked nose, lovely, long-lasting ripe fruit flavours and soft, dusty tannin.

362 CORNAS LA GEYNALE, R. MICHEL 1990 Rhône (F)

£12.50	☞ WSO	↻ e, i, j, k

Absolutely classic. Deep colour; a delicious jammy nose; lovely, long lasting liquorice, violets and berry flavours. A great wine.

363 RIDGE GEYSERVILLE ZINFANDEL 1991 Sonoma (Cal)

£13.25	☞ ADN BH CPW DBY GEL JN LAV NI OD SOM WIN	
		↻ e, i, j, k, m

Luscious, long and warming, with a beautiful, sweet fruit nose. A rich cocktail of nutmeg, cinnamon, vanilla spice and ripe, plummy fruit.

364	**CHATEAUNEUF DU PAPE, CHATEAU DE BEAUCASTEL 1988** Rhône (F)
£13.25	☞ ADN CEB COK DBY GH GON HOT HVW JN LV PON RBS SEB
TAN WAC WCE WTL	🌓 e, i, j, k

Mature, mushroomy, farmyardy nose, rich, earthy flavours, and plenty of berry fruit and green pepper to add complexity. Fascinating, organic stuff from the 'Château Latour of Châteauneuf'.

365	**PENFOLDS MAGILL ESTATE SHIRAZ 1988** South Australia (Aus)
£13.25	☞ ABY ADN AF AUC BOO BU CHE CPW CWW DBW DBY ECK HOU
JAG JEH LWE OD POR SAF SOM TH WR	🌓 b, c, j, m

Penfolds Grange's younger brother: creamy, mellow and succulent, with a hint of blackcurrant Spangles.

366	**COTE ROTIE SEIGNEUR DU MAUGIRON, DELAS FRERES 1987** Rhône (F)
£13.50	☞ EVI FV	🌓 b, c, e, j

From a light vintage, a soft, fruity wine with a minty spicy nose.

367	**CORNAS, AUGUSTE CLAPE 1990** Rhône (F)
£15.00	☞ DBY GON OD YAP	🌓 e, i, j, k

From the best-respected producer in Cornas: a strapping young wine with a full, peppery, blackcurrant nose and flavour. This one has everything, including potential for the future.

368	**COTE ROTIE, EMILE CHAMPET 1990** Rhône (F)
£15.25	☞ OD YAP	🌓 e, i, j, m

Fresh and juicy with loads of concentrated, smoky, berry fruit. Leave for a few years – if you have the patience.

369	**JADE MOUNTAIN SYRAH, DOUGLAS DANIELAK 1990** Sonoma (Cal)
£15.99	☞ CEB ECK M&V MWW RD SAN SOM	🌓 e, i, j, k

Stunning wine, with a superb, perfumed, peppery nose and creamy oak.

370	**YARRA YERING SHIRAZ NO.2 1990** Yarra Valley (Aus)
£16.50	☞ ADN AF BEN BH CHF ECK FV NI NY OD R SOM
	🌓 e, i, j, k

Australian in its ripeness, but with a cedary flavour like a top class claret. Spicy, rich and mouthfilling.

371	**COTE ROTIE, GERIN 1990** Rhône (F)
£16.99	☞ BU TH WR WTR	🌓 e, i, j, k, m

A brilliant blend of spicy fruit and subtle oak. Peppery, creamy and intensely berryish.

372	**CLOS DE MOGADOR, COSTER DE SIURANA 1989** Priorato (Sp)
£19.95	☞ MOR NI	🌓 e, i, j, k, m

A Spanish answer to the wines of the Rhône. Rich, deep and intense, with a strong blackcurrant flavour.

Beaujolais

Beaujolais prices have begun to return to slightly more normal levels, after the madness of the past few years, but it is still impossible to find very much that is worth buying for less than a fiver. Which is why we are so delighted to have found a really good, affordable alternative from Australia which ought to give the Beaujolais makers a little food for thought. The pricier Beaujolais *crus* we've recommended really are worth paying a little extra for.

(Arg) = Argentina; (Au) = Austria; (Aus) = Australia; (Bul) = Bulgaria; (Cal) = California; (Ch) = Chile;; (F) = France; (G) = Germany; (Gr) = Greece; (Hun) = Hungary; (Is) = Israel; (It) = Italy; (Mad) = Madeira; (Mex) = Mexico; (NZ) = New Zealand; (P) = Portugal; (SA) = South Africa; (Slo) = Slovakia; (Sp) = Spain; (UK) = United Kingdom; (US) = USA, excluding California

373	TARRANGO, BROWN BROTHERS 1992 Milawa (Aus)	
£4.99	AB ABY AMA AUC BTH CWS DBY DIR GNW HOU LWE MWW	
NAD NRW SAN VDV W WOC WRW		b, c, j, k

Aussie Beaujolais! Lovely vivid colour, with an almost floral, orangey nose. The flavour is orangey too, with more than a hint of boiled sweets.

374	BEAUJOLAIS VILLAGES, JEAN-LOUIS REVILLON 1991 Beaujolais (F)	
£5.49	VT	e, i, j, k

Delicious, deep, inky purple wine with plenty of black cherry flavour.

375	MACON-BRAY, DOMAINE DE LA COMBE, HENRI LAFARGE 1991 Burgundy (F)	
£5.79	BU TH WR	e, i, j, k, m

An unusual example of a wine which is often all-too forgettable. Lovely and gutsy, with loads of summer pudding fruit.

376	BROUILLY, GEORGES DUBOEUF 1991 Burgundy (F)	
£5.99	G L&W SAF	b, c, d, e, j

Typical, fresh raspberry/redcurrancy wine. Beaujolais as it ought to be.

377	CHENAS, DOMAINE DE CHASSIGNOL, JACQUES DEPAGNEUX 1992 Beaujolais (F)	
£5.99	BOO DBY HOU TOJ WES WNS	b, c, d, j

Mouthwateringly fruity, real Beaujolais. Tastes of ripe strawberries with a hint of bubble-gum.

378	JULIENAS, CHATEAU DES CAPITANS, SARRAU 1991 Beaujolais (F)	
£6.45	JS	b, c, i, j

Serious, quite old-fashioned Beaujolais, with big, mulberryish flavours.

379	FLEURIE, CLOS DE LA CHAPELLE DES BOIS, FERNAND VERPOIX 1991 Beaujolais (F)	
£7.25	A CPW	b, c, e, j

Supple and interesting with vibrant fruit, and length and depth to develop.

380	COTE DE BROUILLY, DOMAINE DE LA VOUTE DES CROZES 1991 Beaujolais (F)	
£7.45	L&W	b, c, e, j

A very youthful, archetypical Beaujolais; deep purple and full of floral appeal. Richly fruity, with a bit of spice.

381	CHENAS, LOUIS CHAMPAGNON 1991 Beaujolais (F)	
£7.50	CPW M&V NI SPG	b, e, i, j, m

Wonderfully aromatic Beaujolais with loads of intense fruit flavour.

Burgundy and other Pinot Noirs

Just as red Burgundy makers are benefitting from a series of good vintages denied to Bordeaux, Pinot Noir makers in the New World are perfecting their art quicker than the French would never have dreamed.

382	MACON ROUGE, LES VIGNERONS A IGE 1992 Burgundy (F)	
£3.89	SAF	b, c, j, m

Soft, plummy wine with rich, summery flavours.

383	MACON SUPERIEUR, CHAMPCLOS, PHILIPPE ANTOINE 1991 Burgundy (F)	
£4.25	VIL	c, e, i, j

Middleweight, unusually well made Mâcon with smooth, ripe, spicy fruit.

384	STRATFORD PINOT NOIR (Cal)	
£4.89	VW	e, i, j

From the maker of the Zinfandel which was last year's Red Wine of the Year. Clean, smooth, stylish and packed with ripe raspberry fruit.

385 HAUTES COTES DE BEAUNE, TETE DU CUVEE, CAVES DES HAUTES COTES 1990 Burgundy (F)

£5.95	☛ DIR GI W	🍶 e, i, j, m

Young wine with classic Pinot raspberry flavour with a dash of oak.

386 MARSANNAY, JEAN GARNIER 1989 Burgundy (F)

£6.35	☛ G	🍶 b, c, e, j

From a recently created appellation just outside Dijon. Attractive, light, redcurranty wine.

387 CAMERON PINOT NOIR Willamette Valley (US)

£6.98	☛ BI PON WCE	🍶 e, i, j

One of Oregon's best producers has made this ripe, slightly oaky, mulberryish wine. A match for many Burgundy villages.

388 SAFEWAY BEAUNE, LUC JAVELOT 1989 Burgundy (F)

£6.99	☛ SAF	🍶 c, e, j

From Labouré Roi under another name, a middleweight wine with the characteristic rose-petal and raspberry smell and flavour of Beaune.

389 HAMILTON-RUSSELL PINOT NOIR, WALKER BAY 1991 Walker Bay (SA)

£7.25	☛ AF AV BH CAP COK COR COR CPS CPW CVR CWS DBY DIR EBA HEM JEH JFD L&W LEA LV LWE MM POR PRW RBS RIB RTW TAN VLW WAW WOC	🍶 e, i, j, m

Advertising mogul Tim Hamilton-Russell more or less invented South African Pinot Noir in the continent's southernmost vineyard. A substantial wine with smoky-meaty flavours and sweet fruit.

390 BOURGOGNE PINOT NOIR, DOMAINE JEAN MARC MOREY 1990 Burgundy (F)

£7.99	☛ D	🍶 b, c, e, j

Classy, with soft mellow fruit and toasty oak. Real Côte de Beaune style.

391 BOURGOGNE PINOT NOIR, DOMAINE PARENT 1990 Burgundy (F)

£7.99	☛ CAC CVR ES GHS GRT H&D LWE OD TAN	🍶 e, i, j, m

Domaine Parent is the oldest family winery in France. This is an intense, characterful, very typical, raspberryish Pinot.

392 SAFEWAY NUITS ST. GEORGES, LABOURE-ROI 1990 Burgundy (F)

£8.99	☛ SAF	🍶 e, i, j, q

Young wine with lots of potential. Good depth of easy-drinking fruit and vanilla oak.

393 SANCERRE ROUGE, A DEZAT 1990 Loire (F)

£9.10	☛ BBR CPS CPW JN SHJ TAN	🍶 e, i, j

Lovely, fresh Pinot Noir, with ripe fruit and spicy oak.

394 COLDSTREAM HILLS PINOT NOIR 1992 Yarra Valley (Aus)

£9.45	☛ AB AUC BWC CPW CVR CWS HW JAR JN PON POR TO	🍶 e, i, j, k

James Halliday, lawyer, wine writer, taster and maker extraordinary, has produced a wonderful cocktail of floral perfume, raspberries, strawberries, peppery spice and sweet oak. Delicious now but worth waiting for.

395 STONIER'S MERRICKS PINOT NOIR 1991 Mornington Peninsula (Aus)

£9.99	☛ LWE WAW	🍶 c, e, j

Gentle wine, smooth and light, with oak, spice and blackberry flavours and a creamy finish.

☛	For an explanation of the stockist abbreviations, see page 16
🍶	For an explanation of food style codes, see page 67

396 SAINTSBURY PINOT NOIR 1991 Carneros (Cal)

£10.29	☛ ADN BH BI FUL J&B TO	🍷 c, e, j

From California's top Pinophiles: a soft, light and well balanced young wine with a future. Plenty of fruit, pepper and mint.

397 MERCUREY, 1ER CRU, CLOS DE MYGLANDS, FAIVELEY 1991 Burgundy (F)

£10.99	☛ AB FUL FV VLW	🍷 c, e, j, m

Made by Faivelay, one of Burgundy's most reliable merchants. Lovely soft, savoury wine with lots of lush fruit, good acidity and length.

398 MONTHELIE, JAFFELIN 1990 Burgundy (F)

£10.99	☛ C&A GNW GRT JAV OD RIB	🍷 e, i, j

From the village neighbouring Volnay, this is a fruity, oaky wine which needs another couple of years.

399 SAVIGNY LES BEAUNE, 1ER CRU AUX GUETTES, DOMAINE PAVELOT 1989 Burgundy (F)

£11.39	☛ D DD	🍷 e, i, j, k

A classy wine from an underrated village. Earthy, rich and ripe with some firm tannin in the background.

400 NEUDORF VINEYARDS MOUTERE PINOT NOIR 1991 Nelson (NZ)

£11.75	☛ ADN BH CHF NI RAM SOM	🍷 e, i, j, k

A very distinctive wine from a little-known region of the South Island of New Zealand. Young, complex and well-made, with fragrant, fruity flavours and hints of bitter chocolate.

401 FIXIN, LOUIS JADOT 1989 Burgundy (F)

£13.69	☛ BU TH WR	🍷 c, e, j

An unusually delicate wine from a village known for tougher fare. Very typical Burgundy with a long finish.

402 BEAUNE 1ER CRU TEURONS, DOMAINE ROSSIGNOL TRAPET 1990 Burgundy (F)

£13.75	☛ ABY CT FV	🍷 e, i, j

Beautiful, deep and long wine with intense, complex, fruit salad flavours and lots of fresh, wild raspberries.

403 NUITS SAINT GEORGES, DOMAINE DE L'ARLOT 1990 Burgundy (F)

£15.00	☛ ABY HR JAR L&W	🍷 e, i, j, k

Exotically heady and rich, with complex, spicy licorice flavours. Great new-wave Burgundy.

404 ROBERT MONDAVI RESERVE PINOT NOIR 1988 Napa Valley (Cal)

£16.50	☛ BEN CWW LV MM MZ RIB WOC	🍷 e, i, j, k, m

A complex wine with lovely, rich fruitcake nose and flavour. Brilliant.

405 BEAUNE 1ER CRU EPENOTTES, VALLET FRERES 1989 Burgundy (F)

£17.50	☛ COK DBY ECK NRW POR TOJ WGW	🍷 e, i, j, m

Serious, traditional Burgundy with mature raspberry fruit and oak. Quite lean and well worth keeping.

406 NUITS ST GEORGES 1ER CRU 'LES PRULIERS', DOMAINE LUCIEN BOILLOT ET FILS 1990 Burgundy (F)

£19.95	☛ BI CT	🍷 e, i, j, k

Oaky, rich, and ripe, with a fascinating herby note. To keep.

407 GEVREY CHAMBERTIN, DOMAINE ALAIN BURGUET, VIEILLES VIGNES 1988 Burgundy (F)

£20.75	☛ D HR	🍷 e, i, j, k

Rich, fleshy Burgundy with unusual intensity. Long and juicy with super, summer fruit and gamey, spicy complexity.

408 NUITS ST GEORGES 'CLOS DE L'ARLOT', DOMAINE DE L'ARLOT 1988 Burgundy (F)

| £22.95 | ☛ ABY BWI HOT HR L&W | ʊ e, i, j, k |

From a tiny punchbowl vineyard: a fine, complex wine with a rich, berry nose and multi-layered tastes of summer fruits, hung game and spice.

409 CORTON CLOS DU ROY, DUBREUIL FONTAINE 1990 Burgundy (F)

| £25.50 | ☛ ABY H&H TRW | ʊ c, e, j |

Supple and complex; lovely, pure fruit balanced by sweet oak.

Italian reds

We are still being asked to subsidize designer labels, but the wines have never tasted better - and there are more good, affordable examples on offer. Mind you, we've also found a great *Italian-style* wine from Mexico...

410 CORTENOVA MERLOT, PASQUA 1991 Grave Friuli (It)

| £2.95 | ☛ G MWW VW | ʊ e, i, j, k |

Juicy and refreshing, peppery, spicy wine with lots of tannin.

411 TESCO INTERNATIONAL WINEMAKER BASILICATA ROSSO, JACQUES LURTON 1992 Basilicata (It)

| £2.99 | ☛ TO | ʊ e, i, j, k, m |

Made by Jacques Lurton of Bordeaux (and just about everywhere else), this is characterful stuff with concentrated ripe fruit.

412 TESCO MONICA DI SARDEGNA, DOLIANOVA Sardinia (It)

| £3.29 | ☛ TO | ʊ c, e, i, j |

Soft and supple wine with good fruit and a gentle, fresh bite.

413 MONTEPULCIANO D'ABRUZZO, DOC, UMANI RONCHI 1991 Marches (It)

| £3.99 | ☛ BU CEL CPS CWS CWW GLY GRT JAG JN LV PON SAC TDS TH UBC V&C VIL VW WL WOI WR | ʊ e, i, j, k |

Extraordinary value wine with tobaccoey, woody, spicy flavours.

414 DOLCETTO D'ASTI, ARALDICA 1992 Piedmont (It)

| £4.15 | ☛ ABY BEN BOO CNL CPW CWI DBY EE HPD LEA NRW NY OD POR RAM SAF SAN SOM V&C WCE WGW | ʊ e, i, j, m |

Juicy, ripe, long and inspiring, with an unusual blackberry flavour.

415 VALPOLICELLA CLASSICO, MASI 1991 Veneto (It)

| £4.75 | ☛ AB ABY CPY CUM DBY DIR G&M NY OD WBM | |
| | | ʊ d, e, j |

Fresh young cherryish Valpolicella. Why doesn't it all taste like this?

416 SALICE SALENTINO RISERVA, AZ. AG. TAURINO 1988 Puglia (It)

| £5.25 | ☛ CWS G LAV SAF SAN V&C WIN WOC | ʊ e, j, k |

Rich, blackcurranty and ripe cherryish, with green pepper freshness.

417 TESCO CHIANTI CLASSICO RISERVA, CASTELLI DE GREVEPESA 1988 Tuscany (It)

| £5.49 | ☛ TO | ʊ c, j, q |

Easy-going wine, full of the intense flavours of morello cherries.

418 VERNACULUM ZOCCOLANTI-PERGOLA, VILLA LIGI 1992 Umbria (It)

| £6.79 | ☛ ABY DAL SAN V&C PON | ʊ c, j, m |

Extraordinary wine, with a raspberry nose and dry, strawberry flavour.

(Arg) = Argentina; (Au) = Austria; (Aus) = Australia; (Bul) = Bulgaria; (Cal) = California; (Ch) = Chile;; (F) = France; (G) = Germany; (Gr) = Greece; (Hun) = Hungary; (Is) = Israel; (It) = Italy; (Mad) = Madeira; (Mex) = Mexico; (NZ) = New Zealand; (P) = Portugal; (SA) = South Africa; (Slo) = Slovakia; (Sp) = Spain; (UK) = United Kingdom; (US) = USA, excluding California

419 BARBERA D'ALBA VIGNOTA, CONTERNO E FANTINO 1991 Piedmont (It)

£7.20	☛ LAV SAN WIN	♡ c, d, e, j

Light yet ripe, with a tremendous depth of sweet, cherryish fruit.

420 SANTO TOMAS BARBERA (Mex)

£7.85	☛ ECK	♡ e, i, j, k

Classic Italian style from Mexico! Spicy, with flavours of vanilla and cherry.

421 SER GIOVETO, VINO DA TAVOLA, ROCCA DELLE MACIE 1989 Tuscany (It)

£7.85	☛ AB CWS JN UBC V&C WL	♡ e, i, k

Mature wine with fascinating flavours of tomatoes, herbs and spices.

422 CHIANTI CLASSICO, ISOLE E OLENA 1990 Tuscany (It)

£8.29	☛ ABY ADN BEN BOO CEB CWI DBY ECK GI GON GRT HAM HEM HLV HOT HOU HVW HW JN LEA NRW NY PON POR RAM RD RTW SAN SEB UBC V&C WCE WGW WSO	♡ e, i, j, k, m

Superstar Chianti with berry fruit, peppery tannin. Should develop well.

423 CARMIGNANO, CAPEZZANA 1987 Tuscany (It)

£8.75	☛ ABY BWS CNL ECK HAM LEF NRW RTW V&C	♡ e, j, q

A very quaffable cross between Italian Cabernet and Chianti.

424 DOLCETTO D'ALBA CORSINI, MASCARELLO 1991 Piedmont (It)

£8.99	☛ BOO BU DBY EVI GON OD PHI PON RD THP V&C WCE WGW	♡ e, i, j

A wine with a future. Rich and full of plummy fruit, with a delicious, buttery, flowery style.

425 LE SASSINE, LE RAGOSE 1988 Veneto (It)

£8.99	☛ AF LWE PHI V&C	♡ e, i, j, k

Mature and complex, with nuts, ripe fruit and gentle tannic finish.

426 FREISA DELLE LANGHE, G D VAJRA 1990 Piedmont (It)

£9.49	☛ ABY ECK FWC GON V&C WCE WGW	♡ e, i, j, k

Made from a very unusual grape, this is packed with the intense flavours of cherries and black grapes.

427 CUMARO ROSSO CONERO, UMANI RONCHI 1989 Marches (It)

£9.50	☛ AMA BH BTH C&B CHF DBY FWC GNW HEM JN LV MM RD UBC V&C	♡ e, j, k

Rich, ripe, warm country wine. Attractive, fruity and well-balanced.

428 BRIC MILEUI, ASCHERI 1990 Piedmont (It)

£9.99	☛ ABY BOO CWI D DBW DBY EVI NY OD POR SOM V&C WCE	♡ e, i, j, m

Dense, rich, sweetly fruity wine opening out wonderfully in the mouth.

429 BAROLO RISERVA, BORGOGNO 1985 Piedmont (It)

£10.99	☛ HPD P RBS THP V&C	♡ e, i, j, m

Classic, very old fashioned Barolo from a good vintage. Still pretty tannic, but with plenty of tobaccoey fruit. One for the traditionalists.

430 RUBESCO RISERVA MONTICCHIO, LUNGAROTTI 1980 Umbria (It)

£14.95	☛ V&C	♡ e, i, j, k

Classic, Italian flavours, a tarry, coffee nose and loads of black cherries.

431 CABREO VIGNETO IL BORGO, RUFFINO 1987 Tuscany (It)

£18.95	☛ V&C	♡ e, i, j, k

Meaty, packed with soft ripe fruit. Needs food and/or time.

432 RECIOTO DELLA VALPOLICELLA, CASAL DEI RONCHI MASI 1988 Veneto (It)

£19.50	☛ AB DBY V&C	♡ e, i, j, k

Sweet, rich, very ripe, full and concentrated, with a characteristic bitter finish.

Iberian reds

Revolutions take place at varying speeds. The dragging of Spain's wine industry from a haven of obstinate conservatism into the 20th century is taking a very long time - especially compared to the speed at which Languedoc Roussillon is transforming itself into the Napa Valley of France. But modern winemaking and attitudes are being introduced - as they are in Portugal, thanks to the keenness of a couple of highly ambitious Australians.

433   LEZIRIA VINHO TINTO, VEGA CO-OPERATIVE ALMEIRIM 1992 Almeirim (P)

| £2.59 | ☛ AB BU G OD TDS TH VW WR | ℧ e, i, j, k |

Aromatic and spicy young wine which is doing for Portugal today what Mateus did 30 years ago.

434   SAINSBURY'S DO CAMPO TINTO, JP VINHOS Terras do Sado (P)

| £2.95 | ☛ JS | ℧ e, i, j |

Wonderful, rich, purple, Beaujolais-style by Australian-born Peter Bright.

435   SAINSBURY'S ARRUDA (P)

| £2.95 | ☛ JS | ℧ e, j, q, r |

Spicy, characterful berryish young red. Perfect for parties.

436   SAFEWAY CARINENA, BODEGAS COOP SAN VALERO 1988 Aragon (Sp)

| £3.35 | ☛ SAF | ℧ c, e, j, q, r |

Easy-drinking wine with lots of full, ripe, almost sweet fruit.

437   CISMEIRA DOURO 1991 Douro (P)

| £3.59 | ☛ CHF CUM EVI HAM VW WGW | ℧ b, c, e, j |

Wonderful, flavourful soft fruity wine. Full of youthful vigour.

438   ALBOR RIOJA TINTO, BODEGAS & BEBIDAS 1991 Rioja (Sp)

| £3.75 | ☛ BOO BU DBY ECK FV HOU HVW JCK NRW PHI POR TDS TH TOJ |
| | TRE WGW WOC WR | ℧ c, e, j, q |

Joint Red Wine of the Year

From the bodega which brought you the more traditional Campo Viejo, this is brilliantly-made, easy-drinking wine, with loads of plummy-strawberryish young Tempranillo flavour. Proof that Rioja doesn't have to have oak. _NOTHING SPECIAL FOR ME MORE OF merlot_

439   BORBA, ADEGA CO-OPERATIVE DE BORBA 1991 Douro (P)

| £3.99 | ☛ AB COK MOR OD RAV TO VW WCE | ℧ e, i, j, k |

Interesting, smooth yet spicy wine, with lots of berry fruit.

440   TESCO TORO RED, FARINAS 1990 Toro (Sp)

| £3.99 | ☛ TO | ℧ e, i, j, k |

Dry, intense, full-bodied wine with plenty of sweet oak and blackcurrant fruit, and a rich, long finish.

441   SOMERFIELD RIOJA TINTO 1989 Rioja (Sp)

| £3.99 | ☛ G | ℧ e, i, j, k |

Soft, traditional Rioja with rich mature, rather solid, plummy fruit.

442   VALDEMAR RIOJA TINTO, MARTINEZ BUJANDA 1992 Rioja (Sp)

| £4.49 | ☛ BU DBY JN TH WR WSC | ℧ e, i, j, k, m |

Dark purple, powerful wine with plenty of fruit, wood and tannin. The new face of Rioja and a wine to teach many a St Emilion a lesson.

| ☛ | For an explanation of the stockist abbreviations, see page 16 |
| ℧ | For an explanation of food style codes, see page 67 |

443	QUINTA DE LA ROSA RED TABLE WINE 1991 Douro (P)	
£4.75	☛ AF BBR CWM GEL HAM LV LWE M&V NY PON RAV SAN SOM THC WCE WGW WRK	🍷 e, i, j, k

More Aussie winemaking, from former Dows Port-maker, David Baverstock. Young, spicy, and peppery with a touch of cream, a lovely, smoky, oaky bouquet and a good firm finish.

444	PERIQUITA, J M DA FONSECA 1990 (P)	
£4.79	☛ AMA BOO BU CHF DBY EE EVI G&M MFW NY OD POR RAE RBS RWC SHG SWB TAN TO WBM WL WOC WR WRW WWT	🍷 e, i, j, k, m

Peppery, characterful (old) woody stuff, made from a grape unknown outside Portugal.

445	MEIA PIPA, J P VINHOS 1989 (P)	
£4.99	☛ BU OD TH WR	🍷 b, c, e, j

Light and pleasing with a delicate colour, clean structure and good finish.

446	TERRAS DEL REI RESERVA, CO-OP AGRICOLA DE REGUENGOS DE MONSARAZ 1988 Alentejo (Sp)	
£4.99	☛ D	🍷 e, i, j, k

Powerful, sweet oaky wine, with soft, gentle fruit and spice.

447	CAMPO VIEJO RIOJA RESERVA 1987 Rioja (Sp)	
£5.25	☛ AMA BEN BOO BU CEL CPS DBY ECK GRT HOU HVW MOR MRN OD POR TDS TH TOJ TRE WBM WGW WOC WR	🍷 e, i, j, k, m

Flavours of redcurrants, well integrated with vanilla and oak. Smooth and mature. Drink it now.

448	CARTUXA, FUNDACO E ALMEIDA 1989 Evora (P)	
£5.99	☛ BOO BU CWS DBY POR TH WGW WR	🍷 e, i, j, k

Deep ruby; full-bodied with a vanilla nose, sweet briary attack and dry finish.

449	ESPORAO, HERDADE DE ESPORAO 1989 Alentejo (P)	
£5.99	☛ OD	🍷 e, j, m

Another success from David Baverstock. Youthful, creamy, fruit-packed wine, with a long finish.

450	YLLERA, VINO DE MESA, SAT LOS CURRO 1988 Ribera del Duero (Sp)	
£6.79	☛ AF AMW BOO BU DBY LWE PHI POR RAM RBS RIB TH VDV WBM WR	🍷 e, j, k

Lovely, maturing wine, full of soft, deep fruit. Not for keeping.

451	COTO DE IMAZ RIOJA RESERVA 1985 Rioja (Sp)	
£6.89	☛ D JCK TRE	🍷 e, j, k, m

Mature and full of mulberry fruit, chewy tannins and balanced acidity.

452	BARON DE LEY RIOJA RESERVA 1987 Rioja (Sp)	
£6.95	☛ BU PON TH WR	🍷 c, e, j

Classy, soft and long with plummy, fruitcake flavour and a gentle finish.

453	JOAO PATO TINTO, VINHO DE MESA 1990 Bairrada (P)	
£6.99	☛ BOO BU TH WGW WR	🍷 e, i, j

From one of Portugal's top producers: a bright ruby wine, with a perfumed, rich, berry-fruit nose, and noticeable vanilla and oak.

454	125 ANIVERSARIO NAVARRA GRAN RESERVA, BODEGAS JULIAN CHIVITE 1985 Navarra (Sp)	
£8.50	☛ COK CWI DIR RTW	🍷 e, i, j, k

Characterful, full-bodied, with strawberry flavours and plenty of spicy fruit. Should be drunk soon.

*455-99 TORRES GRAN SANGREDETORO
Garnacha and another local red. Full-bodied and flavoured
V. Good* ✓

455 REMELLURI RIOJA CRIANZA 1989 Rioja (Sp)		
£9.25	☛ ADN BI MOR TAN	🍷 e, i, j

Appealing, youthful wine with ripe, full, chewy, cooked fruit flavours. Needs a few years to become a classic.

Muscats

Hedonists of the world unite! This section is for everyone who admits to enjoying the sort of wine the Health Fascists most heartily despise. Yes, these are richly indulgent, alcoholic and *sweet*. And highly recommendable.

456 SAINSBURYS MUSCAT DE ST JEAN DE MINERVOIS, VAL D'ORBIEU Midi (F)		
£2.99	☛ JS	🍷 o, q

Light straw-coloured with raisiny fruits and enough lemony-limey acidity to match the honeyed sweetness.

457 SAFEWAY MOSCATEL DE VALENCIA, GANDIA Central (Sp)		
£3.09	☛ SAF	🍷 n, o

Very powerful, intense wine, packed with flavours of honey, marmalade, fruit and spice.

458 MUSCAT OF PATRAS, ACHAIA CLAUSS (Gr)		
£3.79	☛ AMA MWW WOC	🍷 n, o

Intense, woody and fruity, with lemons and oranges. Rich, flavoursome and distinctive.

459 SAMOS NECTAR, SAMOS CO-OPERATIVE 1983 Samos (Gr)		
£5.75	☛ NI WCE	🍷 n, o

Concentrated, sweet and honeyed with flavours of raisins and lemons. Gloriously old-fashioned wine.

460 MOSCATEL PALIDO, MALAGA, SCHOLTZ HERMANOS SA Malaga (Sp)		
£6.67	☛ AF L&S	🍷 n, o, p, q

Rich, thick, raisiny flavours coat the mouth with toffee and caramel. A lovely, nursery treat for adults.

461 STANTON & KILLEEN RUTHERGLEN LIQUEUR MUSCAT Rutherglen (Aus)		
£10.25	☛ ABY AF AMW AUC BOO BU COK DAL DBY HOU HPD HVW LEA	
	LV LWE NI NY PHI PON POR RAE RAM SAN TH WCE WR	
		🍷 n, o, p, q

Intense and powerful dark Muscat, with a concentrated toffee nose, and mature caramel-and-raisin flavours. A proven aphrodisiac.

462 CAMPBELLS RUTHERGLEN LIQUEUR MUSCAT Rutherglen (Aus)		
£11.50	☛ ABB AF AMW AUC BNK BOO CNL CPW CVR DAL DBY HPD LWE	
	NI PHI PMR POR RAM RBS RD RIB WOM	🍷 n, o, q

Subtly complex with rich flavours of orange, crème brûlée and vanilla.

Botrytis and all that rot

More indulgent fare – this time in the form of wines made from grapes picked late and, ideally, affected by noble rot. This benevolent fungus which affects certain types of grape, in certain vineyards, and in certain years, gives wines an extraordinary intense flavour reminiscent of dried apricots.

463 SAINSBURYS AUSLESE BEREICH MITTELHAARDT, QMP, SICHEL 1990 Rhine (G)

£2.59	☛ JS	🍷 n, o

Intense and raisiny-rich, with fresh grapefruity acidity. Great value.

464 MONBAZILLAC DOMAINE DU HAUT RAULY, ALARD 1990 Bordeaux (F)

£3.49	☛ CWS	🍷 n, o

Luscious wine, full of peaches and mandarins, with good balancing acidity.

465 CHATEAU VALENTIN STE CROIX DU MONT, 1992 Bordeaux (F)

£3.99	☛ WMK	🍷 n, o

Honey and nuts, with good, tangy acidity. A great value alternative to Sauternes.

466 DOMAINE DE GARBES, PREMIERES COTES DE BORDEAUX 1990 Bordeaux (F)

£5.45	☛ G	🍷 n, o, q

Lovely, soft, honeyed wine with plenty of broad, ripe, fruit flavours.

467 VIN SANTO BROLIO ESTATE, BARONE RICASOLI 1984 Tuscany (It)

£5.70	☛ DBY ECK WGW	🍷 e, i, j, k

Italian 'sherry'; nutty, fruity and complex, with a strong orange flavour and dry finish. Perfect for dunking nut cookies.

468 NELSON LATE HARVEST RHINE RIESLING, SEIFRIED 1991 Nelson (NZ)

£6.50	☛ AF BBR BH CWS FNZ FWC GI HEM HVW HW JCK LEA LWE RBS RDWAW WSC WWT	🍷 n, o, q

Like liquid lemon-meringue-pie, with intense honey and lemon flavours.

469 CHATEAU DE BERBEC, PREMIERES COTES DE BORDEAUX 1989 Bordeaux (F)

£6.50	☛ BU NI OD RHV TH WR	🍷 n, o, q

Honeyed, mouthfilling wine with fresh, grassy acidity.

470 MONBAZILLAC, CHATEAU THEULET, SCEA ALARD 1990 Bordeaux (F)

£7.25	☛ BH CIW EE RBS	🍷 n, o

Rich and juicy, with toffee, peaches and almonds and just enough oak.

471 NEDERBURG WEISSER RIESLING NOBLE LATE HARVEST 1989 Paarl (SA)

£7.99	☛ CAP LWE	🍷 n, o

A complex blend of apricot, butterscotch and Old English marmalade.

472 NEETHLINGSHOF WEISSER RIESLING NOBLE LATE HARVEST 1991 (SA)

£8.75	☛ AB CAP DBY EVI FWC J&B LWE	🍷 n, o

Peachy, apricotty wine; luscious and very long.

473 CHATEAU DE ROLLAND, BARSAC 1990 Bordeaux (F)

£9.25	☛ MWW WRW	🍷 n, o

Rich, golden wine with a seductive honey nose and rich, thick, honeyed apricot flavours. A hint of grapefruit saves it from being cloying.

474 DINDARELLO, MACULAN 1992 Veneto (It)

£9.50	☛ CWI ODV&C	🍷 n, o

Fascinating wine with flavours of rhubarb and lemon. Very sweet and concentrated, but not in the least cloying.

475 BINGER BUBENSTUCK EHRENFELSER BEERENAUSLESE, LEOFF 1989 Rheinhessen (G)

£9.99	☛ WMK	🍷 n, o

Grapes, apricots and lychees. Very up-front. Very tasty.

476 KALLSTADER SAUMAGEN BEERENAUSLESE, WEINGUT UNDERICH 1990 Kallstader (G)

| £11.99 | ☛ NY | 🍴 n, o |

Tropical-fruit on the nose, luscious, full fruit and soft, balancing acidity.

477 DOMAINE DE NAYS-LABASSERE, JURANCON 1990 South West (F)

| £11.99 | ☛ VT | 🍴 n, o, q |

Pineappley, lemony-orangey wine from one of France's most traditional appellations.

478 MOULIN TOUCHAIS, COTEAUX DU LAYON 1983 Loire (F)

| £12.00 | ☛ MM MWW | 🍴 n, o |

Interesting, mature wine with flavours of apples, nuts and bananas.

479 VOUVRAY MOELLEUX, CLOS DU BOURG, GASTON HUET 1990 Loire (F)

| £21.75 | ☛ BI CPS JN L&W SHJ WSO | 🍴 n, o |

Big, rich, traditional Chenin Blanc, with flavours of apples, pears, honey and butterscotch.

Sherry

Every year, when preparing the *Guide* we dream of a day when sherry will retrieve its place in the affections of British wine drinkers. Sadly, that day seems as far off as ever; sales continue to drop and an increasing amount of dull, tiring sherry inevitably hangs around the shops. Take our advice; buy our recommendations - and try to be sure to get them from merchants with as brisk a trade as possible. That way, you should be sure to enjoy dry sherry at its fresh, tangy best.

480 TANNERS MARISCAL MANZANILLA, VINICOLA HIDALGO Jerez (Sp)

| £5.86 | ☛ TAN | 🍴 a, b, c |

Typically salty with a fresh, tangy, satisfying, long lasting flavour.

481 HIDALGO AMONTILLADO NAPOLEON Jerez (Sp)

| £6.50 | ☛ ADN CWM FUL G&M JN MFW MWW SHJ WBM WOC WOI |
| WSO | | 🍴 m, n, s |

Chocolate-scented with intense nutty flavours and a long dry finish.

482 LUSTAU OLD EAST INDIA, EMILIO LUSTAU Jerez (Sp)

| £8.99 | ☛ BBR CVR EVI FUL JEH MM POR | 🍴 n, o, q |

Wonderful wine with an intensely sweet burnt-caramel flavour.

483 1796 RICH OLD OLOROSO Jerez (Sp)

| £9.50 | ☛ AMA CWW FUL HV JAG JEH MM THP TP WOM |
| | | 🍴 n, o, q |

Rich and caramelly sherry, intensely concentrated, with dollops of sweet fruit and excellent acidity. Rich and delicious.

484 MATUSALEM, GONZALEZ BYASS Jerez (Sp)

| £18.99 | ☛ AB ADN AF AMA BEN BNK BU CEL CNL COK CWS DAL |
| DBW DBY EVI FUL JAG JEH JN L&S LAV LWE MM MTL NI OD PHI RAE |
| RBS RWC SAC SAF STW TH THP UBC V&C VLW WBM WOC WR |
| | | 🍴 n, o, q, s |

Rich, nutty, sweet-yet-dry classic, with gloriously long flavours of raisins, chocolate and caramel.

☛   For an explanation of the stockist abbreviations, see page 16
🍴   For an explanation of food style codes, see page 67

485 OSBORNE Y CIA PEDRO XIMENEZ Jerez (Sp)

£18.99	☛ BAR BH HEM	🍷 n, o, q

An extraordinary, ultra-concentrated, syrupy, wonderfully sweet and spicy wine, with plums and toffee apples.

Port and other fortified wines

The sort of wine English gentlemen used to drink, in the days when they were built differently and had room for a pint or two of port or Madeira after they'd polished off the claret and hock. Today, there are far fewer takers, which is a great pity because these are some of the most delicious wines in the world.

486 RIVESALTES, VIEILLE RESERVE, LES PRODUCTEURS DU MONT TAUCH 1980 Midi (F)

£7.20	☛ BU JEH STW WR	🍷 m, n

Lovely hedonistic Muscat with flavours of crème caramel and sweet oak.

487 TOKAJI ASZU 3 PUTTONYOS, TOKAJI-HEGYALA SCHLUMBERGER 1981 Tokaji (Hun)

£7.75	☛ A BAR BH CFT DBY DIR ES JFD RAV ROD SHG V&C WBM WGW WOM	🍷 m, n, o

Stylish, rich and balanced wine, smelling of honeycomb and butterscotch and tasting smooth and raisiny.

488 OLD TRAFFORD TAWNY, B. SEPPELT & SONS South East Australia (Aus)

£7.75	☛ ABY AMW BU COK DAL DBY HOU LWE NY PHI POR TH WR	🍷 m, n, q

Nutty Aussie 'port' with a rich, figgy, fruitcake quality.

489 CHURCHILL GRAHAM FINEST VINTAGE CHARACTER Douro (P)

£8.75	☛ ABY BH BWS COK CPW CVR D DBY EE FWC GH HEM HW LEA NAD PLA RAM RHV SV SV TAN WAC WSC	🍷 m, q

A rich purple classic with deep, serious flavours and a touch of tannin. An unusually good example of this style.

490 BOAL 5 YEAR OLD, D'OLIVEIRA (Mad)

£8.99	☛ G&M L&W SHJ WBM WOM	🍷 m, n, q

Lovely tangy, orangey-walnutty wine.

491 DOWS CRUSTED PORT BOTTLED 1987 Douro (P)

£10.75	☛ ABB AF BOO CPW L&W LWE NRW POR SEB VIL W WOC	🍷 m, q

A very classy alternative to Vintage Port. Concentrated damson and plum fruit. Needs decanting – and keeping.

492 COLHEITA, A A CALEM & FILHO 1985 Douro (P)

£10.99	☛ ABY CNL ECK OD TOJ V&C WSC	🍷 m, q

Deliciously spicy tawny, with lingering rich, raisiny fruit-and-nut flavours.

493 HENRIQUES & HENRIQUES 10 YEAR OLD VERDELHO (Mad)

£12.49	☛ DBY HAM MTL	🍷 m, q

Sheer extravagance. Nutty and intense, with a soft, toffee Bovril nose, mature flavours of spices and fruit cake and a hint of chocolate.

494 WARRE'S TRADITIONAL LBV 1981 Douro (P)

£12.99	☛ AB ABB ADN AMW BI BOO CAC CNL CPS CUM DIR EVI FV GEL GI HHC L&W MM OD POR RHV RIB SWB TAN VIL W WCE WOC WOI	🍷 m, q

'Traditional' means that unlike most LBV, this hasn't been filtered, so you'll need a decanter. Sweet, maturing and very classy.

495 GALWAY PIPE OLD TAWNY, YALUMBA WINERY Barossa Valley (Aus)

£13.50	☛ AUC BH LAV NY PHI RBS WCE WIN WOC	ひ m, q

Oaky, walnutty nose with aromas of candied orange and lemon peel. A sweet, lingering, rich and delicious wine with a hint of caramel.

496 TAYLOR'S TEN YEAR OLD TAWNY Douro (P)

£14.50	☛ ADN BEN BU CEL D DBY ES EVI FV JAV L&W MM MTL SHG SHJ
	TAN TH THP TP TRE V&C WOC WOM WR WRK WRW WTL
	ひ m, q

Bags of intense flavours of raisiny fruit and nuts. Drink it the way its makers sometimes savour it: well chilled on a warm summer afternoon.

497 NIEPOORT COLHEITA 1983 Douro (P)

£17.75	☛ BI BTH CWS DBW GON RAE WGW	ひ m, q

Great stuff - a single vintage wood-aged port from one of the best exponents of the style. Light, with delicate, mature character.

498 QUINTA DO VESUVIO VINTAGE PORT 1990 Douro (P)

£22.50	☛ ADN AF C&B CNL COK D DAL DIR GEL L&W LWE NI RTW V&C
	WOC WWT	ひ m, q

Big, chewy, inky, blackberryish stuff from a recently launched estate.

499 RUTHERFORD MILES MALVASIA SOLERA 1863 (Mad)

£45.00	☛ BU LV TH WR	ひ m, q

Wonderfully warm and enticing on the nose, with a hint of caramel. Deliciously rich and sweet, with lovely tangy fruit, coffee, raisins and dates, a fantastic texture and a long finish.

Low and non-alcohol wines

The Holy Grail of low alcohol wine remains stubbornly unattainable for most would-be producers. On balance, we'd almost always recommend a blend of fruit juice and mineral water instead of most lo-alc wine, but we're delighted to say that we've found one exception to the poor quality rule.

500 ELECTRA, QUADY WINERY 1991 Madera County (Cal)

£4.99	☛ ABY DBY JN MWW NI	ひ p, o

From the makers of the wonderful high-alcohol Essensia. Smells of gladioli; tastes rich and peary. Far from your Everage wine.

(Arg) = Argentina; (Au) = Austria; (Aus) = Australia; (Bul) = Bulgaria; (Cal) = California; (Ch) = Chile;; (F) = France; (G) = Germany; (Gr) = Greece; (Hun) = Hungary; (Is) = Israel; (It) = Italy; (Mad) = Madeira; (Mex) = Mexico; (NZ) = New Zealand; (P) = Portugal; (SA) = South Africa; (Slo) = Slovakia; (Sp) = Spain; (UK) = United Kingdom; (US) = USA, excluding California

THE STOCKISTS

ABB | Abbey Cellars

The Abbey, Preston Road, Yeovil, Somerset BA21 3AR (Tel 0935 76228 Fax 0935 410368).
Opening Hours: Tues-Fri 11.30am-6.00pm, Sat 10.00am-3.00pm. **Delivery:** free within 20 miles.
Tastings: occasional in-store. **Discounts:** negotiable on quantity.

Wine buyers who were previously required to buy from Abbey by the case, can now pick and choose single bottles from the excellent and innovative range of French Country, Rhône, New World and fine wines available by the bottle at their new retail outlet, Chard Fine Wines.

3	£5.99	SEGURA VIUDAS CAVA BRUT RESERVA Cava (Sp)
33	£28.85	BOLLINGER GRANDE ANNEE 1985 Champagne (F)
74	£4.99	PENFOLDS KOONUNGA HILL CHARDONNAY 1992 SE Australia (Aus)
79	£5.99	ROSEMOUNT CHARDONNAY 1992 Hunter Valley (Aus)
140	£4.79	CHATEAU LA BERTRANDE, AC BORDEAUX 1992 Bordeaux (F)
154	£5.99	VERDELHO, WYNDHAM ESTATE 1991 South East Australia (Aus)
244	£2.99	RUSSE CABERNET CINSAULT (Bul)
256	£4.49	HARDYS NOTTAGE HILL CABERNET SAUVIGNON 1991 South Australia (Aus)
272	£6.99	ROUGE HOMME CABERNET/SHIRAZ 1988 Coonawarra (Aus)
288	£7.29	CABERNET SAUVIGNON, BODEGA Y CAVAS DE WEINERT 1985 Mendoza (Arg)
346	£7.89	CHATEAU MUSAR, 1986 Bekaa Valley (Leb)
351	£8.39	QUIVIRA ZINFANDEL 1989 Sonoma (Cal)
462	£10.34	CAMPBELLS RUTHERGLEN LIQUEUR MUSCAT Rutherglen (Aus)
491	£11.49	DOWS CRUSTED PORT BOTTLED 1987 Douro (P)
494	£13.39	WARRE'S TRADITIONAL LBV 1981 Douro (P

ADN | Adnams Wine Merchants

The Crown, High Street, Southwold, Suffolk IP18 6DP (Tel 0502 724222 Fax 0502 724805).
Opening Hours: Southwold Mon-Sat 10am-6.30 pm; Norwich Mon-Sat 9 am-9 pm. **Delivery:** free locally, nationally for 2 cases or more. **Tastings:** in store tastings and tutored events. **Discounts:** 5% for 12 cases or more, £3 per case collection discount.

East of England and By-the Case/By Mail Wine Merchant of the Year

This is one of the most respected merchants in the country, so there was relief when the similarly popular Haughton Fine Wines needed a saviour, and found one in Simon Loftus. With the Haughtons' Australian and regional French wines on board, the new list offers an extraordinary range of characterful wines from just about everywhere. Adnams bin end sales are legendary, as are its sample cases, beer, kitchen ware, ties and Loftus's excellent book on Puligny Montrachet. Readers of the *Guide* are offered a special price on the new Adnams cricket-cum-wine-taster's blazer. Just say Bobby Jeaux sent you.

11	£7.70	MONTANA LINDAUER BRUT (NZ)
16	£8.75	YALUMBA SPARKLING CABERNET CUVEE PRESTIGE South East Australia (Aus)
20	£7.95	OMAR KHAYYAM, CHAMPAGNE INDIA 1987 Maharashtra (Ind)
24	£10.60	GREEN POINT, DOMAINE CHANDON 1990 Yarra Valley (Aus)

26	£13.95	LE MESNIL BLANC DE BLANCS Champagne (F)
32	£18.20	CHAMPAGNE HENRI BILLIOT Champagne (F)
33	£29.90	BOLLINGER GRANDE ANNEE 1985 Champagne (F)
43	£3.95	COTES DE ST MONT WHITE, PLAIMONT 1991 South West (F)
51	£4.95	CHARDONNAY 'VIRGINIE', VIN DE PAYS D'OC, SARL DOMAINE VIRGINIE LIEURAN 1992 Midi (F)
56	£5.40	SUNNYCLIFF CHARDONNAY 1992 Victoria (Aus)
65	£39.50	JERMANN PINOT BIANCO 1991 Friuli Venezia Giulia (It)
70	£4.55	TIMARA WHITE, MONTANA 1991 (NZ)
72	£4.20	CHASAN, DOMAINE SABLEYROLLE, VIN DE PAYS D'OC 1992 Midi (F)
74	£5.20	PENFOLDS KOONUNGA HILL CHARDONNAY 1992 South East Australia (Aus)
91	£7.95	MARQUES DE MURRIETA RIOJA RESERVA BLANCO 1987 Rioja (Sp)
98	£8.65	LOCAL GROWERS SEMILLON, ROCKFORD 1989 Barossa Valley (Aus)
105	£9.20	CULLENS SAUVIGNON BLANC 1991 Margaret River (Aus)
109	£11.20	MACON CLESSE, DOMAINE DE LA BONGRAN, J. THEVENET 1990 Burgundy (F)
110	£11.45	POMINO IL BENEFIZIO, MARCHESI DE FRESCOBALDI 1990 Tuscany (It)
112	£11.50	ELSTON CHARDONNAY, TE MATA ESTATE 1991 Hawkes Bay (NZ)
115	£14.75	NEWTON UNFILTERED CHARDONNAY 1990 Napa Valley (Cal)
119	£16.85	ROBERT MONDAVI RESERVE CHARDONNAY 1988 Napa Valley (Cal)
142	£4.75	OZIDOC SAUVIGNON, VIN DE PAYS D'OC, J & F LURTON 1992 Midi (F)
160	£7.65	VERNACCIA DI S. GIMIGNANO, PODERI MONTENIDOLI 1991 Tuscany (It)
161	£7.20	JACKSON ESTATE SAUVIGNON BLANC 1992 Marlborough (NZ)
162	£7.20	SELAKS MARLBOROUGH SAUVIGNON BLANC 1991 Marlborough (NZ)
183	£9.25	ARNEIS ROERO, MALVIRA 1992 Piedmont (It)
168	£8.40	SANCERRE LES ROCHES, DOMAINE VACHERON 1992 Loire (F)
188	£6.45	PETER LEHMANN SEMILLON 1992 Barossa Valley (Aus)
233	£3.75	MAS DE FIGARO VIN DE PAYS DE L'HERAULT, AIME GUIBERT 1992 Midi (F)
235	£4.95	DAVID WYNN DRY RED 1992 Eden Valley (Aus)
240	£9.50	MADIRAN, MONTUS, ALAIN BRUMONT 1990 South West (F)
263	£4.50	MERCHANT VINTNERS CLARET, PETER A SICHEL Bordeaux (F)
269	£5.50	MONTANA CABERNET SAUVIGNON 1991 Marlborough (NZ)
291	£7.50	CHATEAU LA TOUR HAUT-CAUSSAN, MEDOC 1989 Bordeaux (F)
309	£13.25	NEWTON MERLOT 1990 Napa Valley (Cal)
343	£7.20	CUVEE DE L'ECU, CHATEAU DU GRAND MOULAS 1992 Rhône (F)
346	£8.25	CHATEAU MUSAR, 1986 Bekaa Valley (Leb)
351	£8.95	QUIVIRA ZINFANDEL 1989 Sonoma (Cal)
353	£9.25	DAVID WYNN PATRIARCH SHIRAZ 1991 Eden Valley (Aus)
361	£11.70	GEORGIA'S PADDOCK, JASPER HILL SHIRAZ 1990 Victoria (Aus)
363	£14.50	RIDGE GEYSERVILLE ZINFANDEL 1991 Sonoma (Cal)
364	£13.50	CHATEAUNEUF DU PAPE, CHATEAU DE BEAUCASTEL 1988 Rhône (F)
365	£13.20	PENFOLDS MAGILL ESTATE SHIRAZ 1988 South Australia (Aus)
370	£16.95	YARRA YERING SHIRAZ NO.2 1990 Yarra Valley (Aus)
396	£7.20	SAINTSBURY PINOT NOIR 1991 Carneros (Cal)
400	£12.95	NEUDORF VINEYARDS MOUTERE PINOT NOIR 1991 Nelson (NZ)
422	£8.65	CHIANTI CLASSICO, ISOLE E OLENA 1990 Tuscany (It)
455	£8.45	REMELLURI RIOJA CRIANZA 1989 Rioja (Sp)
481	£6.20	HIDALGO AMONTILLADO NAPOLEON Jerez (Sp)
484	£19.95	MATUSALEM, GONZALEZ BYASS Jerez (Sp)
494	£13.45	WARRE'S TRADITIONAL LBV 1981 Douro (P)
496	£15.20	TAYLOR'S TEN YEAR OLD TAWNY Douro (P)
498	£20.20	QUINTA DO VESUVIO VINTAGE PORT 1990 Douro (P)

DAL	David Alexander

69 Queen St, Maidenhead, Berkshire SL6 1LT (Tel 0628 30295 Fax 0628 30295). **Opening Hours**: Mon 10am-7pm, Tues-Thurs 10am-8.30pm, Fri/Sat 10am-9pm, Sun 12-2pm. **Delivery:** free within

10 miles and/ or the M4 corridor. **Tastings:** in-store and tutored events. **Discounts:** 5% on a case with cash or cheque.

The mostly French list seems pretty modest but on closer examination reveals some real treats: the black cherry fruit of the '89 Dom de Raguenières Bourgueil (£5.89), excellent value '90 Château de Pitray, Côtes de Castillon (£4.99), and 'the mother of all S. Rhônes', '90 Domaine des Anges Cuvée Spéciale (£7.99). There's also a chance to sample wines from the young German genius Dr Loosen: possibly the best Riesling in the world.

45	£4.69	NOBILO WHITE CLOUD 1992 (NZ)
46	£4.39	CHARDONNAY DEL PIEMONTE, ARALDICA 1992 Piedmont (It)
51	£4.99	CHARDONNAY 'VIRGINIE', VIN DE PAYS D'OC, SARL DOMAINE VIRGINIE LIEURAN 1992 Midi (F)
57	£6.15	CHABLIS, LOUIS ALEXANDRE 1992 Burgundy (F)
77	£4.99	SALISBURY ESTATE CHARDONNAY 1992 South East Australia (Aus)
83	£6.69	GROVE MILL SAUVIGNON 1992 Blenheim (NZ)
144	£4.49	COTEAUX DE LANGUEDOC PICPOUL DE PINET, DUC DE MORNY 1991 Midi (F)
266	£4.99	SALISBURY ESTATE CABERNET SAUVIGNON 1991 South East Australia (Aus)
272	£6.65	ROUGE HOMME CABERNET/SHIRAZ, COONAWARRA 1988 Coonawarra (Aus)
418	£6.79	VERNACULUM ZOCCOLANTI-PERGOLA, VILLA LIGI 1992 Umbria (It)
461	£10.89	STANTON & KILLEEN RUTHERGLEN LIQUEUR MUSCAT Rutherglen (Aus)
462	£10.89	CAMPBELLS RUTHERGLEN LIQUEUR MUSCAT Rutherglen (Aus)
484	£19.99	MATUSALEM, GONZALEZ BYASS Jerez (Sp)
488	£7.79	OLD TRAFFORD TAWNY, B. SEPPELT & SONS South East Australia (Aus)
498	£24.00	QUINTA DO VESUVIO VINTAGE PORT 1990 Douro (P)

AMA | Amathus

377 Green Lanes, Palmers Green, London N13 4JG (Tel 081-886 3787 Fax 081-882 1273). **Opening Hours:**Mon-Thurs 9.30am-9pm, Fri/Sat 9.30am-9.30pm, Sun 12-2.30pm. **Also 97 Muswell Hill Broadway, London N10. Delivery:** free within the London area. **Tastings:** occasional in-store. **Discounts:** approx 10% on a case, collection discount for quantity.

'We blind taste like for like' when buying. Well, Harry Georgiou's taste buds are clearly in working order, judging by a selection of wines which includes Umani Ronchi's Cumaro, Ochoa's Tempranillo and Château Coucheroy. Even so, we'd love to have been around when he blind tasted the Sanatogen, Sanatogen Iron and Wincarnis.

3	£5.99	SEGURA VIUDAS CAVA BRUT RESERVA Cava (Sp)
5	£5.99	GRAND DUCHESS RUSSIAN SPARKLING WINE, Ukraine
11	£6.69	MONTANA LINDAUER BRUT (NZ)
14	£5.69	ANGAS BRUT CLASSIC, YALUMBA WINERY South East Australia (Aus)
20	£7.49	OMAR KHAYYAM, CHAMPAGNE INDIA 1987 Maharashtra (Ind)
33	£28.99	BOLLINGER GRANDE ANNEE 1985 Champagne (F)
53	£5.39	'CASAL DI SERRA' VERDICCHIO CLASSICO, UMANI RONCHI 1991 Marches (It)
70	£3.99	TIMARA WHITE, MONTANA 1991 (NZ)
71	£4.65	LUGANA, SANTI 1991 North (It)
74	£4.99	PENFOLDS KOONUNGA HILL CHARDONNAY 1992 South East Australia (Aus)
79	£5.69	ROSEMOUNT CHARDONNAY 1992 Hunter Valley (Aus)
80	£5.99	CHATEAU REYNELLA STONY HILL CHARDONNAY 1990 South Australia (Aus)
81	£6.89	CATHEDRAL CELLARS CHARDONNAY, KWV 1991 Coastal Region (SA)
91	£7.49	MARQUES DE MURRIETA RIOJA RESERVA BLANCO 1987 Rioja (Sp)
112	£11.99	ELSTON CHARDONNAY, TE MATA ESTATE 1991 Hawkes Bay (NZ)
169	£8.49	HUNTERS MARLBOROUGH SAUVIGNON BLANC 1992 Marlborough (NZ)

244	£2.75	RUSSE CABERNET CINSAULT (Bul)
250	£3.69	STAMBOLOVO RESERVE MERLOT 1987 (Bul)
256	£4.39	HARDYS NOTTAGE HILL CABERNET SAUVIGNON 1991 South Australia (Aus)
259	£4.49	GLEN ELLEN CABERNET SAUVIGNON 1989 (Cal)
269	£4.99	MONTANA CABERNET SAUVIGNON 1991 Marlborough (NZ)
281	£5.99	CHATEAU BONNET OAK AGED, A LURTON 1990 Bordeaux (F)
298	£9.99	LINDEMANS ST GEORGE CABERNET SAUVIGNON 1989 Coonawarra (Aus)
346	£7.49	CHATEAU MUSAR, 1986 Bekaa Valley (Leb)
373	£4.99	TARRANGO, BROWN BROTHERS 1992 Milawa (Aus)
427	£10.69	CUMARO ROSSO CONERO, UMANI RONCHI 1989 Marches (It)
444	£4.39	PERIQUITA, J M DA FONSECA 1990 (P)
447	£5.49	CAMPO VIEJO RIOJA RESERVA 1987 Rioja (Sp)
458	£3.69	MUSCAT OF PATRAS, ACHAIA CLAUSS Greece
483	£8.79	1796 RICH OLD OLOROSO Jerez (Sp)
484	£15.95	MATUSALEM, GONZALEZ BYASS Jerez (Sp)

AMW | Amey's Wines

83 Melford Road, Sudbury, Suffolk CO10 6JT (Tel 0787 77144) **Opening Hours**: Tues-Sat 10am-7pm. **Delivery:** free within 20 miles. **Tastings:** in-store. **Discounts:** 5% on a mixed case.

Mr & Mrs Amey's Australian list has grown to include such top quality smaller growers such as Wirra Wirra, Mountadam, Dromana and the extraordinary Tasmanian organic wine from Buchanan. We were also pleased to see the full range from Moondah Brook. Italy's good too. The Tuscan Villa di Capezzana wines or a rare Puglian Chardonnay (£4.99) will do us nicely.

22	£9.49	MAYERLING CREMANT D'ALSACE, CAVE VINICOLE DE TURCKHEIM Alsace (F)
57	£5.99	CHABLIS, LOUIS ALEXANDRE 1992 Burgundy (F)
61	£6.49	LUGANA CA'DEI FRATI 1992 Brescia (It)
77	£4.99	SALISBURY ESTATE CHARDONNAY 1992 South East Australia (Aus)
79	£6.19	ROSEMOUNT CHARDONNAY 1992 Hunter Valley (Aus)
80	£6.49	CHATEAU REYNELLA STONY HILL CHARDONNAY 1990 South Australia (Aus)
83	£6.79	GROVE MILL SAUVIGNON 1992 Blenheim (NZ)
91	£7.99	MARQUES DE MURRIETA RIOJA RESERVA BLANCO 1987 Rioja (Sp)
112	£11.99	ELSTON CHARDONNAY, TE MATA ESTATE 1991 Hawkes Bay (NZ)
134	£4.19	DOMAINE DE MAUBET VIN DE PAYS DES COTES DE GASCOGNE, FONTAN 1992 South West (F)
146	£5.49	HARDY'S MOONDAH BROOK ESTATE CHENIN BLANC 1992 Gingin, (W Aus)
162	£6.49	SELAKS MARLBOROUGH SAUVIGNON BLANC 1991 Marlborough (NZ)
182	£6.89	GEWURZTRAMINER D'ALSACE, CAVE VINICOLE DE TURCKHEIM 1992 Alsace (F)
238	£6.59	CHATEAU DE LASTOURS CORBIERES, FUT DE CHENE 1989 Midi (F)
256	£4.69	HARDYS NOTTAGE HILL CABERNET SAUVIGNON 1991 South Australia (Aus)
266	£4.99	SALISBURY ESTATE CABERNET SAUVIGNON 1991 South East Australia (Aus)
270	£5.49	HARDY'S MOONDAH BROOK ESTATE CABERNET SAUVIGNON 1989 Gingin (W Aus)
272	£5.49	ROUGE HOMME CABERNET/SHIRAZ, COONAWARRA 1988 Coonawarra (Aus)
273	£5.79	TALTARNI FIDDLEBACK TERRACE 1990 Pyrenees (Aus)
293	£8.99	THE ANGELUS CABERNET SAUVIGNON, WIRRA WIRRA 1991 S Australia (Aus)
294	£8.99	CHATEAU DE ANNEREAUX, LALANDE DE POMEROL 1989 Bordeaux (F)
330	£3.99	VIN DE PAYS DES COLLINES RHODANIENNES CEPAGE SYRAH, CAVE DE TAIN L'HERMITAGE Rhône (F)
335	£4.99	COTES DU RHONE DOMAINE DE TERRE BRULEE, CAVE DE VIGNERONS DE RASTEAU 1990 Rhône (F)
348	£8.29	ROSEMOUNT SHOW RESERVE SYRAH 1990 McLaren Vale (Aus)
450	£6.99	YLLERA, VINO DE MESA, SAT LOS CURRO 1988 Ribera del Duero (Sp)

461	£10.49	STANTON & KILLEEN RUTHERGLEN LIQUEUR MUSCAT Rutherglen (Aus)
462	£12.49	CAMPBELLS RUTHERGLEN LIQUEUR MUSCAT Rutherglen (Aus)
488	£7.49	OLD TRAFFORD TAWNY, B. SEPPELT & SONS South East Australia (Aus)
494	£13.49	WARRE'S TRADITIONAL LBV 1981 Douro (P)

| LAV | Les Amis du Vin |

430 High Road, London, NW10 2HA (Tel 081-451 0469 Fax 081-459 4473). **Opening Hours**: Mon-Fri 9.15am-5.15pm, 24 hour hotline: 081 451 0469/1135/0981. Shop:Mon-Fri 10.30am-7pm. **Delivery:** nationally 3 cases plus. **Tastings:** in-store and tutored events. **Discounts:** 5% on an unmixed case.

This set up incorporates two London fine wine shops (Les Amis du Vin and The Winery), The Wine Growers Association and a mail order company. The excellent list slants towards California and Italy, with all the big names (some available *en primeur*). Not the cheapest wines but some of the most impressive.

16	£7.95	YALUMBA SPARKLING CABERNET CUVEE PRESTIGE South East Australia (Aus)
25	£10.95	CROSER METHODE TRADITIONNELLE, PETALUMA 1990 Adelaide Hills (Aus)
87	£6.95	BARREL FERMENTED CHARDONNAY, ROTHBURY 1992 Hunter Valley (Aus)
91	£9.50	MARQUES DE MURRIETA RIOJA RESERVA BLANCO 1987 Rioja (Sp)
95	£8.95	BARREL SELECT CHARDONNAY, FETZER 1991 Mendocino County (Cal)
100	£8.95	FIRESTONE CHARDONNAY 1990 (Cal)
106	£8.95	EDNA VALLEY CHARDONNAY 1990 Edna Valley (Cal)
107	£12.95	ACACIA CHARDONNAY, THE CHALONE GROUP 1989 Carneros (Cal)
110	£10.50	POMINO IL BENEFIZIO, MARCHESI DE FRESCOBALDI 1990 Tuscany (It)
117	£14.50	RIDGE CHARDONNAY 1990 St Cruz (Cal)
222	£9.95	CHATEAU DE LA GRILLE, CHINON ROSE, A GOSSET 1992 Loire (F)
229	£3.50	VAL DU TORGAN, LES PRODUCTEURS DU MONT TAUCH Midi (F)
268	£5.75	BEL ARBORS MERLOT, FETZER VINEYARDS 1991 Mendocino County (Cal)
269	£5.75	MONTANA CABERNET SAUVIGNON 1991 Marlborough (NZ)
282	£5.95	VALLEY OAKS CABERNET SAUVIGNON, FETZER 1990 Mendocino County (Cal)
295	£8.95	FETZER BARREL SELECT CABERNET SAUVIGNON 1989 Mendocino County (Cal)
303	£9.95	PETALUMA COONAWARRA RED 1988 Coonawarra (Aus)
315	£14.95	MORMORETO CABERNET SAUVIGNON PREDICATO DI BITURICA, VINO DA TAVOLA, MARCHESI DE FRESCOBALDI 1988 Tuscany (It)
336	£4.95	ZINFANDEL, FETZER VINEYARDS 1990 Mendocino County (Cal)
337	£5.75	GALWAY SHIRAZ, YALUMBA WINERY 1991 Barossa Valley (Aus)
346	£7.75	CHATEAU MUSAR, 1986 BEKAA VALLEY (LEB)
349	£7.95	ZINFANDEL, DRY CREEK VINEYARDS 1990 Sonoma (Cal)
363	£11.25	RIDGE GEYSERVILLE ZINFANDEL 1991 Sonoma (Cal)
416	£5.35	SALICE SALENTINO RISERVA, AZ. AG. TAURINO 1988 Puglia (It)
419	£6.95	BARBERA D'ALBA VIGNOTA, CONTERNO E FANTINO 1991 Piedmont (It)
484	£25.95	MATUSALEM, GONZALEZ BYASS Jerez (Sp)
495	£12.95	GALWAY PIPE OLD TAWNY, YALUMBA WINERY Barossa Valley (Aus)

| JAV | John Arkell Vintners |

Kingsdown Brewery, Hyde Road, Stratton St Margaret, Swindon, Wiltshire SN2 6RU (Tel 0793 823026 Fax 0793 828864). **Opening Hours**: Mon-Fri 9am-5.30pm. **Delivery:** free locally. **Tastings:** in-store and tutored events. **Discounts:** 2.5% on a case.

Set up 30 odd years ago to supply its own pubs, Arkells is now a thriving wholesale/retail business in its own right. A traditional northern hemisphere merchant at heart, concentrating on Bordeaux, Burgundy and the Loire, they've headed south, picking up, en route, '86 Cuvaison Zinfandel, '89 Los Vascos Cabernet, '90 Mount Helen Chardonnay and five Kiwis from Babich.

17	£8.58	BOUVET LADUBAY SAUMUR BRUT Loire (F)
33	£29.90	BOLLINGER GRANDE ANNEE 1985 Champagne (F)
44	£4.57	CHARDONNAY, VINO DA TAVOLA, CA DONINI 1992 Triveneto (It)
168	£10.13	SANCERRE LES ROCHES, DOMAINE VACHERON 1992 Loire (F)
172	£9.39	SANCERRE MD, H. BOURGEOIS 1991 Loire (F)
269	£6.26	MONTANA CABERNET SAUVIGNON 1991 Marlborough (NZ)
320	£26.26	CHATEAU PICHON LONGUEVILLE BARON, PAUILLAC 1990 Bordeaux (F)
322	£26.26	CHATEAU LYNCH-BAGES, PAUILLAC 1989 Bordeaux (F)
398	£9.44	MONTHELIE, JAFFELIN 1990 Burgundy (F)
496	£14.21	TAYLOR'S TEN YEAR OLD TAWNY Douro (P)

JAR | John Armit Wines

5 Royalty Studios, 105 Lancaster Road, London W11 1QF, (Tel 071 727 6846 Fax 071 727 7133) **Opening Hours:** Mon-Fri 9am-6pm. **Delivery:** free with 3 cases or more. **Tastings:** samples opened regularly in store. **Discounts:** special mail order offers.

Wine List of the Year

John Armit's stylish list – sorry, 'catalogue'– looks less glossy than the 1992 edition ('it may have given the impression that we are expensive') but now has many more wines at under £6, including an unusually good Muscadet from Clos de Beauregard. California (Ravenswood) and Australia (Nicholson River) are increasingly well represented by wines not found everywhere else, but Mr A's heart is still in Burgundy (*chez* Leflaive, Ponsot and Lamy-Pillot) and Bordeaux (especially in the Right Bank).

233	£4.00	MAS DE FIGARO VIN DE PAYS DE L'HERAULT, AIME GUIBERT 1992 Midi (F)
288	£9.83	CABERNET SAUVIGNON, BODEGA Y CAVAS DE WEINERT 1985 Mendoza (Arg)
394	£10.00	COLDSTREAM HILLS PINOT NOIR 1992 Yarra Valley (Aus)
403	£19.58	NUITS SAINT GEORGES, DOMAINE DE L'ARLOT 1990 Burgundy (F)

AK | Arriba Kettle & Co

Buckle St, Honeybourne, Evesham, Worcester, Worcestershire WR11 5QB (Tel 0386 833024 Fax 0386 833541). **Opening Hours:** by appointment. **Delivery:** free nationally. **Tastings:** samples opened occasionally. Discounts: £2 per case collection discount.

Hispanophile-turned-'Loireophile', Barry Kettle offers an interesting cross-section of wines from small family domaines from Muscadet to Menetou, including the Vouvrays of Domaine Brisbarre, Prince Poniatowski and the luscious sweet Coteaux de Layons from Domaine des Barres, all of which Mr K ships himself. Watch out also for his Spring *en primeur* offers.

A | Asda Stores Ltd

Asda House, Southbank, Great Wilson Street, Leeds, West Yorkshire LS11 5AD (Tel 0532 435435 Fax 0532 418666). **Opening Hours**: Generally Mon-Fri 9am-8pm, Sat 8.30am-8pm. **Tastings:** in-store at selected branches.

'Going Places' Wine Merchant of the Year

Quietly building up strength, Philip Clive and his team have created a range
of wines which could teach one or two supposedly more 'up-market' chains
a thing or two. Regional France is especially well covered (particularly the
less expensive areas of the Rhône) and there is a welcome burgeoning of
organic wines on the list. We were most impressed by the appearance of
producers like Val di Suga, Bürklin-Wolf and Domaine Bunan.

9	£6.99	EDMOND MAZURE VINTAGE BRUT, SEAVIEW 1990 South East Australia (Aus)
23	£8.99	SCHARFFENBERGER BRUT Mendocino County (Cal)
42	£3.75	ASDA CHARDONNAY, VIN DE PAYS D'OC, SKALLI Midi (F)
58	£6.69	ASDA CHABLIS, G. MOTHE 1991 Burgundy (F)
113	£11.99	PULIGNY MONTRACHET, LOUIS CARILLON ET FILS 1991 Burgundy (F)
151	£4.99	MUSCADET DE SEVRE ET MAINE, GUY BOSSARD 1992 Loire (F)
157	£5.99	LUGANA SANTA CRISTINA, VIGNETO MASSONI 1991 Lombardy (It)
167	£7.75	POUILLY FUME, DOMAINE COULBOIS, PATRICK COULBOIS 1991 Loire (F)
196	£3.99	DENBIES ENGLISH WINE 1991 Surrey (UK)
243	£2.89	ASDA MERLOT, VIN DE PAYS D'OC, SKALLI Midi (F)
256	£3.99	HARDYS NOTTAGE HILL CABERNET SAUVIGNON 1991 South Australia (Aus)
269	£4.99	MONTANA CABERNET SAUVIGNON 1991 Marlborough (NZ)
379	£6.85	FLEURIE, CLOS DE LA CHAPELLE DES BOIS, F VERPOIX 1991 Beaujolais (F)
487	£6.99	TOKAJI ASZU 3 PUTTONYOS, TOKAJI-HEGYALA SCHLUMBERGER 1981 (Hun)

AUC | Australian Wine Centre

Down Under, South Australia House, 50 The Strand, London WC2N (Tel 071 925 0751 Fax 071 839
9021). **Opening Hours**: Mon-Fri 10.00am-7.00pm, Sat 10.00am-4.00pm. **Delivery:** free. **Tastings:**
samples opened regularly. **Discounts:** 5% collection discount on a case.

Craig Smith's description of the 'option paralysis' which afflicts some of his
customers is not surprising when you're faced with the most comprehensive
range of Aussie wines around. Apart from the inevitable big names, Smith is
constantly sourcing new wines from small and unknown domaines. It's worth
being on the mailing list - if only to be in on the annual May mega-tasting.

9	£6.99	EDMOND MAZURE VINTAGE BRUT, SEAVIEW 1990 South East Australia (Aus)
24	£9.99	GREEN POINT, DOMAINE CHANDON 1990 Yarra Valley (Aus)
25	£14.99	CROSER METHODE TRADITIONNELLE, PETALUMA 1990 Adelaide Hills (Aus)
64	£8.69	TASMANIAN WINE COMPANY CHARDONNAY, PIPER'S BROOK 1991 (Aus)
77	£4.99	SALISBURY ESTATE CHARDONNAY 1992 South East Australia (Aus)
80	£6.49	CHATEAU REYNELLA STONY HILL CHARDONNAY 1990 South Australia (Aus)
93	£7.99	SEMILLON, STEPHEN HENSCHKE 1991 Adelaide Hills (Aus)
98	£7.99	LOCAL GROWERS SEMILLON, ROCKFORD 1989 Barossa Valley (Aus)
99	£8.99	KRONDORF SHOW RESERVE CHARDONNAY 1991 Barossa Valley (Aus)
218	£5.49	MOUNT HURTLE GRENACHE ROSE, GEOFF MERRILL 1992 McLaren Vale (Aus)
266	£4.99	SALISBURY ESTATE CABERNET SAUVIGNON 1991 South East Australia (Aus)
293	£8.99	THE ANGELUS CABERNET SAUVIGNON, WIRRA WIRRA 1991 S Australia (Aus)
298	£9.99	LINDEMANS ST GEORGE CABERNET SAUVIGNON 1989 Coonawarra (Aus)
303	£11.49	PETALUMA COONAWARRA RED 1988 Coonawarra (Aus)
305	£11.49	CYRIL HENSCHKE CABERNET SAUVIGNON, HENSCHKE 1988 Adelaide Hills (Aus)
350	£7.69	BROKENWOOD SHIRAZ 1991 South East Australia (Aus)
352	£8.49	PENLEY ESTATE SHIRAZ/CABERNET SAUVIGNON 1990 Coonawarra (Aus)
359	£9.99	LAWSON'S SHIRAZ, ORLANDO WINES PTY LTD 1987 South Australia (Aus)
365	£15.99	PENFOLDS MAGILL ESTATE SHIRAZ 1988 South Australia (Aus)
373	£5.49	TARRANGO, BROWN BROTHERS 1992 Milawa (Aus)
394	£9.99	COLDSTREAM HILLS PINOT NOIR 1992 Yarra Valley (Aus)
461	£9.99	STANTON & KILLEEN RUTHERGLEN LIQUEUR MUSCAT Rutherglen (Aus)

| 462 | £9.99 | CAMPBELLS RUTHERGLEN LIQUEUR MUSCAT Rutherglen (Aus) |
| 495 | £11.99 | GALWAY PIPE OLD TAWNY, YALUMBA WINERY Barossa Valley (Aus) |

| AV | Averys of Bristol |

7 Park Street, Bristol, BS1 5NG (Tel 0272 214141 Fax 0272 221729). **Opening Hours**: Mon-Sat 9.00am-7.00pm, Sunday, Bank Holidays 12-3pm. **Delivery:** free nat for 2 cases or more. **Tastings:** in-store and tutored events. **Discounts:** dependent on quantity.

While most wine merchants complain about government policy in 1993, John Avery reminds us that things were worse in 1793, when his company was founded. Britain had just gone to war with France and Spain, causing some supply difficulties. The wines of these countries are now well-represented, but should European relations deteriorate, alternative sources include South Africa, New Zealand and even Canada. California is perhaps their prime speciality, with top names Swanson, Sonoma Cutrer and Far Niente to tempt those without a care.

11	£8.93	MONTANA LINDAUER BRUT (NZ)
33	£28.70	BOLLINGER GRANDE ANNEE 1985 Champagne (F)
45	£3.99	NOBILO WHITE CLOUD 1992 (NZ)
108	£10.00	SWANSON CHARDONNAY, NAPA VALLEY 1990 Napa Valley (Cal)
272	£4.99	ROUGE HOMME CABERNET/SHIRAZ, COONAWARRA 1988 Coonawarra (Aus)
275	£5.49	RUSTENBERG MERLOT, STELLENBOSCH 1991 Stellenbosch (SA)
322	£33.04	CHATEAU LYNCH-BAGES, PAUILLAC 1989 Bordeaux (F)
346	£9.42	CHATEAU MUSAR, 1986 Bekaa Valley (Leb)
389	£6.99	HAMILTON-RUSSELL PINOT NOIR, WALKER BAY 1991 Walker Bay (SA)

| BH | B H Wines |

Boustead Hill House, Boustead Hill, Burgh-by-Sands, Carlisle, Cumbria CA5 6AA (Tel 0228 576711). **Opening Hours**: all reasonable hours. **Delivery:** free locally. **Tastings:** in store and tutored events.

Richard and Linda Neville's enthusiasm for wine and food is clear from their list – and their slimmer volumes on Australia (Mountadam, Pikes, Charles Melton, Yarra Yering, with some older vintages on offer too) and California (Saintsbury, Ridge, Newton). The Rhône, Spain, Italy, Burgundy, Bordeaux and Champagne have been whittled down to a fine, affordable minimum, with some good, small producers. In between buying wines, the Nevilles teach wine at Newcastle University, advise restaurants and hotels, write for local newspapers, run their wine society, and, we wouldn't be surprised, clutch giant bottles while bungy-jumping off Sca Fell.

14	£8.35	ANGAS BRUT CLASSIC, YALUMBA WINERY South East Australia (Aus)
20	£8.50	OMAR KHAYYAM, CHAMPAGNE INDIA 1987 Maharashtra (Ind)
21	£9.95	SPARKLING VOUVRAY, CHEVALIER DE MONCONTOUR Loire (F)
25	£11.60	CROSER METHODE TRADITIONNELLE, PETALUMA 1990 Adelaide Hills (Aus)
33	£30.00	BOLLINGER GRANDE ANNEE 1985 Champagne (F)
53	£5.30	'CASAL DI SERRA' VERDICCHIO CLASSICO, UMANI RONCHI 1991 Marches (It)
64	£12.40	TASMANIAN WINE COMPANY CHARDONNAY, PIPER'S BROOK 1991 (Aus)
91	£7.50	MARQUES DE MURRIETA RIOJA RESERVA BLANCO 1987 Rioja (Sp)
95	£8.20	BARREL SELECT CHARDONNAY, FETZER 1991 Mendocino County (Cal)
99	£9.30	KRONDORF SHOW RESERVE CHARDONNAY 1991 Barossa Valley (Aus)

100	£9.60	FIRESTONE CHARDONNAY 1990 (Cal)
106	£9.20	EDNA VALLEY CHARDONNAY 1990 Edna Valley (Cal)
107	£13.75	ACACIA CHARDONNAY, THE CHALONE GROUP 1989 Carneros (Cal)
110	£10.75	POMINO IL BENEFIZIO, MARCHESI DE FRESCOBALDI 1990 Tuscany (It)
112	£12.50	ELSTON CHARDONNAY, TE MATA ESTATE 1991 Hawkes Bay (NZ)
115	£13.60	NEWTON UNFILTERED CHARDONNAY 1990 Napa Valley (Cal)
117	£8.20	RIDGE CHARDONNAY 1990 St Cruz (Cal)
155	£6.10	ROTHBURY SAUVIGNON BLANC 1992 Marlborough (NZ)
168	£9.25	SANCERRE LES ROCHES, DOMAINE VACHERON 1992 Loire (F)
218	£6.10	MOUNT HURTLE GRENACHE ROSE, GEOFF MERRILL 1992 McLaren Vale (Aus)
268	£5.70	BEL ARBORS MERLOT, FETZER VINEYARDS 1991 Mendocino County (Cal)
269	£5.00	MONTANA CABERNET SAUVIGNON 1991 Marlborough (NZ)
272	£5.10	ROUGE HOMME CABERNET/SHIRAZ, COONAWARRA 1988 Coonawarra (Aus)
273	£5.35	TALTARNI FIDDLEBACK TERRACE 1990 Pyrenees (Aus)
275	£5.35	RUSTENBERG MERLOT, STELLENBOSCH 1991 Stellenbosch (SA)
282	£6.25	VALLEY OAKS CABERNET SAUVIGNON, FETZER 1990 Mendocino County (Cal)
295	£9.15	FETZER BARREL SELECT CABERNET SAUVIGNON 1989 Mendocino County (Cal)
303	£10.10	PETALUMA COONAWARRA RED 1988 Coonawarra (Aus)
309	£12.50	NEWTON MERLOT 1990 Napa Valley (Cal)
346	£7.50	CHATEAU MUSAR, 1986 Bekaa Valley (Leb)
348	£8.15	ROSEMOUNT SHOW RESERVE SYRAH 1990 McLaren Vale (Aus)
349	£8.10	ZINFANDEL, DRY CREEK VINEYARDS 1990 Sonoma (Cal)
353	£8.75	DAVID WYNN PATRIARCH SHIRAZ 1991 Eden Valley (Aus)
363	£14.50	RIDGE GEYSERVILLE ZINFANDEL 1990 Sonoma (Cal)
370	£15.90	YARRA YERING SHIRAZ NO.2 1990 Yarra Valley (Aus)
389	£6.75	HAMILTON-RUSSELL PINOT NOIR, WALKER BAY 1991 Walker Bay (SA)
396	£10.95	SAINTSBURY PINOT NOIR 1991 Carneros (Cal)
400	£11.45	NEUDORF VINEYARDS MOUTERE PINOT NOIR 1991 Nelson (NZ)
427	£9.35	CUMARO ROSSO CONERO, UMANI RONCHI 1989 Marches (It)
470	£6.85	MONBAZILLAC, CHATEAU THEULET, SCEA ALARD 1990 Bordeaux (F)
485	£18.00	OSBORNE Y CIA PEDRO XIMENEZ Jerez (Sp)
487	£8.20	TOKAJI ASZU 3 PUTTONYOS, TOKAJI-HEGYALA SCHLUMBERGER 1981 (Hun)
489	£8.50	CHURCHILL GRAHAM FINEST VINTAGE CHARACTER Douro (P)
495	£13.60	GALWAY PIPE OLD TAWNY, YALUMBA WINERY Barossa Valley (Aus)

DBW | David Baker Wines

4 Derwen Road, Bridgend, Mid Glamorgan CF31 1LE (Tel 0656 650732 Fax 0656 656606). **Opening Hours:** Mon-Sat 9am-6pm. **Delivery:** free locally. **Tastings:** in-store. **Discounts:** 5% per case.

If you want to know the wine ask a policeman. Ex-Superintendant Baker and BT Manager Watkins continue to titilate the tastebuds of South Wales in their search for 'the best new and traditional wines on the market'.

46	£4.75	CHARDONNAY DEL PIEMONTE, ARALDICA 1992 Piedmont (It)
82	£6.95	CARIAD GWIN DA O GYMRU BACCHUS/REICHSTEINER, LLANERCH VINEYARD 1990 Glamorgan (Wales)
288	£6.99	CABERNET SAUVIGNON, BODEGA Y CAVAS DE WEINERT 1985 Mendoza (Arg)
321	£22.99	ORNELLAIA 1990 Tuscany (It)
346	£9.49	CHATEAU MUSAR, 1986 Bekaa Valley (Leb)
348	£7.99	ROSEMOUNT SHOW RESERVE SYRAH 1990 McLaren Vale (Aus)
365	£5.25	PENFOLDS MAGILL ESTATE SHIRAZ 1988 South Australia (Aus)
428	£9.99	BRIC MILEUI, ASCHERI 1990 Piedmont (It)
484	£18.99	MATUSALEM, GONZALEZ BYASS Jerez (Sp)
497	£19.29	NIEPOORT COLHEITA 1983 Douro (P)

BAL	Ballantynes of Cowbridge

Stallancourt House, Llanblethian, Cowbridge, South Glamorgan CF7 7SU (Tel 0446 773044 Fax 0446 775253). **Opening Hours**: office Mon-Sat 9am-6pm, plus 24 hour answerphone, shop: Mon-Sat 10am-6.15pm. **Delivery**: free nationally. **Tastings**: in-store.

Peter Ballantyne started a mail order business in the 70's selling French wines from small growers. In the '80s he realised it was more profitable to sell 'finer' Bordeaux, Rhônes and Burgundies. In the '90's he has opted for a blend of fine and country wines whilst expanding the Italian and New World range. This has obviously paid off as Mr B is opening a 'prestigious shop' with a range of 300+ wines, such as Trapet, Cullens, Henschke, Isole e Olena ...

BLS	Balls Brothers Ltd

313 Cambridge Heath Road, London E2 9LQ (Tel 071 739 6466 Fax 071 729 0258). **Opening Hours**: Mon-Sat 10am-6pm. **Delivery**: free nationally for 2 cases or more. **Tastings**: in store . **Discounts**: 5% per case, £3.50 per case collection discount.

Jack of all trades...? Balls Brothers' wine bars afford their pin-striped customers the opportunity to taste through the range, including older vintages, before rushing to Bethnal Green to place an order; and the food angle is exploited in regular 'Gourmet Dinners'. Check out their list for Jane Mitchell wines from Australia and the well-priced Southern French Domaine Virginie Chardonnay.

ABA	Adam Bancroft Assocs

4-7 Great Pulteney St, London W1R 3DF (Tel 071-434 9919 Fax 071-494 2186). **Opening Hours**: Mon-Fri 9.30am-6pm. **Delivery**: free locally, nationally for 3 or more cases. **Tastings**: samples opened regularly in store.

Adam Bancroft specialises in small French domaines we thought were well kept secrets. Top Rhônes include J.Luc Colombo's Cornas and Collines de Laure, Andre Perret's Condrieu and some juicy little numbers from the Ardèche. Burgundies are a passion, with rarities aplenty, such as red and white Domaine des Deux Roches and Morgon from Calot.

BWS	The Barnes Wine Shop

51 Barnes High St, London SW13 9LN (Tel 081-878 8643 Fax 081- 876 9621). **Opening Hours**: Mon-Sat 9.30am-8.30pm Sun 12-2pm. **Delivery**: free locally. **Tastings**: in store, plus tastings and tutored events.

Still one of the focal points of Barnes's village life, Francis Murray's shop is riding out the storm though, as he says, devaluation and recession have made it more difficult than ever to sell fine wine. Attention has shifted towards more affordable fare from France and Italy, but the influence of James Rogers on Mr M's buying is still evident and there are plenty of worthwhile wines at every price level, including the hard-to-find Corioles from Australia.

11	£7.45	MONTANA LINDAUER BRUT (NZ)
53	£5.95	'CASAL DI SERRA' VERDICCHIO CLASSICO, UMANI RONCHI 1991 Marches (It)
150	£5.45	KONOCTI SAUVIGNON BLANC 1991 LAKE COUNTY (CAL)

197	£4.49	BADEN DRY, BADISCHER WINZERKELLER Baden (G)
218	£5.95	MOUNT HURTLE GRENACHE ROSE, GEOFF MERRILL 1992 McLaren Vale (Aus)
346	£8.45	CHATEAU MUSAR, 1986 Bekaa Valley (Leb)
352	£9.75	PENLEY ESTATE SHIRAZ/CABERNET SAUVIGNON 1990 Coonawarra (Aus)
423	£9.45	CARMIGNANO, CAPEZZANA 1987 Tuscany (It)
489	£9.95	CHURCHILL GRAHAM FINEST VINTAGE CHARACTER Douro (P)

AB | Augustus Barnett Ltd

3 The Maltings, Wetmore Road, Burton-on-Trent, Staffordshire DE14 1SE (Tel 0283 512550 Fax 0283 67595). **Opening Hours**: Mon-Sat 10am-10pm, Sun 12-3pm, 7-10pm. **Delivery**: free locally. **Tastings**: samples opened regularly plus in-store tastings. **Discounts**: 10% per case, 5% per mixed case.

The (we believe) imminent purchase of this chain by Victoria Wine might enable the combined force to sort out its rag-bag of smart and scruffy shops and Augustus Barnett's confusion over its role in vinous society. Under Dr Caroline Gilby, however, the latter chain has introduced such recommendable wines as the Mexican LA Cetto reds and some very skilfully chosen examples from southern France. Finding these in the truly horrible technicolour price list or in some of the lesser shops is, shall we say, challenging.

11	£6.99	MONTANA LINDAUER BRUT (NZ)
14	£7.79	ANGAS BRUT CLASSIC, YALUMBA WINERY South East Australia (Aus)
24	£9.99	GREEN POINT, DOMAINE CHANDON 1990 Yarra Valley (Aus)
43	£3.99	COTES DE ST MONT WHITE, PLAIMONT 1991 South West (F)
44	£3.99	CHARDONNAY, VINO DA TAVOLA, CA DONINI 1992 Triveneto (It)
70	£3.99	TIMARA WHITE, MONTANA 1991 (NZ)
74	£4.99	PENFOLDS KOONUNGA HILL CHARDONNAY 1992 South East Australia (Aus)
121	£17.99	ARARIMU CHARDONNAY, MATUA VALLEY 1991 Gisborne (NZ)
178	£4.49	CORBANS DRY WHITE RIESLING 1991 Marlborough (NZ)
179	£3.99	NEETHLINGSHOF GEWURZTRAMINER 1991 Stellenbosch (SA)
218	£6.49	MOUNT HURTLE GRENACHE ROSE, GEOFF MERRILL 1992 McLaren Vale (Aus)
237	£5.49	CUVEE MYTHIQUE, VIN DE PAYS D'OC, VAL D'ORBIEU 1990 Midi (F)
250	£3.89	STAMBOLOVO RESERVE MERLOT 1987 (Bul)
256	£3.99	HARDYS NOTTAGE HILL CABERNET SAUVIGNON 1991 South Australia (Aus)
268	£4.99	BEL ARBORS MERLOT, FETZER VINEYARDS 1991 Mendocino County (Cal)
269	£4.99	MONTANA CABERNET SAUVIGNON 1991 Marlborough (NZ)
271	£5.29	CHATEAU TIMBERLAY, R. GIRAUD 1990 Bordeaux (F)
282	£5.99	VALLEY OAKS CABERNET SAUVIGNON, FETZER 1990 Mendocino County (Cal)
318	£17.99	ARARIMU CABERNET SAUVIGNON, MATUA VALLEY 1991 (NZ)
319	£17.99	CHATEAU LASCOMBES, MARGAUX 1988 Bordeaux (F)
327	£3.59	DOMAINE DE L'AMEILLAUD, VIN DE PAYS, N. THOMPSON 1992 Midi (F)
346	£7.85	CHATEAU MUSAR, BEKAA VALLEY 1986 Bekaa Valley (Leb)
373	£4.99	TARRANGO, BROWN BROTHERS 1992 Milawa (Aus)
394	£9.49	COLDSTREAM HILLS PINOT NOIR 1992 Yarra Valley (Aus)
397	£10.99	MERCUREY, 1ER CRU, CLOS DE MYGLANDS, FAIVELEY 1991 Burgundy (F)
415	£4.19	VALPOLICELLA CLASSICO, MASI 1991 Veneto (It)
421	£8.45	SER GIOVETO, VINO DA TAVOLA, ROCCA DELLE MACIE 1989 Tuscany (It)
432	£9.89	RECIOTO DELLA VALPOLICELLA, CASAL DEI RONCHI MASI 1988 Veneto (It)
433	£2.69	LEZIRIA VINHO TINTO, VEGA CO-OPERATIVE ALMEIRIM 1992 Almeirim (P)
439	£3.59	BORBA, ADEGA CO-OPERATIVA DE BORBA 1991 Douro (P)
472	£6.99	NEETHLINGSHOF WEISSER RIESLING NOBLE LATE HARVEST 1991 (SA)
484	£18.45	MATUSALEM, GONZALEZ BYASS Jerez (Sp)
494	£10.75	WARRE'S TRADITIONAL LBV 1981 Douro (P)

BAR	Barwell & Jones

Barwell House, 24 Fore Street, Ipswich, Suffolk IP4 1JU (Tel 0473 232322 Fax 0473 280381).

By the time the *Guide* appears, this country firm should have undergone a management buy-out and turned its attention almost entirely to selling exclusive lines of wines wholesale. The Bacchante Wine Club will continue with free membership. Watch this space.

299	£10.70	MEERLUST MERLOT, STELLENBOSCH 1986 Stellenbosch (SA)
485	£18.75	OSBORNE Y CIA PEDRO XIMENEZ Jerez (Sp)
487	£8.50	TOKAJI ASZU 3 PUTTONYOS, TOKAJI-HEGYALA SCHLUMBERGER 1981 (Hun)

BFI	Bedford Fine Wines Ltd

Faulkeners Farm, The Marsh, Carlton, Bedford, Bedfordshire MK43 7JU (Tel 0234 721153 Fax 0234 721145). **Opening Hours:** phone for details. **Delivery:** free within 10 miles. **Tastings:** regular in-store. **Discounts:** on some wines, over £80 collection discount.

By the case only – but who's to complain, when you can make up a mixed dozen from a set of good individual Burgundy domaines, Guigal's fabled La Landonne, Chateaux Palmer or Cheval Blanc.

BEN	Bennetts Wine & Spirits Merchants

High St, Chipping Camden, Glos GL55 6AG, (Tel/Fax 0386 840392). **Opening Hours:** Mon-Fri 9am-1pm, 2-5.30pm, Sat 9am-5.30pm. **Delivery:** free nationally. **Tastings:** samples opened regularly, plus tutored events. **Discounts:** 5% per case, 7.5% 5-10 cases, 10% on 10 cases or more.

Classy stuff indeed. Charles Bennett's list goes from the sublime (quality) to ridiculously reasonable prices with a fine range of classic Bordeaux and small domaine Burgundies, plus some treats in the Rhône, Tuscany and Piedmont. But it is the new world list which is really dazzling, with superstars such as Petaluma, Cape Mentelle, Bannockburn, Yarra Yering, Qupe, Bonny Doon and Ridge.

25	£12.95	CROSER METHODE TRADITIONNELLE, PETALUMA 1990 Adelaide Hills (Aus)
33	£30.95	BOLLINGER GRANDE ANNEE 1985 Champagne (F)
46	£4.85	CHARDONNAY DEL PIEMONTE, ARALDICA 1992 Piedmont (It)
74	£5.60	PENFOLDS KOONUNGA HILL CHARDONNAY 1992 South East Australia (Aus)
77	£5.30	SALISBURY ESTATE CHARDONNAY 1992 South East Australia (Aus)
79	£6.45	ROSEMOUNT CHARDONNAY 1992 Hunter Valley (Aus)
87	£7.25	BARREL FERMENTED CHARDONNAY, ROTHBURY 1992 Hunter Valley (Aus)
91	£8.40	MARQUES DE MURRIETA RIOJA RESERVA BLANCO 1987 Rioja (Sp)
104	£10.45	CHARDONNAY, JANE HUNTER'S WINES 1991 Marlborough (NZ)
106	£10.95	EDNA VALLEY CHARDONNAY 1990 Edna Valley (Cal)
117	£17.95	RIDGE CHARDONNAY 1990 St Cruz (Cal)
119	£17.60	ROBERT MONDAVI RESERVE CHARDONNAY 1988 Napa Valley (Cal)
134	£4.55	DOMAINE DE MAUBET VIN DE PAYS DES COTES DE GASCOGNE, FONTAN 1992 South West (F)
162	£6.99	SELAKS MARLBOROUGH SAUVIGNON BLANC 1991 Marlborough (NZ)
168	£10.75	SANCERRE LES ROCHES, DOMAINE VACHERON 1992 Loire (F)
168	£10.75	SANCERRE LES ROCHES, DOMAINE VACHERON 1992 Loire (F)
169	£9.60	HUNTERS MARLBOROUGH SAUVIGNON BLANC 1993 Marlborough (NZ)
266	£5.30	SALISBURY ESTATE CABERNET SAUVIGNON 1991 South East Australia (Aus)
273	£8.15	TALTARNI FIDDLEBACK TERRACE 1990 Pyrenees (Aus)

282	£7.45	VALLEY OAKS CABERNET SAUVIGNON, FETZER 1990 Mendocino County (Cal)
294	£9.75	CHATEAU DE ANNEREAUX, LALANDE DE POMEROL 1989 Bordeaux (F)
303	£11.45	PETALUMA COONAWARRA RED 1988 Coonawarra (Aus)
321	£25.70	ORNELLAIA 1990 Tuscany (It)
346	£8.40	CHATEAU MUSAR, 1986 Bekaa Valley (Leb)
370	£17.95	YARRA YERING SHIRAZ NO.2 1990 Yarra Valley (Aus)
404	£17.60	ROBERT MONDAVI RESERVE PINOT NOIR 1988 Napa Valley (Cal)
414	£4.50	DOLCETTO D'ASTI, ARALDICA 1992 Piedmont (It)
422	£9.75	CHIANTI CLASSICO, ISOLE E OLENA 1990 Tuscany (It)
447	£6.50	CAMPO VIEJO RIOJA RESERVA 1987 Rioja (Sp)
484	£18.75	MATUSALEM, GONZALEZ BYASS Jerez (Sp)
496	£15.75	TAYLOR'S TEN YEAR OLD TAWNY Douro (P)

BWC | Berkmanns Wine Cellar/ Le Nez Rouge

12 Brewery Road, London N7 9NH (Tel 609 4711). **Opening Hours**: Mon-Fri 9am-5.30pm, Sat 10am-2pm. **Delivery:** free for 3 cases or more within the London postal area and M25. **Tastings:** tutored events. **Discounts:** £1 per case collection discount.

Despite the arrival of some fine Argentinian wines from Norton Estate – 'absolutely lethal' according to Joseph Berkmann – and the Yarra Valley wines of Coldstream Hills, Berkmann (which incorporates Le Nez Rouge wine club), has faithfully stuck to 'what it knows best', meaning France, and particularly Burgundy. There are Duboeuf Beaujolais galore, while Côte d'Or fans will be drawn to the wares of Fougeray de Beauclair, Hudelot-Noëllat, Etienne Sauzet and Méo Camuzet. The claret list contains both big names and reasonable prices, and if you're after France's best Champagne lookalike, there's the excellent Charles de Fère.

79	£6.20	ROSEMOUNT CHARDONNAY 1992 Hunter Valley (AUS)
156	£6.40	MUSCADET CHATEAU DU CLERAY, SAUVION ET FILS 1992 Loire (F)
394	£7.82	COLDSTREAM HILLS PINOT NOIR 1992 Yarra Valley (AUS)

BBR | Berry Bros & Rudd Ltd

3 St James St, London SW1A 1EG (Tel 071 396 9600 Fax 071-396 9611).**Opening Hours**: London:Mon-Fri 9am-5.30pm,Sat Dec only;Basingstoke:Mon-Fri 9am- 5pm, Sat 9am-1pm, 24hr: 071 396 9644. **Delivery:** free locally, nationally for 1 case or more. **Tastings:** in store. **Discounts:** 3% on 3-5 cases, 5% on 5-10 cases, 7.5% on 10 cases or more.

German Specialist Wine Merchant of the Year

Step back 250 years and enter the museum-like premises on St James Street. Berry's 'continues to offer an ever increasing breadth of choice' (which we take to mean a gentle shift away from 'old-fashioned' reds with which they were associated). The chunky little list, complete with maps, covers the very best of Bordeaux, Burgundy and unsung German greats, as well as a super section on 'everyday drinkers' (£4-5), many of which are the firm's 'own label'.

33	£34.00	BOLLINGER GRANDE ANNEE 1985 Champagne (F)
150	£6.70	KONOCTI SAUVIGNON BLANC 1991 LAKE COUNTY (CAL)
169	£9.95	HUNTERS MARLBOROUGH SAUVIGNON BLANC 1992 Marlborough (NZ)
174	£13.80	POUILLY FUME, DE LADOUCETTE 1990 Loire (F)
293	£9.60	THE ANGELUS CABERNET SAUVIGNON, WIRRA WIRRA 1991 S Australia (Aus)
336	£7.30	ZINFANDEL, FETZER VINEYARDS 1990 Mendocino County (Cal)

342	£8.07	PETER LEHMANN 'CLANCY'S RED' 1990 Barossa Valley (Aus)
393	£9.50	SANCERRE ROUGE, A DEZAT 1990 Loire (F)
443	£4.95	QUINTA DE LA ROSA RED TABLE WINE 1991 Douro (P)
468	£7.50H	NELSON LATE HARVEST RHINE RIESLING, SEIFRIED 1991 Nelson (NZ)
482	£11.45	LUSTAU OLD EAST INDIA, EMILIO LUSTAU Jerez (Sp)

BI	**Bibendum Wine Ltd / Yorkshire Fine Wines**

113 Regents Park Road, London, London NW1 8UR (Tel 071 722 5577 Fax 071 722 7354).
Opening Hours: Mon-Sat 10am-8pm. **Delivery**: free within the M25. **Tastings**: regular in store, plus tutored events. **Discounts**: by negotiation; regular promotions.

Can one specialise in virtually everything? The boys in bow ties from Bibendum see no inconsistency in claiming 17 separate areas of specialisation. There is an enticing array of individual Burgundy and Rhône domaines, a starry Italian range; and, with the arrival of Chalk Hill, an impressive American selection. Simon Farr has also addressed areas of previous weakness, expanding the Australian range, developing some new house wines and, for the first time ever, putting a Liebfraumilch on his list!

8	£6.95	DOMINIQUE CHARNAY BLANC DE BLANCS 1989 Burgundy (F)
32	£18.98	CHAMPAGNE HENRI BILLIOT Champagne (F)
33	£29.00	BOLLINGER GRANDE ANNEE 1985 Champagne (F)
34	£45.00	CHAMPAGNE LOUISE POMMERY VINTAGE ROSE 1988 Champagne (F)
83	£6.95	VERNACCIA DI S. GIMIGNANO, PODERI MONTENIDOLI 1991 Tuscany (It)
91	£8.95	MARQUES DE MURRIETA RIOJA RESERVA BLANCO 1987 Rioja (Sp)
96	£8.85	VALLEY VINEYARDS FUME BLANC 1991 Berkshire (UK)
111	£11.95	CHALK HILL CHARDONNAY 1991 Sonoma (Cal)
143	£4.99	SANTA RITA RESERVA SAUVIGNON 1993 Maule (Ch)
145	£4.98	VERDICCHIO DEI CASTELLI DI JESI, BRUNORI 1991 (It)
150	£5.39	KONOCTI SAUVIGNON BLANC 1991 Lake County (Cal)
160	£6.95	GROVE MILL SAUVIGNON 1992 Blenheim (NZ)
183	£7.35	ARNEIS ROERO, MALVIRA 1992 Piedmont (It)
184	£9.30	PINOT GRIGIO, LA VIARTE 1991 Friuli Venezia Giulia (It)
251	£3.98	LA SERRE CABERNET SAUVIGNON, VIN DE PAYS D'OC 1991 Midi (F)
323	£35.00	CHATEAU COS D'ESTOURNEL, ST ESTEPHE 1982 Bordeaux (F)
387	£6.98	CAMERON PINOT NOIR Willamette ValleyUSA
396	£9.50	SAINTSBURY PINOT NOIR 1991 Carneros (Cal)
406	£22.00	NUITS ST GEORGES 1ER CRU 'LES PRULIERS', DOMAINE LUCIEN BOILLOT ET FILS 1990 Burgundy (F)
455	£8.98	REMELLURI RIOJA CRIANZA 1989 Rioja (Sp)
479	£22.95	VOUVRAY MOELLEUX, CLOS DU BOURG, GASTON HUET 1990 Loire (F)
494	£13.50	WARRE'S TRADITIONAL LBV 1981 Douro (P)
497	£16.95	NIEPOORT COLHEITA 1983 Douro (P)

BE	**Bin Ends (London)**

56 Lambs Conduit Street, London, WC1 7PJ (Tel 071 405 3106). **Opening Hours:** Mon-Sat 11am-9pm, Sun 12-3pm & 7-9pm. **Delivery:** free locally. **Tastings:** samples opened regularly plus in-store tastings. Discounts:10% per case (still wine) plus promotions.

Having benefitted from the recent ready availability of bankrupt stock, the self-styled 'pirates of the wine trade' have closed all but one of their London shops and focused their attention on Oxford, Cambridge, Peterborough and Southampton. A sign that the recession may really be over after all?

BN	Bin Ends (Rotherham)

Toone House & Cellars, 83-85 Badsley Moor Lane, Rotherham, S. Yorks, S65 2PH (Tel 0709 36771). **Opening Hours**:Mon-Fri 9.30am-5.30pm, Sat 9.30am-12.30pm. **Delivery**: free locally. **Tastings**: regular in-store and tutored events. **Discounts**: 5% per mixed case, 7.5% on 2 or more.

Patrick Toone is aware that duty-free shopping proves attractive for cheaper wines, though he does remind customers of the hidden cost of 'broken motor springs'. Therefore he is increasing his stocks of finer and rarer wines – the sort of wines you won't find on sale in Calais. Examples that caught our eye included '83 Priorato from Masia Barril, magnums of '83 Sapin Moulin à Vent and Borgogno Barolos back to 1947.

BTH	E H Booth & Co

4-6 Fishergate, Preston, Lancs PR1 3LJ (Tel 0772 51701 Fax 0772 204316). **Opening Hours:** generally Mon-Sat 9am-5pm (some stores open until 8pm). **Tastings**: regular in-store. **Discounts:** 10% per case/mixed case over £3 per bottle.

North of England Wine Merchant of the Year

While Sainsbury's freely admits its lack of interest in up-grading consumer drinking habits, Edwin Booth offers customers of his regional supermarkets a range which such delights as Vega Sicilia, two vintages of Opus One, Krug Clos de Mesnil, Petrus, Mouton, Latour, Romanée Conti and Sassicaia. However, it begins with fairly priced and well-chosen Gascognes and Turckheim Alsaces. We know whose attitude we find most laudable.

3	£5.95	SEGURA VIUDAS CAVA BRUT RESERVA Cava (Sp)
11	£6.95	MONTANA LINDAUER BRUT (NZ)
33	£29.95	BOLLINGER GRANDE ANNEE 1985 Champagne (F)
44	£3.95	CHARDONNAY, VINO DA TAVOLA, CA DONINI 1992 Triveneto (It)
53	£4.99	'CASAL DI SERRA' VERDICCHIO CLASSICO, UMANI RONCHI 1991 Marches (It)
79	£5.99	ROSEMOUNT CHARDONNAY 1992 Hunter Valley (Aus)
98	£7.95	LOCAL GROWERS SEMILLON, ROCKFORD 1989 Barossa Valley (Aus)
160	£6.49	GROVE MILL SAUVIGNON 1992 Blenheim (NZ)
161	£6.49	JACKSON ESTATE SAUVIGNON BLANC 1992 Marlborough (NZ)
182	£5.99	GEWURZTRAMINER D'ALSACE, CAVE VINICOLE DE TURCKHEIM 1992 Alsace (F)
196	£3.99	DENBIES ENGLISH WINE 1991 Surrey (UK)
197	£3.39	BADEN DRY, BADISCHER WINZERKELLER Baden (G)
264	£4.99	BUZET TRADITION, LES VIGNERONS DE BUZET 1988 South West (F)
269	£4.99	MONTANA CABERNET SAUVIGNON 1991 Marlborough (NZ)
325	£2.99	CASA DEL CAMPO SYRAH, BODEGAS SANTA ANA 1992 Mendoza (Arg)
346	£7.69	CHATEAU MUSAR, 1986 Bekaa Valley (Leb)
373	£4.99	TARRANGO, BROWN BROTHERS 1992 Milawa (Aus)
427	£8.49	CUMARO ROSSO CONERO, UMANI RONCHI 1989 Marches (It)
497	£17.95	NIEPOORT COLHEITA 1983 Douro (P)

BOO	Booths of Stockport

62 Heaton Moor Road, Stockport, Cheshire SK4 4NZ (Tel 061 432 3309 Fax 061 432 3309). **Opening Hours:** Mon-Fri 9am-7pm, Sat 9am-5.30pm. **Delivery:** free nationally. **Tastings**: in store and tutored events. **Discounts:**10% per case or mixed case.

'We still manage to squeeze in a range of over 500 wines in a space for 300' says

John Booth. Every nook and cranny is filled with wines carefully and enthusiastically chosen by himself and sold by his brother Graham. Though there are over 50 wines from Australia, these boys are Latin lovers too. Watch out for their old peppery Portuguesers (JM da Fonseca/J. Pires), juicy Piedmonts, super Tuscans, high-class Spaniards and hot Mexicans.

5	£6.20	GRAND DUCHESS RUSSIAN SPARKLING WINE, Ukraine
20	£8.60	OMAR KHAYYAM, CHAMPAGNE INDIA 1987 Maharashtra (Ind)
46	£4.60	CHARDONNAY DEL PIEMONTE, ARALDICA 1992 Piedmont (It)
57	£5.50	CHABLIS, LOUIS ALEXANDRE 1992 Burgundy (F)
61	£6.80	LUGANA CA'DEI FRATI 1992 Brescia (It)
64	£7.95	TASMANIAN WINE COMPANY CHARDONNAY, PIPER'S BROOK 1991 (Aus)
74	£4.99	PENFOLDS KOONUNGA HILL CHARDONNAY 1992 South East Australia (Aus)
77	£4.80	SALISBURY ESTATE CHARDONNAY 1992 South East Australia (Aus)
80	£6.40	CHATEAU REYNELLA STONY HILL CHARDONNAY 1990 South Australia (Aus)
91	£7.60	MARQUES DE MURRIETA RIOJA RESERVA BLANCO 1987 Rioja (Sp)
146	£5.90	HARDY'S MOONDAH BROOK ESTATE CHENIN BLANC 1992 Gingin, Western Australia (Aus)
160	£6.70	GROVE MILL SAUVIGNON 1992 Blenheim (NZ)
161	£7.50	JACKSON ESTATE SAUVIGNON BLANC 1992 Marlborough (NZ)
164	£7.80	MENETOU SALON LES MOROGUES HENRI PELLE 1992 Loire (F)
188	£5.50	PETER LEHMANN SEMILLON 1992 Barossa Valley (Aus)
189	£7.95	LAGAR DE CERVERA, RIAS BAIXAS, LAGAR DE FORNELOSSA 1992 Galicia (Sp)
218	£6.25	MOUNT HURTLE GRENACHE ROSE, GEOFF MERRILL 1992 McLaren Vale (Aus)
237	£5.50	CUVEE MYTHIQUE, VIN DE PAYS D'OC, VAL D'ORBIEU 1990 Midi (F)
238	£5.95	CHATEAU DE LASTOURS CORBIERES, FUT DE CHENE 1989 Midi (F)
266	£4.80	SALISBURY ESTATE CABERNET SAUVIGNON 1991 South East Australia (Aus)
270	£5.90	HARDY'S MOONDAH BROOK ESTATE CABERNET SAUVIGNON 1989 Gingin, Western Australia (Aus)
273	£5.50	TALTARNI FIDDLEBACK TERRACE 1990 Pyrenees (Aus)
298	£9.95	LINDEMANS ST GEORGE CABERNET SAUVIGNON 1989 Coonawarra (Aus)
299	£10.30	MEERLUST MERLOT, STELLENBOSCH 1986 Stellenbosch (SA)
321	£21.65	ORNELLAIA 1990 Tuscany (It)
326	£3.55	RESPLANDY MOUVEDRE, VIN DE PAYS D'OC, VAL D'ORBIEU 1990 Midi (F)
342	£6.65	PETER LEHMANN 'CLANCY'S RED' 1990 Barossa Valley (Aus)
346	£7.95	CHATEAU MUSAR, 1986 Bekaa Valley (Leb)
348	£8.40	ROSEMOUNT SHOW RESERVE SYRAH 1990 McLaren Vale (Aus)
350	£9.40	BROKENWOOD SHIRAZ 1991 South East Australia (Aus)
353	£8.90	DAVID WYNN PATRIARCH SHIRAZ 1991 Eden Valley (Aus)
365	£12.95	PENFOLDS MAGILL ESTATE SHIRAZ 1988 South Australia (Aus)
377	£5.85	CHENAS, DOMAINE DE CHASSIGNOL, JACQUES DEPAGNEUX 1992 Beaujolais (F)
414	£4.50	DOLCETTO D'ASTI, ARALDICA 1992 Piedmont (It)
422	£7.95	CHIANTI CLASSICO, ISOLE E OLENA 1990 Tuscany (It)
424	£6.95	DOLCETTO D'ALBA CORSINI, MASCARELLO 1991 Piedmont (It)
428	£9.99	BRIC MILEUI, ASCHERI 1990 Piedmont (It)
438	£3.65	ALBOR RIOJA TINTO, BODEGAS & BEBIDAS 1991 Rioja (Sp)
444	£4.30	PERIQUITA, J M DA FONSECA 1990 (P)
447	£5.85	CAMPO VIEJO RIOJA RESERVA 1987 Rioja (Sp)
448	£6.20	CARTUXA, FUNDACO E ALMEIDA 1989 Evora (P)
450	£6.95	YLLERA, VINO DE MESA, SAT LOS CURRO 1988 Ribera del Duero (Sp)
453	£9.25	JOAO PATO TINTO, BAIRRADA 1990 Bairrada (P)
461	£10.80	STANTON & KILLEEN RUTHERGLEN LIQUEUR MUSCAT Rutherglen (Aus)
462	£13.50	CAMPBELLS RUTHERGLEN LIQUEUR MUSCAT Rutherglen (Aus)
491	£9.90	DOWS CRUSTED PORT BOTTLED 1987 Douro (P)
494	£6.45H	WARRE'S TRADITIONAL LBV 1981 Douro (P)

| BD | **Bordeaux Direct** |

New Aquitaine House, Paddock Road, Reading, Berkshire RG4 0JY (Tel 0734 481718 Fax 0734 461953). **Opening Hours**: Mon-Fri 10.30am-7pm, Thurs 10.30am-8pm, Sat 9am-6pm. **Delivery:** free nationally over £50. **Tastings:** samples opened regularly, plus in-store tastings and tutored events. **Discounts:** special offers and bulk deals.

Every year we do our best to untangle the relationship between this five-branch retailer and mail order company and the *Sunday Times* Wine Club. We remain confused ('many wines and offers are common to both – although they also have exclusive wines and deals. The buying team is the same').

94   £8.29   **VINAVIUS CHARDONNAY, DOMAINE DES COUSSERGUES, VIN DE PAYS D'OC 1991 Midi (F)**

| BGC | **Borg Castel** |

Samlesbury Mill, Goosefoot Lane, Samlesbury Bottom, Preston, Lancashire PR5 0RN (Tel 0254 852128 Fax 0254 852128). **Opening Hours**: Mon-Fri 10am-5pm, Thurs evening: 7-9.30pm, first Sunday in the month 12am-4pm. **Delivery:** free within 30 miles. **Tastings:** regular in-store. **Discounts:** on 3 or more cases.

A weird and wonderful selection concentrating on Bordeaux and Burgundy, with some interesting bin ends, including '64 Echezeaux from Chanson, a 1985 Quincy and the gloriously out-of-fashion Mafoux Red Sparkling Burgundy.

| BNK | **The Bottleneck** |

7/9 Charlotte St, Broadstairs, Kent CT10 1LR (Tel 0843 861095). **Opening Hours**: Mon-Sat 9am-9pm, Sun 12-2pm, 7-9pm. **Delivery:** free locally. **Tastings:** regular in-store and tutored events. **Discounts:** 5% per mixed case, negotiable on higher quantities.

At the grand old age of five, a recesssion and a few accolades under their belt Chris & Lin Beckett are nowadays counting on Australian, New Zealand, Chilean and East European wines to keep the wheels turning, though they keep up fine wine appearances with some excellent '83 and '85 Bordeaux. Any Kentish men or maids wishing to be further informed should join the newly formed Beckett Wine Appreciation group. (Will no one rid me of this wine..?)

11	£6.99	**MONTANA LINDAUER BRUT (NZ)**
57	£5.99	**CHABLIS, LOUIS ALEXANDRE 1992 Burgundy (F)**
64	£8.49	**TASMANIAN WINE COMPANY CHARDONNAY, PIPER'S BROOK 1991 (Aus)**
70	£3.99	**TIMARA WHITE, MONTANA 1991 (NZ)**
269	£4.99	**MONTANA CABERNET SAUVIGNON 1991 Marlborough (NZ)**
346	£7.95	**CHATEAU MUSAR, 1986 Bekaa Valley (Leb)**
462	£9.95	**CAMPBELLS RUTHERGLEN LIQUEUR MUSCAT Rutherglen (Aus)**
484	£18.99	**MATUSALEM, GONZALEZ BYASS Jerez (Sp)**

| BU | **Bottoms Up** |

Sefton House, 42 Church Road, Welwyn Garden City, Hertfordshire AL8 6LE (Tel 0707 328244 Fax 0707 371398). **Opening Hours**: Mon-Sat 10am-10pm; Sundays vary. **Discounts:** £.60 per case collection discount.

Following the publication of its second designer list (including a piece by the editor of the *Guide*), and 18 months after becoming part of the Thresher empire, this chain of 'high street wine warehouses' is one of the most exciting things to happen to wine in Britain for some time. The staff are cast in the Oddbins/Majestic mould and the promise is never to be undersold!

Bottoms Up stock virtually all the Thresher Wines, plus the following:-

84	£6.99	**COVA DA URSA CHARDONNAY 1991 Terras do Sado (P)**
92	£7.99	MONTANA CHURCH ROAD CHARDONNAY 1991 (NZ)
96	£7.49	**VALLEY VINEYARDS FUME BLANC 1991 Berkshire (UK)**
112	£11.99	**ELSTON CHARDONNAY, TE MATA ESTATE 1991 Hawkes Bay (NZ)**
115	£16.65	**NEWTON UNFILTERED CHARDONNAY 1990 Napa Valley (Cal)**
240	£9.99	MADIRAN, MONTUS, ALAIN BRUMONT 1990 South West (F)
300	£9.99	L'ABEILLE DE FIEUZAL, PESSAC LEOGNAN 1990 Bordeaux (F)
310	£12.99	**LE CARILLON DE L'ANGELUS, ST EMILION 1990 Bordeaux (F)**
312	£13.49	**RESERVE DE LA COMTESSE, PAUILLAC 1987 Bordeaux (F)**
360	£10.99	**ST JOSEPH L'OLIVAIE, P COURSODON 1991 Rhône (F)**
424	£6.99	DOLCETTO D'ALBA CORSINI, MASCARELLO 1991 Piedmont (It)
444	£4.15	**PERIQUITA, J M DA FONSECA 1990 (P)**
486	£7.99	**RIVESALTES, VIEILLE RESERVE, PRODUCTEURS DU MONT TAUCH 1980 Midi (F)**

BRO	Broad Street Wine Co

Emscote Mill, Wharf Street, Warwick, Warwickshire CU34 5LB (Tel 0926 493951 Fax 0926 495345). **Opening Hours:** Mon-Fri 9am-6pm, Sat 9am-1pm. **Delivery:** free locally. **Tastings:** occasional in-store plus tutored events. **Discounts:** £1.60 per case, other discounts negotiable.

The specialist area is Vintage Brandies; but a broad's gotta live, so there's also a good range of classic French wines and an extraordinary selection from New Zealand, including Rongopai, Aotea, Vidal, Cloudy Bay, Redwood Valley and the incredible Ata Rangi Pinot Noir.

BWI	Bute Wines

Mount Stuart, Rothesay, Isle of Bute, Argyll & Bute PA20 9LP (Tel 0700 502730 Fax 0700 505313). **Opening Hours:** Mon-Fri 7.30am-5pm (often available weekends too). Also on 071-937 1629.

Fresh from her appearance on television's 'Vintners' Tales', the charming Marchioness has been organising dinners and tastings nationwide, teaching the uninitiated and fending off the media. But she's still found time to stray beyond Bordeaux and Burgundy (of which she still has many old vintages) to include Bonny Doon, '86 Kirri Billi Merlot and four vintages of Sassicaia and to list such 'Bute's Bin Ends' as '75 Chalone Pinot Noir and '78 Grange Hermitage. There's also an appropriate fizz on offer called Angus Brut. What an Australian might call a 'bute' wine, presumably.

33	£30.03	**BOLLINGER GRANDE ANNEE 1985 Champagne (F)**
124	£29.05	**NUITS ST GEORGES CLOS DE L'ARLOT BLANC, DOMAINE DE L'ARLOT 1990 Burgundy (F)**
160	£6.94	**GROVE MILL SAUVIGNON 1992 Blenheim (NZ)**
195	£3.99	**HOCK TAFELWEIN, RUDOLF MULLER Rheinhessen (G)**
296	£9.03	**CHATEAU TOUR DU HAUT MOULIN, HAUT MEDOC 1985 Bordeaux (F)**
311	£14.65	**CHATEAU CISSAC, HAUT-MEDOC 1982 Bordeaux (F)**
320	£20.59	**CHATEAU PICHON LONGUEVILLE BARON, PAUILLAC 1990 Bordeaux (F)**

322	£25.44	CHATEAU LYNCH-BAGES, PAUILLAC 1989 Bordeaux (F)
323	£39.68	CHATEAU COS D'ESTOURNEL, ST ESTEPHE 1982 Bordeaux (F)
408	£22.88	NUITS ST GEORGES 'CLOS DE L'ARLOT', DOMAINE DE L'ARLOT 1988 Burgundy (F)

BUT | The Butlers Wine Cellar

247 Queens Park Road, Brighton, Sussex BN2 2XJ (Tel 0273 698724 Fax 0273 622761). **Opening Hours:** Tues/Wed 9am-5.30pm, Thurs-Sat 9am-7pm. **Delivery:** free within 10 miles.

Brighton breezy wine lovers should relish this Aladdin's cave of everyday drinking from South Africa, Australia and France and special offers (Gevrey Chambertin at £9.50 – if you don't mind the anonymity of the producer, and the 1973 vintage), Russian wines, Bordeaux and Burgundy back to the 40's.

| 57 | £5.95 | CHABLIS, LOUIS ALEXANDRE 1992 Burgundy (F) |
| 163 | £8.75 | BOURGOGNE ALIGOTE, VALLET FRERES 1990 Burgundy (F) |

ABY | Anthony Byrne Fine Wines Ltd

88 High St, Ramsey, Huntingdon, Cambridgeshire PE17 1BS (Tel 0487 814555 Fax 0487 814962). **Opening Hours:** Mon-Sat 9am-5.30pm. **Delivery:** free nationally for 2 or more cases. **Tastings:** tutored events. **Discounts:** collection discount, dependent on quantity.

Mr Byrne's biggest fans are some of the best chefs and sommeliers in Britain. They appreciate wines classy enough to stand alongside really good cooking. The 1993 *Guide*'s Centre of England Wine Merchant of the Year did as well as ever in this year's Challenge, scoring a higher hit-rate than any other entrant. With strikers like Domaine de l'Arlot and Zind Humbrecht , that's hardly surprising, but he's chosen the other players – Franciscan, Palliser, Fetzer, Isole e Olena, Gagnard Delagrange – just as well.

11	£7.03	MONTANA LINDAUER BRUT (NZ)
12	£8.79	TOURAINE ROSE BRUT, CAVES DES VITICULTEURS DE VOUVRAY Loire (F)
25	£11.95	CROSER METHODE TRADITIONNELLE, PETALUMA 1990 Adelaide Hills (Aus)
28	£16.80	DRAPPIER BLANC DE BLANCS CHAMPAGNE Champagne (F)
33	£30.67	BOLLINGER GRANDE ANNEE 1985 Champagne (F)
34	£46.59	CHAMPAGNE LOUISE POMMERY VINTAGE ROSE 1988 Champagne (F)
43	£3.84	COTES DE ST MONT WHITE, PLAIMONT 1991 South West (F)
46	£4.55	CHARDONNAY DEL PIEMONTE, ARALDICA 1992 Piedmont (It)
61	£6.74	LUGANA CA'DEI FRATI 1992 Brescia (It)
64	£8.34	TASMANIAN WINE COMPANY CHARDONNAY, PIPER'S BROOK 1991 (Aus)
73	£4.27	COTES DE SAINT MONT CUVEE PRESTIGE BLANC, A DAGUIN 1991 S West (F)
74	£5.09	PENFOLDS KOONUNGA HILL CHARDONNAY 1992 South East Australia (Aus)
79	£6.20	ROSEMOUNT CHARDONNAY 1992 Hunter Valley (Aus)
80	£6.22	CHATEAU REYNELLA STONY HILL CHARDONNAY 1990 South Australia (Aus)
81	£7.20	CATHEDRAL CELLARS CHARDONNAY, KWV 1991 Coastal Region (SA)
88	£7.20	BOURGOGNE BLANC, HENRI CLERC 1991 Burgundy (F)
95	£7.90	BARREL SELECT CHARDONNAY, FETZER 1991 Mendocino County (Cal)
112	£10.42	ELSTON CHARDONNAY, TE MATA ESTATE 1991 Hawkes Bay (NZ)
122	£18.75	PULIGNY MONTRACHET 1ER CRU FOLATIERES, HENRI CLERC 1991 Burgundy (F)
124	£28.47	NUITS ST GEORGES CLOS DE L'ARLOT BLANC, DOMAINE DE L'ARLOT 1990 Burgundy (F)
143	£4.94	SANTA RITA RESERVA SAUVIGNON 1993 Maule (Ch)
146	£5.16	HARDY'S MOONDAH BROOK ESTATE CHENIN BLANC 1992 Gingin, Western Australia (Aus)

166	£7.36	TERRES BLANCHES BLANC, AIX EN PROVENCE LES BAUX, NOEL MICHELIN 1992 Midi (F)
171	£9.90	POGGIO ALLE GAZZE, TENUTA DELL'ORNELLAIA 1991 Tuscany (It)
186	£20.98	TOKAY PINOT GRIS VIELLES VIGNES, ZIND HUMBRECHT 1990 Alsace (F)
190	£10.48	MUSCAT, DOMAINE ZIND HUMBRECHT 1991 Alsace (F)
194	£3.91	TOLLANA DRY WHITE 1992 South East Australia (Aus)
211	£17.75	RIESLING HERRENWEG VENDANGE TARDIVE, ZIND HUMBRECHT 1990 Alsace (F)
219	£5.92	ROSE ARGI D'ANSA, LES MAÎTRES VIGNERONS D'IROULEGUY 1992 S West (F)
221	£7.36	TERRES BLANCHES VIN ROSE 1992 Midi (F)
268	£5.64	BEL ARBORS MERLOT, FETZER VINEYARDS 1991 Mendocino County (Cal)
269	£5.19	MONTANA CABERNET SAUVIGNON 1991 Marlborough (NZ)
270	£5.16	HARDY'S MOONDAH BROOK ESTATE CABERNET SAUVIGNON 1989 Gingin, Western Australia (Aus)
279	£5.98	MICHEL LYNCH BORDEAUX ROUGE, COMPAGNIE MEDOCAINE 1989 Bordeaux (F)
282	£6.17	FETZER VALLEY OAKS CABERNET SAUVIGNON 1990 Mendocino County (Cal)
294	£9.47	CHATEAU DE ANNEREAUX, LALANDE DE POMEROL 1989 Bordeaux (F)
295	£8.80	FETZER BARREL SELECT CABERNET SAUVIGNON 1989 Mendocino County (Cal)
298	£9.93	LINDEMANS ST GEORGE CABERNET SAUVIGNON 1989 Coonawarra (Aus)
303	£10.32	PETALUMA COONAWARRA RED 1988 Coonawarra (Aus)
312	£16.96	RESERVE DE LA COMTESSE, PAUILLAC 1987 Bordeaux (F)
317	£18.46	CHATEAU HAUT BAGES AVEROUS, PAUILLAC 1988 Bordeaux (F)
321	£23.40	ORNELLAIA 1990 Tuscany (It)
336	£5.19	ZINFANDEL, FETZER VINEYARDS 1990 Mendocino County (Cal)
346	£7.90	CHATEAU MUSAR, 1986 Bekaa Valley (Leb)
365	£12.66	PENFOLDS MAGILL ESTATE SHIRAZ 1988 South Australia (Aus)
373	£4.85	TARRANGO, BROWN BROTHERS 1992 Milawa (Aus)
402	£14.65	BEAUNE 1ER CRU TEURONS, DOMAINE ROSSIGNOL TRAPET 1990 Burgundy (F)
403	£15.12	NUITS SAINT GEORGES, DOMAINE DE L'ARLOT 1990 Burgundy (F)
408	£23.79	NUITS ST GEORGES 'CLOS DE L'ARLOT', DOM. DE L'ARLOT 1988 Burgundy (F)
409	£26.20	CORTON CLOS DU ROY, DUBREUIL FONTAINE 1990 Burgundy (F)
414	£4.54	DOLCETTO D'ASTI, ARALDICA 1992 Piedmont (It)
415	£4.98	VALPOLICELLA CLASSICO, MASI 1991 Veneto (It)
418	£7.03	VERNACULUM ZOCCOLANTI-PERGOLA, VILLA LIGI 1992 Umbria (It)
422	£8.82	CHIANTI CLASSICO, ISOLE E OLENA 1990 Tuscany (It)
423	£8.53	CARMIGNANO, CAPEZZANA 1987 Tuscany (It)
426	£9.41	FREISA DELLE LANGHE, G D VAJRA 1990 Piedmont (It)
428	£10.22	BRIC MILEUI, ASCHERI 1990 Piedmont (It)
461	£11.42	STANTON & KILLEEN RUTHERGLEN LIQUEUR MUSCAT Rutherglen (Aus)
488	£7.66	OLD TRAFFORD TAWNY, B. SEPPELT & SONS South East Australia (Aus)
489	£9.78	CHURCHILL GRAHAM FINEST VINTAGE CHARACTER Douro (P)
492	£12.10	COLHEITA, A A CALEM & FILHO 1985 Douro (P)
500	£6.86	ELECTRA, QUADY WINERY 1991 Madera County (Cal)

| **DBY** | D Byrne & Co |

Victoria Buildings, 12 King Street, Clitheroe, Lancashire BB7 2EP (Tel 0200 23152). **Opening Hours:** Mon,Tues,Wed,Sat 8.30am-6pm, Thurs/Fri 8.30am-8pm. **Delivery:** free within 20 miles. **Tastings:** Regular in-store and tutored. Discounts: £1.20 per mixed case.

Recently taken over by great-grandsons A & P Byrne, this family owned business has changed only in keeping up with current drinking habits. Andrew and Philip are currently looking to expand the already well represented areas of Italy and Australia (Prunotto, Ceretto, Masi; Piper's Brook, Leeuwin, Stonier's Merricks) and are 'dabnosed' at sniffing out 'wine bargains and bin ends to be had in these hard times'. Drop in on their lovely old shop and cellars for a snoop at the thousand different wines therein.

11	£6.69	MONTANA LINDAUER BRUT (NZ)
17	£7.99	BOUVET LADUBAY SAUMUR BRUT Loire (F)
20	£7.99	OMAR KHAYYAM, CHAMPAGNE INDIA 1987 Maharashtra (Ind)
22	£8.09	MAYERLING CREMANT D'ALSACE, CAVE VINICOLE DE TURCKHEIM Alsace (F)
24	£9.89	GREEN POINT, DOMAINE CHANDON 1990 Yarra Valley (Aus)
33	£26.69	BOLLINGER GRANDE ANNEE 1985 Champagne (F)
45	£4.09	NOBILO WHITE CLOUD 1992 (NZ)
46	£3.89	CHARDONNAY DEL PIEMONTE, ARALDICA 1992 Piedmont (It)
53	£5.09	'CASAL DI SERRA' VERDICCHIO CLASSICO, UMANI RONCHI 1991 Marches (It)
54	£5.75	MONTES UNOAKED CHARDONNAY, DISCOVER WINES LTDA 1993 Curico (Ch)
57	£5.39	CHABLIS, LOUIS ALEXANDRE 1992 Burgundy (F)
61	£5.59	LUGANA CA'DEI FRATI 1992 Brescia (It)
64	£7.45	TASMANIAN WINE COMPANY CHARDONNAY, PIPER'S BROOK 1991 (Aus)
70	£3.99	TIMARA WHITE, MONTANA 1991 (NZ)
74	£4.89	PENFOLDS KOONUNGA HILL CHARDONNAY 1992 South East Australia (Aus)
80	£5.99	CHATEAU REYNELLA STONY HILL CHARDONNAY 1990 South Australia (Aus)
81	£7.49	CATHEDRAL CELLARS CHARDONNAY, KWV 1991 Coastal Region (SA)
87	£6.15	BARREL FERMENTED CHARDONNAY, ROTHBURY 1992 Hunter Valley (Aus)
91	£7.89	MARQUES DE MURRIETA RIOJA RESERVA BLANCO 1987 Rioja (Sp)
98	£7.85	LOCAL GROWERS SEMILLON, ROCKFORD 1989 Barossa Valley (Aus)
99	£9.19	KRONDORF SHOW RESERVE CHARDONNAY 1991 Barossa Valley (Aus)
101	£9.39	VIEUX CHATEAU GAUBERT, GRAVES 1991 Bordeaux (F)
104	£8.69	CHARDONNAY, JANE HUNTER'S WINES 1991 Marlborough (NZ)
108	£9.18	SWANSON CHARDONNAY, NAPA VALLEY 1990 Napa Valley (Cal)
112	£11.79	ELSTON CHARDONNAY, TE MATA ESTATE 1991 Hawkes Bay (NZ)
119	£16.25	ROBERT MONDAVI RESERVE CHARDONNAY 1988 Napa Valley (Cal)
123	£19.15	TORRES MILMANDA CHARDONNAY 1991 Penedes (Sp)
134	£3.79	DOMAINE DE MAUBET VIN DE PAYS DES COTES DE GASCOGNE, FONTAN 1992 South West (F)
144	£4.39	COTEAUX DE LANGUEDOC PICPOUL DE PINET, DUC DE MORNY 1991 Midi (F)
146	£4.99	HARDY'S MOONDAH BROOK ESTATE CHENIN BLANC 1992 Gingin, Western (Aus)
149	£5.79	ZONNEBLOEM BLANC DE BLANC, STELLENBOSCH FARMERS WINERY 1991 Coastal Region (SA)
156	£5.89	MUSCADET CHATEAU DU CLERAY, SAUVION ET FILS 1992 Loire (F)
162	£6.99	SELAKS MARLBOROUGH SAUVIGNON BLANC 1991 Marlborough (NZ)
163	£7.25	BOURGOGNE ALIGOTE, VALLET FRERES 1990 Burgundy (F)
164	£7.49	MENETOU SALON LES MOROGUES HENRI PELLE 1992 Loire (F)
169	£8.05	HUNTERS MARLBOROUGH SAUVIGNON BLANC 1992 Marlborough (NZ)
171	£9.08	POGGIO ALLE GAZZE, TENUTA DELL'ORNELLAIA 1991 Tuscany (It)
174	£10.29	POUILLY FUME, DE LADOUCETTE 1990 Loire (F)
182	£6.39	GEWURZTRAMINER D'ALSACE, CAVE VINICOLE DE TURCKHEIM 1992 Alsace (F)
188	£4.99	PETER LEHMANN SEMILLON 1992 Barossa Valley (Aus)
218	£5.59	MOUNT HURTLE GRENACHE ROSE, GEOFF MERRILL 1992 McLaren Vale (Aus)
238	£5.85	CHATEAU DE LASTOURS CORBIERES, FUT DE CHENE 1989 Midi (F)
244	£2.69	RUSSE CABERNET CINSAULT (Bul)
250	£3.15	STAMBOLOVO RESERVE MERLOT 1987 (Bul)
256	£3.99	HARDYS NOTTAGE HILL CABERNET SAUVIGNON 1991 South Australia (Aus)
269	£4.79	MONTANA CABERNET SAUVIGNON 1991 Marlborough (NZ)
272	£4.99	ROUGE HOMME CABERNET/SHIRAZ, COONAWARRA 1988 Coonawarra (Aus)
275	£6.59	RUSTENBERG MERLOT, STELLENBOSCH 1991 Stellenbosch (SA)
279	£5.99	MICHEL LYNCH BORDEAUX ROUGE, COMPAGNIE MEDOCAINE 1989 Bordeaux (F)
281	£5.99	CHATEAU BONNET OAK AGED, A LURTON 1990 Bordeaux (F)
291	£9.79	CHATEAU LA TOUR HAUT-CAUSSAN, MEDOC 1989 Bordeaux (F)
294	£8.09	CHATEAU DE ANNEREAUX, LALANDE DE POMEROL 1989 Bordeaux (F)
299	£9.69	MEERLUST MERLOT, STELLENBOSCH 1986 Stellenbosch (SA)
301	£10.09	CHATEAU LA TOUR DE PEZ, ST ESTEPHE 1990 Bordeaux (F)

303	£10.49	PETALUMA COONAWARRA RED 1988 Coonawarra (Aus)
305	£10.45	CYRIL HENSCHKE CABERNET SAUVIGNON, HENSCHKE 1988 Adelaide Hills (Aus)
330	£3.89	VIN DE PAYS DES COLLINES RHODANIENNES CEPAGE SYRAH, CAVE DE TAIN L'HERMITAGE Rhône (F)
335	£4.49	COTES DU RHONE DOMAINE DE TERRE BRULEE, CAVE DE VIGNERONS DE RASTEAU 1990 Rhône (F)
336	£7.89	ZINFANDEL, FETZER VINEYARDS 1990 Mendocino County (Cal)
342	£6.09	PETER LEHMANN 'CLANCY'S RED' 1990 Barossa Valley (Aus)
346	£7.19	CHATEAU MUSAR, 1986 Bekaa Valley (Leb)
348	£8.59	ROSEMOUNT SHOW RESERVE SYRAH 1990 McLaren Vale (Aus)
356	£9.89	CHATEAUNEUF DU PAPE, DOMAINE ANDRE BRUNEL 1989 Rhône (F)
363	£9.99	RIDGE GEYSERVILLE ZINFANDEL 1991 Sonoma (Cal)
364	£10.99	CHATEAUNEUF DU PAPE, CHATEAU DE BEAUCASTEL 1988 Rhône (F)
365	£16.89	PENFOLDS MAGILL ESTATE SHIRAZ 1988 South Australia (Aus)
367	£13.99	CORNAS, AUGUSTE CLAPE 1990 Rhône (F)
373	£4.95	TARRANGO, BROWN BROTHERS 1992 Milawa (Aus)
377	£5.49	CHENAS, DOMAINE DE CHASSIGNOL, J DEPAGNEUX 1992 Beaujolais (F)
389	£6.39	HAMILTON-RUSSELL PINOT NOIR, WALKER BAY 1991 Walker Bay (SA)
405	£16.69	BEAUNE 1ER CRU EPENOTTES, VALLET FRERES 1989 Burgundy (F)
414	£3.79	DOLCETTO D'ASTI, ARALDICA 1992 Piedmont (It)
415	£4.54	VALPOLICELLA CLASSICO, MASI 1991 Veneto (It)
422	£7.79	CHIANTI CLASSICO, ISOLE E OLENA 1990 Tuscany (It)
424	£7.09	DOLCETTO D'ALBA CORSINI, MASCARELLO 1991 Piedmont (It)
427	£8.99	CUMARO ROSSO CONERO, UMANI RONCHI 1989 Marches (It)
428	£9.39	BRIC MILEUI, ASCHERI 1990 Piedmont (It)
432	£20.49	RECIOTO DELLA VALPOLICELLA, CASAL DEI RONCHI MASI 1988 Veneto (It)
438	£3.39	ALBOR RIOJA TINTO, BODEGAS & BEBIDAS 1991 Rioja (Sp)
442	£5.29	VALDEMAR RIOJA TINTO, MARTINEZ BUJANDA 1992 Rioja (Sp)
444	£4.09	PERIQUITA, J M DA FONSECA 1990 (P)
447	£5.39	CAMPO VIEJO RIOJA RESERVA 1987 Rioja (Sp)
448	£10.09	CARTUXA, FUNDACO E ALMEIDA 1989 Evora (P)
450	£6.49	YLLERA, VINO DE MESA, SAT LOS CURRO 1988 Ribera del Duero (Sp)
461	£9.19	STANTON & KILLEEN RUTHERGLEN LIQUEUR MUSCAT Rutherglen (Aus)
462	£11.59	CAMPBELLS RUTHERGLEN LIQUEUR MUSCAT Rutherglen (Aus)
467	£5.59H	VIN SANTO BROLIO ESTATE, BARONE RICASOLI 1984 Tuscany (It)
472	£7.70H	NEETHLINGSHOF WEISSER RIESLING NOBLE LATE HARVEST 1991 (SA)
484	£17.00	MATUSALEM, GONZALEZ BYASS Jerez (Sp)
487	£7.39	TOKAJI ASZU 3 PUTTONYOS, TOKAJI-HEGYALA SCHLUMBERGER 1981 (Hun)
488	£6.99	OLD TRAFFORD TAWNY, B. SEPPELT & SONS South East Australia (Aus)
489	£8.59	CHURCHILL GRAHAM FINEST VINTAGE CHARACTER Douro (P)
493	£10.29	HENRIQUES & HENRIQUES 10 YEAR OLD VERDELHO Madeira
496	£12.39	TAYLOR'S TEN YEAR OLD TAWNY Douro (P)
500	£5.65H	ELECTRA, QUADY WINERY 1991 Madera County (Cal)

CPS	CPA's Wine Ltd

44 Queens Road, Mumbles, Swansea, SA3 4AN, (Tel/Fax 0792 360707). **Opening Hours:** Mon, Wed, Thurs, Fri 2-6.30pm, Sat 10am-6pm. **Delivery:** free locally. **Tastings:** tutored events. **Discounts:** 5% per case.

Caroline, Paul & Andrew (C,P & A) have been operating now for two years. Their wine list is short and sweet, dry and sparkling with such high spots as '90 Chablis (JP Grossot), '85 St Joseph (Coursodon) and '89 Mount Edestone Shiraz (Henschke), plus a few local wines from the Llanerch Vineyard, Cardiff. At least one of the trio is always around to listen to, learn from and advise a growing band of faithful followers.

82	£6.45	CARIAD GWIN DA O GYMRU BACCHUS/REICHSTEINER, LLANERCH VINEYARD 1990 Glamorgan (UK)
155	£6.25	ROTHBURY SAUVIGNON BLANC 1992 Marlborough (NZ)
274	£6.70	CHATEAU THIEULEY AC BORDEAUX ROUGE 1989 Bordeaux (F)
282	£6.75	VALLEY OAKS CABERNET SAUVIGNON, FETZER 1990 Mendocino County (Cal)
285	£7.95	CHINON, COULY-DUTHEIL 1990 Loire (F)
296	£10.45	CHATEAU TOUR DU HAUT MOULIN, HAUT MEDOC 1985 Bordeaux (F)
336	£5.50	ZINFANDEL, FETZER VINEYARDS 1990 Mendocino County (Cal)
389	£7.95	HAMILTON-RUSSELL PINOT NOIR, WALKER BAY 1991 Walker Bay (SA)
393	£9.95	SANCERRE ROUGE, A DEZAT 1990 Loire (F)
413	£3.65	MONTEPULCIANO D'ABRUZZO, UMANI RONCHI 1991 Marches (It)
447	£5.75	CAMPO VIEJO RIOJA RESERVA 1987 Rioja (Sp)
479	£21.30	VOUVRAY MOELLEUX, CLOS DU BOURG, GASTON HUET 1990 Loire (F)
494	£12.95	WARRE'S TRADITIONAL LBV 1981 Douro (P)

CAC | Cachet Wines

Lysander Close, Clifton Moor, York, N. Yorkshire YO3 4XB (Tel 0904 690090 Fax 0904 691184). **Opening Hours:** Mon-Fri 8.30am-5.30pm, Sat 9am-1pm. **Delivery:** free within 50 miles. **Tastings:** occasional in-store, plus tutored events.

Graham Coverdale presents a reliable compendium from around the world in which he avoids the big boys in favour of interesting small producers such as the Jurançon from Clos Guirouil, St Veran and Pouilly Fuissé from 'la famille Corsin' and rich, honeyed Aussie Semillon from Simon Hackett.

57	£5.99	CHABLIS, LOUIS ALEXANDRE 1992 Burgundy (F)
61	£6.49	LUGANA CA'DEI FRATI 1992 Brescia (It)
273	£5.59	TALTARNI FIDDLEBACK TERRACE 1990 Pyrenees (Aus)
281	£6.45	CHATEAU BONNET OAK AGED, A LURTON 1990 Bordeaux (F)
330	£3.85	VIN DE PAYS DES COLLINES RHODANIENNES CEPAGE SYRAH, CAVE DE TAIN L'HERMITAGE Rhône (F)
336	£5.59	ZINFANDEL, FETZER VINEYARDS 1990 Mendocino County (Cal)
346	£7.99	CHATEAU MUSAR, 1986 Bekaa Valley (Leb)
391	£7.99	BOURGOGNE PINOT NOIR, DOMAINE PARENT 1990 Burgundy (F)
494	£13.65	WARRE'S TRADITIONAL LBV 1981 Douro (P)

CAP | Cape Province Wines

1 The Broadway, Kingston Road, Staines, Middlesex TW18 1AT (Tel 0784 451860 Fax 0784 469267). **Opening Hours:** Mon-Sat 9am-9pm. **Delivery:** nationally at cost. **Tastings:** regular in-store. **Discounts:** special offers plus collection discount on sliding scale.

While other merchants have only recently jumped on the South African bandwagon, buying KWV from the first rep who walks through their door, Peter Loose has been trying to get it rolling for 20 years, and his latest list is packed with such exotic names as Neethlingshof, Zonnebloem, Beyerskloof and Groot Constantia. Well worth a visit.

4	£5.82	NEDERBURG 1ER CUVEE BRUT Paarl (SA)
81	£6.42	CATHEDRAL CELLARS CHARDONNAY, KWV 1991 Coastal Region (SA)
89	£7.82	CHARDONNAY BATELEUR, DANIE DE WET 1991 Robertson (SA)
149	£5.22	ZONNEBLOEM BLANC DE BLANC, STELLENBOSCH FARMERS WINERY 1991 Coastal Region (SA)
179	£4.02	NEETHLINGSHOF GEWÜRZTRAMINER 1991 Stellenbosch (SA)

299	£10.83	MEERLUST MERLOT, STELLENBOSCH 1986 Stellenbosch (SA)
341	£6.28	KANONKOP PINOTAGE, VAN LOVEREN 1989 Stellenbosch (SA)
389	£7.08	HAMILTON-RUSSELL PINOT NOIR, WALKER BAY 1991 Walker Bay (SA)
471	£7.29	NEDERBURG WEISSER RIESLING NOBLE LATE HARVEST 1989 Paarl (SA)
472	£8.22	NEETHLINGSHOF WEISSER RIESLING NOBLE LATE HARVEST

CWI | A Case of Wine

Harford, Nr. Pumpsaint, Llanwrda, Dyfed SA19 8DT (Tel 05585 671 Fax 05585 671). **Opening Hours:** Mon-Sat 9am-8pm. **Delivery:** free within Dyfed. **Tastings:** regular in-store and tutored events. **Discounts:** 2.5% per unmixed case.

Since our last report, Farmer Dentten has lost his sheep and sold out to Signor Aldo Steccanella and Signora Jennifer Taylor. They also run an Italian restaurant attached to the shop (the multi-talented Aldo is wine buyer and chef). Needless to say the list now has an Italian slant, with a trio of whites from Puiatti, a single-vineyard '90 Dolcetto from Vajra and '90 Barolo Bric Mileui, Ascheri. With pud or cheese try the unctuous '90 Pieropan Recioto di Soave. Francophiles don't fret, there's an off-beat range of inexpensive French country wines (most at £4-6) for you too.

46	£4.50	CHARDONNAY DEL PIEMONTE, ARALDICA 1992 Piedmont (It)
61	£7.15	LUGANA CA'DEI FRATI 1992 Brescia (It)
171	£9.95	POGGIO ALLE GAZZE, TENUTA DELL'ORNELLAIA 1991 Tuscany (It)
321	£22.50	ORNELLAIA 1990 Tuscany (It)
346	£8.15	CHATEAU MUSAR, 1986 Bekaa Valley (Leb)
414	£4.55	DOLCETTO D'ASTI, ARALDICA 1992 Piedmont (It)
422	£8.75	CHIANTI CLASSICO, ISOLE E OLENA 1990 Tuscany (It)
428	£10.55	BRIC MILEUI, ASCHERI 1990 Piedmont (It)
454	£9.50	125 ANIVERSARIO NAVARRA GRAN RESERVA, JULIAN CHIVITE 1985 Navarra (Sp)
474	£8.95	DINDARELLO, MACULAN 1992 Veneto (It)

CVR | The Celtic Vintner Ltd

73 Derwen Fawr Rd, Sketty, Swansea, West Glamorgan SA2 8DR (Tel 0792 206661 Fax 0792 296671). **Opening Hours:** Mon-Fri 9am-6pm or by appointment. **Delivery:** free locally. **Tastings:** regular in-store tastings. **Discounts:** on bulk purchases.

Welsh Wine Merchant of the Year

The idea of having your business taken over and then being allowed to run it in the way you want to, without financial or administrative problems, is one that I'm sure many wine retailers currently dream about. The dream came true for Brian Johnson, following the departure of his daughter from Swansea. A local drink company stepped in with support and left the Johnson family to '... buy, produce lists and sell on a person-to-person basis ... what they like best and are best at'. The new incarnation of Celtic will hopefully be as rewarding a place to visit as the old, and a draft wine list includes the Austrians of Fritz Solomon and Kattus, clarets ranging from the fine Château Bauduc up to the First Growths, and a long list of half bottles. We wait for further developments with great interest.

7	£8.70	CREMANT DE BOURGOGNE, LES CAVES DE VIRE 1989 Burgundy (F)
48	£5.06	CHAIS BAUMIERE, CHARDONNAY VIN DE PAYS D'OC 1990 MIDI (F)
57	£5.88	CHABLIS, LOUIS ALEXANDRE 1992 Burgundy (F)

76	£5.41	CHARDONNAY VIN DE PAYS D'OC, H RYMAN 1992 Midi (F)
79	£5.88	ROSEMOUNT CHARDONNAY 1992 HUNTER VALLEY (AUS)
80	£6.70	CHATEAU REYNELLA STONY HILL CHARDONNAY 1990 South Australia (Aus)
106	£9.76	EDNA VALLEY CHARDONNAY 1992 Edna Valley (Cal)
119	£16.45	ROBERT MONDAVI RESERVE CHARDONNAY 1988 Napa Valley (Cal)
123	£19.98	TORRES MILMANDA CHARDONNAY 1991 PENEDES SPAIN
134	£4.12	DOMAINE DE MAUBET VIN DE PAYS DES COTES DE GASCOGNE, FONTAN 1992 South West (F)
141	£5.17	CUVEE DE CEPAGE SAUVIGNON, DOMAINE DU BREUIL 1992 Loire (F)
146	£4.59	HARDY'S MOONDAH BROOK ESTATE CHENIN BLANC 1992 Gingin, Western Australia (Aus)
154	£5.53	VERDELHO, WYNDHAM ESTATE 1991 South East Australia (Aus)
155	£6.35	ROTHBURY SAUVIGNON BLANC 1992 Marlborough (NZ)
161	6.58	JACKSON ESTATE SAUVIGNON BLANC 1992 Marlborough (NZ)
162	6.35	SELAKS MARLBOROUGH SAUVIGNON BLANC 1991 Marlborough (NZ)
164	8.11	MENETOU SALON LES MOROGUES HENRI PELLE 1992 Loire (F)
238	£6.29	CHATEAU DE LASTOURS CORBIERES, FUT DE CHENE 1989 Midi (F)
244	£2.82	RUSSE CABERNET CINSAULT (Bul)
250	£3.65	STAMBOLOVO RESERVE MERLOT 1987 (Bul)
256	£4.82	HARDYS NOTTAGE HILL CABERNET SAUVIGNON 1991 South Australia (Aus)
270	£4.82	HARDY'S MOONDAH BROOK ESTATE CABERNET SAUVIGNON 1989 Gingin, Western Australia (Aus)
282	£6.47	VALLEY OAKS CABERNET SAUVIGNON, FETZER 1990 Mendocino County (Cal)
288	£8.23	CABERNET SAUVIGNON, BODEGA Y CAVAS DE WEINERT 1985 Mendoza (Arg)
294	£9.40	CHATEAU DE ANNEREAUX, LALANDE DE POMEROL 1989 Bordeaux (F)
335	£4.94	COTES DU RHONE DOMAINE DE TERRE BRULEE, CAVE DE VIGNERONS DE RASTEAU 1990 Rhone (F)
336	£5.41	ZINFANDEL, FETZER VINEYARDS 1990 Mendocino County (Cal)
345	£8.82	ST JOSEPH, CAVES DE SAINT DESIRAT 1989 Rhone (F)
346	£7.05	CHATEAU MUSAR, 1986 Bekaa Valley (Leb)
389	£6.82	HAMILTON-RUSSELL PINOT NOIR, WALKER BAY 1991 Walker Bay (SA)
391	£7.64	BOURGOGNE PINOT NOIR, DOMAINE PARENT 1990 Burgundy (F)
394	£8.23	COLDSTREAM HILLS PINOT NOIR 1992 Yarra Valley (Aus)
462	£4.41	CAMPBELLS RUTHERGLEN LIQUEUR MUSCAT Rutherglen (Aus)
469	£7.29	CHATEAU DE BERBEC, PREMIERES COTES DE BORDEAUX 1989 Bordeaux (F)
482	£8.46	LUSTAU OLD EAST INDIA, EMILIO LUSTAU Jerez (Sp)
489	£8.52	CHURCHILL GRAHAM FINEST VINTAGE CHARACTER Douro (P)

C&A | Chennell & Armstrong Ltd

Manor Lane, Shipton Road, York, YO3 6TX, (Tel 0904 647991 Fax 0904 612445). **Opening Hours:** Mon-Fri 9am-5pm. **Delivery:** free nationally. **Tastings:** tutored events. **Discounts:** 40p per case collection discount, plus others for quantity.

With nearly 180 years under its belt, this independent family business was originally London-based(City gent turned Yorkshire Lad). Wines are mostly French and all from reliable, if sometimes predictable producers (La Chablisienne, Louis Latour, Hugel). It's quite refreshing to find very little New World wine, though this is the place to find Best's, Victoria. Try one of their tasting selections: 'The Latin Case' or a 'A Dinner Party' perhaps. Music lovers might, however, prefer a night in with the 'Country & South Western'.

33	£27.00	BOLLINGER GRANDE ANNEE 1985 Champagne (F)
45	£4.54	NOBILO WHITE CLOUD 1992 (NZ)
53	£6.14	'CASAL DI SERRA' VERDICCHIO CLASSICO, UMANI RONCHI 1991 Marches (It)
74	£5.25	PENFOLDS KOONUNGA HILL CHARDONNAY 1992 South East Australia (Aus)

100	£10.53	FIRESTONE CHARDONNAY 1990 (Cal)
269	£5.29	MONTANA CABERNET SAUVIGNON 1991 Marlborough (NZ)
288	£7.02	CABERNET SAUVIGNON, BODEGA Y CAVAS DE WEINERT 1985 Mendoza (Arg)
346	£7.78	CHATEAU MUSAR, 1986 Bekaa Valley (Leb)
398	£11.99	MONTHELIE, JAFFELIN 1990 Burgundy (F)

| CHF | Chippendale Fine Wines |

15 Manor Square, Otley, W. Yorks W21 3AP (Tel 0943 850633 Fax 0943 850633). **Opening Hours:** Mon,Tues,Thurs, Fri 10am-5.45pm, Sat 9.30am-5pm. **Delivery:** free within 15 miles. **Tastings:** regular in-store. **Discounts:** 5% on 1-5 cases, 7% on 6 or more.

Planning to stay in with a good book? Pick up the latest copy of Mike Pollard's wine list. Historian, radical, cynic, and comedian as well as a jolly good wine buyer, his vinous plot begins in Australia with Tim Adams, Pike's, Cullens and the little known Peel Estate, then gradually takes you around the world (through a large, enjoyable chapter in France and a refreshing stop in New Zealand). Finally you arrive at the Newton Vineyard in California for a glass of pure, unadulterated, unfiltered Chardonnay.

19	£8.50	CHAPIN ROSE, SAUMUR, CHAPIN & LANDAIS Loire (F)
72	£4.35	CHASAN, DOMAINE SABLEYROLLE, VIN DE PAYS D'OC 1992 Midi (F)
105	£10.39	CULLENS SAUVIGNON BLANC 1991 Margaret River (Aus)
115	£13.95	NEWTON UNFILTERED CHARDONNAY 1990 Napa Valley (Cal)
142	£4.75	OZIDOC SAUVIGNON, VIN DE PAYS D'OC, J & F LURTON 1992 Midi (F)
168	£8.75	SANCERRE LES ROCHES, DOMAINE VACHERON 1992 Loire (F)
188	£5.99	PETER LEHMANN SEMILLON 1992 Barossa Valley (Aus)
233	£3.65	MAS DE FIGARO VIN DE PAYS DE L'HERAULT, AIME GUIBERT 1992 Midi (F)
235	£4.89	DAVID WYNN DRY RED 1992 Eden Valley (Aus)
244	£2.79	RUSSE CABERNET CINSAULT (Bul)
309	£13.15	NEWTON MERLOT 1990 Napa Valley (Cal)
346	£7.65	CHATEAU MUSAR, 1986 Bekaa Valley (Leb)
353	£8.95	DAVID WYNN PATRIARCH SHIRAZ 1991 Eden Valley (Aus)
370	£16.35	YARRA YERING SHIRAZ NO.2 1990 Yarra Valley (Aus)
400	£11.85	NEUDORF VINEYARDS MOUTERE PINOT NOIR 1991 Nelson (NZ)
427	£9.85	CUMARO ROSSO CONERO, UMANI RONCHI 1989 Marches (It)
437	£3.59	CISMEIRA DOURO 1991 Douro (P)
444	£4.49	PERIQUITA, J M DA FONSECA 1990 (P)

| CC | Chiswick Cellar |

84 Chiswick High Road, London W4 1SY (Tel 081 994 7989). **Opening Hours:** Mon-Thurs 10am-10.30pm, Fri, Sat 10am-11pm, Sun 12-3pm,7-10.30pm. **Delivery:** free locally. **Tastings:** regular in store. **Discounts:**10% on large orders.

If you are running late en route to a party in Shepherds Bush, then fear not, these chaps are open until 10pm, even on Sundays, and are sure to have something decent. Super Italians (we refer to the proprietors as well as the wines) with a smattering from France and Australia.

| CIW | City Wines Ltd |

221 Queens Road, Norwich, Norfolk NR1 3AE (Tel 0603 660741 Fax 0603 617967). **Opening Hours**: Mon-Sat 9am-9pm, Sun 12-2pm, 7-9pm. Also 305 Aylsham Rd, Norwich. **Delivery:** free within 5

miles. **Tastings:** in-store occasionally plus tutored events. **Discounts:** 5% per case and unmixed case.

Tertia Bell is always on hand to offer 'expert advice' on a fine selection of Juracons, '90 Chablis 'Vielx Vignes', Trapiche's '88 Malbee (not Mr Bumble but a Malbec we suspect) or Nebbiolo's other half, Nebbiola. May we therefore reciprocate with a few spelling lessons? This year 'You deserve to try these wines' brings us value for money with '92 Flame Tree Cabernet/ Merlot (£4.49) and the '88 Chianti Classico Geografico (ignore the NV Chianti Geographico Classico. It's the same wine).

33	£31.99	BOLLINGER GRANDE ANNEE 1985 Champagne (F)
74	£5.45	PENFOLDS KOONUNGA HILL CHARDONNAY 1992 South East Australia (Aus)
79	£6.49	ROSEMOUNT CHARDONNAY 1992 Hunter Valley (Aus)
269	£5.79	MONTANA CABERNET SAUVIGNON 1991 Marlborough (NZ)
470	£7.79	MONBAZILLAC, CHATEAU THEULET, SCEA ALARD 1990 Bordeaux (F)

CRC   The Claret Club

Unit 3, Station Yard, Hungerford, Berks RG17 0DY (Tel 0488 683238 Fax 0488 684919). **Delivery:** nationally at cost. **Tastings:** tutored and organised events. **Discounts:** special offers.

Launched early in 1993 with much fanfare, The Claret Club is what developed out of the *en primeur* scheme and regularly mailed offers of The Hungerford Wine Company. Members will receive a series of in-depth Châteaux profiles and have a chance to buy the wines, as well as other fine wines from around the world. Since there are very few overheads involved, the profit margins will apparently be low and prices keen. Members also have the chance to buy and sell their own wine through the club's newsletters, with the Club taking 14.1% commission on all wines sold. Cynics might suggest that £45 a year membership fee (or £2,000 for GOLD membership) to find out what Anthony Barton's favourite piece of music is, and to get a free binder for your Clive Coates newsletters is a little stiff. They might consider that fee and nod knowingly when Nick Davies says, 'The Claret Club (unlike other existing wine clubs) has no need to sell a single bottle of wine.' But then the *Guide* has never been known for cynicism.

CWW   Classic Wine Warehouse Ltd

Unit A2, Stadium Industrial Estate, Sealand Road, Chester, CH1 4LU (Tel 0244 390 444 Fax 0244 378980). **Opening Hours:** Mon-Fri 7.30am-6pm, Sat 9am-5pm. **Delivery:** free nationally. **Tastings:** occasional in-store and tutored events. **Discounts:** vary.

James Dean and John Lennon are alive and well and running a thriving wine business in Chester. They obviously like Champagne. A large selection at good prices is headed by Edouard Mass at £11.20. Otherwise their list is safe and reliable, with Burgundies from Joseph Drouhin, Australians from Penfolds and the wines of Santa Rita in Chile. Why change a winning formula?

19	£8.08	CHAPIN ROSE, SAUMUR, CHAPIN & LANDAIS Loire (F)
33	£25.80	BOLLINGER GRANDE ANNEE 1985 Champagne (F)
53	£5.30	'CASAL DI SERRA' VERDICCHIO CLASSICO, UMANI RONCHI 1991 Marches (It)
79	£6.12	ROSEMOUNT CHARDONNAY 1992 Hunter Valley (Aus)
143	£4.70	SANTA RITA RESERVA SAUVIGNON 1993 Maule (Ch)

196	£3.95	DENBIES ENGLISH WINE 1991 Surrey (UK)
276	£5.66	CHATEAU DE LA JAUBERTIE BERGERAC ROUGE, HENRY RYMAN 1990 S West (F)
346	£7.56	CHATEAU MUSAR, 1986 Bekaa Valley (Leb)
365	£13.04	PENFOLDS MAGILL ESTATE SHIRAZ 1988 South Australia (Aus)
404	£16.20	ROBERT MONDAVI RESERVE PINOT NOIR 1988 Napa Valley (Cal)
413	£3.51	MONTEPULCIANO D'ABRUZZO, UMANI RONCHI 1991 Marches (It)
483	£8.18	1796 RICH OLD OLOROSO Jerez (Sp)

CFT | Clifton Cellars

22 The Mall, Clifton, Bristol, Avon (Tel 0272 730287). **Opening Hours:** Mon-Fri 9.30am-6.30pm, **Sat 9am-6pm. Delivery:** free locally. **Tastings:** regular in-store and tutored.

'Surrounded by Oddbins', Alan Wright sensibly ploughs his own, rather different furrow. So, if you want an Israeli red, a Bel Air '55, a 1920 port– or one of the recommended wines below, you've found your Mister Wright.

43	£3.80	COTES DE ST MONT WHITE, PLAIMONT 1991 South West (F)
90	£7.99	YARDEN CHARDONNAY, GOLAN HEIGHTS WINERY 1991 Golan Heights (Is)
169	£8.95	HUNTERS MARLBOROUGH SAUVIGNON BLANC 1992 Marlborough (NZ)
222	£10.04	CHATEAU DE LA GRILLE, CHINON ROSE, A GOSSET 1992 Loire (F)
346	£7.97	CHATEAU MUSAR, 1986 Bekaa Valley (Leb)
487	£8.84	TOKAJI ASZU 3 PUTTONYOS, TOKAJI-HEGYALA SCHLUMBERGER 1981 (Hun)

CNL | Connolly's (Wine Merchants) Ltd

Arch 13, 220 Livery Street, Birmingham, West Midlands B3 1EU (Tel 021 236 9269 Fax 021 233 2339). **Opening Hours**: Mon-Fri 9am-5.30pm (minimum - usually longer), Sat 9.30am-1pm. **Delivery:** free locally. **Tastings:** regular in-store and tutored events. **Discounts:** 10% per mixed case (table wine), 10% collection discount on one or more cases.

Chris Connolly's 'Book of Bacchus' gets smarter every year – as do its contents. There's some very serious wine-buying here, with Rhônes from Gripa, Morgon from Château de Pizay, Burgundy from Pascal, Faiveley and Vallet Freres, and Coonawarra reds from Parker Estate. Fairly priced Bordeaux include '85 Léoville Barton at £18.45 and '88 Haut Bages-Libéral at £11.79. All this and the chance to read yet another piece of Mr C's truly awful poetry.

33	£29.95	BOLLINGER GRANDE ANNEE 1985 Champagne (F)
61	£6.89	LUGANA CA'DEI FRATI 1992 Brescia (It)
160	£6.99	GROVE MILL SAUVIGNON 1992 Blenheim (NZ)
260	£4.80	OLD TRIANGLE CABERNET SAUVIGNON, S. SMITH & SONS 1991 Barossa (Aus)
288	£9.25	CABERNET SAUVIGNON, BODEGA Y CAVAS DE WEINERT 1985 Mendoza (Arg)
346	£7.99	CHATEAU MUSAR, 1986 Bekaa Valley (Leb)
414	£4.35	DOLCETTO D'ASTI, ARALDICA 1992 Piedmont (It)
423	£8.85	CARMIGNANO, CAPEZZANA 1987 Tuscany (It)
462	£5.69	CAMPBELLS RUTHERGLEN LIQUEUR MUSCAT Rutherglen (Aus)
484	£18.99	MATUSALEM, GONZALEZ BYASS Jerez (Sp)
492	£10.95	COLHEITA, A A CALEM & FILHO 1985 Douro (P)
494	£12.29	WARRE'S TRADITIONAL LBV 1981 Douro (P)
498	£22.50	QUINTA DO VESUVIO VINTAGE PORT 1990 Douro (P)

COK	Corkscrew Wines

Arch 5, Viaduct Estate, Carlisle, Cumbria CA2 5BN (Tel 0228 43033 Fax 0228 43033). **Opening Hours**: Mon-Sat 10am-6pm. **Delivery:** free locally. **Tastings:** regular in-store tastings. **Discounts:** 5% mixed case, on bottle free on a case.

Laurie Scott tries 'to match the wines to the customer and vice versa' which, to judge by the successful wines in this year's International Wine Challenge, shouldn't be too difficult. There's some very careful wine buying going on here, with good value bottles pretty well across the board, from Louis Alexandre Chablis at £5.99 to the rare Ngatarawa Cabernet-Merlot from New Zealand.

11	£6.99	MONTANA LINDAUER BRUT (NZ)
46	£4.29	CHARDONNAY DEL PIEMONTE, ARALDICA 1992 Piedmont (It)
57	£5.99	CHABLIS, LOUIS ALEXANDRE 1992 Burgundy (F)
64	£8.50	TASMANIAN WINE COMPANY CHARDONNAY, PIPER'S BROOK 1991 (Aus)
74	£4.99	PENFOLDS KOONUNGA HILL CHARDONNAY 1992 South East Australia (Aus)
79	£6.89	ROSEMOUNT CHARDONNAY 1992 Hunter Valley (Aus)
134	£3.99	DOMAINE DE MAUBET VIN DE PAYS DES COTES DE GASCOGNE, FONTAN 1992 South West (F)
246	£3.65	DUNAVAR CONNOSSEUR COLLECTION MERLOT, DANUBIANA BONYHAD 1990 Szekszard (Hun)
260	£4.50	OLD TRIANGLE CABERNET SAUVIGNON, S. SMITH & SONS 1991 Barossa (Aus)
272	£5.45	ROUGE HOMME CABERNET/SHIRAZ, COONAWARRA 1988 Coonawarra (Aus)
330	£3.99	VIN DE PAYS DES COLLINES RHODANIENNES CEPAGE SYRAH, CAVE DE TAIN L'HERMITAGE Rhône (F)
335	£4.99	COTES DU RHONE DOMAINE DE TERRE BRULEE, CAVE DE VIGNERONS DE RASTEAU 1990 Rhône (F)
342	£6.99	PETER LEHMANN 'CLANCY'S RED' 1990 Barossa Valley (Aus)
346	£7.35	CHATEAU MUSAR, 1986 Bekaa Valley (Leb)
364	£13.50	CHATEAUNEUF DU PAPE, CHATEAU DE BEAUCASTEL 1988 Rhône (F)
389	£6.99	HAMILTON-RUSSELL PINOT NOIR, WALKER BAY 1991 Walker Bay (SA)
405	£18.75	BEAUNE 1ER CRU EPENOTTES, VALLET FRERES 1989 Burgundy (F)
439	£4.75	BORBA, ADEGA CO-OPERATIVA DE BORBA 1991 Douro (P)
454	£7.99	125 ANIVERSARIO NAVARRA GRAN RESERVA, JULIAN CHIVITE 1985 Navarra (Sp)
461	£11.25	STANTON & KILLEEN RUTHERGLEN LIQUEUR MUSCAT Rutherglen (Aus)
484	£19.95	MATUSALEM, GONZALEZ BYASS Jerez (Sp)
488	£7.95	OLD TRAFFORD TAWNY, B. SEPPELT & SONS South East Australia (Aus)
489	£9.25	CHURCHILL GRAHAM FINEST VINTAGE CHARACTER Douro (P)
498	£25.00	QUINTA DO VESUVIO VINTAGE PORT 1990 Douro (P)

COR	Corn Road Vintners

Bridge Street, Rothbury, Morpeth, Northumberland NE65 7SE (Tel/Fax 0669 20240). **Opening Hours**: Mon-Fri 8.30am-6pm, Sat 8.30am-1pm, plus 24 hour answer service. **Delivery:** free within 35 miles. **Tastings:** tutored events. **Discounts:** by arrangement.

A new entry into the *Guide*, Corn Road Vintners began because Graham Hodgson could not find any decent wine for his Rothbury restaurant. His list is a perfect riposte to those second rate merchants he was sick of dealing with: clearly and concisely it demystifies wine, while still conveying real enthusiasm. Wines are listed by grape variety, starting with the classics and moving on to an exotic mixed bag, including Auxerrois, Chasan, and even Marechal Foch. Finally, he showcases agencies like Viarengo from Piedmont, offering Grignolino and Gavi as well as Barbera and Barolo.

99	£8.90	KRONDORF SHOW RESERVE CHARDONNAY 1991 Barossa Valley (Aus)
266	£5.15	SALISBURY ESTATE CABERNET SAUVIGNON 1991 South East Australia (Aus)
275	£5.32	RUSTENBERG MERLOT, STELLENBOSCH 1991 Stellenbosch (SA)
341	£5.15	KANONKOP PINOTAGE, VAN LOVEREN 1989 Stellenbosch (SA)
389	£6.75	HAMILTON-RUSSELL PINOT NOIR, WALKER BAY 1991 Walker Bay (SA)

C&B | Corney & Barrow Ltd

12 Helmet Row, London EC1V 3QJ (Tel 071 251 4051 Fax 071 608 1373). **Opening Hours**: Kensington:Mon-Sat 10.30am-8pm. Also: Belvoir House, High Street, Newmarket. **Delivery:** free locally, nationally for 3 or more cases (4 in Scotland). **Tastings:** regular in-store and tutored events.

In last year's *Guide*, we described this wine merchant as 'club like' and 'daunting'. We apologise unreservedly. Corney & Barrow not only welcome new customers warmly, they even take the trouble to send them a smart booklet unravelling the mysteries of wine, including how to open a bottle. When you've just received your allocation of Château Petrus and Domaine de la Romanée Conti, you will find this information invaluable. If you are after more modest fare C&B can help out there too – with a growing, recession-conscious range of French regional wines to sip at while reading your Lloyds bill.

33	£30.29	BOLLINGER GRANDE ANNEE 1985 Champagne (F)
53	£5.95	'CASAL DI SERRA' VERDICCHIO CLASSICO, UMANI RONCHI 1991 Marches (It)
77	£6.25	SALISBURY ESTATE CHARDONNAY 1992 South East Australia (Aus)
103	£9.22	RULLY 1ER CRU, RABOURCE, OLIVIER LEFLAIVE 1991 Burgundy (F)
148	£5.29	BERGERAC, LA COMBE DE GRINOU 1992 South West (F)
283	£6.64	MONTAGNE ST. EMILION, CHATEAU BERTIN 1989 Bordeaux (F)
292	£10.81	COLUMBIA CREST MERLOT, STIMSON LANE 1989 Washington State (US)
302	£10.40	CHATEAU DE LAMARQUE, HAUT MEDOC 1990 Bordeaux (F)
321	£27.55	ORNELLAIA 1990 Tuscany (It)
427	£11.25	CUMARO ROSSO CONERO, UMANI RONCHI 1989 Marches (It)
498	£27.80	QUINTA DO VESUVIO VINTAGE PORT 1990 Douro (P)

CWM | Cornwall Wine Merchants Ltd

Chapel Rd, Tuckingmill, Camborne, Cornwall TR14 8QY (Tel 0209 715765 Fax 0209 612321) **Opening Hours:** Mon-Fri 9am-5pm. **Delivery:** free within 100 miles. **Tastings:** regular in store plus tutored events.

Nick Richards is sticking to his guns: 'as always our emphasis is on value for money and variety rather than big names.' Hence a list bursting with 'little name' producers. New this year are Australians Willespie (Margaret River) and McGuigan Bros (Hunter Valley) plus Te Kairanga's fresh, delicate whites and raspberry Pinot Noir from Martinborough, New Zealand. Mr Richards has also made the most of low prices and invested in some Burgundy.

45	£4.39	NOBILO WHITE CLOUD 1992 (NZ)
182	£5.99	GEWURZTRAMINER D'ALSACE, CAVE VINICOLE DE TURCKHEIM 1992 Alsace (F)
330	£3.99	VIN DE PAYS DES COLLINES RHODANIENNES CEPAGE SYRAH, CAVE DE TAIN L'HERMITAGE Rhône (F)
443	£4.79	QUINTA DE LA ROSA RED TABLE WINE 1991 Douro (P)
481	£5.99	HIDALGO AMONTILLADO NAPOLEON Jerez (Sp)

CWS | The Co-operative Wholesale Society

PO Box 53, New Century House, Manchester M60 4ES (Tel 061-834 1212 Fax 061-839 2616) **Opening Hours**: vary (average: Mon-Sat 8am-8pm). **Tastings**: in-store plus tutored and organised events.

Arabella Woodrow MW and her recently promoted associate Paul Bastard were deservingly short-listed for this year's Going Places award. The message of good wine is getting through and even the scruffiest shop ought to be able to sell you a drinkable bottle. But their ambitions run higher; they want the superstores to compete with more centralised supermarkets, which is why, during National Wine Week, Ms Woodrow dashed around the country holding tastings with the zeal of a vinous Billy Graham.

11	£6.99	MONTANA LINDAUER BRUT (NZ)
20	£6.29	OMAR KHAYYAM, CHAMPAGNE INDIA 1987 Maharashtra (Ind)
24	£9.95	GREEN POINT, DOMAINE CHANDON 1990 Yarra Valley (Aus)
39	£3.29	CHARDONNAY GYONGYOS, HUGH RYMAN 1992 (Hun)
44	£3.85	CHARDONNAY, VINO DA TAVOLA, CA DONINI 1992 Triveneto (It)
45	£3.79	NOBILO WHITE CLOUD 1992 (NZ)
70	£3.99	TIMARA WHITE, MONTANA 1991 (NZ)
81	£5.99	CATHEDRAL CELLARS CHARDONNAY, KWV 1991 Coastal Region (SA)
89	£7.49	CHARDONNAY BATELEUR, DANIE DE WET 1991 Robertson (SA)
99	£8.49	KRONDORF SHOW RESERVE CHARDONNAY 1991 Barossa Valley (Aus)
123	£16.95	TORRES MILMANDA CHARDONNAY 1991 Penedes (Sp)
146	£4.99	HARDY'S MOONDAH BROOK ESTATE CHENIN BLANC 1992 Gingin, (W Aus)
196	£3.99	DENBIES ENGLISH WINE 1991 Surrey (UK)
197	£3.69	BADEN DRY, BADISCHER WINZERKELLER Baden (G)
200	£3.75	COOP KABINETT, QMP RHEINHESSEN, ST URSULA 1989 Rheinhessen (G)
239	£5.35	CAHORS, PRINCE PROBUS, J. L. BALDES 1988 South West (F)
245	£3.25	COOP CALIFORNIA RUBY CABERNET, P. FLEMMING FRANCE (Cal)
256	£3.99	HARDYS NOTTAGE HILL CABERNET SAUVIGNON 1991 South Australia (Aus)
262	£4.75	COOP AUSTRALIAN CABERNET SAUVIGNON, BERRI ESTATES 1989 (S Aus)
311	£9.99	CHATEAU CISSAC, HAUT-MEDOC 1982 Bordeaux (F)
346	£7.49	CHATEAU MUSAR, 1986 Bekaa Valley (Leb)
373	£4.49	TARRANGO, BROWN BROTHERS 1992 Milawa (Aus)
389	£6.49	HAMILTON-RUSSELL PINOT NOIR, WALKER BAY 1991 Walker Bay (SA)
394	£7.99	COLDSTREAM HILLS PINOT NOIR 1992 Yarra Valley (Aus)
413	£3.55	MONTEPULCIANO D'ABRUZZO, UMANI RONCHI 1991 Marches (It)
416	£4.99	SALICE SALENTINO RISERVA, AZ. AG. TAURINO 1988 Puglia (It)
421	£6.99	SER GIOVETO, VINO DA TAVOLA, ROCCA DELLE MACIE 1989 Tuscany (It)
448	£5.49	CARTUXA, FUNDACO E ALMEIDA 1989 Evora (P)
464	£3.49	MONBAZILLAC DOMAINE DU HAUT RAULY, ALARD 1990 Bordeaux (F)
468	£5.69	NELSON LATE HARVEST RHINE RIESLING, SEIFRIED 1991 Nelson (NZ)
484	£17.29	MATUSALEM, GONZALEZ BYASS Jerez (Sp)
497	£19.25	NIEPOORT COLHEITA 1983 Douro (P)

CEB | Croque en Bouche

221 Wells Road, Malvern Wells, Worcester, WR14 4HF, (Tel 0684 565612). **Opening Hours**: any reasonable hour by telephone appointment. **Delivery:** free over £350.

This restaurant-cum-merchant list only appears every five years; hardly surprising when you consider the amount of work that has gone into it. Robin Jones sells by the case only, which at least helps limit your choice to 12 bottles. But how can anyone choose, when there are 50 top Côte Rôties, 5 Condrieus, rare St Joseph, '76 Grange Hermitage and '62 white Marques de Murrieta on offer?

11	£6.60	MONTANA LINDAUER BRUT (NZ)
20	£8.80	OMAR KHAYYAM, CHAMPAGNE INDIA 1987 Maharashtra (Ind)
30	£19.00	CHAMPAGNE JACQUESSON BLANC DE BLANCS Champagne (F)
33	£30.29	BOLLINGER GRANDE ANNEE 1985 Champagne (F)
45	£3.95	NOBILO WHITE CLOUD 1992 (NZ)
79	£5.70	ROSEMOUNT CHARDONNAY 1992 Hunter Valley (Aus)
119	£15.00	ROBERT MONDAVI RESERVE CHARDONNAY 1988 Napa Valley (Cal)
272	£5.20	ROUGE HOMME CABERNET/SHIRAZ, COONAWARRA 1988 Coonawarra (Aus)
292	£8.60	COLUMBIA CREST MERLOT, STIMSON LANE 1989 Washington State (US)
303	£12.50	PETALUMA COONAWARRA RED 1988 Coonawarra (Aus)
348	£8.60	ROSEMOUNT SHOW RESERVE SYRAH 1990 McLaren Vale (Aus)
358	£11.20	FROG'S LEAP ZINFANDEL 1990 Napa Valley (Cal)
364	£12.90	CHATEAUNEUF DU PAPE, CHATEAU DE BEAUCASTEL 1988 Rhône (F)
369	£16.20	JADE MOUNTAIN SYRAH, DOUGLAS DANIELAK 1990 Sonoma (Cal)
422	£8.80	CHIANTI CLASSICO, ISOLE E OLENA 1990 Tuscany (It)

CUM | The Cumbrian Cellar

1 St Andrew's Square, Penrith, Cumbria CA11 7AN (Tel 0768 63664). **Opening Hours:** Mon-Sat 9am-5.30pm. **Delivery:** free locally. **Tastings:** occasional in-store. **Discounts:** 5% per mixed case, 50p per case collection discount.

This list reminds us of the Around the World in 80 Wines tasting organised by *WINE* Magazine for National Wine Week. Where would you like to go? Russia, China, Brazil, Peru or a trip round ancient Greece? Closer to home you can take in several regions of France, Spain and Italy. Kenneth Gear recommends you stop off for a wee dram of one of his many single malts on the way.

79	£6.85	ROSEMOUNT CHARDONNAY 1992 Hunter Valley (Aus)
151	£7.15	MUSCADET DE SEVRE ET MAINE, GUY BOSSARD 1992 Loire (F)
197	£4.55	BADEN DRY, BADISCHER WINZERKELLER Baden (G)
346	£8.50	CHATEAU MUSAR, 1986 Bekaa Valley (Leb)
415	£5.10	VALPOLICELLA CLASSICO, MASI 1991 Veneto (It)
437	£4.20	CISMEIRA DOURO 1991 Douro (P)
494	£12.90	WARRE'S TRADITIONAL LBV 1981 Douro (P)

D | Davisons Wine Merchants

7 Aberdeen Rd, Croydon, Surrey CR0 1EQ (Tel 081 681 3222 Fax 081 760 0390). **Opening Hours**: average: Mon-Sat 10am-2pm, 5-10pm, Sun 12-2pm, 7-9pm. **Delivery:** free locally. **Tastings:** regular in-store. **Discounts:** 8.5% per mixed or unmixed case.

Regional Chain Wine Merchant of the Year

Which British merchant can offer Châteaux Lynch Bages, Talbot and La Lagune '78, '79, '81, '82, '83, '85, '86, '88, '89 and '90? Which stocks over 3000 cases of Grahams and Taylors vintage port? Which has 1500 cases of '82 classed growth claret 'gently maturing for the next generation'? Despite our efforts to spread the word, Davisons remains one of the best kept secrets of the wine world: a chain of 79 shops, with wines ranging from the well-chosen and inexpensive, to first class mature stuff – often at prices lower than you'd pay at auction.

11	£6.99	MONTANA LINDAUER BRUT (NZ)
45	£4.25	NOBILO WHITE CLOUD 1992 (NZ)
54	£5.59	MONTES UNOAKED CHARDONNAY, DISCOVER WINES LTDA 1993 Curico (Ch)

74	£4.99	PENFOLDS KOONUNGA HILL CHARDONNAY 1992 South East Australia (Aus)
79	£5.99	ROSEMOUNT CHARDONNAY 1992 Hunter Valley (Aus)
91	£7.89	MARQUES DE MURRIETA RIOJA RESERVA BLANCO 1987 Rioja (Sp)
99	£8.99	KRONDORF SHOW RESERVE CHARDONNAY 1991 Barossa Valley (Aus)
154	£5.85	VERDELHO, WYNDHAM ESTATE 1991 South East Australia (Aus)
161	£6.99	JACKSON ESTATE SAUVIGNON BLANC 1992 Marlborough (NZ)
256	£3.99	HARDYS NOTTAGE HILL CABERNET SAUVIGNON 1991 South Australia (Aus)
271	£5.35	CHATEAU TIMBERLAY, R. GIRAUD 1990 Bordeaux (F)
314	£15.95	DOMAINE DE L'EGLISE, POMEROL 1985 Bordeaux (F)
323	£49.95	CHATEAU COS D'ESTOURNEL, ST ESTEPHE 1982 Bordeaux (F)
346	£8.25	CHATEAU MUSAR, 1986 Bekaa Valley (Leb)
390	£7.99	BOURGOGNE PINOT NOIR, DOMAINE JEAN MARC MOREY 1990 Burgundy (F)
399	£10.45	SAVIGNY LES BEAUNE, 1ER CRU AUX GUETTES, DOM. PAVELOT 1989 Burgundy (F)
407	£19.95	GEVREY CHAMBERTIN, ALAIN BURGUET, VIEILLES VIGNES 1988 Burgundy (F)
428	£10.95	BRIC MILEUI, ASCHERI 1990 Piedmont (It)
446	£4.99	TERRAS DEL REI RESERVA, CO-OP AGRICOLA DE REGUENGOS DE MONSARAZ 1988 Alentejo (P)
451	£6.75	COTO DE IMAZ RIOJA RESERVA 1985 Rioja (Sp)
489	£8.39	CHURCHILL GRAHAM FINEST VINTAGE CHARACTER Douro (P)
496	£14.45	TAYLOR'S TEN YEAR OLD TAWNY Douro (P)
498	£20.00	QUINTA DO VESUVIO VINTAGE PORT 1990 Douro (P)

ROD | Rodney Densem Wines

Stapeley Bank, London Road, Nantwich, Cheshire CW5 7JW (Tel 0270 623665 Fax 0270 624062) **Opening Hours:** Mon, Tues 10am-6pm, Weds-Fri 9am-6pm, Sat 9am-5.30pm. **Delivery:** free within 30 miles. **Tastings:** regular in-store plus tutored events. **Discounts:** 5% per mixed case plus offers.

After 20 years as a French specialist, Rodney Densem really knows his oignons. 'Grandes Marques' Fizz and Cru Classé Bordeaux are to the fore, but Austraphiles are offered a choice of big names and small domaines, including St Halletts 'Old Block Shiraz' and Buckleys plummy Grenache.

24	£9.95	GREEN POINT, DOMAINE CHANDON 1990 Yarra Valley (Aus)
33	£30.79	BOLLINGER GRANDE ANNEE 1985 Champagne (F)
34	£39.59	CHAMPAGNE LOUISE POMMERY VINTAGE ROSE 1988 Champagne (F)
64	£9.35	TASMANIAN WINE COMPANY CHARDONNAY, PIPER'S BROOK 1991 (Aus)
99	£6.99	KRONDORF SHOW RESERVE CHARDONNAY 1991 Barossa Valley (Aus)
112	£13.60	ELSTON CHARDONNAY, TE MATA ESTATE 1991 Hawkes Bay (NZ)
231	£3.69	MISTY MOORING RED, ANGOVES (Aus)
273	£6.35	TALTARNI FIDDLEBACK TERRACE 1990 Pyrenees (Aus)
294	£10.99	CHATEAU DE ANNEREAUX, LALANDE DE POMEROL 1989 Bordeaux (F)
342	£7.79	PETER LEHMANN 'CLANCY'S RED' 1990 Barossa Valley (Aus)
487	£11.15	TOKAJI ASZU 3 PUTTONYOS, TOKAJI-HEGYALA SCHLUMBERGER 1981 (Hun)

DIR | Direct Wine Shipments

5/7 Corporation Square, Belfast, Antrim BT1 3AJ (Tel 0232 238700 Fax 0232 240202). **Opening Hours:** Mon-Wed 9.30am-6.30pm, Thurs 9.30am-8.00pm, Fri 9.30am-6.30pm, Sat10am-5pm. **Delivery:** free locally. **Tastings:** regular in-store and tutored. **Discounts:** 7.5% per case, 5% per mixed case, frequent 10% offers.

Northern Ireland Wine Merchant of the Year

Follow the signs for the Belfast Sea Cat, get lost, and eventually you'll find this stately vinous pleasure dome. Kevin McAlindon offers his customers a wide range of first class wines, including white Burgundies from Domaine Leflaive, Australians from Brown Brothers and some exciting Italians (Lungarotti's Rubesco '79 for £12.95 is either a mis-print or a bargain). He also runs a wine appreciation course and organises theme dinners, hosted by the likes of Jean Hugel and Marc Chapoutier.

3	£5.46	SEGURA VIUDAS CAVA BRUT RESERVA Cava (Sp)
20	£8.50	OMAR KHAYYAM, CHAMPAGNE INDIA 1987 Maharashtra (Ind)
33	£29.83	BOLLINGER GRANDE ANNEE 1985 Champagne (F)
95	£9.45	BARREL SELECT CHARDONNAY, FETZER 1991 Mendocino County (Cal)
123	£17.05	TORRES MILMANDA CHARDONNAY 1991 Penedes (Sp)
144	£3.79	COTEAUX DE LANGUEDOC PICPOUL DE PINET, DUC DE MORNY 1991 Midi (F)
169	£8.07	HUNTERS MARLBOROUGH SAUVIGNON BLANC 1992 Marlborough (NZ)
295	£10.74	FETZER BARREL SELECT CABERNET SAUVIGNON 1989 Mendocino County (Cal)
344	£7.55	CROZES HERMITAGE LA PETITE RUCHE, CHAPOUTIER 1991 Rhône (F)
346	£7.55	CHATEAU MUSAR, 1986 Bekaa Valley (Leb)
349	£9.45	ZINFANDEL, DRY CREEK VINEYARDS 1990 Sonoma (Cal)
373	£4.25	TARRANGO, BROWN BROTHERS 1992 Milawa (Aus)
385	£5.69	HAUTES COTES DE BEAUNE, TETE DU CUVEE, CAVES DES HAUTES COTES 1990 Burgundy (F)
389	£7.84	HAMILTON-RUSSELL PINOT NOIR, WALKER BAY 1991 Walker Bay (SA)
415	£4.74	VALPOLICELLA CLASSICO, MASI 1991 Veneto (It)
454	£8.50	125 ANIVERSARIO NAVARRA GRAN RESERVA, CHIVITE 1985 Navarra (Sp)
487	£6.64	TOKAJI ASZU 3 PUTTONYOS, TOKAJI-HEGYALA SCHLUMBERGER 1981 (Hun)
494	£12.30	WARRE'S TRADITIONAL LBV 1981 Douro (P)
498	£16.63	QUINTA DO VESUVIO VINTAGE PORT 1990 Douro (P)

DD | Domaine Direct

29 Wilmington Square, London WC1X 0EG (Tel 071 837 1142 Fax 071 837 8605). **Opening Hours**: Mon-Fri 7.30am-5.30pm, plus 24 hour answerphone service. **Delivery:** free in London for 1 or more cases, nationally for 3 or more. **Tastings:** tutored events.

Simon Taylor-Gill's firm used to concentrate exclusively on Burgundy. Then he discovered the New World and began to address it just as seriously. The result is a very classy collection of the best of both Worlds.

| 307 | £9.81 | LEEUWIN ESTATE CABERNET SAUVIGNON 1986 Margaret River (Aus) |
| 399 | £12.34 | SAVIGNY LES BEAUNE, 1ER CRU AUX GUETTES, DOMAINE PAVELOT 1989 Burgundy (F) |

EE | Eaton Elliot Wine Merchant

15 London Road, Alderley Edge, Cheshire SK9 7JT (Tel 0625 582354 Fax 0625 586404). **Opening Hours:** Mon 10am-6.30pm, Tues-Fri 10am-8.30pm, Sat 9.30am-7pm. Also at The Fox, Oddington, Nr Moreton-in-Marsh, Gloucestershire GL56 0UR. (Tel 0451 870555). **Delivery:** free locally. **Tastings:** in-store. **Discounts:** 5% per case.

With the demise of Willoughby's in Wilmslow, Eaton Elliot would seem to have this affluent corner of Cheshire to themselves. They continue to woo their customers with good service and some very exciting wines. Nebbiolo from the Produttori del Barbaresco at £5.70 is one of many bargains. They also stock High Weald English Vineyard, a wine that tastes like good Pouilly Fumé – very useful for humbling loud buffs who think they can taste blind.

33	£30.90	BOLLINGER GRANDE ANNEE 1985 Champagne (F)
46	£4.20	CHARDONNAY DEL PIEMONTE, ARALDICA 1992 Piedmont (It)
79	£6.10	ROSEMOUNT CHARDONNAY 1992 Hunter Valley (Aus)
91	£7.55	MARQUES DE MURRIETA RIOJA RESERVA BLANCO 1987 Rioja (Sp)
168	£9.50	SANCERRE LES ROCHES, DOMAINE VACHERON 1992 Loire (F)
174	£12.15	POUILLY FUME, DE LADOUCETTE 1990 Loire (F)
229	£3.50	VAL DU TORGAN, LES PRODUCTEURS DU MONT TAUCH Midi (F)
414	£4.10	DOLCETTO D'ASTI, ARALDICA 1992 Piedmont (It)
444	£4.85	PERIQUITA, J M DA FONSECA 1990 (P)
470	£6.95	MONBAZILLAC, CHATEAU THEULET, SCEA ALARD 1990 Bordeaux (F)
489	£9.30	CHURCHILL GRAHAM FINEST VINTAGE CHARACTER Douro (P)

| ECK | Eckington Wines |

2 Ravencar Road, Eckington, Sheffield S31 9GJ, (Tel 0246 433213 Fax 0246 433213). **Opening Hours**: 'open all hours'. **Delivery**: free locally. **Tastings**: held regularly. **Discounts**: negotiable.

Dr Andrew Loughran offers his customers perhaps the ultimate in personal service: armed with an extensive database, he will search for any wine requested, and pinpoint the best price available in the UK. Meanwhile he holds stocks of those he particularly recommends — a superb selection, including Hamilton Russell Pinot Noir and Tasmania Wine Company Chardonnay.

11	£7.25	MONTANA LINDAUER BRUT (NZ)
15	£8.49	DEINHARD LILA RIESLING BRUT, SEKT Mittelrhein (G)
20	£7.25	OMAR KHAYYAM, CHAMPAGNE INDIA 1987 Maharashtra (Ind)
22	£8.59	MAYERLING CREMANT D'ALSACE, CAVE VINICOLE DE TURCKHEIM Alsace (F)
28	£16.99	DRAPPIER BLANC DE BLANCS CHAMPAGNE Champagne (F)
51	£4.99	CHARDONNAY 'VIRGINIE', VIN DE PAYS D'OC, SARL DOMAINE VIRGINIE LIEURAN 1992 Midi (F)
57	£5.95	CHABLIS, LOUIS ALEXANDRE 1992 Burgundy (F)
74	£4.94	PENFOLDS KOONUNGA HILL CHARDONNAY 1992 South East Australia (Aus)
80	£5.99	CHATEAU REYNELLA STONY HILL CHARDONNAY 1990 South Australia (Aus)
81	£5.99	CATHEDRAL CELLARS CHARDONNAY, KWV 1991 Coastal Region (SA)
90	£7.40	YARDEN CHARDONNAY, GOLAN HEIGHTS WINERY 1991 Golan Heights (Is)
91	£6.99	MARQUES DE MURRIETA RIOJA RESERVA BLANCO 1987 Rioja (Sp)
115	£13.49	NEWTON UNFILTERED CHARDONNAY 1990 Napa Valley (Cal)
116	£15.30	CHATEAU DE SENEJAC WHITE BORDEAUX 1989 Bordeaux (F)
143	£4.59	SANTA RITA RESERVA SAUVIGNON 1993 Maule (Ch)
146	£4.95	HARDY'S MOONDAH BROOK ESTATE CHENIN BLANC 1992 Gingin, (W Aus)
154	£5.99	VERDELHO, WYNDHAM ESTATE 1991 South East Australia (Aus)
163	£7.35	BOURGOGNE ALIGOTE, VALLET FRERES 1990 Burgundy (F)
164	£7.55	MENETOU SALON LES MOROGUES HENRI PELLE 1992 Loire (F)
180	£4.99	NEIL ELLIS INGLEWOOD GEWURZTRAMINER 1992 (SA)
182	£5.99	GEWURZTRAMINER D'ALSACE, CAVE VINICOLE DE TURCKHEIM 1992 Alsace (F)
188	£5.49	PETER LEHMANN SEMILLON 1992 Barossa Valley (Aus)
194	£3.96	TOLLANA DRY WHITE 1992 South East Australia (Aus)
218	£5.89	MOUNT HURTLE GRENACHE ROSE, GEOFF MERRILL 1992 McLaren Vale (Aus)
238	£5.95	CHATEAU DE LASTOURS CORBIERES, FUT DE CHENE 1989 Midi (F)
244	£2.65	RUSSE CABERNET CINSAULT (Bul)
250	£3.50	STAMBOLOVO RESERVE MERLOT 1987 (Bul)
256	£4.45	HARDYS NOTTAGE HILL CABERNET SAUVIGNON 1991 South Australia (Aus)
257	£4.40	SEAVIEW CABERNET SAUVIGNON/SHIRAZ 1990 South East Australia (Aus)
269	£5.49	MONTANA CABERNET SAUVIGNON 1991 Marlborough (NZ)
270	£4.95	HARDY'S MOONDAH BROOK ESTATE CABERNET SAUVIGNON 1989 Gingin (W Aus)
272	£4.95	ROUGE HOMME CABERNET/SHIRAZ, COONAWARRA 1988 Coonawarra (Aus)

273	£4.99	TALTARNI FIDDLEBACK TERRACE 1990 Pyrenees (Aus)
292	£8.46	COLUMBIA CREST MERLOT, STIMSON LANE 1989 Washington State (US)
296	£7.39	CHATEAU TOUR DU HAUT MOULIN, HAUT MEDOC 1985 Bordeaux (F)
298	£9.28	LINDEMANS ST GEORGE CABERNET SAUVIGNON 1989 Coonawarra (Aus)
299	£9.50	MEERLUST MERLOT, STELLENBOSCH 1986 Stellenbosch (SA)
308	£10.95	CHATEAU CANTERMERLE, HAUT MEDOC 1987 Bordeaux (F)
309	£12.29	NEWTON MERLOT 1990 Napa Valley (Cal)
335	£4.59	COTES DU RHONE DOMAINE DE TERRE BRULEE, CAVE DE VIGNERONS DE RASTEAU 1990 Rhône (F)
342	£6.69	PETER LEHMANN 'CLANCY'S RED' 1990 Barossa Valley (Aus)
346	£6.99	CHATEAU MUSAR, 1986 Bekaa Valley (Leb)
365	£12.42	PENFOLDS MAGILL ESTATE SHIRAZ 1988 South Australia (Aus)
369	£15.90	JADE MOUNTAIN SYRAH, DOUGLAS DANIELAK 1990 Sonoma (Cal)
370	£15.39	YARRA YERING SHIRAZ NO.2 1990 Yarra Valley (Aus)
405	£16.89	BEAUNE 1ER CRU EPENOTTES, VALLET FRERES 1989 Burgundy (F)
420	£7.85	SANTO TOMAS BARBERA (Mex)
422	£7.99	CHIANTI CLASSICO, ISOLE E OLENA 1990 Tuscany (It)
423	£7.99	CARMIGNANO, CAPEZZANA 1987 Tuscany (It)
426	£6.55	FREISA DELLE LANGHE, G D VAJRA 1990 Piedmont (It)
438	£3.75	ALBOR RIOJA TINTO, BODEGAS & BEBIDAS 1991 Rioja (Sp)
447	£5.49	CAMPO VIEJO RIOJA RESERVA 1987 Rioja (Sp)
467	£5.75	VIN SANTO BROLIO ESTATE, BARONE RICASOLI 1984 Tuscany (It)
492	£10.85	COLHEITA, A A CALEM & FILHO 1985 Douro (P)

EP | Eldridge Pope & Co plc

Weymouth Ave, Dorchester, Dorset DT1 1QT (Tel 0305 251251 Fax 0305 258300). **Opening Hours:** Mon-Sat 9am-1pm, 2-5.30pm, varying half days. **Delivery:** free nationally for 2 or more cases. **Tastings:** regular in-store and tutored/theme events. **Discounts:** 5% per mixed case.

A 160 year old traditional merchant committed to 'old fashioned principles – good service, good quality, and value for money'. The chocolate coloured list, full of mainly Old World delights, has an incredible range of Petits Châteaux and mind blowing Burgundies, many from growers exclusive to EP. Still in France, the country wines (complete with map) are astonishing. The '88 Abbaye de Valmagne (1/3 each Syrah, Mourvèdre and Grenache) at £4.47, or the '91 white Montravel Ch le Bondieu (£4.52) are super value.

EBA | Ben Ellis & Associates Ltd

Brockham Wine Cellars, Wheelers Lane, Brockham, Surrey RH3 3HJ (Tel 0737 842160 Fax 0737 843210). **Opening Hours**: Mon-Fri 9am-6.30pm, Sat 9am-1pm. **Delivery:** free within central London. **Tastings:** regular in-store plus tutored and theme events.

'The core of our business remains traditional...with value in the £5-8 bracket.' The former includes an impressive choice of Bordeaux, ('90 Pichon Baron, '89 Calon Segur) domaine Burgundies (Comtes Lafon, Daniel Rion) and Northern Rhône (Dervieux, Faurie), while the latter (which includes the greater part of the list) inevitably relies more heavily on the New World, with Tarrawarra Chardonnay, Hollick Cabernet Merlot, Rockford, Shiraz, Vavasour Sauvignon, Qupe Mourvêdre and Cameron Pinot Noir.

77	£4.99	SALISBURY ESTATE CHARDONNAY 1992 South East Australia (Aus)
141	£4.75	CUVEE DE CEPAGE SAUVIGNON, DOMAINE DU BREUIL 1992 Loire (F)
189	£8.03	LAGAR DE CERVERA, RIAS BAIXAS, LAGAR DE FORNELOSSA 1992 Galicia (Sp)

272	£5.43	ROUGE HOMME CABERNET/SHIRAZ, COONAWARRA 1988 Coonawarra (Aus)
320	£20.56	CHATEAU PICHON LONGUEVILLE BARON, PAUILLAC 1990 Bordeaux (F)
330	£4.11	VIN DE PAYS DES COLLINES RHODANIENNES CEPAGE SYRAH, CAVE DE TAIN L'HERMITAGE Rhone (F)
389	£7.20	HAMILTON-RUSSELL PINOT NOIR, WALKER BAY 1991 Walker Bay (SA)

EVI | Evingtons Wine Merchants

120 Evington Rd, Leicester LE2 1HH (Tel 0533 542702). **Opening Hours:** Mon-Sat 9.30am-6pm.
Delivery: free within 20 miles. **Tastings:** regular in-store tastings plus themed and tutored events.
Discounts: 5% on 1-3 cases, 7.5% on 4-9 cases, 10% on 10 or over (check).

Nearly 70 years on the job and Evingtons are still going strong, despite pressure from local supermarkets. Their concise list includes such finds as the '89 La Parrina from Italy, whites from the new world (Grove Mill, Houghtons) and rare sweeties from the Loire. A comprehensive Rhône line up includes some seven Chateauneufs du Pape.

11	£7.19	MONTANA LINDAUER BRUT (NZ)
15	£7.80	DEINHARD LILA RIESLING BRUT, SEKT Mittelrhein (G)
33	£31.20	BOLLINGER GRANDE ANNEE 1985 Champagne (F)
46	£12.45	CHARDONNAY DEL PIEMONTE, ARALDICA 1992 Piedmont (It)
74	£5.35	PENFOLDS KOONUNGA HILL CHARDONNAY 1992 South East Australia (Aus)
91	£8.70	MARQUES DE MURRIETA RIOJA RESERVA BLANCO 1987 Rioja (Sp)
160	£7.10	GROVE MILL SAUVIGNON 1992 Blenheim (NZ)
269	£5.29	MONTANA CABERNET SAUVIGNON 1991 Marlborough (NZ)
311	£13.45	CHATEAU CISSAC, HAUT-MEDOC 1982 Bordeaux (F)
332	£4.05	VIN DE PAY DES COLLINES RHODANIENNES SYRAH, VERRIER 1990 Rhône (F)
366	£15.50	COTE ROTIE SEIGNEUR DU MAUGIRON, DELAS FRERES 1987 Rhône (F)
424	£8.50	DOLCETTO D'ALBA CORSINI, MASCARELLO 1991 Piedmont (It)
428	£9.90	BRIC MILEUI, ASCHERI 1990 Piedmont (It)
437	£3.85	CISMEIRA DOURO 1991 Douro (P)
444	£4.65	PERIQUITA, J M DA FONSECA 1990 (P)
472	£8.80H	NEETHLINGSHOF WEISSER RIESLING NOBLE LATE HARVEST 1991 (SA)
482	£8.65	LUSTAU OLD EAST INDIA, EMILIO LUSTAU Jerez (Sp)
484	£19.90	MATUSALEM, GONZALEZ BYASS Jerez (Sp)
494	£13.49	WARRE'S TRADITIONAL LBV 1981 Douro (P)
496	£14.89	TAYLOR'S TEN YEAR OLD TAWNY Douro (P)

PEY | Philip Eyres Wine Merchant

The Cellars, Coleshill, Amersham, Bucks HP7 OLS (Tel 0494 433823 Fax 0494 431349)
Opening Hours: telephone Mon-Fri 8am-10pm, Sat, Sun answerphone. **Delivery:** free locally.
Tastings: samples opened occasionally in store.

A posse of respected wine traders have joined Philip Eyres, tracking down customers in the Home Counties for his impressive portfolio of wines. The range is broad, with Champagne Le Mesnil, Gentaz Côte Rôtie, Trapiche from Argentina, and South African stars Hamilton Russell and Kanonkop. Yet the real passion here is Germany — offerings include Dr Loosen, Bassermann-Jordan and Von Schubert. As ever, the wine names read like the monkey's first typing lesson, but taste like nectar.

FAR	Farr Vintners Ltd

19 Sussex Street, London SW1V 4RR (Tel 071 828 1960 Fax 071 828 3500). **Opening Hours**: Mon-Fri 10am-6pm. **Tastings:** tutored events. **Discounts:** variable over £2,000.

In an age when Great Britain is sounding increasingly like a misnomer, London remains the centre of the world fine wine market, and Farr Vintners are as responsible for this as anyone. Even the French buy their wine here, attracted by the fair prices and incomparable range of stock: current bargains include '61 Lynch Bages for £80 and '37 Moulin Touchais for £55 (all their prices are ex-vat). Stephen Browett and Lindsay Hamilton will even give a discount if you spend more than £2,000 – pretty generous given their average sale is £3,000. Definite candidates for the Queen's award for exports.

311	£12.25	CHATEAU CISSAC, HAUT-MEDOC 1982 Bordeaux (F)
323	£38.18	CHATEAU COS D'ESTOURNEL, ST ESTEPHE 1982 Bordeaux (F)

FV	Fernlea Vintners

7 Fernlea Road, Balham, London SW12 7RT (Tel 081 673 0053 Fax 081 673 3559). **Opening Hours**: Mon-Sat 9.30am-5.30pm. **Delivery:** free for over 10 cases. **Tastings:** samples opened regularly. **Discounts:** 'glass of wine!'

Balham possesses a new 'Gateway to the South' in the form of Fernlea Vintners. The range is suitably unusual, featuring the Mexican wines of L A Cetto and a good selection from Austria. Equally unusual is Peter Godden's collection discount: 'Probably a nice glass of wine'. Domaine Delas Condrieu should make the journey worthwhile.

25	£13.70	CROSER METHODE TRADITIONNELLE, PETALUMA 1990 Adelaide Hills (Aus)
33	£28.98	BOLLINGER GRANDE ANNEE 1985 Champagne (F)
79	£6.61	ROSEMOUNT CHARDONNAY 1992 Hunter Valley (Aus)
97	£8.35	WAIPARA SPRINGS CHARDONNAY 1991 Canterbury (NZ)
105	£10.16	CULLENS SAUVIGNON BLANC 1991 Margaret River (Aus)
119	£16.75	ROBERT MONDAVI RESERVE CHARDONNAY 1988 Napa Valley (Cal)
160	£5.94	GROVE MILL SAUVIGNON 1992 Blenheim (NZ)
162	£7.70	SELAKS MARLBOROUGH SAUVIGNON BLANC 1991 Marlborough (NZ)
172	£10.15	SANCERRE MD, H. BOURGEOIS 1991 Loire (F)
174	£11.37	POUILLY FUME, DE LADOUCETTE 1990 Loire (F)
278	£6.11	GOUNDREY LANGTON CABERNET/MERLOT 1991 Mount Barker (Aus)
295	£10.77	FETZER BARREL SELECT CABERNET SAUVIGNON 1989 Mendocino County (Cal)
323	£35.84	CHATEAU COS D'ESTOURNEL, ST ESTEPHE 1982 Bordeaux (F)
349	£9.48	ZINFANDEL, DRY CREEK VINEYARDS 1990 Sonoma (Cal)
353	£9.11	DAVID WYNN PATRIARCH SHIRAZ 1991 Eden Valley (Aus)
366	£11.44	COTE ROTIE SEIGNEUR DU MAUGIRON, DELAS FRERES 1987 Rhone (F)
370	£16.08	YARRA YERING SHIRAZ NO.2 1990 Yarra Valley (Aus)
397	£11.38	MERCUREY, 1ER CRU, CLOS DE MYGLANDS, FAIVELEY 1991 Burgundy (F)
402	£13.00	BEAUNE 1ER CRU TEURONS, DOMAINE ROSSIGNOL TRAPET 1990 Burgundy (F)
438	£4.40	ALBOR RIOJA TINTO, BODEGAS & BEBIDAS 1991 Rioja (Sp)
496	£13.31	TAYLOR'S TEN YEAR OLD TAWNY Douro (P)

AF	Alexr Findlater & Co

Heveningham High House, Nr Halesworth, Suffolk, IP19 0EA, (Tel 0986 798274 Fax 0986 798694) **Opening Hours**: Mon-Sat 10am-6pm. **Delivery:** free nationally. **Tastings:** occasionally in store.

'We shall always follow quality not price, and then justify our price on taste.'
An appropriate attitude for an ex-accountant we feel, and one which is fully
spported (sic) by Alexr (sic) Findlater's rather eclectic list. From ZD Californians
to the Mission wines from New Zealand and Tim Adams's brilliant
Australians, there's an enticing collection of New World wines while
Burgundy, Germany and Italy are similarly well covered in Europe. Altogethr
rathr good.

4	£5.49	NEDERBURG 1ER CUVEE BRUT Paarl (SA)
5	£6.95	GRAND DUCHESS RUSSIAN SPARKLING WINE, Ukraine
11	£6.50	MONTANA LINDAUER BRUT (NZ)
24	£9.95	GREEN POINT, DOMAINE CHANDON 1990 Yarra Valley (Aus)
33	£28.95	BOLLINGER GRANDE ANNEE 1985 Champagne (F)
74	£4.95	PENFOLDS KOONUNGA HILL CHARDONNAY 1992 South East Australia (Aus)
79	£5.79	ROSEMOUNT CHARDONNAY 1992 Hunter Valley (Aus)
160	£6.59	GROVE MILL SAUVIGNON 1992 Blenheim (NZ)
92	£7.50	MONTANA CHURCH ROAD CHARDONNAY 1991 (NZ)
95	£9.20	BARREL SELECT CHARDONNAY, FETZER 1991 Mendocino County (Cal)
97	£8.99	WAIPARA SPRINGS CHARDONNAY 1991 Canterbury (NZ)
100	£10.80	FIRESTONE CHARDONNAY 1990 (Cal)
104	£9.80	CHARDONNAY, JANE HUNTER'S WINES 1991 Marlborough (NZ)
112	£12.95	ELSTON CHARDONNAY, TE MATA ESTATE 1991 Hawkes Bay (NZ)
116	£16.95	CHATEAU DE SENEJAC WHITE BORDEAUX 1989 Bordeaux (F)
159	£6.65	SAUVIGNON BLANC, VILLIERA 1992 Paarl (SA)
169	£7.99	HUNTERS MARLBOROUGH SAUVIGNON BLANC 1992 Marlborough (NZ)
180	£5.35	NEIL ELLIS INGLEWOOD GEWURZTRAMINER 1992 (SA)
229	£2.99	VAL DU TORGAN, LES PRODUCTEURS DU MONT TAUCH Midi (F)
257	£4.50	SEAVIEW CABERNET SAUVIGNON/SHIRAZ 1990 South East Australia (Aus)
267	£5.60	KANONKOP KADETTE, STELLENBOSCH 1991 Stellenbosch (SA)
269	£4.95	MONTANA CABERNET SAUVIGNON 1991 Marlborough (NZ)
299	£9.75	MEERLUST MERLOT, STELLENBOSCH 1986 Stellenbosch (SA)
303	£10.95	PETALUMA COONAWARRA RED 1988 Coonawarra (Aus)
348	£7.95	ROSEMOUNT SHOW RESERVE SYRAH 1990 McLaren Vale (Aus)
365	£13.45	PENFOLDS MAGILL ESTATE SHIRAZ 1988 South Australia (Aus)
370	£16.70	YARRA YERING SHIRAZ NO.2 1990 Yarra Valley (Aus)
389	£6.95	HAMILTON-RUSSELL PINOT NOIR, WALKER BAY 1991 Walker Bay (SA)
425	£5.89	LE SASSINE, LE RAGOSE 1988 Veneto (It)
443	£4.50	QUINTA DE LA ROSA RED TABLE WINE 1991 Douro (P)
450	£6.75	YLLERA, VINO DE MESA, SAT LOS CURRO 1988 Ribera del Duero (Sp)
460	£7.70	MOSCATEL PALIDO, MALAGA, SCHOLTZ HERMANOS SA Malaga (Sp)
461	£9.59	STANTON & KILLEEN RUTHERGLEN LIQUEUR MUSCAT Rutherglen (Aus)
462	£9.95	CAMPBELLS RUTHERGLEN LIQUEUR MUSCAT Rutherglen (Aus)
468	£5.99	NELSON LATE HARVEST RHINE RIESLING, SEIFRIED 1991 Nelson (NZ)
484	£18.45	MATUSALEM, GONZALEZ BYASS Jerez (Sp)
491	£10.85	DOWS CRUSTED PORT BOTTLED 1987 Douro (P)
498	£19.95	QUINTA DO VESUVIO VINTAGE PORT 1990 Douro (P)

FDL	Findlater Mackie Todd & Co Ltd

Deer Park Road, Merton Abbey, London SW19 3TU (Tel 081 543 0966 Fax 081 543 2415). **Opening
Hours:** Mon-Fri 9am-5pm. **Delivery:** free nationally for 3 or more cases.

The big news here is the surprise purchase of this mail order operation by
Waitrose whose buyers are now choosing and pricing the wines — which,
as far as we can see, has had an entirely beneficial effect. There are some
unusual wines here – including the Goldwater Estate Chardonnay from

New Zealand – and some good mixed cases. Beware though that by-the-case prices (often identical to by-the-bottle prices elsewhere) now exclude carriage. What's that about 'Never knowingly undersold'?

FNZ	Fine Wines of New Zealand Ltd

PO Box 476, London NW5 2NZ (Tel 071 482 0093 Fax 071 267 8400),**Opening Hours**: 24 hour answerphone. **Delivery:** nationally at cost. **Discounts:** £5 collection discount per case.

Margaret Harvey has swapped her pharmacy Phd for an MW and continues to provide a range of N Z wines from 'the north of North Island to the South of South Island', including a host of small producers (and in New Zealand, that means small). Going from north to south we suggest St Nesbit, Mills Reef, Mission (founded in 1840, it's the oldest vineyard in NZ), Ata Ranghi, (the richest most concentrated Pinot Noirs, Cabernet & Merlots), Waipara Springs and Rippon, the most southern vineyard situated in the earthquake stricken plains of Otago.

160	£5.95	GROVE MILL SAUVIGNON 1992 Blenheim (NZ)
220	£6.95	VIDAL MERLOT ROSE 1992 Hawkes Bay (NZ)
468	£7.25	NELSON LATE HARVEST RHINE RIESLING, SEIFRIED 1991 Nelson (NZ)

LEF	Le Fleming Wines

9 Longcroft Avenue, Harpenden, Herts AL5 2RB (Tel 0582 760125). **Opening Hours**: 24 hours answering service. **Delivery:** free within 25 miles. **Tastings:** regularly in-store. **Discounts:** 5% 'occasionally'.

Cherry Jenkins has definitely earned the title 'Purveyor of Fine New World Wines to the Cognoscenti of Hertfordshire'. A list featuring Schinus Molle, David Wynn and Newton is further strengthened by wines from Mount Langhi Ghiran and Charles Melton. Meanwhile in France, Daniel Rion Burgundies and Les Terraces de Guilhem (the second wine of Mas de Daumas Gassac) provide evidence of an ever-improving list.

24	£10.49	GREEN POINT, DOMAINE CHANDON 1990 Yarra Valley (Aus)
61	£6.16	LUGANA CA'DEI FRATI 1992 Brescia (It)
188	£5.50	PETER LEHMANN SEMILLON 1992 Barossa Valley (Aus)
309	£10.00	NEWTON MERLOT 1990 Napa Valley (Cal)
346	£7.12	CHATEAU MUSAR, 1986 Bekaa Valley (Leb)
423	£7.57	CARMIGNANO, CAPEZZANA 1987 Tuscany (It)

JFD	John Ford Wines

8 Richardson Road, Hove, East Sussex BN3 5RB (Tel 0273 735891). **Opening Hours**: Mon-Sat 9am-9pm, Sun 12-2pm, 7-9pm. **Delivery:** free within 10 miles. **Tastings:** regularly in-store. **Discounts:** 10% per case for cash or cheque.

After spells in retail with Peter Dominic and Thresher, Liz Rollings took over John Ford Wines with her husband Ken in August 1992. 'We hope to establish a reputation for service, reliability, good humour and gentle advice.' They now have a monthly newsletter and regular informal tastings in the shop, with plans to set up a more formal tasting programme. Will the first wines be from the healthy South African range, featuring Stellenryck, Hamilton-Russell and Meerendal, or will they be from the sensibly chosen and priced claret range? Contact the shop for more details.

20	£8.99	OMAR KHAYYAM, CHAMPAGNE INDIA 1987 Maharashtra (Ind)
45	£5.09	NOBILO WHITE CLOUD 1992 (NZ)
250	£4.19	STAMBOLOVO RESERVE MERLOT 1987 (Bul)
290	£9.59	CHATEAU BISTON BRILLETTE, CRU BOURGEOIS MOULIS 1989 Bordeaux (F)
292	£9.19	COLUMBIA CREST MERLOT, STIMSON LANE 1989 Washington State (US)
336	£5.99	ZINFANDEL, FETZER VINEYARDS 1990 Mendocino County (Cal)
389	£8.09	HAMILTON-RUSSELL PINOT NOIR, WALKER BAY 1991 Walker Bay (SA)
487	£7.99	TOKAJI ASZU 3 PUTTONYOS, TOKAJI-HEGYALA SCHLUMBERGER 1981 (Hun)

F&M | Fortnum & Mason

181 Piccadilly, London W1A 1ER (Tel 071 734 8040 Fax 071 437 3278). **Opening Hours**: Mon-Sat 9.30-6pm. **Delivery**: free within the M25. **Tastings**: in-store, plus tutored. **Discounts**: 5% for 1-4 cases; 7.5% for 5-9 cases, 10% for 10 cases.

Annette Duce's achievement since arriving at Fortnums has been to expand the list into the New World, and include the more innovative producers of Europe, while making the ever-stylish department more accessible. This is still the place to pick and choose from 14 port shippers or decide whether to buy a '45 Lynch Bages at £250, to pay the extra £150 for the '26 Lafite - or stick to the own-label Corbières at £3.95.

JFR | John Frazier Ltd

Stirling Road, Cranmore Industrial Estate, Shirley, Solihull, West Midlands B90 4XD (Tel 021 704 3415 Fax 021 711 2710). **Opening Hours**: Mon-Sat 10am-10pm, Sun 12-2pm, 7-10pm. **Delivery:** free within 30 miles. **Tastings**: occasionally in-store, plus tutored.

If John Frazier become a doctor (his handwriting certainly qualifies him) he would no doubt prescribe a regular dose of New World wine. And his five shops would make excellent pharmacies, stocked as they are with wines from Cuvaison, C J Pask, Taltarni and Moss Wood. If the condition is serious, try '83 Grange Hermitage – has medicine ever tasted so good?

FWC | The Fulham Road Wine Centre

899-901 Fulham Rd, London SW6 5HU (Tel 071 736 7009 Fax 071 736 6648). **Opening Hours**: Mon-Sat 10am-9pm. **Delivery:** free locally, nationally at cost. **Tastings:** regularly in-store, plus tutored events and dinners. **Discounts:** 5% per mixed case.

Declaring an interest (parts of the *Guide* were compiled in the office here and Robert Joseph is a regular lecturer at the Centre's Wine School), we have no hesitation in recommending this as an unusually good source of friendly, down-to-earth service and excellent advice. The shop is packed with maps, books, and gadgets etc as well as a small but carefully chosen range of wines. Look out for a good choice from Slovakia, plenty of unusual Australians and Kiwis, and a quickly changing Fine Wine section that includes some of the shop's best bargains. Canny Fulhamites make the Centre a regular haunt on Saturdays when bottles are always open for tasting.

11	£7.95	MONTANA LINDAUER BRUT (NZ)
23	£12.95	SCHARFFENBERGER BRUT Mendocino County (Cal)
53	£5.95	'CASAL DI SERRA' VERDICCHIO CLASSICO, UMANI RONCHI 1991 Marches (It)
63	£7.99	LA MONT NORMAN, VIN DE PAYS 1993 (F)
64	£8.95	TASMANIAN WINE COMPANY CHARDONNAY, PIPER'S BROOK 1991 (Aus)
91	£8.95	MARQUES DE MURRIETA RIOJA RESERVA BLANCO 1987 Rioja (Sp)
154	£6.45	VERDELHO, WYNDHAM ESTATE 1991 South East Australia (Aus)
228	£3.75	FRANKOVKA, VINO NITRA 1991 Pezinok Slovakia
248	£3.95	SLOVAKIAN CABERNET SAUVIGNON, VINA NITRA 1992 (SLO)
266	£4.95	SALISBURY ESTATE CABERNET SAUVIGNON 1991 South East Australia (Aus)
279	£6.85	MICHEL LYNCH BORDEAUX ROUGE, COMPAGNIE MEDOCAINE 1989 Bordeaux (F)
316	£15.95	LAUREL GLEN CABERNET SAUVIGNON 1987 Sonoma (Cal)
322	£26.50	CHATEAU LYNCH-BAGES, PAUILLAC 1989 Bordeaux (F)
323	£48.50	CHATEAU COS D'ESTOURNEL, ST ESTEPHE 1982 Bordeaux (F)
346	£8.45	CHATEAU MUSAR, 1986 Bekaa Valley (Leb)
426	£9.55	FREISA DELLE LANGHE, G D VAJRA 1990 Piedmont (It)
427	£9.95	CUMARO ROSSO CONERO, UMANI RONCHI 1989 Marches (It)
468	£6.95	NELSON LATE HARVEST RHINE RIESLING, SEIFRIED 1991 Nelson (NZ)
472	£8.95	NEETHLINGSHOF WEISSER RIESLING NOBLE LATE HARVEST 1991 (SA)
489	£9.85	CHURCHILL GRAHAM FINEST VINTAGE CHARACTER Douro (P)

FUL | Fuller Smith & Turner plc

Griffin Brewery, Chiswick Lane South, Chiswick, London W4 2QB (Tel 081 994 3691 Fax 081 995 0230). **Opening Hours:** Mon-Sat 9.30am-9.30pm, Sun 12-3pm, 7-9pm. **Delivery:** free locally. **Tastings:** regularly in-store. **Discounts:** free bottle with every mixed case. Other discounts negotiable.

Alistair Llewellyn-Smith is determined to keep up the momentum of the last few years. Most of the wine sold is under £4 a bottle, but those on a bigger budget can splash out on Roumier '89 Chambolle Musigny and '87 Grange. Recent trips to Italy and California should strengthen these areas of previous weakness, and the well-trained Fullers managers have smart newly-fitted shops in which to showcase this commendable range.

24	£9.99	GREEN POINT, DOMAINE CHANDON 1990 Yarra Valley (Aus)
33	£29.75	BOLLINGER GRANDE ANNEE 1985 Champagne (F)
39	£3.49	CHARDONNAY GYONGYOS, HUGH RYMAN 1992 (Hun)
43	£3.99	COTES DE ST MONT WHITE, PLAIMONT 1991 South West (F)
53	£5.35	'CASAL DI SERRA' VERDICCHIO CLASSICO, UMANI RONCHI 1991 Marches (It)
64	£8.99	TASMANIAN WINE COMPANY CHARDONNAY, PIPER'S BROOK 1991 (Aus)
74	£4.99	PENFOLDS KOONUNGA HILL CHARDONNAY 1992 South East Australia (Aus)
76	£5.95	CHARDONNAY VIN DE PAYS D'OC, H RYMAN 1992 Midi (F)
79	£6.10	ROSEMOUNT CHARDONNAY 1992 Hunter Valley (Aus)
182	£5.89	GEWURZTRAMINER D'ALSACE, CAVE VINICOLE DE TURCKHEIM 1992 Alsace (F)
256	£3.99	HARDYS NOTTAGE HILL CABERNET SAUVIGNON 1991 South Australia (Aus)
269	£4.99	MONTANA CABERNET SAUVIGNON 1991 Marlborough (NZ)
272	£4.99	ROUGE HOMME CABERNET/SHIRAZ, COONAWARRA 1988 Coonawarra (Aus)
346	£7.95	CHATEAU MUSAR, 1986 Bekaa Valley (Leb)
396	£8.49	SAINTSBURY PINOT NOIR 1991 Carneros (Cal)
397	£10.99	MERCUREY, 1ER CRU, CLOS DE MYGLANDS, FAIVELEY 1991 Burgundy (F)
481	£5.55	HIDALGO AMONTILLADO NAPOLEON Jerez (Sp)
482	£8.59	LUSTAU OLD EAST INDIA, EMILIO LUSTAU Jerez (Sp)
483	£9.99	1796 RICH OLD OLOROSO Jerez (Sp)
484	£16.99	MATUSALEM, GONZALEZ BYASS Jerez (Sp)

MFW	Marcus Fyfe Wines

Unit 3, Lorne Street, Lochgilphead, Argyll PA31 8LU (Tel 0546 603646 Fax 0546 606233). **Opening Hours:** Mon-Thurs 9.30am-7pm, Fri 9.30am-8pm, Sat 10am-7pm. **Delivery:** free within 5 miles. **Tastings:** occasional in-store. **Discounts:** 5% on 1-3 cases; 10% on 3 cases or more.

As the holiday season hots up, so does Marcus Fyfe's turnover – as the yachties glide through the Western Isles, odds are they'll stop off and load up with Médoc or a local Argyll malt. This year sees some interesting new arrivals in Lochgilphead, including Domaine Vieux Télégraphe's delicious leftovers in the form of 'Les Marrons' (£5.79) and a great alternative to Barolo, an '83 Gattinara Riserva from L & I Nervi (£7.39). There's often a bargain on the Fine Wine list, too; this time you can sail way with magnum of '83 Ch Cissac for £12.90.

11	£6.99	MONTANA LINDAUER BRUT (NZ)
44	£4.99	PERIQUITA, J M DA FONSECA 1990 (P)
481	£7.99	HIDALGO AMONTILLADO NAPOLEON Jerez (Sp)

GBY	Elizabeth Gabay and Partners

25 Cottenham Drive, Wimbledon, London SW20 0TD (Tel 081-947 1661 Fax 081-947 4601). **Opening Hours:** usually staffed during office hours, otherwise 24-hour answering service. **Delivery:** free locally. **Tastings:** occasional in-store.

Elizabeth Gabay is a self-proclaimed food and wine expert. When she's not researching, writing, tasting and tutoring, she's touring France, seeking new wines for her customers. Her speciality is Provence and her comprehensive listings prove she really knows her stuff. Italy, too, is well covered, from Nino Negri's '89 Barbera from Valtellina, to the perfumed white '90 Ramitello made from the local Falanghina variety. Gabay & Co have also achieved the first 'cool climate' Australian selection we've seen.

GLY	Gallery Wines

14 Dungiven Road, Londonderry BT47 1BW (Tel 0504 48762 Fax 0504 42481). **Opening Hours:** Mon-Sat 11.30am-9pm. **Delivery:** free locally. **Tastings:** regular in-store. **Discounts:** 10% per case.

Londonderry's wine guru Bernard O'Kane now runs annual wine classes, that are well worth attending. Since 50% of the local population currently drink no wine at all, his zeal might just prove good business in the long run.

74	£5.79	PENFOLDS KOONUNGA HILL CHARDONNAY 1992 South East Australia (Aus)
79	£6.99	ROSEMOUNT CHARDONNAY 1992 Hunter Valley (Aus)
133	£4.29	NOGALES SAUVIGNON BLANC, DISCOVER WINES LTDA 1993 Curico (Ch)
244	£2.99	RUSSE CABERNET CINSAULT (Bul)
259	£4.99	GLEN ELLEN CABERNET SAUVIGNON 1989 (Cal)
282	£6.99	VALLEY OAKS CABERNET SAUVIGNON, FETZER 1990 Mendocino County (Cal)
346	£9.49	CHATEAU MUSAR, 1986 Bekaa Valley (Leb)
413	£4.49	MONTEPULCIANO D'ABRUZZO, UMANI RONCHI 1991 Marches (It)

GDS	Garrards Wine & Spirit Merchants

Mayo House, 49 Main Street, Cockermouth, Cumbria CA13 9JS (Tel 0900 823592). **Opening Hours:**

Mon-Tues 9.30am-5.45pm, Wed-Sat 9.30am-8pm. **Delivery**: free locally. **Tastings**: occasional in-store. **Discounts**: 5%per case.

Garrards proclaim themselves 'your astonishing good fortune', but it is Christopher and Joyce Garrard who are lucky, having remained in the *Guide* after committing the cardinal sin of listing wines without producer names. However, there were extenuating circumstances, the list being a temporary reaction to the 'force majeure' of currency devaluation. Where mentioned, the producers seemed a pretty reliable bunch, and the excellent sherry list justified giving these Cockermouth miscreants one more chance.

G	**Gateway Foodmarkets Ltd**

Hawkfield Business Park, Whitchurch Lane, Bristol, Avon BS14 0TJ (Tel 0272 359359 Fax 0272 780 629). **Opening Hours**: Mon-Sat 8.30am-6pm. **Tastings**: regular in-store.

The innovation that gained Gateway the 'Going Places' award in last year's *Guide* has slowed over the past 12 months, but some great wines are still available, with '90 Jaffelin Meursault and '88 Haut-Marbuzet the absolute summit. For thriftier folk, the French country range has expanded, while the Somerfield Rioja Crianza from Bodegas Almenar is good value, too. As we go to press, 60 new wines from Italy, Australia, Portugal, Chile and South Africa are being introduced and, with more than 60 Gateways turned into more upmarket Somerfield stores, the chain should continue to go places.

11	£7.99	MONTANA LINDAUER BRUT (NZ)
12	£6.35	TOURAINE ROSE BRUT, CAVES DES VITICULTEURS DE VOUVRAY Loire (F)
24	£9.99	GREEN POINT, DOMAINE CHANDON 1990 Yarra Valley (Aus)
46	£3.69	CHARDONNAY DEL PIEMONTE, ARALDICA 1992 Piedmont (It)
48	£4.75	CHAIS BAUMIERE, CHARDONNAY VIN DE PAYS D'OC 1990 Midi (F)
59	£6.75	PETIT CHABLIS, GOULLEY 1991 Burgundy (F)
60	£6.95	SOMERFIELD CHABLIS, LA CHABLISIENNE 1990 Burgundy (F)
68	£3.19	SOMERFIELD AUSTRALIAN DRY WHITE (Aus)
74	£4.99	PENFOLDS KOONUNGA HILL CHARDONNAY 1992 South East Australia (Aus)
146	£5.49	HARDY'S MOONDAH BROOK ESTATE CHENIN BLANC 1992 Gingin, Western Australia (Aus)
182	£5.99	GEWURZTRAMINER D'ALSACE, CAVE VINICOLE DE TURCKHEIM 1992 Alsace (F)
191	£2.39	GATEWAY HOCK, RUDOLF MULLER Rhein (G)
197	£3.25	BADEN DRY, BADISCHER WINZERKELLER Baden (G)
230	£3.39	SOMERFIELD CALIFORNIAN DRY RED (Cal)
250	£3.49	STAMBOLOVO RESERVE MERLOT 1987 (Bul)
257	£3.99	SEAVIEW CABERNET SAUVIGNON/SHIRAZ 1990 South East Australia (Aus)
259	£4.45	GLEN ELLEN CABERNET SAUVIGNON 1989 (Cal)
264	£3.85	BUZET TRADITION, LES VIGNERONS DE BUZET 1988 South West (F)
346	£7.99	CHATEAU MUSAR, 1986 Bekaa Valley (Leb)
376	£5.69	BROUILLY, GEORGES DUBOEUF 1991 Burgundy (F)
386	£6.35	MARSANNAY, JEAN GARNIER 1989 Burgundy (F)
410	£2.89	CORTENOVA MERLOT, PASQUA 1991 Grave Friuli (It)
416	£4.99	SALICE SALENTINO RISERVA, AZ. AG. TAURINO 1988 Puglia (It)
433	£2.39	LEZIRIA VINHO TINTO, VEGA CO-OPERATIVE ALMEIRIM 1992 Almeirim (P)
441	£3.99	SOMERFIELD RIOJA TINTO 1989 Rioja (Sp)
466	£5.45	DOMAINE DE GARBES, PREMIERES COTES DE BORDEAUX 1990 Bordeaux (F)

| GON | Gauntleys of Nottingham |

4 High St, Exchange Arcade, Nottingham NG1 2ET (Tel 0602 417973 Fax 0602 509519); **Opening Hours:** Mon-Sat 9am-5.30pm. **Tastings:** regular in-store and tutored events. **Discounts:** variable.

Last year's Rhône Specialist of the Year, Gauntleys is a wonderful firm secreted beneath a haven for cigarophiles. There are, of course, Rhônes galore, ranging from Gramenon's rare Viognier Côtes du Rhône to Guigal's even rarer La Landonne Côte Rôtie, but the Burgundies (Burguet, Bachelet, Rion, Lafon et al) and Alsaces (Ostertag, Zind Humbrecht, Weinbach) are almost as splendid. With glories like these, who needs the New World?

33	£30.00	BOLLINGER GRANDE ANNEE 1985 Champagne (F)
272	£5.75	ROUGE HOMME CABERNET/SHIRAZ, COONAWARRA 1988 Coonawarra (Aus)
356	£11.00	CHATEAUNEUF DU PAPE, DOMAINE ANDRE BRUNEL 1989 Rhône (F)
364	£15.00	CHATEAUNEUF DU PAPE, CHATEAU DE BEAUCASTEL 1988 Rhône (F)
367	£15.00	CORNAS, AUGUSTE CLAPE 1990 Rhône (F)
422	£8.00	CHIANTI CLASSICO, ISOLE E OLENA 1990 Tuscany (It)
424	£7.90	DOLCETTO D'ALBA CORSINI, MASCARELLO 1991 Piedmont (It)
426	£8.50	FREISA DELLE LANGHE, G D VAJRA 1990 Piedmont (It)
497	£20.00	NIERPOORT COLHEITA 1983 Douro (P)

| GEL | Gelston Castle Fine Wines |

Castle Douglas, Scotland DG7 1QE (Tel 0556 3012 Fax 0556 4183). **Opening Hours:** Mon-Fri 9am-7pm. **Delivery:** free for orders over £150. **Tastings:** regular samples. **Discounts:** £2 per case collection discount; 5% on 10 cases champagne; 5% per case or 10% on two cases other wines.

Due to our publishing deadline, we missed Alexander Scott's entertaining 1993 list. No doubt there was plenty of wit and sound advice. Germany is still the number-one hot spot, with some small parcels of wine from top vintages and producers giving tremendous value at £6.50-£8. Drinking beautifully now, and for the next 20 years, is Bürklin-Wolff's '88 Ruppertsberger Riesling (£6.95). Burgundy, too, is well covered and features only single-domaine wines. Concentrating on some serious producers has created a small but quality-packed Rhône listing; five wines from the Cornas-based Syrah genius J Lionnet include the rare white St Péray.

43	£4.00	COTES DE ST MONT WHITE, PLAIMONT 1991 South West (F)
307	£9.95	LEEUWIN ESTATE CABERNET SAUVIGNON 1986 Margaret River (Aus)
326	£3.95	RESPLANDY MOURVEDRE, VIN DE PAYS D'OC, VAL D'ORBIEU 1990 Midi (F)
346	£7.50	CHATEAU MUSAR, 1986 Bekaa Valley (Leb)
363	£13.25	RIDGE GEYSERVILLE ZINFANDEL 1991 Sonoma (Cal)
443	£4.75	QUINTA DE LA ROSA RED TABLE WINE 1991 Douro (P)
494	£13.50	WARRE'S TRADITIONAL LBV 1981 Douro (P)
498	£21.67	QUINTA DO VESUVIO VINTAGE PORT 1990 Douro (P)

| JAG | J A Glass |

11 High Street, Dysart, Kirkcaldy, Fife, Scotland (Tel 0592 651850). **Opening Hours:** Mon-Sat 9am-6pm (Wed 9am-12.30pm). **Delivery:** free on larger orders. **Tastings:** tutored. **Discount:** special rates on mixed cases.

A newcomer to the *Guide*, with a shortish list which nevertheless provides all that one could want from a local merchant. Léoville Barton, Wolf Blass,

Chapoutier and Torres are all reliable names worth seeking out, while more eclectic producers such as Cuvaison and Bert Simon get a look in from time to time.

11	£6.79	MONTANA LINDAUER BRUT (NZ)
33	£27.99	BOLLINGER GRANDE ANNEE 1985 Champagne (F)
44	£3.79	CHARDONNAY, VINO DA TAVOLA, CA DONINI 1992 Triveneto (It)
45	£3.99	NOBILO WHITE CLOUD 1992 (NZ)
53	£4.99	'CASAL DI SERRA' VERDICCHIO CLASSICO, UMANI RONCHI 1991 Marches (It)
74	£4.99	PENFOLDS KOONUNGA HILL CHARDONNAY 1992 South East Australia (Aus)
256	£4.49	HARDYS NOTTAGE HILL CABERNET SAUVIGNON 1991 South Australia (Aus)
259	£4.49	GLEN ELLEN CABERNET SAUVIGNON 1989 (Cal)
269	£4.79	MONTANA CABERNET SAUVIGNON 1991 Marlborough (NZ)
272	£4.99	ROUGE HOMME CABERNET/SHIRAZ, COONAWARRA 1988 Coonawarra (Aus)
298	£9.99	LINDEMANS ST GEORGE CABERNET SAUVIGNON 1989 Coonawarra (Aus)
365	£12.99	PENFOLDS MAGILL ESTATE SHIRAZ 1988 South Australia (Aus)
413	£3.49	MONTEPULCIANO D'ABRUZZO, UMANI RONCHI 1991 Marches (It)
483	£8.59	1796 RICH OLD OLOROSO Jerez (Sp)
484	£16.99	MATUSALEM, GONZALEZ BYASS Jerez (Sp)

MG	Matthew Gloag & Son Ltd

Bordeaux House, 33 Kinnoull Street, Perth, Tayside PH1 5EU (Tel 0738 21101 Fax 0738 28167). **Opening Hours:** Mon-Fri 9am-5pm. **Delivery**: free. **Tastings**: regular in-store and tutored events. **Discounts**: 5% per case collection discount.

This well-established merchant, perhaps more famous for its Grouse, now offers its shop and mail-order customers a tempting array of small grower Burgundies to complement the high-quality Bordeaux and Rhône sections. But Gillian Lloyd is no blinkered Francophile; Australia, New Zealand and South Africa are all well represented in a good broad list.

GH	Goedhuis & Co Ltd

6 Rudolf Place, Miles Street, London SW8 1RP (Tel 071-793 7900 Fax 071-793 7170). **Opening Hours:** Mon-Fri 8.30am-6.30pm. **Tastings**: regular in-store.

Michel Colin, Jean Marc Boillot, Paul Pernot, Laurent Ponsot, Michel Lafarge…to anyone with even the sketchiest knowledge of real Burgundy, these names mean business – as does the debonnair Mr Goedhuis. He *does* sell wines that don't come out of the top drawer of Bordeaux and Burgundy – but he also knows how conservative his City and Japanese clients can be. A merchant worth dealing with – if only for the seductive bin ends lists.

164	£7.25	MENETOU SALON LES MOROGUES HENRI PELLE 1992 Loire (F)
296	£10.83	CHATEAU TOUR DU HAUT MOULIN, HAUT MEDOC 1985 Bordeaux (F)
312	£20.58	RESERVE DE LA COMTESSE, PAUILLAC 1987 Bordeaux (F)
322	£25.50	CHATEAU LYNCH-BAGES, PAUILLAC 1989 Bordeaux (F)
364	£12.33	CHATEAUNEUF DU PAPE, CHATEAU DE BEAUCASTEL 1988 Rhône (F)
489	£9.15	CHURCHILL GRAHAM FINEST VINTAGE CHARACTER Douro (P)

G&M	Gordon & Macphail

George House, Boroughbriggs Road, Elgin, Moray IV30 1JY (Tel 0343 545111 Fax 0343 54 155).

Opening Hours: Mon-Fri 9am-5.15pm, Sat 9am-5pm; closed Weds pm. **Delivery**: free within 30 miles. **Tastings**: regular in-store. **Discounts**: 5% per half case; 10% per case.

A name all malt whisky buffs should be familiar with, this Elgin-based company has a new speciality: South African wine, with 71 examples at the last count. Otherwise, their list offers reliable names through the merchant vintner's group, and the rare pleasure of a section devoted to Scottish wine.

33	£33.90	BOLLINGER GRANDE ANNEE 1985 Champagne (F)
56	£5.99	SUNNYCLIFF CHARDONNAY 1992 Victoria (Aus)
81	£6.70	CATHEDRAL CELLARS CHARDONNAY, KWV 1991 Coastal Region (SA)
263	£5.70	MERCHANT VINTNERS CLARET, PETER A SICHEL Bordeaux (F)
269	£5.90	MONTANA CABERNET SAUVIGNON 1991 Marlborough (NZ)
311	£38.60M	CHATEAU CISSAC, HAUT-MEDOC 1982 Bordeaux (F)
346	£9.30	CHATEAU MUSAR, 1986 Bekaa Valley (Leb)
415	£5.65	VALPOLICELLA CLASSICO, MASI 1991 Veneto (It)
444	£5.30	PERIQUITA, J M DA FONSECA 1990 (P)
481	£7.25	HIDALGO AMONTILLADO NAPOLEON Jerez (Sp)
490	£9.65	BOAL 5 YEAR OLD, D'OLIVEIRA (Mad)

GI | Grape Ideas

3/5 Hythe Bridge St, Oxford, Oxon OX1 2EW (Tel 0865 722137 Fax 0865 791594). **Opening Hours:** Mon-Sat 10am-7pm. **Delivery**: free locally. **Tastings**: occasional in-store. **Discounts**: 5% per unmixed case; 2.5% per mixed case.

'No customer should become bored drinking the same old wine all the time,' is the philosophy shared by David Stevens MW and son Alistair. They're always on the lookout for the new and exciting and this year it's two Niagara Creek wines – a Cabernet Sauvignon and Chardonnay Colombard (£3.99) and a red and white from Plantagent Mount Barker in Western Australia (£4.95). For a safe bet, listen for 'his masters choice'– wines personally recommended by the master (of wine) himself.

33	£30.50	BOLLINGER GRANDE ANNEE 1985 Champagne (F)
43	£3.79	COTES DE ST MONT WHITE, PLAIMONT 1991 South West (F)
96	£4.95	VALLEY VINEYARDS FUME BLANC 1991 Berkshire (UK)
113	£16.50	PULIGNY MONTRACHET, LOUIS CARILLON ET FILS 1991 Burgundy (F)
146	£5.25	HARDY'S MOONDAH BROOK ESTATE CHENIN BLANC 1992 Gingin, Western Australia (Aus)
149	£5.99	ZONNEBLOEM BLANC DE BLANC, STELLENBOSCH FARMERS WINERY 1991 Coastal Region (SA)
154	£5.35	VERDELHO, WYNDHAM ESTATE 1991 South East Australia (Aus)
168	£7.50	SANCERRE LES ROCHES, DOMAINE VACHERON 1992 Loire (F)
232	£3.29	DOMAINE DE ST LAURENT, VIN DE PAYS DES COTEAUX DU LIBRON 1991 Midi (F)
270	£5.25	HARDY'S MOONDAH BROOK ESTATE CABERNET SAUVIGNON 1989 Gingin, Western Australia (Aus)
288	£7.35	CABERNET SAUVIGNON, BODEGA Y CAVAS DE WEINERT 1985 Mendoza (Arg)
294	£8.95	CHATEAU DE ANNEREAUX, LALANDE DE POMEROL 1989 Bordeaux (F)
336	£5.90	ZINFANDEL, FETZER VINEYARDS 1990 Mendocino County (Cal)
346	£7.95	CHATEAU MUSAR, 1986 Bekaa Valley (Leb)
385	£5.95	HAUTES COTES DE BEAUNE, TETE DU CUVEE, CAVES DES HAUTES COTES 1990 Burgundy (F)
422	£6.95	CHIANTI CLASSICO, ISOLE E OLENA 1990 Tuscany (It)
468	£6.75H	NELSON LATE HARVEST RHINE RIESLING, SEIFRIED 1991 Nelson (NZ)
494	£14.40	WARRE'S TRADITIONAL LBV 1981 Douro (P)

GEW | Great English Wines/Harvest Group

Clocktower Mews, Stanlake Park, Twyford, Reading, Berks RG10 0BN (Tel 0734 344290 Fax 0734 320914). **Opening Hours:** phone for details. **Delivery**: free locally. **Tastings**: regular in-store , and tutored events. **Discounts:** 5-10%, depending on quantity.

This set-up is the result of an unusual arrangement between a young Australian winemaker (John Worontschak) and an English wine specialist (Maurice Moore, of Great English Wines). It involves 10 wineries from around the country who all consult the expert Mr Worontschak. So if it's Reading red, Berkshire Botrytis or Glastonbury Fumé you're after, you know who to call.

GNW | The Great Northern Wine Co

Granary Wharf, The Canal Basin, Leeds, Yorkshire LS1 4BR (Tel 0532 461200 Fax 0532 461209). **Opening Hours:** Leeds: Mon-Sat 9am-6pm, Ripon: Mon-Thurs 9am-6pm, Fri 9am-7pm, Sat 9am-6pm. **Delivery**: free locally. **Tastings**: regular in-store, plus tutored events.

Undaunted by the arrival of Bibendum (at Yorkshire Fine Wines), Gavin Barlow and John Senior have now opened a second branch in Ripon, offering the same winning combination of good service and a wide range of interesting wines. Their New World selection is particularly good, with close on 30 Australian producers and 15 Californians to choose from. Our only complaint is that the list is designed more for staff than customers.

53	£5.25	'CASAL DI SERRA' VERDICCHIO CLASSICO, UMANI RONCHI 1991 Marches (It)
74	£4.99	PENFOLDS KOONUNGA HILL CHARDONNAY 1992 South East Australia (Aus)
91	£7.91	MARQUES DE MURRIETA RIOJA RESERVA BLANCO 1987 Rioja (Sp)
101	£10.98	VIEUX CHATEAU GAUBERT, GRAVES 1991 Bordeaux (F)
112	£9.99	ELSTON CHARDONNAY, TE MATA ESTATE 1991 Hawkes Bay (NZ)
157	£5.49	LUGANA SANTA CRISTINA, VIGNETO MASSONI 1991 Lombardy (It)
164	£7.15	MENETOU SALON LES MOROGUES HENRI PELLE 1992 Loire (F)
168	£8.95	SANCERRE LES ROCHES, DOMAINE VACHERON 1992 Loire (F)
194	£3.55	TOLLANA DRY WHITE 1992 South East Australia (Aus)
216	£4.91	CHATEAU TOUR DES GENDRES BERGERAC ROSE 1992 South West (F)
218	£6.25	MOUNT HURTLE GRENACHE ROSE, GEOFF MERRILL 1992 McLaren Vale (Aus)
238	£6.00	CHATEAU DE LASTOURS CORBIERES, FUT DE CHENE 1989 Midi (F)
272	£5.50	ROUGE HOMME CABERNET/SHIRAZ, COONAWARRA 1988 Coonawarra (Aus)
282	£6.71	VALLEY OAKS CABERNET SAUVIGNON, FETZER 1990 Mendocino County (Cal)
285	£6.66	CHINON, COULY-DUTHEIL 1990 Loire (F)
346	£7.92	CHATEAU MUSAR, 1986 Bekaa Valley (Leb)
373	£4.99	TARRANGO, BROWN BROTHERS 1992 Milawa (Aus)
398	£11.95	MONTHELIE, JAFFELIN 1990 Burgundy (F)
427	£9.78	CUMARO ROSSO CONERO, UMANI RONCHI 1989 Marches (It)

GRT | Great Western Wine Company

2-3 Mile End, London Road, Bath, Avon BA1 6PT (Tel 0225 446009 Fax 0225 442139). **Opening Hours:** Mon-Fri 9am-7pm, Sat 10am-7pm. **Delivery**: free within 20 miles. **Tastings**: regular in-store, plus tutored events.

While everyone else follows the trail Down Under, Messrs Addis & Nordberg have turned to less well-known parts of France. From the Cevennes, Cataluna, Thongue & Thau come inspiring small domaine wines, some made from classic Syrah and Chardonnay, others from local grapes like the Rolle, Terret and Mourvedre. Beyond France there's a Marlborough Chardonnay from Almuth Lorentz, three vintages of some super Moldovans and a fat, citrussy '90 Beaujolais Blanc from the unsung Bernard Dalicieux.

61	£6.75	LUGANA CA'DEI FRATI 1992 Brescia (It)
79	£6.29	ROSEMOUNT CHARDONNAY 1992 Hunter Valley (Aus)
101	£7.99	VIEUX CHATEAU GAUBERT, GRAVES 1991 Bordeaux (F)
134	£3.99	DOMAINE DE MAUBET VIN DE PAYS DES COTES DE GASCOGNE, FONTAN 1992 South West (F)
182	£6.79	GEWURZTRAMINER D'ALSACE, CAVE VINICOLE DE TURCKHEIM 1992 Alsace (F)
216	£4.70	CHATEAU TOUR DES GENDRES BERGERAC ROSE 1992 South West (F)
274	£5.69	CHATEAU THIEULEY AC BORDEAUX ROUGE 1989 Bordeaux (F)
278	£5.80	GOUNDREY LANGTON CABERNET/MERLOT 1991 Mount Barker (Aus)
287	£7.75	KENDALL-JACKSON CABERNET SAUVIGNON 1989 (Cal)
313	£15.65	CLOS DU CLOCHER, POMEROL, BOUROTTE 1989 Bordeaux (F)
318	£14.00	ARARIMU CABERNET SAUVIGNON, MATUA VALLEY 1991 (NZ)
346	£7.80	CHATEAU MUSAR, 1986 Bekaa Valley (Leb)
348	£8.50	ROSEMOUNT SHOW RESERVE SYRAH 1990 McLaren Vale (Aus)
391	£7.90	BOURGOGNE PINOT NOIR, DOMAINE PARENT 1990 Burgundy (F)
398	£10.99	MONTHELIE, JAFFELIN 1990 Burgundy (F)
413	£3.99	MONTEPULCIANO D'ABRUZZO, UMANI RONCHI 1991 Marches (It)
422	£8.45	CHIANTI CLASSICO, ISOLE E OLENA 1990 Tuscany (It)
447	£5.99	CAMPO VIEJO RIOJA RESERVA 1987 Rioja (Sp)

PTR | Peter Green & Co

37a/b Warrender Park Rd, Edinburgh, Midlothian EH9 1HJ (Tel 031-229 5925). **Opening Hours:** Mon-Fri 9.30am-6.30pm Sat 9.30am-7pm. **Delivery**: free locally. **Tastings**: occasional samples. **Discounts**: 5% on unmixed cases.

There are two Romers in this corner shop – Michael and Douglas – who between them buy up such serious wines as the set of Chenins from Brédif, Baumard's Savennières and four vintages of his Quarts de Chaumes. Australia is represented by Cape Mentelle and Pirammima, and the highly appropriate (for local customers) Bannockburn and Piper's Brook. For the true English gent and noble Scot respectively, there's a fine range of claret going back to '61 and an A-Z of 100 single malts.

GRO | Grog Blossom

66 Notting Hill Gate, London W11 3HT (Tel 071-792 3834); 253 West End Lane, London NW6 1XN (Tel 071-794 7808); 160 High Road, London N2 9AS (081-883 3588). **Opening Hours:** 10am-10pm. **Delivery**: free locally. **Tastings**: regular in-store. **Discounts**: 5% per case.

Paul O'Connor must have some pretty useful contacts because he specialises in finding parcels of exciting wines, Champagnes and beers at attractive prices and passing the bargains on to customers. Consequently he does not issue a list, but it's always worth a visit to see what's in stock. Paul guarantees satisfaction, whether you want beer (over 250 at last count), Italian or Australian wine, or something from South America.

PGR	Patrick Grubb Selections

Orchard Lea House, Steeple Aston, Bicester, Oxon OX6 3RT (Tel 0869 40229 Fax 0869 40867). **Opening Hours:** 24-hour answerphone. **Tastings**: occasional in-store.

Patrick Grubb is a traditional country wine merchant, offering his Oxford-shire customers a predominantly French list (with reassuring names like Louis Latour, Bouchard Père et Fils, and Château Léoville-Barton), as well as considerable knowledge and experience. At the same time, he also imports the wines of Preston Vineyards in Sonoma, along with his favour-ite, Zonnebloem, from the Cape.

HLV	Halves Ltd

Wood Yard, off Corve Street, Ludlow, Shropshire SY8 2PX (Tel 0584 877866 Fax 0584 877677). **Opening Hours:** Mon-Fri 8am-6pm, Sat 10am-1pm; Stratford-upon-Avon: Mon-Fri 8am-7pm, Sat 9am-2pm, or by arrangement. **Delivery**: free. **Tastings**: tutored events. **Discounts**: 4% per case; 7.5% on mixed cases.

If you are planning to spend and drink less, or to cram as many wines into one sitting as possible, then Halves could be your answer. Tim Jackson has more than 200 half-bottles to choose from: Georges Vernay's Condrieu, Guigal's '85 Brune et Blonde, Boillot's '88 Puligny Montrachet…But you don't have to spend a fortune. French country, Australian & New Zealand wines are now available at Tim Jackson's new retail wine warehouse. The difficulty is convincing producers to bother with halves – and to price them reasonably. Obviously, all the prices below are for half-bottles.

33	£15.18	BOLLINGER GRANDE ANNEE 1985 Champagne (F)
74	£3.44	PENFOLDS KOONUNGA HILL CHARDONNAY 1992 South East Australia (Aus)
79	£4.32	ROSEMOUNT CHARDONNAY 1992 Hunter Valley (Aus)
106	£6.84	EDNA VALLEY CHARDONNAY 1990 Edna Valley (Cal)
110	£3.82	POMINO IL BENEFIZIO, MARCHESI DE FRESCOBALDI 1990 Tuscany (It)
273	£3.67	TALTARNI FIDDLEBACK TERRACE 1990 Pyrenees (Aus)
285	£4.29	CHINON, COULY-DUTHEIL 1990 Loire (F)
422	£5.70	CHIANTI CLASSICO, ISOLE E OLENA 1990 Tuscany (It)

HAM	Hampden Wine Co

Jordan's Courtyard, 8 Upper High Street, Thame, Oxon OX9 3ER, (Tel 084 421 3251 Fax 084 426 1100). **Opening Hours:** Mon-Wed, Sat 9am-5pm; Thurs-Fri 9am-5.30pm. **Delivery**: 15 miles. **Tastings**: occasional in-store, plus tutored events. **Discounts**: 5% on mixed cases.

Times have been tough for Lance Foyster and Co, but any merchant with this approach to wine buying deserves to succeed. Every area is precisely covered, with prices starting at just over £3 a bottle and including such delights as Dr Loosen's Rieslings. Is this Britain's best 8-page wine list?

33	£23.50	BOLLINGER GRANDE ANNEE 1985 Champagne (F)
77	£4.95	SALISBURY ESTATE CHARDONNAY 1992 South East Australia (Aus)
79	£6.50	ROSEMOUNT CHARDONNAY 1992 Hunter Valley (Aus)
266	£4.95	SALISBURY ESTATE CABERNET SAUVIGNON 1991 South East Australia (Aus)
272	£5.70	ROUGE HOMME CABERNET/SHIRAZ, COONAWARRA 1988 Coonawarra (Aus)
422	£7.65	CHIANTI CLASSICO, ISOLE E OLENA 1990 Tuscany (It)
423	£8.30	CARMIGNANO, CAPEZZANA 1987 Tuscany (It)

437	£3.45	CISMEIRA DOURO 1991 Douro (P)
443	£4.95	QUINTA DE LA ROSA RED TABLE WINE 1991 Douro (P)
493	£15.50	HENRIQUES & HENRIQUES 10 YEAR OLD VERDELHO Madeira

HFV | Harcourt Fine Wine

3 Harcourt Street, London W1H 1DS (Tel 071-723 7202 Fax 071-723 8085). **Opening Hours:** Mon-Fri 9.30 am-5.30pm, Sat 11.30 am-4.30pm. **Delivery:** free locally. **Tastings:** regular in-store. **Discounts:** 5% or more per case.

Harcourt stocks shelf upon shelf of English wines, including many which have risen above the level of 'green and occasionally pleasant' to gain the recognition they deserve. At the same time, under the alias Eau de Vie, Harcourt offers a list of Armagnacs covering virtually every vintage back to the last century – perfect if you've run out of ideas for birthday presents.

HPD | Harpenden Wines

68 High St, Harpenden, Hertfordshire AL5 2SP (Tel 0582 765605 Fax 0923 252718). **Opening Hours:** Mon-Fri 10am-10pm, Sat 9am-10pm, Sun 12-3pm, 7-9pm. **Delivery:** 10 miles. **Tastings:** regular in-store tastings. **Discounts:** 7.5% per case; 5% per mixed case.

Paul Beaton is kind enough to mark his organic wines 'suitable for Veggies' (V) 'and Vegans' (VE) for which neither eggs nor fishscales have been used as fining agents. Top organics include the Alsace '90 Pinot Blanc, Pierre Frick, '89 NZ Millton Vineyard Chenin, '89 Dom Richaume Syrah or Cabernet and the David Wynn Eden Ridge range. For carnivores, there are nine Petits Châteaux Bordeaux under a tenner, or the big Kiwi Coleraine Cab/Merlot '90. Fish-eaters should try the '92 Pierro Semillon/Sauvignon.

14	£8.99	ANGAS BRUT CLASSIC, YALUMBA WINERY South East Australia (Aus)
20	£7.29	OMAR KHAYYAM, CHAMPAGNE INDIA 1987 Maharashtra (Ind)
33	£28.49	BOLLINGER GRANDE ANNEE 1985 Champagne (F)
112	£12.95	ELSTON CHARDONNAY, TE MATA ESTATE 1991 Hawkes Bay (NZ)
134	£4.45	DOMAINE DE MAUBET VIN DE PAYS DES COTES DE GASCOGNE, FONTAN 1992 South West (F)
161	£6.95	JACKSON ESTATE SAUVIGNON BLANC 1992 Marlborough (NZ)
311	£21.25	CHATEAU CISSAC, HAUT-MEDOC 1982 Bordeaux (F)
337	£6.49	GALWAY SHIRAZ, YALUMBA WINERY 1991 Barossa Valley (Aus)
414	£4.75	DOLCETTO D'ASTI, ARALDICA 1992 Piedmont (It)
429	£11.49	BAROLO RISERVA, BORGOGNO 1985 Piedmont (It)
461	£9.95	STANTON & KILLEEN RUTHERGLEN LIQUEUR MUSCAT Rutherglen (Aus)
462	£5.59	CAMPBELLS RUTHERGLEN LIQUEUR MUSCAT Rutherglen (Aus)

GHS | Gerard Harris Fine Wines

2 Green End St, Aston Clinton, Aylesbury, Bucks HP22 5HP (Tel 0296 631041 Fax 0296 631250). **Opening Hours:** Mon-Wed 9.30am-6.30pm, Thurs-Sat 9.30am-8pm. **Delivery:** free within 20 miles. **Tastings:** regular in-store.

This fine wine merchant shares its premises and wine list with the Bell Inn (a Relais & Châteaux), whose well-fed customers can't resist picking up a bottle of what they've just enjoyed with lunch. There's a classic spread of good Bordeaux châteaux, mainly small Burgundy domaines (Parent,

Voarick), plus inexpensive French regionals and good Aussies. Locals will be pleased to hear of the Fine Wine Society; life membership is a mere £15.

17	£9.00	**BOUVET LADUBAY SAUMUR BRUT Loire (F)**
33	£32.85	**BOLLINGER GRANDE ANNEE 1985 Champagne (F)**
45	£5.25	**NOBILO WHITE CLOUD 1992 (NZ)**
53	£5.95	**'CASAL DI SERRA' VERDICCHIO CLASSICO, UMANI RONCHI 1991 Marches (It)**
110	£14.30	**POMINO IL BENEFIZIO, MARCHESI DE FRESCOBALDI 1990 Tuscany (It)**
112	£12.95	**ELSTON CHARDONNAY, TE MATA ESTATE 1991 Hawkes Bay (NZ)**
269	£5.70	**MONTANA CABERNET SAUVIGNON 1991 Marlborough (NZ)**
288	£8.20	**CABERNET SAUVIGNON, BODEGA Y CAVAS DE WEINERT 1985 Mendoza (Arg)**
346	£8.55	**CHATEAU MUSAR, 1986 Bekaa Valley (Leb)**
391	£9.20	**BOURGOGNE PINOT NOIR, DOMAINE PARENT 1990 Burgundy (F)**

ROG	Roger Harris Wines

Loke Farm, Weston Longville, Norfolk NR9 5LG (Tel 0603 880171 Fax 0603 880291). **Opening Hours:** 9am-5pm Mon-Fri. **Delivery**: free. **Discounts**: £2 per case off 2 cases or more; £4 per case off 10 cases or more.

Roger Harris is truly in love with everything Beaujolais – he'll even help you arrange a holiday there, and he's one of the few people who can convincingly speak about different Beaujolais crus as individual areas. Interestingly, since Duboeuf moved into supermarkets, smaller merchants are moving over to lesser-known producers. This could be Mr Harris's finest hour.

RHV	Richard Harvey Wines

Bucknowle House, Bucknowle, Wareham, Dorset BH20 5PQ (Tel 0929 480352). **Opening Hours:** Mon-Fri 9am-6pm. **Delivery**: free locally. **Tastings**: occasional samples.

Richard Harvey sells Australian wines for up to £2 a bottle less than his Dorset competitors. The only catch is that you have to pick them up from his recently opened La Maison du Vin in Cherbourg. Back home, he still specialises in French wines, though Germany does get a look in. Move over 'flying winemakers', it's time for the 'ferrying winemerchant'.

26	£17.50	**LE MESNIL BLANC DE BLANCS Champagne (F)**
272	£4.75	**ROUGE HOMME CABERNET/SHIRAZ, COONAWARRA 1988 Coonawarra (Aus)**
278	£6.50	**GOUNDREY LANGTON CABERNET/MERLOT 1991 Mount Barker (Aus)**
288	£7.95	**CABERNET SAUVIGNON, BODEGA Y CAVAS DE WEINERT 1985 Mendoza (Arg)**
469	£5.50	**CHATEAU DE BERBEC, PREMIERES COTES DE BORDEAUX 1989 Bordeaux (F)**
489	£9.25	**CHURCHILL GRAHAM FINEST VINTAGE CHARACTER Douro (P)**
494	£13.50	**WARRE'S TRADITIONAL LBV 1981 Douro (P)**

HV	John Harvey & Sons

31 Denmark St, Bristol BS1 5DQ (Tel 0272 268882 Fax 0272 253378). **Opening Hours:** Mon-Fri 9.30am-6pm, Sat 9.30am-1pm. **Tastings**: occasional tutored events.

Following the decision by owners Allied to dismantle the larger aspects of its wholesale business, this 500 year-old company has shifted focus to its smaller customers. The original premises have been revamped to allow tastings, particularly of Harveys' specialities, Bordeaux and fortified wines.

| 33 | £32.87 | BOLLINGER GRANDE ANNEE 1985 Champagne (F) |
| 483 | £9.17 | 1796 RICH OLD OLOROSO Jerez (Sp) |

| **HHC** | **Haynes, Hanson & Clarke** |

17 Lettice St, London SW6 4EH (Tel 071-736 7878 Fax 071-371 5887). **Opening Hours:** Mon-Sat 9.30am-7pm. **Delivery:** free for 5 or more cases. **Tastings:** regular in-store tastings. **Discounts:** 10% per case.

A long list of quality small producers and a commitment to service help this merchant go from strength to strength. Names like Roumier, Grivot and Rossignol-Trapet ensure Haynes, Hanson & Clarke's continued status as Burgundy specialists, while Kistler, Cape Mentelle and Green Point will appeal to those with an insatiable desire for New World novelty.

24	£9.99	GREEN POINT, DOMAINE CHANDON 1990 Yarra Valley (Aus)
33	£32.30	BOLLINGER GRANDE ANNEE 1985 Champagne (F)
43	£3.95	COTES DE ST MONT WHITE, PLAIMONT 1991 South West (F)
56	£5.40	SUNNYCLIFF CHARDONNAY 1992 Victoria (Aus)
79	£6.60	ROSEMOUNT CHARDONNAY 1992 Hunter Valley (Aus)
160	£6.99	GROVE MILL SAUVIGNON 1992 Blenheim (NZ)
164	£8.45	MENETOU SALON LES MOROGUES HENRI PELLE 1992 Loire (F)
174	£12.80	POUILLY FUME, DE LADOUCETTE 1990 Loire (F)
263	£4.45	MERCHANT VINTNERS CLARET, PETER A SICHEL Bordeaux (F)
271	£5.60	CHATEAU TIMBERLAY, R GIRAUD 1990 Bordeaux (F)
494	£13.60	WARRE'S TRADITIONAL LBV 1981 Douro (P)

| **H&H** | **Hector & Honorez Wines Ltd** |

7 East Street, Kimbolton, Cambridgeshire PE18 0HJ (Tel 0480 861444 Fax 0480 861646). **Opening Hours:** Mon-Sat 9.30am-5.30pm. **Delivery:** free locally. **Tastings:** occasional samples and in-store. **Discounts:** 7.5% per case.

Despite their whacky name, a quick glance at this merchant's list proves they take their wines very seriously, with producers like Didier Dagueneau, Joseph Roty and Pierro in Western Australia. They've even managed to get hold of some usually unobtainable Châteauneuf from Henri Bonneau.

113	£16.90	PULIGNY MONTRACHET, LOUIS CARILLON ET FILS 1991 Burgundy (F)
164	£7.25	MENETOU SALON LES MOROGUES HENRI PELLE 1992 Loire (F)
232	£3.50	DOMAINE DE ST LAURENT, VIN DE PAYS DES COTEAUX DU LIBRON 1991 Midi (F)
239	£9.25	CAHORS, PRINCE PROBUS, JL. BALDES 1988 South West (F)
240	£9.90	MADIRAN, MONTUS, ALAIN BRUMONT 1990 South West (F)
285	£6.95	CHINON, COULY-DUTHEIL 1990 Loire (F)
350	£7.25	BROKENWOOD SHIRAZ 1991 South East Australia (Aus)
409	£27.00	CORTON CLOS DU ROY, DUBREUIL FONTAINE 1990 Burgundy (F)

| **HW** | **Hedley Wright & Co Ltd** |

The Country Wine Cellars, 10-11 Twyford Centre, London Road, Bishops Stortford, Hertfordshire CM23 3YT (Tel 0279 506512 Fax 0279 657462). **Opening Hours:** Mon-Wed 9am-6pm, Thurs-Fri 10am-7pm, Sat 10am-6pm. **Delivery:** free locally. **Tastings:** regular in-store, plus tutored events. **Discounts:** 5% for regular customers.

Based in the heart of the Old World, this traditional country merchant focuses firmly on the New World, with wines like the Montes range from Chile and Jackson Estate from New Zealand, the country in which Martin Wright found his most exciting discovery – the Daniel Le Brun sparklers.

54	£4.99	MONTES UNOAKED CHARDONNAY, DISCOVER WINES LTDA 1993 Curico (Ch)
79	£6.95	ROSEMOUNT CHARDONNAY 1992 Hunter Valley (Aus)
89	£8.95	CHARDONNAY BATELEUR, DANIE DE WET 1991 Robertson (SA)
161	£6.99	JACKSON ESTATE SAUVIGNON BLANC 1992 Marlborough (NZ)
222	£10.50	CHATEAU DE LA GRILLE, CHINON ROSE, A GOSSET 1992 Loire (F)
273	£5.95	TALTARNI FIDDLEBACK TERRACE 1990 Pyrenees (Aus)
280	£6.85	J WILE & SON CABERNET SAUVIGNON 1987 Napa Valley (Cal)
348	£9.75	ROSEMOUNT SHOW RESERVE SYRAH 1990 McLaren Vale (Aus)
394	£9.45	COLDSTREAM HILLS PINOT NOIR 1992 Yarra Valley (Aus)
422	£7.90	CHIANTI CLASSICO, ISOLE E OLENA 1990 Tuscany (It)
468	£7.75	NELSON LATE HARVEST RHINE RIESLING, SEIFRIED 1991 Nelson (NZ)
489	£9.50	CHURCHILL GRAHAM FINEST VINTAGE CHARACTER Douro (P)

DHM	Douglas Henn-Macrae

81 Mackenders Lane, Eccles, Aylesford, Kent ME20 7JA (Tel 0622 710952 Fax 0622 791203). **Opening Hours:** 24-hour answerphone. **Delivery:** free for 10 or more cases. **Tastings:** occasional samples.

Asked why he specialises in obscure wines from Germany and Texas, Douglas Henn-Macrae points out that he speaks both languages – and, perhaps more relevantly, that there is 'no point duplicating what lots of other people are already doing'. It is certainly true that no supermarket sells Texan Emerald Riesling. Tasting notes such as 'weird…a pronounced alcohol burn at the back of the throat' may give a clue as to why.

HEM	The Hermitage

124 Fortis Green Road, London N10 3DU, (Tel 081 365 2122 Fax 081 442 0439). **Opening Hours:** Mon-Sat 10.30am-8pm, Sun 12-2.30pm. **Delivery:** free locally. **Tastings:** regular samples. **Discounts:** 5% collection discount; 5% per case.

Joint Small Independent Merchant of the Year

A real Mary Poppins' carpetbag of a shop. Quite how Gill Reynolds manages to squeeze 700 brilliant wines into this space remains a mystery. There's Huët, Beaucastel, Mascarello, Pesquera and Ridge, to name just a few, and prices are very fair. Hardened drinkers can find vintage Armagnac and Malt Whisky, either of which ought to help the medicine go down a treat.

20	£7.99	OMAR KHAYYAM, CHAMPAGNE INDIA 1987 Maharashtra (Ind)
22	£8.99	MAYERLING CREMANT D'ALSACE, CAVE VINICOLE DE TURCKHEIM Alsace (F)
25	£13.99	CROSER METHODE TRADITIONNELLE, PETALUMA WNERY 1990 Adelaide Hills (Aus)
53	£5.65	'CASAL DI SERRA' VERDICCHIO CLASSICO, UMANI RONCHI 1991 Marches (It)
59	£8.95	PETIT CHABLIS, GOULLEY 1991 Burgundy (F)
61	£6.45	LUGANA CA'DEI FRATI 1992 Brescia (It)
64	£8.45	TASMANIAN WINE COMPANY CHARDONNAY, PIPER'S BROOK 1991 (Aus)
74	£4.99	PENFOLDS KOONUNGA HILL CHARDONNAY 1992 South East Australia (Aus)
91	£7.91	MARQUES DE MURRIETA RIOJA RESERVA BLANCO 1987 Rioja (Sp)

97	£8.99	WAIPARA SPRINGS CHARDONNAY 1991 Canterbury (NZ)
189	£8.35	LAGAR DE CERVERA, RIAS BAIXAS, LAGAR DE FORNELOSSA 1992 Galicia (Sp)
265	£4.95	ERRAZURIZ CABERNET SAUVIGNON, MAULE 1991 Maule (Ch)
346	£7.95	CHATEAU MUSAR, 1986 Bekaa Valley (Leb)
353	£9.45	DAVID WYNN PATRIARCH SHIRAZ 1991 Eden Valley (Aus)
389	£6.99	HAMILTON-RUSSELL PINOT NOIR, WALKER BAY 1991 Walker Bay (SA)
422	£8.45	CHIANTI CLASSICO, ISOLE E OLENA 1990 Tuscany (It)
427	£9.99	CUMARO ROSSO CONERO, UMANI RONCHI 1989 Marches (It)
468	£6.25	NELSON LATE HARVEST RHINE RIESLING, SEIFRIED 1991 Nelson (NZ)
485	£20.00	OSBORNE Y CIA PEDRO XIMENEZ Jerez (Sp)
489	£9.45	CHURCHILL GRAHAM FINEST VINTAGE CHARACTER Douro (P)

H&D | Hicks & Don

Blandford St Mary, Dorset DT11 9LS (Tel 0258 456040 Fax 0258 450147). **Opening Hours:** Mon-Fri 9am-5pm, plus 24-hour answerphone service. **Delivery**: free for 3 or more cases. **Tasting**: tutored events.

Messrs Hicks & Don like to buy 'quality wines which are good examples of their type'. Concentrating mainly on Bordeaux and Burgundy, though with some very tempting wines from the South-west, their list is full of surprising wines and producers including '92 Reuilly Sauvignon Henri Beurdin, a '92 Viognier from Francois Monier in the southern Rhône, De Jessy Saumur Brut and, from Italy, the interesting '91 Chardonnay dei Vinattieri and Ca dei Frati's '91 Vigna Brolettino. Watch out for the French country wines, too.

33	£29.32	BOLLINGER GRANDE ANNEE 1985 Champagne (F)
170	£9.23	SAUVIGNON BLANC, KENWOOD 1991 Sonoma (Cal)
391	£8.78	BOURGOGNE PINOT NOIR, DOMAINE PARENT 1990 Burgundy (F)

JEH | J E Hogg

61 Cumberland St, Edinburgh EH3 6RA (Tel/Fax 031-556 4025). **Opening Hours:** Mon-Tues, Thurs-Fri 9am-1pm, 2.30pm-6pm; Wed, Sat 9am-1 pm. **Delivery**: free locally. **Tastings**: occasional samples.

Evidently a lover of Alsace and a rare supporter of top-quality German estates, Jim Hogg is just as good at Bordeaux (dry red and sticky white). We're sure he'd shoehorn a few more New World wine wines into his tiny store, but he has to leave a little space for the 70 malt whiskies, 60 sherries, eight vintages of La Chapelle, plus fine teas and coffees.

3	£5.47	SEGURA VIUDAS CAVA BRUT RESERVA Cava (Sp)
4	£6.33	NEDERBURG 1ER CUVEE BRUT Paarl (SA)
15	£6.78	DEINHARD LILA RIESLING BRUT, SEKT Mittelrhein (G)
24	£9.49	GREEN POINT, DOMAINE CHANDON 1990 Yarra Valley (Aus)
33	£26.55	BOLLINGER GRANDE ANNEE 1985 Champagne (F)
91	£6.53	MARQUES DE MURRIETA RIOJA RESERVA BLANCO 1987 Rioja (Sp)
100	£8.99	FIRESTONE CHARDONNAY 1990 (Cal)
106	£8.65	EDNA VALLEY CHARDONNAY 1990 Edna Valley (Cal)
174	£10.28	POUILLY FUME, DE LADOUCETTE 1990 Loire (F)
197	£3.61	BADEN DRY, BADISCHER WINZERKELLER Baden (G)
229	£2.82	VAL DU TORGAN, LES PRODUCTEURS DU MONT TAUCH Midi (F)
259	£4.19	GLEN ELLEN CABERNET SAUVIGNON 1989 (Cal)
273	£5.49	TALTARNI FIDDLEBACK TERRACE 1990 Pyrenees (Aus)
297	£9.37	CHATEAU NOTTON, MARGAUX 1988 Bordeaux (F)

342	£6.41	PETER LEHMANN 'CLANCY'S RED' 1990 Barossa Valley (Aus)
365	£12.34	PENFOLDS MAGILL ESTATE SHIRAZ 1988 South Australia (Aus)
389	£6.17	HAMILTON-RUSSELL PINOT NOIR, WALKER BAY 1991 Walker Bay (SA)
482	£7.57	LUSTAU OLD EAST INDIA, EMILIO LUSTAU Jerez (Sp)
483	£8.40	1796 RICH OLD OLOROSO Jerez (Sp)
484	£16.99	MATUSALEM, GONZALEZ BYASS Jerez (Sp)
486	£6.84	RIVESALTES, VIEILLE RESERVE, LES PRODUCTEURS DU MONT TAUCH 1980 Midi (F)

HOL | Holland Park Wine Co

12 Portland Road, London W11 4LA (Tel 071-221 9614 Fax 071-221 9613). **Opening Hours:** Mon-Fri 10am-8.30pm, Sat 9am-8.30pm. **Delivery**: free within the M25 and nationally for orders over £100. **Tastings**: regular in-store and tutored events. **Discounts**: 5% per case.

James Handford and Co's attractive little list is full of wines for every occasion and they'll soon trot out a few for under £5, including '91 Domaine des Terriers Syrah (£4.49) and '90 Graacher Münzlay Riesling (£4.74). To celebrate the savings, grab a bottle of the rich, nutty, appley Ch de Chenonceau, one of the wines exclusive to the establishment.

20	£8.40	OMAR KHAYYAM, CHAMPAGNE INDIA 1987 Maharashtra (Ind)
33	£31.95	BOLLINGER GRANDE ANNEE 1985 Champagne (F)
98	£9.49	LOCAL GROWERS SEMILLON, ROCKFORD 1989 Barossa Valley (Aus)
104	£10.49	CHARDONNAY, JANE HUNTER'S WINES 1991 Marlborough (NZ)
169	£9.99	HUNTERS MARLBOROUGH SAUVIGNON BLANC 1992 Marlborough (NZ)
174	£12.95	POUILLY FUME, DE LADOUCETTE 1990 Loire (F)
182	£6.75	GEWURZTRAMINER D'ALSACE, CAVE VINICOLE DE TURCKHEIM 1992 Alsace (F)
231	£4.79	MISTY MOORING RED, ANGOVES (Aus)
256	£4.95	HARDYS NOTTAGE HILL CABERNET SAUVIGNON 1991 South Australia (Aus)
273	£5.95	TALTARNI FIDDLEBACK TERRACE 1990 Pyrenees (Aus)
286	£7.49	STONIER'S WINERY SELECTION CABERNETS 1991 Mornington Peninsula (Aus)
288	£7.99	CABERNET SAUVIGNON, BODEGA Y CAVAS DE WEINERT 1985 Mendoza (Arg)

HOU | Hoult's Wine Merchants

10 Viaduct St, Huddersfield, West Yorkshire HD1 5BL (Tel 0484 510700 Fax 0484 510712). **Opening Hours:** Mon-Sat 9am-6pm. **Delivery**: free locally. **Tastings**: regular in-store. **Discounts**: 5% per mixed case.

David Hoult views his Huddersfield railway arch, Château Hoult, as a fun, Oddbins-style shop. There's a broad range of Aussies and he has been quick to see the potential in Italy. Our advice: produce a proper list, and don't forget that large wine-producing country at the other end of the Chunnel.

11	£6.99	MONTANA LINDAUER BRUT (NZ)
20	£7.95	OMAR KHAYYAM, CHAMPAGNE INDIA 1987 Maharashtra (Ind)
33	£29.99	BOLLINGER GRANDE ANNEE 1985 Champagne (F)
57	£5.99	CHABLIS, LOUIS ALEXANDRE 1992 Burgundy (F)
61	£6.99	LUGANA CA'DEI FRATI 1992 Brescia (It)
74	£4.99	PENFOLDS KOONUNGA HILL CHARDONNAY 1992 South East Australia (Aus)
77	£4.99	SALISBURY ESTATE CHARDONNAY 1992 South East Australia (Aus)
79	£5.99	ROSEMOUNT CHARDONNAY 1992 Hunter Valley (Aus)
80	£5.99	CHATEAU REYNELLA STONY HILL CHARDONNAY 1990 South Australia (Aus)
99	£9.99	KRONDORF SHOW RESERVE CHARDONNAY 1991 Barossa Valley (Aus)

134	£3.99	DOMAINE DE MAUBET VIN DE PAYS DES COTES DE GASCOGNE, FONTAN 1992 South West (F)
146	£4.99	HARDY'S MOONDAH BROOK ESTATE CHENIN BLANC 1992 Gingin, Western Australia (Aus)
161	£6.99	JACKSON ESTATE SAUVIGNON BLANC 1992 Marlborough (NZ)
171	£9.99	POGGIO ALLE GAZZE, TENUTA DELL'ORNELLAIA 1991 Tuscany (It)
194	£3.29	TOLLANA DRY WHITE 1992 South East Australia (Aus)
238	£6.99	CHATEAU DE LASTOURS CORBIERES, FUT DE CHENE 1989 Midi (F)
256	£3.99	HARDYS NOTTAGE HILL CABERNET SAUVIGNON 1991 South Australia (Aus)
257	£3.99	SEAVIEW CABERNET SAUVIGNON/SHIRAZ 1990 South East Australia (Aus)
266	£4.99	SALISBURY ESTATE CABERNET SAUVIGNON 1991 South East Australia (Aus)
269	£4.99	MONTANA CABERNET SAUVIGNON 1991 Marlborough (NZ)
270	£5.99	HARDY'S MOONDAH BROOK ESTATE CABERNET SAUVIGNON 1989 Gingin, Western Australia (Aus)
298	£9.99	LINDEMANS ST GEORGE CABERNET SAUVIGNON 1989 Coonawarra (Aus)
321	£22.99	ORNELLAIA 1990 Tuscany (It)
342	£6.99	PETER LEHMANN 'CLANCY'S RED' 1990 Barossa Valley (Aus)
346	£7.99	CHATEAU MUSAR, 1986 Bekaa Valley (Leb)
348	£7.99	ROSEMOUNT SHOW RESERVE SYRAH 1990 McLaren Vale (Aus)
365	£12.99	PENFOLDS MAGILL ESTATE SHIRAZ 1988 South Australia (Aus)
373	£4.99	TARRANGO, BROWN BROTHERS 1992 Milawa (Aus)
377	£6.99	CHENAS, DOMAINE DE CHASSIGNOL, J DEPAGNEUX 1992 Beaujolais (F)
422	£8.50	CHIANTI CLASSICO, ISOLE E OLENA 1990 Tuscany (It)
438	£3.75	ALBOR RIOJA TINTO, BODEGAS & BEBIDAS 1991 Rioja (Sp)
447	£6.99	CAMPO VIEJO RIOJA RESERVA 1987 Rioja (Sp)
461	£5.49H	STANTON & KILLEEN RUTHERGLEN LIQUEUR MUSCAT Rutherglen (Aus)
462	£5.49H	CAMPBELLS RUTHERGLEN LIQUEUR MUSCAT Rutherglen (Aus)
488	£8.99	OLD TRAFFORD TAWNY, B SEPPELT & SONS South East Australia (Aus)

HOT	House of Townend

Red Duster House, 101 York Street, Hull, Humberside HU2 0QX (Tel 0482 26891 Fax 0482 587042). **Opening Hours:** Mon-Sat 10am-10pm, Sun hours vary. **Delivery**: free within 60 miles. **Tastings**: regular in-store, plus tutored events.

This traditional chain has recently acquired a local hotel-restaurant and converted it into a large cave (stalactites et al) packed with more than 500 wines. This year sees a vastly improved New World list (save California, a combination of Gallo and Opus One). Townend's passion, though, is Bordeaux, with a range of fine vintages from *les Grands et les Petits châteaux*. The magnum of '86 Ch d'Angludet is pretty good value at £24.40.

33	£33.95	BOLLINGER GRANDE ANNEE 1985 Champagne (F)
346	£8.99	CHATEAU MUSAR, 1986 Bekaa Valley (Leb)
364	£12.75	CHATEAUNEUF DU PAPE, CHATEAU DE BEAUCASTEL 1988 Rhône (F)
408	£21.70	NUITS ST GEORGES 'CLOS DE L'ARLOT', DOM. DE L'ARLOT 1988 Burgundy (F)
422	£7.99	CHIANTI CLASSICO, ISOLE E OLENA 1990 Tuscany (It)

HUD	Hudsons Fine Wines

17 Lacy Road, Putney, London SW15 1NH (Tel 081-780 1567). **Opening Hours:** Mon-Sat 9am-9pm, Sun 12-3pm. **Delivery**: free locally. **Tastings**: regular samples.

Nine months after opening their lovely little shop in a Putney side-street with 300 highly varied wines, this Anglo-French team is already hoping to open up more outlets by the end of '94. Lovers of cheese and wine could experiment enjoyably with Burgundies from Parent, Engel and Rousseau and Italians such as '90 Carignano de Sulcis & Ceppi Storici and stock from their sister shop Truckles & Truffles.

HUN	Hungerford Wine Co

Unit 3, Station Yard, Hungerford, Berks, RG17 0DY (Tel 0488 683238 Fax 0488 684919). **Opening Hours:** Mon-Sat 9am-5.30pm. **Tastings:** regular in-store, pllus tutored events. **Discounts:** varied.

Nick Davies' company has undergone big upheavals in the past year, with the regular *en primeur* and fine wine offers now being dealt with through The Claret Club (qv). The Hungerford Wine Company continues to store wine and operate the retail business in Hungerford High Street, hopefully offering callers rather more instant access to their purchases than has hitherto been enjoyed by some *en primeur* customers. The shop's main speciality (surprise, surprise) is claret, ranging from 1989 Château Gerbay (£4.95), to 1983 Château Petrus (£170). For weightlifters there are imperials (six litres) of 1988 Château Filhot. The rest are less weighty, although Hugel Alsace, Mount Helen Aussies and Jaffelin Burgundies won't disappoint.

17	£8.75	BOUVÉT LADUBAY SAUMUR BRUT Loire (F)
174	£13.15	POUILLY FUME, DE LADOUCETTE 1990 Loire (F)
322	£28.50	CHATEAU LYNCH-BAGES, PAUILLAC 1989 Bordeaux (F)

TOJ	Tony Jeffries Wines

69 Edith Street, Northampton, NW1 5EP (Tel 0604 22375). **Opening Hours:** Tues-Fri 10am-3pm, Sat 9am-5pm. **Delivery:** free locally. **Tastings:** regular in-store, plus tutored events. **Discounts:** 10% per case cash; 5% per case credit card.

Tony Jeffries is, by his own admission, a 'recent convert to Rhône wines', who's 'learning fast'. Well, with wines from Jamet, new wave Chapoutiers and Château de Beaucastel, he's well on his way to a degree – along with the ones he might have got for New Zealand (Vidal, Vavasour, Palliser and Mission), Australia and South Africa. Thoroughly impressive. Alpha-plus.

11	£6.95	MONTANA LINDAUER BRUT (NZ)
57	£5.75	CHABLIS, LOUIS ALEXANDRE 1992 Burgundy (F)
79	£5.95	ROSEMOUNT CHARDONNAY 1992 Hunter Valley (Aus)
80	£5.99	CHATEAU REYNELLA STONY HILL CHARDONNAY 1990 South Australia (Aus)
112	£12.25	ELSTON CHARDONNAY, TE MATA ESTATE 1991 Hawkes Bay (NZ)
146	£4.99	HARDY'S MOONDAH BROOK ESTATE CHENIN BLANC 1992 Gingin, Western Australia (Aus)
163	£7.55	BOURGOGNE ALIGOTE, VALLET FRERES 1990 Burgundy (F)
250	£5.85	STAMBOLOVO RESERVE MERLOT 1987 (Bul)
256	£4.25	HARDYS NOTTAGE HILL CABERNET SAUVIGNON 1991 South Australia (Aus)
257	£4.45	SEAVIEW CABERNET SAUVIGNON/SHIRAZ 1990 South East Australia (Aus)
269	£4.99	MONTANA CABERNET SAUVIGNON 1991 Marlborough (NZ)
270	£4.99	HARDY'S MOONDAH BROOK ESTATE CABERNET SAUVIGNON 1989 Gingin, Western Australia (Aus)
330	£3.85	VIN DE PAYS DES COLLINES RHODANIENNES CEPAGE SYRAH, CAVE DE TAIN L'HERMITAGE Rhône (F)
335	£4.70	COTES DU RHONE DOMAINE DE TERRE BRULEE, CAVE DE VIGNERONS DE RASTEAU 1990 Rhône (F)

336	£4.95	ZINFANDEL, FETZER VINEYARDS 1990 Mendocino County (Cal)
348	£7.95	ROSEMOUNT SHOW RESERVE SYRAH 1990 McLaren Vale (Aus)
353	£9.25	DAVID WYNN PATRIARCH SHIRAZ 1991 Eden Valley (Aus)
377	£5.85	CHENAS, DOMAINE DE CHASSIGNOL, J DEPAGNEUX 1992 Beaujolais (F)
405	£17.35	BEAUNE 1ER CRU EPENOTTES, VALLET FRERES 1989 Burgundy (F)
438	£3.55	ALBOR RIOJA TINTO, BODEGAS & BEBIDAS 1991 Rioja (Sp)
447	£5.65	CAMPO VIEJO RIOJA RESERVA 1987 Rioja (Sp)
492	£10.95	COLHEITA, A A CALEM & FILHO 1985 Douro (P)

JOB | Jeroboams

51 Elizabeth St, London SW1W 9PP (Tel 071-823 5623 Fax 071-495 3314). **Opening Hours:** both shops: Mon-Fri 9am-6pm, Elizabeth Street: Sat 9am-2pm, Bute Street: 9am-6pm. **Delivery**: free locally. **Tastings**: occasional in-store. **Discounts**: 5% or more per case.

Whether it's cheese, charcuterie or wines you're after, there's tons of choice here. Sue Raymond's wines are 'carefully chosen to complement the cheeses'. We're less certain about Burgundy from Pierre Andre (aka La Reine Pédauque) than we are about the unctuous stickies; Jurançon Moelleux, Muscats from Beaumes de Venise (P Perrin), Rutherglen (Brown Bros) and California (Quady's), but we'd still queue to join Sue's Cheese Club.

SHJ | SH Jones & Co Ltd

27 High Street, Banbury, Oxon OX16 8EW (Tel 0295 251179 Fax 0295 272352). **Opening Hours:** Mon-Fri 8.30am-5.30pm, Sat 9am-5pm. **Delivery**: free locally. **Tastings**: regular in-store. **Discounts**: 7.5% mixed case; 5% per case (not fine).

More than 100 years old, this family-run business continues to flourish in 'the Garden of England', as Derek Jones calls his turf. Burgundy remains a speciality, with Savigny from Camus-Bruchon, St Aubin from Prudhon, and top white wine Domaines Leflaive and Colin. The Rhône list also merits mention – not least for Vieux Télégraphe back to 1980, and some fine older Guigal reds, including his Côte Rôtie Brune et Blonde '78. Mitchells (Clare Valley) and Palliser Estate ensure excitement for New World fanatics.

11	£6.95	MONTANA LINDAUER BRUT (NZ)
24	£10.35	GREEN POINT, DOMAINE CHANDON 1990 Yarra Valley (Aus)
26	£16.85	LE MESNIL BLANC DE BLANCS Champagne (F)
32	£18.90	CHAMPAGNE HENRI BILLIOT Champagne (F)
43	£3.65	COTES DE ST MONT WHITE, PLAIMONT 1991 South West (F)
51	£4.89	CHARDONNAY 'VIRGINIE', VIN DE PAYS D'OC, SARL DOMAINE VIRGINIE LIEURAN 1992 Midi (F)
56	£5.15	SUNNYCLIFF CHARDONNAY 1992 Victoria (Aus)
194	£4.05	TOLLANA DRY WHITE 1992 South East Australia (Aus)
263	£4.25	MERCHANT VINTNERS CLARET, PETER A SICHEL Bordeaux (F)
269	£4.99	MONTANA CABERNET SAUVIGNON 1991 Marlborough (NZ)
288	£9.00	CABERNET SAUVIGNON, BODEGA Y CAVAS DE WEINERT 1985 Mendoza (Arg)
393	£9.05	SANCERRE ROUGE, A DEZAT 1990 Loire (F)
479	£12.30	VOUVRAY MOELLEUX, CLOS DU BOURG, GASTON HUET 1990 Loire (F)
481	£5.65	HIDALGO AMONTILLADO NAPOLEON Jerez (Sp)
490	£8.70	BOAL 5 YEAR OLD, D'OLIVEIRA (Mad)
496	£13.80	TAYLOR'S TEN YEAR OLD TAWNY Douro (P)

J&B	Justerini & Brooks Ltd

61 St James St, London SW1A 1LZ (Tel 071-493 8721 Fax 071-499 4653). **Opening Hours:** Mon-Fri 9am-5.30pm, Sats in December (London) 9am-1pm. **Delivery:** free nationally, min 2 cases. **Tastings:** tutored events. **Discounts:** £1 per case 2-4 cases; £2 per case 5-7 cases; £3 per case 8-plus cases.

Rhône Specialist of the Year

For a traditional wine merchant, J&B are ahead of their time. Besides splendid Bordeaux, Burgundy and Loire from small, top-class producers, there are eight vintages of the most exciting Rhône wines we've encountered; tiny, scarcely-seen producers from Côte Rôtie (Clusel-Roch), Cornas (Jean Lionnet), St Joseph (Andre Perret, Gaillard), Crozes Hermitage (Etienne Pochon) and a large choice of even rarer whites. Congratulations also to Hew Blair for getting hold of Brokenwood from Australia and the cool-climate aromatic wines from Scotchmans Hill in Victoria.

17	£7.45	BOUVET LADUBAY SAUMUR BRUT Loire (F)
26	£11.50	LE MESNIL BLANC DE BLANCS Champagne (F)
33	£29.00	BOLLINGER GRANDE ANNEE 1985 Champagne (F)
51	£4.80	CHARDONNAY 'VIRGINIE', VIN DE PAYS D'OC, SARL DOMAINE VIRGINIE LIEURAN 1992 Midi (F)
74	£5.90	PENFOLDS KOONUNGA HILL CHARDONNAY 1992 South East Australia (Aus)
79	£6.95	ROSEMOUNT CHARDONNAY 1992 Hunter Valley (Aus)
91	£8.90	MARQUES DE MURRIETA RIOJA RESERVA BLANCO 1987 Rioja (Sp)
109	£11.20	MACON CLESSE, DOMAINE DE LA BONGRAN, J. THEVENET 1990 Burgundy (F)
161	£6.95	JACKSON ESTATE SAUVIGNON BLANC 1992 Marlborough (NZ)
204	£6.91	ERDENER TREPPCHEN RIESLING KABINETT, MONCHHOF 1989 Mosel Saar Ruwer (G)
306	£11.95	HUSCH CABERNET SAUVIGNON NORTHFIELD SELECTION 1988 Mendocino County (Cal)
312	£9.60	RESERVE DE LA COMTESSE, PAUILLAC 1987 Bordeaux (F)
313	£15.95	CLOS DU CLOCHER, POMEROL, BOUROTTE 1989 Bordeaux (F)
322	£29.00	CHATEAU LYNCH-BAGES, PAUILLAC 1989 Bordeaux (F)
336	£6.55	ZINFANDEL, FETZER VINEYARDS 1990 Mendocino County (Cal)
355	£9.80	ST JOSEPH GRISIERES, A PERRET 1990 Rhône (F)
396	£10.95	SAINTSBURY PINOT NOIR 1991 Carneros (Cal)
472	£9.90	NEETHLINGSHOF WEISSER RIESLING NOBLE LATE HARVEST 1991 (SA)

JCK	J C Karn

Cheltenham Cellars, 7 Lansdown Place, Cheltenham, Gloucestershire GL50 2HU (Tel 0242 513265). **Opening Hours:** Mon-Fri 9am-6pm; Sat 9am-1.30pm. **Delivery:** free locally. **Tastings:** occasional in-store, plus tutored events. **Discounts:** 5% per case.

This small merchant was established just after the battle of Waterloo. It specialises in small lots of well-priced quality wines, many scooped from liquidated businesses, so there's a tendency to sell out fast – but there's plenty more where that came from, according to Richard Gooch. 'Our clientèle look forward to a regular novelty,' he says, so he presents his wine with a mixture of 'entertainment and information'. An all-round performer.

4	£6.49	NEDERBURG 1ER CUVEE BRUT Paarl (SA)
11	£6.99	MONTANA LINDAUER BRUT (NZ)
70	£3.99	TIMARA WHITE, MONTANA 1991 (NZ)
169	£9.49	HUNTERS MARLBOROUGH SAUVIGNON BLANC 1992 Marlborough (NZ)

178	£3.99	CORBANS DRY WHITE RIESLING 1991 Marlborough (NZ)
269	£4.99	MONTANA CABERNET SAUVIGNON 1991 Marlborough (NZ)
294	£9.59	CHATEAU DE ANNEREAUX, LALANDE DE POMEROL 1989 Bordeaux (F)
359	£10.89	LAWSON'S SHIRAZ, ORLANDO WINES PTY LTD 1987 South Australia (Aus)
438	£3.98	ALBOR RIOJA TINTO, BODEGAS & BEBIDAS 1991 Rioja (Sp)
451	£6.89	COTO DE IMAZ RIOJA RESERVA 1985 Rioja (Sp)
468	£6.49	NELSON LATE HARVEST RHINE RIESLING, SEIFRIED 1991 Nelson (NZ)

K&B | King & Barnes Ltd

The Horsham Brewery, 18 Bishopric, Horsham, West Sussex RH12 1QP (Tel 0403 270470 Fax 0403 270570). **Opening Hours:** Mon -Sat 9am-5.30pm. **Delivery**: free locally. **Tastings**: regular in-store and tutored events. **Discounts**: 5% per case (wine); 2.5% per case (fort. wine, spirits).

Following the recession and a couple of bad European vintages Simon Deakin feels 'it's high time we all had a break'. So relax and take your pick from his glossy green list (complete with maps) covering all four corners of the globe. France and Australia are strong points, but if you're feeling adventurous try a Mexican red or Moldovan white.

KS | Kwiksave / Liquor Save

Warren Drive, Prestatyn, Clywd, LL19 7HV (Tel 0745 887111 Fax 0745 882504). **Opening Hours:** Mon-Sat 8.30am-5.30pm (late opening 8pm selected stores).

Only last year, most people who cared about what they drank, thought of Kwiksave – if at all – as a chain of miserable-looking shops selling cheap Lieb and Lambrusco. The revolution came with the arrival of Angela Muir, a Master of Wine famous for bullying Spaniards, French and Slovakians into making better wine for all sorts of British retailers. Ms Muir's influence is already evident in highly drinkable wines from southern France and one of the few worthwhile cheap own-label Champagnes. More impressively, she's found a drinkable £2.99 Californian.

| 35 | £2.67 | PELICAN BAY SEMILLON (Aus) |

L&W | Lay & Wheeler Ltd

6 Culver St West, Colchester, Essex CO1 1JA (Tel 0206 764446 Fax 0206 560002). **Opening Hours**: Wine Market Mon-Sat 8am-8pm; Culver Street Mon-Sat 8.30am-5.30pm. **Delivery**: free within 60 miles for 2 or more cases. **Tastings**: regular in-store, plus tutored events. **Discounts**: 5% on 10 or more cases; cash and carry prices.

Lay & Wheeler continue to offer not only an extraordinary list of wines, but convey an enthusiasm that really makes you want to buy a case of everything. However, if your cellars are full, why not try one of their wine workshops – tastings with a difference. Recent highlights were Champange Krug, 10 vintages of Château Latour and the wines of Domaine de la Romanée Conti. Look out for their regular newsletters to see exactly what's on offer.

11	£7.34	MONTANA LINDAUER BRUT (NZ)
24	£10.69	GREEN POINT, DOMAINE CHANDON 1990 Yarra Valley (Aus)
29	£17.55	'J' JORDAN 1987 Sonoma (Cal)

33	£28.95	BOLLINGER GRANDE ANNEE 1985 Champagne (F)
43	£3.98	COTES DE ST MONT WHITE, PLAIMONT 1991 South West (F)
51	£4.99	CHARDONNAY 'VIRGINIE', VIN DE PAYS D'OC, SARL DOMAINE VIRGINIE LIEURAN 1992 Midi (F)
56	£4.99	SUNNYCLIFF CHARDONNAY 1992 Victoria (Aus)
93	£7.74	SEMILLON, STEPHEN HENSCHKE 1991 Adelaide Hills (Aus)
112	£11.95	ELSTON CHARDONNAY, TE MATA ESTATE 1991 Hawkes Bay (NZ)
114	£14.65	HOWELL MOUNTAIN CHARDONNAY, PETER MICHAEL 1990 Napa Valley (Cal)
161	£7.29	JACKSON ESTATE SAUVIGNON BLANC 1992 Marlborough (NZ)
218	£5.86	MOUNT HURTLE GRENACHE ROSE, GEOFF MERRILL 1992 McLaren Vale (Aus)
263	£4.21	MERCHANT VINTNERS CLARET, PETER A SICHEL Bordeaux (F)
276	£6.24	CHATEAU DE LA JAUBERTIE BERGERAC ROUGE, HENRY RYMAN 1990 S West (F)
305	£10.65	CYRIL HENSCHKE CABERNET SAUVIGNON, HENSCHKE 1988 Adelaide Hills (Aus)
321	£20.95	ORNELLAIA 1990 Tuscany (It)
322	£24.95	CHATEAU LYNCH-BAGES, PAUILLAC 1989 Bordeaux (F)
346	£7.99	CHATEAU MUSAR, 1986 Bekaa Valley (Leb)
352	£8.85	PENLEY ESTATE SHIRAZ/CABERNET SAUVIGNON 1990 Coonawarra (Aus)
358	£10.30	FROG'S LEAP ZINFANDEL 1990 Napa Valley (Cal)
376	£6.65	BROUILLY, GEORGES DUBOEUF 1991 Burgundy (F)
380	£7.45	COTE DE BROUILLY, DOMAINE DE LA VOUTE DES CROZES 1991 Beaujolais (F)
389	£6.99	HAMILTON-RUSSELL PINOT NOIR, WALKER BAY 1991 Walker Bay (SA)
403	£14.65	NUITS SAINT GEORGES, DOMAINE DE L'ARLOT 1990 Burgundy (F)
408	£21.50	NUITS ST GEORGES 'CLOS DE L'ARLOT', DOM. DE L'ARLOT 1988 Burgundy (F)
479	£21.64	VOUVRAY MOELLEUX, CLOS DU BOURG, GASTON HUET 1990 Loire (F)
490	£8.68	BOAL 5 YEAR OLD, D'OLIVEIRA (Mad)
491	£11.74	DOWS CRUSTED PORT BOTTLED 1987 Douro (P)
494	£13.59	WARRE'S TRADITIONAL LBV 1981 Douro (P)
496	£13.69	TAYLOR'S TEN YEAR OLD TAWNY Douro (P)
498	£20.00	QUINTA DO VESUVIO VINTAGE PORT 1990 Douro (P)

L&S	Laymont & Shaw Ltd

The Old Chapel, Millpool, Truro, Cornwall TR1 1EX (Tel 0872 70545 Fax 0872 223005). **Opening Hours:** Mon-Fri 9am-5pm. **Delivery**: free nationally. **Tastings**: occasional in-store, plus tutored events. **Discounts**: various.

Many wine buyers find Spain a little too much like hard work, so we should be grateful that Laymont & Shaw have stuck to their guns, because their list provides ample evidence of real quality and value in Spanish wine. The amusingly-named Don John is a bargain at £3.50, while those untroubled by financial worries can assemble a mixed case of Vega Sicilia, with vintages back to 1962. They also offer Spanish olives, olive oils and vinegars, plus the odd recipe idea so we can all lead the Hispanic good life.

91	£7.93	MARQUES DE MURRIETA RIOJA RESERVA BLANCO 1987 Rioja (Sp)
189	£7.43	LAGAR DE CERVERA, RIAS BAIXAS, LAGAR DE FORNELOSSA 1992 Galicia (Sp)
460	£6.67	MOSCATEL PALIDO, MALAGA, SCHOLTZ HERMANOS SA Malaga (Sp)
484	£19.23	MATUSALEM, GONZALEZ BYASS Jerez (Sp)

LAY	Laytons Wine Merchants Ltd

20 Midland Road, London NW1 2AD (Tel 071-388 5081 Fax 071-383 7419). **Opening Hours:** Mon-Fri 9.30am-8pm, Sat 10am-4pm. **Delivery**: free nationally. **Tastings:** regular in-store. **Discounts:** 15% per case from Andre Simon shops; collection discount on orders over £117.50.

Graham Chidgey succeeds in being decidedly modern yet charmingly old-fashioned. Hence his range includes Taltarni, Tui Vale, and Rancho Sisquoc from the New World, plus some unpronounceable Moldovans, as well as 'Jolly Good Claret' at £4.75 a bottle. The Burgundy selection is a case in point – own-label bottlings from Ropiteau alongside the best individual domaines (Dujac, Pousse d'Or, Sauzet etc). And if you prefer not to crawl the kerbs of Kings Cross looking for Laytons' head office, the same wines are sold in the firm's Andre Simon shops.

LEA	Lea & Sandeman Co Ltd

301 Fulham Rd, London SW10 9QH (Tel 071- 376 4767 Fax 071- 351 0275). **Opening Hours:** Mon-Sat 9.30am-8.30pm. Also 211 Kensington Church Street, London W8 (Tel 071 221 1982). **Delivery:** free over £120. **Tastings:** regular in-store. **Discounts:** 5-12.5% per case.

Being bang opposite Oddbins is obviously good for business, as C Lea and P Sandeman have recently opened up another stylish outlet, this time opposite Kensington Place Restaurant. Their wonderful selection of wines brings together the innovative and affordable with the utmost in prestige and class. Small domaines are a speciality, as are occasional offers of wonderful hand-painted trays. Among the rarer finds is the smoky, blackberry-and-coffee Côte Rôtie from Clusel Roch.

33	£27.61	BOLLINGER GRANDE ANNEE 1985 Champagne (F)	
106	£9.99	EDNA VALLEY CHARDONNAY 1990 Edna Valley (Cal)	
108	£9.95	SWANSON CHARDONNAY, NAPA VALLEY 1990 Napa Valley (Cal)	
171	£9.40	POGGIO ALLE GAZZE, TENUTA DELL'ORNELLAIA 1991 Tuscany (It)	
180	£5.61	NEIL ELLIS INGLEWOOD GEWURZTRAMINER 1992 (SA)	
216	£4.64	CHATEAU TOUR DES GENDRES BERGERAC ROSE 1992 South West (F)	
272	£5.58	ROUGE HOMME CABERNET/SHIRAZ, COONAWARRA 1988 Coonawarra (Aus)	
273	£5.64	TALTARNI FIDDLEBACK TERRACE 1990 Pyrenees (Aus)	
295	£9.93	FETZER BARREL SELECT CABERNET SAUVIGNON 1989 Mendocino County (Cal)	
321	£22.48	ORNELLAIA 1990 Tuscany (It)	
389	£6.99	HAMILTON-RUSSELL PINOT NOIR, WALKER BAY 1991 Walker Bay (SA)	
414	£4.31	DOLCETTO D'ASTI, ARALDICA 1992 Piedmont (It)	
422	£8.35	CHIANTI CLASSICO, ISOLE E OLENA 1990 Tuscany (It)	
461	£5.58	STANTON & KILLEEN RUTHERGLEN LIQUEUR MUSCAT Rutherglen (Aus)	
468	£6.46	NELSON LATE HARVEST RHINE RIESLING, SEIFRIED 1991 Nelson (NZ)	
489	£8.95	CHURCHILL GRAHAM FINEST VINTAGE CHARACTER Douro (P)	

LES	CRS Ltd - Leos

29 Dantzic St, Manchester, M4 4BA (Tel 061-832 8152 Fax 061-834 4056). **Opening Hours:** Mon-Sat 8am-6pm, plus late night and Sundays in some stores. **Tastings:** occasional in-store.

Stand by to be confused: Leos (Co-operative Retail Services) is related to the Co-op (Wholesale Services) and sells some of the same wines (own-label Alsace for example) but generally does its own, more upmarket thing. They do some really good wines, including Montana Sauvignon Blanc, Erazuriz Don Maximiano Cabernet and Chateau Cissac '82, a favourite with El Vino habitués. On the other hand, Leos also sells E&J Gallo Chardonnay, a wine more appropriate to Leos' new, more downmarket, Pioneer stores.

OWL	OW Loeb & Co Ltd

64 Southwark Bridge Rd, London SE1 0AS (Tel 071-928 7750 Fax 071-928 1855). **Opening Hours:** Mon-Fri 9am-5.30pm. **Discounts**: £1 per case.

This shipper has been trading since 1874; 120 years on and we manage to feature them in this year's *Guide*! Their stylish list, based on traditional areas of France and Germany, is packed with small, top class domaines, many of which are exclusivities, eg Burgundy; Domaine Dujac, Armand Rousseau, Rhône; Jaboulet, J Reynaud's Ch Rayas/Fonsalette/Pignan, Alsace; Mme Théo Faller, and Pfalz's Bürklin-Wolff. The potentially bewildering sections on Burgundy and Germany make excellent reading, thanks to the explanatory introductions, full vintage charts, individual producer profiles and even a German glossary!

LWE	London Wine Emporium Ltd

86 Goding Street, Vauxhall, London SE11 5AW (Tel 071-587 1302 Fax 071-587 0982). **Opening Hours:** Mon-Fri 10am-7pm, Sat 10am- 5pm, Sun 11am- 4pm. **Delivery**: free nationally for 3 or more cases. **Tastings**: regular in-store.

A brilliant selection of Antipodeans, including museum pieces such as the 1965 Lindemans shiraz and red sparklers which show what they gain with age. But that's not all: there's an expertly chosen range of South Africans, plus cosmopolitan offerings from Moldova, Turkey and Greece. Pop down there on a Sunday, and keep an eye out for the rare Ata Rangi reds.

4	£5.49	NEDERBURG 1ER CUVEE BRUT Paarl (SA)
5	£6.99	GRAND DUCHESS RUSSIAN SPARKLING WINE, Ukraine
6	£6.69	LE GRAND PAVILLON DE BOSCHENDAL, CUVEE BRUT BLANC DE BLANCS Paarl (SA)
11	£6.79	MONTANA LINDAUER BRUT (NZ)
20	£8.59	OMAR KHAYYAM, CHAMPAGNE INDIA 1987 Maharashtra (Ind)
24	£9.99	GREEN POINT, DOMAINE CHANDON 1990 Yarra Valley (Aus)
30	£18.99	CHAMPAGNE JACQUESSON BLANC DE BLANCS Champagne (F)
79	£5.69	ROSEMOUNT CHARDONNAY 1992 Hunter Valley (Aus)
92	£7.79	MONTANA CHURCH ROAD CHARDONNAY 1991 (NZ)
97	£6.99	WAIPARA SPRINGS CHARDONNAY 1991 Canterbury (NZ)
104	£9.75	CHARDONNAY, JANE HUNTER'S WINES 1991 Marlborough (NZ)
112	£12.79	ELSTON CHARDONNAY, TE MATA ESTATE 1991 Hawkes Bay (NZ)
116	£14.99	CHATEAU DE SENEJAC WHITE BORDEAUX 1989 Bordeaux (F)
159	£6.69	SAUVIGNON BLANC, VILLIERA 1992 Paarl (SA)
160	£6.59	GROVE MILL SAUVIGNON 1992 Blenheim (NZ)
169	£8.99	HUNTERS MARLBOROUGH SAUVIGNON BLANC 1992 Marlborough (NZ)
179	£4.29	NEETHLINGSHOF GEWÜRZTRAMINER 1991 Stellenbosch (SA)
180	£5.35	NEIL ELLIS INGLEWOOD GEWURZTRAMINER 1992 (SA)
229	£2.99	VAL DU TORGAN, LES PRODUCTEURS DU MONT TAUCH Midi (F)
259	£4.79	GLEN ELLEN CABERNET SAUVIGNON 1989 (Cal)
275	£4.49	RUSTENBERG MERLOT, STELLENBOSCH 1991 Stellenbosch (SA)
286	£8.39	STONIER'S WINERY SELECTION CABERNETS 1991 Mornington Peninsula (Aus)
299	£10.49	MEERLUST MERLOT, STELLENBOSCH 1986 Stellenbosch (SA)
346	£7.49	CHATEAU MUSAR, 1986 Bekaa Valley (Leb)
348	£7.99	ROSEMOUNT SHOW RESERVE SYRAH 1990 McLaren Vale (Aus)
350	£8.49	BROKENWOOD SHIRAZ 1991 South East Australia (Aus)
365	£12.99	PENFOLDS MAGILL ESTATE SHIRAZ 1988 South Australia (Aus)
373	£4.99	TARRANGO, BROWN BROTHERS 1992 Milawa (Aus)
389	£6.99	HAMILTON-RUSSELL PINOT NOIR, WALKER BAY 1991 Walker Bay (SA)
391	£8.99	BOURGOGNE PINOT NOIR, DOMAINE PARENT 1990 Burgundy (F)

395	£10.99	STONIER'S MERRICKS PINOT NOIR 1991 Mornington Peninsula (Aus)
425	£8.79	LE SASSINE, LE RAGOSE 1988 Veneto (It)
443	£4.79	QUINTA DE LA ROSA RED TABLE WINE 1991 Douro (P)
450	£6.75	YLLERA, VINO DE MESA, SAT LOS CURRO 1988 Ribera del Duero (Sp)
461	£9.59	STANTON & KILLEEN RUTHERGLEN LIQUEUR MUSCAT Rutherglen (Aus)
462	£9.99	CAMPBELLS RUTHERGLEN LIQUEUR MUSCAT Rutherglen (Aus)
468	£5.99	NELSON LATE HARVEST RHINE RIESLING, SEIFRIED 1991 Nelson (NZ)
471	£8.75	NEDERBURG WEISSER RIESLING NOBLE LATE HARVEST 1989 Paarl (SA)
472	£8.49	NEETHLINGSHOF WEISSER RIESLING NOBLE LATE HARVEST 1991 (SA)
484	£15.99	MATUSALEM, GONZALEZ BYASS Jerez (Sp)
488	£6.99	OLD TRAFFORD TAWNY, B. SEPPELT & SONS South East Australia (Aus)
491	£10.49	DOWS CRUSTED PORT BOTTLED 1987 Douro (P)
498	£20.39	QUINTA DO VESUVIO VINTAGE PORT 1990 Douro (P)

LWL	London Wine Ltd

Chelsea Wharf, 15 Lots Road, London, SW10 0QF (Tel 071-351 6856 Fax 071-351 0030). **Opening Hours:** Mon-Fri 9am-9pm, Sat 10am-7pm, Sun 12-3pm. **Delivery:** free locally. **Discounts:** 5% per case.

One of the first wine warehouses, London Wine continues to thrive at its riverside base near Chelsea Wharf, site of the *1993 International Wine Challenge*. Its range is solid rather than exciting but, as Ted Farmer says, over the past year, the firm has 'returned to its warehouse origins', concentrating on job lots such as a Chevalier Montrachet '85 at £96 a case and Château Climens '81 for £12 a bottle, plus budget-priced batches of more basic fare. In other words, London Wine is rather less Limited than it was.

WL	William Low & Company plc

PO Box 73, Baird Ave, Dundee, Tayside DD1 9NF (Tel 0382 814022 Fax 0382 811420). **Opening Hours:** Mon-Weds 9am-8pm, Thurs-Fri 9am-9pm, Sat 9am-6pm, Sun 10am-5pm. **Tastings:** regular in-store. **Discounts:** 1 free bottle with selected cases.

Wine is increasingly the order of the day in northern climes, according to Wm Low's buyer Kevin Wilson. His wine department is one year old, and growing fast. Now with trained, helpful staff and a range of 300 or so wines, including a few exclusivities, it's little wonder the supermarket chain is confident enough to open six more stores, with well-stocked wine sections.

24	£9.95	GREEN POINT, DOMAINE CHANDON 1990 Yarra Valley (Aus)
44	£3.79	CHARDONNAY, VINO DA TAVOLA, CA DONINI 1992 Triveneto (It)
70	£3.99	TIMARA WHITE, MONTANA 1991 (NZ)
74	£4.99	PENFOLDS KOONUNGA HILL CHARDONNAY 1992 South East Australia (Aus)
133	£3.79	NOGALES SAUVIGNON BLANC, DISCOVER WINES LTDA 1993 Curico (Ch)
146	£4.49	HARDY'S MOONDAH BROOK ESTATE CHENIN BLANC 1992 Gingin, Western Australia (Aus)
179	£4.99	NEETHLINGSHOF GEWURZTRAMINER 1991 Stellenbosch (SA)
212	£3.49	CLAIRET DE GASTON, BORDEAUX, PETER A. SICHEL Bordeaux (F)
233	£3.49	MAS DE FIGARO VIN DE PAYS DE L'HERAULT, AIME GUIBERT 1992 Midi (F)
235	£4.39	DAVID WYNN DRY RED 1992 Eden Valley (Aus)
256	£3.99	HARDYS NOTTAGE HILL CABERNET SAUVIGNON 1991 South Australia (Aus)
269	£4.99	MONTANA CABERNET SAUVIGNON 1991 Marlborough (NZ)
282	£5.49	VALLEY OAKS CABERNET SAUVIGNON, FETZER 1990 Mendocino County (Cal)

298	£9.95	LINDEMANS ST GEORGE CABERNET SAUVIGNON 1989 Coonawarra (Aus)
413	£3.69	MONTEPULCIANO D'ABRUZZO, UMANI RONCHI 1991 Marches (It)
421	£7.49	SER GIOVETO, VINO DA TAVOLA, ROCCA DELLE MACIE 1989 Tuscany (It)
444	£4.79	PERIQUITA, J M DA FONSECA 1990 (P)

MWW | Majestic Wine Warehouses

Odhams Trading Estate, St Albans Road, Watford, Hertfordshire WD2 5RE (Tel 0923 816999 Fax 0923 819105). **Opening Hours:** Mon-Sat 10am-8pm, Sun 10am-6pm. **Delivery**: free within 5 miles. **Tastings**: regular in-store.

Heading back to the good old days, Majestic is clearly comfortable in its new livery and with its (slightly less new) management. Champagne is a speciality (and one in which Majestic competes head-on with Oddbins), but there's a growing range of good value regional wines, and all sorts of highly commendable tastings with some of the world's top producers. The only criticism we'd make is that there are still too many wines on the adequate side of exciting. Taste before you buy – or follow our recommendations.

24	£9.99	GREEN POINT, DOMAINE CHANDON 1990 Yarra Valley (Aus)
33	29.95	BOLLINGER GRANDE ANNEE 1985 Champagne (F)
39	£3.39	CHARDONNAY GYONGYOS, HUGH RYMAN 1992 (Hun)
74	£4.99	PENFOLDS KOONUNGA HILL CHARDONNAY 1992 South East Australia (Aus)
76	£4.99	CHARDONNAY VIN DE PAYS D'OC, H RYMAN 1992 Midi (F)
85	£4.99	COTES DE BEAUNE, LABOURE-ROI 1991 Burgundy (F)
131	£3.79	DOMAINE DE ROBINSON VIN DE PAYS DES COTES DE GASCOGNE 1992 South West (F)
137	£3.99	BORDEAUX BLANC, RAOUL JOHNSTON 1992 Bordeaux (F)
168	£8.99	SANCERRE LES ROCHES, DOMAINE VACHERON 1992 Loire (F)
231	£2.99	MISTY MOORING RED, ANGOVES (Aus)
261	£4.69	CLARET, RAOUL JOHNSTON Bordeaux (F)
287	£7.99	KENDALL-JACKSON CABERNET SAUVIGNON 1989 (Cal)
329	£3.99	MONASTERE DE TRIGNAN COTEAUX DU LANGUEDOC 1991 Midi (F)
334	£5.99	STRATFORD ZINFANDEL (Cal)
344	£6.99	CROZES HERMITAGE LA PETITE RUCHE, CHAPOUTIER 1991 Rhône (F)
346	£7.49	CHATEAU MUSAR, 1986 Bekaa Valley (Leb)
369	£16.99	JADE MOUNTAIN SYRAH, DOUGLAS DANIELAK 1990 Sonoma (Cal)
373	£4.50	TARRANGO, BROWN BROTHERS 1992 Milawa (Aus)
410	£2.99	CORTENOVA MERLOT, PASQUA 1991 Grave Friuli (It)
458	£3.99	MUSCAT OF PATRAS, ACHAIA CLAUSS (Gre)
473	£7.99	CHATEAU DE ROLLAND, BARSAC 1990 Bordeaux (F)
478	£9.99	MOULIN TOUCHAIS, COTEAUX DU LAYON 1983 Loire (F)
481	£6.49	HIDALGO AMONTILLADO NAPOLEON Jerez (Sp)
500	£3.99	ELECTRA, QUADY WINERY 1991 Madera County (Cal)

MAR | Marco's Wines

13 Ferrier Street, London, SW18 1SN (Tel 081-871 4944 Fax 081-871 2265). **Opening Hours:** Warehouse: Mon-Sat 10am-8pm, Sun 12-3pm, Stores Mon-Sat 10am-10pm, Sun 12-3pm, 7-10pm. **Delivery**: free within 2 miles. **Tastings**: regular in-store. **Discounts**: 10% per case public; 15% per case trade.

As regular customers of this establishment, we thought it only right to include them this year. In 1981, lease in hand, the young and ambitious

Marco Attard opened his first 'hole in the wall' off-licence, spending the night there, sleeping bag on pallet. 13 years on, the hard work has paid off. He now has four branches, two wine warehouses (one in SW18, the other in Calais) and 200-odd wines to choose from. The staff are cheerful, and even at 10pm keep you entertained after everyone else has gone home.

M&S | Marks & Spencer plc

47 Baker Street, London W1A 1DN (Tel 071 268 8580 Fax 071 268 2674). **Opening Hours:** vary. **Tastings**: regular in store. **Discounts**: 12 bottles for the price of 11.

One of the more active supporters of National Wine Week, with specially trained staff at work in all of its stores, M&S's latest improvement is a food-and-wine matching computer system. The range, however, remains what it has long been – unexcitingly commendable, with lots of over-familiar names such as Lindemans Bin 65, Mondavi Woodbridge and Duboeuf Beaujolais. There are signs of innovation in a Jan Boland Coetzee and Neil Ellis co-production from South Africa, and in new wines from Domaine Virginie in southern France, but these too are on offer elsewhere in the High Street. We'd like to see the people who dream up all those exciting sandwiches and underwear send some of their imagination along the corridor.

297   £9.99   CHATEAU NOTTON, MARGAUX 1988 Bordeaux (F)

MC | Master Cellar

7 Aberdeen Rd, Croydon, mailing address: 73 South End Croydon, CR0 1BF, Surrey CR0 1EQ (Tel 081 686 9989 Fax 081 760 0390). **Opening Hours:** Tues-Fri 10am-7pm, Sat 10am-6pm, Sun 10am-2pm. **Tastings**: regular in-store. **Discounts**: 8.5% per case, extra 2.5% for more than 10 cases.

A wine warehouse with a few differences: there are mature fine and rare wines. As an offshoot from the Davisons chain of off-licences, there's a great deal of choice, from Lambrusco to Latour, Puligny to Penfolds, new lines, bin-ends and genuine bargains (the Grivot '83 Vosne Romanée at £12.95 has gone up just 25p from last year!) A good reason to go to Croydon.

DX | Mayfair Cellars

14 Rushworth Street, London SE1 0RB (Tel 071-928 8899 Fax 071-401 8041). **Opening Hours:** Mon-Fri 9am-5pm. **Delivery**: free locally. **Tastings**: regular samples. **Discounts**: variable.

They might have dropped their very '80s name *Drinkx*, but the list is designed for surviving yuppies still addicted to the good life. Kicking off with a Bordeaux section packed with classed growths and top Pomerol, it includes a large and glossy spread on Champagne Jacquesson, and finishes with a tempting array of cigars. They will even sell you a humidor for £97.50 (ex-VAT). As they say, 'Les Miserables – certainly not a description for us'.

30   £18.25   CHAMPAGNE JACQUESSON BLANC DE BLANCS Champagne (F)
160   £6.99   GROVE MILL SAUVIGNON 1992 Blenheim (NZ)

| MYS | Mayor Sworder & Co Ltd |

381 Kennington Road, London SE11 4PT (Tel 071-735 0385 Fax 071-735 0341). **Opening Hours:** Mon-Fri 8.30am-5.30pm. **Delivery**: free within M25. **Tastings**: regular in-store. **Discounts**: variable.

Celebrating his firm's 90th birthday by taking over Russell & McIver, Martin Everett MW is quietly disproving its traditionalist image by exploring all sorts of new areas. He has, however, dug not Down Under but deeper into France to find excellent country wines, and interesting Rhônes to complete his existing well-conceived list.

| MCL | McLeod's |

11 Bridge St, Louth, Lincs LN11 0DR (Tel 0507 601094 Fax 0507 608412). **Opening Hours:** Mon-Sun 10am-8.30pm. **Delivery**: free within 15 miles. **Tastings**: occasional in-store. **Discounts**: 5% per case; 10% on 2 or more cases.

Stuart McLeod seems to be working on commission for the Louth tourist board, to judge by the publicity he gives this beautiful Lincolnshire town. And his shop does the town proud: refurbished in the prevailing Georgian style, it is packed with interesting wine and food, including more than 200 cheeses. Stuart does not produce a wine list, believing instead that his stock should complement whatever exciting foods are currently available. Thus, the arrival of some delicious Chinese pancakes will prompt the purchase of a few cases of Tsingsao Chardonnay.

| MM | Michael Menzel Wines |

297-299 Eccleshall Rd, Sheffield, S. Yorks S11 8NX (Tel 0742 683557 Fax 0742 671267). **Opening Hours:** Mon-Sat 10am-9pm, Sun 12-2pm, 7-9pm. **Delivery**: free within 50 miles. **Tastings**: occasional in-store. **Discounts**: approx 10% per case.

Mr Menzel prides himself on the good relations he has with many of his suppliers. Obviously he has a way with the French, judging by the array of J Drouhin, Louis Latour, Faiveley, de Vogüe and recent Chapoutier wines on his list. There are some fine vintages of top-flight Bordeaux too: '83 Margaux, '85 Cheval Blanc, '79 Gruaud Larose… Then there are the will-they-never-die? Borgognos from Piedmont and such noble old Spaniards as the '52 Castillo Ygay red and '75 Vega Sicilia Unico. One of the few merchants to have five Bandols from Domaines Ott. Watch this space for Menzel's Wine Bar.

3	£6.85	SEGURA VIUDAS CAVA BRUT RESERVA CAVA (Sp)
17	£9.40	BOUVET LADUBAY SAUMUR BRUT Loire (F)
20	£8.59	OMAR KHAYYAM, CHAMPAGNE INDIA 1987 Maharashtra (Ind)
33	£29.99	BOLLINGER GRANDE ANNEE 1985 Champagne (F)
45	£4.99	NOBILO WHITE CLOUD 1992 (NZ)
53	£6.99	'CASAL DI SERRA' VERDICCHIO CLASSICO, UMANI RONCHI 1991 Marches (It)
65	£11.95	JERMANN PINOT BIANCO 1991 Friuli Venezia Giulia (It)
79	£6.99	ROSEMOUNT CHARDONNAY 1992 Hunter Valley (Aus)
91	£9.05	MARQUES DE MURRIETA RIOJA RESERVA BLANCO 1987 Rioja (Sp)
110	£7.35	POMINO IL BENEFIZIO, MARCHESI DE FRESCOBALDI 1990 Tuscany (It)
119	£17.95	ROBERT MONDAVI RESERVE CHARDONNAY 1988 Napa Valley (Cal)
120	£17.35	CRICHTON HALL CHARDONNAY 1991 Napa Valley (Cal)

123	£23.95	TORRES MILMANDA CHARDONNAY 1991 Penedes (Sp)
174	£12.80	POUILLY FUME, DE LADOUCETTE 1990 Loire (F)
197	£4.99	BADEN DRY, BADISCHER WINZERKELLER Baden (G)
311	£11.75	CHATEAU CISSAC, HAUT-MEDOC 1982 Bordeaux (F)
346	£8.40	CHATEAU MUSAR, 1986 Bekaa Valley (Leb)
389	£8.10	HAMILTON-RUSSELL PINOT NOIR, WALKER BAY 1991 Walker Bay (SA)
404	£17.95	ROBERT MONDAVI RESERVE PINOT NOIR 1988 Napa Valley (Cal)
427	£8.25	CUMARO ROSSO CONERO, UMANI RONCHI 1989 Marches (It)
478	£19.00	MOULIN TOUCHAIS, COTEAUX DU LAYON 1983 Loire (F)
482	£9.99	LUSTAU OLD EAST INDIA, EMILIO LUSTAU Jerez (Sp)
483	£10.98	1796 RICH OLD OLOROSO Jerez (Sp)
484	£22.00	MATUSALEM, GONZALEZ BYASS Jerez (Sp)
494	£13.59	WARRE'S TRADITIONAL LBV 1981 Douro (P)
496	£15.25	TAYLOR'S TEN YEAR OLD TAWNY Douro (P)

MTL | Mitchells Wine Merchants Ltd

354 Meadowhead, Sheffield, S. Yorkshire S8 7UJ (Tel 0742 745587 Fax 0742 748481). **Opening Hours:** Mon-Sat 8.30am-10pm, Sun 12-3pm, 7-9pm. **Delivery**: free locally. **Tastings**: regular in-store. **Discounts**: 2.5% mixed case; 5% case.

Spain is the obvious passion of John Mitchell and Dave Marriott, Sheffield's amiable toreadors of wine. In addition to stocking at least seven Gran Reserva Riojas, including the excellent Marques de Murrieta 1975, they dream of opening an Iberian bar in the middle of their shop ('Half a San Miguel revitalises the shopping'). Unfortunately there's little room, crammed as their premises are with wine bargains from all over the world, more than 140 malt whiskies and John and Dave's larger-than-life personalities.

20	£7.99	OMAR KHAYYAM, CHAMPAGNE INDIA 1987 Maharashtra (Ind)
33	£30.45	BOLLINGER GRANDE ANNEE 1985 Champagne (F)
70	£4.19	TIMARA WHITE, MONTANA 1991 (NZ)
180	£5.49	NEIL ELLIS INGLEWOOD GEWURZTRAMINER 1992 (SA)
269	£5.95	MONTANA CABERNET SAUVIGNON 1991 Marlborough (NZ)
319	£24.95	CHATEAU LASCOMBES, MARGAUX 1988 Bordeaux (F)
346	£7.99	CHATEAU MUSAR, 1986 Bekaa Valley (Leb)
484	£18.95	MATUSALEM, GONZALEZ BYASS Jerez (Sp)
493	£12.49	HENRIQUES & HENRIQUES 10 YEAR OLD VERDELHO Madeira
496	£13.95	TAYLOR'S TEN YEAR OLD TAWNY Douro (P)

MOR | Moreno Wine Importers

2 Norfolk Place, London W2 1QN (Tel 071-706 3055 Fax 071-724 3813). **Opening Hours:** both shops: Mon-Fri 10am-9pm, Norfolk Place: Sat 10am-8pm, Marylands Rd: Sat 10am-9pm, Sun 12-2pm. **Delivery**: free locally. **Tastings**: regular samples. **Discounts**: 5% per case/collection discount.

Manuel Moreno has flirted with the more commercial wines of Chile, but his heart remains with his roots – in Spain. Trendsetters looking to get ahead of the pack should hurry down to Moreno and get acquainted with the wines of Somontano, Toro, and Extremadura. The wine list also includes valuable information about Rioja vintages and ageing regulations, so a quick browse will set you up as the Hispanic expert at any dinner table.

| 78 | £5.65 | CHARDONNAY BARREL FERMENTED, VINAS DEL VERO 1991 Somontano (Sp) |
| 91 | £7.99 | MARQUES DE MURRIETA RIOJA RESERVA BLANCO 1987 Rioja (Sp) |

147	£4.99	CASABLANCA WHITE LABEL SAUVIGNON BLANC 1992 (Ch)
153	£5.00	MARQUES DE ALELLA CLASSICO 1992 Alella (Sp)
189	£8.00	LAGAR DE CERVERA, RIAS BAIXAS, LAGAR DE FORNELOSSA 1992 Galicia (Sp)
372	£20.65	CLOS DE MOGADOR, COSTER DE SIURANA 1989 Priorato (Sp)
439	£5.99	BORBA, ADEGA CO-OPERATIVA DE BORBA 1991 Douro (P)
447	£6.75	CAMPO VIEJO RIOJA RESERVA 1987 Rioja (Sp)
455	£9.99	REMELLURI RIOJA CRIANZA 1989 Rioja (Sp)

M&V | Morris & Verdin Ltd

28 Churton St, London SW1V 2LP (Tel 071 630 8888 Fax 071 630 6227). **Opening Hours:** Mon-Fri 8am-6pm. **Delivery:** free locally. **Tastings:** occasional in-store.

Do independent merchants have a *raison d'etre* in the 1990s? Jasper Morris proves the answer is 'yes', with a range that reveals careful appraisal of the market as well as superb buying. The domaine-bottled Burgundies are still the envy of other merchants, while the addition of Frog's Leap strengthens an already formidable line-up of top quality Californian wines and, with Au Bon Climat and Bonny Doon, means that Mr M now sells wines from three of the only West Coast wineries with a proven sense of humour.

33	£29.00	BOLLINGER GRANDE ANNEE 1985 Champagne (F)
51	£4.90	CHARDONNAY 'VIRGINIE', VIN DE PAYS D'OC, SARL DOMAINE VIRGINIE LIEURAN 1992 MIDI (F)
116	£14.00	CHATEAU DE SENEJAC WHITE BORDEAUX 1989 Bordeaux (F)
164	£7.40	MENETOU SALON LES MOROGUES HENRI PELLE 1992 Loire (F)
260	£4.90	OLD TRIANGLE CABERNET SAUVIGNON, S. SMITH & SONS 1991 Barossa (Aus)
291	£7.90	CHATEAU LA TOUR HAUT-CAUSSAN, MEDOC 1989 Bordeaux (F)
357	£9.50	QUPE SYRAH, BOB LINDQUIST 1991 Central Coast (Cal)
358	£9.90	FROG'S LEAP ZINFANDEL 1990 Napa Valley (Cal)
369	£15.00	JADE MOUNTAIN SYRAH, DOUGLAS DANIELAK 1990 Sonoma (Cal)
381	£7.40	CHENAS, LOUIS CHAMPAGNON 1991 Beaujolais (F)
443	£4.50	QUINTA DE LA ROSA RED TABLE WINE 1991 Douro (P)

MRN | Wm Morrison Supermarkets

41 Industrial Estate, Wakefield, N Yorks WF2 0XF, (Tel 0924 870000 Fax 0924 821260). **Opening Hours:** vary (generally 9am-8pm). **Tastings:** occasional in-store.

The sight of a happy shopping bag yelling 'More reasons to shop at Morrisons' is one few Southerners have ever witnessed. What a pity, and what a pity, too, that there aren't more regional supermarkets offering such good wines (and fresh fish, according to the Deputy Editor's mother) as this Northern firm. While their range is not as large as some supermarkets, it is well-chosen, with Jamieson's Run, Guy Saget, Cousiño Macul, Domaine de la Baume and L A Cetto all names worth pushing the trolley towards.

20	£6.99	OMAR KHAYYAM, CHAMPAGNE INDIA 1987 Maharashtra (Ind)
70	£3.99	TIMARA WHITE, MONTANA 1991 (NZ)
81	£5.99	CATHEDRAL CELLARS CHARDONNAY, KWV 1991 Coastal Region (SA)
91	£7.49	MARQUES DE MURRIETA RIOJA RESERVA BLANCO 1987 Rioja (Sp)
250	£3.49	STAMBOLOVO RESERVE MERLOT 1987 (Bul)
447	£5.25	CAMPO VIEJO RIOJA RESERVA 1987 Rioja (Sp)

NAD | The Nadder Wine Co. Ltd

Hussars House, 2 Netherhampton Rd, Harnham, Salisbury, Wiltshire SP2 8HE (Tel 0722 325418 Fax 0722 421617). **Opening Hours:** Mon-Fri 9am-7pm, Sat 10am-3pm. **Delivery:** free within 50 miles. **Tastings:** regular in-store tastings. **Discounts:** 2.5% collection discount. 5%, 7.5% and 10%. respectively on purchases over £100, £500 and £1,000.

Even sleepy Wiltshire is no longer a safe haven for wine snobs. The straight-talking Chris Gilbey describes wines as 'guzzlers', often at 'silly' prices, with advice like 'Grab it!' plus some further advice to John Major that we prefer not to print. And Chris is no snob himself when it comes to buying wines – he stocks the Yuppie-sounding Los Porches from Spain at decidedly post-80s £2.95. Also tempting are such value-for-money Aussies as Tisdall and Salisbury Estate.

79	£5.99	ROSEMOUNT CHARDONNAY 1992 Hunter Valley (Aus)
85	£6.99	COTES DE BEAUNE, LABOURE-ROI 1991 Burgundy (F)
104	£9.85	CHARDONNAY, JANE HUNTER'S WINES 1991 Marlborough (NZ)
169	£8.99	HUNTERS MARLBOROUGH SAUVIGNON BLANC 1992 Marlborough (NZ)
231	£3.49	MISTY MOORING RED, ANGOVES (Aus)
299	£10.25	MEERLUST MERLOT, STELLENBOSCH 1986 Stellenbosch (SA)
348	£7.99	ROSEMOUNT SHOW RESERVE SYRAH 1990 McLaren Vale (Aus)
373	£4.95	TARRANGO, BROWN BROTHERS 1992 Milawa (Aus)
489	£9.75	CHURCHILL GRAHAM FINEST VINTAGE CHARACTER Douro (P)

JN | James Nicholson Wine Merchant

27a Killyleagh Street, Crossgar, County Down Northern Ireland BT30 9DG (Tel 0396 830091 Fax 0396 830028) **Opening Hours:** Mon-Sat 10am-7pm. **Delivery:** free. **Tastings:** regular in-store and tutored events. **Discounts:** up to 10% per case.

Hors de combat from this year's regional award, but in as good a shape as ever. The Burgundy list still relies quite heavily on Drouhin, but names such as Jean Marc Boillot (Pommard), Michel Colin (Chassagne) and Alain Guyard (Gevrey) have now crept in. Lingenfelder, J J Prum and Schloss Reinhartshausen now illuminate the German selection, while the subtle trio of Heemskerk, Bannockburn and Cape Mentelle all show that there is more to Australia than 'Tits-Up-Front' Chardonnay. And, for non-Ulstermen, the company now services Eire and offers free delivery throughout the UK.

14	£5.69	ANGAS BRUT CLASSIC, YALUMBA WINERY S.E. Australia (Aus)
17	£8.35	BOUVET LADUBAY SAUMUR BRUT Loire (F)
25	£12.50	CROSER METHODE TRADITIONNELLE, PETALUMA WINERY 1990 Adelaide Hills (Aus)
53	£4.99	'CASAL DI SERRA' VERDICCHIO CLASSICO, DOC, UMANI RONCHI 1991 Marches (It)
79	£5.85	ROSEMOUNT CHARDONNAY 1992 Hunter Valley (Aus)
91	£8.49	MARQUES DE MURRIETA RIOJA RESERVA BLANCO 1987 Rioja (Sp)
95	£9.85	BARREL SELECT CHARDONNAY, FETZER VINEYARDS 1991 Mendocino County (Cal)
146	£4.79	OXFORD LANDING SAUVIGNON BLANC, YALUMBA WINERY 1992 S. Australia (Aus)
215	£4.40	VALDEMAR ROSADA, MARTINEZ BUJANDA 1992 Rioja (Sp)
232	£3.79	DOMAINE DE ST LAURENT, VIN DE PAYS DES COTEAUX DU LIBRON 1991 Midi (F)
237	£5.85	CUVEE MYTHIQUE, VIN DE PAYS D'OC, VAL D'ORBIEU 1990 Midi (F)
276	£5.65	CHATEAU DE LA JAUBERTIE BERGERAC ROUGE, HENRY RYMAN 1990 South West (F)
281	£5.99	CHATEAU BONNET OAK AGED, A LURTON 1990 Bordeaux (F)
295	£9.99	FETZER BARREL SELECT CABERNET SAUVIGNON 1989 Mendocino County (Cal)
299	£9.95	MEERLUST MERLOT, STELLENBOSCH 1986 Stellenbosch (SA)

303	£11.99	PETALUMA COONAWARRA RED 1988 Coonawarra (Aus)
346	£7.80	CHATEAU MUSAR, 1986 Bekaa Valley (Leb)
348	£8.60	ROSEMOUNT SHOW RESERVE SYRAH 1990 McLaren Vale (Aus)
363	£11.55	RIDGE GEYSERVILLE ZINFANDEL 1991 Sonoma (Cal)
364	£14.99	CHATEAUNEUF DU PAPE, CHATEAU DE BEAUCASTEL 1988 Rhône (F)
393	£8.39	SANCERRE ROUGE, A DEZAT 1990 Loire (F)
394	£9.40	COLDSTREAM HILLS PINOT NOIR 1992 Yarra Valley (Aus)
413	£3.99	MONTEPULCIANO D'ABRUZZO, DOC, UMANI RONCHI 1991 Marches (It)
421	£8.30	SER GIOVETO, VINO DA TAVOLA, ROCCA DELLE MACIE 1989 Tuscany (It)
422	£9.39	CHIANTI CLASSICO, ISOLE E OLENA 1990 Tuscany (It)
427	£11.35	CUMARO ROSSO CONERO, UMANI RONCHI 1989 Marches (It)
442	£3.99	VALDEMAR RIOJA TINTO, MARTINEZ BUJANDA 1992 Rioja (Sp)
479	£14.65	VOUVRAY MOELLEUX, CLOS DU BOURG, GASTON HUET 1990 Loire (F)
481	£6.30	HIDALGO AMONTILLADO NAPOLEON Jerez (Sp)
484	£17.95	MATUSALEM, GONZALEZ BYASS Jerez (Sp)
500	£4.75	ELECTRA, QUADY WINERY 1991 Madera County (Cal)

N&P | Nickolls & Perks Ltd

37 High St, Stourbridge, West Midlands DY8 1TA (Tel 0384 394518 Fax 0384 440786). **Opening Hours:** Mon-Thurs 9am-6pm, Fri 9am-9pm, Sat 9am-6pm. **Delivery:** free locally. **Tastings:** regular in-store and tutored events, plus wine club. **Discounts:** 10% on case price.

It's good to hear William Gardener shouting out above the gloom. 'We are enjoying a period of exceptional value for money among the world's fine mature wines and able to supply our private fine wine enthusiasts with exceptional wine at practically half-price.' There are some good, everyday wines but a glance at the fine wine list shows what has attracted customers from over 25 countries: claret, Burgundy and port dating back to 1904.

NIC | Nicolas UK Ltd

71 Abingdon Road, London W8 6AW (Tel 071-937 3996 Fax 071-937 0209). **Opening Hours:** Mon-Sat 10am-10pm. **Delivery:** free locally. **Tastings:** regular in-store. **Discounts:** 5% per case.

This, the only French wine chain anyone has heard of, is not the cheapest place to buy wine in France. Which may explain why Nicolas isn't actually the cheapest place to buy wine in Britain either. The shops are an authentically stylish (not to say snooty) slice of Gallic life, however, with French-trained staff and French regional wines unavailable elsewhere. Le Nouveau Monde is less comprehensively covered. *Bien sur!*

17	£10.50	BOUVET LADUBAY SAUMUR BRUT Loire (F)
18	£9.85	CREMANT DE LOIRE ROSE, CAVE DES VIGNERONS DE SAUMUR Loire (F)
22	£10.99	MAYERLING CREMANT D'ALSACE, CAVE VINICOLE DE TURCKHEIM Alsace (F)
24	£10.50	GREEN POINT, DOMAINE CHANDON 1990 Yarra Valley (Aus)
33	£32.30	BOLLINGER GRANDE ANNEE 1985 CHAMPAGNE (F)
43	£4.99	COTES DE ST MONT WHITE, PLAIMONT 1991 South West (F)
87	£7.95	BARREL FERMENTED CHARDONNAY, ROTHBURY ESTATE 1992 Hunter Valley (Aus)
177	£11.40	SAVENNIERES, CHATEAU D'EPIRE, LUC BIZARD 1990 Loire (F)
229	£4.25	VAL DU TORGAN, LES PRODUCTEURS DU MONT TAUCH Midi (F)
304	£9.99	LES FIEFS DE LAGRANGE, ST JULIEN 1989 Bordeaux (F)
330	£4.90	VIN DE PAYS DES COLLINES RHODANIENNES CEPAGE SYRAH, CAVE DE TAIN L'HERMITAGE Rhône (F)
346	£8.50	CHATEAU MUSAR, 1986 Bekaa Valley (Leb)

NRW | Noble Rot Wine Warehouse Ltd

18 Market Street, Bromsgrove, Worcestershire B61 8DA (Tel 0527 575606 Fax 0527 574091). **Opening Hours:** Mon-Fri 10am-7pm, Sat 9.30am-6.30pm. **Delivery:** within 15 miles. **Tastings:** regular in-store and tutored events, plus wine club. **Discounts:** regular special offers.

Julie Wyres describes her place as 'a vinous cocktail of safe bets plus a dash of imagination' which she says works well on the Midlands palate. As realists, she and her colleagues took the decision to sacrifice their vinous pet desires and offer steadfast everyday drinking styles at £3-5 with frequent new arrivals to try. There are grand tastings, charity nights and wine seminars, all of which help to boost sales of recommendable sparkling and late harvest wines which might remain glued to other merchants' shelves.

20	£8.99	OMAR KHAYYAM, CHAMPAGNE INDIA 1987 Maharashtra India
22	£8.99	MAYERLING CREMANT D'ALSACE, CAVE VINICOLE DE TURCKHEIM Alsace (F)
46	£3.99	CHARDONNAY DEL PIEMONTE, ARALDICA 1992 Piedmont (It)
57	£5.95	CHABLIS, LOUIS ALEXANDRE 1992 Burgundy (F)
61	£6.49	LUGANA CA'DEI FRATI 1992 Brescia (It)
74	£4.99	PENFOLDS KOONUNGA HILL CHARDONNAY 1992 S.E. Australia (Aus)
77	£4.89	SALISBURY ESTATE CHARDONNAY 1992 S.E. Australia (Aus)
80	£6.69	CHATEAU REYNELLA STONY HILL CHARDONNAY 1990 S. Australia (Aus)
144	£4.75	COTEAUX DE LANGUEDOC PICPOUL DE PINET, DUC DE MORNY 1991 Midi (F)
164	£7.99	MENETOU SALON LES MOROGUES HENRI PELLE 1992 Loire (F)
182	£6.79	GEWURZTRAMINER D'ALSACE, CAVE VINICOLE DE TURCKHEIM 1992 Alsace (F)
197	£3.75	BADEN DRY, BADISCHER WINZERKELLER Baden (G)
235	£4.49	DAVID WYNN DRY RED 1992 Eden Valley (Aus)
266	£4.89	SALISBURY ESTATE CABERNET SAUVIGNON 1991 S.E. Australia (Aus)
330	£3.95	VIN DE PAYS DES COLLINES RHODANIENNES CEPAGE SYRAH, CAVE DE TAIN L'HERMITAGE Rhône (F)
373	£5.29	TARRANGO, BROWN BROTHERS 1992 Milawa (Aus)
405	£18.99	BEAUNE 1ER CRU EPENOTTES, VALLET FRERES 1989 Burgundy (F)
414	£3.99	DOLCETTO D'ASTI, ARALDICA 1992 Piedmont (It)
422	£8.29	CHIANTI CLASSICO, ISOLE E OLENA 1990 Tuscany (It)
423	£7.49	CARMIGNANO, CAPEZZANA 1987 Tuscany (It)
438	£3.69	ALBOR RIOJA TINTO, BODEGAS & BEBIDAS 1991 Rioja (Sp)
491	£10.99	DOWS CRUSTED PORT BOTTLED 1987 Douro (P)

NI | Nobody Inn

Doddiscombsleigh, Nr Exeter, Devon EX6 7PS (Tel 0647 52394 Fax 0647 52978). **Opening Hours:** Mon-Sat 11am-11pm, Sun 11am-10.30pm.

West of England Wine Merchant of the Year

Not the best known merchant in the west country, but a firm favourite with everyone who has braved the Devon lanes to get to this pub – and to anyone else who has become as submerged as we did in a list which competes with the local telephone directory. Best described as large but perfectly formed, it offers a wealth of choice at all price ranges, from seven different Madirans to five vintages of Opus One (we lost count of the number of sweet wines, a house speciality). As if all this were not enough, there is Nick Borst-Smith's informative and amusing commentary – English sweet wine is 'a miracle made possible by the use of under-arm deodorants'.

28	£9.48	DRAPPIER BLANC DE BLANCS CHAMPAGNE Champagne (F)

38	£9.00	VIN DE PAYS DE L'HERAULT BLANC, SKALLI 1992 Midi (F)
74	£4.99	PENFOLDS KOONUNGA HILL CHARDONNAY 1992 S.E. Australia (Aus)
76	£4.99	CHARDONNAY VIN DE PAYS D'OC, H RYMAN 1992 Midi (F)
96	£8.45	VALLEY VINEYARDS FUME BLANC 1991 Berkshire (UK)
117	£16.00	RIDGE CHARDONNAY 1990 St Cruz (Cal)
123	£19.99	TORRES MILMANDA CHARDONNAY 1991 Penedes (Sp)
146	£4.65	OXFORD LANDING SAUVIGNON BLANC, YALUMBA WINERY 1992 S. AUSTRALIA (AUS)
156	£6.99	MUSCADET CHATEAU DU CLERAY, SAUVION ET FILS 1992 Loire (F)
161	£8.82	JACKSON ESTATE SAUVIGNON BLANC 1992 Marlborough (NZ)
169	£10.19	HUNTERS MARLBOROUGH SAUVIGNON BLANC 1992 Marlborough (NZ)
288	£6.51	CABERNET SAUVIGNON, BODEGA Y CAVAS DE WEINERT 1985 Mendoza (Arg)
305	£10.86	CYRIL HENSCHKE CABERNET SAUVIGNON, STEPHEN HENSCHKE 1988 Adelaide Hills (Aus)
323	£36.60	CHATEAU COS D'ESTOURNEL, ST ESTEPHE 1982 Bordeaux (F)
363	£15.00	RIDGE GEYSERVILLE ZINFANDEL 1991 Sonoma (Cal)
370	£15.49	YARRA YERING SHIRAZ NO.2 1990 Yarra Valley (Aus)
372	£19.20	CLOS DE MOGADOR, COSTER DE SIURANA 1989 Priorato (Sp)
381	£7.93	CHENAS, LOUIS CHAMPAGNON 1991 Beaujolais (F)
400	£11.76	NEUDORF VINEYARDS MOUTERE PINOT NOIR 1991 Nelson (NZ)
445	£5.05	HARDY'S MOONDAH BROOK ESTATE CHENIN BLANC 1992 Gingin, W. Australia (Aus)
459	£6.46	SAMOS NECTAR, SAMOS CO-OPERATIVE 1983 Samos, (Gr)
461	£10.43	STANTON & KILLEEN RUTHERGLEN LIQUEUR MUSCAT Rutherglen (Aus)
462	£4.96	CAMPBELLS RUTHERGLEN LIQUEUR MUSCAT Rutherglen (Aus)
469	£3.48	CHATEAU DE BERBEC, PREMIERES COTES DE BORDEAUX 1989 Bordeaux (F)
484	£20.08	MATUSALEM, GONZALEZ BYASS Jerez (Sp)
498	£22.36	QUINTA DO VESUVIO VINTAGE PORT 1990 Douro (P)
500	£5.26	ELECTRA, QUADY WINERY 1991 Madera County (Cal)

RN	Rex Norris Wine Merchants

50 Queens Rd, Haywards Heath, West Sussex RH16 1EE (Tel 0444 454756). **Opening Hours:** Mon-Sat 9am-7pm. **Delivery:** free within 5 miles. **Tastings:** regular in-store tastings. **Discounts:** 10% per case.

Kelvin Pretty and Rex Norris sell good value wine from anywhere in the world, especially if it can be sold for £3.50-5.50, but their heart is really in Europe, in regions like the Collines Rhodaniennes and Faugères, where they find a 'wider choice of alternative flavours to Chardonnay and Shiraz'.

57	£5.99	CHABLIS, LOUIS ALEXANDRE 1992 Burgundy (F)
182	£6.99	GEWURZTRAMINER D'ALSACE, CAVE VINICOLE DE TURCKHEIM 1992 Alsace (F)
238	£6.65	CHATEAU DE LASTOURS CORBIERES, FUT DE CHENE 1989 Midi (F)
330	£4.15	VIN DE PAYS DES COLLINES RHODANIENNES CEPAGE SYRAH, CAVE DE TAIN L'HERMITAGE Rhône (F)

OD	Oddbins Ltd

31-33 Weir Rd, London SW19 8UG (Tel 081-944 4400 Fax 081-944 4411). **Opening Hours:** Mon-Sat 10am-9pm. Sun 12-3pm, 7-9 pm. **Delivery:** free locally. **Tastings:** regular in-store tastings. tutored events. On request. **Discounts:** 5% per case pus regular quantity discounts on Champagne.

National Chain and Spanish Merchant of the Year

Rather than resting on its laurels, Oddbins has set off to conquer pastures new. 'Fine wine' is a new enthusiasm, so the best shops are now the place to look for such rarities as Guigal's La Mouline, 1990 clarets at little more than their 1991 *en primeur* prices and obscure Penfolds bins the world has never seen. Then there's the range of whacky own-label wines (look out for the extraordinary 'Vanishing Point' label); a quarterly (not quite sufficiently Oddbinnsy) newsletter called *The Catalyst* and brave new ranges of wines from Germany, Spain and New Zealand. The Oddbins list remains a Steadmanised joy, though the words are worth reading, too. And if this is not enough, there's an Oddbins Australian Wine Tour on which you can compare the real thing with all those Steadman illustrations.

3	£5.99	SEGURA VIUDAS CAVA BRUT RESERVA Cava (Sp)
9	£8.99	EDMOND MAZURE VINTAGE BRUT, SEAVIEW 1990 S.E. Australia (Aus)
11	£6.99	MONTANA LINDAUER BRUT (NZ)
14	£6.99	ANGAS BRUT CLASSIC, YALUMBA WINERY S.E. Australia (Aus)
16	£7.49	YALUMBA SPARKLING CABERNET CUVEE PRESTIGE S.E. Australia (Aus)
24	£10.50	GREEN POINT, DOMAINE CHANDON 1990 Yarra Valley (Aus)
25	£10.49	CROSER METHODE TRADITIONNELLE, PETALUMA WINERY 1990 Adelaide Hills (Aus)
33	£29.95	BOLLINGER GRANDE ANNEE 1985 Champagne (F)
69	£3.49	TOLLEYS PEDARE CHENIN COLOMBARD 1990 S. Australia (Aus)
70	£3.99	TIMARA WHITE, MONTANA 1991 (NZ)
74	£4.95	PENFOLDS KOONUNGA HILL CHARDONNAY 1992 S.E. Australia (Aus)
76	£3.99	CHARDONNAY VIN DE PAYS D'OC, H RYMAN 1992 Midi (F)
77	£4.69	SALISBURY ESTATE CHARDONNAY 1992 S.E. Australia (Aus)
80	£5.99	CHATEAU REYNELLA STONY HILL CHARDONNAY 1990 S. Australia (Aus)
84	£6.99	COVA DA URSA CHARDONNAY 1991 Terras do Sado (P)
92	£7.99	MONTANA CHURCH ROAD CHARDONNAY 1991 (NZ)
98	£8.99	LOCAL GROWERS SEMILLON, ROCKFORD 1989 Barossa Valley (Aus)
99	£7.99	KRONDORF SHOW RESERVE CHARDONNAY 1991 Barossa Valley (Aus)
102	£8.99	CHATEAU DOISY-DAENE SEC, BORDEAUX, P. DUBOURDIEU 1990 Bordeaux (F)
117	£13.99	RIDGE CHARDONNAY 1990 St Cruz (Cal)
126	£3.49	VIN DE PAYS D'OC, SUR LIE, J & F LURTON 1992 Midi (F)
133	£3.99	NOGALES SAUVIGNON BLANC, DISCOVER WINES LTDA 1993 Curico (Ch)
135	£3.99	SAUVIGNON BLANC RUEDA, HERMANOS LURTON 1992 Rueda (Sp)
146	£4.69	OXFORD LANDING SAUVIGNON BLANC, YALUMBA WINERY 1992 S. Australia (Aus)
193	£2.99	RHINE RIESLING GREAT PLAIN, MOR WINERY 1992 Mor, Hungary
257	£3.99	SEAVIEW CABERNET SAUVIGNON/SHIRAZ 1990 S.E. Australia (Aus)
269	£4.99	MONTANA CABERNET SAUVIGNON 1991 Marlborough (NZ)
274	£5.39	CHATEAU THIEULEY AC BORDEAUX ROUGE 1989 Bordeaux (F)
282	£5.99	VALLEY OAKS CABERNET SAUVIGNON, FETZER VINEYARDS 1990 Mendocino County (Cal)
293	£7.99	THE ANGELUS CABERNET SAUVIGNON, WIRRA WIRRA 1991 S. Australia (Aus)
295	£8.99	FETZER BARREL SELECT CABERNET SAUVIGNON 1989 Mendocino County (Cal)
298	£9.99	LINDEMANS ST GEORGE CABERNET SAUVIGNON 1989 Coonawarra (Aus)
303	£9.99	PETALUMA COONAWARRA RED 1988 Coonawarra (Aus)
320	£19.99	CHATEAU PICHON LONGUEVILLE BARON, PAUILLAC 1990 Bordeaux (F)
330	£3.99	VIN DE PAYS DES COLLINES RHODANIENNES CEPAGE SYRAH, CAVE DE TAIN L'HERMITAGE Rhône (F)
336	£4.99	ZINFANDEL, FETZER VINEYARDS 1990 Mendocino County (Cal)
342	£6.49	PETER LEHMANN 'CLANCY'S RED' 1990 Barossa Valley (Aus)
344	£7.49	CROZES HERMITAGE LA PETITE RUCHE, CHAPOUTIER 1991 Rhône (F)
354	£8.75	CHATEAUNEUF DU PAPE, PIERRE ANDRE 1990 Rhône (F)
357	£9.99	QUPE SYRAH, BOB LINDQUIST 1991 Central Coast (Cal)
363	£11.99	RIDGE GEYSERVILLE ZINFANDEL 1991 Sonoma (Cal)
365	£12.49	PENFOLDS MAGILL ESTATE SHIRAZ 1988 S. Australia (Aus)
367	£16.49	CORNAS, AUGUSTE CLAPE 1990 Rhône (F)
368	£16.99	COTE ROTIE, EMILE CHAMPET 1990 Rhône (F)

370	£14.99	YARRA YERING SHIRAZ NO.2 1990 Yarra Valley (Aus)
391	£6.99	BOURGOGNE PINOT NOIR, DOMAINE PARENT 1990 Burgundy (F)
398	£9.99	MONTHELIE, JAFFELIN 1990 Burgundy (F)
414	£3.69	DOLCETTO D'ASTI, ARALDICA 1992 Piedmont (It)
415	£4.49	VALPOLICELLA CLASSICO, MASI 1991 Veneto (It)
424	£9.99	DOLCETTO D'ALBA CORSINI, MASCARELLO 1991 Piedmont (It)
428	£9.99	BRIC MILEUI, ASCHERI 1990 Piedmont (It)
433	£2.49	LEZIRIA VINHO TINTO, VEGA CO-OPERATIVE ALMEIRIM 1992 Almeirim (P)
439	£3.29	BORBA, ADEGA CO-OPERATIVA DE BORBA 1991 Douro (P)
444	£3.99	PERIQUITA, J M DA FONSECA 1990 (P)
445	£4.89	MEIA PIPA, J P VINHOS 1989 (P)
447	£4.99	CAMPO VIEJO RIOJA RESERVA 1987 Rioja (Sp)
449	£5.99	ESPORAO, HERDADE DE ESPORAO 1989 Alentejo (P)
469	£5.99	CHATEAU DE BERBEC, PREMIERES COTES DE BORDEAUX 1989 Bordeaux (F)
474	£9.99	DINDARELLO, MACULAN 1992 Veneto (It)
484	£18.75	MATUSALEM, GONZALEZ BYASS Jerez (Sp)
492	£10.99	COLHEITA, A A CALEM & FILHO 1985 Douro (P)
494	£12.49	WARRE'S TRADITIONAL LBV 1981 Douro (P)

ORG	The Organic Wine Co Ltd

PO Box 81, High Wycombe, Bucks HP13 5QN (Tel 0494 446557 Fax 0494 713030). **Opening Hours:** Mon-Fri 9am-5.30pm, Sat 9am-1pm, plus 24 hour answerphone. **Delivery:** free within 15 miles. **Tastings:** tutored events. **Discounts:** various special offers.

Tony Mason has been forced to review his stock. 'Gone are most of the single-vineyard German wines, seldom so delicious and seldom so unwanted'. Gone too, the Californian winery 'purchased by a retired admiral who, wanting his name on the label, increased prices by 60%.' Still, the wines of Jean Musso (Burgundy), Andre Stentz (Alsace) and Château du Puy (Bordeaux) will all continue to give affordable green pleasure.

151	£5.49	MUSCADET DE SEVRE ET MAINE, GUY BOSSARD 1992 Loire (F)
166	£8.75	TERRES BLANCHES BLANC, AIX EN PROVENCE LES BAUX, NOEL MICHELIN 1992 Midi (F)
217	£4.87	CORBIERES, CHATEAU DE CARAGUILHES, LION FAIVRE 1991 Midi (F)
340	£5.99	COTES DU RHONE, DOMAINE ST. APOLLINAIRE, CUVEE CEPAGE SYRAH, FREDERIC DAUMAS 1990 Rhône (F)

P	Parfrements

68 Cecily Road, Cheylesmore, Coventry, West Midlands CV3 5LA (Tel 0203 503646 Fax 0203 506028). **Opening Hours:** 24-hour answerphone. **Delivery:** nationally at cost. **Tastings:** regular in-store and tutored tastings, plus wine club.

Gerald Gregory has recently reduced his prices by 20% – but introduced a quantity-linked delivery charge, 'penalising clients who only buy one case of plonk'. Mr G's quite right; life's too short! Just think, customers could be imbibing '89 Lastours Corbières, '85 Bannockburn Shiraz,' '92 Jackson Estate Sauvignon. However, those on a tighter budget should check out Mr G's perfectly respectable 'everyday wines'.

54	£6.44	MONTES UNOAKED CHARDONNAY, DISCOVER WINES LTDA 1993 Curico (Ch)
57	£7.06	CHABLIS, LOUIS ALEXANDRE 1992 Burgundy (F)
133	£3.22	NOGALES SAUVIGNON BLANC, DISCOVER WINES LTDA 1993 Curico (Ch)

161	£7.90	JACKSON ESTATE SAUVIGNON BLANC 1992 Marlborough (NZ)
250	£4.88	STAMBOLOVO RESERVE MERLOT 1987 (Bul)
335	£5.98	COTES DU RHONE DOMAINE DE TERRE BRULEE, CAVE DE VIGNERONS DE RASTEAU 1990 Rhône (F)
429	£10.27	BAROLO RISERVA, BORGOGNO 1985 Piedmont (It)

THP | Thos Peatling

Westgate Street, Bury St Edmunds, Suffolk IP33 1QS (Tel 0284 755948 Fax 0284 705795). **Opening Hours:** variable. **Delivery:** free locally. **Tastings:** regular in-store and tutored events. **Discounts:** 5% and up per case.

Bordeaux Merchant of the Year

The wonderful glazed look on the face of the sunflower, bottle in one hand, glass in the other, on the cover of the Summer list implies he has first-hand experience of the superb Bordeaux selection that won Thos Peatling its award. Mind you, this company might have won several other prizes – for its other wines, its beautiful old shops and the quality of the service offered within them. Quite simply, Thos Peatling is a first-class traditional merchant with an up-to-the-minute range of wines.

11	£6.99	MONTANA LINDAUER BRUT (NZ)
24	£9.99	GREEN POINT, DOMAINE CHANDON 1990 Yarra Valley (Aus)
33	£29.99	BOLLINGER GRANDE ANNEE 1985 Champagne (F)
45	£4.95	NOBILO WHITE CLOUD 1992 (NZ)
62	£7.25	MACON VIRE L'ARRIVE VIEILLES VIGNES, CAVES COOPERATIVE A. SARJEANT 1988 Burgundy (F)
99	£9.99	KRONDORF SHOW RESERVE CHARDONNAY 1991 Barossa Valley (Aus)
244	£2.99	RUSSE CABERNET CINSAULT (Bul)
250	£3.99	STAMBOLOVO RESERVE MERLOT 1987 (Bul)
264	£5.35	BUZET TRADITION, LES VIGNERONS DE BUZET 1988 South West (F)
269	£4.99	MONTANA CABERNET SAUVIGNON 1991 Marlborough (NZ)
288	£7.75	CABERNET SAUVIGNON, BODEGA Y CAVAS DE WEINERT 1985 Mendoza (Arg)
291	£7.99	CHATEAU LA TOUR HAUT-CAUSSAN, MEDOC 1989 Bordeaux (F)
308	£11.55	CHATEAU CANTERMERLE, HAUT MEDOC 1987 Bordeaux (F)
319	£13.99	CHATEAU LASCOMBES, MARGAUX 1988 Bordeaux (F)
320	£21.99	CHATEAU PICHON LONGUEVILLE BARON, PAUILLAC 1990 Bordeaux (F)
322	£24.99	CHATEAU LYNCH-BAGES, PAUILLAC 1989 Bordeaux (F)
346	£8.55	CHATEAU MUSAR, 1986 Bekaa Valley (Leb)
424	£7.89	DOLCETTO D'ALBA CORSINI, MASCARELLO 1991 Piedmont (It)
429	£11.15	BAROLO RISERVA, BORGOGNO 1985 Piedmont (It)
483	£9.99	1796 RICH OLD OLOROSO Jerez (Sp)
484	£18.99	MATUSALEM, GONZALEZ BYASS Jerez (Sp)
496	£5.99	TAYLOR'S TEN YEAR OLD TAWNY Douro (P)

PHI | Philglas & Swiggot

21 Northcote Rd, London SW11 1NG (Tel 071-924 4494 Fax 071-585 0049). **Opening Hours:** Tues-Sat 10am-9.30pm. Sun 12-3pm, 7pm-9pm. Mon 5pm-9.30pm. **Delivery:** free within 4 miles. **Tastings:** regular in-store plus tutored events. **Discounts:** 5% per mixed case.

This whacky specialist has Battersea buzzing. Mike & Karen Rogers seek out value wines from the Antipodes – and from 'Old World producers breaking with tradition to create quality wines' in regions like Languedoc Roussillon.

If they don't suit, you can drown your sorrows in a magnum of '86 Demoiselle de Sociando-Mallet for £12.99, even on a Sunday.

24	£10.50	GREEN POINT, DOMAINE CHANDON 1990 Yarra Valley (Aus)
46	£4.75	CHARDONNAY DEL PIEMONTE, ARALDICA 1992 Piedmont (It)
53	£5.65	'CASAL DI SERRA' VERDICCHIO CLASSICO, DOC, UMANI RONCHI 1991 Marches (It)
57	£6.99	CHABLIS, LOUIS ALEXANDRE 1992 Burgundy (F)
77	£4.55	SALISBURY ESTATE CHARDONNAY 1992 S.E. Australia (Aus)
99	£9.99	KRONDORF SHOW RESERVE CHARDONNAY 1991 Barossa Valley (Aus)
144	£4.99	COTEAUX DE LANGUEDOC PICPOUL DE PINET, DUC DE MORNY 1991 Midi (F)
155	£6.99	ROTHBURY SAUVIGNON BLANC 1992 Marlborough (NZ)
160	£6.99	GROVE MILL SAUVIGNON 1992 Blenheim (NZ)
169	£8.99	HUNTERS MARLBOROUGH SAUVIGNON BLANC 1992 Marlborough (NZ)
182	£6.99	GEWURZTRAMINER D'ALSACE, CAVE VINICOLE DE TURCKHEIM 1992 ALSACE (F)
238	£6.55	CHATEAU DE LASTOURS CORBIERES, FUT DE CHENE 1989 Midi (F)
272	£5.75	ROUGE HOMME CABERNET/SHIRAZ, COONAWARRA 1988 Coonawarra (Aus)
303	£11.99	PETALUMA COONAWARRA RED 1988 Coonawarra (Aus)
305	£13.50	CYRIL HENSCHKE CABERNET SAUVIGNON, STEPHEN HENSCHKE 1988 Adelaide Hills (Aus)
424	£8.99	DOLCETTO D'ALBA CORSINI, MASCARELLO 1991 Piedmont (It)
425	£8.99	LE SASSINE, LE RAGOSE 1988 Veneto (It)
438	£3.99	ALBOR RIOJA TINTO, BODEGAS & BEBIDAS 1991 Rioja (Sp)
450	£7.50	YLLERA, VINO DE MESA, SAT LOS CURRO 1988 Ribera del Duero (Sp)
461	£5.75	STANTON & KILLEEN RUTHERGLEN LIQUEUR MUSCAT Rutherglen (Aus)
462	£5.99	CAMPBELLS RUTHERGLEN LIQUEUR MUSCAT Rutherglen (Aus)
484	£16.99	MATUSALEM, GONZALEZ BYASS Jerez (Sp)
488	£7.55	OLD TRAFFORD TAWNY, B. SEPPELT & SONS S.E. Australia (Aus)
495	£15.99	GALWAY PIPE OLD TAWNY, YALUMBA WINERY Barossa Valley (Aus)

CPW | Christopher Piper Wines Ltd

1 Silver St, Ottery St Mary, Devon EX11 1DB (Tel 0404 814139 Fax 0404 812100). **Opening Hours:** Mon-Fri 8.30am-1pm, 2-6pm. Sat 9am-1pm, 2.30-7pm. **Delivery:** free nationally for over 6 cases; free per case within 20 miles; free in the south-west for over 3 cases, otherwise nationally at cost. **Tastings:** regular in-store and tutored tastings. **Discounts:** various.

The King is dead! Beaujolais enthusiast (he even makes the stuff), Christopher Piper has parted company with Georges Duboeuf, and now stocks a great range of domaine-bottled alternatives. The rest of his list is packed with growers from all over the world. Burgundy features Comte Armand, Tollot Beaut and Sauzet, while his Italian selection features Tenuta dell'Ornellaia and Aldo Conterno. Look out, too, for Piper's new Vins de Pays.

11	£7.58	MONTANA LINDAUER BRUT (NZ)
33	£29.06	BOLLINGER GRANDE ANNEE 1985 Champagne (F)
38	£3.30	VIN DE PAYS DE L'HERAULT BLANC, SKALLI 1992 Midi (F)
74	£2.85H	PENFOLDS KOONUNGA HILL CHARDONNAY, 1992 S.E. Australia (AUS)
85	£8.48	COTES DE BEAUNE, LABOURE-ROI 1991 Burgundy (F)
106	£9.74	EDNA VALLEY CHARDONNAY 1990 Edna Valley (Cal)
110	£11.67	POMINO IL BENEFIZIO, MARCHESI DE FRESCOBALDI 1990 Tuscany (It)
141	£4.84	CUVEE DE CEPAGE SAUVIGNON, DOMAINE DU BREUIL 1992 Loire (F)
156	£5.60	MUSCADET CHATEAU DU CLERAY, SAUVION ET FILS 1992 Loire (F)
160	£6.81	GROVE MILL SAUVIGNON 1992 Blenheim (NZ)
169	£8.83	HUNTERS MARLBOROUGH SAUVIGNON BLANC 1992 Marlborough (NZ)
173	£10.50	POUILLY FUME, TRADITION CULLU, MASSON-BLONDELET 1990 Loire (F)
197	£3.88	BADEN DRY, BADISCHER WINZERKELLER Baden (G)

269	£5.71	MONTANA CABERNET SAUVIGNON 1991 Marlborough (NZ)
321	£21.99	ORNELLAIA 1990 Tuscany (It)
336	£5.69	ZINFANDEL, FETZER VINEYARDS 1990 Mendocino County (Cal)
346	£8.34	CHATEAU MUSAR, BEKAA VALLEY 1986 Bekaa Valley (Leb)
363	£15.26	RIDGE GEYSERVILLE ZINFANDEL 1991 Sonoma (Cal)
365	£13.19	PENFOLDS MAGILL ESTATE SHIRAZ 1988 S. Australia (Aus)
379	£7.69	FLEURIE, CLOS DE LA CHAPELLE DES BOIS, FERNAND VERPOIX 1991 Beaujolais (F)
381	£7.35	CHENAS, LOUIS CHAMPAGNON 1991 Beaujolais (F)
389	£7.49	HAMILTON-RUSSELL PINOT NOIR, 1991 Walker Bay (SA)
393	£9.53	SANCERRE ROUGE, A DEZAT 1990 Loire (F)
394	£9.65	COLDSTREAM HILLS PINOT NOIR 1992 Yarra Valley (Aus)
414	£4.23	DOLCETTO D'ASTI, ARALDICA 1992 Piedmont (It)
415	£4.60	VALPOLICELLA CLASSICO, MASI 1991 Veneto (It)
462	£5.52	CAMPBELLS RUTHERGLEN LIQUEUR MUSCAT Rutherglen (Aus)
489	£9.11	CHURCHILL GRAHAM FINEST VINTAGE CHARACTER Douro (P)
491	£11.48	DOWS CRUSTED PORT BOTTLED 1987 Douro (P)

TP | Terry Platt Wine Merchant

Ferndale Rd, Llandudno Junction, Gwynned LL31 9NT (Tel 0492 592971 Fax 0492 592196). **Opening Hours:** Mon-Fri 8am-5.30pm. **Delivery:** free within 75 miles. **Tastings:** regular in-store and tutored events. **Discounts:** negotiable.

Jeremy Platt's 32-year-old firm offers a straightforward and solid range, with the emphasis on classic French. There are, however, a few newcomers such as Château de Trignon (Gigondas), a Viognier which actually tastes of Viognier, Batasaiolo 's juicy, robust and inexpensive Barbera, Barbaresco and Barolo. and the unusually affordable Napa wines from J Wile.

24	£10.52	GREEN POINT, DOMAINE CHANDON 1990 Yarra Valley (Aus)
33	£26.73	BOLLINGER GRANDE ANNEE 1985 Champagne (F)
78	£5.23	CHARDONNAY BARREL FERMENTED, VINAS DEL VERO, COVISA 1991 Somontano (Sp)
91	£8.21	MARQUES DE MURRIETA RIOJA RESERVA BLANCO 1987 Rioja (Sp)
161	£7.64	JACKSON ESTATE SAUVIGNON BLANC 1992 Marlborough (NZ)
280	£5.86	J WILE & SON CABERNET SAUVIGNON 1987 Napa Valley (Cal)
346	£7.82	CHATEAU MUSAR, 1986 Bekaa Valley (Leb)
483	£9.46	1796 RICH OLD OLOROSO Jerez (Sp)
496	£13.65	TAYLOR'S TEN YEAR OLD TAWNY Douro (P)

PLA | Playford Ros Ltd

Middle Park House, Sowerby, Thirsk YO7 3AH (Tel 0845 526777). **Opening Hours:** Mon-Sat 8am-6pm. **Delivery:** free locally. **Tastings:** tutored. **Discounts:** 5% for cash.

Nigel Munton and Andrew Firth offer Burgundies – including excellent Olivier Leflaives – Trimbach Alsaces, and an array of inexpensive claret. The New World shows careful selection, too, with Klein Constantia, the rare Cloudy Bay Cabernet/Merlot and Pierro Chardonnay. A range of which any Yorkshireman could be proud – as if a Yorkshireman needed a reason.

33	£28.18	BOLLINGER GRANDE ANNEE 1985 Champagne (F)
70	£4.50	TIMARA WHITE, MONTANA 1991 (NZ)
77	£5.23	SALISBURY ESTATE CHARDONNAY 1992 S.E. Australia (Aus)
149	£5.09	ZONNEBLOEM BLANC DE BLANC, STELLENBOSCH FARMERS WINERY 1991 Coastal Region (SA)

266	£5.27	SALISBURY ESTATE CABERNET SAUVIGNON 1991 S.E. Australia (Aus)
288	£8.66	CABERNET SAUVIGNON, BODEGA Y CAVAS DE WEINERT 1985 Mendoza (Arg)
307	£15.62	LEEUWIN ESTATE CABERNET SAUVIGNON 1986 Margaret River (Aus)
346	£7.58	CHATEAU MUSAR, Bekaa Valley 1986 (Leb)
353	£8.72	DAVID WYNN PATRIARCH SHIRAZ 1991 Eden Valley (Aus)
489	£8.48	CHURCHILL GRAHAM FINEST VINTAGE CHARACTER Douro (P)

PON | Le Pont de la Tour

The Butlers Wharf Building, 36D, Shad Thames,, Butlers Wharf, London SE1 2YE (Tel 071-403 2403 Fax 071-403 0267). **Opening Hours:** Mon-Sat 12-8.30pm, Sun 12-3pm. **Delivery:** free locally. **Tastings:** tutored. **Discounts:** 5% per mixed case.

Terence Conran enjoys wine. Pamela Gregory, his wine shop manager enjoys choosing and selling it. As she says, 'The Conran restaurants owe the success of their wine lists to our range of 1,000 wines.' Michelot Nuits St Georges, Dashwood Sauvignon from New Zealand, Château Climens 1983, 1949 and 1928, Vega Sicilia 1968... All commendably Conranish: a combination of style, content and imaginative good taste.

33	£33.50	BOLLINGER GRANDE ANNEE 1985 Champagne (F)
51	£6.45	CHARDONNAY 'VIRGINIE', VIN DE PAYS D'OC, SARL DOMAINE VIRGINIE, LIEURAN 1992 Midi (F)
53	£5.75	'CASAL DI SERRA' VERDICCHIO CLASSICO, DOC, UMANI RONCHI 1991 Marches (It)
65	£13.25	JERMANN PINOT BIANCO 1991 Friuli Venezia Giulia (It)
112	£14.25	ELSTON CHARDONNAY, TE MATA ESTATE 1991 Hawkes Bay (NZ)
123	£23.50	TORRES MILMANDA CHARDONNAY 1991 Penedes (Sp)
171	£9.75	POGGIO ALLE GAZZE, TENUTA DELL'ORNELLAIA 1991 Tuscany (It)
174	£12.75	POUILLY FUME, DE LADOUCETTE 1990 Loire (F)
272	£5.99	ROUGE HOMME CABERNET/SHIRAZ, 1988 Coonawarra (Aus)
299	£10.99	MEERLUST MERLOT, STELLENBOSCH 1986 Stellenbosch (SA)
321	£19.50	ORNELLAIA 1990 Tuscany (It)
352	£9.99	PENLEY ESTATE SHIRAZ/CABERNET SAUVIGNON, Coonawarra 1990 (Aus)
364	£13.95	CHATEAUNEUF DU PAPE, CHATEAU DE BEAUCASTEL 1988 Rhône (F)
387	£9.85	CAMERON PINOT NOIR, Willamette Valley (US)
394	£10.95	COLDSTREAM HILLS PINOT NOIR, 1992 Yarra Valley (Aus)
413	£4.75	MONTEPULCIANO D'ABRUZZO, DOC, UMANI RONCHI 1991 Marches (It)
418	£6.99	VERNACULUM ZOCCOLANTI-PERGOLA, VILLA LIGI 1992 Umbria (It)
422	£8.75	CHIANTI CLASSICO, ISOLE E OLENA, 1990 Tuscany (It)
424	£8.99	DOLCETTO D'ALBA CORSINI, MASCARELLO 1991 Piedmont (It)
443	£4.50	QUINTA DE LA ROSA RED TABLE WINE 1991 Douro (P)
452	£7.25	BARON DE LEY RIOJA RESERVA 1987 Rioja (Sp)
461	£16.00	STANTON & KILLEEN RUTHERGLEN LIQUEUR MUSCAT Rutherglen (Aus)
470	£7.50	MONBAZILLAC, CHATEAU THEULET, SCEA ALARD 1990 Bordeaux (Fr)

POR | The Portland Wine Company

16 North Parade, Sale, Cheshire M33 3JS (Tel 061 962 8752 Fax 061 905 1291). **Opening Hours:** Mon-Sat 10am-10pm, Sun 12-3pm, 7-10pm. **Delivery:** free locally. **Tastings:** tutored events. **Discounts:** 10% per case. 5% per half case.

Geoff Dickinson hasn't been the same since his trip to Australia; apparently he hops everywhere and carries wine in his pouch. His Australian list is exceptional. 40 top wineries including small producers such as Rockford, Allandale, Yarra Yering and (his favourite) Charlie Melton. The Wine Club will allow you to meet (and maybe play cricket with) such Aussie superstar producers as Bob Maclean. Fair drinkum mate.

4	£5.99	NEDERBURG 1ER CUVEE BRUT Paarl (SA)
11	£6.99	MONTANA LINDAUER BRUT (NZ)
20	£7.95	OMAR KHAYYAM, CHAMPAGNE INDIA 1987 Maharashtra India
22	£8.99	MAYERLING CREMANT D'ALSACE, CAVE VINICOLE DE TURCKHEIM Alsace (F)
33	£29.75	BOLLINGER GRANDE ANNEE 1985 CHAMPAGNE (F)
34	£42.95	CHAMPAGNE LOUISE POMMERY VINTAGE ROSE 1988 Champagne (F)
46	£3.99	CHARDONNAY DEL PIEMONTE, ARALDICA 1992 Piedmont (It)
57	£5.99	CHABLIS, LOUIS ALEXANDRE 1992 Burgundy (F)
61	£5.95	LUGANA CA'DEI FRATI 1992 Brescia (It)
64	£8.49	TASMANIAN WINE COMPANY CHARDONNAY, PIPER'S BROOK 1991 Tasmania (Aus)
74	£4.95	PENFOLDS KOONUNGA HILL CHARDONNAY 1992 S.E. Australia (Aus)
79	£5.99	ROSEMOUNT CHARDONNAY 1992 Hunter Valley (Aus)
80	£6.49	CHATEAU REYNELLA STONY HILL CHARDONNAY 1990 S. Australia (Aus)
91	£7.49	MARQUES DE MURRIETA RIOJA RESERVA BLANCO 1987 Rioja (Sp)
104	£8.99	CHARDONNAY, JANE HUNTER'S WINES 1991 Marlborough (NZ)
123	£19.99	TORRES MILMANDA CHARDONNAY 1991 Penedes (Sp)
161	£7.49	JACKSON ESTATE SAUVIGNON BLANC 1992 Marlborough (NZ)
169	£8.39	HUNTERS MARLBOROUGH SAUVIGNON BLANC 1992 Marlborough (NZ)
171	£8.99	POGGIO ALLE GAZZE, TENUTA DELL'ORNELLAIA 1991 Tuscany (It)
182	£6.49	GEWURZTRAMINER D'ALSACE, CAVE VINICOLE DE TURCKHEIM 1992 Alsace (F)
194	£3.59	TOLLANA DRY WHITE 1992 S.E. Australia (Aus)
218	£6.25	MOUNT HURTLE GRENACHE ROSE, GEOFF MERRILL 1992 McLaren Vale (Aus)
237	£5.49	CUVEE MYTHIQUE, VIN DE PAYS D'OC, VAL D'ORBIEU 1990 Midi (F)
238	£6.09	CHATEAU DE LASTOURS CORBIERES, FUT DE CHENE 1989 Midi (F)
266	£4.79	SALISBURY ESTATE CABERNET SAUVIGNON 1991 S.E. Australia (Aus)
269	£4.99	MONTANA CABERNET SAUVIGNON 1991 Marlborough (NZ)
270	£5.95	HARDY'S MOONDAH BROOK ESTATE CABERNET SAUVIGNON 1989 Gingin, W. Australia (Aus)
273	£5.49	TALTARNI FIDDLEBACK TERRACE 1990 Pyrenees (Aus)
298	£8.99	LINDEMANS ST GEORGE CABERNET SAUVIGNON 1989 Coonawarra (Aus)
321	£21.95	ORNELLAIA 1990 Tuscany (It)
326	£3.59	RESPLANDY MOUVEDRE, VIN DE PAYS D'OC, VAL D'ORBIEU 1990 Midi (F)
342	£6.49	PETER LEHMANN 'CLANCY'S RED' 1990 Barossa Valley (Aus)
346	£7.49	CHATEAU MUSAR, 1986 Bekaa Valley (Leb)
348	£7.99	ROSEMOUNT SHOW RESERVE SYRAH 1990 McLaren Vale (Aus)
352	£9.49	PENLEY ESTATE SHIRAZ/CABERNET SAUVIGNON 1990 Coonawarra (Aus)
353	£8.79	DAVID WYNN PATRIARCH SHIRAZ 1991 Eden Valley (Aus)
365	£12.99	PENFOLDS MAGILL ESTATE SHIRAZ 1988 S. Australia (Aus)
389	£6.95	HAMILTON-RUSSELL PINOT NOIR, 1991 Walker Bay (SA)
394	£9.75	COLDSTREAM HILLS PINOT NOIR 1992 Yarra Valley (Aus)
405	£18.49	BEAUNE 1ER CRU EPENOTTES, VALLET FRERES 1989 Burgundy (F)
414	£3.99	DOLCETTO D'ASTI, ARALDICA 1992 Piedmont (It)
422	£7.90	CHIANTI CLASSICO, ISOLE E OLENA 1990 Tuscany (It)
424	£6.99	DOLCETTO D'ALBA CORSINI, MASCARELLO 1991 Piedmont (It)
428	£9.49	BRIC MILEUI, ASCHERI 1990 Piedmont (It)
438	£3.75	ALBOR RIOJA TINTO, BODEGAS & BEBIDAS 1991 Rioja (Sp)
444	£4.19	PERIQUITA, J M DA FONSECA 1990 (P)
445	£5.95	HARDY'S MOONDAH BROOK ESTATE CHENIN BLANC 1992 Gingin, W. Australia (Aus)
447	£5.49	CAMPO VIEJO RIOJA RESERVA 1987 Rioja (Sp)
448	£6.29	CARTUXA, FUNDACO E ALMEIDA 1989 Evora (P)
450	£6.79	YLLERA, VINO DE MESA, SAT LOS CURRO 1988 Ribera del Duero (Sp)
461	£5.75	STANTON & KILLEEN RUTHERGLEN LIQUEUR MUSCAT Rutherglen (Aus)
462	£9.49	CAMPBELLS RUTHERGLEN LIQUEUR MUSCAT Rutherglen (Aus)

482	£10.95	LUSTAU OLD EAST INDIA, EMILIO LUSTAU Jerez (Sp)
488	£7.49	OLD TRAFFORD TAWNY, B. SEPPELT & SONS S.E. Australia (Aus)
491	£9.75	DOWS CRUSTED PORT BOTTLED 1987 Douro (P)
494	£12.95	WARRE'S TRADITIONAL LBV 1981 Douro (P)

PMR   Premier Wine Warehouse

3 Heathmans Rd, London SW6 4TJ (Tel 071-736 9073). **Opening Hours:** Mon-Fri 9am-7.30pm Sat 10am-5.30pm. **Delivery:** free locally. **Tastings:** regular in-store tastings; tutored events on request. **Discounts:** various.

This Fulham wine warehouse is within spitting distance of the bureau where Frankie MacJago, the genius son of the man who invented Bailey's Irish Cream, turns our computer discs into printing film. And Premier really is a wine warehouse – like Majestic used to be, with an ever-changing range of South Africans, Spaniards and southern French wines. Ignore the list which concentrates on the core selection; just pop down the Parson's Green side street – you might even find a Premier Grand Cru.

78	£5.49	CHARDONNAY BARREL FERMENTED, VINAS DEL VERO, COVISA 1991 Somontano (Sp)
79	£5.75	ROSEMOUNT CHARDONNAY 1992 Hunter Valley (Aus)
189	£7.95	LAGAR DE CERVERA, RIAS BAIXAS, LAGAR DE FORNELOSSA 1992 Galicia (Sp)
462	£5.50	CAMPBELLS RUTHERGLEN LIQUEUR MUSCAT Rutherglen (Aus)

PRW   Protea Wines

7a Chesson Road, London W14 9QR (Tel 071-386 7319). **Delivery:** free locally. **Tastings:** occasionally.

A far cry from the pinstripes of St James's, Greg Howard sits in a sports locker-like office in a Springbok top, and dispenses advice about rugby, beer and wine to anyone who will listen. His wine list proves his expertise on one of those subjects. A *Who's Who* of top Cape wineries, it also contains information about climate, geography, grape varities, and appellation laws – a veritable 'bluffer's guide' to this increasingly popular subject.

| 389 | £8.21 | HAMILTON-RUSSELL PINOT NOIR, 1991 Walker Bay (SA) |

PUG   Pugsons of Buxton

Cliff House, 6 Terrace Road, Buxton, Derbyshire SK17 6DR (Tel 0298 77696 Fax 0298 72381). **Opening Hours:** Mon-Sat 9am-5.30pm, Sun 11am-3pm. **Delivery:** free within 10 miles. **Tastings:** tutored, plus organised events. **Discounts:** 5% per mixed case.

'If we were just a wine shop we'd be broke by now,' says Peter Pugson, who attributes his survival to his cheeses and believes small independents have to rely on the best mix of products they can offer. He has recently employed the skills of wine and food expert Debbie Lush to run tutored tastings – including, we hope, such combinations as Marie Claire Robler's crisp '90 Pouilly-sur-Loire and a Dovedale Blue or a Crottin de Chavignol.

| 161 | £6.95 | JACKSON ESTATE SAUVIGNON BLANC 1992 Marlborough (NZ) |

R	R S Wines

32 Vicarage Road, Southville, Bristol, Avon BS3 1PD (Tel 0272 631780 Fax 0272 533797). **Opening Hours:** Mon-Fri 9am-5pm. **Delivery:** free locally. **Tastings:** tutored.

It's easy for wine merchants to stock the likes of Château la Jaubertie, Hardy's and Marqués de Cáceres, but R S also stocks rare delights such as Domaine Bourillon d'Orléans Vouvray, Maroslavac Leger Burgundy and Blewitt Springs Shiraz. And if you're still curious, you could always try the rare 1970 Colares from Antonio Bernardino Paulo da Silva.

80	£6.50	CHATEAU REYNELLA STONY HILL CHARDONNAY 1990 S. Australia (Aus)
91	£7.25	MARQUES DE MURRIETA RIOJA RESERVA BLANCO 1987 Rioja (Sp)
146	£4.50	HARDY'S MOONDAH BROOK ESTATE CHENIN BLANC 1992 Gingin, Western Australia (Aus)
152	£6.40	DOMAINE DE GRANDCHAMP BERGERAC SAUVIGNON BLANC 1992 South West (F)
256	£4.40	HARDYS NOTTAGE HILL CABERNET SAUVIGNON, BRL HARDY WINE CO 1991 S. Australia (Aus)
270	£4.50	HARDY'S MOONDAH BROOK ESTATE CABERNET SAUVIGNON 1989 Gingin, W. Australia (Aus)
281	£6.00	CHATEAU BONNET OAK AGED, A LURTON 1990 Bordeaux (F)
288	£6.95	CABERNET SAUVIGNON, BODEGA Y CAVAS DE WEINERT 1985 Mendoza (Arg)
346	£7.30	CHATEAU MUSAR 1986 Bekaa Valley (Leb)
348	£8.25	ROSEMOUNT SHOW RESERVE SYRAH 1990 McLaren Vale (Aus)
370	£13.70	YARRA YERING SHIRAZ NO.20 1990 Yarra Valley (Aus)

RAE	Raeburn Fine Wines

21/23 Comely Bank Road, Edinburgh, EH4 1DS (Tel 031-332 5166 Fax 031- 332 5166). **Opening Hours:** Mon-Sat 9am-6pm. **Delivery:** free locally. **Tastings:** tutored and organised events. **Discounts:** 2.5% per case. 5% per mixed case.

Scotland Merchant of the Year

'These you have loved' ought to be Zubair Mohamed's theme. His original grocers shop and new outlet somehow contain one of the most impressive, diverse and fascinating ranges in the country, from the the greatest and rarest, to obscure wines you never thought you'd see again. Burgundy is a passion followed by Bordeaux, the Rhône and a number of European-style Californians Zubair imports himself.

24	£9.99	GREEN POINT, DOMAINE CHANDON 1990 Yarra Valley (Aus)
236	£5.99	COTEAUX DU LANGUEDOC, DOMAINE DE L'HORTUS, JEAN ORLIAC 1991 South West (F)
444	£4.99	PERIQUITA, J M DA FONSECA 1990 (P)
461	£9.99	STANTON & KILLEEN RUTHERGLEN LIQUEUR MUSCAT Rutherglen (Aus)
484	£18.75	MATUSALEM, GONZALEZ BYASS Jerez (Sp)
497	£16.50	NIEPOORT COLHEITA 1983 Douro (P)

RAM	The Ramsbottom Victuallers Co Ltd

16-18 Market Place, Ramsbottom, Bury, Lancashire BL0 9HT (Tel 0706 825070). **Opening Hours:** Tues-Fri 10.30am-9pm, Sat 10.30am-5pm, Sun 12-3pm. **Delivery:** free locally. **Tastings:** regular in-store and tutored, plus organised events. **Discounts:** 5% per case.

This is not a food guide, so we won't mention the homemade cassoulet, aromatic capers on their stems (!), Loch Fyne Eels, three dozen single estate olive oils, English cheeses and French chutneys but move instead directly to the 850 wines covering just about every region imaginable. Paret's Burgundies, Clos de L'Arbalestrier organic St Joseph, Ch. Pibarnon from Bandol, seven wines from Zind Humbrecht, and, for lovers of stickies, the '88 Domaine Castéra 100% Petit Manseng and the late harvest '90 Pouilly Fumé (Didier Paboit). For those faithful to the cause, there are two dozen English wines – all the more extraordinary, when you learn that Chris Johnson, the man behind it all, is teetotal.

77	£4.55	SALISBURY ESTATE CHARDONNAY 1992 S.E. Australia (Aus)
91	£7.95	MARQUES DE MURRIETA RIOJA RESERVA BLANCO 1987 Rioja (Sp)
98	£8.59	LOCAL GROWERS SEMILLON, ROCKFORD 1989 Barossa Valley (Aus)
115	£17.15	NEWTON UNFILTERED CHARDONNAY 1990 Napa Valley (Cal)
161	£7.50	JACKSON ESTATE SAUVIGNON BLANC 1992 Marlborough (NZ)
176	£5.45	THAMES VALLEY VINEYARDS SWEET LEA 1990 Berkshire (UK)
186	£14.60	TOKAY PINOT GRIS VIELLES VIGNES, DOMAINE ZIND HUMBRECHT 1990 Alsace (F)
236	£5.99	COTEAUX DU LANGUEDOC, DOMAINE DE L'HORTUS, JEAN ORLIAC 1991 South West (F)
266	£5.65	SALISBURY ESTATE CABERNET SAUVIGNON 1991 S.E. Australia (Aus)
323	£38.50	CHATEAU COS D'ESTOURNEL, ST ESTEPHE 1982 Bordeaux (F)
400	£12.95	NEUDORF VINEYARDS MOUTERE PINOT NOIR 1991 Nelson (NZ)
414	£4.85	DOLCETTO D'ASTI, ARALDICA 1992 Piedmont (It)
422	£8.75	CHIANTI CLASSICO, ISOLE E OLENA 1990 Tuscany (It)
450	£6.89	YLLERA, VINO DE MESA, SAT LOS CURRO 1988 Ribera del Duero (Sp)
461	£10.89	STANTON & KILLEEN RUTHERGLEN LIQUEUR MUSCAT Rutherglen (Aus)
462	£5.75	CAMPBELLS RUTHERGLEN LIQUEUR MUSCAT Rutherglen (Aus)
489	£4.99H	CHURCHILL GRAHAM FINEST VINTAGE CHARACTER Douro (P)

RAV | Ravensbourne Wine

602 Bell House, 49 Greenwich High Road, London SE10 8JL (Tel 081-692 9655 Fax 081-692 9655). **Opening Hours:** Mon-Fr 9am-5pm, Sat 10am-1pm. **Delivery:** free within Greater London. **Tastings:** regular in-store and tutored, plus organised events. **Discounts:** 5% per case.

In the 1980s, 'bespoke' was an over-used synonym for 'expensive', so we don't know why these Welsh ex-pats describe themselves as 'independent bespoke vintners'. They offer a wide selection of fairly priced, lesser known, French regionals, such as Pécharmant and Picpoul de Pinet. They also refer to their excellent tutored tastings as 'wine workshop roadshows' – obviously over-elaborate phrasing is a little indulgence.

11	£7.49	MONTANA LINDAUER BRUT (NZ)
70	£4.25	TIMARA WHITE, MONTANA 1991 (NZ)
151	£6.25	MUSCADET DE SEVRE ET MAINE, GUY BOSSARD 1992 Loire (F)
160	£6.81	GROVE MILL SAUVIGNON 1992 Blenheim (NZ)
197	£3.85	BADEN DRY, BADISCHER WINZERKELLER Baden (G)
269	£5.29	MONTANA CABERNET SAUVIGNON 1991 Marlborough (NZ)
272	£5.25	ROUGE HOMME CABERNET/SHIRAZ, COONAWARRA 1988 Coonawarra (Aus)
278	£5.85	GOUNDREY LANGTON CABERNET/MERLOT 1991 Mount Barker (Aus)
346	£7.95	CHATEAU MUSAR 1986 Bekaa Valley (Leb)
439	£4.39	BORBA, ADEGA CO-OPERATIVA DE BORBA 1991 Douro (P)
443	£3.99	QUINTA DE LA ROSA RED TABLE WINE 1991 Douro (P)
487	£8.45	TOKAJI ASZU 3 PUTTONYOS, TOKAJI-HEGYALA SCHLUMBERGER 1981 Tokaji (Hun)

RD	Reid Wines (1992) Ltd

The Mill, Marsh Lane, Hallatrow, Nr Bristol, Avon BS18 5EB (Tel 0761 452645 Fax 0761 453642).
Opening Hours: Mon-Fri 10.30am-6pm or strictly by appointment. **Delivery:** free within 25 miles and central London. **Tastings:** regular in-store and tutored tastings.

Reid's list is getting longer and the quotations more amusing. Bill Baker kicks off by recommending 'what's good for us': value-for-money wines such as Dom de Meinjarre Madiran and Brumont's Bouscassé white. Further on there are JC Dageneau, Coche Dury, Bonny Doon, Avignonesi (try the '88 I Grifi) and some of the best fine & rare wines in the country; now's the time to order your '45 Bonnezeaux, Réné Lalou. New listings among Baker's dozens include Wairau River (NZ) and Francis Ford Coppola's Niebaum Coppola.

51	£6.00	CHARDONNAY 'VIRGINIE', VIN DE PAYS D'OC, SARL DOMAINE VIRGINIE LIEURAN 1992 Midi (F)
53	£6.05	'CASAL DI SERRA' VERDICCHIO CLASSICO, DOC, UMANI RONCHI 1991 Marches (It)
123	£22.61	TORRES MILMANDA CHARDONNAY 1991 Penedes (Sp)
157	£6.63	LUGANA SANTA CRISTINA, VIGNETO MASSONI 1991 Lombardy (It)
159	£7.05	SAUVIGNON BLANC, VILLIERA 1992 Paarl (SA)
168	£9.40	SANCERRE LES ROCHES, DOMAINE VACHERON 1992 Loire (F)
171	£9.69	POGGIO ALLE GAZZE, TENUTA DELL'ORNELLAIA 1991 Tuscany (It)
240	£9.69	MADIRAN, MONTUS, ALAIN BRUMONT 1990 South West (F)
273	£5.99	TALTARNI FIDDLEBACK TERRACE 1990 Pyrenees (Aus)
288	£9.34	CABERNET SAUVIGNON, BODEGA Y CAVAS DE WEINERT 1985 Mendoza (Arg)
321	£22.50	ORNELLAIA 1990 Tuscany (It)
346	£8.22	CHATEAU MUSAR 1986 Bekaa Valley (Leb)
357	£10.39	QUPE SYRAH, BOB LINDQUIST 1991 Central Coast (Cal)
369	£17.03	JADE MOUNTAIN SYRAH, DOUGLAS DANIELAK 1990 Sonoma (Cal)
422	£8.50	CHIANTI CLASSICO, ISOLE E OLENA 1990 Tuscany (It)
424	£7.63	DOLCETTO D'ALBA CORSINI, MASCARELLO 1991 Piedmont (It)
427	£10.56	CUMARO ROSSO CONERO, UMANI RONCHI 1989 Marches (It)
462	£11.16	CAMPBELLS RUTHERGLEN LIQUEUR MUSCAT Rutherglen (Aus)
468	£6.46H	NELSON LATE HARVEST RHINE RIESLING, SEIFRIED 1991 Nelson (NZ)

RES	La Reserve

56 Walton Street, London SW3 1RB (Tel 07- 589 2020 Fax 071-581 0250). **Opening Hours:** Mon-Sat 9.30am-9pm. **Delivery:** free within 5 miles. **Tastings:** regular in-store and tutored tastings. **Discounts:** 5% or an extra bottle per case.

Five siblings, each with its own separate identity and personality, thanks to the freedom each manager has when buying wine. There is a standard list shared by the whole family, though, including interesting wines from 'just outside' appellations such as the '91 Bourgogne Blanc from Sauzet and the '90 Cuvée Rouge Gorge, from Domaine de Pegau in Châteauneuf. For top-flight, old and rare wines, La Reserve is clearly the favoured son.

RIB | Ribble Vintners Ltd

93-97 Lancaster Road, Preston, Lancashire PR1 2QJ (Tel 0772 884866 Fax 0772 884760). **Opening Hours:** Mon-Sat 10 am-6pm. **Delivery:** free within 20 miles.. **Tastings:** regular in-house and tutored and organised events. **Discounts:** 5% per case.

Thank goodness H Roche & Co survived the recession. We'd certainly mourn the loss of one of the most exciting, innovative lists in the country and the absence of the Big H's fascinating and witty ditties. Due to public demand, wines are now merchandised according to predominant grape variety and style rather than by country. An interesting way to compare styles and producers.

45	£4.39	NOBILO WHITE CLOUD 1992 (NZ)
64	£7.99	TASMANIAN WINE COMPANY CHARDONNAY, PIPER'S BROOK 1991 Tasmania (Aus)
91	£6.99	MARQUES DE MURRIETA RIOJA RESERVA BLANCO 1987 Rioja (Sp)
93	£8.30	SEMILLON, STEPHEN HENSCHKE 1991 Adelaide Hills (Aus)
115	£12.50	NEWTON UNFILTERED CHARDONNAY 1990 Napa Valley (Cal)
119	£15.29	ROBERT MONDAVI RESERVE CHARDONNAY 1988 Napa Valley (Cal)
123	£21.25	TORRES MILMANDA CHARDONNAY 1991 Penedes (Sp)
158	£7.95	MUSCADET CLOS DE LA SABLETTE, MARCEL MARTIN 1990 Loire (F)
162	£7.50	SELAKS MARLBOROUGH SAUVIGNON BLANC 1991 Marlborough (NZ)
172	£9.99	SANCERRE MD, H. BOURGEOIS 1991 Loire (F)
174	£12.50	POUILLY FUME, DE LADOUCETTE 1990 Loire (F)
189	£7.59	LAGAR DE CERVERA, RIAS BAIXAS, LAGAR DE FORNELOSSA 1992 Galicia (Sp)
272	£5.49	ROUGE HOMME CABERNET/SHIRAZ, COONAWARRA 1988 Coonawarra (Aus)
282	£6.50	VALLEY OAKS CABERNET SAUVIGNON, FETZER VINEYARDS 1990 Mendocino County (Cal)
293	£9.49	THE ANGELUS CABERNET SAUVIGNON, WIRRA WIRRA 1991 S. Australia (Aus)
304	£10.99	LES FIEFS DE LAGRANGE, ST JULIEN 1989 Bordeaux (F)
305	£11.50	CYRIL HENSCHKE CABERNET SAUVIGNON, STEPHEN HENSCHKE 1988 Adelaide Hills (Aus)
309	£11.50	NEWTON MERLOT 1990 Napa Valley (Cal)
336	£4.99	ZINFANDEL, FETZER VINEYARDS 1990 Mendocino County (Cal)
344	£7.85	CROZES HERMITAGE LA PETITE RUCHE, CHAPOUTIER 1991 Rhône (F)
346	£6.99	CHATEAU MUSAR 1986 BEKAA VALLEY (LEB)
353	£8.99	DAVID WYNN PATRIARCH SHIRAZ 1991 Eden Valley (Aus)
358	£13.95	FROG'S LEAP ZINFANDEL 1990 Napa Valley (Cal)
389	£6.99	HAMILTON-RUSSELL PINOT NOIR, 1991 Walker Bay (SA)
398	£10.50	MONTHELIE, JAFFELIN 1990 Burgundy (F)
404	£9.49	ROBERT MONDAVI RESERVE PINOT NOIR 1988 Napa Valley (Cal)
450	£6.99	YLLERA, VINO DE MESA, SAT LOS CURRO 1988 Ribera del Duero (Sp)
462	£5.75	CAMPBELLS RUTHERGLEN LIQUEUR MUSCAT Rutherglen (Aus)
494	£9.75	WARRE'S TRADITIONAL LBV 1981 Douro (P)

RWW | Richmond Wine Warehouse

138 Lower Mortlake Rd, Richmond, Surrey TW9 3JZ (Tel 081-948 4196 Fax 081-332 1061). **Opening Hours:** Mon-Sat 10am-7pm. **Delivery:** free locally. **Tastings:** regular in-store. **Discounts:** negotiable.

This is Stephen Addy's 10th year at his converted school, and he's become very popular with his classmates, especially on Saturdays which is 'free tasting day'. He's obviously been studying French, judging by the number of super Bordeaux, Burgundies and French country wines at far from extortionate prices (we spotted the juicy, smoky '90 Domaine des Anges at

£4.99). He's good at geography, too, as the rest of the world, from Australia to Chile, is equally well represented. Top marks.

RWC	Rioja Wine Co Ltd

Argoed House, Llanfwrog, Ruthin, Clwyd LL15 1LG (Tel 0824 703407 Fax 0824 703407)
Opening Hours: 'all hours'. **Delivery:** free nationally. **Tastings:** regular in-store and tutored, plus organised events. **Discounts:** wholsesale prices.

The opening of Roy Mottram-Smale's wine warehouse announced last year was unfortunately, but not surprisingly, postponed. Instead he managed to acquire a second outlet in the West Midlands. Although still a specialist in Iberia, he has recently added to his portfolio several single property French country wines of a quality rarely found in Spain.

113	£9.35	PULIGNY MONTRACHET, DOMAINE LOUIS CARILLON ET FILS 1991 Burgundy (F)
147	£5.99	CASABLANCA WHITE LABEL SAUVIGNON BLANC 1992 (Ch)
153	£5.85	MARQUES DE ALELLA CLASSICO 1992 Alella (Sp)
189	£7.63	LAGAR DE CERVERA, RIAS BAIXAS, LAGAR DE FORNELLOSSA 1992 Galicia (Sp)
326	£3.75	RESPLANDY MOUVEDRE, VIN DE PAYS D'OC, VAL D'ORBIEU 1990 Midi (F)
444	£4.29	PERIQUITA, J M DA FONSECA 1990 (P)
484	£19.89	MATUSALEM, GONZALEZ BYASS Jerez (Sp)

HR	Howard Ripley Fine French Wines

35 Eversley Crescent, London N21 1EL (Tel 081-360 8904 Fax 081-360 8904). **Opening Hours:** Mon-Sat 8am-10pm, Sun 8am-12noon. **Delivery:** free within 5 miles. **Tastings:** tutored events.

Burgundy Specialist of the Year

For Burgundy lovers only. Mr Ripley's appraisal of the '91 vintage (for red) is 'from the more or less good to the superb...each vineyard is particularly well expressed.' This he demonstrates in his latest offerings from Rousseau, Dom. Leroy, which is 'currently outscoring DRC', Dujac and more recently Roumier and Dom Comte Senard (a traditional, big, dark, long-lived style made by the controversial Méthode Accad). For the uninitiated, why not start with the £7.50 '88 Bourgogne from Dom de L'Arlot, which is really the declassified 1er cru Clos de Forêts.

124	£25.85	NUITS ST GEORGES CLOS DE L'ARLOT BLANC, DOMAINE DE L'ARLOT 1990 Burgundy (F)
403	£12.92	NUITS SAINT GEORGES, DOMAINE DE L'ARLOT 1990 Burgundy (F)
407	£21.50	GEVREY CHAMBERTIN, DOMAINE ALAIN BURGUET, VIEILLES VIGNES 1988 Burgundy (F)
408	£22.32	NUITS ST GEORGES 'CLOS DE L'ARLOT', DOMAINE DE L'ARLOT 1988 Burgundy (F)

WRB	Robbs of Hexham

48 Fore Street, Hexham, Northumberland NE46 1NA (Tel 0434 607396). **Opening Hours:** Mon-Thurs 9am-5pm, Fri 9am-7pm, Sat 9am-5.30pm. **Delivery:** free locally. **Tastings:** for customers' club. **Discounts:** 5% per case (10% for club members).

David Hollingsworth likes Australia – and wines like the fat strawberries 'n' tar '91 Penfolds Shiraz/Mataro (£4.79) and the huge St Hugo Cabernet

Sauvignon '88 (£8.95). We'd have liked to have seen a few more whites which weren't made of Chardonnay, but were delighted to discover the zesty Kiwi '91 Vidal Sauvignon.

11	£7.75	MONTANA LINDAUER BRUT (NZ)
74	£5.29	PENFOLDS KOONUNGA HILL CHARDONNAY 1992 S.E. Australia (Aus)
154	£5.99	VERDELHO, WYNDHAM ESTATE 1991 S.E. Australia (Aus)
194	£3.15	TOLLANA DRY WHITE 1992 S.E. Australia (Aus)
269	£5.49	MONTANA CABERNET SAUVIGNON 1991 Marlborough (NZ)
296	£7.39	CHATEAU TOUR DU HAUT MOULIN, HAUT MEDOC 1985 Bordeaux (F)

RBS | Roberson Wine Merchant

348 Kensington High Street, London W14 8NS (Tel 071-371 2121 Fax 071-371 4010). **Opening Hours:** Mon-Sat 10am-8pm, Sun 12-3pm. **Delivery:** free locally. **Tastings:** regular in-store and tutored. **Discounts:** 5% per cases. negotiable on large orders.

Besieged by the new puritanism, it's nice to see those flamboyant cavaliers Cliff Roberson and Chris Donaldson holding out in their sumptuous Kensington palace. But this is definitely not a case of all style and no content – their massive list, with nine pages of Bordeaux alone, reads like a *Who's Who* of the best wine producers in the world. The only problem is choosing a bottle from this incredible range and still getting to dinner before the other guests have gone home.

11	£7.35	MONTANA LINDAUER BRUT (NZ)
17	£8.95	BOUVET LADUBAY SAUMUR BRUT Loire (F)
19	£8.75	CHAPIN ROSE, SAUMUR, CHAPIN & LANDAIS Loire (F)
24	£10.75	GREEN POINT, DOMAINE CHANDON 1990 Yarra Valley (Aus)
25	£12.95	CROSER METHODE TRADITIONNELLE, PETALUMA WINERY 1990 Adelaide Hills (Aus)
33	£29.95	BOLLINGER GRANDE ANNEE 1985 CHAMPAGNE (F)
34	£38.00	CHAMPAGNE LOUISE POMMERY VINTAGE ROSE 1988 Champagne (F)
78	£5.85	CHARDONNAY BARREL FERMENTED, VINAS DEL VERO, COVISA 1991 Somontano (Sp)
106	£10.50	EDNA VALLEY CHARDONNAY 1990 Edna Valley (Cal)
151	£4.95	MUSCADET DE SEVRE ET MAINE, GUY BOSSARD 1992 Loire (F)
174	£12.75	POUILLY FUME, DE LADOUCETTE 1990 Loire (F)
238	£7.75	CHATEAU DE LASTOURS CORBIERES, FUT DE CHENE 1989 Midi (F)
272	£5.75	ROUGE HOMME CABERNET/SHIRAZ, COONAWARRA 1988 Coonawarra (Aus)
282	£6.95	VALLEY OAKS CABERNET SAUVIGNON, FETZER VINEYARDS 1990 Mendocino County (Cal)
288	£7.45	CABERNET SAUVIGNON, BODEGA Y CAVAS DE WEINERT 1985 Mendoza (Arg)
303	£11.50	PETALUMA COONAWARRA RED 1988 Coonawarra (Aus)
311	£18.95	CHATEAU CISSAC, HAUT-MEDOC 1982 Bordeaux (F)
346	£8.50	CHATEAU MUSAR 1986 Bekaa Valley (Leb)
364	£17.50	CHATEAUNEUF DU PAPE, CHATEAU DE BEAUCASTEL 1988 Rhône (F)
389	£7.65	HAMILTON-RUSSELL PINOT NOIR, 1991 Walker Bay (SA)
429	£10.95	BAROLO RISERVA, BORGOGNO 1985 Piedmont (It)
444	£4.95	PERIQUITA, J M DA FONSECA 1990 (P)
450	£7.85	YLLERA, VINO DE MESA, SAT LOS CURRO 1988 Ribera del Duero (Sp)
462	£5.75	CAMPBELLS RUTHERGLEN LIQUEUR MUSCAT Rutherglen (Aus)
468	£6.50H	NELSON LATE HARVEST RHINE RIESLING, SEIFRIED 1991 Nelson (NZ)
470	£7.95	MONBAZILLAC, CHATEAU THEULET, SCEA ALARD 1990 Bordeaux (F)
484	£19.95	MATUSALEM, GONZALEZ BYASS Jerez (Sp)
495	£14.50	GALWAY PIPE OLD TAWNY, YALUMBA WINERY Barossa Valley (Aus)

RTW | The Rose Tree Wine Co

15 Suffolk Parade, Cheltenham, Gloucestershire GL50 2AE (Tel 0242 583732 Fax 0242 222159). **Opening Hours:** Mon-Fri 9am-7pm, Sat 9am-6pm. **Delivery:** free within 30 miles. **Tastings:** tutored. **Discounts:** 5% per case.

Messrs Brown and Maynard's business has been growing now for six years. Despite having to prune down their pretty pink list during the recession they've discovered wines in South West France and in South Africa (Hamilton Russell Chardonnay and Pinot Noir). Their roots, however, still lie in the *terra firma* of some excellent Bordeaux, Burgundy and Loire.

45	£4.82	**NOBILO WHITE CLOUD 1992 (NZ)**
101	£9.20	**VIEUX CHATEAU GAUBERT, GRAVES 1991 Bordeaux (F)**
112	£13.60	**ELSTON CHARDONNAY, TE MATA ESTATE 1991 Hawkes Bay (NZ)**
182	£6.99	**GEWURZTRAMINER D'ALSACE, CAVE VINICOLE DE TURCKHEIM 1992 Alsace (F)**
197	£4.00	**BADEN DRY, BADISCHER WINZERKELLER Baden (G)**
274	£6.12	**CHATEAU THIEULEY AC BORDEAUX ROUGE 1989 Bordeaux (F)**
285	£6.99	**CHINON, COULY-DUTHEIL 1990 Loire (F)**
292	£7.16	**COLUMBIA CREST MERLOT, STIMSON LANE 1989 Washington State USA**
296	£11.25	**CHATEAU TOUR DU HAUT MOULIN, HAUT MEDOC 1985 Bordeaux (F)**
346	£8.50	**CHATEAU MUSAR 1986 Bekaa Valley (Leb)**
389	£7.60	**HAMILTON-RUSSELL PINOT NOIR, 1991 Walker Bay (SA)**
422	£6.95	**CHIANTI CLASSICO, ISOLE E OLENA 1990 Tuscany (It)**
423	£9.20	**CARMIGNANO, CAPEZZANA 1987 Tuscany (It)**
454	£14.56	**125 ANIVERSARIO NAVARRA GRAN RESERVA, BODEGAS JULIAN CHIVITE 1985 Navarra (Sp)**
498	£22.00	**QUINTA DO VESUVIO VINTAGE PORT 1990 Douro (P)**

R&I | Russell & McIver Ltd

The Rectory, St-Mary-at-Hill, Eastcheap, London EC3R 8EE (Tel 071-283 3575 Fax 071-626 6000). **Opening Hours:** Mon-Fri 9am-5.30pm. **Delivery:** free within London. **Tastings:** regular in-store and tutored tastings. **Discounts:** negotiable.

After more than 125 years as 'wine merchants of the City of London' Russell & McIver has, this year, become associated with Mayor Sworder. While we are sorry to see another excellent firm lose its independence, we can think of few merchants with whom it would be more compatible.

SAC | Le Sac a Vin

See La Reserve

33	£33.50	**BOLLINGER GRANDE ANNEE 1985 Champagne (F)**
43	£3.96	**COTES DE ST MONT WHITE, PLAIMONT 1991 South West (F)**
78	£5.50	**CHARDONNAY BARREL FERMENTED, VINAS DEL VERO, COVISA 1991 Somontano (Sp)**
160	£6.95	**GROVE MILL SAUVIGNON 1992 Blenheim (NZ)**
87	£7.95	**BARREL FERMENTED CHARDONNAY, ROTHBURY ESTATE 1992 Hunter Valley (Aus)**
106	£10.75	**EDNA VALLEY CHARDONNAY 1990 Edna Valley (Cal)**
149	£5.95	**ZONNEBLOEM BLANC DE BLANC, STELLENBOSCH FARMERS WINERY 1991 Coastal Region (SA)**
155	£6.95	**ROTHBURY SAUVIGNON BLANC 1992 Marlborough (NZ)**

162	£6.30	SELAKS MARLBOROUGH SAUVIGNON BLANC 1991 Marlborough (NZ)
174	£12.95	POUILLY FUME, DE LADOUCETTE 1990 Loire (F)
222	£10.95	CHATEAU DE LA GRILLE, CHINON ROSE, A GOSSET 1992 Loire (F)
303	£12.50	PETALUMA COONAWARRA RED 1988 Coonawarra (Aus)
336	£6.50	ZINFANDEL, FETZER VINEYARDS 1990 Mendocino County (Cal)
346	£7.50	CHATEAU MUSAR 1986 Bekaa Valley (Leb)
413	£3.95	MONTEPULCIANO D'ABRUZZO, DOC, UMANI RONCHI 1991 Marches (It)

SAF | Safeway Stores plc

Safeway House, 6 Millington Road, Hayes, Middlesex UB3 4AY (Tel 081-848 8744 Fax 081-756 2910). **Opening Hours:** Mon-Sat 8am-8pm, selected stores Sun 10am-4pm. **Tastings:** occasional organised events. **Discounts:** various.

'The Sainsbury of the '90s'. We hope the Safeway buying team won't take that comment as too back-handed a compliment; it refers to the spirit of innovation so evident in this chain's buying. Sainsbury can congratulate itself on having been the first supermarket to get into Moldova; Safeway acted more dramatically in introducing the fresh Young Vatted Merlot and Cabernet which will be the face of all sorts of new Eastern European wines. There's a good own-label fizz, over a dozen English wines, a growing range of organics, and wine buff fare ranging from Coldstream Hills Pinot to second-label clarets. The only possible complaint is that you may have to go searching to find some of these wines…

6	£6.49	LE GRAND PAVILLON DE BOSCHENDAL, CUVEE BRUT BLANC DE BLANCS Paarl (SA)
11	£6.99	MONTANA LINDAUER BRUT (NZ)
27	£14.99	SAFEWAY CHAMPAGNE ALBERT ETIENNE VINTAGE, MASSE 1988 Champagne (F)
39	£3.35	CHARDONNAY GYONGYOS, HUGH RYMAN 1992 (Hun)
40	£3.35	SAFEWAY CHARDONNAY DEL TRIVENETO, G.I.V. 1992 North (It)
41	£3.75	'LE MONFERRINE' CHARDONNAY DEL PIEMONTE, A.V.P. 1992 Piedmont (It)
46	£3.75	CHARDONNAY DEL PIEMONTE, ARALDICA 1992 Piedmont (It)
66	£2.89	SAFEWAY LA MANCHA, RODRIQUEZ & BERGER 1992 Central (Sp)
67	£2.99	SAFEWAY CALIFORNIAN WHITE, HEUBLEIN 1992 (Cal)
71	£3.99	LUGANA, SANTI 1991 North (It)
79	£5.99	ROSEMOUNT CHARDONNAY 1992 Hunter Valley (Aus)
82	£6.49	CARIAD GWIN DA O GYMRU BACCHUS/REICHSTEINER, LLANERCH VINEYARD 1990 Glamorgan Wales
85	£5.99	COTES DE BEAUNE, LABOURE-ROI 1991 Burgundy (F)
86	£6.99	THE MILLTON VINEYARD CHARDONNAY 1992 Gisborne (NZ)
90	£7.49	YARDEN CHARDONNAY, GOLAN HEIGHTS WINERY 1991 Golan Heights (Is)
125	£2.89	BLAYE BLANC, GINESTET 1992 Bordeaux (F)
126	£3.35	VIN DE PAYS D'OC, SUR LIE, J & F LURTON 1992 Midi (F)
127	£3.35	LA COUME DE PEYRE, VIN DE PAYS DES COTES DE GASCOGNE, PLAIMONT 1992 South West (F)
151	£4.99	MUSCADET DE SEVRE ET MAINE, GUY BOSSARD 1992 Loire (F)
182	£5.99	GEWURZTRAMINER D'ALSACE, CAVE VINICOLE DE TURCKHEIM 1992 Alsace (F)
187	£3.15	MORIO MUSKAT, ST URSULA 1992 Rheinpfalz (G)
198	£3.99	SAFEWAY'S STANLAKE, THAMES VALLEY VINEYARDS 1992 (UK)
201	£3.99	SAFEWAY SPATLESE, RHEINHESSEN, FRANZ REH 1990 Rhine (G)
213	£3.65	SYRAH ROSE, 'GASTRONOMIE', VIN DE PAYS D'OC, FORTANT DE (F) 1992 Midi (F)
223	£2.65	HUNGARIAN COUNTRY WINE KEKFRANKOS/ZWEIGELT, VILLANY, ZOLTAN BELLA 1992 (Hun)
224	£2.99	DOMAINE SAPT INOUR, SINCOMAR PARLIER & FERMAUD (Mor)
241	£2.85	YOUNG VATTED MERLOT, RUSSE WINERY 1992 (Bul)
247	£3.49	DOMAINE ANTHEA MERLOT, SERGE ZIGGIOTTI 1992 Midi (F)

249	£3.55	AUSTRALIAN CABERNET SAUVIGNON, RIVERINA WINES 1992 Riverina (Aus)
250	£3.49	STAMBOLOVO RESERVE MERLOT 1987 (Bul)
254	£3.99	CHATEAU CASTERA, BORDEAUX 1991 Bordeaux (F)
256	£3.99	HARDYS NOTTAGE HILL CABERNET SAUVIGNON, BRL HARDY WINE CO 1991 S.Australia (Aus)
267	£5.59	KANONKOP KADETTE, STELLENBOSCH 1991 Stellenbosch (SA)
289	£7.99	DOMAINE RICHEAUME CABERNET SAUVIGNON, COTES DE PROVENCE 1991 Midi (F)
290	£7.99	CHATEAU BISTON BRILLETTE, CRU BOURGEOIS MOULIS 1989 Bordeaux (F)
317	£14.99	CHATEAU HAUT BAGES AVEROUS, PAUILLAC 1988 Bordeaux (F)
325	£3.69	CASA DEL CAMPO SYRAH, BODEGAS SANTA ANA 1992 Mendoza (Arg)
336	£4.99	ZINFANDEL, FETZER VINEYARDS 1990 Mendocino County (Cal)
346	£7.49	CHATEAU MUSAR 1986 Bekaa Valley (Leb)
365	£12.99	PENFOLDS MAGILL ESTATE SHIRAZ 1988 S. Australia (Aus)
376	£5.85	BROUILLY, GEORGES DUBOEUF 1991 Burgundy (F)
382	£3.89	MACON ROUGE, LES VIGNERONS A IGE 1992 Burgundy (F)
388	£6.99	SAFEWAY BEAUNE, LUC JAVELOT 1989 Burgundy (F)
392	£8.99	SAFEWAY NUITS ST. GEORGES, LABOURE-ROI 1990 Burgundy (F)
414	£3.65	DOLCETTO D'ASTI, ARALDICA 1992 Piedmont (It)
416	£4.99	SALICE SALENTINO RISERVA, AZ. AG. TAURINO 1988 Puglia (It)
436	£3.35	SAFEWAY CARIÑENA, BODEGAS COOP SAN VALERO 1988 Aragon (Sp)
457	£3.15	SAFEWAY MOSCATEL DE VALENCIA, GANDIA Central (Sp)
484	£16.49	MATUSALEM, GONZALEZ BYASS Jerez (Sp)

JS	J Sainsbury plc

Stamford House, Stamford Street, London SE1 9LL (Tel 071-921 6000). **Opening Hours:** vary. **Tastings:** occasionally. **Discounts:** various.

After criticism from a number of directions last year, Sainsbury's seem to have regained posession of the ball. The range now includes far fewer disappointments, though stylish shots at the goal are infrequent, too. Interestingly, the chain which once prided itself on competing on level terms with any wine merchant now seems to have decided to concentrate on moderately priced good quality wines. The Vintage Selection logo, once a controversial element on all sorts of labels, is to disappear and there will be almost no higher-priced, own-label wines. Watch out for staff wandering through the wine department wearing Walkmans; they're not listening to Michael Jackson – it's all part of the chain's new on-the-job training scheme.

7	£6.75	CREMANT DE BOURGOGNE, LES CAVES DE VIRE 1989 Burgundy (F)
11	£6.99	MONTANA LINDAUER BRUT (NZ)
14	£5.99	ANGAS BRUT CLASSIC, YALUMBA WINERY S.E. Australia (Aus)
24	£9.95	GREEN POINT, DOMAINE CHANDON 1990 Yarra Valley (Aus)
33	£28.95	BOLLINGER GRANDE ANNEE 1985 Champagne (F)
36	£2.75	SAINSBURYS ROMANIAN SYLVANER, JIDVEI (Rom)
37	£2.95	SAINSBURYS DO CAMPO BRANCO TERRAS DO SADO, J.P. VINHOS (P)
39	£3.35	CHARDONNAY GYONGYOS, HUGH RYMAN 1992 (Hun)
45	£4.25	NOBILO WHITE CLOUD 1992 (NZ)
53	£5.45	'CASAL DI SERRA' VERDICCHIO CLASSICO, DOC, UMANI RONCHI 1991 Marches (It)
74	£4.95	PENFOLDS KOONUNGA HILL CHARDONNAY 1992 S.E. Australia (Aus)
76	£4.95	CHARDONNAY VIN DE PAYS D'OC, H RYMAN 1992 Midi (F)
92	£7.99	MONTANA CHURCH ROAD CHARDONNAY 1991 (NZ)
99	£7.99	KRONDORF SHOW RESERVE CHARDONNAY 1991 Barossa Valley (Aus)
100	£7.49	FIRESTONE CHARDONNAY 1990 (Cal)
✿ 135	£3.99	SAUVIGNON BLANC RUEDA, HERMANOS LURTON 1992 Rueda (Sp)

136	£3.99	SAINSBURY'S NEW ZEALAND SAUVIGNON BLANC FERNHILLS, DELEGATS 1992 Hawkes Bay (NZ)
• 152	£5.95	DOMAINE DE GRANDCHAMP BERGERAC SAUVIGNON BLANC 1992 South West (F)
188	£4.99	PETER LEHMANN SEMILLON 1992 Barossa Valley (Aus)
196	£3.99	DENBIES ENGLISH WINE 1991 Surrey (UK)
212	£2.99	CLAIRET DE GASTON, BORDEAUX, PETER A. SICHEL Bordeaux (F)
214	£3.99	DOMAINE DE LA TUILERIE MERLOT ROSE 1992 Midi (F)
308	£14.39	CHATEAU CANTERMERLE, HAUT MEDOC 1987 Bordeaux (F)
333	£4.55	SAINSBURY'S CROZES HERMITAGE Rhône (F)
342	£6.49	PETER LEHMANN 'CLANCY'S RED' 1990 Barossa Valley (Aus)
346	£7.45	CHATEAU MUSAR, BEKAA VALLEY 1986 Bekaa Valley (Leb)
356	£8.65	CHATEAUNEUF DU PAPE, DOMAINE ANDRE BRUNEL 1989 Rhône (F)
378	£6.45	JULIENAS, CHATEAU DES CAPITANS, SARRAU 1991 Beaujolais (F)
434	£2.95	SAINSBURY'S DO CAMPO TINTO, JP VINHOS Terras do Sado (P)
435	£2.95	SAINSBURY'S ARRUDA (P)
445	£4.99	HARDY'S MOONDAH BROOK ESTATE CHENIN BLANC 1992 Gingin, Western Australia (Aus)
456	£2.99H	SAINSBURY'S MUSCAT DE ST JEAN DE MINERVOIS, VAL D'ORBIEU Midi (F)
463	£2.59H	SAINSBURY'S AUSLESE BEREICH MITTELHAARDT, QMP, SICHEL 1990 Rhine (G)

SAN	Sandiway Wine Co

Chester Road, Sandiway, Cheshire CW8 2NH (Tel 0606 882101). **Opening Hours:** Mon-Fri 9am-1pm, 2-5.30pm, 6.30-10pm (Weds half day), Sat 9am-10pm, Sun 12-2pm, 7-10pm. **Delivery:** free within10 miles. **Tastings:** regular in-store and tutored plus organised events. **Discounts:** 5% per case.

Armed only with wit and palate, Graham Wharmby is transforming his convenience-store-with-an-identity-crisis into a wine and food emporium. How many other villages shops run tastings of Valpolicella and Soave (usually 'about as interesting as the AGM of the Egremont WI') and present Messrs Allegrini and Pieropan in person? Over 50 Italians, top-class (Lafon, Bachelet) Burgundies and Charles Melton and Penley Australians. All good reasons to (as Graham says) 'get rid of your embarrassing surplus money'.

46	£4.08	CHARDONNAY DEL PIEMONTE, ARALDICA 1992 Piedmont (It)
61	£5.95	LUGANA CA'DEI FRATI 1992 Brescia (It)
77	£4.95	SALISBURY ESTATE CHARDONNAY 1992 S.E. Australia (Aus)
79	£6.07	ROSEMOUNT CHARDONNAY 1992 Hunter Valley (Aus)
98	£8.59	LOCAL GROWERS SEMILLON, ROCKFORD 1989 Barossa Valley (Aus)
106	£9.95	EDNA VALLEY CHARDONNAY 1990 Edna Valley (Cal)
266	£4.95	SALISBURY ESTATE CABERNET SAUVIGNON 1991 S.E. Australia (Aus)
272	£5.45	ROUGE HOMME CABERNET/SHIRAZ, 1988 Coonawarra (Aus)
291	£8.95	CHATEAU LA TOUR HAUT-CAUSSAN, MEDOC 1989 Bordeaux (F)
303	£9.95	PETALUMA COONAWARRA RED 1988 Coonawarra (Aus)
346	£7.19	CHATEAU MUSAR, BEKAA VALLEY 1986 BEKAA VALLEY (LEB)
348	£7.99	ROSEMOUNT SHOW RESERVE SYRAH 1990 McLaren Vale (Aus)
369	£15.65	JADE MOUNTAIN SYRAH, DOUGLAS DANIELAK 1990 Sonoma (Cal)
373	£5.29	TARRANGO, BROWN BROTHERS 1992 Milawa (Aus)
414	£4.08	DOLCETTO D'ASTI, ARALDICA 1992 Piedmont (It)
416	£5.10	SALICE SALENTINO RISERVA, AZ. AG. TAURINO 1988 Puglia (It)
418	£6.15	VERNACULUM ZOCCOLANTI-PERGOLA, VILLA LIGI 1992 Umbria (It)
419	£7.47	BARBERA D'ALBA VIGNOTA, CONTERNO E FANTINO 1991 Piedmont (It)
422	£8.25	CHIANTI CLASSICO, ISOLE E OLENA 1990 Tuscany (It)
443	£4.95	QUINTA DE LA ROSA RED TABLE WINE 1991 Douro (P)
461	£5.17H	STANTON & KILLEEN RUTHERGLEN LIQUEUR MUSCAT Rutherglen (Aus)

SWB	Satchells of Burnham Market

North St, Burnham Market, Norfolk PE31 8HG (Tel 0328 738272 Fax 0328 738272). **Opening Hours:** Mon-Fri 9.30am-6pm, Sat 9.30-7pm, seasonal Sundays 12-2pm. **Delivery:** free locally. **Tastings:** regular in-house and tutored tastings plus organised events. **Discounts:** 5-10% per case

Maxwell Graham-Wood is a born optimist. He is 'confident that consumers are becoming more forthright and knowledgeable, which can only be to everyone's benefit'. He intends to ship more of his own wines, steering clear of the obvious. This year sees a cracking range of French country and Italian wines – the La Spinona's '85 Barbaresco is a steal at £7.44. A newcomer to his own-label range is a blended whisky from Glenlivet.

11	£7.84	MONTANA LINDAUER BRUT (NZ)
14	£6.95	ANGAS BRUT CLASSIC, YALUMBA WINERY S.E. Australia (Aus)
33	£31.90	BOLLINGER GRANDE ANNEE 1985 CHAMPAGNE (F)
43	£4.67	COTES DE ST MONT WHITE, PLAIMONT 1991 South West (F)
61	£5.70	LUGANA CA'DEI FRATI 1992 Brescia (It)
73	£4.99	COTES DE SAINT MONT CUVEE PRESTIGE BLANC, ANDRE DAGUIN 1991 South West (F)
79	£6.68	ROSEMOUNT CHARDONNAY 1992 Hunter Valley (Aus)
85	£8.29	COTES DE BEAUNE, LABOURE-ROI 1991 Burgundy (F)
112	£12.81	ELSTON CHARDONNAY, TE MATA ESTATE 1991 Hawkes Bay (NZ)
123	£21.49	TORRES MILMANDA CHARDONNAY 1991 Penedes (Sp)
250	£4.23	STAMBOLOVO RESERVE MERLOT 1987 (Bul)
269	£5.72	MONTANA CABERNET SAUVIGNON 1991 Marlborough (NZ)
323	£40.00	CHATEAU COS D'ESTOURNEL, ST ESTEPHE 1982 Bordeaux (F)
444	£5.81	PERIQUITA, J M DA FONSECA 1990 (P)
494	£14.29	WARRE'S TRADITIONAL LBV 1981 Douro (P)

SEB	Sebastopol Wines

Sebastopol Barn, London Road, Blewbury Nr. Didcot, Oxfordshire OX11 9HB (Tel 0235 850471 Fax 0235 850776). **Opening Hours:** Tues-Sat 10:30am-5.30pm. closed Sun/Mon. **Delivery:** free within10 miles. **Tastings:** regular in-house and tutored plus organised events. **Discounts:** 5% per case.

From Barbara Affleck's barn comes the smoke, pepper, spice and plums of her fine selection of Rhônes, including several vintages of red and white Beaucastel and the monster Cotie Rotie of Bernard Burgaud. Australia-wise new additions include Charles Melton's 9 Popes and Cape Mentelle's big Zin. Along the same lines are JM da Fonseca '86 Camarate and Tinto Velho. A merchant with spice to spare.

74	£5.41	PENFOLDS KOONUNGA HILL CHARDONNAY 1992 S.E. Australia (Aus)
264	£4.73	BUZET TRADITION, LES VIGNERONS DE BUZET 1988 South West (F)
305	£11.50	CYRIL HENSCHKE CABERNET SAUVIGNON, STEPHEN HENSCHKE 1988 Adelaide Hills (Aus)
320	£26.19	CHATEAU PICHON LONGUEVILLE BARON, PAUILLAC 1990 Bordeaux (F)
321	£24.49	ORNELLAIA 1990 Tuscany (It)
322	£26.95	CHATEAU LYNCH-BAGES, PAUILLAC 1989 Bordeaux (F)
364	£11.89	CHATEAUNEUF DU PAPE, CHATEAU DE BEAUCASTEL 1988 Rhône (F)
422	£8.73	CHIANTI CLASSICO, ISOLE E OLENA 1990 Tuscany (It)
491	£12.53	DOWS CRUSTED PORT BOTTLED 1987 Douro (P)

SK	Seckford Wines

2 Betts Ave, Martlesham Heath, Suffolk IP5 7RH (Tel 0473 626681 Fax 0473 626004). **Opening Hours:** Tues-Sat 10am to 6pm (closed Sun Mon). **Delivery:** free locally. **Tastings:** regular in-store and tutored, plus organised events.

Good news for Suffolk slurpers of fine and 'everyday' wine. William Parker's Bordeaux are particularly drinkable, with a number of '85s, '86s and '87s at affordable prices. Excellent value, too, is the Champagne Jeanmaire '83 Rosé at £12.95. Italy's a strong point with Piedmont's best – including Altare, Ascheri and Conterno – but the Antipodes are well covered too. And if you don't like what you bought they'll exchange it (unopened of couse) for something 'more to your taste'.

SEL	Selfridges

400 Oxford St, London W1A 1AB (Tel 071-629 1234 Fax 071-491 1880). **Opening Hours:** Mon-Sat 9.30am-7pm (Thurs to 8pm). **Delivery:** nationally at cost. **Tastings:** regular in-store. **Discounts:** 12 bottles for the price of 11 on most wines.

Selfridges prove that being part of a big smart store does not have to mean being part of a big smart rip-off. New buyer William Longstaff has expanded an already impressive range, working particularly hard on Italy and California (where new arrivals include Matanzas Creek and Quivera). At the same time, prices remain very reasonable, which should prove a comforting thought while you wait for your car to be unclamped outside.

ES	Edward Sheldon

New St, Shipston on Stour, Warwickshire CV36 4EN (Tel 0608 661409 Fax 0608 663166). **Opening Hours:** Mon 9am-5.30pm, Tues-Fri 9am-7pm, Sat 9am-5pm. **Delivery:** free within 30 miles for 2 cases or more. **Tastings:** regular in-store and tutored, plus organised events. **Discounts:** negotiable.

'Purely medicinal' – there's a good excuse for the pharmacist-come-vintner who started this company selling 'medicated wine'. 150 years later, tradition lives on in the form of excellent château-bottled clarets going back to '66 and a good mix of Burgundies. Less traditional is a good choice of New Zealand from Babich, Coopers Creek, and Te Mata but California (all Mondavi) could do with a review. Those, like us, who enjoy sharing good wine should check out the 40 or so wines available in magnums, double magnums and Imperials. Oh, and there's always the chance of meeting a wine-mad thespian from nearby Stratford.

11	£6.99	MONTANA LINDAUER BRUT (NZ)
17	£8.28	BOUVET LADUBAY SAUMUR BRUT Loire (F)
33	£30.16	BOLLINGER GRANDE ANNEE 1985 Champagne (F)
44	£3.97	CHARDONNAY, VINO DA TAVOLA, CA DONINI 1992 Triveneto (It)
45	£4.63	NOBILO WHITE CLOUD 1992 (NZ)
53	£5.21	'CASAL DI SERRA' VERDICCHIO CLASSICO, DOC, UMANI RONCHI 1991 Marches (It)
91	£8.61	MARQUES DE MURRIETA RIOJA RESERVA BLANCO 1987 Rioja (Sp)
112	£11.39	ELSTON CHARDONNAY, TE MATA ESTATE 1991 Hawkes Bay (NZ)
119	£17.18	ROBERT MONDAVI RESERVE CHARDONNAY 1988 Napa Valley (Cal)
269	£4.99	MONTANA CABERNET SAUVIGNON 1991 Marlborough (NZ)
288	£7.24	CABERNET SAUVIGNON, BODEGA Y CAVAS DE WEINERT 1985 Mendoza (Arg)

346	£7.99	CHATEAU MUSAR, BEKAA VALLEY 1986 Bekaa Valley (Leb)
391	£8.08	BOURGOGNE PINOT NOIR, DOMAINE PARENT 1990 Burgundy (F)
487	£7.76	TOKAJI ASZU 3 PUTTONYOS, TOKAJI-HEGYALA SCHLUMBERGER 1981 Tokaji (Hun)
496	£14.19	TAYLOR'S TEN YEAR OLD TAWNY Douro (P)

SHV | Sherborne Vintners

The Old Vicarage, Leigh, Sherborne, Dorset DT9 6HL (Tel 0935 872222 Fax 0935 873094). **Opening Hours:** ring for details. **Delivery:** free within 20 miles. **Tastings:** occasionally, for clubs on request.

Ian Sinnot confesses (ha,ha) to be the 'aficionado autentico' of Spanish wine – take his 'Spanish List par excellence'. There's wine from Muga, Ardanza (don't miss the '85), Pesquera, Vega Sicilia and the unusual Lar de Barros (Extremadura) plus just about every other *barrio* Spain possesses. Life after Spain brings us to the rest of the world and Wine Challenge 'Medalmania'. Every wine's got some award or other, so naturally we highly approve.

SAS | Sherston Wine Company

97 Victoria Street, St Albans, Herts AL1 3TJ (Tel 0727 858841). **Opening Hours:** Tues-Fri 11.30am-7pm, Sat 9.30am-6pm. **Delivery:** free within 20 miles. **Tastings:** regular in-store plus tutored events. **Discounts:** 5% per case, 7% for customers' club members.

Any homesick Roman legionaries still camped in St Albans will find solace in the Sherston Wine Company selection. The flavour there is decidedly Mediterranean, with Italy, southern France, Portugal and Spain (the house speciality) particularly well represented. While many of his competitors have set off to conquer the southern hemisphere, Ernest Jacoby proves that, with wine like the (Australian-made) Quinta de la Rosa from the Upper Douro, the Old World has a bright future as well as an illustrious past.

SV | Smedley Vintners

Rectory Cottage, Lilley, Luton, Bedfordshire LU2 8LU (Tel 0462 768214 Fax 0462 768332). **Opening Hours:** telephone for details. **Delivery:** free within 50 miles. **Tastings:** organised and tutored events. **Discounts:** £1.20 per case.

'We are determined to survive and go on offering good wines at attractive prices,' says Derek Smedley, and so he does if you're willing to buy by the dozen. If you're an indecisive type then entrust yourself to the emphatically non-pushy Mr S and his interesting 'tasting cases', including 'Springbok & Kiwi' and 'Burgundy & Rhône' (which ought to interest those who like the traditional blends of the two).

43	£4.20	COTES DE ST MONT WHITE, PLAIMONT 1991 South West (F)
54	£4.90	MONTES UNOAKED CHARDONNAY, DISCOVER WINES LTDA 1993 Curico (Ch)
79	£5.50	ROSEMOUNT CHARDONNAY 1992 Hunter Valley (Aus)
161	£6.50	JACKSON ESTATE SAUVIGNON BLANC 1992 Marlborough (NZ)
244	£2.88	RUSSE CABERNET CINSAULT (Bul)
273	£5.50	TALTARNI FIDDLEBACK TERRACE 1990 Pyrenees (Aus)
288	£7.50	CABERNET SAUVIGNON, BODEGA Y CAVAS DE WEINERT 1985 Mendoza (Arg)
489	£7.74	CHURCHILL GRAHAM FINEST VINTAGE CHARACTER Douro (P)

SOM | Sommelier Wine Co Ltd

c/o The Grapevine, 23 St George's Esplanade, St Peter Port, Guernsey, Channel Islands (Tel 0481 721677 Fax 0481 716818). **Opening Hours:** Tues-Sat 10am-5:30pm (6pm Fridays). **Delivery:** free locally. **Tastings:** tutored tastings and organised events. **Discounts:** 5% per case.

Oenophiles in tax exile are brilliantly serviced by Richard Allisette and the five fellow enthusiasts with whom he runs this excellent firm. They started after shipping a few cases of Sancerre rosé and now list a mouth-watering selection from all over the globe, including many exciting new additions from Italy and Australia. Each wine on the list is accompanied by an intelligent tasting note and the prices offer yet more temptation to sell up and move to Guernsey.

14	£6.95	ANGAS BRUT CLASSIC, YALUMBA WINERY S.E. Australia (Aus)
16	£6.30	YALUMBA SPARKLING CABERNET CUVEE PRESTIGE S.E. Australia (Aus)
18	£5.50	CREMANT DE LOIRE ROSE, CAVE DES VIGNERONS DE SAUMUR Loire (F)
25	£9.70	CROSER METHODE TRADITIONNELLE, PETALUMA WINERY 1990 Adelaide Hills (Aus)
26	£13.95	LE MESNIL BLANC DE BLANCS Champagne (F)
46	£4.08	CHARDONNAY DEL PIEMONTE, ARALDICA 1992 Piedmont (It)
51	£4.25	CHARDONNAY 'VIRGINIE', VIN DE PAYS D'OC, SARL DOMAINE VIRGINIE LIEURAN 1992 Midi (F)
61	£5.70	LUGANA CA'DEI FRATI 1992 Brescia (It)
74	£4.95	PENFOLDS KOONUNGA HILL CHARDONNAY 1992 S.E. Australia (Aus)
95	£7.75	BARREL SELECT CHARDONNAY, FETZER VINEYARDS 1991 Mendocino County (Cal)
115	£12.35	NEWTON UNFILTERED CHARDONNAY 1990 Napa Valley (Cal)
117	£14.70	RIDGE CHARDONNAY 1990 St Cruz (Cal)
155	£5.80	ROTHBURY SAUVIGNON BLANC 1992 Marlborough (NZ)
162	£5.95	SELAKS MARLBOROUGH SAUVIGNON BLANC 1991 Marlborough (NZ)
171	£8.10	POGGIO ALLE GAZZE, TENUTA DELL'ORNELLAIA 1991 Tuscany (It)
172	£9.55	SANCERRE MD, H. BOURGEOIS 1991 Loire (F)
173	£10.60	POUILLY FUME, TRADITION CULLU, MASSON-BLONDELET 1990 Loire (F)
194	£3.45	TOLLANA DRY WHITE 1992 S.E. Australia (Aus)
222	£7.85	CHATEAU DE LA GRILLE, CHINON ROSE, A GOSSET 1992 Loire (F)
235	£3.95	DAVID WYNN DRY RED 1992 Eden Valley (Aus)
273	£4.95	TALTARNI FIDDLEBACK TERRACE 1990 Pyrenees (Aus)
274	£4.40	CHATEAU THIEULEY AC BORDEAUX ROUGE 1989 Bordeaux (F)
277	£5.30	SAUMUR, CHATEAU FOUQUET, PAUL FILLIATREAU 1990 Loire (F)
295	£8.60	FETZER BARREL SELECT CABERNET SAUVIGNON 1989 Mendocino County (Cal)
298	£8.95	LINDEMANS ST GEORGE CABERNET SAUVIGNON 1989 Coonawarra (Aus)
303	£9.45	PETALUMA COONAWARRA RED 1988 Coonawarra (Aus)
309	£11.40	NEWTON MERLOT 1990 Napa Valley (Cal)
321	£19.30	ORNELLAIA 1990 Tuscany (It)
336	£4.95	ZINFANDEL, FETZER VINEYARDS 1990 Mendocino County (Cal)
353	£7.85	DAVID WYNN PATRIARCH SHIRAZ 1991 Eden Valley (Aus)
357	£9.35	QUPE SYRAH, BOB LINDQUIST 1991 Central Coast (Cal)
358	£9.85	FROG'S LEAP ZINFANDEL 1990 Napa Valley (Cal)
363	£13.50	RIDGE GEYSERVILLE ZINFANDEL 1991 Sonoma (Cal)
365	£11.70	PENFOLDS MAGILL ESTATE SHIRAZ 1988 S. Australia (Aus)
369	£13.95	JADE MOUNTAIN SYRAH, DOUGLAS DANIELAK 1990 Sonoma (Cal)
370	£14.45	YARRA YERING SHIRAZ NO.2 1990 Yarra Valley (Aus)
400	£10.40	NEUDORF VINEYARDS MOUTERE PINOT NOIR 1991 Nelson (NZ)
414	£4.08	DOLCETTO D'ASTI, ARALDICA 1992 Piedmont (It)
428	£8.40	BRIC MILEUI, ASCHERI 1990 Piedmont (It)
443	£4.15	QUINTA DE LA ROSA RED TABLE WINE 1991 Douro (P)

SPR	Spar UK Ltd

32-40 Headstone Drive, Harrow, Middx HA3 5QT (Tel 081- 863 5511 Fax 081- 863 0603). **Opening Hours:** vary. **Delivery:** at the discretion of the manager. **Tastings:** tutored, plus organised events.

Since much of what each Spar stocks is at the individual retailers' discretion, it's difficult to generalise about the 2,000- plus licensed outlets. Still, Philippa Carr MW and Liz Aked, formerly of Asda, know their stuff, so the majority of the range will certainly be drinkable, even if all the wines don't rise to the heights of the Baron Villeneuve de Cantemerle or the Chablis from La Chablisienne. Both buyers also deserve credit for introducing Spar customers to adventurous new wines from Slovakia.

227	£3.09	SPAR COTEAUX DU LANGUEDOC Midi (F)
228	£2.99	FRANKOVKA, VINO NITRA 1991 Pezinok Slovakia

SPG	Springfield Wines

Springfield Mill, Norman Road, Denby Dale, Huddersfield, West Yorkshire HD8 8TH (Tel 0484 864929 Fax 0484 861761). **Opening Hours:** Mon-Weds 9.30am-5.30pm, Thurs/Fri 9.30am-6.30pm, Sat 9am-5pm. **Delivery:** free locally. **Tastings:** regular in-house and tutored, plus special events. **Discounts:** 5% per case (cash & cheque).

Judging by their long list of little-known producers, Mesdames Brook and Higgs know their way around France. Their list of French Country wines makes intriguing reading, with such curios as Arbois Papillette Rosé Brut and Pinot-Ploussard, both of which might even take some looking for in Paris, let alone Huddersfield. Non-Francophiles might be more interested in similarly off-beat offerings from Russia, Greece and Cyprus.

10	£6.99	ARBOIS-PUPILLIN, PAPILLETTE BLANC BRUT, FRUITIERE VINICOLE DE PUPILLIN Jura (F)
28	£18.99	DRAPPIER BLANC DE BLANCS CHAMPAGNE Champagne (F)
260	£4.65	OLD TRIANGLE CABERNET SAUVIGNON, S. SMITH & SONS 1991 Barossa Valley (Aus)
263	£4.75	MERCHANT VINTNERS CLARET, PETER A SICHEL Bordeaux (F)
346	£7.80	CHATEAU MUSAR, BEKAA VALLEY 1986 Bekaa Valley (Leb)
381	£6.35	CHENAS, LOUIS CHAMPAGNON 1991 Beaujolais (F)

FSW	Frank E Stainton

3 Berrys Yard, Finkle Street, Kendal, Cumbria LA9 4AB (Tel 0539 731886 Fax 0539 730396). **Opening Hours:** Mon-Sat 8.30am-6pm. **Delivery:** free within 30 miles. **Tastings:** occasional tutored. **Discounts:** 5% per unsplit case (cash or cheque).

Frank Stainton suggests that you peruse his list with an 'opened' bottle of wine at your side – either an attempt to prove that business and pleasure can be mixed, or a subtle way of increasing his customers' average spend. Certainly the list includes a number of wines that would fit either bill: Mosel from S A Prum, Taltarni and Aotea from the Antipodes, as well as a whole page of famous name clarets. Frank would probably feel even happier if you chose the Yquem 1985.

STW	Stewarts Wine Barrels

224 Castlereagh Rd, Belfast, Antrim BT5 5HZ (Tel 0232 704434 Fax 0232 799008). **Opening Hours:** most branches Mon-Sat 9.30am-9.00pm. **Tastings:** regular in-store and tutored, plus organised events. **Discounts:** 10% per case.

We London wimps have it easy, being surrounded by more wine shops than we can possibly want. But in Northern Ireland, the choice is much more limited, and wine lovers have to be much more diligent in their searching. Still, there's always Stewarts, offering large ranges of ports, sherries, South Africans, French country wines and a whole stack of Labouré-Roi Burgundies.

11	£7.99	MONTANA LINDAUER BRUT (NZ)
47	£4.69	WHITE BURGUNDY, LABOURE-ROI 1991 Burgundy (F)
76	£4.99	CHARDONNAY VIN DE PAYS D'OC, H RYMAN 1992 Midi (F)
85	£5.65	COTES DE BEAUNE, LABOURE-ROI 1991 Burgundy (F)
89	£6.99	CHARDONNAY BATELEUR, DANIE DE WET 1991 Robertson (SA)
132	£3.99	SAUVIGNON BLANC, VREDENDAL COOP 1991 (SA)
158	£5.39	MUSCADET CLOS DE LA SABLETTE, MARCEL MARTIN 1990 Loire (F)
175	£3.59	SAUVIGNON SEMILLON, MONDRAGON 1991 Santiago (Ch)
195	£3.19	HOCK TAFELWEIN, RUDOLF MULLER Rheinhessen (G)
202	£4.25	DANIE DE WET SINGLE ESTATE RHINE RIESLING RESERVE 1991 Robertson (SA)
229	£3.39	VAL DU TORGAN, LES PRODUCTEURS DU MONT TAUCH Midi (F)
258	£4.99	DOMAINE DE RIVOYRE CABERNET SAUVIGNON, H RYMAN 1990 Midi (F)
259	£4.99	GLEN ELLEN CABERNET SAUVIGNON 1989 (Cal)
267	£4.99	KANONKOP KADETTE, STELLENBOSCH 1991 Stellenbosch (SA)
269	£5.99	MONTANA CABERNET SAUVIGNON 1991 Marlborough (NZ)
304	£11.99	LES FIEFS DE LAGRANGE, ST JULIEN 1989 Bordeaux (F)
341	£7.59	KANONKOP PINOTAGE, VAN LOVEREN 1989 Stellenbosch (SA)
484	£17.00	MATUSALEM, GONZALEZ BYASS Jerez (Sp)
486	£5.99	RIVESALTES, VIEILLE RESERVE, LES PRODUCTEURS DU MONT TAUCH 1980 Midi (F)

SUM	Summerlee Wines Ltd

64 High St, Earls Barton, Northampton NN6 0JG (Tel 0604 810488 Fax 0604 810488). **Opening Hours:** Mon-Fri 9am-2pm **Delivery:** free within 80 miles for 2 cases; free nationally for 5 cases. **Tastings:** organised events.

Freddy Price states that Summerlee 'do not list a Liebfraumilch... But we do stock and we can supply these on demand.' This sums up the problem with being a German wine specialist: his list is full of delicious, and often underpriced, wines from Schloss Saarstein, Max Ferd. Richter and Paul Anheuser, but the market wants cheap sugared sewage water. However, the self-interested among us are not complaining, for we only have to share Freddy's excellent range with a few Oxbridge dons who haven't yet heard that German wine is out of fashion.

205	£7.24	SAARSTEINER RIESLING KABINETT, SCHLOSS SAARSTEIN 1990 Mosel Saar Ruwer (G)
209	£12.11	NEIDERHAUSER FELSEN REISLING AUSLESE, PAUL ANHEUSER 1989 Nahe (G)
210	£12.36	JOHANNISBERGER ERNTEBRINGER RIESLING KABINETT, BALTHASAR RESS 1990 Rheingau (G)

DWL | The Sunday Times Wine Club

New Aquitaine House, Paddock Road, Reading, Berkshire RG4 0JY (Tel 0734 481713 Fax 0734 461953). **Opening Hours:** Club:Mon-Fri 9am-7pm,Sat/Sun 10am-4pm (credit card orders 0734 472288) Shop: Mon-Fri 9am-5.30pm (8pm Thurs),Sat 9am-6pm. **Delivery:** nationally over £50. **Tastings:** regular in-store and tutored, plus organised events.

Tony Laithwaite promises that all sorts of interesting things are being cooked up here. Well, we'll see. For the moment, we can only repeat our comments of previous years: we love the annual get-together at the Horticultural Hall (and the chance it gave this time to compare wines with some of the things they're supposed to smell and taste of); we admire the wine tours and the printed material. The only thing that lets it all down is the value for money offered by the wines. Comparison with the Wine Society does the Sunday Times Wine Club no favours.

94 £8.29 **VINAVIUS CHARDONNAY, DOMAINE DES COUSSERGUES, VIN DE PAYS D'OC 1991 Midi (F)**

T&W | T & W Wines

51 King St, Thetford, Norfolk, IP24 2AU, (Tel 0842 765646 Fax 0842 766407). **Opening Hours:** Mon -Fri 9.30am-5.30pm. Sat 9.30am-1pm. **Delivery:** free within 15 miles. **Tastings:** regular in-store and tutored, plus organised events.

Fine & Rare Specialist of the Year

The East Anglian merchant which *not* everyone has heard of, T& W continue to offer an extraordinary selection of fine and rare wines and a unique range of top-flight Californians. Their list kicks off with a treat for those who like necrophilia but only in small doses – a selection of over 300 half bottles with vintages back to 1928. In full bottles the choice includes 1971 Gaja Barbaresco and 1955 Jaboulet Côte Rôtie. At the other end of the maturity scale, 1990 Burgundies from Rossignol-Trapet are offered *en-primeur*, and the New World section features the latest releases from Kent Rasmussen and Taltarni, while born-again hedonists will want to worship at the shrine of St Willi of Opitz.

185 £10.28 **PINOT BLANC LATE HARVEST SPATLESE DRY, THE OPITZ WINERY 1990 (Au)**

TAN | Tanners Wines Ltd

26 Wyle Cop, Shrewsbury, Shropshire SY1 1XD, (Tel 0743 232400 Fax 0743 344401). **Opening Hours:** Mon - Sat 9am - 6pm **Delivery:** free locally and nationally for orders over £75. **Tastings:** regular in-store and tutored, plus organised events. **Discounts:** 5% per case, 7.5% on 10 cases.

In 1925 Tanners were described as 'well known to many agriculturalists, sportsmen and others, not only in Shrewsbury but throughout the county of Shropshire'. Nowadays this family firm is known to a broader cross section of people all over the country. Tanners are proud of their 150 years of trading, and continue to appeal to traditionalists with a range of Bordeaux and Burgundy, and their excellent service. At the same time, they offer a distinctly modern selection of New World wines, including Tim Adams from Australia and a laager of South Africans led by Hamilton Russell.

20	£7.80	OMAR KHAYYAM, CHAMPAGNE INDIA 1987 Maharashtra (India)
33	£29.65	BOLLINGER GRANDE ANNEE 1985 CHAMPAGNE (F)
43	£4.15	COTES DE ST MONT WHITE, PLAIMONT 1991 South West (F)
45	£4.95	NOBILO WHITE CLOUD 1992 (NZ)
51	£4.99	CHARDONNAY 'VIRGINIE', VIN DE PAYS D'OC, SARL DOMAINE VIRGINIE LIEURAN 1992 Midi (F)
56	£5.68	SUNNYCLIFF CHARDONNAY 1992 Victoria (Aus)
61	£7.09	LUGANA CA'DEI FRATI 1992 Brescia (It)
74	£5.25	PENFOLDS KOONUNGA HILL CHARDONNAY 1992 S.E. Australia (Aus)
91	£8.05	MARQUES DE MURRIETA RIOJA RESERVA BLANCO 1987 Rioja (Sp)
153	£6.74	MARQUES DE ALELLA CLASSICO 1992 Alella (Sp)
161	£6.99	JACKSON ESTATE SAUVIGNON BLANC 1992 Marlborough (NZ)
195	£3.36	HOCK TAFELWEIN, RUDOLF MULLER Rheinhessen (G)
232	£3.68	DOMAINE DE ST LAURENT, VIN DE PAYS DES COTEAUX DU LIBRON 1991 Midi (F)
250	£3.95	STAMBOLOVO RESERVE MERLOT 1987 (Bul)
299	£11.90	MEERLUST MERLOT, STELLENBOSCH 1986 Stellenbosch (SA)
312	£11.86	RESERVE DE LA COMTESSE, PAUILLAC 1987 Bordeaux (F)
328	£4.05	CEPAGE SYRAH, DOMAINE LA CONDAMINE L'EVEQUE 1991 Midi (F)
343	£7.39	CUVEE DE L'ECU, CHATEAU DU GRAND MOULAS 1992 Rhône (F)
344	£7.50	CROZES HERMITAGE LA PETITE RUCHE, CHAPOUTIER 1991 Rhône (F)
346	£7.40	CHATEAU MUSAR 1986 Bekaa Valley (Leb)
364	£13.60	CHATEAUNEUF DU PAPE, CHATEAU DE BEAUCASTEL 1988 Rhône (F)
389	£7.30	HAMILTON-RUSSELL PINOT NOIR, 1991 Walker Bay (SA)
391	£7.99	BOURGOGNE PINOT NOIR, DOMAINE PARENT 1990 Burgundy (F)
393	£9.19	SANCERRE ROUGE, A DEZAT 1990 Loire (F)
444	£4.97	PERIQUITA, J M DA FONSECA 1990 (P)
455	£8.99	REMELLURI RIOJA CRIANZA 1989 Rioja (Sp)
480	£5.86	TANNERS MARISCAL MANZANILLA, VINICOLA HIDALGO Jerez (Sp)
489	£9.25	CHURCHILL GRAHAM FINEST VINTAGE CHARACTER Douro (P)
494	£13.32	WARRE'S TRADITIONAL LBV 1981 Douro (P)
496	£15.69	TAYLOR'S TEN YEAR OLD TAWNY Douro (P)

CT	**Charles Taylor Wines Ltd**

64 Alexandra Road, Epsom, Surrey KT17 4BZ (Tel 0372 728330 Fax 0372 724833). **Opening Hours:** Mon-Fri 8am-6pm plus 24- hour answerphone. **Delivery:** nationally at cost. **Tastings:** organised and tutored events.

Charles Taylor's list begins with Ancien Domaine Auffray in Chablis, which is apt for a company run by the youngest ever Master of Wine who takes pride in selling a broad range of the most old fashioned Burgundies still being made. To some, this might induce nightmares about volatile acidity and illegal additions of Algerian wine, but a quick tasting of Rossignol-Trapet will prove that Charles' missionary zeal is not misguided. He also knows that man cannot live on Burgundy alone and offers two interesting (if old-fashioned) Australian wineries, Redbank from Victoria and Evans & Tate from the Margaret River area in Western Australia.

101	£7.35	VIEUX CHATEAU GAUBERT, GRAVES 1991 Bordeaux (F)
113	£13.65	PULIGNY MONTRACHET, DOMAINE LOUIS CARILLON ET FILS 1991 Burgundy (F)
118	£15.60	CHASSAGNE-MONTRACHET 1ER CRU, 'LES CHAMPS GAIN', DOMAINE JEAN PILLOT ET FILS 1991 Burgundy (F)
139	£4.50	MUSCADET DOMAINE DES DEUX RIVES, D. HARDY & C. LUNEAU 1990 Loire (F)
181	£5.30	ALSACE PINOT BLANC, DOMAINE JEAN-LUC MADER 1990 Alsace (F)
274	£5.30	CHATEAU THIEULEY AC BORDEAUX ROUGE 1989 Bordeaux (F)
296	£8.35	CHATEAU TOUR DU HAUT MOULIN, HAUT MEDOC 1985 Bordeaux (F)

320	£16.00	CHATEAU PICHON LONGUEVILLE BARON, PAUILLAC 1990 Bordeaux (F)
322	£26.00	CHATEAU LYNCH-BAGES, PAUILLAC 1989 Bordeaux (F)
323	£36.00	CHATEAU COS D'ESTOURNEL, ST ESTEPHE 1982 Bordeaux (F)
338	£5.35	CROZES HERMITAGE ROUGE, JEAN-MARIE BORJA 1990 Rhône (F)
402	£13.65	BEAUNE 1ER CRU TEURONS, DOMAINE ROSSIGNOL TRAPET 1990 Burgundy (F)
406	£17.55	NUITS ST GEORGES 1ER CRU 'LES PRULIERS', DOMAINE LUCIEN BOILLOT ET FILS 1990 Burgundy (F)

TO	Tesco Stores plc

Wine Dept (Rear of Tesco Old House), Delamere Rd, Cheshunt, Hertfordshire EN8 9SL (Tel 0992 32222 Fax 0992 624299). **Opening Hours:** vary. **Tastings:** tutored and organised events. **Discounts:** various.

Always in the frame for the Supermarket of the Year award, Tesco is still out there like Avis, trying harder, despite a year which 'depressed the most optimistic of us', as Stephen Clarke says. 'No matter how delicious and good value a wine we offer, customers are only interested in buying bargains'. Those customers are well served, but they really ought to take advantage of some of Tesco's other, most excitingly-chosen wines around. While M&S were pretending to have had Robert Mondavi make a widely available wine exclusively for them, Tesco really did contract Jacques Lurton to produce genuinely exclusive cuvées for them in three continents. The focus now, though, is on communication. Watch out for all sorts of informative stuff on bottles, shelves and in leaflets.

1	£4.69	TESCO PROSECCO SPUMANTE, ZONIN Piedmont (It)
2	£5.89	TESCO MARTINI ASTI SPUMANTE, CASTELVERO Piedmont (It)
5	£5.79	GRAND DUCHESS RUSSIAN SPARKLING WINE (Ukraine)
7	£6.99	CREMANT DE BOURGOGNE, LES CAVES DE VIRE 1989 Burgundy (F)
11	£6.99	MONTANA LINDAUER BRUT (NZ)
18	£7.59	CREMANT DE LOIRE ROSE, CAVE DES VIGNERONS DE SAUMUR Loire (F)
21	£7.99	SPARKLING VOUVRAY, CHEVALIER DE MONCONTOUR Loire (F)
24	£9.99	GREEN POINT, DOMAINE CHANDON 1990 Yarra Valley (Aus)
50	£4.99	TESCO MACON BLANC VILLAGE, LES CAVES DE VIRE 1992 Burgundy (F)
55	£5.49	TESCO CHABLIS, LA CHABLISIENNE 1992 Burgundy (F)
70	£3.99	TIMARA WHITE, MONTANA 1991 (NZ)
74	£4.99	PENFOLDS KOONUNGA HILL CHARDONNAY 1992 S.E. Australia (Aus)
79	£5.89	ROSEMOUNT CHARDONNAY 1992 Hunter Valley (Aus)
84	£6.99	COVA DA URSA CHARDONNAY 1991 Terras do Sado (P)
111	£9.99	CHALK HILL CHARDONNAY 1991 Sonoma (Cal)
126	£2.99	VIN DE PAYS D'OC, SUR LIE, J & F LURTON 1992 Midi (F)
128	£3.39	TESCO SAUVIGNON BLANC, UNIVITIS Bordeaux (F)
129	£3.49	TESCO NURAGUS, DOLIANOVA Sardinia (It)
161	£6.99	JACKSON ESTATE SAUVIGNON BLANC 1992 Marlborough (NZ)
192	£2.79	TESCO DRY HOCK, TAFELWEIN, ZIMMERMAN GRAFF Rhein (G)
196	£3.99	DENBIES ENGLISH WINE 1991 Surrey (UK)
199	£2.39	TESCO HOCK, DEUTSCHES WEINTOR (G)
203	£4.49	TESCO KLOSTER STEINWEILER SPATLESE, QMP, DEUTSCHES WEINTOR Rheinpfalz (G)
226	£2.99	TESCO AUSTRALIAN RED, PENFOLDS S. Australia (Aus)
234	£4.65	DOMAINE DES BAUMELLES ROUGE, COTES DE LUBERON, VAL JOANIS 1991 Rhône (F)
242	£2.85	TESCO BULGARIAN CABERNET SAUVIGNON, LOVICO Suhindol (Bul)
252	£3.99	TESCO NEW ZEALAND CABERNET MERLOT, COOKS NEW ZEALAND WINE CO 1990 Gisborne (NZ)

253	£3.99	TESCO AUSTRALIAN CABERNET SAUVIGNON, MILDARA Mildura (Aus)
255	£3.99	TESCO MEXICAN CABERNET SAUVIGNON, L A CETTO 1988 Mexico
269	£4.99	MONTANA CABERNET SAUVIGNON 1991 Marlborough (NZ)
308	£14.99	CHATEAU CANTERMERLE, HAUT MEDOC 1987 Bordeaux (F)
324	£2.95	TESCO COTES DU RHONE, MICHEL BERNARD Rhône (F)
334	£3.99	STRATFORD ZINFANDEL (Cal)
394	£7.99	COLDSTREAM HILLS PINOT NOIR 1992 Yarra Valley (Aus)
396	£10.99	SAINTSBURY PINOT NOIR 1991 Carneros (Cal)
411	£2.99	TESCO INTERNATIONAL WINEMAKER BASILICATA ROSSO, JACQUES LURTON 1992 Basilicata (It)
412	£3.29	TESCO MONICA DI SARDEGNA, DOLIANOVA Sardinia (It)
417	£5.49	TESCO CHIANTI CLASSICO RISERVA, CASTELLI DE GREVEPESA 1988 Tuscany (It)
439	£3.35	BORBA, ADEGA CO-OPERATIVA DE BORBA 1991 Douro (P)
440	£3.99	TESCO TORO RED, FARINAS 1990 Toro (Sp)
444	£3.99	PERIQUITA, J M DA FONSECA 1990 (P)
445	£4.99	HARDY'S MOONDAH BROOK ESTATE CHENIN BLANC 1992 Gingin, Western Australia (Aus)

| **TH** | **Thresher Wine Shops** |

Sefton House, 42 Church Road, Welwyn Garden City, Hertfordshire AL8 6PJ (Tel 0707 328244 Fax 0707 371398). **Opening Hours:** Mon-Sat 10am-10.30pm, Sundays vary. **Delivery:** nationally where possible. **Tastings:** participate in organised events. **Discounts:** none, but various special offers.

To anyone who can remember the Thresher of a few years ago, the chain today is almost unrecognizable. Kim Tidy and his team do a remarkable job of wine buying; the only criticism which can be made is that sometimes they buy too many wines of a particular style, occasionally obscuring the wood with a plethora of trees. But, judging by the International Wine Challenge results, the wines in the best Thresher Wine Shops are easily good enough to place Thresher in the running for this year's top prize. Our judges remaining reservation, however, was the one voiced last year: until the (unashamedly beer-oriented) Drink Stores from Thresher (which only stock our recommended wines marked with an *) take on their own identity, Thresher itself cannot really compete for the award won by its sister chain, Wine Rack.

Wines marked with an * are available in Drink Stores from Thresher. Much of the rest of the range is also to be found in Wine Rack shops.

3	£6.09	SEGURA VIUDAS CAVA BRUT RESERVA Cava (Sp)
11	£6.99	MONTANA LINDAUER BRUT (NZ)
22*	£8.99	MAYERLING CREMANT D'ALSACE, CAVE VINICOLE DE TURCKHEIM Alsace (F)
26	£14.29	LE MESNIL BLANC DE BLANCS Champagne (F)
28	£16.25	DRAPPIER BLANC DE BLANCS CHAMPAGNE Champagne (F)
33	£30.25	BOLLINGER GRANDE ANNEE 1985 CHAMPAGNE (F)
39*	£3.35	CHARDONNAY GYONGYOS, HUGH RYMAN 1992 (Hun)
52	£4.99	DOMAINE DES DEUX RUISSEAUX CHARDONNAY, SKALLI 1991 Midi (F)
57*	£5.99	CHABLIS, LOUIS ALEXANDRE 1992 Burgundy (F)
59	£6.59	PETIT CHABLIS, GOULLEY 1991 Burgundy (F)
70*	£3.99	TIMARA WHITE, MONTANA 1991 (NZ)
74	£4.99	PENFOLDS KOONUNGA HILL CHARDONNAY 1992 S.E. Australia (Aus)
79*	£5.99	ROSEMOUNT CHARDONNAY 1992 Hunter Valley (Aus)
91	£7.49	MARQUES DE MURRIETA RIOJA RESERVA BLANCO 1987 Rioja (Sp)
97	£9.29	WAIPARA SPRINGS CHARDONNAY 1991 Canterbury (NZ)
104	£9.99	CHARDONNAY, JANE HUNTER'S WINES 1991 Marlborough (NZ)

106	£9.99	EDNA VALLEY CHARDONNAY 1990 Edna Valley (Cal)
107	£8.99	ACACIA CHARDONNAY, THE CHALONE GROUP 1989 Carneros (Cal)
111	£11.49	CHALK HILL CHARDONNAY 1991 Sonoma (Cal)
150	£5.49	KONOCTI SAUVIGNON BLANC 1991 LAKE COUNTY (CAL)
165	£7.99	KATNOOK ESTATE SAUVIGNON BLANC 1992 COONAWARRA (AUS)
161	£6.99	JACKSON ESTATE SAUVIGNON BLANC 1992 Marlborough (NZ)
162	£6.99	SELAKS MARLBOROUGH SAUVIGNON BLANC 1991 Marlborough (NZ)
164	£7.25	MENETOU SALON LES MOROGUES HENRI PELLE 1992 Loire (F)
169	£8.99	HUNTERS MARLBOROUGH SAUVIGNON BLANC 1992 Marlborough (NZ)
182*	£5.99	GEWURZTRAMINER D'ALSACE, CAVE VINICOLE DE TURCKHEIM 1992 Alsace (F)
189	£8.49	LAGAR DE CERVERA, RIAS BAIXAS, LAGAR DE FORNELOSSA 1992 Galicia (Sp)
194*	£3.29	TOLLANA DRY WHITE 1992 S.E. Australia (Aus)
206	£7.29	WINKELER HASENSPRUNG RIESLING KABINETT, BARON VON BRENTANO 1990 Rheingau (G)
207	£8.99	KREUZNACHER BRUCKES RIESLING AUSLESE, SCHLOSS VON PLETTENBERG 1989 Nahe (G)
208	£9.99	TRITTENHEIMER APOTHEKE RIESLING AUSLESE, GRANS FASSIAN 1989 Mosel Saar Ruwer (G)
215	£3.99	VALDEMAR ROSADA, MARTINEZ BUJANDA 1992 Rioja (Sp)
229*	£2.99	VAL DU TORGAN, LES PRODUCTEURS DU MONT TAUCH Midi (F)
236	£4.99	COTEAUX DU LANGUEDOC, DOMAINE DE L'HORTUS, JEAN ORLIAC 1991 South West (F)
238	£6.29	CHATEAU DE LASTOURS CORBIERES, FUT DE CHENE 1989 Midi (F)
244*	£2.85	RUSSE CABERNET CINSAULT (Bul)
250*	£3.89	STAMBOLOVO RESERVE MERLOT 1987 (Bul)
258	£3.99	DOMAINE DE RIVOYRE CABERNET SAUVIGNON, H RYMAN 1990 Midi (F)
269*	£4.99	MONTANA CABERNET SAUVIGNON 1991 Marlborough (NZ)
281	£6.29	CHATEAU BONNET OAK AGED, A LURTON 1990 Bordeaux (F)
298	£9.99	LINDEMANS ST GEORGE CABERNET SAUVIGNON 1989 Coonawarra (Aus)
303	£9.99	PETALUMA COONAWARRA RED 1988 Coonawarra (Aus)
317	£14.99	CHATEAU HAUT BAGES AVEROUS, PAUILLAC 1988 Bordeaux (F)
346	£8.19	CHATEAU MUSAR, BEKAA VALLEY 1986 BEKAA VALLEY (LEB)
347	£7.99	ST. JOSEPH, COTE DIANE, CAVE CO-OPERATIVE DE ST. DESIRAT 1989 Rhône (F)
348	£8.69	ROSEMOUNT SHOW RESERVE SYRAH 1990 McLaren Vale (Aus)
353	£9.99	DAVID WYNN PATRIARCH SHIRAZ 1991 Eden Valley (Aus)
365	£12.99	PENFOLDS MAGILL ESTATE SHIRAZ 1988 S. Australia (Aus)
371	£17.99	COTE ROTIE, GERIN 1990 Rhône (F)
375	£5.79	MACON-BRAY, DOMAINE DE LA COMBE, HENRI LAFARGE 1991 Burgundy (F)
401	£13.69	FIXIN, LOUIS JADOT 1989 Burgundy (F)
413*	£3.89	MONTEPULCIANO D'ABRUZZO, DOC, UMANI RONCHI 1991 Marches (It)
433*	£2.55	LEZIRIA VINHO TINTO, VEGA CO-OPERATIVE ALMEIRIM 1992 Almeirim (P)
438*	£3.89	ALBOR RIOJA TINTO, BODEGAS & BEBIDAS 1991 Rioja (Sp)
442	£3.99	VALDEMAR RIOJA TINTO, MARTINEZ BUJANDA 1992 Rioja (Sp)
445	£4.99	MEIA PIPA, J P VINHOS 1989 (P)
447*	£4.99	CAMPO VIEJO RIOJA RESERVA 1987 Rioja (Sp)
448	£5.99	CARTUXA, FUNDACO E ALMEIDA 1989 Evora (P)
450	£5.99	YLLERA, VINO DE MESA, SAT LOS CURRO 1988 Ribera del Duero (Sp)
452	£6.95	BARON DE LEY RIOJA RESERVA 1987 Rioja (Sp)
453	£5.99	JOAO PATO TINTO, BAIRRADA 1990 Bairrada (P)
461	£5.49	STANTON & KILLEEN RUTHERGLEN LIQUEUR MUSCAT Rutherglen (Aus)
469	£6.79	CHATEAU DE BERBEC, PREMIERES COTES DE BORDEAUX 1989 Bordeaux (F)
484	£18.99	MATUSALEM, GONZALEZ BYASS Jerez (Sp)
488	£7.99	OLD TRAFFORD TAWNY, B. SEPPELT & SONS S.E. Australia (Aus)
496	£15.69	TAYLOR'S TEN YEAR OLD TAWNY Douro (P)
499	£39.00	RUTHERFORD MILES MALVASIA SOLERA 1863 Madeira

| MAD | Madeleine Trehearne Partners |

20 New End Square, London NW3 1LN (Tel 071- 435 6310 Fax 071- 794 8816). **Opening Hours:** 24 hrs, 7 days a week. **Delivery:** free within 5 miles. **Tastings:** tutored and organised events. **Discounts:** 5% on over 5 cases.

When she is not teaching English, Madeleine Trehearne's attention is clearly turned to the French. From her Hampstead cottage she sells a range of interesting small domaine wines, mainly from the SouthWest, Loire and Bordeaux. Perfect accompaniments to her smoked trout and salmon, cheeses and truffles.

| TRE | Tremaynes. |

40a Bell Street, Henley on Thames, Oxon RG9 2BG (Tel 0491 575061). **Opening Hours:** Mon-Fri 10am-8pm, Sat 9am-8pm, Sun 12-2pm. **Delivery:** free within 15 miles. **Tastings:** regular in-store and tutored, plus organised events. **Discounts:** negotiable.

A perfectly reasonable selection of wines from France, Italy and Germany without producers, so we can't tell them from Adam or Yves (or Klaus for that matter). The Aussies and Kiwis we recognised instantly: Mitchelton, Tyrells, Oyster Bay, Delegat's but we had to guess again at the Periquita '82 and Camarate '87, JM da Fonseca perhaps? Luckily the Ch Les Ormes de Pez '82 (£20) speaks for itself.

33	£31.00	BOLLINGER GRANDE ANNEE 1985 CHAMPAGNE (F)
100	£11.50	FIRESTONE CHARDONNAY 1990 (Cal)
167	£10.00	POUILLY FUME, DOMAINE COULBOIS, PATRICK COULBOIS 1991 Loire (F)
197	£4.40	BADEN DRY, BADISCHER WINZERKELLER Baden (G)
438	£3.90	ALBOR RIOJA TINTO, BODEGAS & BEBIDAS 1991 Rioja (Sp)
447	£6.20	CAMPO VIEJO RIOJA RESERVA 1987 Rioja (Sp)
451	£7.00	COTO DE IMAZ RIOJA RESERVA 1985 Rioja (Sp)
496	£15.70	TAYLOR'S TEN YEAR OLD TAWNY Douro (P)

| TRW | Trinity Wine |

82A Acre Lane, London SW2 5QN (Tel 071-326 4540). **Opening Hours:** 10.30am-10.30pm **Delivery:** free locally. **Tastings:** regular in-store and tutored, plus organised outside events.

It's all change at Trinity: they have moved offices and dropped Bordeaux completely. What remains reassuringly familiar is their excellent and competitively priced range of Burgundy. Recent coups have included the St Vincent de Brixton banquet and the 'Masters Selection', an offer of wines from Monnier and Javillier in Meursault, Dubreuil-Fontaine's Cortons and some interesting reds from Trapet, including his 1976 Latricières-Chambertin for £30. Burgundy does indeed flow in the streets of Brixton!

| 409 | £23.50 | CORTON CLOS DU ROY, DUBREUIL FONTAINE 1990 Burgundy (F) |

| TVW | Turville Valley Wines |

The Firs, Potter Row, Great Missenden, Bucks HP16 9LT (Tel 02406 8818 Fax 02406 8832) **Opening Hours:** Mon-Sat 9am-5:30pm **Delivery:** free within 5 miles and in Central London. **Tastings:** tutored tastings and organised events.

As recession-hit customers are forced to clear out their cellars, more and more exotic treasures appear on the Turville Valley list: 1961 Latour, Yquem back to 1939, a quadruple-magnum of 1976 Romanée Conti, 1973 Grange Hermitage. One is reminded of a Jeffrey Archer novel – lots of famous names dropped on every page; an entertaining read, but not really believable.

UBC | Ubiquitous Chip

12 Ashton Lane, Glasgow G12 8SJ (Tel 041- 334 5007). **Opening Hours:** Mon-Fri 12-10pm, Sat 11am-10pm **Delivery:** free locally. **Tastings:** regular in-store and tutored.

This is still Glasgow's hottest-spot for eating, drinking and vinous 'take-aways'. This year the latest addition to the business – the wine shop – celebrates its tenth year. The wines in store are as praiseworthy and diverse as ever. The finest Bordeaux (you name it they've got it), Burgundy (Leroy, Jobard, Rollin's '87 Corton Charlemagne in mags) and Rhône (Guigal, Paul Avril, Multier's '90 Condrieu) the best of Italy and Spain and a New World extravaganza for Chalone, Shafer, Chardonnay, Shiraz, Sauvignon, Semillon supporters. Not you? Then a Singleton, Speyburn, Strathisla or Chimay should serve.

32	£19.10	CHAMPAGNE HENRI BILLIOT Champagne (F)
44	£3.95	CHARDONNAY, VINO DA TAVOLA, CA DONINI 1992 Triveneto (It)
169	£8.40	HUNTERS MARLBOROUGH SAUVIGNON BLANC 1992 Marlborough (NZ)
174	£6.95H	POUILLY FUME, DE LADOUCETTE 1990 LOIRE (F)
244	£2.99	RUSSE CABERNET CINSAULT (Bul)
295	£12.70	FETZER BARREL SELECT CABERNET SAUVIGNON 1989 Mendocino County (Cal)
413	£4.15	MONTEPULCIANO D'ABRUZZO, DOC, UMANI RONCHI 1991 Marches (It)
421	£7.30	SER GIOVETO, VINO DA TAVOLA, ROCCA DELLE MACIE 1989 Tuscany (It)
422	£5.80H	CHIANTI CLASSICO, ISOLE E OLENA 1990 TUSCANY (IT)
427	£10.20	CUMARO ROSSO CONERO, UMANI RONCHI 1989 Marches (It)
484	£16.99	MATUSALEM, GONZALEZ BYASS Jerez (Sp)

U | Unwins Wine Merchants

Birchwood House, Victoria Road, Dartford, Kent DA1 5AJ (Tel 0322 272711 Fax 0322 294469). **Opening Hours:** Majority Mon-Sat 10am-10pm, Sun 12-2pm, 7pm-9.30pm. **Delivery:** free locally. **Tastings:** regular in-store and tutored, plus organised events. **Discounts:** 10% on mixed cases.

Hang on a moment, Taylor's '77, Kumeu River Chardonnay, Haut Brion, Margaux, Latour, Mouton (three vintages of each), isn't this Unwins, the seed people? Well those wines may not be in your local branch, but they can be ordered, and '83 Mouton by-the-bottle at £45 is cheap. If only the rest of the Unwins list were as interesting... But elsewhere in the range, more care must be taken, particularly in the rather limp German and Californian selections and Bichot-dominated Burgundies. We wish Unwins a very happy 150th anniversary and hope that in the coming year, the heights to which the port and claret selections rise can be achieved across the board.

11	£7.65	MONTANA LINDAUER BRUT (NZ)
22	£7.99	MAYERLING CREMANT D'ALSACE, CAVE VINICOLE DE TURCKHEIM Alsace (F)
33	£32.95	BOLLINGER GRANDE ANNEE 1985 CHAMPAGNE (F)
74	£5.49	PENFOLDS KOONUNGA HILL CHARDONNAY 1992 S.E. Australia (Aus)

79	£6.99	ROSEMOUNT CHARDONNAY 1992 Hunter Valley (Aus)
168	£9.49	SANCERRE LES ROCHES, DOMAINE VACHERON 1992 Loire (F)
182	£5.99	GEWURZTRAMINER D'ALSACE, CAVE VINICOLE DE TURCKHEIM 1992 Alsace (F)

V&C | Valvona & Crolla Ltd

19 Elm Row, Edinburgh, EH7 4AA (Tel 031 556 6066 Fax 031 556 1668). **Opening Hours:** Mon - Sat 8.30am-6pm, Thurs/Fri until 7.30pm. **Delivery:** local orders over £25.00 **Tastings:** regular in-store and tutored, plus organised events. **Discounts:** 5% on mixed cases.

Italian Specialist of the Year

If more Italian restaurants received the Valvona and Crolla list, the world would be a better place. This company has tried as hard as anyone to rid us of the plague of filthy Italian wines. The fact that they are located in 'the North of the British Isles' (Philip Contini's phrase, not ours) is no excuse to ignore them. Indeed, with free delivery of eight or more cases, the problem is not which eight to choose, but which eight not to choose, from this definitive range of Italian goodies.

13	£7.69	BERLUCCHI BIANCO IMPERIALE, VINO DA TAVOLA, GUIDO BERLUCCHI Lombardy (It)
33	£32.00	BOLLINGER GRANDE ANNEE 1985 Champagne (F)
44	£3.99	CHARDONNAY, VINO DA TAVOLA, CA DONINI 1992 Triveneto (It)
46	£4.39	CHARDONNAY DEL PIEMONTE, ARALDICA 1992 Piedmont (It)
53	£5.39	'CASAL DI SERRA' VERDICCHIO CLASSICO, DOC, UMANI RONCHI 1991 Marches (It)
61	£6.69	LUGANA CA'DEI FRATI 1992 Brescia (It)
65	£10.59	JERMANN PINOT BIANCO 1991 Friuli Venezia Giulia (It)
110	£12.99	POMINO IL BENEFIZIO, MARCHESI DE FRESCOBALDI 1990 Tuscany (It)
157	£6.99	LUGANA SANTA CRISTINA, VIGNETO MASSONI 1991 Lombardy (It)
171	£9.79	POGGIO ALLE GAZZE, TENUTA DELL'ORNELLAIA 1991 Tuscany (It)
315	£17.95	MORMORETO CABERNET SAUVIGNON PREDICATO DI BITURICA, VINO DA TAVOLA, MARCHESI DE FRESCOBALDI 1988 Tuscany (It)
321	£23.99	ORNELLAIA 1990 Tuscany (It)
413	£3.99	MONTEPULCIANO D'ABRUZZO, DOC, UMANI RONCHI 1991 Marches (It)
414	£4.39	DOLCETTO D'ASTI, ARALDICA 1992 Piedmont (It)
416	£4.99	SALICE SALENTINO RISERVA, AZ. AG. TAURINO 1988 Puglia (It)
418	£6.89	VERNACULUM ZOCCOLANTI-PERGOLA, VILLA LIGI 1992 Umbria (It)
421	£7.65	SER GIOVETO, VINO DA TAVOLA, ROCCA DELLE MACIE 1989 Tuscany (It)
422	£8.45	CHIANTI CLASSICO, ISOLE E OLENA 1990 Tuscany (It)
423	£8.59	CARMIGNANO, CAPEZZANA 1987 Tuscany (It)
424	£7.89	DOLCETTO D'ALBA CORSINI, MASCARELLO 1991 Piedmont (It)
425	£8.99	LE SASSINE, LE RAGOSE 1988 Veneto (It)
426	£8.99	FREISA DELLE LANGHE, G D VAJRA 1990 Piedmont (It)
427	£9.69	CUMARO ROSSO CONERO, UMANI RONCHI 1989 Marches (It)
428	£10.49	BRIC MILEUI, ASCHERI 1990 Piedmont (It)
429	£10.99	BAROLO RISERVA, BORGOGNO 1985 Piedmont (It)
430	£14.95	RUBESCO RISERVA MONTICCHIO, LUNGAROTTI 1980 Umbria (It)
431	£18.95	CABREO VIGNETO IL BORGO, RUFFINO 1987 Tuscany (It)
432	£18.95	RECIOTO DELLA VALPOLICELLA, CASAL DEI RONCHI MASI 1988 Veneto (It)
474	£7.69H	DINDARELLO, MACULAN 1992 Veneto (It)
484	£18.99	MATUSALEM, GONZALEZ BYASS Jerez (Sp)
487	£7.69	TOKAJI ASZU 3 PUTTONYOS, TOKAJI-HEGYALA SCHLUMBERGER 1981 Tokaji (Hun)
492	£6.59	COLHEITA, A A CALEM & FILHO 1985 Douro (P)
496	£14.89	TAYLOR'S TEN YEAR OLD TAWNY Douro (P)
498	£23.00	QUINTA DO VESUVIO VINTAGE PORT 1990 Douro (P)

HVW	Helen Verdcourt

Spring Cottage, Kimbers Lane, Maidenhead, Berkshire SL6 2QP (Tel 0628 25577). **Opening Hours:** anytime – with help of answerphone. **Delivery:** free locally. **Tastings:** tutored tastings and organised events. **Discounts:** 5% per case.

Joint Small Independent Merchant of the Year

Despite the efforts of politicians and economists who've done their best to sabotage the efforts of businesses like hers, Ms Verdcourt's crowd-pulling vinous one-woman-band plays on – especially in Australia, New Zealand and the Rhône. 'How long can it last?' she wonders as she sets off to give another tutored tasting, deliver another wedding-load of Champagne or case of waiting-list Cloudy Bay. As long, we reply, as she continues to supply Berks, Bucks and Surrey with such delights as '90 Ridge Paso Robles Zinfandel (£8.50), '90 Coudoulet de Beaucastel (£6.90), and '92 Pierro Semillon/Sauvignon (£7.10) at such reasonable prices.

11	£6.85	MONTANA LINDAUER BRUT (NZ)
53	£5.50	'CASAL DI SERRA' VERDICCHIO CLASSICO, DOC, UMANI RONCHI 1991 Marches (It)
64	£7.90	TASMANIAN WINE COMPANY CHARDONNAY, PIPER'S BROOK 1991 Tasmania (Aus)
70	£4.10	TIMARA WHITE, MONTANA 1991 (NZ)
74	£4.95	PENFOLDS KOONUNGA HILL CHARDONNAY 1992 S.E. Australia (Aus)
79	£6.00	ROSEMOUNT CHARDONNAY 1992 Hunter Valley (Aus)
91	£7.40	MARQUES DE MURRIETA RIOJA RESERVA BLANCO 1987 Rioja (Sp)
104	£9.25	CHARDONNAY, JANE HUNTER'S WINES 1991 Marlborough (NZ)
117	£15.25	RIDGE CHARDONNAY 1990 St Cruz (Cal)
155	£6.10	ROTHBURY SAUVIGNON BLANC 1992 Marlborough (NZ)
162	£5.70	SELAKS MARLBOROUGH SAUVIGNON BLANC 1991 Marlborough (NZ)
164	£7.90	MENETOU SALON LES MOROGUES HENRI PELLE 1992 Loire (F)
169	£8.45	HUNTERS MARLBOROUGH SAUVIGNON BLANC 1992 Marlborough (NZ)
182	£5.60	GEWURZTRAMINER D'ALSACE, CAVE VINICOLE DE TURCKHEIM 1992 Alsace (F)
257	£4.50	SEAVIEW CABERNET SAUVIGNON/SHIRAZ 1990 S.E. Australia (Aus)
269	£5.00	MONTANA CABERNET SAUVIGNON 1991 Marlborough (NZ)
281	£6.00	CHATEAU BONNET OAK AGED, A LURTON 1990 Bordeaux (F)
282	£6.65	VALLEY OAKS CABERNET SAUVIGNON, FETZER VINEYARDS 1990 Mendocino County (Cal)
298	£9.85	LINDEMANS ST GEORGE CABERNET SAUVIGNON 1989 Coonawarra (Aus)
309	£10.90	NEWTON MERLOT 1990 Napa Valley (Cal)
330	£3.90	VIN DE PAYS DES COLLINES RHODANIENNES CEPAGE SYRAH, CAVE DE TAIN L'HERMITAGE Rhône (F)
336	£5.55	ZINFANDEL, FETZER VINEYARDS 1990 Mendocino County (Cal)
348	£8.00	ROSEMOUNT SHOW RESERVE SYRAH 1990 McLaren Vale (Aus)
348	£8.00	ROSEMOUNT SHOW RESERVE SYRAH 1990 McLaren Vale (Aus)
353	£8.25	DAVID WYNN PATRIARCH SHIRAZ 1991 Eden Valley (Aus)
364	£11.10	CHATEAUNEUF DU PAPE, CHATEAU DE BEAUCASTEL 1988 Rhône (F)
422	£7.90	CHIANTI CLASSICO, ISOLE E OLENA 1990 Tuscany (It)
438	£3.55	ALBOR RIOJA TINTO, BODEGAS & BEBIDAS 1991 Rioja (Sp)
447	£5.90	CAMPO VIEJO RIOJA RESERVA 1987 Rioja (Sp)
461	£9.80	STANTON & KILLEEN RUTHERGLEN LIQUEUR MUSCAT Rutherglen (Aus)

VW	Victoria Wine

Brook House, Chertsey Road, Woking, Surrey GU21 5BE (Tel 0483 715066 Fax 0483 755234) **Opening Hours:** majority Mon-Sat 10am to 10pm, Sundays vary. **Delivery:** Nationally at cost. **Tastings:** tutored tastings, customers' club. **Discounts:** 5% mixed cases, 7 for 6 on Champagne.

Girding its loins to accommodate Augustus Barnett, Victoria Wine has continued to develop its range, and to concentrate its attention on training the staff in its best shops. Regional France has become an area of particular strength, but this chain deserves credit for successfully pioneering styles where others have failed. Last year's Red Wine of the Year, the Stratford Zinfandel from California has, for example, been joined by a Pinot Noir from the same winery selling at under a fiver – a price at which most Californians claim it to be impossible to produce almost anything drinkable. Victoria Wine is also the only place to buy the stunning 1986 Vintage Champagne, this year's joint Sparkling Wine of the Year.

11	£6.99	MONTANA LINDAUER BRUT (NZ)
24	£9.99	GREEN POINT, DOMAINE CHANDON 1990 Yarra Valley (Aus)
31	£18.59	VICTORIA WINE VINTAGE CHAMPAGNE 1986 Champagne (F)
33	£31.99	BOLLINGER GRANDE ANNEE 1985 CHAMPAGNE (F)
38	£2.99	VIN DE PAYS DE L'HERAULT BLANC, SKALLI 1992 Midi (F)
45	£3.99	NOBILO WHITE CLOUD 1992 (NZ)
46	£3.79	CHARDONNAY DEL PIEMONTE, ARALDICA 1992 Piedmont (It)
53	£6.09	'CASAL DI SERRA' VERDICCHIO CLASSICO, DOC, UMANI RONCHI 1991 Marches (It)
74	£4.99	PENFOLDS KOONUNGA HILL CHARDONNAY 1992 S.E. Australia (Aus)
74	£4.99	PENFOLDS KOONUNGA HILL CHARDONNAY 1992 S.E. Australia (Aus)
75	£4.99	BOURGOGNE CHARDONNAY, BOISSET 1992 Burgundy (F)
79	£6.15	ROSEMOUNT CHARDONNAY 1992 Hunter Valley (Aus)
91	£7.99	MARQUES DE MURRIETA RIOJA RESERVA BLANCO 1987 Rioja (Sp)
126	£3.69	VIN DE PAYS D'OC, SUR LIE, J & F LURTON 1992 Midi (F)
130	£3.59	GAILLAC CAVE DE LABASTIDE DE LEVIS 1992 South West (F)
213	£3.79	SYRAH ROSE, 'GASTRONOMIE', VIN DE PAYS D'OC, FORTANT DE FRANCE 1992 Midi (F)
225	£2.99	VICTORIA WINE FRENCH FULL RED, SKALLI Midi (F)
228	£2.99	FRANKOVKA, VINO NITRA 1991 Pezinok Slovakia
246	£2.99	DUNAVAR CONNOSSEUR COLLECTION MERLOT, DANUBIANA BONYHAD 1990 Szekszard (Hun)
248	£3.29	SLOVAKIAN CABERNET SAUVIGNON, VINA NITRA 1992 (Slovakia)
258	£4.29	DOMAINE DE RIVOYRE CABERNET SAUVIGNON, H RYMAN 1990 Midi (F)
265	£4.79	ERRAZURIZ CABERNET SAUVIGNON, MAULE 1991 Maule (Ch)
269	£4.99	MONTANA CABERNET SAUVIGNON 1991 Marlborough (NZ)
284	£6.79	CHATEAU CARIGNAN, PREMIERES COTES DE BORDEAUX 1990 Bordeaux (F)
334	£4.65	STRATFORD ZINFANDEL (Cal)
384	£4.89	STRATFORD PINOT NOIR (Cal)
410	£2.99	CORTENOVA MERLOT, PASQUA 1991 Grave Friuli (It)
413	£3.69	MONTEPULCIANO D'ABRUZZO, DOC, UMANI RONCHI 1991 Marches (It)
433	£2.59	LEZIRIA VINHO TINTO, VEGA CO-OPERATIVE ALMEIRIM 1992 Almeirim (P)
437	£3.09	CISMEIRA DOURO 1991 Douro (P)
439	£3.49	BORBA, ADEGA CO-OPERATIVA DE BORBA 1991 Douro (P)

LV	La Vigneronne

105 Old Brompton Rd, London SW7 3LE (Tel 071 589 6113 Fax 071 581 2983). **Opening Hours:** Mon-Fri 10am-9pm, Sat 10am-7pm. **Delivery:** free locally. **Tastings:** organised tutored events and for customers' club. **Discounts:** 5% per case.

Specialising in the best, the rarest, the most mature and more often than not the fairly expensive, Liz and Mike Berry as independent merchants have the awful task of selecting and tasting most of these wines themselves *sur place*. Out of their 1,000 wines most are ready to drink ('Our clientele is buying for immediate drinking'). For those in search of more everyday tipples there are some well chosen inexpensive French (Liz is author of a book on Languedoc Roussilon) and a line-up of classy Aussies and Californians at around £10. Quality guaranteed.

24	£9.95	GREEN POINT, DOMAINE CHANDON 1990 Yarra Valley (Aus)
53	£6.45	'CASAL DI SERRA' VERDICCHIO CLASSICO, DOC, UMANI RONCHI 1991 Marches (It)
350	£9.95	BROKENWOOD SHIRAZ 1991 S.E. Australia (Aus)
364	£16.95	CHATEAUNEUF DU PAPE, CHATEAU DE BEAUCASTEL 1988 Rhône (F)
389	£7.95	HAMILTON-RUSSELL PINOT NOIR, 1991 Walker Bay (SA)
404	£18.95	ROBERT MONDAVI RESERVE PINOT NOIR 1988 Napa Valley (Cal)
413	£4.95	MONTEPULCIANO D'ABRUZZO, DOC, UMANI RONCHI 1991 Marches (It)
427	£12.50	CUMARO ROSSO CONERO, UMANI RONCHI 1989 Marches (It)
443	£4.95	QUINTA DE LA ROSA RED TABLE WINE 1991 Douro (P)
461	£6.99	STANTON & KILLEEN RUTHERGLEN LIQUEUR MUSCAT Rutherglen (Aus)
499	£65.00	RUTHERFORD MILES MALVASIA SOLERA 1863 Madeira (P)

VIL | Village Wines

6 Mill Row, High Street, Bexley, Kent DA5 1LA (Tel 0322 558772 Fax 0322 558772). **Opening Hours:** Mon to Fri 10am-6pm, Sat 10am to 5pm, Sun (Christmas only) 11am to 4pm. **Delivery:** free locally. **Tastings:** regular in-store and tutored, organised events. **Discounts:** 5% on orders over £250.

The unfashionability of German wines must annoy these Men of Kent, who have done as much as anyone to promote that country's quality wines, both red and white. But their customers aren't complaining because prices for good wines remain remarkably low. Even at £19.49 a half bottle, Sebastiani's Mehringer Zellerberg Riesling Eiswein looks like a bargain. Other areas of the list offer good value as well; there are lots of interesting French regionals, and the eastern European section includes some eclectic Moldavan reds.

54	£4.99	MONTES UNOAKED CHARDONNAY, DISCOVER WINES LTDA 1993 Curico (Ch)
65	£12.95	JERMANN PINOT BIANCO 1991 Friuli Venezia Giulia (It)
160	£6.99	GROVE MILL SAUVIGNON 1992 Blenheim (NZ)
101	£7.95	VIEUX CHATEAU GAUBERT, GRAVES 1991 Bordeaux (F)
140	£4.69	CHATEAU LA BERTRANDE, AC BORDEAUX 1992 Bordeaux (F)
197	£3.95	BADEN DRY, BADISCHER WINZERKELLER Baden (G)
292	£7.25	COLUMBIA CREST MERLOT, STIMSON LANE 1989 Washington State (US)
297	£10.89	CHATEAU NOTTON, MARGAUX 1988 Bordeaux (F)
383	£4.25	MACON SUPERIEUR, CHAMPCLOS, PHILIPPE ANTOINE 1991 Burgundy (F)
413	£3.98	MONTEPULCIANO D'ABRUZZO, DOC, UMANI RONCHI 1991 Marches (It)
491	£11.89	DOWS CRUSTED PORT BOTTLED 1987 Douro (P)
494	£13.98	WARRE'S TRADITIONAL LBV 1981 Douro (P)

VLW | Villeneuve Wines Ltd

27 Northgate, Peebles, Scotland, EH45 8RX (Tel 0721 722500 Fax 0721 729922). **Opening Hours:** Mon-Weds 10am-7pm, Thurs 10 am-8pm, Fri 10am-9pm, Sat 9am-9pm. **Delivery:** free within 50 miles. **Tastings:** regular in-store and tutored, plus organised events. **Discounts:** 5% per case.

The cover of the Villeneuve list is alarmingly reminiscent of a surrealist nightmare, but the selection inside shouldn't scare anyone. There are a host of reliable – if not always inspiring – producers: Faiveley, Chapoutier, and Château de Sours from France, Torres from Spain, KWV from South Africa and Montana from New Zealand. Rising stars from less fashionable areas are showcased too – Bredif from Vouvray, Domaine de Trevallon from Les Baux, Pieropan from Soave and Trapiche from Argentina. And to ensure your dreams are sweet, try a nightcap from the three-page Malt Whisky list.

11	£6.99	MONTANA LINDAUER BRUT (NZ)
44	£3.99	CHARDONNAY, VINO DA TAVOLA, CA DONINI 1992 Triveneto (It)
45	£3.99	NOBILO WHITE CLOUD 1992 (NZ)
46	£3.99	CHARDONNAY DEL PIEMONTE, ARALDICA 1992 Piedmont (It)
48	£3.99	CHAIS BAUMIERE, CHARDONNAY VIN DE PAYS D'OC 1990 Midi (F)
61	£5.99	LUGANA CA'DEI FRATI 1992 Brescia (It)
65	£10.95	JERMANN PINOT BIANCO 1991 Friuli Venezia Giulia (It)
74	£4.99	PENFOLDS KOONUNGA HILL CHARDONNAY 1992 S.E. Australia (Aus)
79	£5.99	ROSEMOUNT CHARDONNAY 1992 Hunter Valley (Aus)
91	£7.49	MARQUES DE MURRIETA RIOJA RESERVA BLANCO 1987 Rioja (Sp)
100	£8.29	FIRESTONE CHARDONNAY 1990 (Cal)
104	£8.75	CHARDONNAY, JANE HUNTER'S WINES 1991 Marlborough (NZ)
169	£8.79	HUNTERS MARLBOROUGH SAUVIGNON BLANC 1992 Marlborough (NZ)
174	£10.95	POUILLY FUME, DE LADOUCETTE 1990 Loire (F)
194	£5.99	TOLLANA DRY WHITE 1992 S.E. Australia (Aus)
229	£2.99	VAL DU TORGAN, LES PRODUCTEURS DU MONT TAUCH Midi (F)
250	£5.85	STAMBOLOVO RESERVE MERLOT 1987 (Bul)
259	£4.49	GLEN ELLEN CABERNET SAUVIGNON 1989 (Cal)
269	£4.99	MONTANA CABERNET SAUVIGNON 1991 Marlborough (NZ)
282	£6.69	VALLEY OAKS CABERNET SAUVIGNON, FETZER VINEYARDS 1990 Mendocino County (Cal)
311	£12.95	CHATEAU CISSAC, HAUT-MEDOC 1982 Bordeaux (F)
321	£23.99	ORNELLAIA 1990 Tuscany (It)
330	£4.25	VIN DE PAYS DES COLLINES RHODANIENNES CEPAGE SYRAH, CAVE DE TAIN L'HERMITAGE Rhône (F)
336	£5.79	ZINFANDEL, FETZER VINEYARDS 1990 Mendocino County (Cal)
344	£7.99	CROZES HERMITAGE LA PETITE RUCHE, CHAPOUTIER 1991 Rhône (F)
389	£6.99	HAMILTON-RUSSELL PINOT NOIR, 1991 Walker Bay (SA)
397	£9.95	MERCUREY, 1ER CRU, CLOS DE MYGLANDS, FAIVELEY 1991 Burgundy (F)
484	£17.99	MATUSALEM, GONZALEZ BYASS Jerez (Sp)

VDV	Vin du Van

Colthups, The Street, Appledore, Kent TN26 2BX (Tel 023383 727). **Opening Hours:** 9am-6pm 7 days. **Delivery:** free locally. **Discounts:** 5-10% on 2-10 cases

It is hard to know exactly what is going on in sleepy Appledore. As far as we can tell from Vin du Van's own reports, a mysterious godfather-like figure called El Supremo is zipping around Kent in a flying corkscrew, delivering wines selected by Doris, Stanley the Cat MW, and an Australian relative who says 'Ripper!' a lot. Their list is filled with top quality Spanish and Antipodean wines at daft (low) prices, accompanied by tasting notes such as 'humungous', 'so full of flavour there was only room for a tiny label', and 'sporran-pleasingly tasty. Hoots!'. Don't run out of gas, El Supremo, the wine trade needs you.

74	£4.75	PENFOLDS KOONUNGA HILL CHARDONNAY 1992 S.E. Australia (Aus)
155	£5.90	ROTHBURY SAUVIGNON BLANC 1992 Marlborough (NZ)
188	£5.25	PETER LEHMANN SEMILLON 1992 Barossa Valley (Aus)
235	£4.75	DAVID WYNN DRY RED 1992 Eden Valley (Aus)
257	£4.20	SEAVIEW CABERNET SAUVIGNON/SHIRAZ 1990 S.E. Australia (Aus)
260	£4.21	OLD TRIANGLE CABERNET SAUVIGNON, S. SMITH & SONS 1991 Barossa Valley (Aus)

265	£4.95	ERRAZURIZ CABERNET SAUVIGNON, MAULE 1991 Maule (Ch)
337	£5.25	GALWAY SHIRAZ, YALUMBA WINERY 1991 Barossa Valley (Aus)
339	£5.99	BOTOBOLAR VINEYARD SHIRAZ, GIL WAHLQUIST 1990 Mudgee (Aus)
342	£6.40	PETER LEHMANN 'CLANCY'S RED' 1990 Barossa Valley (Aus)
346	£6.95	CHATEAU MUSAR, 1986 Bekaa Valley (Leb)
373	£4.99	TARRANGO, BROWN BROTHERS 1992 Milawa (Aus)
450	£5.80	YLLERA, VINO DE MESA, SAT LOS CURRO 1988 Ribera del Duero (Sp)

VER | Vinceremos Wines & Spirits Ltd

65 Raglan Road, Leeds, West Yorkshire LS2 9D2 (Tel 0532 431691 Fax 0532 431693). **Opening Hours:** Mon-Fri 9am-5.30pm, other times by arrangement. **Delivery:** free nationally on 5 cases. **Tastings:** tutored only. **Discounts:** 5% for 5 cases.

Jerry and Jem, as their names would suggest, are committed believers in – and promoters of – organic wine, but they're as fussy about quality as they are about greenness. Which explains the presence on their list of wines like Domaine Richeaume from Provence and Millton from New Zealand. Beyond these, there is a non-organic section too, including offerings from India, Lebanon, Morocco, Ukraine and – why not? – Zimbabwe.

20	£8.30	OMAR KHAYYAM, CHAMPAGNE INDIA 1987 Maharashtra India
86	£6.99	THE MILLTON VINEYARD CHARDONNAY 1992 Gisborne (NZ)
151	£5.35	MUSCADET DE SEVRE ET MAINE, GUY BOSSARD 1992 Loire (F)
217	£4.75	CORBIERES, CHATEAU DE CARAGUILHES, LION FAIVRE 1991 Midi (F)
289	£7.99	DOMAINE RICHEAUME CABERNET SAUVIGNON, COTES DE PROVENCE 1991 Midi (F)
354	£9.95	CHATEAUNEUF DU PAPE, PIERRE ANDRE 1990 Rhône (F)

VT | The Vine Trail

5 Surrey Road, Bishopston, Bristol, Avon B57 9DJ (Tel / Fax 0272 423946). **Opening Hours:** 'All hours'. **Delivery:** free locally. **Tastings:** regular in-store. **Discounts:** 2% on 8 cases, 3% on 20 cases.

Nick Brookes has been on the trail for wines from small French family run domaines now for a few years and has built up an exclusive, slightly off beat list of quality wines at very acceptable prices. Watch out for the Madiran Vieilles Vignes from Dom. des Bories and well priced fizz from Ay (home of Bollinger) with four years' bottle-age.

| 374 | £5.49 | BEAUJOLAIS VILLAGES, JEAN-LOUIS REVILLON 1991 Beaujolais (F) |
| 477 | £11.99 | DOMAINE DE NAYS-LABASSERE, JURANCON 1990 South West (F) |

VR | Vintage Roots

Sheeplands Farm, Wargrave Road, Wargrave, Berkshire RG10 8DT (Tel 0734 401222 Fax 0734 404814). **Opening Hours:** Mon-Fri 9am-6pm, plus 24 hour answerphone. **Delivery:** free within 30 miles; free nationally on 5 cases. **Tastings:** Occasionally and on request. **Discounts:** 5% on 5 cases.

Recent EEC legislation means that all organic produce is now certified as such, so you really know what you're getting. Messrs Palmer, Piggott & Ms. Belsh go one step further by offering a separate vegetarian wine list. We liked the sound of the '89 Veggie Viognier. For those confessing to 'Zins' there's a couple of highly praised '90s. English Sedlescombe 'Sur Lie' is a more recommendable effort at the Muscadet style, and we'd certainly go for the organic Tasmanians from Buchanan.

151	£5.45	MUSCADET DE SEVRE ET MAINE, GUY BOSSARD 1992 Loire (F)
166	£8.30	TERRES BLANCHES BLANC, AIX EN PROVENCE LES BAUX, NOEL MICHELIN 1992 Midi (F)
217	£4.99	CORBIERES, CHATEAU DE CARAGUILHES, LION FAIVRE 1991 Midi (F)
221	£7.95	TERRES BLANCHES VIN ROSE 1992 Midi (F)
339	£5.55	BOTOBOLAR VINEYARD SHIRAZ, GIL WAHLQUIST 1990 Mudgee (Aus)
340	£5.99	COTES DU RHONE, DOMAINE ST. APOLLINAIRE, CUVEE CEPAGE SYRAH, FREDERIC DAUMAS 1990 Rhône (F)
354	£9.50	. CHATEAUNEUF DU PAPE, PIERRE ANDRE 1990 Rhône (F)

W	Waitrose Ltd

Doncastle Rd, South Industrial Area, Bracknell, Berkshire RG12 8YA (Tel 0344 424680 Fax 0344 488195). **Opening Hours:** Mon, Tues 8.30am-6pm, Wed, Thurs 8.30am-8pm, Fri 8.30am-9pm, Sat 8.30am-6pm. **Tastings:** occasionally **Discounts:** 5% per case.

Supermarket of the Year

Short-listed every year for this award, Waitrose finally wrested it from some very vigorous competition after what all of our judges felt was a year when its range had taken on new strengths. In many ways, of course, it is hard to compare this employee-owned chain with its neighbours in the High Street. Waitrose, for instance, almost uniquely refuses to break the law by opening on Sundays and complies with its own 'founder's rules' which simultaneously bar it from advertising or promoting itself and taking part in competitions like the *International Wine Challenge*. Despite its absence from the *Challenge*, the judges recognised that, behind the scenes in Waitrose's Bracknell tasting rooms, there is some really dynamic wine buying being done across the board and some exemplary staff training being offered. Very well chosen wines at very fair prices.

24	£9.95	GREEN POINT, DOMAINE CHANDON 1990 Yarra Valley (Aus)
48	£4.49	CHAIS BAUMIERE, CHARDONNAY VIN DE PAYS D'OC 1990 Midi (F)
74	£4.95	PENFOLDS KOONUNGA HILL CHARDONNAY 1992 S.E. Australia (Aus)
125	£2.99	BLAYE BLANC, GINESTET 1992 Bordeaux (F)
146	£4.79	OXFORD LANDING SAUVIGNON BLANC, YALUMBA WINERY 1992 S. Australia (Aus)
161	£6.95	JACKSON ESTATE SAUVIGNON BLANC 1992 Marlborough (NZ)
187	£2.79	MORIO MUSKAT, ST URSULA 1992 Rheinpfalz (G)
197	£3.25	BADEN DRY, BADISCHER WINZERKELLER Baden (G)
269	£4.99	MONTANA CABERNET SAUVIGNON 1991 Marlborough (NZ)
282	£5.95	VALLEY OAKS CABERNET SAUVIGNON, FETZER VINEYARDS 1990 Mendocino County (Cal)
345	£7.85	ST JOSEPH, CAVES DE SAINT DESIRAT 1989 Rhône (F)
346	£7.45	CHATEAU MUSAR, 1986 Bekaa Valley (Leb)
373	£4.45	TARRANGO, BROWN BROTHERS 1992 Milawa (Aus)
385	£6.50	HAUTES COTES DE BEAUNE, TETE DU CUVEE, CAVES DES HAUTES COTES 1990 Burgundy (F)
491	£9.95	DOWS CRUSTED PORT BOTTLED 1987 Douro (P)
494	£12.50	WARRE'S TRADITIONAL LBV 1981 Douro (P)

WAW | Waterloo Wine Co Ltd

57a to 61 Lant Street, Borough, London SE1 1QL (Tel 071 403 7967 Fax 071 357 6976). **Opening Hours:** Mon-Fri 10am-6.30pm / Sat 10am-5pm. **Delivery:** free locally **Tastings:** regular in-store and tutored.

Between visits to his own vineyard in Waipara, Paul Tutton finds enough time to run a first rate wine company in the murky depths of SE1. His New Zealand links give Waterloo the agency for the excellent Waipara Springs Winery, as well as Stoniers Merricks from Australia. The Old World is not forgotten in an extensive wine list – a well priced French Regional section boasts five different red Corbières alone, and the Loire range, headed by Gaston Huët, puts most of its rivals to shame.

3	£30.70	BOLLINGER GRANDE ANNEE 1985 CHAMPAGNE (F)
97	£8.05	WAIPARA SPRINGS CHARDONNAY 1991 Canterbury (NZ)
194	£3.55	TOLLANA DRY WHITE 1992 S.E. Australia (Aus)
269	£5.76	MONTANA CABERNET SAUVIGNON 1991 Marlborough (NZ)
272	£5.47	ROUGE HOMME CABERNET/SHIRAZ, 1988 Coonawarra (Aus)
285	£5.95	CHINON, COULY-DUTHEIL 1990 Loire (F)
286	£6.89	STONIER'S WINERY SELECTION CABERNETS 1991 Mornington Peninsula (Aus)
389	£6.99	HAMILTON-RUSSELL PINOT NOIR, 1991 Walker Bay (SA)
395	£8.95	STONIER'S MERRICKS PINOT NOIR 1991 Mornington Peninsula (Aus)
468	£5.72	NELSON LATE HARVEST RHINE RIESLING, SEIFRIED 1991 Nelson (NZ)

WAC | Waters of Coventry Ltd

Collins Road, Heathcote, Warwick, Warwickshire CV34 6TF (Tel 0926 888889 Fax 0926 887416) **Opening Hours:** Mon-Fri 9am-5pm, Sat 9am-12.30pm. **Delivery:** free within 30 miles. **Discounts:** various.

Nearly two-hundred years old, and recently relocated to nearby Warwick, Waters is admittedly a wholesaler-cum-retailer (this is a useful source for 10-litre bag-in-box Montague Liebfraumilch) but its range contains such welcome names as Bürklin Wolf, Tiefenbrunner and Jacques Germain in Burgundy. The claret list is shallower than it initially seems (when you set aside the magnums and halves) but even with VAT excluded from prices, there are such good buys to be found as Lynch Bages 1985 at under £25.

33	£26.46	BOLLINGER GRANDE ANNEE 1985 CHAMPAGNE (F)
161	£5.93	JACKSON ESTATE SAUVIGNON BLANC 1992 Marlborough (NZ)
166	£7.38	TERRES BLANCHES BLANC, AIX EN PROVENCE LES BAUX, NOEL MICHELIN 1992 Midi (F)
221	£6.91	TERRES BLANCHES VIN ROSE 1992 Midi (F)
273	£5.50	TALTARNI FIDDLEBACK TERRACE 1990 Pyrenees (Aus)
285	£5.99	CHINON, COULY-DUTHEIL 1990 Loire (F)
364	£17.59	CHATEAUNEUF DU PAPE, CHATEAU DE BEAUCASTEL 1988 Rhône (F)
489	£8.01	CHURCHILL GRAHAM FINEST VINTAGE CHARACTER Douro (P)

WEP | The Welshpool Wine Company

20 Severn St, Welshpool, Powys, Mid-Wales.(Tel 0938 553243) **Opening Hours:** Mon-Fri 9.30am - 8.30pm. **Delivery:** free locally. **Tastings:** regularly in-store.

A newly established retail arm of the Raisin Social wholesaling business,

Welshpool's strengths lie mainly in France and, as the list below show, South Africa. Burgundies come from Ropiteau and Maurice Chenu, Loires come from Prince Poniatowski, while the list of lesser-known Bordeaux Châteaux is worth rifling for the likes of Château la Gorce (Médoc) and Château de Parenchère (Bordeaux Supérieur).

89	£6.99	CHARDONNAY BATELEUR, DANIE DE WET 1991 Robertson (SA)
132	£3.99	SAUVIGNON BLANC, VREDENDAL COOP 1991 (SA)
267	£4.99	KANONKOP KADETTE, STELLENBOSCH 1991 Stellenbosch (SA)
341	£7.99	KANONKOP PINOTAGE, VAN LOVEREN 1989 Stellenbosch (SA)

WES | Wessex Wines

197 St Andrews Rd, Bridport, Dorset DT6 3BT (Tel 0308 23400). **Opening Hours:** Mon-Sat 8.30am - 9.30pm. **Delivery:** free within 20 miles. **Tastings:** regular in-store. **Discounts:** 5% per case, 7.5% on 7 cases.

As one might imagine from his name, Mike Farmer understands the conservative tastes of his Dorset customers, and offers them a down-to-earth selection featuring reliable names like Duboeuf, Laboure Roi and CVNE. Yet we suspect he quietly yearns for a revolution in wine tastes – particularly away from Chardonnay and Cabernet Sauvignon towards less commercial varietals. Infiltrators into his list include an Australian Grenache and two different Riesling/Chenin Blanc blends.

57	£5.73	CHABLIS, LOUIS ALEXANDRE 1992 Burgundy (F)
79	£5.99	ROSEMOUNT CHARDONNAY 1992 Hunter Valley (Aus)
178	£4.19	CORBANS DRY WHITE RIESLING 1991 Marlborough (NZ)
182	£6.49	GEWURZTRAMINER D'ALSACE, CAVE VINICOLE DE TURCKHEIM 1992 Alsace (F)
244	£2.89	RUSSE CABERNET CINSAULT (Bul)
268	£5.38	BEL ARBORS MERLOT, FETZER VINEYARDS 1991 Mendocino County (Cal)
330	£3.91	VIN DE PAYS DES COLLINES RHODANIENNES CEPAGE SYRAH, CAVE DE TAIN L'HERMITAGE Rhône (F)
346	£6.85	CHATEAU MUSAR, 1986 Bekaa Valley (Leb)
377	£6.07	CHENAS, DOMAINE DE CHASSIGNOL, JACQUES DEPAGNEUX 1992 Beaujolais (F)

WHC | Whiclar & Gordon Wines Ltd

The Bunker, Glebelands, Vincent Lane, Dorking, Surrey RH4 3YZ (Tel 0306 885711 Fax 0306 740053). **Opening Hours:** Mon-Fri 9am-5.30pm, Sat 9am-4pm. **Delivery:** free within 10 miles. **Tastings:** regular in-store and tutored, plus organised events. **Discounts:** 5% on mixed cases

New to the Guide, this company's Wine Bunker is a welcome change to the kind in which Surrey's golfers normally find themselves. The amusingly illustrated list showcases good large producers: Hardy's from Australia (W&G's parent company), California's Franciscan and the Cave de Buxy in Burgundy. Unsurprisingly Hardy's French Domaine de la Baume features among a strong set of regional wines, while, as good neighbours, W&G offer prize winners from the nearby Denbies Wine Estate.

WWT | Whitebridge Wines

Unit 21, Whitebridge Estate, Stone, Staffordshire ST15 8LQ (Tel 0785 817229 Fax 0785 811181)

Opening Hours: Mon-Fri 9am-5.30pm, Sat 9.30am-1pm. **Delivery:** free locally. **Tastings:** regularly in-store. **Discounts:** 5% on mixed cases.

Since its takeover five years ago by two Oxbridge graduates (plenty of drinking practice) Whitebridge has quadrupled its turnover and 'become one of the leading wine warehouses in the Midlands'. Whereas others are 'slimming down' their lists, Francis Peel has upped his by 100 new lines! The emphasis here is on value for money, but there are some welcome rarities, such as a '92 'Grain Sauvage' Jurançon sec for £4.99, or '87 Van Gogh label (!) Bandol for £6.99 and Beresford's '90 McLaren Vale Chardonnay.

33	£29.35	BOLLINGER GRANDE ANNEE 1985 CHAMPAGNE (F)
272	£5.75	ROUGE HOMME CABERNET/SHIRAZ, COONAWARRA 1988 Coonawarra (Aus)
346	£7.98	CHATEAU MUSAR, 1986 Bekaa Valley (Leb)
444	£4.99	PERIQUITA, J M DA FONSECA 1990 (P)
468	£5.99	NELSON LATE HARVEST RHINE RIESLING, SEIFRIED 1991 Nelson (NZ)
498	£20.00	QUINTA DO VESUVIO VINTAGE PORT 1990 Douro (P)

WOC	**Whitesides of Clitheroe Ltd**

Shawbridge St, Clitheroe, Lancashire BB7 1NA (Tel 0200 22281 Fax 0200 27129). **Opening Hours:** Mon-Sat 9am-5.30pm. **Delivery:** free within 50 miles. **Tastings:** organised tutored events. **Discounts:** 5% per case.

This town obviously is big enough for both of them because, like D Byrne, Whitesides continue to flourish. Traditionalists are well served with Bordeaux, from house claret at £3.99 to Château Margaux 1983 (definitely the wine of the vintage). The New World selection continues to expand, now covering 18 different Australian wineries and good names from New Zealand, California and even New York State. As for the large malt whisky list, that includes the intriguingly named As We Get It.

11	£6.65	MONTANA LINDAUER BRUT (NZ)
33	£24.50	BOLLINGER GRANDE ANNEE 1985 Champagne (F)
44	£3.99	CHARDONNAY, VINO DA TAVOLA, CA DONINI 1992 Triveneto (It)
45	£4.35	NOBILO WHITE CLOUD 1992 (NZ)
48	£4.75	CHAIS BAUMIERE, CHARDONNAY VIN DE PAYS D'OC 1990 Midi (F)
70	£3.99	TIMARA WHITE, MONTANA 1991 (NZ)
74	£4.99	PENFOLDS KOONUNGA HILL CHARDONNAY 1992 S.E. Australia (Aus)
79	£5.99	ROSEMOUNT CHARDONNAY 1992 Hunter Valley (Aus)
91	£7.75	MARQUES DE MURRIETA RIOJA RESERVA BLANCO 1987 Rioja (Sp)
119	£13.35	ROBERT MONDAVI RESERVE CHARDONNAY 1988 Napa Valley (Cal)
123	£19.99	TORRES MILMANDA CHARDONNAY 1989 Penedes (Sp)
154	£5.45	VERDELHO, WYNDHAM ESTATE 1991 S.E. Australia (Aus)
155	£5.99	ROTHBURY SAUVIGNON BLANC 1992 Marlborough (NZ)
161	£6.49	JACKSON ESTATE SAUVIGNON BLANC 1992 Marlborough (NZ)
174	£11.45	POUILLY FUME, DE LADOUCETTE 1990 Loire (F)
194	£3.19	TOLLANA DRY WHITE 1992 S.E. Australia (Aus)
272	£5.35	ROUGE HOMME CABERNET/SHIRAZ, 1988 Coonawarra (Aus)
273	£4.99	TALTARNI FIDDLEBACK TERRACE 1990 Pyrenees (Aus)
336	£5.39	ZINFANDEL, FETZER VINEYARDS 1990 Mendocino County (Cal)
346	£7.55	CHATEAU MUSAR, 1986 Bekaa Valley (Leb)
373	£4.45	TARRANGO, BROWN BROTHERS 1992 Milawa (Aus)
389	£6.85	HAMILTON-RUSSELL PINOT NOIR, 1991 Walker Bay (SA)
404	£15.75	ROBERT MONDAVI RESERVE PINOT NOIR 1988 Napa Valley (Cal)
416	£5.35	SALICE SALENTINO RISERVA, AZ. AG. TAURINO 1988 Puglia (It)

438	£3.69	ALBOR RIOJA TINTO, BODEGAS & BEBIDAS 1991 Rioja (Sp)
444	£4.29	PERIQUITA, J M DA FONSECA 1990 (P)
447	£5.55	CAMPO VIEJO RIOJA RESERVA 1987 Rioja (Sp)
458	£3.59	MUSCAT OF PATRAS, ACHAIA CLAUSS (Gr)
481	£4.99	HIDALGO AMONTILLADO NAPOLEON Jerez (Sp)
484	£17.50	MATUSALEM, GONZALEZ BYASS Jerez (Sp)
491	£9.19	DOWS CRUSTED PORT BOTTLED 1987 Douro (P)
494	£11.49	WARRE'S TRADITIONAL LBV 1981 Douro (P)
495	£13.35	GALWAY PIPE OLD TAWNY, YALUMBA WINERY Barossa Valley (Aus)
496	£12.59	TAYLOR'S TEN YEAR OLD TAWNY Douro (P)
498	£20.00	QUINTA DO VESUVIO VINTAGE PORT 1990 Douro (P)

WTL | Whittalls Wines

Darlaston Rd, Walsall, West Midlands WS2 9SQ (Tel 0922 36161 Fax 0922 36167). **Opening Hours:** Mon-Fri 9am-5.30pm. **Delivery:** free within 10 miles. **Tastings:** regular in-store and tutored, plus organised events.

The wine list of this wholesaler reminds one of the West Midlands in a number of ways: it is large, easy to get lost in, but contains some real beauty. Vinous sightseers will head for Chinon from Couly Dutheil or a Rhône range including Juge Cornas and the Côte Rôties of Rostaing and Barge.

79	£4.95	ROSEMOUNT CHARDONNAY 1992 HUNTER VALLEY (AUS)
161	£5.70	JACKSON ESTATE SAUVIGNON BLANC 1992 Marlborough (NZ)
259	£3.31	GLEN ELLEN CABERNET SAUVIGNON 1989 (Cal)
285	£5.30	CHINON, COULY-DUTHEIL 1990 Loire (F)
364	£9.19	CHATEAUNEUF DU PAPE, CHATEAU DE BEAUCASTEL 1988 Rhône (F)
496	£10.95	TAYLOR'S TEN YEAR OLD TAWNY Douro (P)

WDW | Windrush Wines Ltd

The Ox House, Market Square, Northleach, Cheltenham, Gloucestershire GL5H 3EG (Tel 0451 860680 Fax 0451 801166). **Opening Hours:** shop: Mon-Sat 9am-5:30pm; offices: 9am-6pm, Sat 10am-1pm. **Delivery:** free locally. **Tastings:** regular in-store. **Discounts:** 2.5% for cash.

Centre of England Merchant of the Year

Mark Savage MW can take a hint. If the Government wants to make it difficult for independent merchants in Britain, why not open an office in Paris from which customers can collect their duty-free wines? Stuff like Stag's Leap from California, Eyrie from Oregon and a host of Burgundies (a Savage enthusiasm) plus exciting southern French wines. Back in England Windrush offer first class service and the same wines from new premises in Northleach as well as in their Cirencester shop. The *Guide* does not have a Best British Wine Merchant in France Award. Yet. But if we did, we suspect Mr S would be a strong a contender for that, too.

WBM | Wine Byre Merchants

Burnside, Cupar, Fife, Scotland, KY15 4BH (Tel 0334 53215 Fax 0334 53215) **Opening Hours:** Mon-Sat 9.30-7pm. **Delivery:** free within 30 miles. **Tastings:** regular in-store and tutored, plus organised events. **Discounts:** 5% on mixed cases.

Lance Sharpus-Jones & Co operate from a designer cowshed (or Byre). Inside, 700 wines are housed on rustic wooden shelves, except those at £3; they're in the cattle trough. There are big names (Rosemount, Torres, Antinori) and smaller (and arguably more interesting) fry such as Mascarello, Labégorce Zédé, Trimbach. Alternatively there's Tiger Milk, (a cure for mad cow disease), Moniack's Mead and Dry Seafish (budgies love it).

3	£6.99	SEGURA VIUDAS CAVA BRUT RESERVA Cava (Sp)
11	£6.99	MONTANA LINDAUER BRUT (NZ)
14	£5.79	ANGAS BRUT CLASSIC, YALUMBA WINERY S.E. Australia (Aus)
20	£7.99	OMAR KHAYYAM, CHAMPAGNE INDIA 1987 Maharashtra India
45	£4.49	NOBILO WHITE CLOUD 1992 (NZ)
123	£19.99	TORRES MILMANDA CHARDONNAY 1991 Penedes (Sp)
155	£5.99	ROTHBURY SAUVIGNON BLANC 1992 Marlborough (NZ)
256	£4.25	HARDYS NOTTAGE HILL CABERNET SAUVIGNON, BRL HARDY WINE CO 1991 S.Australia (Aus)
263	£4.69	MERCHANT VINTNERS CLARET, PETER A SICHEL Bordeaux (F)
292	£7.59	COLUMBIA CREST MERLOT, STIMSON LANE 1989 Washington State (US)
415	£5.79	VALPOLICELLA CLASSICO, MASI 1991 Veneto (It)
444	£4.79	PERIQUITA, J M DA FONSECA 1990 (P)
447	£6.99	CAMPO VIEJO RIOJA RESERVA 1987 Rioja (Sp)
450	£8.39	YLLERA, VINO DE MESA, SAT LOS CURRO 1988 Ribera del Duero (Sp)
481	£7.49	HIDALGO AMONTILLADO NAPOLEON Jerez (Sp)
484	£18.99	MATUSALEM, GONZALEZ BYASS Jerez (Sp)
487	£5.35	TOKAJI ASZU 3 PUTTONYOS, TOKAJI-HEGYALA SCHLUMBERGER 1981 Tokaji (Hun)
490	£8.99	BOAL 5 YEAR OLD, D'OLIVEIRA Madeira

| CRL | The Wine Centre/Charles Steevenson Wines |

Russell Street, Tavistock, Devon PL19 8BD (Tel 0822 615985 Fax 0822 617094). **Opening Hours:** Mon-Sat 9am-7pm. **Delivery:** free locally. **Tastings:** regular in-store plus organised events. **Discounts:** 5% on mixed cases.

Charles Steevenson (sic) has been supplying Devon with an unassuming range of super wines for nearly eight years. Although a Francophile at heart we suspect a leap of faith 'down under'. Well chosen Aussies include Plantagenet's '90 Chardonnay from Margaret River, Peter Lehmann's '90 Semillon, and Great Western's '88 Chalambar Shiraz. Nearer home though, try washing down your pastie with a Cornish white from the Tamar Valley.

| WE | The Wine Emporium/Cockburn's of Leith Ltd |

The Wine Emporium, 7 Devon Place, Edinburgh, EH12 5HJ (Tel 031 346 1113 Fax 031 313 2607) **Opening Hours:** Wine Emporium: Mon-Fri 9am-6pm, Sat 10am-6pm, Sunday 11am-5pm. The Retail Shop: Mon-Sat 10am-6pm. **Delivery:** free within Edinburgh. **Tastings:** regular in-store and tutored, plus organised events. **Discounts:** 5% per case.

Scotland's oldest wine merchant offers a range to satisfy the most pernickety fans of the classic regions – Langoa & Léoville Barton, Armand Rousseau, Louis Gisselbrecht, Domaine Les Pallières and Dr Bürklin-Wolf to name but a few. But creeping in among these established faces are some more modern ones, such as Roberto Bava and Taltarni. It all fits in with the philosophy recounted in the Red Burgundy section: '... the key factor is the selection of only the very best growers – all else is a waste of our time and your money!'

WR	**Wine Rack**

Sefton House, 42 Church Road, Welwyn Garden City, Hertfordshire AL8 6LE (Tel 0707 328244 Fax 0707 371398). **Opening Hours:** Mon-Sat 10am-10pm, Sun varies. **Delivery:** free nationally where possible **Tastings:** regular in-store and tutored, plus organised events. **Discounts:** various.

New World Merchant of the Year and Wine Merchant of the Year

It's sometimes difficult to remember that it was only as recently as 1989 that the first five Wine Rack shops were opened. In four years, they have become Britain's most exciting and innovative place to buy anything from French country wines to top clarets (the range currently including over a dozen 'second labels') and almost anything from New Zealand and Alsace. The latter region should benefit further from the new 'Exclusively Alsace' club, which allows members (membership is free) a 5% discount on all Alsatian wines and access to smaller parcels which never make it onto the shelves. Watch out too for Madeiras. Cossart and Gordon Bual 1910 at £80, anyone?

3	£6.09	SEGURA VIUDAS CAVA BRUT RESERVA Cava (Sp)
11	£6.99	MONTANA LINDAUER BRUT (NZ)
22	£8.99	MAYERLING CREMANT D'ALSACE, CAVE VINICOLE DE TURCKHEIM Alsace (F)
26	£14.29	LE MESNIL BLANC DE BLANCS Champagne (F)
28	£16.25	DRAPPIER BLANC DE BLANCS CHAMPAGNE Champagne (F)
33	£30.25	BOLLINGER GRANDE ANNEE 1985 Champagne (F)
39	£3.35	CHARDONNAY GYONGYOS, HUGH RYMAN 1992 (Hun)
52	£4.99	DOMAINE DES DEUX RUISSEAUX CHARDONNAY, SKALLI 1991 Midi (F)
57	£5.99	CHABLIS, LOUIS ALEXANDRE 1992 Burgundy (F)
59	£6.59	PETIT CHABLIS, GOULLEY 1991 Burgundy (F)
70	£3.99	TIMARA WHITE, MONTANA 1991 (NZ)
74	£4.99	PENFOLDS KOONUNGA HILL CHARDONNAY 1992 S.E. Australia (Aus)
79	£5.99	ROSEMOUNT CHARDONNAY 1992 HUNTER VALLEY (AUS)
84	£6.99	COVA DA URSA CHARDONNAY 1991 Terras do Sado (P)
91	£7.49	MARQUES DE MURRIETA RIOJA RESERVA BLANCO 1987 Rioja (Sp)
92	£7.99	MONTANA CHURCH ROAD CHARDONNAY 1991 (NZ)
96	£7.49	VALLEY VINEYARDS FUME BLANC 1991 Berkshire (UK)
97	£9.29	WAIPARA SPRINGS CHARDONNAY 1991 Canterbury (NZ)
104	£9.99	CHARDONNAY, JANE HUNTER'S WINES 1991 Marlborough (NZ)
106	£9.99	EDNA VALLEY CHARDONNAY 1990 Edna Valley (Cal)
107	£9.99	ACACIA CHARDONNAY, THE CHALONE GROUP 1989 Carneros (Cal)
111	£11.49	CHALK HILL CHARDONNAY 1991 Sonoma (Cal)
112	£11.99	ELSTON CHARDONNAY, TE MATA ESTATE 1991 Hawkes Bay (NZ)
115	£16.65	NEWTON UNFILTERED CHARDONNAY 1990 Napa Valley (Cal)
150	£5.49	KONOCTI SAUVIGNON BLANC 1991 Lake County (Cal)
161	£6.99	JACKSON ESTATE SAUVIGNON BLANC 1992 Marlborough (NZ)
162	£6.99	SELAKS MARLBOROUGH SAUVIGNON BLANC 1991 Marlborough (NZ)
164	£6.99	MENETOU SALON LES MOROGUES HENRI PELLE 1992 Loire (F)
165	£7.99	KATNOOK ESTATE SAUVIGNON BLANC 1992 Coonawarra (Aus)
169	£8.99	HUNTERS MARLBOROUGH SAUVIGNON BLANC 1992 Marlborough (NZ)
182	£5.99	GEWURZTRAMINER D'ALSACE, CAVE VINICOLE DE TURCKHEIM 1992 Alsace (F)
186	£13.99	TOKAY PINOT GRIS VIELLES VIGNES, DOMAINE ZIND HUMBRECHT 1990 Alsace (F)
189	£8.49	LAGAR DE CERVERA, RIAS BAIXAS, LAGAR DE FORNELOSSA 1992 Galicia (Sp)
190	£8.49	MUSCAT, DOMAINE ZIND HUMBRECHT 1991 Alsace (F)
194	£3.29	TOLLANA DRY WHITE 1992 S.E. Australia (Aus)
206	£7.29	WINKELER HASENSPRUNG RIESLING KABINETT, BARON VON BRENTANO 1990 Rheingau (G)
207	£8.99	KREUZNACHER BRUCKES RIESLING AUSLESE, SCHLOSS VON PLETTENBERG 1989 Nahe (G)

208	£9.99	TRITTENHEIMER APOTHEKE RIESLING AUSLESE, GRANS FASSIAN 1989 Mosel Saar Ruwer (G)
215	£3.99	VALDEMAR ROSADA, MARTINEZ BUJANDA 1992 Rioja (Sp)
229	£2.99	VAL DU TORGAN, LES PRODUCTEURS DU MONT TAUCH Midi (F)
236	£4.99	COTEAUX DU LANGUEDOC, DOMAINE DE L'HORTUS, JEAN ORLIAC 1991 South West (F)
238	£6.29	CHATEAU DE LASTOURS CORBIERES, FUT DE CHENE 1989 Midi (F)
240	£4.99	MADIRAN, MONTUS, ALAIN BRUMONT 1990 South West (F)
244	£2.85	RUSSE CABERNET CINSAULT (Bul)
250	£3.89	STAMBOLOVO RESERVE MERLOT 1987 (Bul)
258	£3.99	DOMAINE DE RIVOYRE CABERNET SAUVIGNON, H RYMAN 1990 Midi (F)
269	£4.99	MONTANA CABERNET SAUVIGNON 1991 Marlborough (NZ)
281	£6.29	CHATEAU BONNET OAK AGED, A LURTON 1990 Bordeaux (F)
298	£9.99	LINDEMANS ST GEORGE CABERNET SAUVIGNON 1989 Coonawarra (Aus)
300	£9.99	L'ABEILLE DE FIEUZAL, PESSAC LEOGNAN 1990 Bordeaux (F)
303	£9.99	PETALUMA COONAWARRA RED 1988 Coonawarra (Aus)
310	£12.99	LE CARILLON DE L'ANGELUS, ST EMILION 1990 Bordeaux (F)
312	£13.49	RESERVE DE LA COMTESSE, PAUILLAC 1987 Bordeaux (F)
317	£14.99	CHATEAU HAUT BAGES AVEROUS, PAUILLAC 1988 Bordeaux (F)
346	£8.19	CHATEAU MUSAR,1986 Bekaa Valley (Leb)
347	£7.99	ST. JOSEPH, COTE DIANE, CAVE CO-OPERATIVE DE ST. DESIRAT 1989 Rhône (F)
348	£8.69	ROSEMOUNT SHOW RESERVE SYRAH 1990 McLaren Vale (Aus)
353	£9.99	DAVID WYNN PATRIARCH SHIRAZ 1991 Eden Valley (Aus)
365	£12.99	PENFOLDS MAGILL ESTATE SHIRAZ 1988 S. Australia (Aus)
371	£17.99	COTE ROTIE, GERIN 1990 Rhône (F)
375	£5.79	MACON-BRAY, DOMAINE DE LA COMBE, HENRI LAFARGE 1991 Burgundy (F)
401	£13.69	FIXIN, LOUIS JADOT 1989 Burgundy (F)
413	£3.99	MONTEPULCIANO D'ABRUZZO, DOC, UMANI RONCHI 1991 Marches (It)
433	£2.55	LEZIRIA VINHO TINTO, VEGA CO-OPERATIVE ALMEIRIM 1992 Almeirim (P)
438	£3.69	ALBOR RIOJA TINTO, BODEGAS & BEBIDAS 1991 Rioja (Sp)
442	£3.99	VALDEMAR RIOJA TINTO, MARTINEZ BUJANDA 1992 Rioja (Sp)
444	£4.15	PERIQUITA, J M DA FONSECA 1990 (P)
445	£4.99	MEIA PIPA, J P VINHOS 1989 (P)
447	£4.99	CAMPO VIEJO RIOJA RESERVA 1987 Rioja (Sp)
448	£5.99	CARTUXA, FUNDACO E ALMEIDA 1989 Evora (P)
450	£5.99	YLLERA, VINO DE MESA, SAT LOS CURRO 1988 Ribera del Duero (Sp)
452	£6.95	BARON DE LEY RIOJA RESERVA 1987 Rioja (Sp)
453	£5.99	JOAO PATO TINTO, BAIRRADA 1990 Bairrada (P)
461	£5.49	STANTON & KILLEEN RUTHERGLEN LIQUEUR MUSCAT Rutherglen (Aus)
469	£6.79	CHATEAU DE BERBEC, PREMIERES COTES DE BORDEAUX 1989 Bordeaux (F)
484	£18.99	MATUSALEM, GONZALEZ BYASS Jerez (Sp)
486	£7.99	RIVESALTES, VIEILLE RESERVE, LES PRODUCTEURS DU MONT TAUCH 1980 Midi (F)
488	£7.49	OLD TRAFFORD TAWNY, B. SEPPELT & SONS S.E. Australia (Aus)
496	£13.99	TAYLOR'S TEN YEAR OLD TAWNY Douro (P)
499	£39.00	RUTHERFORD MILES MALVASIA SOLERA 1863 Madeira

WSC	The Wine Schoppen Ltd

1 Abbeydale Rd South, Sheffield, S Yorks S7 2QL (Tel 0742 365684 Fax 0742 352171). **Opening Hours:** Mon-Fri 9.30am-6pm, Sat 9.30am-5pm, Barrels & Bottles: Mon-Fri 9am-6pm, Sat 9am-2.15pm. **Delivery:** free within 15 miles. **Tastings:** regular in-store and tutored, plus organised events and customers' club. **Discounts:** 5% upwards per case.

Anne Coghlan's impressive list proves that Germany is again demanding recognition as a source of top quality wine. Add to this a programme of tutored tastings given by the growers themselves, and Sheffield residents should certainly have no excuse to confuse their Rheinpfalz with their Rheinhessen.

5	£6.99	GRAND DUCHESS RUSSIAN SPARKLING WINE (Ukraine)
108	£13.55	SWANSON CHARDONNAY, NAPA VALLEY 1990 Napa Valley (Cal)
149	£5.46	ZONNEBLOEM BLANC DE BLANC, STELLENBOSCH FARMERS WINERY 1991 Coastal Region (SA)
154	£6.35	VERDELHO, WYNDHAM ESTATE 1991 S.E. Australia (Aus)
83	£5.92	VERNACCIA DI S. GIMIGNANO, PODERI MONTENIDOLI 1991 Tuscany (It)
268	£6.74	BEL ARBORS MERLOT, FETZER VINEYARDS 1991 Mendocino County (Cal)
295	£7.20	FETZER BARREL SELECT CABERNET SAUVIGNON 1989 Mendocino County (Cal)
442	£6.59	VALDEMAR RIOJA TINTO, MARTINEZ BUJANDA 1992 Rioja (Sp)
468	£6.87	NELSON LATE HARVEST RHINE RIESLING, SEIFRIED 1991 Nelson (NZ)
489	£9.86	CHURCHILL GRAHAM FINEST VINTAGE CHARACTER Douro (P)
492	£20.99	COLHEITA, A A CALEM & FILHO 1985 Douro (P)

SHG | Wine Shop on the Green

12a Albany Terrace, Haverfordwest, Dyfed SA61 1RH (Tel 0437 766864 Fax 0437 765004) **Opening Hours:** Mon-Sat 10am-6pm (Thurs 10am-1pm). **Delivery:** free within 100 miles. **Tastings:** regular in-store and tutored, plus organised events and customers' club. **Discounts:** 5% on mixed cases.

Having worked for Oddbins and the Australian Wine Bureau, Wendy MacMahon's enthusiasm for Antipodean wines is hardly surprising. She and her partner Mike Llewhellin started up in the middle of the recession and business is booming. 'Australia's a firm favourite with our customers... But the French country wines are becoming more popular'. Champagne is strictly 'Bolli' here, Wendy's baby son's first words...

33	£31.80	BOLLINGER GRANDE ANNEE 1985 CHAMPAGNE (F)
48	£4.89	CHAIS BAUMIERE, CHARDONNAY VIN DE PAYS D'OC 1990 Midi (F)
80	£4.99	CHATEAU REYNELLA STONY HILL CHARDONNAY 1990 S. Australia (Aus)
82	£6.50	CARIAD GWIN DA O GYMRU BACCHUS/REICHSTEINER, LLANERCH VINEYARD 1990 Glamorgan (Wales)
444	£4.29	PERIQUITA, J M DA FONSECA 1990 (P)
487	£8.45	TOKAJI ASZU 3 PUTTONYOS, TOKAJI-HEGYALA SCHLUMBERGER 1981 Tokaji (Hun)
496	£17.90	TAYLOR'S TEN YEAR OLD TAWNY Douro (P)

WSO | The Wine Society

Gunnels Wood Rd, Stevenage, Herts SG1 2BG (Tel 0438 741177 Fax 0438 741392). **Opening Hours:** Mon-Fri 9am-5.30pm, Sat 9am-1pm. **Delivery:** Free nationally. **Tastings:** regular in-store and tutored, plus organised events and customers' club. **Discounts:** £3 per case on collection.

Continuing to confound critics and competitors with an ever-improving selection of wines and exciting new marketing initiatives. France remains the strong point, with everything from Gascogne to Château Lafite 1982, but the New World is not far behind, with Kumeu River, Wirra Wirra, and Ravenswood. Meanwhile the mixed case ideas are inspired (including DIY home tasting kits for budding 'blind' masters), and a new collection point near Calais which allows members to 'beat the Chancellor'.

162	£6.60	SELAKS MARLBOROUGH SAUVIGNON BLANC 1991 Marlborough (NZ)

164	£7.69	MENETOU SALON LES MOROGUES HENRI PELLE 1992 Loire (F)
174	£12.04	POUILLY FUME, DE LADOUCETTE 1990 Loire (F)
293	£9.25	THE ANGELUS CABERNET SAUVIGNON, WIRRA WIRRA 1991 S. Australia (Aus)
327	£3.95	DOMAINE DE L'AMEILLAUD, VIN DE PAYS, N. THOMPSON 1992 Midi (F)
328	£3.75	CEPAGE SYRAH, DOMAINE LA CONDAMINE L'EVEQUE 1991 Midi (F)
362	£12.50	CORNAS LA GEYNALE, R. MICHEL 1990 Rhône (F)
479	£22.75	VOUVRAY MOELLEUX, CLOS DU BOURG, GASTON HUET 1990 Loire (F)
481	£6.29	HIDALGO AMONTILLADO NAPOLEON Jerez (Sp)

WTR | The Wine Treasury Ltd

143 Ebury Street, London SW1W 9QN (Tel 071 730 6774 Fax 071 823 6402). **Opening Hours:** Mon-Fri 9am-6pm. **Delivery:** free nationally on 4 cases. **Tastings:** tutored, plus organised events and customers' club. **Discounts:** 'generous for quantity!'.

The Wine Treasury's chancellor, Neville Blech, has strong views about the current obsession with price-pointing, and what he considers to be its effect on wine quality. Unfortunately we can't print them! However his list indicates his position clearly – never mind the prices (which are ex-VAT and as such pretty unhelpful) feel the quality. And his range of Californians and Burgundies is certainly well chosen. Try the Rollin Corton Charlemagne versus Kistler McCrae Vineyard for the Chardonnay experience of a lifetime.

138	£4.45	RESPLANDY SAUVIGNON BLANC, VIN DE PAYS D'OC, VAL D'ORBIEU 1992 Midi (F)
140	£4.55	CHATEAU LA BERTRANDE, AC BORDEAUX 1992 Bordeaux (F)
189	£6.80	LAGAR DE CERVERA, RIAS BAIXAS, LAGAR DE FORNELOSSA 1992 Galicia (Sp)
320	£20.25	CHATEAU PICHON LONGUEVILLE BARON, PAUILLAC 1990 Bordeaux (F)
326	£3.72	RESPLANDY MOUVEDRE, VIN DE PAYS D'OC, VAL D'ORBIEU 1990 Midi (F)
352	£8.47	PENLEY ESTATE SHIRAZ/CABERNET SAUVIGNON, 1990 Coonawarra (Aus)
371	£14.12	COTE ROTIE, GERIN 1990 Rhône (F)

WCE | Winecellars

153-155 Wandsworth High St, London, SW18 4JB (Tel 081 871 3979 Fax 081 874 8380) **Opening Hours:** Mon-Fri 11.30am-8.30pm, Sat 10.30-8.30pm. **Delivery:** free per case within M25; nationally for 2 cases. **Tastings:** regular in-store and tutored, plus organised events. **Discounts:** £3.60 per case on collection; £1 per case on 5 or more delivered cases.

London / South-East Merchant of the Year and Joint Wine Merchant of the Year

Winecellars' tasting for the trade and press is one of the key dates of the vinous year. The reason the tastings work so well is the combination of cherished old friends and exciting new acquaintances from Italy and – increasingly – from a growing range of other countries. All show that Messrs Gleave and Belfrage (et al) are not afraid of flavour in their wines. It was this range and the way the wines are presented, both in the Wandsworth shop and in the splendid list which won Winecellars these two awards.

24	£10.25	GREEN POINT, DOMAINE CHANDON 1990 Yarra Valley (Aus)
33	£28.25	BOLLINGER GRANDE ANNEE 1985 CHAMPAGNE (F)
46	£4.49	CHARDONNAY DEL PIEMONTE, ARALDICA 1992 Piedmont (It)
57	£5.99	CHABLIS, LOUIS ALEXANDRE 1992 Burgundy (F)
61	£6.79	LUGANA CA'DEI FRATI 1992 Brescia (It)
77	£4.95	SALISBURY ESTATE CHARDONNAY 1992 S.E. Australia (Aus)

91	£8.39	MARQUES DE MURRIETA RIOJA RESERVA BLANCO 1987 Rioja (Sp)
98	£8.99	LOCAL GROWERS SEMILLON, ROCKFORD 1989 Barossa Valley (Aus)
106	£10.25	EDNA VALLEY CHARDONNAY 1990 Edna Valley (Cal)
113	£21.99	PULIGNY MONTRACHET, DOMAINE LOUIS CARILLON ET FILS 1991 Burgundy (F)
144	£5.25	COTEAUX DE LANGUEDOC PICPOUL DE PINET, DUC DE MORNY 1991 Midi (F)
155	£6.39	ROTHBURY SAUVIGNON BLANC 1992 Marlborough (NZ)
171	£9.99	POGGIO ALLE GAZZE, TENUTA DELL'ORNELLAIA 1991 Tuscany (It)
182	£6.45	GEWURZTRAMINER D'ALSACE, CAVE VINICOLE DE TURCKHEIM 1992 Alsace (F)
197	£3.99	BADEN DRY, BADISCHER WINZERKELLER Baden (G)
266	£4.95	SALISBURY ESTATE CABERNET SAUVIGNON 1991 S.E. Australia (Aus)
305	£12.55	CYRIL HENSCHKE CABERNET SAUVIGNON, STEPHEN HENSCHKE 1988 Adelaide Hills (Aus)
321	£23.85	ORNELLAIA 1990 Tuscany (It)
330	£3.99	VIN DE PAYS DES COLLINES RHODANIENNES CEPAGE SYRAH, CAVE DE TAIN L'HERMITAGE Rhône (F)
364	£12.75	CHATEAUNEUF DU PAPE, CHATEAU DE BEAUCASTEL 1988 Rhône (F)
387	£6.99	CAMERON PINOT NOIR Willamette Valley USA
414	£4.35	DOLCETTO D'ASTI, ARALDICA 1992 Piedmont (It)
422	£8.95	CHIANTI CLASSICO, ISOLE E OLENA 1990 Tuscany (It)
424	£7.69	DOLCETTO D'ALBA CORSINI, MASCARELLO 1991 Piedmont (It)
426	£9.49	FREISA DELLE LANGHE, G D VAJRA 1990 Piedmont (It)
428	£9.95	BRIC MILEUI, ASCHERI 1990 Piedmont (It)
439	£4.25	BORBA, ADEGA CO-OPERATIVA DE BORBA 1991 Douro (P)
443	£4.99	QUINTA DE LA ROSA RED TABLE WINE 1991 Douro (P)
459	£5.25	SAMOS NECTAR, SAMOS CO-OPERATIVE 1983 Samos (Gr)
461	£5.95	STANTON & KILLEEN RUTHERGLEN LIQUEUR MUSCAT Rutherglen (Aus)
494	£12.95	WARRE'S TRADITIONAL LBV 1981 Douro (P)
495	£14.25	GALWAY PIPE OLD TAWNY, YALUMBA WINERY Barossa Valley (Aus)

| WMK | Winemark Wine Merchant |

3 Duncrue Place, Belfast, Northern Ireland BT3 9BU (Tel 0232 746274 Fax 0232 748022). **Opening Hours:** Mon-Sat 9:30am-9pm. **Delivery:** free locally. **Tastings:** regular in-store and tutored, plus organised events and customers' club.

With 72 shops, and a steadily improving selection of wines, this northern Irish chain has unobtrusively become one of the strongest in the British Isles. The range is not homogenous. Burgundies are weak, but there are delightful German wines from Muller Catoir and Grans-Fassian. Spain and Portugal are stronger – as is regional France which includes some excellent vins de pays. Winemark's own-label wines are also often far better than their slightly unprepossessing name and labels might lead you to suppose.

331	£3.99	CHATEAU DE MALIJAY, COTES DU RHONE, DOMAINE VITICOLES LISTEL C.S.M. 1990 Rhône (F)
465	£3.99	CHATEAU VALENTIN STE CROIX DU MONT, 1992 Bordeaux (F)
475	£9.99	BINGER BUBENSTUCK EHRENFELSER BEERENAUSLESE, LEOFF 1989 Rheinhessen (G)

| WIN | The Winery |

4 Clifton Road, Maida Vale, London W9 1SS (Tel 071 286 6475). **Opening Hours:** The Winery: Mon-Fri 10.30am-8.30pm, Sat 10am-6.30. Les Amis Du Vin Mon-Fri 10:30am to 7pm. **Delivery:** free locally. **Tastings:** regular in-store.

The wines which are now dispensed in this Maida Vale shop may be as efficacious as the remedies sold when it was an apothecary in the early years of this century. The range of Champagne is as impressive as any in London, and the Californian, Italian and French range benefits from the Winery being the retail arm of wholesalers, Geoffrey Roberts Agencies. A trip to the Winery could be just what the doctor ordered.

14	£8.25	ANGAS BRUT CLASSIC, YALUMBA WINERY S.E. Australia (Aus)
16	£7.95	YALUMBA SPARKLING CABERNET CUVEE PRESTIGE S.E. Australia (Aus)
25	£10.95	CROSER METHODE TRADITIONNELLE, PETALUMA WINERY 1990 Adelaide Hills (Aus)
33	£29.50	BOLLINGER GRANDE ANNEE 1985 Champagne (F)
87	£6.95	BARREL FERMENTED CHARDONNAY, ROTHBURY ESTATE 1992 Hunter Valley (Aus)
91	£9.50	MARQUES DE MURRIETA RIOJA RESERVA BLANCO 1987 Rioja (Sp)
95	£8.95	BARREL SELECT CHARDONNAY, FETZER VINEYARDS 1991 Mendocino County (Cal)
96	£10.95	VALLEY VINEYARDS FUME BLANC 1991 Berkshire (UK)
100	£8.95	FIRESTONE CHARDONNAY 1990 (Cal)
106	£8.99	EDNA VALLEY CHARDONNAY 1990 Edna Valley (Cal)
107	£12.95	ACACIA CHARDONNAY, THE CHALONE GROUP 1989 Carneros (Cal)
110	£10.50	POMINO IL BENEFIZIO, MARCHESI DE FRESCOBALDI 1990 Tuscany (It)
112	£12.95	ELSTON CHARDONNAY, TE MATA ESTATE 1991 Hawkes Bay (NZ)
117	£14.50	RIDGE CHARDONNAY 1990 St Cruz (Cal)
146	£4.85	OXFORD LANDING SAUVIGNON BLANC, YALUMBA WINERY 1992 S. Australia (Aus)
155	£5.95	ROTHBURY SAUVIGNON BLANC 1992 Marlborough (NZ)
222	£9.95	CHATEAU DE LA GRILLE, CHINON ROSE, A GOSSET 1992 Loire (F)
268	£5.75	BEL ARBORS MERLOT, FETZER VINEYARDS 1991 Mendocino County (Cal)
269	£5.75	MONTANA CABERNET SAUVIGNON 1991 Marlborough (NZ)
282	£5.95	VALLEY OAKS CABERNET SAUVIGNON, FETZER VINEYARDS 1990 Mendocino County (Cal)
295	£8.95	FETZER BARREL SELECT CABERNET SAUVIGNON 1989 Mendocino County (Cal)
297	£7.95	CHATEAU NOTTON, MARGAUX 1988 Bordeaux (F)
303	£9.99	PETALUMA COONAWARRA RED 1988 Coonawarra (Aus)
315	£14.95	MORMORETO CABERNET SAUVIGNON PREDICATO DI BITURICA, VINO DA TAVOLA, MARCHESI DE FRESCOBALDI 1988 Tuscany (It)
336	£4.95	ZINFANDEL, FETZER VINEYARDS 1990 Mendocino County (Cal)
337	£5.75	GALWAY SHIRAZ, YALUMBA WINERY 1991 Barossa Valley (Aus)
346	£7.75	CHATEAU MUSAR, BEKAA VALLEY 1986 BEKAA VALLEY (LEB)
349	£7.95	ZINFANDEL, DRY CREEK VINEYARDS 1990 Sonoma (Cal)
363	£11.25	RIDGE GEYSERVILLE ZINFANDEL 1991 Sonoma (Cal)
416	£5.35	SALICE SALENTINO RISERVA, AZ. AG. TAURINO 1988 Puglia (It)
419	£6.95	BARBERA D'ALBA VIGNOTA, CONTERNO E FANTINO 1991 Piedmont (It)
495	£12.95	GALWAY PIPE OLD TAWNY, YALUMBA WINERY Barossa Valley (Aus)

WOI	Wines of Interest

46 Burlington Rd, Ipswich, Suffolk IP1 2HZ (Tel 0473 215752 Fax 0473 280275). **Opening Hours:** Mon-Fri 9am-6pm, Sat 9am-1pm. **Delivery:** free locally. **Tastings:** regular in-store and tutored, plus organised events. **Discounts:** 5% on mixed cases

A brave name in the age of the Trades Description Act, but Tim Voelker continues to justify it with a nicely balanced list. Highlights include Rocca Rubia from Sardinia, and the wines of Wirra Wirra in Australia. In the fine wine list, we found Château Branaire Ducru 1982 for £22.50, a good price for what one influential American termed a 'gustatory smorgasbord'.

| 26 | £18.75 | LE MESNIL BLANC DE BLANCS Champagne (F) |
| 53 | £5.45 | 'CASAL DI SERRA' VERDICCHIO CLASSICO, DOC, UMANI RONCHI 1991 Marches (It) |

88	£7.80	BOURGOGNE BLANC, HENRI CLERC 1991 Burgundy (F)
141	£4.75	CUVEE DE CEPAGE SAUVIGNON, DOMAINE DU BREUIL 1992 Loire (F)
162	£6.75	SELAKS MARLBOROUGH SAUVIGNON BLANC 1991 Marlborough (NZ)
250	£4.99	STAMBOLOVO RESERVE MERLOT 1987 (Bul)
266	£4.99	SALISBURY ESTATE CABERNET SAUVIGNON 1991 S.E. Australia (Aus)
293	£8.85	THE ANGELUS CABERNET SAUVIGNON, WIRRA WIRRA 1991 S. Australia (Aus)
413	£3.89	MONTEPULCIANO D'ABRUZZO, DOC, UMANI RONCHI 1991 Marches (It)
481	£6.25	HIDALGO AMONTILLADO NAPOLEON Jerez (Sp)
494	£13.50	WARRE'S TRADITIONAL LBV 1981 Douro (P)

WNS Winos Wine Shop

63 George St, Oldham, Lancs OL1 1LX (Tel 061 652 9396). **Opening Hours:** Mon-Sat 9am-6pm. **Delivery:** free within 30 miles. **Tastings:** tutored. **Discounts:** 5% on mixed cases.

Philip Garratt and Stephen Whitehead, the two winos in question, must have been at the meths when they settled on their prices: reliable house wine Cuvée Jean Paul for £2.50, Italian star Ceppi Storici for £4.25. Buy a case and you get a further 5% off. The best news of all, particularly for Oldham's bag ladies, is that payment methods accepted include 'Access, Visa and Barter!'

19	£7.45	CHAPIN ROSE, SAUMUR, CHAPIN & LANDAIS Loire (F)
20	£7.75	OMAR KHAYYAM, CHAMPAGNE INDIA 1987 Maharashtra India
22	£8.95	MAYERLING CREMANT D'ALSACE, CAVE VINICOLE DE TURCKHEIM Alsace (F)
45	£5.45	NOBILO WHITE CLOUD 1992 (NZ)
79	£5.65	ROSEMOUNT CHARDONNAY 1992 Hunter Valley (Aus)
99	£9.25	KRONDORF SHOW RESERVE CHARDONNAY 1991 Barossa Valley (Aus)
182	£6.75	GEWURZTRAMINER D'ALSACE, CAVE VINICOLE DE TURCKHEIM 1992 Alsace (F)
266	£4.85	SALISBURY ESTATE CABERNET SAUVIGNON 1991 S.E. Australia (Aus)
272	£4.95	ROUGE HOMME CABERNET/SHIRAZ, 1988 Coonawarra (Aus)
346	£6.95	CHATEAU MUSAR, BEKAA VALLEY 1986 BEKAA VALLEY (LEB)
348	£7.95	ROSEMOUNT SHOW RESERVE SYRAH 1990 McLaren Vale (Aus)
377	£6.25	CHENAS, DOMAINE DE CHASSIGNOL, JACQUES DEPAGNEUX 1992 Beaujolais (F)

MAW M & A Winter

181 High Rd, Chigwell, Essex IG7 6NU (Tel 081 500 2074 Fax 081 500 1956). **Opening Hours:** Mon-Fri 9am-9pm, (closed Mon pm), Sat 9am-10pm. **Delivery:** free within 5 miles. **Tastings:** occasionally, plus theme dinners/events. **Discounts:** 10% per case.

Canny wine buyers know that although John Winter's shop stocks several delicous everyday drinking wines, the bargains are to be be found on the mailing list. Customers can take advantage of Mr W's frugal 10% wholesale profit margin on wines like 1977 Grahams at £16.45, 1963 Croft at £35.25. Quantities are limited, so order early – or you might suffer from the discontent of Winter.

WGW Woodgate Wines

Woodgate Farm, Lowick, Nr Ulverston, Cumbria LA12 8ES (Tel 0229 85637). **Opening Hours:** Mon-Fri 9am-5pm, weekends by appointment **Delivery:** free within Cumbria. **Tastings:** occasionally. **Discounts:** wholesale.

The barn which used to house cows and sheep is now the home for Bill

Towers's hobby-turned-business. Vallet Frères, the Jura wines of Boilley and country wines from Châteaux le Raz and Lastours are more interesting than the Rudolf Muller Germans. Bill has recently augmented his Italian range, while outside Europe, Moss Wood and Hunters are worth seeking out.

22	£8.90	MAYERLING CREMANT D'ALSACE, CAVE VINICOLE DE TURCKHEIM Alsace (F)
46	£3.95	CHARDONNAY DEL PIEMONTE, ARALDICA 1992 Piedmont (It)
57	£5.55	CHABLIS, LOUIS ALEXANDRE 1992 Burgundy (F)
59	£6.70	PETIT CHABLIS, GOULLEY 1991 Burgundy (F)
61	£5.90	LUGANA CA'DEI FRATI 1992 Brescia (It)
77	£4.70	SALISBURY ESTATE CHARDONNAY 1992 S.E. Australia (Aus)
134	£3.90	DOMAINE DE MAUBET VIN DE PAYS DES COTES DE GASCOGNE, FONTAN 1992 South West (F)
144	£4.50	COTEAUX DE LANGUEDOC PICPOUL DE PINET, DUC DE MORNY 1991 Midi (F)
163	£7.25	BOURGOGNE ALIGOTÉ, VALLET FRERES 1990 Burgundy (F)
164	£7.75	MENETOU SALON LES MOROGUES HENRI PELLE 1992 Loire (F)
171	£8.70	POGGIO ALLE GAZZE, TENUTA DELL'ORNELLAIA 1991 Tuscany (It)
182	£6.30	GEWURZTRAMINER D'ALSACE, CAVE VINICOLE DE TURCKHEIM 1992 Alsace (F)
238	£6.50	CHATEAU DE LASTOURS CORBIERES, FUT DE CHENE 1989 Midi (F)
266	£4.70	SALISBURY ESTATE CABERNET SAUVIGNON 1991 S.E. Australia (Aus)
299	£10.00	MEERLUST MERLOT, STELLENBOSCH 1986 Stellenbosch (SA)
301	£10.25	CHATEAU LA TOUR DE PEZ, ST ESTEPHE 1990 Bordeaux (F)
321	£19.00	ORNELLAIA 1990 Tuscany (It)
330	£3.75	VIN DE PAYS DES COLLINES RHODANIENNES CEPAGE SYRAH, CAVE DE TAIN L'HERMITAGE Rhône (F)
335	£4.70	COTES DU RHONE DOMAINE DE TERRE BRULEE, CAVE DE VIGNERONS DE RASTEAU 1990 Rhône (F)
405	£15.50	BEAUNE 1ER CRU EPENOTTES, VALLET FRERES 1989 Burgundy (F)
414	£3.85	DOLCETTO D'ASTI, ARALDICA 1992 Piedmont (It)
422	£9.80	CHIANTI CLASSICO, ISOLE E OLENA 1990 Tuscany (It)
424	£5.40	DOLCETTO D'ALBA CORSINI, MASCARELLO 1991 Piedmont (It)
426	£8.25	FREISA DELLE LANGHE, G D VAJRA 1990 Piedmont (It)
437	£3.20	CISMEIRA DOURO 1991 Douro (P)
438	£3.50	ALBOR RIOJA TINTO, BODEGAS & BEBIDAS 1991 Rioja (Sp)
443	£4.80	QUINTA DE LA ROSA RED TABLE WINE 1991 Douro (P)
447	£5.60	CAMPO VIEJO RIOJA RESERVA 1987 Rioja (Sp)
448	£5.65	CARTUXA, FUNDACO E ALMEIDA 1989 Evora (P)
453	£8.50	JOAO PATO TINTO, BAIRRADA 1990 Bairrada (P)
467	£5.60	VIN SANTO BROLIO ESTATE, BARONE RICASOLI 1984 Tuscany (It)
487	£7.90	TOKAJI ASZU 3 PUTTONYOS, TOKAJI-HEGYALA SCHLUMBERGER 1981 Tokaji (Hun)
497	£16.50	NIEPOORT COLHEITA 1983 Douro (P)

WRW	**The Wright Wine Co**

The Old Smithy, Raikes Road, Skipton, North Yorkshire BD23 1NP (Tel 0756 700886 Fax 0756 798580). **Opening Hours:** Mon-Sat 9am-6pm. **Delivery:** free within 35 miles. **Tastings:** wines open in-store. **Discounts:** 5% on mixed cases

A lovely little, stone-walled, wine-clad establishment with excellent Bordeaux at under a fiver, the rare '88 St Joseph white from Bernard Grippat, and one of the few Pinotages which doesn't speak Afrikaans. This one's a Kiwi from Nobilo. We also loved the choice of Wallabies (smaller Australian producers) and the older vintages, formerly the property of less fortunate merchants. Lots of halves for the quality-not-quantity seekers.

3	£6.75	SEGURA VIUDAS CAVA BRUT RESERVA Cava (Sp)

33	£29.80	BOLLINGER GRANDE ANNEE 1985 Champagne (F)
64	£8.60	TASMANIAN WINE COMPANY CHARDONNAY, PIPER'S BROOK 1991 Tasmania (Aus)
79	£6.50	ROSEMOUNT CHARDONNAY 1992 Hunter Valley (Aus)
90	£8.35	YARDEN CHARDONNAY, GOLAN HEIGHTS WINERY 1991 Golan Heights (Is)
91	£8.00	MARQUES DE MURRIETA RIOJA RESERVA BLANCO 1987 Rioja (Sp)
218	£6.65	MOUNT HURTLE GRENACHE ROSE, GEOFF MERRILL 1992 McLaren Vale (Aus)
272	£5.75	ROUGE HOMME CABERNET/SHIRAZ,1988 Coonawarra (Aus)
278	£6.60	GOUNDREY LANGTON CABERNET/MERLOT 1991 Mount Barker (Aus)
311	£14.90	CHATEAU CISSAC, HAUT-MEDOC 1982 Bordeaux (F)
346	£8.20	CHATEAU MUSAR, 1986 Bekaa Valley (Leb)
373	£5.25	TARRANGO, BROWN BROTHERS 1992 Milawa (Aus)
444	£4.70	PERIQUITA, J M DA FONSECA 1990 (P)
473	£11.60	CHATEAU DE ROLLAND, BARSAC 1990 Bordeaux (F)
496	£13.50	TAYLOR'S TEN YEAR OLD TAWNY Douro (P)

PWY | Peter Wylie Fine Wines

Plymtree Manor, Plymtree, Devon EX15 2LE (Tel 08847 555 Fax 08847 557). **Opening Hours:** Mon-Fri 9.30am-6pm. **Delivery:** free in London for 3 or more cases.

The wines here could tell a tale or two, with vintages spanning over a period of 110 years. Six monarchs later the 1890 Lafite is still going strong as are its successors 1902 & 1912 Mouton Rothschild, the 1937 Marquis de Terme (to recall a love affair which led to an abdication) or the more reliable 1937 Rayne Vigneau. Ultimately there's the longest lived lady of all: 1953 Margaux. Moving into more modern times of high inflation the Petrus '90 will set you back £2,590 a case. Mr Wylie also 'needs your wine' (discerning vintages only) so its worth re-checking your cellar or Granny's garden shed.

YAP | Yapp Brothers

The Old Brewery, Mere, Wiltshire BA12 6DY (Tel 0747 860423 Fax 0747 860929). **Opening Hours:** Mon-Fri 9am-5pm / Sat 9am-1pm. **Delivery:** free nationally for 2 cases. **Tastings:** regular in-store and tutored, plus organised events. **Discounts:** various on collected and bulk orders.

Robin Yapp's wine 'book' reads like a trip along the Loire, the Rhône or one of their tributaries, allowing you to taste and meet producers like Gerard Chave, A. Graillot and Auguste Clape – and discover the shy sparkling Marsanne from St Peray, the black cherry reds from the Loire and the liquoricey ink of Provencal Mourvêdre. There's Chenin galore: Jasnières, Savennières, Montlouis, Quarts de Chaume ranging from the steely dry or gentle fizz to 'the sweet and truly transcendental'. It seems that every particular French vinous experience is here in Wiltshire.

18	£8.25	CREMANT DE LOIRE ROSE, CAVE DES VIGNERONS DE SAUMUR Loire (F)
30	£17.25	CHAMPAGNE JACQUESSON BLANC DE BLANCS Champagne (F)
49	£4.95	ORLEANAIS, COVIFRUIT 1992 Loire (F)
177	£8.35	SAVENNIERES, CHATEAU D'EPIRE, LUC BIZARD 1990 Loire (F)
277	£6.75	SAUMUR, CHATEAU FOUQUET, PAUL FILLIATREAU 1990 Loire (F)
338	£6.50	CROZES HERMITAGE ROUGE, JEAN-MARIE BORJA 1990 Rhône (F)
347	£9.25	ST. JOSEPH, COTE DIANE, CAVE CO-OPERATIVE DE ST. DESIRAT 1989 Rhône (F)
367	£16.75	CORNAS, AUGUSTE CLAPE 1990 Rhône (F)
368	£15.75	COTE ROTIE, EMILE CHAMPET 1990 Rhône (F)

NY | Noel Young Wines

56 High Street, Trumpington, Cambridge, Cambs CB2 2LS (Tel 0223 844744 Fax 0223 844736).
Opening Hours: Mon-Sat 10am-9pm, Sun 12-2pm. **Delivery:** free within 25 miles. **Tastings:** regular in-store and tutored, plus organised events. **Discounts:** 5-10% per case.

Noel Young gives his staff regular tests on their wine knowledge. Judging by the wines listed below – just a small selection from Mr Young's range – his employees should have some most enjoyable tasting practice. As with many small merchants, the range changes too quickly for any list to be current for too long, so it's worth being on his mailing list.

3	£6.39	SEGURA VIUDAS CAVA BRUT RESERVA Cava (Sp)
16	£8.49	YALUMBA SPARKLING CABERNET CUVEE PRESTIGE S.E. Australia (Aus)
33	£14.99H	BOLLINGER GRANDE ANNEE 1985 Champagne (F)
46	£3.99	CHARDONNAY DEL PIEMONTE, ARALDICA 1992 Piedmont (It)
54	£5.49	MONTES UNOAKED CHARDONNAY, DISCOVER WINES LTDA 1993 Curico (Ch)
61	£6.39	LUGANA CA'DEI FRATI 1992 Brescia (It)
77	£4.99	SALISBURY ESTATE CHARDONNAY 1992 S.E. Australia (Aus)
160	£6.99	GROVE MILL SAUVIGNON 1992 Blenheim (NZ)
91	£7.69	MARQUES DE MURRIETA RIOJA RESERVA BLANCO 1987 Rioja (Sp)
98	£8.99	LOCAL GROWERS SEMILLON, ROCKFORD 1989 Barossa Valley (Aus)
104	£9.69	CHARDONNAY, JANE HUNTER'S WINES 1991 Marlborough (NZ)
112	£11.59	ELSTON CHARDONNAY, TE MATA ESTATE 1991 Hawkes Bay (NZ)
147	£4.39	CASABLANCA WHITE LABEL SAUVIGNON BLANC 1992 (Ch)
153	£5.99	MARQUES DE ALELLA CLASSICO 1992 Alella (Sp)
161	£6.99	JACKSON ESTATE SAUVIGNON BLANC 1992 Marlborough (NZ)
164	£7.99	MENETOU SALON LES MOROGUES HENRI PELLE 1992 Loire (F)
166	£8.99	TERRES BLANCHES BLANC, AIX EN PROVENCE LES BAUX, NOEL MICHELIN 1992 Midi (F)
169	£8.99	HUNTERS MARLBOROUGH SAUVIGNON BLANC 1992 Marlborough (NZ)
189	£7.99	LAGAR DE CERVERA, RIAS BAIXAS, LAGAR DE FORNELOSSA 1992 Galicia (Sp)
233	£3.79	MAS DE FIGARO VIN DE PAYS DE L'HERAULT, AIME GUIBERT 1992 Midi (F)
235	£4.89	DAVID WYNN DRY RED 1992 Eden Valley (Aus)
240	£10.99	MADIRAN, MONTUS, ALAIN BRUMONT 1990 South West (F)
266	£4.99	SALISBURY ESTATE CABERNET SAUVIGNON 1991 S.E. Australia (Aus)
273	£5.59	TALTARNI FIDDLEBACK TERRACE 1990 Pyrenees (Aus)
292	£7.99	COLUMBIA CREST MERLOT, STIMSON LANE 1989 Washington State (US)
321	£23.00	ORNELLAIA 1990 Tuscany (It)
339	£6.99	BOTOBOLAR VINEYARD SHIRAZ, GIL WAHLQUIST 1990 Mudgee (Aus)
346	£7.69	CHATEAU MUSAR 1986 BEKAA VALLEY (LEB)
350	£8.49	BROKENWOOD SHIRAZ 1991 S.E. Australia (Aus)
352	£9.19	PENLEY ESTATE SHIRAZ/CABERNET SAUVIGNON, 1990 Coonawarra (Aus)
353	£8.99	DAVID WYNN PATRIARCH SHIRAZ 1991 Eden Valley (Aus)
357	£9.69	QUPE SYRAH, BOB LINDQUIST 1991 Central Coast (Cal)
370	£16.59	YARRA YERING SHIRAZ NO.2 1990 Yarra Valley (Aus)
414	£3.79	DOLCETTO D'ASTI, ARALDICA 1992 Piedmont (It)
415	£4.49	VALPOLICELLA CLASSICO, MASI 1991 Veneto (It)
422	£8.39	CHIANTI CLASSICO, ISOLE E OLENA 1990 Tuscany (It)
428	£9.69	BRIC MILEUI, ASCHERI 1990 Piedmont (It)
443	£4.79	QUINTA DE LA ROSA RED TABLE WINE 1991 Douro (P)
444	£4.39	PERIQUITA, J M DA FONSECA 1990 (P)
461	£9.59	STANTON & KILLEEN RUTHERGLEN LIQUEUR MUSCAT Rutherglen (Aus)
476	£11.99	KALLSTADER SAUMAGEN BEERENAUSLESE, WEINGUT UNDERICH 1990 Kallstader (G)
488	£8.99	OLD TRAFFORD TAWNY, B. SEPPELT & SONS S.E. Australia (Aus)
495	£13.99	GALWAY PIPE OLD TAWNY, YALUMBA WINERY Barossa Valley (Aus)

MERCHANTS' SERVICES AND SPECIALITIES

The two charts on the following pages have proved popular with those readers who requested an at-a-glance guide to the overall style of the merchants we recommend in later pages.

Should you have an acquired taste for, or perhaps have been newly introduced to and enjoyed the wines of a particular area, the chart on p.254 listing those merchants which consider this area to be their 'speciality' field will point the way towards the source of further examples. The chart summarising services offered to customers on p.244 has also, as we hoped, been a salutary lesson to those firms – particularly those in the High Street – who, with a little more effort, could make marked improvements in the range of services they offer.

Though of course one would not expect a supermarket, say, to be able to offer the individual service available at a specialist wine merchant, there are cases where the High Street merchant that has trained its staff to be informed and helpful can be a far more attractive proposition to customers than the intimidatingly snooty specialist where one doesn't dare ask such vital questions as 'Should I drink it now, or wait?' for fear of being thought ignorant.

Notes for merchants' services chart (p.244)

STYLE OF BUSINESS

It is sometimes difficult to pin merchants down and ask them to define their style of business clearly. Wine warehouses sell by the bottle, supermarkets run their own wine clubs and mail-order-only firms run in-store tastings. The information presented to us is the description given to us by each company, to which we would add the following interpretations.

National High Street: a large chain of off-licences covering a very substantial part of Britain – for example, Victoria Wine.

Regional High Street: a smaller chain confined to a particular region. In general, these should offer a more specialist approach to selling wine. Awards in this category are always fiercely fought.

Wine club: either mail-order only, or a merchant with some sort of scheme (for which there may or may not be a fee) whereby members receive, for example, regular newsletters, priority on wine orders, discounts, invitations to tastings etc.

Wine warehouse: this once indicated a by-the-case-only operation, and though this still holds true for some, the term has become much looser, often being used simply to decribe the general atmosphere of the shop.

BY-THE-BOTTLE

It can be infuriating, having trawled round a so-called wine warehouse dutifully making up a case, to discover that you could have bought only the bottle you needed for Sunday lunch after all. And the '12 or nothing' rule can be equally frustrating when you simply fancy trying a bottle of something new. However, most by-the-case outlets allow that case to be mixed, which gives a lot more pleasure in the choosing and drinking than a dozen frantic stops at the late-night grocers that happens to be on your way home from work.

CREDIT CARDS

Many small merchants would rather offer customers a discount for a cheque or cash than accept credit cards, so saving themselves the paperwork and the commission levied by the credit card companies. Worth enquiring.

ACCOUNT FACILITIES

Personal account facilities are available at the merchant's discretion. References are usually needed.

DELIVERY

L = free local delivery; N = free national delivery, though in many cases a premium is paid for this service – that is, the price of wines delivered 'free' may be rather high. Firms that acknowledge this – eg Adnams, The Wine Society – offer a 'collection discount'. More detailed information can be found in the firms' individual entries.

CELLARAGE

The firm has, or has access to, secure, temperature-controlled storage for customers' wines. Charges vary.

INVESTMENT ADVICE

Advice on wines to lay down for future drinking or profit will be freely available. Many firms in this category have their own cellar schemes whereby customers are informed of and/or assisted to take advantage of special purchases.

EN PRIMEUR

The firm will regularly offer and advise on *en primeur* (in-the-barrel) purchases and make all the necessary arrangements.

PARTY PLANNING

The reverse of the 'investment' coin; the company will give sensible and economical advice on wine styles, quantities per person, etc. Particularly valuable if the company also offers 'sale or return'.

TASTINGS

'In-store' means that informal tastings of opened or promoted wines take place, often on an ad hoc basis, so luck will prevail. 'Ticketed/tutored' tastings imply a more organised event, though you will not necessarily be charged a fee to attend. Fuller details may appear under companies' individual entries.

When contemplating a major purchase, any good specialist merchant should, except in the case of the most expensive wines, be more than happy to open a bottle for tasting purposes.

THE STOCKISTS' CODES

For easy reference the stockists' codes are shown on both the left and right hand sides of the charts.

		Nat. High Street	Reg. High Street	Ind. Merchant	Wine Club	Supermarket
ABB	Abbey Cellars			•		
ADN	Adnams Wine Merchants			•		
DAL	David Alexander			•		
AMA	Amathus			•		
AMW	Amey's Wines			•		
LAV	Les Amis du Vin					
JAV	John Arkell Vintners			•		
JAR	John Armit Wines			•		
AK	Arriba Kettle & Co			•		
A	Asda Stores Ltd					•
AUC	Australian Wine Centre			•	•	
AV	Averys of Bristol			•	•	
BH	BH Wines			•	•	
DBW	David Baker Wines			•	•	
BAL	Ballantynes of Cowbridge			•		
BLS	Balls Brothers Ltd			•		
ABA	Adam Bancroft Assocs			•		
BWS	The Barnes Wine Shop			•		
AB	Augustus Barnett Ltd	•				
BAR	Barwell & Jones					
BFI	Bedford Fine Wines Ltd			•		
BEN	Bennetts Wine & Spirits Merchants			•		
BWC	Berkmann/Le Nez Rouge			•		
BBR	Berry Bros & Rudd Ltd			•		
BI	Bibendum Wine Ltd			•		
BE	Bin Ends (London)			•		
BN	Bin Ends (Rotherham)			•		
BTH	EH Booth & Co					•
BOO	Booths of Stockport			•		
BD	Bordeaux Direct			•	•	
BGC	Borg Castel			•		
BNK	The Bottleneck			•		
BU	Bottoms Up	•				•
BRO	Broad Street Wine Co			•		
BWI	Bute Wines			•		
BUT	The Butlers Wine Cellar			•		
ABY	Anthony Byrne Fine Wines Ltd			•		
DBY	D Byrne & Co			•		
CPS	CPA's Wine Ltd			•		
CAC	Cachet Wines			•		
CAP	Cape Province Wines			•		
CWI	A Case of Wine			•		
CVR	The Celtic Vintner Ltd			•		
C&A	Chennell & Armstrong Ltd			•		
CHF	Chippendale Fine Wines			•		
CC	Chiswick Cellar			•		
CIW	City Wines Ltd			•		
CRC	The Claret Club				•	
CWW	Classic Wine Warehouses Ltd			•		
CFT	Clifton Cellars			•		

Wine W'House	By The Bottle	No. of Branches	Credit Cards	Own Charge Card	Account Facilities	Mail Order	Delivery	Coll. Discount	Cellarage	Invest. Advice	En Primeur	Free Glass Loan	Glass Loan	Ice	Party Planning	Gift Mailing	Books	In-Store Tastings	Tutored Tastings	Stockist code
•		1	•		•	•	L					•		•	•	•				ABB
•	•	3	•		•	•		•		•	•	•		•	•	•	•	•	•	ADN
	•	1	•		•	•	L			•	•	•		•	•	•			•	DAL
	•	2	•		•	•	L					•		•	•				•	AMA
	•	1	•		•	•	L					•							•	AMW
	•	2	•	•	•	•				•				•	•	•	•		•	LAV
	•	1	•		•	•	L		•		•	•		•	•	•	•		•	JAV
	•	1	•		•	•	L	•	•	•	•				•				•	JAR
	•	1	•		•	•	L	•											•	AK
	•	202	•		•		N	•				•							•	A
	•	1	•		•	•	L			•	•	•		•	•	•		•	•	AUC
	•	1	•		•	•	L					•							•	AV
		1	•		•	•				•	•	•		•	•	•			•	BH
	•	1	•		•	•	L			•	•	•		•	•	•			•	DBW
	•	1	•		•			•		•		•		•	•	•	•		•	BAL
	•	1	•		•	•	L	•		•		•	•		•	•	•		•	BLS
	•	1	•		•	•	L	•		•				•	•	•	•		•	ABA
	•	1	•		•	•	L	•		•				•	•	•	•		•	BWS
	•	543	•		•	•	L			•				•	•	•			•	AB
	•	3	•		•	•	L					•		•	•	•			•	BAR
	•	1	•		•	•	L					•							•	BFI
	•	1	•		•	•	N	•		•									•	BEN
	•	1	•		•	•	N	•		•	•								•	BWC
	•	1	•		•	•	L	•		•	•			•	•	•			•	BBR
•	•	1	•		•	•	L					•		•	•	•			•	BI
	•	1	•		•	•	L												•	BE
	•	1	•		•	•	L												•	BN
	•	21	•		•	•						•							•	BTH
	•	1	•		•	•								•					•	BOO
	•	5	•		•	•	L					•		•	•	•			•	BD
•	•	1	•		•	•	L	•		•		•			•	•			•	BGC
	•	60	•		•		L					•						•		BNK
	•	1	•		•															BU
	•	1	•		•	•	L	•		•		•							•	BRO
	•	1	•		•	•			•		•	•			•				•	BWI
	•	1	•		•	•													•	BUT
	•	1	•		•	•	L	•											•	ABY
	•	1	•		•	•	L			•		•							•	DBY
	•	1	•		•	•	L			•		•			•	•		•	•	CPS
	•	1	•		•	•						•			•				•	CAC
	•	1	•		•		•		•			•			•			•	•	CAP
	•	1	•		•	•	L						•					•	•	CWI
	•	1	•		•	•	L			•		•			•			•	•	CVR
	•	1	•		•	•	L	•		•		•			•			•	•	C&A
	•	1	•		•	•	L											•	•	CHF
	•	1	•		•	•	L			•		•		•				•	•	CC
	•	1	•		•	•	L						•	•	•			•	•	CIW
	•	1	•		•														•	CRC
•	•	1	•		•	•	L	•		•		•		•	•	•			•	CWW
	•	1	•		•		L		•		•		•			•			•	CFT

		Nat. High Street	Reg. High Street	Ind. Merchant	Wine Club	Supermarket
CNL	Connolly's (Wine Merchants) Ltd			•		
COK	Corkscrew Wines			•		
COR	Corn Road Vintners			•		
C&B	Corney & Barrow Ltd			•		
CWM	Cornwall Wine Merchants Ltd			•		
CWS	The Co-operative Wholesale Society					•
CEB	Croque en Bouche					
CUM	The Cumbrian Cellar			•		
D	Davisons Wine Merchants		•			
ROD	Rodney Densem Wines			•		
DIR	Direct Wine Shipments			•		
DD	Domaine Direct			•		
EE	Eaton Elliot Wine Merchant			•		
ECK	Eckington Wines			•	•	
EP	Eldridge Pope & Co plc			•		
EBA	Ben Ellis & Associates Ltd			•		
EVI	Evingtons Wine Merchants			•	•	
PEY	Philip Eyres Wine Merchant			•		
FAR	Farr Vintners Ltd			•		
FV	Fernlea Vintners			•		
AF	Alexr Findlater & Co			•		
FDL	Findlater Mackie Todd & Co Ltd					
FNZ	Fine Wines of New Zealand Ltd					
LEF	Le Fleming Wines			•		
JFD	John Ford Wines					
F&M	Fortnum & Mason			•		
JFR	John Frazier Ltd			•		
FWC	The Fulham Road Wine Centre			•	•	
FUL	Fuller Smith & Turner plc		•			
MFW	Marcus Fyfe Wines			•		
GBY	Elizabeth Gabay and Partners					
GLY	Gallery Wines			•	•	
GDS	Garrards Wine & Spirit Merchants			•		
G	Gateway Foodmarkets Ltd					•
GON	Gauntleys of Nottingham			•		
GEL	Gelston Castle Fine Wines			•		
JAG	JA Glass			•		
MG	Matthew Gloag & Son Ltd			•	•	
GH	Goedhuis & Co Ltd			•		
G&M	Gordon & Macphail			•		
GI	Grape Ideas			•		
GEW	Great English Wines/Harvest Group					
GNW	The Great Northern Wine Co			•	•	
GRT	Great Western Wine Company			•		
PTR	Peter Green & Co			•		
GRO	Grog Blossom			•		
PGR	Patrick Grubb Selections			•		
HLV	Halves Ltd			•		
HAM	Hampden Wine Co			•		
HFV	Harcourt Fine Wine			•		

Wine W'House	By The Bottle	No. of Branches	Credit Cards	Own Charge Card	Account Facilities	Mail Order	Delivery	Coll. Discount	Cellarage	Invest. Advice	En Primeur	Free Glass Loan	Glass Loan	Ice	Party Planning	Gift Mailing	Books	In-Store Tastings	Tutored Tastings	Stockist code
	•	1	•		•	•					•	•		•		•	•	•	•	CNL
•	•	1	•		•	•	L								•	•	•		•	COK
		1	•		•	•						•		•	•	•			•	COR
		2	•		•	•	N		•	•	•	•			•	•			•	C&B
		1	•		•	•	L			•	•	•				•			•	CWM
		2000	•	•		•						•						•	•	CWS
		1	•			•		•	•							•				CEB
	•	1	•		•	•	L	•	•						•	•			•	CUM
	•	79	•		•	•	L					•					•		•	D
		1	•		•	•	L			•	•					•	•		•	ROD
•	•	1	•		•	•	L								•	•			•	DIR
		1	•		•	•				•	•								•	DD
		1	•		•	•	L					•			•	•	•		•	EE
		1	•		•	•	L					•	•						•	ECK
	•	9	•		•	•	L		•			•					•		•	EP
•		1	•		•	•	L			•	•				•	•			•	EBA
		1	•		•	•	L					•			•	•	•		•	EVI
		1	•		•	•				•	•					•			•	PEY
	•	1	•		•	•				•	•	•					•		•	FAR
•		1	•		•	•	L	•		•	•				•					FV
		1	•		•	•				•	•	•			•	•	•			AF
		1	•		•	•		•		•	•	•			•	•				FDL
		1	•		•	•					•								•	FNZ
		1	•		•	•	L					•			•	•			•	LEF
		1	•		•	•			•		•					•			•	JFD
		1	•	•	•	•				•	•				•	•			•	F&M
	•	5	•		•	•	L			•	•	•							•	JFR
		1	•		•	•	L					•	•		•	•	•		•	FWC
	•	60	•		•	•	L					•			•				•	FUL
		1	•		•	•						•			•					MFW
		1	•		•	•													•	GBY
	•	1	•		•	•	L						•	•	•	•	•		•	GLY
	•	1	•		•	•	L						•	•	•	•	•		•	GDS
		650	•		•	•											•		•	G
		1	•		•	•				•	•						•		•	GON
		1	•		•	•	L	•	•	•	•				•					GEL
		1	•		•	•	L			•						•			•	JAG
	•	1	•		•	•	N	•		•						•			•	MG
		1	•		•	•				•						•	•		•	GH
		1	•		•	•				•	•					•		•	•	G&M
		1	•		•	•	L			•					•				•	GI
		1	•		•	•	L					•			•	•			•	GEW
•		1	•		•	•	L								•	•	•		•	GNW
•		1	•		•	•	L			•	•				•	•			•	GRT
	•	1	•		•	•	L			•	•								•	PTR
		3	•		•	•	L			•							•			GRO
	•	1	•		•	•			•							•				PGR
	•	1	•	•	•	•										•				HLV
	•	1	•		•	•						•								HAM
		1	•		•	•	L			•				•	•	•		•		HFV

		Nat. High Street	Reg. High Street	Ind. Merchant	Wine Club	Supermarket
HPD	Harpenden Wines			•		
GHS	Gerard Harris Fine Wines			•	•	
ROG	Roger Harris Wines			•		
RHV	Richard Harvey Wines			•		
HV	John Harvey & Sons					
HHC	Haynes, Hanson & Clarke			•		
H&H	Hector & Honorez Wines Ltd			•		
HW	Hedley Wright & Co Ltd			•		
DHM	Douglas Henn-Macrae			•		
HEM	The Hermitage			•		
H&D	Hicks & Don			•		
JEH	JE Hogg			•		
HOL	Holland Park Wine Co			•		
HOU	Hoult's Wine Merchants			•		
HOT	House of Townend			•	•	
HUD	Hudsons Fine Wines			•	•	
HUN	Hungerford Wine Co			•		
TOJ	Tony Jeffries Wines			•		
JOB	Jeroboams			•		
SHJ	S H Jones & Co Ltd			•		
J&B	Justerini & Brooks Ltd			•		
JCK	JC Karn			•		
K&B	King & Barnes Ltd			•	•	
KS	Kwiksave					•
L&W	Lay & Wheeler Ltd			•		
L&S	Laymont & Shaw Ltd			•		
LAY	Laytons Wine Merchants Ltd			•		
LEA	Lea & Sandeman Co Ltd		•	•		
LES	CRS Ltd/Leos					•
OWL	OW Loeb & Co Ltd			•		
LWE	London Wine Emporium Ltd			•		
LWL	London Wine Ltd			•		
WL	William Low & Company plc					•
MWW	Majestic Wine Warehouses					
MAR	Marco's Wines					
M&S	Marks & Spencer plc	•				
MC	Master Cellar					
DX	Mayfair Cellars			•		
MYS	Mayor Sworder & Co Ltd			•		
MCL	McLeod's			•		
MM	Michael Menzel Wines			•		
MTL	Mitchells Wine Merchants Ltd			•	•	
MOR	Moreno Wine Importers			•		
M&V	Morris & Verdin Ltd			•		
MRN	Wm Morrison Supermarkets					•
NAD	The Nadder Wine Co. Ltd			•		
JN	James Nicholson Wine Merchant			•		
N&P	Nickolls & Perks Ltd			•		
NIC	Nicolas UK Ltd	•				
NRW	Noble Rot Wine Warehouse Ltd			•		

Wine W'House	By The Bottle	No. of Branches	Credit Cards	Own Charge Card	Account Facilities	Mail Order	Delivery	Coll. Discount	Cellarage	Invest. Advice	En Primeur	Free Glass Loan	Glass Loan	Ice	Party Planning	Gift Mailing	Books	In-Store Tastings	Tutored Tastings	Stockist code
	•	1	•				L											•		HPD
	•	1	•	•	•	•									•		•	•	•	GHS
	•	1	•	•	•	•	N				•				•					ROG
	•	1	•		•	•	L		y	•	•	•			•					RHV
	•	1	•																	HV
	•	1	•			•	N	•							•	•		•		HHC
	•	1	•				L			•					•			•		H&H
•	•	1	•				L			•			•		•	•		•		HW
	•	1	•			•				•								•		DHM
	•	1	•			•	L	•										•		HEM
	•	1	•			•				•	•	•				•		•		H&D
	•	1	•		•	•	L								•			•		JEH
•	•	1	•		•	•	L		•	•	•			•	•	•	•	•	•	HOL
	•	14	•			•					•			•	•	•	•		•	•	HOT
	•	1	•		•	•	L							•	•	•		•	•	HUD
	•	1	•		•	•			•	•	•				•	•		•	•	HUN
	•	1	•				L			•								•	•	TOJ
	•	1	•				L									•				JOB
	•	1	•		•	•	L	•		•	•			•	•	•	•	•	•	SHJ
	•	2	•		•	•	L		•	•	•				•			•		J&B
	•	1	•		•	•	L					•			•	•				JCK
	•	1	•				L										•	•	•	K&B
	•	726	•																	KS
•	•	1	•		•	•	L	•		•			•		•		•	•	•	L&W
	•	1	•		•	•	L								•			•	•	L&S
•		31	•		•	•	L	•		•	•			•	•	•		•	•	LAY
	•	2	•		•	•	N			•	•	•			•	•		•		LEA
	•	457	•															•		LES
	•	1	•			•														OWL
•	•	1	•		•	•	L				•							•		LWE
•	•	1	•		•	•	L			•								•		LWL
	•	66	•												•	•		•	•	WL
•	•	42	•		•	•	L							•	•	•		•	•	MWW
•	•	5	•		•	•	L							•	•			•	•	MAR
	•	280	•	•	•	•												•		M&S
•	•	1	•		•	•			•		•			•	•			•		MC
	•	1	•		•	•	L	•	•	•	•			•	•	•		•		DX
	•	1	•		•	•	L		•	•	•				•			•	•	MYS
	•	1	•			•	L							•						MCL
	•	1	•		•	•	L							•	•		•			MM
	•	2	•		•	•	L				•			•	•	•		•	•	MTL
	•	2	•		•	•	L	•						•	•			•	•	MOR
	•	1	•		•	•	L		•	•					•			•		M&V
	•	77	•							•					•			•		MRN
•	•	1	•		•	•	L	•		•					•	•		•	•	NAD
	•	1	•		•	•				•	•			•	•	•		•	•	JN
	•	1	•		•	•	L			•				•	•	•	•	•	•	N&P
	•	9	•		•	•	L			•	•			•	•			•	•	NIC
•	•	1	•		•	•	L			•				•	•		•	•	•	NRW

		Nat. High Street	Reg. High Street	Ind. Merchant	Wine Club	Supermarket
NI	Nobody Inn			•		
RN	Rex Norris Wine Merchants			•		
OD	Oddbins Ltd	•				
ORG	The Organic Wine Co Ltd			•		
P	Parfrements			•		
THP	Thos Peatling		•			
PHI	Philglas & Swiggot			•		
CPW	Christopher Piper Wines Ltd			•		
TP	Terry Platt Wine Merchant			•		
PLA	Playford Ros Ltd			•		
PON	Le Pont de la Tour			•		
POR	The Portland Wine Company			•		
PMR	Premier Wine Warehouse			•		
PRW	Protea Wines			•		
PUG	Pugsons of Buxton			•		
R	RS Wines			•		
RAE	Raeburn Fine Wines			•		
RAM	The Ramsbottom Victuallers Co Ltd			•		
RAV	Ravensbourne Wine			•		
RD	Reid Wines (1992) Ltd			•		
RES	La Reserve			•	•	
RIB	Ribble Vintners Ltd			•		
RWW	Richmond Wine Warehouse			•		
RWC	Rioja Wine Co Ltd			•		
HR	Howard Ripley Fine French Wines			•		
WRB	Robbs of Hexham				•	
RBS	Roberson Wine Merchant			•		
RTW	The Rose Tree Wine Co			•		
R&I	Russell & McIver Ltd			•		
SAC	Le Sac a Vin			•		
SAF	Safeway Stores plc					•
JS	J Sainsbury Plc					•
SAN	Sandiway Wine Co			•		
SWB	Satchells of Burnham Market			•		
SEB	Sebastopol Wines			•		
SK	Seckford Wines			•		
SEL	Selfridges					
ES	Edward Sheldon			•		
SHV	Sherborne Vintners			•		
SAS	Sherston Wines			•		
SV	Smedley Vintners			•		
SOM	Sommelier Wine Co Ltd			•		
SPR	Spar UK Ltd	•				
SPG	Springfield Wines			•		
FSW	Frank E Stainton			•		
STW	Stewarts Wine Barrels	•	•			
SUM	Summerlee Wines Ltd			•		
DWL	The Sunday Times Wine Club			•	•	
SUP	Supergrape Ltd			•	•	
T&W	T&W Wines			•		

Wine W'House	By The Bottle	No. of Branches	Credit Cards	Own Charge Card	Account Facilities	Mail Order	Delivery	Coll. Discount	Cellarage	Invest. Advice	En Primeur	Free Glass Loan	Glass Loan	Ice	Party Planning	Gift Mailing	Books	In-Store Tastings	Tutored Tastings	Stockist code
	•	1	•		•		L						•			•		•	•	NI
	•	1	•		•		L						•		•			•		RN
	•	177	•				L				•				•	•			•	OD
		1	•		•	•	L	•					•			•		•	•	ORG
		1	•		•	•							•		•	•		•	•	P
		28	•		•	•	N		•		•		•	•	•	•		•	•	THP
	•	1	•		•		L						•			•		•	•	PHI
		1	•		•	•	N	•	•	•	•		•			•		•	•	CPW
		1	•		•	•	L						•			•			•	TP
		1	•													•				PLA
	•	1	•				L						•			•			•	PON
	•	3	•		•		L				•		•		•	•		•	•	POR
•		1	•		•	•	L			•			•	•	•	•			•	PMR
		1	•				L						•							PRW
	•	1	•		•	•	L				•		•			•			•	PUG
		1	•		•		L			•	•		•			•				R
	•	2	•		•		L		•		•		•						•	RAE
	•	1	•				L												•	RAM
	•	1	•		•	•	L	•			•		•		•	•			•	RAV
		4	•		•	•					•		•		•	•		•	•	RD
	•	1	•		•	•		•		•	•		•		•	•		•	•	RES
	•	1	•		•		L	•			•		•			•			•	RIB
•		1	•		•	•	L				•		•		•	•			•	RWW
		1	•				L						•		•	•		•	•	RWC
		1	•		•	•														HR
	•	1	•	•	•	•	L				•								•	WRB
	•	1	•		•		L				•		•		•	•		•	•	RBS
	•	1	•		•		L		•		•		•		•	•		•	•	RTW
			•		•		L		•				•		•	•			•	R&I
		5	•		•		L	•	•				•			•	•		•	SAC
	•	2483	•										•				•			SAF
	•	327	•													•	•			JS
		1	•		•	•	L				•		•		•	•		•	•	SAN
	•	1	•		•	•	L	•			•		•		•	•		•	•	SWB
•		1	•		•	•	L				•		•			•		•	•	SEB
		1	•	•	•	•					•		•			•		•	•	SK
		1	•		•	•					•	•				•		•	•	SEL
		1	•		•	•					•		•							ES
	•	1	•								•		•			•			•	SHV
		1	•		•		L				•		•		•			•	•	SAS
	•	1	•		•		L		•	•	•				•	•			•	SV
		1	•	•	•		L						•		•					SOM
		2000						•					•		•	•			•	SPR
	•	1	•		•	•	L				•		•		•	•		•	•	SPG
	•	1	•		•	•	L				•		•		•	•		•	•	FSW
•		50	•		•	•							•		•			•	•	STW
	•	1	•		•		L			•	•		•		•				•	SUM
	•	1	•		•						•		•		•			•	•	DWL
	•	1	•		•	•	L				•				•	•			•	SUP
	•	1	•		•	•	N			•	•		•			•		•	•	T&W

		Nat. High Street	Reg. High Street	Ind. Merchant	Wine Club	Supermarket
TAN	Tanners Wines Ltd			•		
CT	Charles Taylor Wines Ltd			•		
TO	Tesco Stores plc					•
TH	Thresher Wine Shops		•			
MAD	Madeleine Trehearne Partners			•		
TRE	Tremaynes			•		
TRW	Trinity Wine			•		
TVW	Turville Valley Wines			•		
UBC	Ubiquitous Chip			•		
U	Unwins Wine Merchants		•			
V&C	Valvona & Crolla Ltd			•		
HVW	Helen Verdcourt			•	•	
VW	Victoria Wine	•				
LV	La Vigneronne			•		
VIL	Village Wines			•		
VLW	Villeneuve Wines Ltd			•	•	
VDV	Vin du Van					
VER	Vinceremos Wines & Spirits Ltd					
VT	The Vine Trail			•		
VR	Vintage Roots			•		
W	Waitrose Ltd					•
WAW	Waterloo Wine Co Ltd			•		
WAC	Waters of Coventry Ltd			•		
WEP	The Welshpool Wine Co			•		
WES	Wessex Wines			•		
WHC	Whiclar & Gordon Wines Ltd			•		
WWT	Whitebridge Wines			•		
WOC	Whitesides of Clitheroe Ltd			•		
WTL	Whittalls Wines			•		
WDW	Windrush Wines Ltd			•		
WBM	Wine Byre Merchants			•	•	
CRL	The Wine Centre/Charles Steevenson Wines			•		
WE	Wine Emporium/Cockburn's of Leith Ltd			•	•	
WR	Wine Rack		•			
WSC	The Wine Schoppen Ltd			•		
SHG	Wine Shop on the Green			•		
WSO	The Wine Society			•	•	
WTR	The Wine Treasury Ltd			•		
WCE	Winecellars			•		
WMK	Winemark Wine Merchant		•	•		
WIN	The Winery			•		
WOI	Wines of Interest			•		
WNS	Winos Wine Shop			•		
MAW	M & A Winter			•		
WGW	Woodgate Wines			•		
WRW	The Wright Wine Co			•		
PWY	Peter Wylie Fine Wines			•		
YAP	Yapp Brothers			•		
NY	Noel Young Wines			•		

Wine W'House	By The Bottle	No. of Branches	Credit Cards	Own Charge Card	Account Facilities	Mail Order	Delivery	Coll. Discount	Cellarage	Invest. Advice	En Primeur	Free Glass Loan	Glass Loan	Ice	Party Planning	Gift Mailing	Books	In-Store Tastings	Tutored Tastings	Stockist code
	•	6	•							•	•			•	•	•	•	•	•	TAN
		1	•			•	•			•	•								•	CT
	•	401	•			•											•		•	TO
	•	870	•			•	N					•		•	•	•			•	TH
		1	•			•	L			•	•	•			•	•	•		•	MAD
	•	1	•			•	L			•					•	•		•	•	TRE
		1	•		•	•	L								•	•	•		•	TRW
		1	•			•	L		•		•		•	•		•	•	•	•	TVW
	•	300	•			•	L				•				•	•		•	•	UBC
		1	•		•	•	•												•	U
		1	•			•	L									•			•	V&C
		973	•									•	•		•	•				HVW
		1	•			•	L			•					•	•		•	•	VW
•		1	•			•	L						•		•	•		•	•	LV
	•	1	•			•				•		•		•	•	•			•	VIL
	•	1	•		•	•					•		•	•		•			•	VLW
		1																		VDV
		1	•			•	L								•	•			•	VER
		1	•			•	L	•	•			•		•	•	•		•	•	VT
		1	•		•	•	•	•					•			•				VR
	•	107	•								•			•	•	•				W
		1	•				L			•		•		•		•		•	•	WAW
		1	•			•								•		•			•	WAC
		1	•			•	L			•					•			•	•	WEP
		1	•			•	L	•				•			•			•	•	WES
•		1	•							•	•		•		•	•		•	•	WHC
•	•	1	•			•	L					•			•	•			•	WWT
	•	1	•			•	L							•	•	•			•	WOC
•		1	•		•	•	L			•						•			•	WTL
•	•	2	•			•	L			•				•	•	•		•	•	WDW
	•	1	•			•	L			•	•					•		•	•	WBM
•	•	1	•			•				•	•			•	•	•		•	•	CRL
		118	•			•	N					•			•	•		•		WE
		11	•			•	L			•	•				•	•		•		WR
		1	•			•	L						•		•	•	•		•	WSC
		1	•			•		•	•	•	•			•	•	•		•	•	SHG
		1	•			•				•	•				•	•			•	WSO
		2	•			•	L	•		•	•			•	•	•	•	•	•	WTR
	•	72	•			•	L					•			•	•			•	WCE
	•	2	•			•	L			•					•	•		•	•	WMK
	•	1	•			•		•							•	•			•	WIN
	•	1	•			•	L			•				•	•	•			•	WOI
	•	1	•		•	•				•	•					•		•		WNS
	•	1	•									•			•	•	•			MAW
	•	1									•				•	•	•			WGW
	•	1	•		•	•	L	•	•						•	•				WRW
	•	1	•		•	•	L	•							•	•		•	•	PWY
	•	1			•	•	L								•			•		YAP
	•	1	•			•	L				•		•		•			•		NY

		Bordeaux	Burgundy	Rhône	Loire	Alsace
ABB	Abbey Cellars					
ADN	Adnams Wine Merchants				•	
DAL	David Alexander		•			
AMA	Amathus					
AMW	Amey's Wines					
LAV	Les Amis du Vin					
JAV	John Arkell Vintners	•				
JAR	John Armit Wines	•	•			
AK	Arriba Kettle & Co				•	
A	Asda Stores Ltd		•			
AUC	Australian Wine Centre					
AV	Averys of Bristol	•	•			
BH	BH Wines					
DBW	David Baker Wines	•				
BAL	Ballantynes of Cowbridge	•	•			
BLS	Balls Brothers Ltd	•	•	•		
ABA	Adam Bancroft Assocs		•	•	•	
BWS	The Barnes Wine Shop					
AB	Augustus Barnett Ltd					
BAR	Barwell & Jones					
BFI	Bedford Fine Wines Ltd					
BEN	Bennetts Wine & Spirits Merchants	•	•			•
BWC	Berkmann/Le Nez Rouge	•	•			
BBR	Berry Bros & Rudd Ltd	•	•	•	•	•
BI	Bibendum Wine Ltd	•	•	•	•	•
BE	Bin Ends (London)					
BN	Bin Ends (Rotherham)					
BTH	EH Booth & Co					
BOO	Booths of Stockport					
BD	Bordeaux Direct					
BGC	Borg Castel					
BNK	The Bottleneck					
BU	Bottoms Up					
BRO	Broad Street Wine Co					
BWI	Bute Wines	•	•	•		•
BUT	The Butlers Wine Cellar	•	•	•		•
ABY	Anthony Byrne Fine Wines Ltd		•			•
DBY	D Byrne & Co	•		•	•	•
CPS	CPA's Wine Ltd					
CAC	Cachet Wines					
CAP	Cape Province Wines					
CWI	A Case of Wine					
CVR	The Celtic Vintner Ltd				•	
C&A	Chennell & Armstrong Ltd					
CHF	Chippendale Fine Wines					
CC	Chiswick Cellar	•	•		•	
CIW	City Wines Ltd					
CRC	Claret Club	•				
CWW	Classic Wine Warehouses Ltd					
CFT	Clifton Cellars	•				

Champagne	French Reg.	Germany	Spain	Portugal	Italy	Australia	New Zealand	California	Other U.S.	South America	South Africa	England	Sherry	Port	Madeira	Organic	Fine/Old Wines	Malt Whisky	Half Bottles	Stockist code
	•					•											•			ABB
		•				•	•										•			ADN
																		•		DAL
					•		•													AMA
•	•					•	•	•									•			AMW
							•										•			LAV
									•								•			JAV
																	•			JAR
													•							AK
						•														A
						•	•			•							•			AUC
											•									AV
																				BH
																				DBW
•	•					•	•										•			BAL
						•	•													BLS
											•									ABA
							•													BWS
											•									AB
											•		•							BAR
•					•	•	•	•									•			BFI
																				BEN
•	•	•											•	•			•		•	BWC
•	•				•		•						•	•			•		•	BBR
•	•												•	•			•			BI
•													•	•			•			BE
													•	•			•			BN
				•	•	•								•						BTH
	•																			BOO
																				BD
																				BGC
•	•				•		•								•				•	BNK
																				BU
	•																•			BRO
													•				•			BWI
	•																•		•	BUT
	•	•	•		•	•	•						•				•		•	ABY
																				DBY
											•									CPS
																				CAC
																•				CAP
	•				•	•			•											CWI
	•					•	•													CVR
						•														C&A
•	•	•			•						•		•						•	CHF
																				CC
																				CIW
																		•			CRC
•																			•	CWW
																			•	CFT

		Bordeaux	Burgundy	Rhône	Loire	Alsace
CNL	Connolly's (Wine Merchants) Ltd					
COK	Corkscrew Wines			•		
COR	Corn Road Vintners					
C&B	Corney & Barrow Ltd	•				
CWM	Cornwall Wine Merchants Ltd					
CWS	The Co-operative Wholesale Society					
CEB	Croque en Bouche			•		
CUM	The Cumbrian Cellar					
D	Davisons Wine Merchants	•	•			
ROD	Rodney Densem Wines					
DIR	Direct Wine Shipments					
DD	Domaine Direct		•			
EE	Eaton Elliot Wine Merchant					
ECK	Eckington Wines					
EP	Eldridge Pope & Co plc	•	•		•	•
EBA	Ben Ellis & Associates Ltd					
EVI	Evingtons Wine Merchants			•		
PEY	Philip Eyres Wine Merchant	•				
FAR	Farr Vintners Ltd	•	•	•		
FV	Fernlea Vintners					
AF	Alexr Findlater & Co		•			
FDL	Findlater Mackie Todd & Co Ltd					
FNZ	Fine Wines of New Zealand Ltd					
LEF	Le Fleming Wines					
JFD	John Ford Wines					
F&M	Fortnum & Mason	•	•	•	•	•
JFR	John Frazier Ltd					
FWC	The Fulham Road Wine Centre	•				
FUL	Fuller Smith & Turner plc					
MFW	Marcus Fyfe Wines					
GBY	Elizabeth Gabay and Partners					
GLY	Gallery Wines					
GDS	Garrards Wine & Spirit Merchants					
G	Gateway Foodmarkets Ltd					
GON	Gauntleys of Nottingham			•	•	•
GEL	Gelston Castle Fine Wines	•	•	•		
JAG	JA Glass					
MG	Matthew Gloag & Son Ltd					
GH	Goedhuis & Co Ltd	•	•			
G&M	Gordon & Macphail					
GI	Grape Ideas				•	
GEW	Great English Wines/Harvest Group					
GNW	The Great Northern Wine Co					
GRT	Great Western Wine Company					
PTR	Peter Green & Co	•			•	•
GRO	Grog Blossom					
PGR	Patrick Grubb Selections	•				
HLV	Halves Ltd					
HAM	Hampden Wine Co				•	•
HFV	Harcourt Fine Wine					

Champagne	French Reg.	Germany	Spain	Portugal	Italy	Australia	New Zealand	California	Other U.S.	South America	South Africa	England	Sherry	Port	Madeira	Organic	Fine/Old Wines	Malt Whisky	Half Bottles	Stockist code
	•																•			CNL
						•														COK
																				COR
																	•			C&B
																	•			CWM
																				CWS
					•	•							•				•			CEB
						•											•		•	CUM
					•									•			•			D
																	•			ROD
																	•			DIR
																	•			DD
																				EE
						•														ECK
	•	•											•				•		•	EP
																	•			EBA
		•											•				•			EVI
											•			•						PEY
														•			•			FAR
•																				FV
					•	•	•				•									AF
																			•	FDL
																				FNZ
																				LEF
•		•			•															JFD
													•				•		•	F&M
	•																			JFR
																	•			FWC
																				FUL
	•																			MFW
		•																		GBY
													•						•	GLY
																	•		•	GDS
														•						G
		•																		GON
																	•			GEL
																			•	JAG
																				MG
																	•			GH
											•								•	G&M
	•		•		•				•											GI
										•										GEW
					•															GNW
	•																			GRT
	•				•	•	•			•	•		•	•	•	•	•	•		PTR
					•	•														GRO
														•	•					PGR
		•		•									•	•			•			HLV
•	•	•	•		•												•			HAM
		•									•									HFV

		Bordeaux	Burgundy	Rhône	Loire	Alsace
HPD	Harpenden Wines					
GHS	Gerard Harris Fine Wines					
ROG	Roger Harris Wines		•			
RHV	Richard Harvey Wines		•			
HV	John Harvey & Sons	•				
HHC	Haynes, Hanson & Clarke		•			
H&H	Hector & Honorez Wines Ltd			•	•	•
HW	Hedley Wright & Co Ltd				•	
DHM	Douglas Henn-Macrae					
HEM	The Hermitage					
H&D	Hicks & Don					
JEH	JE Hogg					
HOL	Holland Park Wine Co	•	•		•	•
HOU	Hoult's Wine Merchants					
HOT	House of Townend		•			
HUD	Hudsons Fine Wines					
HUN	Hungerford Wine Co	•				
TOJ	Tony Jeffries Wines					
JOB	Jeroboams					
SHJ	SH Jones & Co Ltd	•	•	•		
J&B	Justerini & Brooks Ltd	•	•	•		
JCK	JC Karn					
K&B	King & Barnes Ltd					
KS	Kwiksave					
L&W	Lay & Wheeler Ltd	•	•	•	•	•
L&S	Laymont & Shaw Ltd					
LAY	Laytons Wine Merchants Ltd		•			
LEA	Lea & Sandeman Co Ltd	•	•	•	•	•
LES	CRS Ltd/Leos					
OWL	OW Loeb & Co Ltd	•	•	•		•
LWE	London Wine Emporium Ltd					
LWL	London Wine Ltd					
WL	William Low & Company plc					
MWW	Majestic Wine Warehouses					
MAR	Marco's Wines					
M&S	Marks & Spencer plc					
MC	Master Cellar	•	•			
DX	Mayfair Cellars					
MYS	Mayor Sworder & Co Ltd					
MCL	McLeod's					
MM	Michael Menzel Wines		•	•	•	•
MTL	Mitchells Wine Merchants Ltd					
MOR	Moreno Wine Importers					
M&V	Morris & Verdin Ltd		•			
MRN	Wm Morrison Supermarkets					
NAD	The Nadder Wine Co. Ltd					
JN	James Nicholson Wine Merchant	•				
N&P	Nickolls & Perks Ltd					
NIC	Nicolas UK Ltd	•	•	•		•
NRW	Noble Rot Wine Warehouse Ltd					

Champagne	French Reg.	Germany	Spain	Portugal	Italy	Australia	New Zealand	California	Other U.S.	South America	South Africa	England	Sherry	Port	Madeira	Organic	Fine/Old Wines	Malt Whisky	Half Bottles	Stockist code
																				HPD
																				GHS
	•																			ROG
	•																•			RHV
													•	•						HV
																				HHC
	•																•		•	H&H
		•					•			•	•		•	•						HW
									•											DHM
					•	•	•													HEM
																				H&D
•		•				•	•													HOL
																			•	HOU
																				HOT
																				HUD
			•																	HUN
•																				TOJ
	•																		•	JOB
	•												•	•			•	•	•	SHJ
																	•			J&B
																				JCK
																				K&B
•	•	•			•				•				•	•			•		•	L&W
			•																	L&S
																				LAY
•	•					•							•	•			•	•	•	LEA
																				LES
																				OWL
																				LWE
	•					•														LWL
	•																			WL
																				MWW
																				MAR
																				M&S
																				MC
																				DX
																				MYS
																				MCL
•					•								•				•		•	MM
•		•			•									•					•	MTL
		•																		MOR
							•													M&V
																				MRN
																			•	NAD
	•																			JN
																				N&P
•	•																•			NIC
																				NRW

		Bordeaux	Burgundy	Rhône	Loire	Alsace
NI	Nobody Inn					•
RN	Rex Norris Wine Merchants					
OD	Oddbins Ltd	•		•		
ORG	The Organic Wine Co Ltd					
P	Parfrements					
THP	Thos Peatling	•				
PHI	Philglas & Swiggot					
CPW	Christopher Piper Wines Ltd	•	•	•		
TP	Terry Platt Wine Merchant	•	•	•	•	
PLA	Playford Ros Ltd					
PON	Le Pont de la Tour	•	•			
POR	The Portland Wine Company					
PMR	Premier Wine Warehouse					
PRW	Protea Wines					
PUG	Pugsons of Buxton				•	
R	RS Wines	•	•		•	
RAE	Raeburn Fine Wines	•	•			
RAM	The Ramsbottom Victuallers Co Ltd					•
RAV	Ravensbourne Wine					
RD	Reid Wines (1992) Ltd	•				•
RES	La Reserve	•	•	•	•	•
RIB	Ribble Vintners Ltd			•		
RWW	Richmond Wine Warehouse	•	•			
RWC	Rioja Wine Co Ltd		•		•	
HR	Howard Ripley Fine French Wines		•			
WRB	Robbs of Hexham					
RBS	Roberson Wine Merchant	•				
RTW	The Rose Tree Wine Co	•	•		•	
R&I	Russell & McIver Ltd					
SAC	Le Sac a Vin		•			
SAF	Safeway Stores plc					
JS	J Sainsbury Plc					
SAN	Sandiway Wine Co					
SWB	Satchells of Burnham Market					
SEB	Sebastopol Wines	•		•		•
SK	Seckford Wines	•	•			
SEL	Selfridges					
ES	Edward Sheldon	•				
SHV	Sherborne Vintners					
SAS	Sherston Wines					
SV	Smedley Vintners					
SOM	Sommelier Wine Co Ltd					
SPR	Spar UK Ltd					
SPG	Springfield Wines					•
FSW	Frank E Stainton					
STW	Stewarts Wine Barrels					
SUM	Summerlee Wines Ltd					
DWL	The Sunday Times Wine Club					
SUP	Supergrape Ltd	•				
T&W	T&W Wines		•	•		•

	Champagne	French Reg.	Germany	Spain	Portugal	Italy	Australia	New Zealand	California	Other U.S.	South America	South Africa	England	Sherry	Port	Madeira	Organic	Fine/Old Wines	Malt Whisky	Half Bottles	Stockist code
													•							•	NI
		•	•	•		•			•		•										RN
																				•	OD
																	•				ORG
					•																P
															•			•			THP
		•																			PHI
		•																		•	CPW
						•		•													TP
																		•			PLA
						•															PON
				•																	POR
															•						PMR
												•									PRW
		•				•															PUG
																		•			R
														•	•			•		•	RAE
		•				•				•							•				RAM
		•				•												•	•	•	RAV
	•					•												•		•	RD
		•					•		•									•	•		RES
							•														RIB
	•			•		•					•			•	•			•			RWW
												•		•	•			•			RWC
																					HR
																				•	WRB
						•											•		•	RBS
						•	•											•			RTW
		•																•			R&I
	•																	•			SAC
																	•				SAF
																					JS
						•	•														SAN
		•																•			SWB
						•															SEB
	•						•		•						•			•		•	SK
	•												•	•	•			•			SEL
					•																ES
																					SHV
																					SAS
		•					•	•	•												SV
																					SOM
																					SPR
						•														•	SPG
																					FSW
																					STW
																					SUM
		•																			DWL
	•					•									•						SUP
	•					•			•							•		•		•	T&W

		Bordeaux	Burgundy	Rhône	Loire	Alsace
TAN	Tanners Wines Ltd					
CT	Charles Taylor Wines Ltd	•	•	•	•	
TO	Tesco Stores plc					
TH	Thresher Wine Shops	•				
MAD	Madeleine Trehearne Partners		•			
TRE	Tremaynes	•				•
TRW	Trinity Wine		•			
TVW	Turville Valley Wines	•	•	•		•
UBC	Ubiquitous Chip	•		•	•	
U	Unwins Wine Merchants	•				
V&C	Valvona & Crolla Ltd					
HVW	Helen Verdcourt			•		
VW	Victoria Wine	•				
LV	La Vigneronne			•	•	•
VIL	Village Wines					
VLW	Villeneuve Wines Ltd			•		
VDV	Vin du Van					
VER	Vinceremos Wines & Spirits Ltd					
VT	The Vine Trail					
VR	Vintage Roots					
W	Waitrose Ltd					
WAW	Waterloo Wine Co Ltd				•	
WAC	Waters of Coventry Ltd					
WEP	The Welshpool Wine Company	•	•			
WES	Wessex Wines					
WHC	Whiclar & Gordon Wines Ltd	•				
WWT	Whitebridge Wines					
WOC	Whitesides of Clitheroe Ltd					
WTL	Whittalls Wines					
WDW	Windrush Wines Ltd					
WBM	Wine Byre Merchants	•			•	
CRL	The Wine Centre/Charles Steevenson Wines					
WE	Wine Emporium/Cockburn's of Leith Ltd					
WR	Wine Rack					•
WSC	The Wine Schoppen Ltd					•
SHG	Wine Shop on the Green		•			
WSO	The Wine Society					
WTR	The Wine Treasury Ltd		•	•		
WCE	Winecellars					
WMK	Winemark Wine Merchant					
WIN	The Winery					
WOI	Wines of Interest					
WNS	Winos Wine Shop					
MAW	M&A Winter	•	•			
WGW	Woodgate Wines					
WRW	The Wright Wine Co					
PWY	Peter Wylie Fine Wines	•	•			
YAP	Yapp Brothers			•	•	•
NY	Noel Young Wines					

Champagne	French Reg.	Germany	Spain	Portugal	Italy	Australia	New Zealand	California	Other U.S.	South America	South Africa	England	Sherry	Port	Madeira	Organic	Fine/Old Wines	Malt Whisky	Half Bottles	Stockist code
	•		•										•				•			TAN
				•	•															CT
	•		•																•	TO
	•																			TH
					•															MAD
											•				•				•	TRE
															•		•			TRW
						•	•	•			•						•	•		TVW
																		•	•	UBC
																			•	U
																				V&C
		•																		HVW
	•													•						VW
	•										•						•		•	LV
					•															VIL
	•										•								•	VLW
	•															•				VDV
	•															•				VER
																	•			VT
																	•			VR
	•																			W
	•																			WAW
																				WAC
																				WEP
											•									WES
						•														WHC
																				WWT
																				WOC
									•											WTL
•																				WDW
	•	•							•	•			•	•	•		•	•		WBM
	•	•																		CRL
		•				•														WE
		•		•	•	•														WR
																				WSC
																				SHG
					•															WSO
					•												•			WTR
																				WCE
					•	•		•												WMK
																	•		•	WIN
																				WOI
																				WNS
•															•		•	•		MAW
																	•			WGW
•																	•	•	•	WRW
														•	•		•			PWY
																				YAP
					•															NY

The Vintages

Quality ranges from 1-10, from the worst to the greatest respectively. Please note that these marks are all generalisations – good producers make good wine in bad years and bad producers can make even good years a disaster. For fuller details on specific regions, consult the A-Z section.

	BORDEAUX RED	BORDEAUX WHITE – SWEET	BURGUNDY RED	BURGUNDY WHITE	RHONE RED	GERMANY WHITE	ITALY RED	SPAIN RIOJA	AUSTRALIA WHITE	AUSTRALIA RED	CALIFORNIA RED	PORT
1992	6△	6△	6△	7△	6△	7△	6△	5△	7△	7△	8△	
1991	6△	7△	8△	8△	8△	9△	8△	8△	9△	9△	7△	8△
1990	8△	9△	10△	8△	9△	9△	8△	8△	9▲	9△	9△	
1989	10△	9△	10△	9△	9△	9▲	7△	8△	6△	6▲	7△	
1988	8△	9△	9△	8▲	8△	8▲	9△	6△	8▲	8▲	7▲	
1987	6●	5△	8▲	7●	6△	7▲	7△	7▲	8●	8●	8▲	
1986	8△	8△	7●	8▲	7▲	7●	7▲	6△	7●	8▲	8▲	
1985	8▲	7△	9▲	7▲	8●	8▲	10●	7▲	8●	8▲	9▲	10△
1984	5●	3●	5▼	7●	6●	5●	5●	5●	8▼	8▲	8▲	
1983	7▲	9△	7▲	6●	9▲	9●	9●	7●		7●	6▼	9△
1982	9▲	4●	5●	6●	7●	5▼	8●	9●		8●	7●	7▲
1981	7●	6▲	4▼	8●	6●	6▼	7●	8●			6▼	5●
1980	5●	5●	8●	6●	6●	5▼	7●	5▽			7▼	8▲
1979	7●	7●	7●	8●	7●	6▼	8▼	4▽			7▼	7▽
1978	8▲	4▼	8●	8▼	10▼	3▽	7▼	8▼				8▲
1977	4▼	2▼	4▽	6▼	4▼	4▼	7▼	3▽				10△
1976	6●	8●	7▼	5▼	7●	8●	4▽	7▽				7▲
1975	7●	8●	2▽	5▽	3▽	8●	6▽	8▼				7●
1974	4▽	★	3▽	4▽	4▽	★	6▽	4▽				4▼
1973	3▽	3▼	3▽	4▽	5▼	★	4▽	8▼				
1972	3▽	★	8●	8▼	5▼	★	3▽	3▽				
1971	6▼	8●	9●	8▼	9●	10▼	8▼	4▽				
1970	8●	6▼	6▼	6▼	7▼	★	8▼	9▼				9▲
1969	★	3▽	8▼	8▼	8▼	★	7▽	7▽				
1968	★	★	★	★	★	★	6▽	8▽				
1967	5▼	7●	5▽	5▼	7▼	★	7▼	6▽				7▼
1966	7●	4▼	7▼	7▽	8▼	★	4▽	7▽				9●
1965	★	★	★	★	★	★	★	★				
1964	★	★	8▼	9▼	8▼	★	8▽	9▽				
1963	★	★	★	★	★	★	★	★				10●
1962	6▼	8▼	6▽	8▽	8▼	★	★	★				
1961	10●	7▼	★	★	9▼	★	★	★				

△ Still needs keeping   ▼ Should be drunk soon
▲ Can be drunk but will improve   ▽ Probably over the hill
● Drinking now   ★ Bad year/don't buy/past it

Reproduced by kind permission of WINE Magazine

INDEX TO WINES

Wines that appear in bold type are particularly recommended.
Those that appear printed in red are the *Guide*'s Wines of The Year